New Challenges for Documentary

from your bookseller or THE UNIVERSITY OF CALIFORNIA PRESS, Berkeley, CA 94720

New Challenges for Documentary

Edited by

Alan Rosenthal

University of California Press

Berkeley / Los Angeles / London

University of California Press
Berkeley and Los Angeles, California

University of California Press, Ltd.
London, England

**Library of Congress Cataloging-in-Publication
Data**

New challenges for documentary.

  Includes bibliographies and index.
  1. Moving-pictures, Documentary. 2. Documentary
television programs. I. Rosenthal, Alan, 1936–
PN1995.9.D6N377   1988   791.43'53   86-24944
ISBN 0-520-05725-2 (alk. paper)
ISBN 0-520-05724-4 (pbk. : alk paper)

Printed in the United States of America

    4   5   6   7   8   9

For Larry Solomon
my friend and partner
who has taught me so much about film

Contents

Acknowledgments

First, my thanks to all the authors who appear in this book and who allowed me to reprint their articles. In this category special thanks are due to Pat Aufderheide, Patricia Erens, Larry Lichty, and Linda Williams, all of whom went out of their way to amend and rewrite their articles at my request so as to focus them more specifically on the needs of this book.

A special debt is also owed to Fred Friendly, Craig Gilbert, Ann Kaplan, D. B. Jones, and Dai Vaughan. In these cases, the authors and/or their publishers allowed me to make selections from certain articles whose length prevented their publication in full. This excerpting of articles is not a practice I like, but it was forced on me by limitations of space. I very much appreciate having been allowed to make such selections and to have been trusted to exercise my judgment in these matters.

I also want to thank Pamela Yates very much. I accosted her at a terrible time, when she was in the middle of a film crisis and working against a deadline. Nevertheless, she took time out to show me her films and to discuss them at length. These gestures are remembered.

Thanks are also due to Anna Katoff, who did all the typing of the manuscript, to Christine Rimon and the staff of the American Cultural Center, Jerusalem, who helped me research articles and assisted me with all my photocopying, and to Anne Canright for her skillful editing. I would also like to acknowledge the help of Chuck Kleinhans, Noel Carroll, and Gerry O'Grady. All three sent me extremely helpful background papers and also pointed me in the direction of other articles they thought would be of assistance in shaping the book.

I discussed the concept of this book with many friends over about two years, but six people above all others guided my steps and made invaluable contributions. Both John Katz of York University, Toronto, and Jerry Kuehl were in at the very beginning. Both encouraged me at great length via the international mails, and both provided useful criticism regarding specific chapters.

Three other people who helped me enormously were Henry Breitrose of Stanford University, Jay Ruby of Temple University, and Brian Winston of New York University. All three are old friends, and all three went through all the chapter introductions carefully, helping me with their expertise, provoking some new ideas, and wisely challenging some of my rasher statements.

As usual, my overall guiding light was Ernest Callenbach. This is the third book on which he has given me editorial help, and his humor, wit, impeccable judgment, and immense enthusiasm were invaluable all along the way. To all the above five and to him my thanks and gratitude.

Grateful acknowledgment is also made to the following sources for their permission to reprint the articles in this anthology:

"Documentary: I Think We Are in Trouble," reprinted from *Sight and Sound* 48, no. 1 (Winter 1978/79), by permission of Brian Winston and *Sight and Sound*.

"Television Documentary Usage," from chapters 3 and 4 of *Television Documentary Usage*, copyright © British Film Institute, 1976. Reprinted by permission of the British Film Institute.

"The Voice of Documentary," from *Film Quarterly* 36, no. 3 (Spring 1983), copyright © 1983 by the Regents of the University of California. Reprinted by permission of the Regents and Bill Nichols.

"The Image Mirrored: Reflexivity and the Documentary Film," reprinted from the *Journal of the University Film Association* 29, no. 1 (Fall 1977), by permission of Jay Ruby and the *Journal of the University Film and Video Association*.

"Theories and Strategies of the Feminist Documentary," reprinted from *Millennium Film Journal*, no. 12 (Fall–Winter 1982/83). This article appeared in a revised version in E. Ann Kaplan, *Women and Film: Both Sides of the Camera* (London: Methuen, 1983).

"Truth Claims," reprinted from *Sight and Sound* 50, no. 4 (Autumn 1981), by permission of Jerry Kuehl and *Sight and Sound*.

"Getting It Right," reprinted from *Sight and Sound* 51, no. 1 (Winter 1981/82), by permission of *Sight and Sound*.

"The Canadian Film Board Unit B," from *Movies and Memoranda*, copyright © Canadian Film Institute, 1981. Reprinted by permission of D. B. Jones and the Canadian Film Institute.

"Filming the Cultural Revolution," reprinted from *Jump Cut*, no. 12/13 (1976), by permission of Thomas Waugh and *Jump Cut*.

"History Is the Theme of All My Films: An Interview with Emile de Antonio," reprinted from *Cineaste* 12, no. 2 (Spring 1982), by permission of *Cineaste*.

"Wiseman's *Model* and the Documentary Project: Toward a Radical Film Practice," from *Film Quarterly* 37, no. 2 (Winter 1983/84), copyright © 1984 by the Regents of the University of California. Reprinted by permission of the Regents and Dan Armstrong.

"Reflections on *An American Family*," reprinted from *Studies in Visual Communication* 8, no. 1 (Winter 1982), copyright © 1981 by the Annenberg School of Communications. All rights reserved. Used by permission of *Studies in Visual Communication*.

"*Two Laws* from Australia, One White, One Black," from *Film Quarterly* 36, no. 3 (Spring 1983), copyright © 1983 by the Regents of the University of California. Reprinted by permission of the Regents and James Roy MacBean.

"The Politics of Documentary," reprinted from *Cineaste* 11, no. 3 (Summer 1981), by permission of *Cineaste*.

"Ultimately We Are All Outsiders: The Ethics of Documentary Filming," reprinted from the *Journal of the University Film Association* 28, no. 1 (Winter 1976), by permission of Calvin Pryluck and the *Journal of the University Film and Video Association*.

"The Tradition of the Victim in Griersonian Documentary," reprinted from *Image Ethics: The Moral and Legal Rights of Subjects in Film and Television*, ed. Larry Gross, John Katz, and Jay Ruby (in press). Used by permission of the author and the editors.

"The Prosecutor," from *The Camera Age* (New York: Penguin, 1982). Reprinted by permission of Michael J. Arlen.

"*No Lies*: Direct Cinema as Rape," reprinted from the *Journal of the University Film Association* 29, no. 1 (Fall 1977), by permission of Vivian C. Sobchack and the *Journal of the University Film and Video Association*.

"Media Power: The Double Bind," reprinted from *Journal of Communication* 24, no. 4 (Autumn 1974), by permission of Stuart Hall and *Journal of Communication*.

"How TV Covers War," reprinted by permission of *The New Republic*, copyright © 1983 The New Republic Inc.

"The McCarthy Broadcast," from *Due to Circumstances Beyond Our Control* (New York: Vintage Books, 1968). Reprinted by permission of Fred Friendly.

"An Independent with the Networks," reprinted from *Studies in Visual Communication* 8, no. 1 (Winter 1982), copyright © 1981 by the Annenberg School of Communications. All rights reserved. Used by permission of *Studies in Visual Communication*.

"*Blacks Britannica*: A Clear Case of Censorship," reprinted from *Jump Cut*, no. 21 (1978), by permission of Peter Biskind and *Jump Cut*.

"New Boy: An Independent with Israel TV," from *Journal of the University Film Association* 33, no. 4 (Fall 1981), copyright © 1981 by Alan Rosenthal. Used by permission of the author.

"History on the Public Screen I," by Donald Watt, and "History on the Public Screen II," by Jerry Kuehl, reprinted from *The Historian and Film*, ed. Paul Smith (Cambridge: Cambridge University Press, 1976), by permission of Cambridge University Press and the authors.

"Narration, Invention, and History," reprinted from *Cineaste* 12, no. 2 (Spring 1982), by permission of *Cineaste*.

"World War II—Soviet Style," from *Commentary*, May 1979. All rights reserved. Reprinted by permission of *Commentary* and the author.

"*The Sorrow and the Pity*: France and Her Political Myths," from *Film and Revolution* (Bloomington: Indiana University Press, 1972). Reprinted by permission of James Roy MacBean and the Indiana University Press.

"Ireland—Two Nations," reprinted from *Sight and Sound* 50, no. 1 (Winter 1980/81), by permission of *Sight and Sound*.

"The Good Fight," copyright © 1984 by Pat Aufderheide. Used by permission of the author.

" 'Vietnam: A Television History': Media Research and Some Comments," copyright © 1985 by Larry Lichty.

"Direct Cinema: The Third Decade," reprinted from *Sight and Sound* 52, no. 4 (Autumn 1983), by permission of Brian Winston and *Sight and Sound*.

"De interpretatione," from *Film Quarterly* 30, no. 4 (Summer 1977), copyright © 1977 by the Regents of the University of California. Reprinted by permission of the Regents.

"Phantom India," from *Film Quarterly* 27, no. 4 (Summer 1974), copyright © 1974 by the Regents of the University of California. Reprinted by permission of the Regents and Todd Gitlin.

"*When the Mountains Tremble*: An Interview with Pamela Yates," from *Film Quarterly* 39, no. 1 (Fall 1985), copyright © 1985 by the Regents of the University of California. Reprinted by permission of the Regents.

"Women's Documentary Filmmaking: The Personal Is Political," from *Women Artists' News* 1, no. 3 (Fall 1981), revised and updated for this anthology. Used by permission of *Women Artists' News* and Patricia Erens.

"*What You Take for Granted*," copyright © 1984 by Linda Williams. Used by permission of the author.

"*Word Is Out*" and "*Gay U.S.A.*," from *Film Quarterly* 32, no. 2 (Winter 1978/79), copyright © 1978 by the Regents of the University of California. Reprinted by permission of the Regents and Lee Atwell.

"*Hiroshima-Nagasaki*: The Case of the A-Bomb Footage," from *Studies in Visual Communication* 8, no. 1 (Winter 1982), copyright © 1980 by Erik Barnouw. Used by permission of *Studies in Visual Communication* and the author.

"*The War Game*: An Interview with Peter Watkins," from *The New Documentary in Action* (Berkeley and Los Angeles: University of California Press,

1971), copyright © 1971 by the Regents of the University of California. Used by permission of the Regents and Alan Rosenthal.

For illustrations I would like to acknowledge my debt to Granada Television, Joan Churchill, The National Film Board of Canada, Emile de Antonio, Fred Wiseman and Oliver Kool, Craig Gilbert, The British Broadcasting Corporation, DeMott/Kreines Films, and Skylight Pictures.

General Introduction

The aim of *New Challenges for Documentary* is to look at the dominant questions and controversies confronting documentary today. It attempts to do this by assembling a very diverse and provocative collection of writings on documentary that, taken together, give a broad overview of the key problems in the field. Most of the articles in this volume have been written since 1975, and they focus on documentary since that time. Occasionally, however, earlier articles have been included because their subject matter helps illuminate the present.

The major concern of this book is whether documentary has a function to perform as we approach the latter part of the century. The emphasis is on major documentary issues: Where is documentary going? How should it go? What subjects should it be covering? How should filmmakers act? What form should documentary take? How can documentary be relevant to major social and political issues of the 1980s and 1990s? The book attempts to stimulate discussion and thinking by raising questions and focusing the debate. The challenge is where we go from here, and my hope is that the book will provide a few maps and a few suggestions.

Why is it vital to meet that challenge? One answer is that in the mid-1980s there is a feeling that documentary is in the doldrums and that unless the form can be revitalized or reenergized it will swiftly lose any general or social impact it ever had. This gloomy prognostication has been a recurring theme in documentary literature since the late 1970s. Thus, the decline of the documentary was the main thrust of an article in the *Columbia Journalism Review* in 1979;[1] it was discussed by Pat Aufderheide and George Stoney in articles for *American Film*[2] and *Sightlines*;[3] and it was the subject of a special report,

"Does the Documentary Have a Future?," compiled by Peter Biskind for *American Film* in 1982.[4]

The present gloom contrasts strongly with the mood of the early 1960s, when the possibilities of *cinéma vérité*, the rise of the film schools, the gradual movement of women into documentary, and the strength of network television documentaries created what now seems a golden age of nonfiction film. Today, in the mid-1980s, the mood—at least in the United States—seems very different.

The major problems are easily listed. *Cinéma vérité*, as a challenging and inspiring form, seems exhausted. The subjects for documentary also seem increasingly hackneyed. Everything appears to have been done, from major wars to family histories. While the documentary output of the commercial networks is diminishing, filmmakers seem to regard the possibilities of public television with little joy. Funding remains a major problem for independent filmmakers, while access by outsiders to the networks is still extremely difficult. Finally, the audience itself seems to be losing what little interest it had in documentary as a media form.

These grave comments on the present are usually coupled with dire forecasts for the future. How true is it all? Is the fate of documentary signed, sealed, and delivered? One aim of this book is to investigate this supposed crisis so we can proceed more confidently into the future; another, broader purpose is to discuss some theoretical issues and other topics that have been ignored in the past and to open up new areas for documentary research.

Luckily, a lot of pioneering has already been done. One bright spark in this gloomy picture of documentary is the number of people now writing seriously about documentary concerns, despite the tendency of film theorists such as Christian Metz to relegate nonfiction film to a very minor place in the film hierarchy. Since 1969 we have witnessed the publication of two histories of documentary, three casebooks, two anthologies, and a number of special-topic books, such as Stephen Mamber's *Cinéma Vérité in America*.[5] A number of excellent magazines have also emerged, including *Cineaste, Film Library Quarterly, The Independent, Jump Cut, Film Quarterly, Screen,* and *Sightlines,* all of which make irregular but serious efforts to survey the documentary field.

Despite this tremendous intellectual ferment, a sense of focus has, in the main, been absent since the days of John Grierson and Paul Rotha. Both Grierson and Rotha wrote extensive polemics exploring the why and wherefore of documentary.[6] In contrast, the two recent anthologies by Lewis Jacobs and Richard Barsam,[7] though useful as documentary companion readers, concentrate on reviews of interesting films rather than on the theory of documentary practice. My hope is that *New Challenges for Documentary* will revive the debate on ideas. When the ideas are clear, let us hope that inspiration will follow.

The concept for this collection originated in the 1970s, when I was working on two documentary interview books that eventually appeared as *The New Documentary in Action* and *The Documentary Conscience*.[8] My interest at the time was to explore *how* documentaries were made and what problems confronted the filmmaker at every point in the work process. However, as I interviewed people, I found topics arising that I had never really considered before. Thus, it was impossible to talk to Ellen Hovde about *Grey Gardens* without talking about ethics; nor could I discuss *Cathy Come Home* with Jeremy Sandford without discussing the function and purpose of documentary drama. Again and again, interviewees would bring up the same points. Unfortunately, we would touch on these peripheral topics for five minutes, then leave them hanging. As I began to get the broad picture, I realized there were a number of serious theoretical issues in documentary that had been neglected in the past and that called for major formal discussion. So, gradually, this book was born.

New Challenges for Documentary is divided into six parts and deals with four main topics: theory, form, and text; the purpose, methods, and ethical position of the filmmaker; documentary and television; and the subjects of documentary. Part I, concerned mainly with form and text, brings together some of the post-Griersonian thinking about documentary theory. Although much time has been spent in defining documentary film—as if it was something concrete instead of a loose concept—the literature on theory, structure, and organization is surprisingly sparse, in contrast to the massive output relating to narrative-film theory.

Before 1970, one would have been hard put to find anyone writing seriously about documentary theory outside of the well-thumbed texts of Grierson and Rotha and a few translated pieces of Dziga Vertov. Today, however, a host of new critics, including Bill Nichols, Dai Vaughan, Brian Winston, Julia Lesage, E. Ann Kaplan, and Chuck Kleinhans, are asking incisive questions about how documentary works, how it signifies, and what the practical and theoretical implications in choice of narrative, assembly, and form are. Although facets of these major areas of theory are explored in Part I, many subjects could not be dealt with in depth. The most serious of these, the semantics of the image, is touched on in a number of articles, but much more serious discussion of this question is called for.

After theory, a main concern of the book is filmmaking practice. Who *is* the filmmaker? How does he or she work? What are the filmmaker's responsibilities and relationship to the documentary subject, and what are the constraints of making a film? Parts II and III provide discussion of the thoughts, beliefs, and practices of a few key filmmakers, from the members of the Canadian National Film Board's Unit B to Joris Ivens and Emile de Antonio. Besides showing the trials and tribulations of the filmmakers, these sections deal also with ethics in filmmaking. This issue, raised loud and clear as a result of such films as *Marjoe* and *Salesman*, is discussed here with great clarity by writers and directors such as Calvin Pryluck, Jay Ruby, and Craig Gilbert.

Part IV deals with television as the main medium by which documentary reaches, and by implication can affect, a mass audience. Here I have tried to raise questions concerning television power, access, ideas, censorship, and funding, with the aim of providing a picture of how television, particularly American television, looks on documentary. A theoretical article by Stuart Hall opens the section, however, providing an introduction to the power structure and constraints of television. This general subject of the "unseen rules" is important to documentary but lies outside the scope of this book. For those wishing to explore further, I would recommend *On Television* by Stuart Hood,[9] which looks at how the words and images of television are chosen and how TV organizations are linked to the central power of the state.

The last two parts of the book deal with documentary subject matter, in particular history and current social and political themes. Part V includes some discussion of the work of independents and their predilection for oral and biographic histories, but its main concern is with series histories such as "Ireland" and "Vietnam." Part VI is devoted almost entirely to the work and concerns of independent filmmakers, focusing on the growth of radical and political filmmaking in the past twenty years and on the issues raised by the feminist movement, the gay movement, the wars in Central America, and nuclear disarmament.

Though the book is divided into discrete subjects, discussions naturally and inevitably overlap. Thus, Brian Winston's article on the future of *vérité* in Part VI is also extremely relevant to Part I, with its focus on form. Similarly, E. Ann Kaplan's discussion of women and film theory at the start of the book could equally well have followed on and amplified Patricia Erens's article on feminist filmmakers in Part VI. The articles about de Antonio, Watkins, Robert Drew, and Israel television could likewise have been placed elsewhere. Occasionally I mention such a cross-reference possibility in a specific part introduction, but generally I leave it to the reader to determine the broader context for individual essays.

Although all books demand that choices be made, the anthologist's task is especially difficult. With luck there are more good articles than can fit, but this ideal situation is both a blessing and a curse: a blessing because there is so much good material to choose from, a curse because so much of value has to be dropped for want of space. I read a tremendous number of articles in making the current selection, so a brief word on choice is needed.

Besides looking for the best and most interesting articles of the past few years, I also decided to avoid, as far as possible, anthologizing well-known essays that could easily be found elsewhere, including such excellent articles as "Fascinating Fascism" by Susan Sontag and "Toward New Goals in Documentary" by Arthur Barron. This desire to avoid duplication also meant leaving out a number of articles on radical filmmaking, since *Jump Cut* was preparing a special anthology devoted to that topic, edited by Thomas Waugh.

Once I had narrowed the field, I also set up guidelines for readability and intellectual rigor. The readability element is, for me, a *sine qua non*, especially in regard to film theory, which runs the danger of a certain self-inflicted marginalization—that is, elitism so extreme that the message becomes inaccessible to the ordinary film viewer. At the same time, intellectual rigor is necessary to provide the basis for and to stimulate and provoke argument and discussion. I should perhaps add here that in a few cases I strongly disagree with the attitudes and conclusions writers put forward. But, as Mao said, let a thousand flowers bloom.

For the sake of clarity, I have concentrated almost exclusively on North American documentary. At first I wanted to say more about British and European filmmaking, but almost every article I looked at needed another article to explain its references. For example, I omitted a very good article by Anthony Smith on filming the Northern Ireland conflict because of the subject's unfamiliarity to most Americans. However, I have occasionally taken the liberty of including an article that is only tangential to documentary, such as Mark Crispin Miller's piece on how television covers war and Stuart Hall's essay on media power. These articles provide a fuller background-picture against which to place the documentary discussion.

One tries to be complete, but I was surprised to find, even after a great deal of searching, that there are still a number of essential documentary topics that are hardly discussed. The most serious of these omissions, alluded to a number of times in this anthology, is the almost complete absence of any meaningful discussion of the documentary audience.

Grierson may sometimes have been patronizing, but he was always concerned with audience and effect. This is true of Humphrey Jennings as well. Today the discussion of audience is usually confined to a few left-wing filmmakers concerned with using film as an organizing tool for radical debate and social action. Again, while the theorists talk about truth and objectivity, such discussion is usually done in the abstract, without any attention given to the viewer's role in the matter.

Two subjects cry out for more research and discourse: one is audience perception, the second, effect and action. Both are related to reception theory, a conceptual attempt to understand the position of the audience. Work on how the audience understands a film would add a new dimension to the debate on truth and objectivity. Work on effect would clarify what documentaries really do in terms of propaganda and attitude change. Now, media effects and attitude change are not exactly new subjects. The two-step theory of change and the uses and gratifications theory have both been around for years and are in every beginning text on social psychology. Possibly the time has come to start applying these theories to documentary, but I am not sure. I suspect that we would end up with more mystification than ever.

Another topic surprisingly absent from most discussion is the issue of *new* documentary forms. Nichols's "The Voice of Documentary" and MacBean's *"Two Laws"* in this volume begin to open up the topic, but the debate could go much further. What discussion there is, for instance in drama documentary, tends to be reactive rather than exploratory. This is in sad contrast to the excitement that surrounded the birth of *cinéma vérité* and that greeted Watkins's *Culloden*, which grafted the immediacy of current-affairs news techniques onto a historical drama to give a vital sense of place and reality, and Allan King's *A Married Couple*, which explored the possibility of turning a *cinéma vérité* situation into a structured fiction.

One of the complaints of the mid-1980s, already mentioned, is that the documentary form is moribund. In his article "Invention, Narration, and History," Jeffrey Youdelman discusses the deadening effect of the "talking heads" documentary, a problem that Patricia Erens also mentions with regard to women's films. Yet here and there one does see innovation, as in Jill Godmilow's *Far from Poland*, Leo Hurwitz's *Dialogue with a Woman Departed*, Meredith Monk's *Ellis Island*, or Mitchell Block's *No Lies*. This volume includes two articles that focus on important innovators in form: Linda Williams explores the marvelous shades and possibilities of Michelle Citron's work, and Vivian Sobchack looks at the work of Mitchell Block. But these are only isolated articles. Lacking is general work that will try to deduce or suggest where documentary can go from here. And this work is essential in effecting a revitalization of documentary form, without which, I seriously think, the documentary is doomed.

The last of the missing topics that came to my mind, though I am sure there are many more, has to do with the implications of new Super 8mm and video techniques for documentary, techniques that change weekly, if not daily.[10] Yet for the most part, the potential of these new tools and new possibilities for the documentarist seems to be ignored. Here, too, lies an area ripe for exploration and experimentation.

One can talk about documentary from a hundred viewpoints. In the end one has to ask, Does it really matter, or are we merely dealing with interesting but abstract academic questions? Personally, I think documentary is essential to our society, and only when the issues of the medium are clarified will it become evident how the form can work best for the general good of the society.

The last challenge, then, may be the challenge of function—to determine what documentary should be doing and how it can best be used to ameliorate society and bring about positive social change. The key function of documentary, as I see it, is to explore the hard, awkward questions more deeply and more critically than other branches of the media do (or can). Independent filmmaking thus becomes vitally important, because it affords the necessary diversity of non–status quo viewpoints, and it allows exactly those questions to be asked that are too difficult for the networks.

In other words, the key function of documentary is to set the agenda and define the most important issues for public debate. Thus, I conclude this volume with a discussion of documentary and nuclear war. Clearly the most important issue of our time, nuclear warfare must remain at the center of public debate—and documentaries are playing a crucial part in keeping it there.

The role of documentary, then, is to continue to ask the hard, often disturbing questions so pertinent to our age. If documentary can do that, and can do that in a revitalized and more dynamic form, then the challenge will have been met and documentary will be able to move confidently into the future.

September 1986

Notes

1. Marvin Barrett, "TV Diplomacy and Other Broadcast Quandaries," *Columbia Journalism Review*, May–June 1979, pp. 69–80.

2. Pat Aufderheide, "Public Television's Prime Time Politics," *American Film* 8 (April 1983): 53–58.

3. George C. Stoney, "The Future of Documentary," *Sightlines* (Fall–Winter 1983/84): 10–12.

4. Peter Biskind, "Does Documentary Have a Future?" *American Film* 7 (April 1982): 57–64.

5. Stephen Mamber, *Cinéma Vérité in America* (Cambridge, Mass.: MIT Press, 1974).

6. John Grierson, *Grierson on Documentary*, ed. H. Forsyth Hardy (New York: Harcourt Brace, 1947), and Paul Rotha, *Documentary Film* (New York: Hastings House, 1952).

7. Lewis Jacobs, *The Documentary Tradition* (New York: Hopkinson and Blake, 1969), and Richard Meran Barsam, *Nonfiction Film: Theory and Criticism* (New York: E. P. Dutton, 1976).

8. Alan Rosenthal, *The New Documentary in Action* (Berkeley and Los Angeles: University of California Press, 1971), and Alan Rosenthal, *The Documentary Conscience* (Berkeley and Los Angeles: University of California Press, 1980).

9. Stuart Hood, *On Television* (London: Pluto Press, 1980).

10. See, in particular, the Super 8mm work of John Chapman in the film *In the Name of the People*, about El Salvador.

Part I

Documentary Structures: Theory, Shape, and Form

Introduction

The pieces assembled in this first section examine some of the main theoretical issues of documentary raised in the past decade. There has, of course, always been serious theoretical discussion about documentary, from the Lef arena and John Grierson onward, but it is interesting to note the change in emphasis over the years.

The Grierson and Paul Rotha–inspired trend focused on intention, purpose, and audience. Again and again their writings emphasize (often in a rather patronizing way) the social and educational goals of documentary. In the 1960s, however, came a clear change of emphasis. With *cinéma vérité* and the growth of film schools, the discussion centered on two intertwined realms. The first was concerned with the future of *vérité*—what could and should it be doing, and how did it differ from old-style filming? The second revolved around practical matters—the importance of film training, possibilities of the new lightweight technology, the place of documentary outside the networks, and cooperative group filmmaking.

What typifies the past ten years has been increasing attention to theoretical issues in documentary as opposed to the practical, everyday problems of filmmaking. This invasion of theory has been led mainly by left-wing structuralists and semiologists, inspired by such theorists as Christian Metz, Claude Lévi-Strauss, Jean Louis Comolli, Roland Barthes, and Louis Althusser and published in the pages of *Jump Cut, Screen, The Velvet Light Trap, Women and Film*, and *Film Quarterly*.

The new theoreticians, by taking nothing for granted, have shocked many complacent documentarists out of their easy, unquestioning acceptance of the form. They have asked hard, confusing questions. They tend to assume from the start that film is a language, with a grammar and semantics. They have challenged preconceived notions of how documentary is seen and have in fact brought into question the very notion that documentary is something special and very different from fiction.

Discussion now tends to center on the film form itself and film language rather than on societal concerns. Now, almost for the first time since the essays of Dziga Vertov, serious attention is being focused not on documentary's (mythical) "reality" but on its *form*. Thus the discussion has ranged from examining the implications of Fred Wiseman's editing scheme[1] to the fictional aspects of *Harlan County, U.S.A.*[2] What is being attempted, in essence, and as a relatively new approach, is a close textual analysis of documentary in an attempt to strip the form of myths that have accumulated over the years—for example, that documentary is "truer" than the standard fiction entertainment film.

This first section takes up a number of key issues. These include questions of form, method, objectivity, narrative style, ideology, reflexivity, and the problems and possibilities of documentary drama. I chose Brian Winston's "I Think We Are in Trouble" to set the scene because in a clear, readable, and very down-to-earth way he puts his finger very precisely on some of the basic issues: the relationship of truth and fiction in many of the films of the past; the nature of structure and storytelling in the form; the purpose of documentary; the problem of *vérité*; and the relationship between filmmaker and subject, including the right to institute a documentary probe. The later sections by Dai Vaughan, Bill Nichols, Ann Kaplan, and Jay Ruby apply a fraction closer to formal textual considerations. They discuss methods of discourse, TV forms, image ideology, cultural assumptions, theory in regard to new feminist films, reflexivity, objectivity and truth, and the seen and unseen manipulations and biases of the director. Finally, Jerry Kuehl and Elizabeth Sussex round off the section with two articles on drama documentary as seen from an English perspective, with Kuehl severely criticizing the form and Sussex endorsing its use.

Though the recent theoretical discussions have ranged far and wide, one central point emerges: a great many critics think that "all is suspect" within the form. At first that seems heresy. A strong and widely held assumption in the past was that documentary has a special claim to the truth—that is why we make documentaries and why people watch them. This claim is now under severe attack by many theoreticians, who argue that semiology and structuralism have shown that the documentary film, like the feature film, uses signifying practices that, structured like language, are already symbolic. Hence, all film, including documentary, is ultimately "fiction."[3]

The idea that intrinsically there can be no truth in documentary allies itself very quickly with attacks on the concept of objectivity. There can be no objectivity, it is said, only highly personalized subjective statements by the filmmaker. This is one of the central theses of Colin MacArthur's *Television and History*⁴ and is continually stressed by Eileen McGarry. MacArthur argues, mainly with reference to British television, that the filmmaker is totally caught up in his or her ideological system and cannot see the world as it really is or as those *outside* the system see it. McGarry puts it another way: "Images are structured in time and space in a series of patterns arranged to the filmmaker's view of the world, which often reflect the dominant codes through which a culture apprehends reality."⁵

The attack on documentary's claim to truth and objectivity is reinforced by some of the following arguments: Documentary depends on selection and is manipulated by political codes, by the presence of the director, by the style of shooting, by the cutting. Everything depends on a subjective choice—objectivity is impossible. Again, the distance between the fiction film and the documentary is lessened because the latter is dependent on so many methods of the former, such as reconstruction, dominant and evolving central characters, occasional parallel editing, and a tension and climax resolution structure. In short, objectivity is nothing but a pose, and documentary in the end has little to do with the real world but is merely another social fiction.

I don't really subscribe to this view. We are all, Marxists included, caught up in our various cultural and ideological systems. No one is outside, and if only the outside view can have any value or objectivity, then let us say a cheerful goodbye to creative work and criticism, not just in film but in most of the arts. Again, when Metz suggests that all films are fictions because they are representations—that is to say, the train is on the screen and not literally in the screening room—then we have simply left the world of commonsense language for semantic hairsplitting, which is of doubtful utility. Noel Carroll provides an interesting discussion around the "no truth–no objectivity" argument in an excellent paper on nonfiction film. He writes: "The possibility of objectivity in the nonfiction film is denied because such films involve selection . . . interpretation . . . manipulation . . . point of view, and prompt commentators to reclassify such films as subjective. Yet if these arguments have any force, the lectures and texts of history and science will have to be their victims as well."⁶ Most serious historians, of course, claim objectivity, yet the writing of history is extremely ideological—why else the constant rewriting and reinterpretation of historial events? So in history, as in film, the debate goes on.

However, to bring this discussion down to earth, it must be remembered that few filmmakers, from Flaherty onward, have ever claimed total objectivity. Most have started, one way or another, from the premise that their work is an *interpretation* of reality or, as Grierson stresses, "a *creative*" treatment of actuality. For a while in the 1960s the claims of a few *vérité* apologists to show "total truth" may have pushed the interpretive school of filmmakers into the background. If so, the modern "all is fiction" school of critics can be seen as an overreaction to the *vérité* arguments, which were flimsy to begin with.

Further on in his paper, Carroll has some comments on documentary method that are valuable for their clarity and common sense:

> In any given field of research or argument there are patterns of reasoning, routines for assessing evidence, means for weighing evidence, and standards for observation . . . that are shared by practitioners in the field. Abiding by these established practices is, at any given time, believed to be the best method for getting at the truth. . . . We call a piece of research objective in the light of its adherence to the practice of reasoning and evidence gathering in a particular field.[7]

The cine-Marxists will argue that Carroll's definition is shot through with ideology. They would say, for example, that the criteria for belief in certain established practices are highly dependent on one's culture . . . and cultures differ. Nevertheless, I see the above as a good approach to the whole question of trust and disbelief regarding the arguments and the methods of documentary filmmakers.

Theoreticians suffer from three problems. One is their tendency to push a point too far, putting them in danger of throwing the baby out with the bathwater. The second is their use of a writing style that is often difficult to understand and that, as I have already suggested, sometimes sinks into a self-inflicted marginalization. The third, and most serious, problem is their failure to talk about film in a way that affects practice. Insofar as the theoreticians' work brings us closer to a deeper understanding not only of documentary method and structure but also the implications of cultural anomalies, style, fads, ideology, and image in the documentary form, it is all to the good. But at some point theory should affect practice. So far, the theoretical work has been generally shunned or dismissed as irrelevant by most working filmmakers and has failed to produce or inspire films that have had any significant effect on audiences.

I am also disturbed by the fact that while certain subjects have been done to death by the critics, vast areas of documentary interest still go relatively unexplored. I include here the whole question of documentary *authority* and *trust*. Exceptions to the dearth of work on this subject are articles by Dai Vaughan, whose essay on TV documentary is contained in this volume, and Colin MacArthur's extremely provocative monograph on television and history.[8]

Another interesting topic waiting to be researched is that of emotion versus reason in documentary construction. This is a topic widely discussed with regard to television news gathering, but it is almost totally absent in documentary analysis. Yet it is an important area for investigation, particularly because so many documentaries, from *Seeing Red* to *The Battle of Chile*, rely on high emotional appeal rather than on a cool, more detached analytical approach.

One topic above all is glaring in its omission from recent discussion, and that is the question of audience and effect. Most concerned documentary filmmakers work with two clear, if unstated, purposes in mind: to witness and to affect.[9] To witness is to say, "Look—this happened, pay attention." To affect is to move the audience, to hope that the film will cause emotional, political, and social change.

Given this second purpose, aimed toward action, one would assume that theorists would continually come back to two questions: Can and do documentaries cause change? If so, what is the best form to use to accomplish such change? The questions are there, but documentary critics, and indeed sociologists and psychologists as well, answer them with a deafening silence.

I suspect that many writers on documentary and film have their roots and education in literature and semiology and that they manifest a certain wariness of the social sciences and communications theory. This means that the work of Carl Hovland, Elihu Katz, Paul Lazarsfeld, and Kendal and Woolf and the Payne Fund studies on attitude and opinion change are, for many, totally foreign territory. However, one should add that today there are many students of the social sciences who no longer find Lazarsfeld or the theories on attitude change either fashionable or useful. This is a pity, because I think the application of communications theory to questions of audience attitude, reception, and action in documentary might open up very interesting vistas for research.

The question whether documentaries cause change and under what circumstances is open. Most documentarists believe in change via film, but in practice, such change is hard to substantiate. If one assumes, theoretically, that under certain circumstances documentaries can cause change, then a very practical question for the documentarist would be what documentary method, form, or structure causes the fastest and most enduring change for a specific audience. Again, the question is met with almost total silence.

Unfortunately, form seems to be discussed almost entirely in terms of aesthetics rather than purpose. In this context, calls for *change* in the documentary form are constant.[10] The documentary is perceived as being tired, formula bound, sticking to old authoritarian methods, too reliant on witnesses and authoritarian presenters, nonpoetic, and nonexperimental. Godard's films and *Hour of the Furnaces* are cited as examples to follow; a film like Jill Godmilow's *Far from Poland* is lauded for its innovation and for its fusion of documentary reality and fiction.

Aesthetic innovation for its own sake may be a worthy goal, but I think the discussion becomes more interesting when related to purpose. Many critics of traditional documentary assume that new forms will escape the old traps of "identification," male-centered pleasure/gratification obsessions, and so on, and, by galvanizing and stirring an audience to greater action, will open the way to a new, more liberated life. I consider these implicit assumptions highly suspect—we clearly need research to prove or disprove the affective powers of documentary.

Another subject virtually ignored by American critics is that of documentary drama, or docudrama. In England the discussion has proliferated,[11] possibly because filmmakers there have made many more serious attempts to use the form, including *Cathy Come Home*, *Strike*, and *Invasion*. Efforts in the United States, however, seem to be limited to biographic entertainments, such as *Sadat*, *Golda Meir*, and *Roots*, with certain interesting exceptions, such as *Skokie*, *Blind Ambition,* and *The Missiles of October*.

Documentary drama has a long history, studded with some of the most famous names and films in the documentary pantheon, from Harry Watt's *North Sea* and Humphrey Jennings's *Fires Were Started* through the work of Willard Van Dyke and Leo Hurwitz to, more recently, Peter Watkins's *The War Game*, Ken Loach's *Cathy Come Home*, and Chris Rallings's films for the BBC. This body of work has raised certain theoretical problems that can be put fairly simply: Where is the center of truth in this form, and how believable or how suspect is it? As suggested earlier, one of the underlying assumptions and attractions of documentary is that it is supposed to be more honest and accurate than fiction. As Brian Winston puts it, "On the basis of Grierson's notion of a separate form, we have established a hierarchy of truth in film whereby documentary stands higher than fiction."[12] In documentary drama, however, whole areas seem to be opening up where fiction is presented as fact, as reality. I would argue that in most cases the fusion of drama and documentary raises few problems. The audience clearly perceives, for the most part, what is fact and what is fiction and where license with fact has been taken. But there are obviously situations where the mixing of fact with fiction and dramatizations masquerading as documentary can be dangerous and misleading.

Broadly speaking, I think that two elements combine to create such a problematic situation. First, the audience has to totally or almost completely misread the fiction as fact. Second, the subject being presented must be one that can, or is meant to, affect our social or political actions and attitudes in the present in a fairly important way.

Given these two elements, I find few problems with *North Sea, Golda Meir*, or *Roots*. However, Richard Attenborough's *Gandhi* disturbs me profoundly with its simplistic picture of a martyr and superficial recounting of history, much in the same way that *October* and *The End of St. Petersburg* disturbed some of the better critics almost sixty years ago.

The confused boundary lines between fiction and fact can be seen in three recent, highly publicized television presentations, *Washington Behind Closed Doors*, Anthony Thomas's *Death of a Princess*, and *The Atlanta Child Murders*. *Washington* was fiction, but nevertheless was clearly based on Nixon's Watergate years. It was this assumed claim to authenticity that made it special. However, within the program, *unproved* rumor about Kennedy's involvement with the CIA assassination schemes was casually paired with Nixon's *proved* inclination to indulge in illegal activities.[13] In ATV's *Death of a Princess*, the execution of a Saudi Arabian princess and her lover—a true-to-life event—was mixed with a highly problematic picture of behavior among the Saudi Arabian elite. It was even more difficult for an audience to untangle truth from fiction here than in the *Washington* case.

The third example of the mingling of fact with fiction is CBS's *The Atlanta Child Murders*. First screened in February 1985, the film cast doubt on the just conviction of the man found guilty of two of the twenty-eight slayings that shocked Atlanta between 1979 and 1981. CBS called the film a "fact-based drama," but many residents of Atlanta claimed that the film totally distorted the truth. CBS finally agreed to label the film as containing "some fiction." In an editorial comment on the film, the *New York Times* wrote:

> "Fact-based drama" not only defrauds the news but assaults it, hit and run. The dramatists never stay around for rebuttal or new facts. Mayor Andy Young of Atlanta was appearing on CBS News all this week objecting to the film's portrayal of events. But dissension gets no part in a docudrama. And if new evidence were to turn up next week, only CBS News would be left to clean up after CBS Entertainments. . . . Does no one in charge of television care enough about either news or fiction to halt this corruption?[14]

Given the problems surrounding documentary drama, what is its appeal to the serious filmmaker? Leslie Woodhead, the creator of some of the most interesting documentaries shown on English television, sees it as a form of last resort. "It is a way of doing things where ordinary documentary cannot cope . . . a way of telling a story that would be impossible by conventional documentary methods." What is the impossible story? For Woodhead it has ranged from the Russian invasion of Czechoslovakia, in *Invasion*, to *Strike*, about the Solidarity Movement in the Lenin shipyards in Gdansk. Woodhead's aim has been to recreate history as accurately as possible; his method has been summed up by David Boulton, one of his scriptwriters: "No invented characters, no invented names, no dramatic devices owing more to the writer's (or director's) creative imagination than to the impeccable record of *what actually happened*. For us, the dramatised documentary is an exercise in journalism, not dramatic art."[15]

If we approve the method stated by Boulton and assume that it is bolstered by years of research, high-grade source materials such as diaries and interviews, and intense verification of facts, the question remains, How do we let the audience know all of this? A possible answer is that given by Robert Vas in *The Issue Should Be Avoided* and by Jill Godmilow in *Far from Poland*: both use signposting, which clearly indicates the source of authority for what is happening on the screen. This technique is certainly feasible, though an alternative might be a form of filmic footnotes to go with the credits.

All these discussions on documentary form and the practicability of the documentary idea itself are timely and invigorating. Some necessary demythologizing has taken place, and documentary is the better for it. However, one element has been missing, which, although not really necessary to formal criticism, should inform all serious theoretical discussion—and that is the audience.

Films are made for people—to be seen, absorbed, enjoyed, and acted upon. Formal discussion of documentary as fiction is all very well, but at some point attention must be directed to audience perception. Clearly, the sophistication level of the audience has changed immensely since the beginnings of documentary in the 1930s. Viewers are not as befuddled as theoreticians would make them out to be. Most viewers do not for one moment imagine that there are clear windows on history, and they do not generally confuse drama with actual documentary. Most people who take a serious interest in documentary are aware of the artifices of editing and selection and know that what they see is a producer's vague approximation of what actually happened.

One can theorize away, but my suspicion is that the audience will continue to accept documentary as somehow "truer" than fiction. They may grow more aware of the artifice, the means of selection, the biases, and the constraints— and all to the good. However, I suspect that they will continue to see documentary as a special genre, a useful tool that provides some clear and necessary observations about the world, occasionally even stirring them to action. This may be because of the audience's trust in the integrity of certain documentary makers, such as Ed Murrow in the past and Bill Moyers today. It may be an ingrained habit formed over the years. Whatever the reasons for the attitude and the trust, I believe both are still there. And it is this audience perception and outlook that, we must hope, continues to inspire and motivate the documentarist.

Notes

1. Bill Nichols, "Frederick Wiseman's Documentaries: Theory and Structure," in Nichols, *Ideology and the Image: Social Representation in the Cinema and Other Media* (Bloomington: Indiana University Press, 1981).

2. E. Ann Kaplan, "The Documentary Form," *Jump Cut*, no. 15 (1977): 11.

3. Ibid.

4. Colin MacArthur, *Television and History* (London: British Film Institute, 1978).

5. Eileen McGarry, "Documentary Realism and Women's Cinema," *Women in Film* 2 (Summer 1975): 50.

6. Noel Carroll, "From Real to Reel: Entangled in Nonfiction Film," in *Philosophy Looks at Film*, ed. Dale Jamieson (New York: Oxford University Press, 1983), p. 27.

7. Ibid., p. 30.

8. MacArthur, *Television and History*.

9. On this subject see also Chuck Kleinhans, "Forms, Politics, Makers, and Contexts: Basic Issues for a Theory of Radical Political Documentary," unpublished paper, Chicago, 1984, and Alan Rosenthal, *The Documentary Conscience* (Berkeley and Los Angeles: University of California Press, 1980).

10. The Flaherty International Film Seminar 1984 is a good example, where the traditional authoritarian documentary with commentator was continually denounced from the floor.

11. For a fuller discussion, see John Caughie, "Progressive Television and Documentary Drama," *Screen* 21 (1980): 21–31; Jerry Kuehl, "The Motives for Making Drama Documentary," *Vision* 14 (April 1978); and Chris Ralling, "What Is Television Doing to History?," *The Listener*, Jan. 17, 1980.

12. Brian Winston, "I Think We Are in Trouble," *Sight and Sound* 48 (Winter 1978/79): 3.

13. See also Michael Arlen, "Adrift in Docudrama," *The Camera Age* (New York: Penguin Books, 1981), p. 276.

14. *New York Times*, Feb. 10, 1985, p. B10.

15. David Boulton, *Invasion: A Writer's Perspective* (Manchester: Granada Television Pamphlet, 1981).

Documentary: I Think We Are in Trouble

Brian Winston

It all begins with this: "Of course, *Moana*, being a visual account of events in the daily life of a Polynesian youth and his family, has documentary value." Thus wrote Grierson in a review of Flaherty's second classic that was published by the *New York Sun* on 8 February 1926. This is generally taken to be the first time the word "documentary" was used in connection with film. Of course, what we understand by that term precedes Grierson's coining of it. The cinema began with documentary material, but audiences rapidly became bored with babies eating breakfast, trains arriving at stations, and workers leaving factories. Audiences in the 1890s required of the new medium what they expected of older media—stories, narratives with beginnings, middles, climaxes, denouements, and ends. And it was the fiction film that was to provide for this age-old want. Only when Flaherty began to structure his actuality material so that it too might satisfy those needs could Grierson and others detect a new form and name it "documentary." But the need for structure implicitly contradicts the notion of unstructured actuality. The idea of documentary, then and now, is sustained by simply ignoring this contradiction. Paul Rotha therefore could sum it up thus: "Documentary's essence lies in the dramatization of actual material."

For over half a century we have been happy to accept this. But of late a growing sophistication has begun to question the very basis on which the idea of documentary rests. Given the need to decide for a camera to be present; the deals that must be done with those who are to be filmed; the effect of the camera's presence; the decision when to film and when not; how to light, what lens to use, and where to stand; where to position microphones—one can legitimately begin to query what is "actual" in Rotha's "actual material."

And then the crucial work of molding the film into a culturally satisfying shape—the need to ignore the sequence of rushes, to crosscut, to build climaxes, to remove or add sound, to add commentary and music, titles—raises further questions as to how much of the "actual" can be left when the process of "dramatization" is complete.

These doubts are not obscure academic ones without relevance to the film-maker and his or her audience. On the basis of Grierson's notion of a separate form we have established a hierarchy of truth in film whereby documentary (in its narrow sense, but also current affairs and news) stands higher than fiction. If it is the case that that hierarchy is built on shifting sand, then the legitimacy of whole areas of work crumbles; and, further, the moral and ethical problems facing the filmmaker are dramatically increased.

By the late 1940s the crude idea of separating documentary from fiction had received many knocks. From the very beginning filmmakers had been quizzed about their working methods. Was it right to get Nanook freezing inside his roofless igloo so that the interior could be naturally lit? Did Aran men still fish for shark? But, more important, the strain of adapting a studio-based technology for the very different work of documentary filming had led to regular reconstruction practices. Thus, real mail sorters sort mail in a faked rail coach in a studio because the technology would not allow *Night Mail* to be made *in situ*. Harry Watt recalls that "we couldn't afford what they have in feature films—that is, a rocker set . . . so all we could do was to move by hand, out of picture, certain things like balls of string hanging down, make them sway regularly to give the impression of the train moving, and get the chaps to sway a little bit."

Since the exotic subject matter of early documentaries (Persian nomads, Eskimos, Polynesians, and the rest) had given way to a quite conscious political desire to document the filmmakers' own societies, subjects like *Night Mail* were constantly requiring fiction film solutions. By 1948 the notion of "actual material" had to be drastically refined. A definition of documentary film of that year states that it is "all methods of recording on celluloid any aspect of reality interpreted either by factual shooting or by sincere and justifiable re-construction, so as to appeal either to reason or emotion, for the purpose of stimulating the desire for, and the widening of human knowledge and under-standing, and of truthfully posing problems and their solutions in the spheres of economics, culture, and human relations." *Brief Encounter*, anybody?

What has happened here, in effect, is that since documentaries required the same technology as features, the resultant confusion could only be unscrambled by calling the purpose of the filmmakers and the responses of audiences into the balance. It had become less a question of how and what things appeared on the screen but rather why they were there. As Arthur Schlesinger, Jr., said, "The line between the documentary and the fiction film is tenuous indeed.

Both are artifacts; both are contrivances. Both are created by editing and selection. Both, wittingly or not, embody a viewpoint. The fact that one eschews and the other employs professional actors becomes in the end an economic detail." And not even this last little distinction can be allowed to stand. Kurosawa made a documentary about women workers in an optical factory during the war, *The Most Beautiful*, in which actresses played the workers—but he did not allow them to wear makeup.

For some the solution to the problem of rediscovering the roots of documentary lay in advancing the technology. Leacock, who had been Flaherty's cameraman on *Louisiana Story*, struggled through the 1950s to create a portable 16mm sync sound outfit based on the widely used Auricon. Parallel to this, in France the brilliant designer Coutant was developing the first custom-built handholdable self-blimped camera. At the same time, battery-driven tape recorders were developing to the point at which they would render professionally acceptable sound and did not require four people to carry them; and film stocks were not only growing in sensitivity, but their tolerance for being forced in development increased also. Thus by 1960 the technology was at hand to break out of the bind created by using feature-film equipment to make documentaries. Leacock was able to ask, for the first time, that the events being filmed remained more important than the requirements of the filmmakers. It was possible, at last, to "observe" without elaborate, previously agreed-upon arrangements, without directions, without lights.

The acceptance of this technology into the mainstream of broadcast television is something many of us will remember vividly. I can recall seeing in the "World in Action" offices in 1963 *Jane*, a film made by Pennebaker in New York the previous year. It had been shot on Ilford and forced to 1,000 ASA, facts that were simply denied by representatives of the manufacturing company and the labs when we asked them to duplicate the work in England. It was an era when cameramen demanded whether you wanted something shot "properly" or in "wobblyscope" and sound recordists audibly queried the acceptability of mumbles. But this happy season soon passed and technicians mastered the new machines. *Vérité* here became one style of shooting among many, but this was not the case in the United States and France.

Those who had pushed for the gear erected around it a philosophy of documentary purity. In America this meant direct cinema. The filmmakers were to keep their contacts with the subject to an absolute minimum; to be as self-effacing as possible; never, but never, to ask anybody to do anything for the camera. And the final films were to adhere as closely as possible to the actual order of events as filmed; takes were long, and jump cuts were a sign of virile truth in the editing; and, almost above all, there was no commentary, no third voice imposing a frame between subjects and audience. Needless to say, interviews were also *verboten*; ironically, as Colin Young points out, it was "about that same time Jean-Luc Godard started using 'interviews' in his fiction." With the fervor of true believers, the direct-cinema group cast scorn and derision on all who made films purporting to be documentaries in any other way but theirs. The grain had been found—"actual material" as mined from life, fresh and vivid before your very eyes. Yet the need for "dramatization," rooted as it was in millennia of storytelling, had not gone away.

It was a pity that because of our shared language we should have taken cognizance of the Americans before we got around to absorbing the French use of the new technology. For there in the work of Chris Marker, and more particularly in that of the anthropologist Jean Rouch, the nature of the new grail was being more directly questioned. In retrospect, it seems to me that the crucial film in all this is *Chronique d'un été*, made by Rouch and Edgar Morin, a sociologist, in the summer of 1960. Perhaps because of their more strict academic backgrounds they were more aware of the intrinsic difficulties of observation than were the Americans. They understood better the effect of the observer on the observed, and obeying their own notions of what "truths" were possible in the filmmaking process, they resolved that honesty demanded they be visible in the final film.

Chronique is partly about 'the strange tribe that lives in Paris," a reaction by Rouch to radical criticism of the anthropologists' role in cultures other than their own. But more than that, it is a film that directly confronts the difficulty of preserving "the actual," even with the new equipment. At the start, Morin and Rouch talk on camera about trying to get "a type of *cinéma vérité*"—the first time, as far as I am aware, the phrase was recorded. The film's climax, like most of its sequences, is manipulated—created by the filmmakers. They have invited all the participants to see a rough cut (this courtesy, by the way, being no part of direct-cinema practice). The reactions to the cut are then filmed, and the coda consists of Morin and Rouch pacing the halls of the Musée de l'Homme discussing vexed questions as to whether it was right to probe one participant's emotional crisis, or whether another's recall of wartime deportation was real or dramatized for the camera. At the door of the museum, Rouch asks Morin what he thinks. He replies: "I think we are in trouble." The film ends.

It is my contention that Morin was right. We have been in trouble ever since. The new technology did not solve the problems of documentary; rather, it pushed them back to basics. The validity of the documentary idea and the difficulties of making documentaries were not in essence to do with reconstruction. The new technology removed that as a problem for the better part of fifteen years. But the technology did not touch the moral and ethical difficulties of the filmmaker. If anything, the ease with which he or she could penetrate other people's lives increased these problems. And it did not tackle the basic need for all messages to be structured in obedience to cultural codes— to tell stories. Substantially, direct cinema and *cinéma vérité* were made and can be evaluated like any other documentaries. They did not create a new code.

For Rouch and Morin the only possible *vérité* was one that included the filmmaker—as if it were the case that the only subject for documentary film was the making of documentary film. Although this is a *reductio ad absurdum*, since film's ability to record events and to bring witness to bear must count for something, nevertheless it is a healthier and more honest absurdity than some others. The notion that, for instance, film crews can be like "flies on the wall," which is very much what *vérité* has come to mean in Britain, is just as much nonsense.

Thus, in various ways in various countries the new technology allowed rhetorics to be created that sustained the idea of the documentary. So it is still the case that documentary, in the words of Arthur Schlesinger, Jr., "seems an honest, weather-beaten word, conveying the feeling that here, at last, there is no nonsense, no faking, only plain facts." The filmmaker is caught by the public acceptance of the notion of documentary, institutionalized in discrete broadcasting departments, separate union agreements, and the rest. The "crisis," if there is one, has to do with this dilemma. Having established that some films contain a greater degree of a particular sort of truth than others, and having done so on pretty tenuous grounds, can any valid basis for such work now be drawn?

In Britain, *vérité* has become simply a question of long handheld takes, actuality sound, and a certain looseness with the rules of continuity cutting. As such it has joined the whole panoply of techniques that preexisted its introduction—commentary, interviews, graphics, reconstruction, and the rest. But it has caused damage to all of these. Filmmakers are now too often sloppy about construction. Unless the form is dictated in terms of a specific time span, the average weekly television documentary frequently leaps from area to area of its subject matter like a startled fawn. The commentary relies on tired and well-worked (it's-a-long-way-from-this-to-this) links to hold the whole together. The need to mold long *vérité* takes is not in my view a prime cause of this incoherence. Rather, the new technology as a whole has meant a revolution in the way any documentary is made. People do not write documentaries as they used to—like features. Research can often now become simply a question of doing the deal to get inside whatever door needs to be got inside. The rhetoric of direct cinema is used to limit the manipulation once thought necessary to make a coherent and dramatic (with the littlest possible "d") statement. The result is that structure goes out the window and much work is confused and ill thought out. When a documentarist of, say, David Attenborough's experience and standing can make a straightforward look at the London Zoo a shambles, some old-fashioned standards have clearly been lost. And the wonders of *vérité* have offered little to compensate for this loss of rigor.

Direct cinema has, at its best, never fallen into this trap. Wiseman's *Hospital*, for instance, reveals that the standards of storytelling have not changed. The film is structured around sequences of normal, emotionally uncharged activities crosscut with sequences of distress, whereby the former become shorter and the latter longer and more distressful as the film progresses. It is all about as loose and untouched by human film editor as the average Hitchcock. It takes place within a clearly defined cultural frame. It starts with hospital personnel starting an operation. It finishes with them finishing an operation—the patient is dead. And its coda is an old man being turned away, walking down a corridor like a sunsetless Chaplin.

In British terms, when *vérité* is being used more or less (actually, normally less) as the direct cinema intended it to be, as in Tim King's *Casualty* in the "Hospital" series or in Angela Pope's *Best Days?*, there is a similar attention to structure. *Best Days?* starts with assembly and finishes with the school cleaners. *Casualty* obeys a strict time pattern constantly reinforced in shots and commentary. But much other work lacks the rigor of the great documentary tradition because filmmakers have allowed themselves to be duped by the seeming randomness of much direct cinema.

In films that mix techniques, and that is the vast majority, there is an even greater hazard to be faced in the use of bits of *vérité*. Take, for instance (although many more examples are readily available), James Cameron's report on Israel or the "Inside Story" on the British troops in Belize. It is the excuse, if you will, of the easily captured episode that either loosens or destroys the overall shape of the film. In "Inside Story," a soldier is briefly interviewed on the nonavailability of basic materials and is then observed failing to find in the general store the putty he needs. Such a sequence, coming as it does in the midst of a clever commentary—and in a film that is leaping around Belize from base to base, activity to activity—only adds to the hodgepodge. Happenstance is used to cover what could otherwise be a real element in the story. The army's difficulties with material, with provisions, with entertainment, are all treated with different techniques, which are seemingly more-or-less randomly linked. Cameron uses the accident of an Oriental women's group's bus breaking down to say all he has to say about the position of Oriental Jews in Israel. Around such happenstance too many current documentaries fall apart, literally, at the seams.

Happenstance remains a problem even when *vérité* is being used more consistently in a film. *Vérité* in essence invites us, the audience, to consider material as evidence. The "fly on the wall" rhetoric increases this. At its most extreme, it's the tape released by the police for *The Case of Yolande McShane*. (Although John Willis used mixed techniques and a well-constructed form, it is the video element that here concerns us primarily.) The tape, which was obtained by a video camera literally embedded flylike in the wall, was presented both in court and on television as evidence. But it was therefore quite clearly evidence of just one particular event, a meeting between Mrs. McShane and her mother. In this it differed from most *vérité* shooting, which claims to stand not only as specifics but also as examples of general cases. This is true of *Best Days?* and *Casualty*, and as a result the impression that we are spending just one day in the school (or indeed are actually at all times in the school) or the impression that events are happening simultaneously because of crosscutting between different areas in the ward renders the material that much more suspect. Happenstance starts to play too large a part. The fly begins to acquire editorial skills.

Obviously this would be all right if the rhetoric surrounding such programs were different, but it isn't. And it's the rhetoric as often as not that brings down the wrath of participants and others, not the program material itself. If you introduce something as "a fly-on-the-wall view" of a subject, and *Best Days?* was so introduced by David Dimbleby, then even if you are Caesar's wife in terms of obtaining the material, you are still likely to be in trouble.

I do not want to give the impression that all these problems are simply the result of *vérité*. Most have been caused, or at least exacerbated, by the introduction of lightweight equipment, but some have nothing to do with it. Take, for instance, what might be called hidden reconstruction, which is far too common in investigative and general work. Although whole programs or sequences within programs are now commonly identified as being reconstructions, this does not apply to the single shot (as when Mrs. McShane's brother-in-law is seen entering a police station clutching a letter that he actually, one gathers from the commentary, clutched on some previous occasion). Nor does it prevent more general ambiguities, as when, in the first "South African Experience," the school board is shown today, sitting discussing God knows what, while in the commentary Anthony Thomas explains what they, the very same men, had discussed and decided many years before.

It is possible to avoid many of these problems altogether and simply take testimony, as in *Jimmy*. At least we immediately know where we are. There is no pretense that the event would have existed were it not for the camera. This leaves us, as audience, with the problem of evaluating the testimony we are given. Did Jimmy go "Paki-bashing"? At that point in the interview it becomes difficult to know whether Jimmy's admission is true or bravado. The audience becomes jury, but it can, however partially, also assess Michael Whyte's performance as a cross-examiner. With *vérité* this all becomes more vexed.

I watch the unfolding educational disaster of the comprehensive school in *Best Days?* and I am utterly unprepared for the sudden conversation with the university applicants. Nothing in the film up to that point suggests that in such an atmosphere any child can be prepared for university. I begin to assume that the fly is a fully paid up member of the Headmasters' Conference. It could be argued that this is simply because the film has failed to convince as evidence. But even when that claim can be better made, as say, with *Decisions: Steel*, the waterfront is still quite clearly not fully covered. Yet it is significant that the dispute that followed that transmission was about actual managerial processes, not about whether the film had recorded those processes in a fraudulent or incomplete way. Roger Graef has the advantage of an expanded time slot and is prepared to bore the pants off us to make sure we know what goes on, yet he will not acknowledge the limitations of treating observation as fact. Just because he frequently hides under the table or out in the corridor while shooting does not mean he is not there.

On all these grounds it becomes easiest to cope with personalized statements, like James Cameron's on Israel or Anthony Thomas's in "The South African Experience." This willingness to reveal where one is coming from was the distinguishing mark of much of Robert Vas's work. It can be seen too in the best work of journalists like Michael Cockerell and Tom Mangold. And if one can add—as Adrian Cowell did with his careful description of how *Opium Warlords* was actually shot—a reminder of some sort of the filmmaking process, so much the better.

The basic inheritance of *vérité* shooting is that instead of acknowledging the actual processes of filmmaking (as in the *cinéma vérité* model) and the implicit selection and editorializing that filming implies at every stage, elaborate claims are made by filmmakers to take upon themselves the emotional capacity and the brain of the members of the order *Diptera*.

Legitimatization of material does not depend on clearly marking programs as documentary. It does not depend, in fact, on any easy solutions. The old techniques are as valuable as the new if a proper basis for their use can be established. There is no particular virtue in adopting the rhetoric of the strictest proponents of direct cinema. They still manipulate and editorialize. There is no guarantee of some species of realer truth in jump cutting or going to black. (But one thing they did understand: the method, whether as pure as man can make it or as debased as television often requires it, is not suited to all subjects— it needs concreteness and, preferably, almost Greek unities of time and space; it cannot cope too well with grand abstractions.) Equally, there are no advantages in coming clean about provenance or reconstructions. All these are technological or stylistic devices. Of themselves they are neither good nor bad, although they can irritate or confuse. The real issue remains outside technological solutions. It has to do, as it has from the beginning, not with questions of form but rather with issues of purpose.

Narrativity is but one aspect of the need to conform to deep-seated cultural norms. Stories must be told, but about what? Dana's adage about news applies equally well to documentary. Dogs biting men might seem as appropriate, at first sight, to the documentary filmmaker as men biting dogs. But in effect, the demands of narrativity and the concomitant expectations of the audience turn all dog bites around. Because of the nature of television, to film a dog biting a man makes it just as deviant an event when screened as man biting dog.

The proof of this can be found in ethnographic work. At its best, at its most observationally pure, only an anthropologist could love it. The uncut distant observation of quotidian activity or special ritual requires professional training on the part of the audience. For a general, unspecialized group it is repetitive, boring, and incomprehensible. And anyway, most anthropologists are as given to structuring their work according to narrative norms of their own societies as the rest of us. The result is that film has never yielded its promise as an anthropological tool, and it never will. If anything, they are even more hypersensitive about happenstance, selection, lens, and so on. Show them an interminable take of a man in long shot hoeing, and they will complain about the degree of manipulation involved in starting and stopping the camera![1]

So it is that "Disappearing World," apart from looking like very good films to the rest of us, can also win approval from the Royal Anthropological Society. They cannot create an alternative code, so they might as well use the one we all obey. Ethnographic concerns inform many films made about our own society, but few are as rigorous as Richard Broad's undeservedly unremarked film *The Shoot*, about an English gamekeeper's year. And here, as usual, its value as evidence was vitiated by its excellence as film. An exquisite shot of the landscape into which the gamekeeper hero exquisitely places himself, followed by a matched cut to a close-up of the trap he is inspecting, speaks too clearly of a skilled and mannered director at his most elegant. But ethnographic it isn't. Or rather, it is as ethnographic as the average Millais. In other words, hanging around looking at things yields rushes. Molding the rushes into films renders the material suspect as evidence and turns all behavior, most of which is normally unfilmed, into deviant behavior if only by reason of the filming.

Most documentaries have little overt ethnographic purpose. Even the currently fashionable documentary series, concentrating as they do on the world of work, deal in some measure with deviancy. It is the pilot who has never landed on the aircraft carrier before (*The Squadrons Are Coming* in the "Sailor" series), the doctors who do not know what they are doing (*Casualty* in the "Hospital" series), that adds the *frisson* we expect from the screen. And as for the one-offs, it is *60 Seconds of Hatred*, the lifeboat man who did not get on the boat, the juvenile delinquent, the homeless. It is man bites dog—in a word, deviancy.

It is probably fair to suggest that more than Dennis Potter and Philip Purser are increasingly disturbed by and distrustful of this seemingly endless parade of the halt and the blind, the deranged and the dispossessed, on our screens. The justification for this work depends on twin pillars. One is that the film contains a more-or-less truthful account of the subject (which, as I have indicated above, is open to not a few questions). The other is contained in a hodgepodge of ideas involving notions of the public's right to know, the rhetoric of the fourth estate, etc., which together add up to a hallowed element in the liberal philosophy of the state. It should, however, not be forgotten that this corpus of ideas emerged in the very different circumstances of two centuries ago and related to the very different situation of the media then.

Of course, there is no difficulty about the public's right to know, however much more honored in the breach than the observance it might often seem to be. But essentially, it is not (and never has been) the public's right to know that is at issue. It is rather which members of the public have the right to tell— to publish. Liebling once remarked, "Anybody in the ten-million-dollar category is free to buy or found a paper in a great city like New York or Chicago, and anybody with around a million (plus a lot of sporting blood) is free to try it in a place of mediocre size like Worcester, Mass." This is just as true of broadcasting; truer, in fact, because of the government's regulation of the airwaves. The limits on publication rights require considerable circumspection on the part of broadcasters. The care needed becomes all the more important. It certainly cannot be discharged by relying on half-understood nineteenth-century platitudes when the going gets tough. And it becomes even more tricky as long as the documentarist and the broadcasting executive view deviancy of all kinds as instant subject matter.

It is the case that the majority of documentaries deal with social issues and normally concentrate on people in society who are unable to fend for themselves. This inability clearly extends to their dealing with the broadcasters. Broadcasters therefore owe a duty of care to those without whose cooperation they could not work. Too often that care is, in my view, not being properly discharged. Take *Goodbye, Longfellow Road*. The opening with the bailiffs was a salutary demonstration of the casual brutality of officialdom. The investigation of the Housing Trusts and their perhaps improper relations with some local government officials was equally justifiable in simple terms of the public's right to know. But what about the film's heart? What is the moral position of a crew stalking a woman day after day as she searches for a roof and eventually filming her being rushed to the hospital, diseased by her living conditions? To suggest that they intervene (more than their presence already does) reminds one of Buñuel. When Viridiana stops her car so that she can untie an exhausted dog from the axle of a cart, behind her back as she works, and unseen by her, another equally exhausted dog is being pulled by another cart in the opposite direction. It is not the function of film crews to act as an entirely haphazard and arbitrary long stop to the social support systems. Yet, equally, their use of others' experience to create spectacle, however edifying, does not (or certainly should not, in common human terms) leave them untouched.

Edifying is the crucial word here. For the public's right to know implies an assumption about the nature of the audience response. This seems to suggest that if the audience is shown a situation, then public awareness will move to correct it in some way. Even if this were demonstrably the case, which it demonstrably is not, it would still be difficult to justify it in terms of television's mass audience. And the superficiality of much documentary work, encouraged by the *vérité* style, makes it difficult to see how the information given could achieve opinion-changing effects.

Most films lack almost any meaningful analysis of cause. This is a part of the great British documentary tradition, and it has been there from the very start. Of *Drifters* a particularly perceptive contemporary critic wrote: "Remember the contempt Grierson actually had for the marketing of the fish, the regret he seemed to express that the fish, the fruit of the glorious adventure, was bought and sold for money. . . . Grierson dealt with actual industry or occupation but ran away from its social meaning." It can be said that similar inhibitions seem to be built into the agenda for most social documentaries. This seems to be more true of domestic than foreign subjects ("Hong Kong Beat" being a dishonorable exception). Thus Anthony Thomas's examination of Sandra's case in the first "South African Experience" offers a far more coherent attempt to explain the society in which the film is set than do most British counterparts— *Jimmy*, for example. But even Thomas, admittedly under considerable and quite improper pressure from certain quarters, becomes far less clear in his economic analysis of British interests in South Africa in the last of the series.

It is in this sense that films are superficial. The unwillingness to tackle cause certainly contributes to the acceptability of many seemingly contentious social issues as subject matter. The worst that can happen to the system is that the audience will dip into its pocket and donate to shelters for the homeless. (And it is more interesting to note that *Cathy Come Home* was committed rather than that it was a drama documentary.) So I am denying that the television audience's right to know is an automatic justification for the pursuit of social deviancy as subject matter. For after all, is it the U.K. transmission of World in Action's *Year of the Torturer* that has effect, or is it special screenings for the European Council of Ministers?

This is perhaps more clearly seen when one turns from victim documentaries (like *Goodbye, Longfellow Road*) to other aspects of deviancy juicier by far than homelessness. Take the murderers. A public right to know was the implicit justification of *60 Seconds of Hatred*. It was made explicit by the police chief at the end of *The Case of Yolande McShane*. In these programs it is difficult to see what is edifying, or even how public opinion affects the issues one way or the other.

The policeman argued that the McShane case was an example of hidden crime and that showing it would deter. But I would have thought there was an equal chance many more of us might have gotten the idea that bumping off a wealthy senile relative was a piece of cake. It is no longer possible for broadcasters to hide in ignorance of the case on violence, relying on ill-thought-out liberal attitudes on the effects of television. There is a case (and many think it now overwhelming) that for the badly socialized all classes of television messages can be misused—if not as models then more possibly as triggers.

The fact that both these films (thundering good tales, very well told) were good examples of craft deepens the problem. The music sequences in *60 Seconds of Hatred* might well have offered clues as to the murderer's mental attitude. But to do so in such an impressionistic way must move the film from edifying to prurient. And why was so much of the police tape used in *The Case of Yolande McShane?* Was the nuns' search of the mother necessary to the police officers' and the program-makers' justification? Or was it not, rather, simply degrading to the old woman? And would the facts of Mrs. McShane's wartime illegitimate baby. or even her support of Mosley in the period before that, have been admissible evidence in a court of law? (And even if they were, why should they be repeated in a story of attempted matricide?) That the police have mastered video technology should be generally known. But the film was not, in truth, really about that.

In these programs we are getting close to the *News of the World*—only here I see nobody making their apologies and leaving. We are smack in the middle of the *News of the World* with *Chance of a Lifetime—Lifeboat.* Here in long shot, with radio mikes (carefully?) hidden, the man who alone survived the storm of forty years before meets and talks to the man who decided not to go. It was the first time they had spoken to each other since that night. In a previous interview in the film, one of them was asked who was to make the first move. I would not presume to suggest which of them it ought to have been. But of one thing I am absolutely certain—it should not have been YTV, a wholly owned subsidiary of Trident Television. Where in this rank invasion of privacy can be found any vestige of a public right to know?

It is significant that the people one worries for, the people whose hopelessness or guilt is paraded before us, are all less able to defend themselves than those, more powerful, whose rights are more quickly protected. When "The London Programme" has audio tapes of a senior police officer's wife talking to the wife of his chief suspect in quite improper terms, suddenly the IBA is very concerned about the former's privacy. But for Mrs. McShane's mother, Jimmy, the Cornish seamen, there seems to be nae bother.

It would be as well if we started to distinguish between an individual's public and private personae, a feat not unimaginable in English law. People discharging official functions (as in all Roger Graef's work) have a public persona when they are so acting. Other behavior, whether deviant or not, in such people attaches to their private persona. Others might well have almost no public persona except, say, when they are progressing through public places.

If this were made clear, then the filmmakers would better know where they are. The public persona would be susceptible to coverage that could then be easily justified in terms of the public's right to know. In fact, in the interest of freedom of information the public persona should be a lot more susceptible to such coverage than it often is now. But the private persona should attract a clear, limiting, and binding duty of care from the filmmaker.

I have tried to make the following points: documentary has so much in common with fiction that stressing its differences is not only difficult but cannot legitimatize it. The impact of the *vérité* style has resulted in a lessening of the rigor with which films are put together; it has increased the ad hoc element in filming. The constant examination of social problems in a highly personalized and intrusive way (as made possible by the *vérité* style) cannot be justified by the public's right to know. There should be a distinction between public and private personae; and when dealing with the latter, filmmakers should have an absolute duty of care to protect the subject, even, if necessary, from themselves. The release form may be sufficient in law at present, but it will not do for ethics. Above all, perhaps one should stress that filmmakers in documentary are the victims of a rhetoric they have but inherited, but which both on and off the screen they are not at sufficient pains to disown. In this light, the dispute about drama documentaries should be seen for what it is—a dispute about how material is presented, not about what the material presents. For the fact that somewhere on Iona Isle lies buried Macbeth would have become important to *Macbeth* only if the Globe management were to have claimed that all the events the audience was to witness were based on an eyewitness account smuggled out of the castle on bits of parchment by the old man Ross meets in Act 2 Scene 4.

And it is this problem of presentation in documentaries generally that raises most of these issues. Our ability to reason out codes of practice that would allow us properly to discharge a sophisticated and workable notion of documentary in this society is constantly befouled by our unwillingness to tackle the basic issue. Documentaries are constructed artifacts. We know that when we look at the titles of "Hong Kong Beat" or "Sailor." We know it when we come to heap praise or blame on those who make them. But for all other purposes we seem as able as ever to ignore it. To continue to do so "would not be a good plan."

Note

1. This occurred at a recent meeting in Australia of anthropologists, who had watched such a scene in a Rouch film.

Television Documentary Usage

Dai Vaughan

The following excerpts are taken from chapters 3 and 4 of Dai Vaughan's monograph Television Documentary Usage, *published by the British Film Institute in 1976. Vaughan has written extensively on film theory and as an editor has worked on documentaries since the early 1960s, often with Roger Graef. He has also published general criticism, poetry, and fiction.*

I have reprinted chapter 3, "The Reign of Mannerism," in full but have had to limit my extracts from chapter 4, "Vérité," because of shortage of space. In "Vérité," Vaughan begins by discussing the development of the idea of documentary as art and the impact of vérité *techniques on mannerism. He then briefly touches on reflexivity, which is the subject of one of Jay Ruby's articles in this book, mentions the paradocumentary style of "Days of Hope," and pinpoints the different paths taken by French and American* vérité *pioneers.*

Just prior to the second extract Vaughan discusses metareality and the way a photographic image functions not only as icon but also as index. He argues that there is a relationship of causality as well as of resemblance. This leads to a discussion of the differences between the fiction film and documentary, with Vaughan suggesting that "whereas the relation of image to metareality in the fiction film is that of signifier to signified, in documentary it is also—at least in the intention of the maker, though perhaps not necessarily in the perception of the viewer—that of referent to referend."

The Reign of Mannerism

The Early Seventies

Having suggested the way in which, over the span of the 1960s, television was crystallizing a definition of its role in relation to society and hence in relation to film, we must now consider the effects of this definition on documentary usage.

Three years ago, in an unpublished article, I wrote the following paragraphs:

It can scarcely be disputed that television is becalmed in a mannerist phase. Every editor knows exactly where he is expected to cut; and the convention grows that the first cutting point is the best one: for to allow such a point to pass without cutting may be interpreted as laxness. This principle applies not only to action footage but even to talking heads. The interviewee must not be seen to hesitate, grope for words, or add qualifying clauses that would disrupt the crisp pacing of the program. Commentary, which six years ago was considered something of an anachronism, has returned to favor and is being used, not simply to clarify points in the narrative that would not reveal their full significance without it, but to supply wall-to-wall reassurance for the audience, who are held, despite the example of the commercials, to find film language too demanding. The doctrine of "signposting," initially seen as an irreproachable attempt to point up the architecture of a film and to minimize confusion, has now swollen into a grotesque insistence that everything should be explained. The viewer must be told what a talking head is about to say, for fear he may presume to draw his own inferences from what is said.

Clearly the reign of mannerism offers benefits to financiers, since it is a mode of prefabricated-unit construction whose assembly requires little skill; but I do not think I am being unduly paranoid in seeing a correlation between the administrative authoritarianism of a given broadcasting organization and the degree to which it demands procedures that drain the images to alphabetical abstraction and impose interpretations of institutional uniformity. It is as if some principle of hegemony were at issue.

Such arguments are sometimes dismissed as outrageously purist—even elitist—by those who claim that television, as a popular medium, has no right to make unreasonable demands on the patience or intelligence of its viewers, and that to consider film language without reference to its intended public is misguided, since, for example, the requirements of a film made for educational or research purposes are totally different from those of a program designed for entertainment. But it seems to me that a serious element of bad faith inheres in the desire to fix a "target audience" for our films, since this involves an attempt to predict—which rapidly degenerates into an attempt to determine—the reactions of others. It may be insisted that some such movement is performed whenever we try to judge whether a film "works," or when we appeal to our friends for their comments. But in judging whether a film works we are merely trying to estrange ourselves from it sufficiently to gauge what our response to it, as a structure independent of our intentions, would be. The responses of our friends, beyond helping us to achieve this estrangement—for which purpose their mere presence, without comment, is sometimes enough—and beyond answering certain prosaic questions of comprehensibility, can really tell us little. In a field where all the data are subjective, efforts at sampling are efforts to guard against the unexpected: against the discovery of unsignposted pathways through the labyrinth.

The evil of mannerism lies precisely in its appeal to predictability. Reliance on cliché creates patterns of expectation within which the viewer feels cheated if the clichés are not respected. It is a circular system in which we can say only what the viewer expects to hear, since he is trapped in our assumptions as to how he expects it to be said. In such a pass, it is difficult for filmmakers to distinguish between genuine expressive failure and mere failure to conform to dead conventions. Our only alternatives are to swim with the tide or to risk absurdity. But we must resist making assumptions about our audiences: not for fear they may prove erroneous, but for fear they may prove correct. A film should select its own target audience: those people who will accord it a positive response. To try and predetermine this audience is to seek to preempt the freedom of the viewer. The distinction between education and entertainment masks a principle of intellectual divide-and-rule that is aesthetically unsound and morally disreputable.

In Quest of Prose

I had planned to integrate the above paragraphs directly into this study; but on rereading them, I recognize that they no longer entirely do justice to the situation. However, simply to translate them into the past tense would be to imply that mannerism had run its course—which it has not. What is crucial is the connection established between the commercial attitude toward the viewer—the denial of his creativity entailed in seeing him as a quotient, as one unit of a mass—and the impoverishment of film usage. When we say that the executive producer is not empowered to take risks, we mean by "risks" departures from a set of filmic norms that, like the Newspeak dictionary, are becoming more circumscribed and rigid with every year that passes. If the active and structuring element in the viewer's response is to be negated, then our communication must be made to resemble as closely as possible that form that most thoroughly eliminates ambiguity: verbal prose poised for its change of state into mathematics.

What was not sufficiently clear, however, was that this trend toward prose consisted not simply in the imposition of a heavy weight of verbiage upon the picture, but in an attempt to rob even filmic signs of their "motivation" by subordinating them to anterior needs of structure. Film may be said to exhibit a dual nature: as discourse and as metareality. The strategy of television as an institution has been to push the emphasis, in documentary, toward film-as-discourse.

A detailed analysis of the linguistic modes adopted by television would be rewarding. Some hints may be offered. If we switch on our sets and see a man addressing us directly, we know he is a narrator or presenter. If his gaze is directed slightly off-camera, we know he is an interviewee, a talking head. If he is turned away from us by an angle of more than about 15°, he is a part of an action sequence. It is clear that there is a hierarchy of authority implicit in this code. The talking head is permitted to gaze into the sacred sector only through the priestlike intercession of the interviewer; if he speaks directly to the camera, he will create an impression of insolence. Thus, the function of a presenter introducing a documentary—or interpolated within it—is to diminish the authority of the people filmed and to posit the film itself, in contrast to the profilmic reality, as the object of scrutiny: so that what we are aware of watching is not the filmed event but the televised film (of the event). A similar result—an emphasis on the double mediation between ourselves and the reality— is achieved by the use of fades and dissolves and by the superimposition of lettering—traditionally title and credits but, increasingly, all manner of miscellaneous information—upon the image.

Another subtle way in which the reality of what we are seeing may be degraded is through the customary couching of commentary in the present tense. This does not, as is sometimes averred, make for immediacy. It has, rather, two complementary possibilities: one, dependent on a grammatical confusion between the historic present and the present continuous (so that "X happens" means not only "X is happening" but also "X always happens"), is to render abstract the "truth" of the image by imparting to it the status of an eternal verity, outside time; the other is, by eliding the "present" of the event's occurrence with the present of our viewing of the film (so that the commentary seems to describe the film rather than the occurrence), to create a sense of redundancy that usually acts to the disadvantage of the visuals. Where commentary in the past tense acknowledges the historicity of the film as medium, allowing us to construe on it the filmed events, commentary in the present tense implies the film's transparency in its elision of timescales while, in its redundancy, sapping its vigor.

Even the talking head—which, as we have observed, is *vérité* in a sense almost too unavoidable to be interesting—is not immune from the use of techniques that will rob it of its proper significance. Indeed it may, by virtue of its verbal nature, provide a particularly clear example. First of all, the exclusion of hesitancies and qualifications, noted above, diminishes the personality of the speaker in favor of the abstract content of his words. These will then be organized into a structure which was not the structure of his discourse: and the steps of his argument will be used to lead not to his own conclusion, but to a conclusion with which he may not even agree. Early in my career I was told, "You'll have to put this man in, to ensure a fair balance of opinion. If you don't like what he says, you can always cut to a wall being knocked down." What we see here, both with the talking head and with the wall, is their reduction toward the symbolic through submission to a syntax not of their own generation.

It is difficult to know how much of film grammar is culturally acquired and how much represents simply the most (or even the only) reasonable construction a viewer may place on the disposition of sounds and images. I was recently shown a rough cut of a film in which someone saying "The man's a fascist" led directly into a talking head of a government minister. When I commented that this seemed a disagreeably snide way of suggesting that the minister was a fascist, the director replied that he had not noticed, still less intended, this implication. The implication could, nonetheless, be construed on the cut, though my perception of it may be a measure of the degree to which I am schooled in the mannerist idiom. This provides, I think, a sharp illustration of the way in which the use of wide-ranging juxtaposition, and our reliance on such juxtaposition being "picked up" by the viewer, may degenerate into a crude grammar for the articulation of stock responses.

Uniformity

A further way in which the film-as-metareality may be weakened is by the superimposition of levels of discourse quite irrelevant to it. This effect is characteristic of the documentary series, whose episodes are frequently required to exhibit a surface similarity more appropriate to a chain of fast-food restaurants. Thus, in "The World at War"—a series of compilation films varying much in mood and character—the use throughout of the same commentator and music (both in themselves excellent) and the association of this music with a standardized opening title sequence, conspire to suggest that the Second World War had been staged for the benefit of Thames Television.

Another example is offered by the BBC's "The Explorers," a series of documentary dramatizations. Each of these films begins—after a title sequence of monumental tediousness in which it seems to be implied that the actors were cast for their resemblance to paintings of the characters they portrayed, though the paintings are obviously portraits of the actors—with an introduction spoken by David Attenborough in the map room of the Royal Geographical Society, Mr. Attenborough's voice then persisting into the films as narration. Some of the episodes—the more buccaneering ones—do not suffer greatly as a result of this treatment; but others do. A particularly unfortunate victim is David Cobham's *Amundsen*. Here the central character, as written, is a man who entered Arctic exploration out of childhood masochism, who was motivated in the South Pole venture mainly by financial considerations yet who, having tried to compensate for his own errors of judgment by taking unforgivable risks with the lives of his companions, was prepared to demand their obedience in the name of military discipline. This interpretation is sustained by the leading actor in a portrayal of muted lunacy. Yet the harsh outlines are scarcely perceptible beneath the genial enthusiasm of Mr. Attenborough and the map room's stolid furniture of achievement.

If executives genuinely do not understand this criticism, it is because it is the series, rather than its constituents, that presents itself first to their attention (in the form, "Let's do a series on such-and-such"). The films are merely the matter that fleshes out the executives' creativity—otherwise, the merchandise. After all, it is cynically remarked that the American stations will buy anything so long as there are twenty-six of it.

Professionalism

But, in most of the instances so far considered, the discourse to which metareality is subordinated may at least be assumed to possess its own significance and integrity. The decline into mannerism is completed at the point where the imposed syntax, usually in the form of rhythmic structures governing our expectations, exerts so strong a pull as to become itself virtually the object of scrutiny at the expense of the filmic constituents. One film I cut contained a shot of a stripper in a workingmen's club, which I had held for about twenty seconds. I was content to watch the lady undress for a while; but the director said, "That shot isn't doing any work. We must find some voice-over to lay against it." It is perfectly true that "signposting" and the imposition of systems of expectation extrinsic to the material establish common ground on which filmmaker and viewer may meet, confident of each other's purposes; but when the point is reached where a shot of a stripper at the climax of her act is considered incapable of holding the attention of at least 50 percent of the audience, then documentary has surely arrived at a very strange condition. Film is not a pure, symbolic sign system. To articulate it as if it were—as if its grammar were anterior to its imagery, rather than our attribution of sense calling forth the grammar in a gestalt—is to reduce it to such penurious abstraction that the satisfying of prior expectations is all it can do.

It is conceivable that what I have unkindly called the "jazzy" style of the late sixties, with its virtuoso concentration on surface texture and effect, did much to alert middle management to the possibility of assessing films by superficial criteria. The technique—a sort of metronomic sensitivity—is easily mastered. Its appeal to the executive lies in the fact that it not only offers him a ready-made wisdom by which to judge programs whose individual aims and difficulties he may be too busy to consider in due detail, but also, in a self-fulfilling way, satisfies his imposture of knowing what the public wants. What is more disheartening is to recognize that the potential for this development lay in the very qualities that made the documentaries of the early sixties so exciting to work on. The ease with which poetry could be conjured out of juxtaposition, the element of "inspiration to order," appeared to guarantee an endless fund of imaginative vitality while in fact facilitating the subordination of material to extrinsic structures which were to become more inflexible as schedules shrank. Whereas, in the early sixties, a schedule of ten to twelve weeks was considered acceptable for a half-hour documentary, nowadays a standard series (such as "Horizon") will think itself lucky to get more than five weeks for an hour. But, as a fellow editor remarked to me recently: "In those days we were developing the conventions. Now we merely apply them."

It is the technician's pride in his workmanship that leads him to tolerate, and hence perpetuate, this condition. His unwillingness to admit defeat deters him from complaining at the progressive reduction of schedules. He will show that he can do a good job regardless of the difficulties (for if he does not, someone else will). But it can only be done at the expense of originality. There is no time to ask ourselves whether there may not be other ways in which the material could be presented—potentialities to be revealed which our work routines inhibit us from seeing. Haste necessitates the adoption of rules of thumb for calculating the viewer's response, and this in turn requires the adoption of methods to which such calculation is appropriate. Thus again we see how commercial considerations—pared budgets resulting in shorter schedules—lead to the perception of film itself as commerce. This process is mediated through the motives the organization induces in its executives (the need to validate untenable assumptions) and in its technicians (the need to produce work that will be judged acceptable on the basis of these assumptions). It is really not good enough for me to say that we employ the commercial and authoritarian models of communication only as a shorthand, since shorthand is all we have time for. What has happened is that we have adopted toward our own work a mode of sensitivity born of the need of others to pass snap judgment on it. Professionalism is the technician's bad faith.

The Reaction

Mannerism consists in the attempt by film to approximate to the condition of verbal prose. But verbal prose, when addressed by those in authority to those without, is suspect. It is the medium in which lies are told and orders given.

Toward the turn of the decade, a good many technicians became dissatisfied with mannerism and all it stood for. This was in large measure the result of their experience in watching rushes shot on the new, lightweight synchronous equipment. This equipment, because of its unobtrusiveness, could record unrehearsed events without interruption and present them in such a fashion that the time scale of these events, requiring no reconstruction from fragmented elements, was preserved intact. Yet this experience could be preserved for the viewing public only by the abandonment of many traditional documentary usages—specifically, in this context, those of mannerism, with whatever authoritarian assumptions they might conceal. To end with an extract from the same article I quoted at the start of this section:

> The crucial distinction is between the structuring of material in direct response to our perception of its human significance and its structuring to meet a preconception of the responses of others (these responses being perforce allocated by the nature of our consequent methods to the educational, entertainment, or other spheres). Ultimately it is a question of rhythm: of presenting the material in a way that will encourage the viewer to grant it the same manner of attention, detached yet inquisitive, as we ourselves pay to rushes in the viewing theater. What is required is an editing style that will invite a rhythmic response founded not on the rate of satisfaction of prior expectations but on the interest engaged by the shots—a style in which rhythm will be perceived as legitimating the action simply because the action itself will be the prime component of the rhythm. In this way, perhaps, we may succeed in extending to our subjects an existential courtesy matching that which we will extend to our viewers in declining to preempt their interpretations. The editor, having been brought up to understand that less is more, is beginning to complain that more is not enough.

Vérité

Let us say we allow that metareality and referend might be magically assimilated—an assimilation that would, I suppose, render the medium truly transparent—we nonetheless strike problems as soon as we stray from our primitive example. A brick wall, after all, is not much influenced in its behavior by the presence of the camera; and neither, in the old dispensation, would it have required rehearsal: but now that our technology allows the viewer to suppose that the profilmic event (or referend) of what he is seeing is, however intimate or complex it may be, an unrehearsed action, we are faced with the problem of whether or not this action (assuming his supposition to be correct) is sufficiently similar to . . . to what? If we answer, "To what usually happens," we are re-admitting, by the back door, the criterion of typical and general truth.

To enable us to discuss this problem I believe we require a new concept: the "putative event." The putative event is the profilmic event as it would have occurred had the camera and crew not been present. It is, needless to say, a logical absurdity, since it postulates a nonexistent world in which no comparable event might have occurred at all—or, even if it had, there would be no way the degree of its similarity to what did occur could be assessed. In practice, however, there is a gradient of types of event, from the brick wall at one end to the most intimate or clandestine of human interactions at the other, where we may guess at the degree (if not always the manner) of the camera's probable interference, either in prospect or retrospect; and our putative events therefore occupy a vector divergent from this. Thus, the putative event may prove, like the square root of minus one, a concept useful though imaginary.

The profilmic event is known to the filmmakers; the diegesis is the creation of the viewer; and the putative event is not an object of consciousness at all but only a point of reference. The problem of the relation between film and reality may now be approached in two discrete steps: the relation of diegesis to profilmic event (i.e., is what we think we're seeing what really happened?) and the relation of profilmic to putative event (i.e., how much did filming affect it?).

Traditional fiction film is not concerned with the profilmic event, which it negates in the generation of a diegesis from its elements. Here we may assert a true identity between profilmic and putative events—both effaced behind the diegesis—since the activity before the camera existed only to be filmed. Some recent filmmakers, notably Godard, have sought to rupture the naturalism of the diegesis by focusing attention back on the profilmic event (for example, by including three takes of a line spoken by Anna Karina in one shot). But this, since anterior reality is irrelevant to the fiction, risks opening up the gap between the profilmic and the putative, for if a fresh diegesis does not simply reconstitute itself to accommodate the profilmic intrusion, we may begin to ask whether what we are seeing is a filmed event or a *filmed* filmed event, thus slithering into an infinite regression. I raise this question only in order to demonstrate that the making manifest of the filmmakers' activity does not necessarily perform the same function in fiction film as in documentary, since their activities are of a different order.

In traditional documentary, the profilmic event is only partially effaced (effaced only insofar as it is rehearsed or reconstructed) behind a diegesis that is held to mirror a putative event conceived as general or typical—its generality being, in fact, a measure of its distance from the profilmic, since in no other sense than the general can an event be considered putative behind a reconstruction. The impurity of all this has never been in serious doubt; but attempts to narrow the gap between the profilmic and the putative have nonetheless been unceasing and have consisted in the retention of as many common elements—locations, props, personnel, lines of dialogue used verbatim—as possible, whose indexal reference is seen as grounding the diegesis in a reality.[1] Thus, to designate a film "documentary" lies within the jurisdiction of the viewer, and within that of the filmmaker only insofar as he presumes on it, since it implies a construction of the diegesis as indexally related to the profilmic event and this, in turn, as "locating" a putative reality beyond it. We perceive *Western Approaches* as documentary and *Bicycle Thieves* as fiction to the extent that we perceive them as making or not making appeal to a reality anterior to the camera's intervention (the reality we assign to the ships in the former being consequently different in essence from that which we assign to the streets in the latter), and this, as we have seen, is likely to be the extent to which we read its truth as general to the situation or particular to the characters portrayed.

By and large, then, traditional documentary has held the putative at arm's length from the profilmic by a generalism calculated to protect the profilmic from too close a questioning. But there have always been limiting cases, such as Grierson's *Drifters*, whose profilmic elements have seemed sufficiently rudimentary, public, or repetitive to be considered unproblematic, and at the same time have seemed to offer, by virtue of these same qualities, legitimate ground for general inference; and these cases have frequently been seized on as exemplary. Indeed, we may now perhaps rephrase our description of the documentary impulse as: a movement toward mystical union between putative and profilmic events and between profilmic event and diegesis—unions that, though they may be approached, may never be consummated. It is a quest for a medium wholly transparent to the world yet still able to function as discourse.

However, the development of the new equipment, encouraging us to assign indexal significance to film images in a far less coarse fashion, has done more than render obsolete the criterion of general truth that formerly seemed almost definitive of the documentary genre. It has created a situation where, though the attribution of documentary significance remains within the province of the viewer, the relation between profilmic and putative has, with the collapse of the concept of generality, entered a problematic flux. The filmmaker knows better than the viewer (though even he only imperfectly and by a stretch of the imagination) the relation of the profilmic to any putative event; yet assumptions about this relationship must be made by the viewer if the attribution of a purely generalizing or typifying significance is no longer to be considered acceptable. Moreover, if the relation between putative and profilmic is to be seen as projecting the significance of "an individual and real event" into the diegesis, it becomes important that the diegesis, as construed on the images, should bear some congruence with the profilmic event. People start talking about sincerity.

The two traditions we have dubbed *vérité* and observational film constitute different responses to this challenge. *Vérité* seeks to eliminate the putative event as a term by absorbing it into, or identifying it with, the profilmic. If the diegesis is construed as an "observed" reality, then it will make no sense to ask what that reality would have been like had it not been observed. Life with a camera is what the films are about; and the putative event is consigned to limbo in much the same manner as in a fiction film—the difference being that the diegesis, far from effacing the profilmic, founds all its claims on an appeal to it. But this procedure conceals a sleight of hand. It rests on an unacknowledged assumption that no one would trouble to reconstruct or fabricate an event merely to show himself, caught unawares, filming it. It may be argued that this assumption, in the cases of particular filmmakers or particular filmed events, is underpinned by knowledge reaching us through cultural channels extrinsic to the films themselves. But this is unsatisfactory in that it simply sweeps the difficulty under the carpet—the carpet being the question of how, and with what accuracy, we interpret these other cultural messages. Besides, if the films' credibility is to rest on extrinsic factors, why do they go to such trouble to wear their honor on their sleeves?

Of course, all films reach us in a context that labels them as to their supposed nature; but these labels are in fact only indications of the ways they are required to function. There is a story, doubtless apocryphal, that when de Sica was asked how he had persuaded the child in *Bicycle Thieves* to cry so convincingly, he replied, "I hit him." It makes quite a difference to our subjective appreciation of the shot whether we read it iconically, as a child "crying" for motives implied in the narrative, or indexally, as a child "really" crying because he is hurt. The cultural label "feature film," silent on how the effect was achieved, directs us to the former at the possible expense of the latter. That of *"cinéma vérité"* does the reverse.

Observational film, however, seeks to eliminate the profilmic from the system. Recognizing that there is no way the relation of profilmic to diegetic reality may be objectively validated, it rests all its faith in the diegesis as an acceptable—since equally inaccessible—equivalent to the putative event. Thus, the filmmaker will not shrink from initiating interactions (though his honesty will deter him from rehearsing or fabricating them) that may be construed as filmed (profilmic) ones or as unfilmed (putative) ones according to the whim of the viewer; the apparent assumption being that, so long as the filmmaker keeps his house in order, the viewer can be left to make himself at home in it. But though we may shut our eyes to the profilmic, it will not go away. If the diegesis is to be construed in an individual rather than a typified sense, it cannot appeal directly to the putative, since the putative, being only a logical construct, can be located only by inference from the profilmic. In other words, we cannot assess the relation of the film as we see it to what *might* have happened if we eliminate any consideration of what *did* happen. (If we do, we are back in the business of general truths mediated through the understanding of the filmmakers and ratified by the assent of the viewer.) Thus, observational film too makes covert appeal to extrinsic sources of information: not, in this case, information about the filmmakers' ethics serving to validate the relation between profilmic and putative reality, but information about film language serving to validate the relation between diegesis and the profilmic. It assumes a growing sophistication in the viewer's use of the medium.

Finally, in order to establish the limits of the argument, let us acknowledge that such a program as "Candid Camera" may truly be said to achieve identity between the putative and the profilmic. But the use of concealed cameras and microphones, quite apart from any moral qualms its extension to a more serious context might arouse, seems to set strict limits on both the situation of the action and the consequent articulation of the image. It may be that these limits could, in a purely technical sense, be overcome; but one suspects that a more highly articulated style, in shooting and editing, would in fact disperse and dilute the very quality of "actuality"—the subjective assurance of the truth of what we are seeing—on which this program, through its sheer gawkiness, depends. Like newsreel in the old dispensation, "Candid Camera" escapes definition as documentary precisely to the extent that it is unproblematic.

Television *Vérité*

The exploitation of the new equipment in television, when it has not been used simply to add immediacy and bite to such otherwise traditional series as "All in a Day," has given rise to a form of *vérité* usage that, though not without ancestry in such films as *Warrendale*, is fairly distinctive to the medium. Its distinctiveness, moreover, lies in a quality it shares with the paradocumentary drama discussed above: the presentation of a smooth, naturalistic surface not dissimilar from that of a nineteenth-century novel. We may care to ask why, when the stress in most of the arts is on alienation and the disruption of codes, the two most progressive movements in television should arrive at a reinstatement of naturalism[2] (or, not to beg the question, why I should deem such movements progressive).

The answer to this is implicit in what has been said already. Given the nature of the stimulus—the insistence of mannerism on film as prose, leading to a sort of indexal malnutrition—it was only reasonable that television technicians should respond by seeking in the new equipment an opportunity to restore the documentary health of the image. Mannerism is itself a highly disjunctive style—representing, indeed, the debasement of progressive usages. The only way to reunite the image with its indexal sources was to sweep away that accretion of codings that, as we have implied, modulate authority vis-à-vis the viewer into authority vis-à-vis the filmed world.

But we must now ask just what "television *vérité*" entails: how is the naturalism arrived at; what assumptions govern its making; and what options for interpretation does it present to the viewer?

The stated philosophy behind this form of filmmaking, epitomized in the work of Roger Graef, is that portable synchronous equipment has now become so unobtrusive, and the crew needed to operate it so small in number, that events may be observed with a degree of interference that is for all practical purposes—or, let us simply say, for the purposes of the film—negligible. The crucial claim, therefore, is for a much-enhanced identity between profilmic and putative events: for a disparity no greater than would be engendered by the introduction into people's circumstances of a silent, inactive, yet ever-present guest—a familiar, a *memento mori*. This claim, in its pure form, is of course naive, since it disregards the fact that many people, especially in public life, may have strong motives for presenting to the media a specially tailored image of their behavior and may, however busy or prepossessed, succeed in doing so; but it is backed up by a further claim (less widely advertised, to be sure) that such modifications of behavior may frequently be perceived during the editing and either eliminated or shown for what they are.

But if we can agree that a close fit between profilmic and putative is more possible now than formerly, we must proceed to ask how this fact is accommodated in the viewer's response; for some evidence must be supposed to lurk beneath the surface of the naturalism if the claims of these films are to rest on anything more substantial than protestations of the filmmakers' ultimate decency. (The recent Granada series "Decisions" carried a card at the head of each program announcing that nothing had been staged for the camera—an assurance likely, one would have thought, to arouse as many suspicions as it dispelled.)

The television version of *vérité* cuts across the distinctions between "*vérité*" and "observational film" as defined above. Like traditional *vérité*, it requires the assumption of a strong identity between diegetic and profilmic reality; but it goes to no comparable lengths to ensure it. It prefers, rather, to avoid as far as possible the "distractions" caused by the appearance of the equipment in the picture and rejects entirely such devices as the interview, which can help us to assess intuitively our distance from what we are shown. This may be justified on the grounds that a narrowing of the gap between putative and profilmic implies a proportional narrowing between profilmic and diegesis: that is to say, the less the observation has influenced an event, the less important it is that we perceive the event as observed.

But the converse is not true. Our failure to perceive the observation does not in any way guarantee its lack of influence on the event. In its reliance on the unsullied diegesis, television *vérité* resembles what we have called observational film. Yet, unlike that tradition, it rests its claims heavily on a congruence between profilmic and putative which the diegesis can do nothing to substantiate. Thus, while it may be interpreted as assuming a visual sophistication in the viewer, a sophistication, for example, that will protect him from allowing the cutting of shots for "continuity" to weaken his sense of their discrete relation to the profilmic, it may equally be interpreted as an attempt to ditch the profilmic altogether in a spirit of "If we can never achieve transparency, let's behave as if we'd already gotten it." Such an appeal to transparency, though, would insult the viewer, much as does mannerism, by denying his constitutive faculty—that is, by failing to acknowledge that the film's meaning can be, regardless of its provenance, only the meaning which the viewer assigns to it. Yet on the other hand a retreat behind opacity—"Leave the creative integrity to us, and you just be satisfied with the consequences"—would be not only undemocratic but, since the films' "integrity" is their only claim to special significance, self-defeating.

If we ask what transformative assumptions the *vérité* filmmaker is using— assumptions as to how his statements about his work may be transformed into statements appropriate to the viewer's frame of reference (or methodology be discussed as communication, ethics as aesthetics)—we must surely, if we are to make sense of it, postulate something like the following: "The reality that the viewer invests in the diegesis by attributing significance to the images will be, whether or not we assure him of it, in all reasonable senses congruent with the reality of the profilmic events; or at least, will probably be congruent in the same measure as the profilmic is congruent with the putative." Thus, the seeming transparency is resolved as a superimposition of two congruences, more or less matching (though there is no knowing when they may slip).

This is not to deny that alternative strategies are available to the viewer. He may infer a claim to transparency where none is intended and either take his diegesis on trust or condemn it as an imposture. He may be so committed to an indexal reading that he will decline to construct a diegesis altogether, preferring to perceive the individual shots as data—that is, as "evidence" for some broader construction of his own. Or he may choose to construe the film entirely on the iconic level: a procedure assumed, I think, by those who argue that since all film is artifice, all methods are justified. (This, by eliminating from the viewer's response any transformative assumptions about the film's ethics, reduces *vérité* to a question of acting—to one means among others for getting good performances.) But still, our "transformation" at least shows a way in which, without too much bending of likelihood, our films may be assumed to achieve their intended significance; and it has the grace to affirm this not as an imperative but as a probability.

This probability is clearly strengthened by any assumptions we may make as to the viewer's visual sophistication or his persuasion, from other sources, of the filmmakers' probity; but, unless we are happy to be left with films that people must be told how to watch, we will acknowledge that our "transformation" still grounds any claim to distinctive verity firmly within the freedom of the beholder. Further, I think we must admit that our transformative assumption diminishes sharply in credibility as we move from the metareality of the filmic elements to the absorption of this metareality into a complex diegetic structure. The credence we as viewers allow these films depends very much on the extent to which they are seen to mistrust the inherited grammars of film discourse. And this is a matter of degree. Television *vérité* is, aesthetically, a house built on sand. It will stay up all right; but only if the sand receives constant attention.

Notes

1. For Vaughan, *index* presupposes the anterior reality of what is being signified, whereas the icon and the symbol conjure up phantoms. The symbol may seem to be elusive, but common consent agrees to its meaning. *Indexical* suggests to Vaughan "pertaining to" (rather than functioning as) indexes (rather than indices).—A.R.

2. By "naturalism" I mean adherence to a uniform system of conventions not called into question from within.

The Voice of Documentary

Bill Nichols

It is worth insisting that the strategies and styles deployed in documentary, like those of narrative film, change; they have a history. And they have changed for much the same reasons: the dominant modes of expository discourse change; the arena of ideological contestation shifts. The comfortably accepted realism of one generation seems like artifice to the next. New strategies must constantly be fabricated to re-present "things as they are" and still others to contest this very representation.

In the history of documentary we can identify at least four major styles, each with distinctive formal and ideological qualities.[1] In this article I propose to examine the limitations and strengths of these strategies, with particular attention to one that is both the newest and in some ways the oldest of them all.[2]

The direct-address style of the Griersonian tradition (or, in its most excessive form, the March of Time's "voice of God") was the first thoroughly worked out mode of documentary. As befitted a school whose purposes were over- whelmingly didactic, it employed a supposedly authoritative yet often pre- sumptuous off-screen narration. In many cases this narration effectively dom- inated the visuals, though it could be, in films like *Night Mail* or *Listen to Britain*, poetic and evocative. After World War II, the Griersonian mode fell into disfavor (for reasons I will come back to later), and it has little contemporary currency—except for television news, game and talk shows, ads, and docu- mentary specials.

Its successor, *cinéma vérité*, promised an increase in the "reality effect" with its directness, immediacy, and impression of capturing untampered events in the everyday lives of particular people. Films like *Chronicle of a Summer, Le joli mai, Lonely Boy, Back-Breaking Leaf, Primary*, and *The Chair* built on the new technical possibilities offered by portable cameras and sound recorders, which could produce synchronous dialogue under location conditions. In pure *cinéma vérité* films, the style seeks to become "transparent" in the same mode as the classical Hollywood style—capturing people in action, and letting the viewer come to conclusions about them unaided by any implicit or explicit commentary.

Sometimes mesmerizing, frequently perplexing, such films seldom offered the sense of history, context, or perspective that viewers seek. And so in the past decade we have seen a third style that incorporates direct address (characters or narrator speaking directly to the viewer), usually in the form of the interview. In a host of political and feminist films, witness-participants step before the camera to tell their story. Sometimes profoundly revealing, sometimes fragmented and incomplete, such films have provided the central model for contemporary documentary. But as a strategy and a form, the interview-oriented film has problems of its own.

More recently, a fourth phase seems to have begun, with films moving toward more complex forms where epistemological and aesthetic assumptions become more visible. These new self-reflexive documentaries mix observational passages with interviews, the voice-over of the filmmaker with intertitles, making patently clear what has been implicit all along: documentaries always were forms of re-presentation, never clear windows onto "reality"; the filmmaker was always a participant-witness and an active fabricator of meaning, a producer of cinematic discourse rather than a neutral or all-knowing reporter of the way things truly are.

Ironically, film theory has been of little help in this recent evolution, despite the enormous contribution of recent theory to questions of the production of meaning in narrative forms. In documentary the most advanced, modernist work draws its inspiration less from poststructuralist models of discourse than from the working procedures of documentation and validation practiced by ethnographic filmmakers. And as far as the influence of film history goes, the figure of Dziga Vertov now looms much larger than that of either Flaherty or Grierson.

I do not intend to argue that self-reflexive documentary represents a pinnacle or solution in any ultimate sense. It is, however, in the process of evolving alternatives that seem, in our present historical context, less obviously problematic than the strategies of commentary, *vérité*, or the interview. These new forms may, like their predecessors, come to seem more "natural" or even "realistic" for a time. But the success of every form breeds its own overthrow: it limits, omits, disavows, represses (as well as represents). In time, new necessities bring new formal inventions.

As suggested above, in the evolution of documentary the contestation among forms has centered on the question of "voice." By voice I mean something narrower than style: that which conveys to us a sense of a text's social point of view, of how it is speaking to us and how it is organizing the materials it is presenting to us. In this sense, voice is not restricted to any one code or feature, such as dialogue or spoken commentary. Voice is perhaps akin to that intangible, moirélike pattern formed by the unique interaction of all a film's codes, and it applies to all modes of documentary.

Far too many contemporary filmmakers appear to have lost their voice. Politically, they forfeit their own voice for that of others (usually characters recruited to the film and interviewed). Formally, they disavow the complexities of voice, and discourse, for the apparent simplicities of faithful observation or respectful representation, the treacherous simplicities of an unquestioned empiricism (the world and its truths exist; they need only be dusted off and reported). Many documentarists would appear to believe what fiction-filmmakers only feign to believe, or openly question: that filmmaking creates an objective representation of the way things really are. Such documentaries use the magical template of verisimilitude without the storyteller's open resort to artifice. Very few seem prepared to admit through the very tissue and texture of their work that all filmmaking is a form of discourse fabricating its effects, impressions, and point of view.

Yet it especially behooves the documentary filmmaker to acknowledge what she or he is actually doing. Not in order to be accepted as modernist for the sake of being modernist, but to fashion documentaries that may more closely correspond to a contemporary understanding of our position within the world so that effective political/formal strategies for describing and challenging that position can emerge. Strategies and techniques for doing so already exist. In documentary they seem to derive most directly from *The Man with a Movie Camera* and *Chronique d'un été* and are vividly exemplified in David and Judith MacDougall's Turkana trilogy (*Lorang's Way, Wedding Camels, A Wife Among Wives*). But before discussing this tendency further, we should first examine the strengths and limitations of *cinéma vérité* and the interview-based film. They are well represented by two recent and highly successful films: *Soldier Girls* and *Rosie the Riveter*.

Soldier Girls presents a contemporary situation: basic army training as experienced by women volunteers. Purely indirect or observational, *Soldier Girls* provides no spoken commentary, no interviews or titles, and like Fred Wiseman's films, it arouses considerable controversy about its point of view. One viewer at Filmex interjected, "How on earth did they get the army to let them make such an incredibly anti-army film?" What struck that viewer as powerful criticism, though, may strike another as an honest portrayal of the tough-minded discipline necessary to learn to defend oneself, to survive in harsh environments, to kill. As in Wiseman's films, organizational strategies establish a preferred reading—in this case, one that favors the personal over the political, that seeks out and celebrates the irruptions of individual feeling and conscience in the face of institutional constraint, that rewrites historical process as the expression of an indomitable human essence whatever the circumstance. But these strategies, complex and subtle like those of realist fiction, tend to ascribe to the historical material itself meanings that in fact are an effect of the film's style or voice, just as fiction's strategies invite us to believe that "life" is like the imaginary world inhabited by its characters.

A precredit sequence of training exercises that follows three women volunteers ends with a freeze-frame and iris-in to isolate the face of each woman. Similar to classic Hollywood-style vignettes used to identify key actors, this sequence inaugurates a set of strategies that links *Soldier Girls* with a large part of American *cinéma vérité* (*Primary, Salesman, An American Family,* the "Middletown" series). It is characterized by a romantic individualism and a dramatic, fictionlike structure, but employing "found" stories rather than the wholly invented ones of Hollywood. Scenes in which Private Hall oversees punishment for Private Alvarez and in which the women recruits are awakened and prepare their beds for Drill Sergeant Abing's inspection prompt an impression of looking in on a world unmarked by our, or the camera's, act of gazing. And those rare moments in which the camera or person behind it is acknowledged certify more forcefully that other moments of "pure observation" capture the social presentation of self we too would have witnessed had we actually been there to see for ourselves. When *Soldier Girls'* narrativelike tale culminates in a shattering moment of character revelation, it seems to be a happy coincidence of dramatic structure and historical events unfolding. In as extraordinary an epiphany as any in all of *vérité,* tough-minded Drill Sergeant Abing breaks down and confesses to Private Hall how much of his own humanity and soul has been destroyed by his experience in Vietnam. By such means, the film transcends the social and political categories that it shows but refuses to name. Instead of the personal becoming political, the political becomes personal.

We never hear the voice of the filmmaker or a narrator trying to persuade us of this romantic humanism. Instead, the film's structure relies heavily on classical narrative procedures, among them: (1) a chronology of apparent causality that reveals how each of the three women recruits resolves the conflict between her own sense of individuality and army discipline; (2) shots organized into dramatically revelatory scenes that only acknowledge the camera as participant-observer near the film's end, when one of the recruits embraces the filmmakers as she leaves the training base, discharged for her "failure" to fit in; and (3) excellent performances from characters who "play themselves" without any inhibiting self-consciousness. (The phenomenon of filming individuals who play themselves in a manner strongly reminiscent of the performances of professional actors in fiction could be the subject of an extended study in its own right.) These procedures allow purely observational documentaries to asymptotically narrow the gap between a fabricated realism and the apparent capture of reality itself that so facinated André Bazin.

This gap may also be looked at as a gap between evidence and argument.[3] One of the peculiar fascinations of film is precisely that it so easily conflates the two. Documentary displays a tension arising from the attempt to make statements about life that are quite general, while necessarily using sounds and images that bear the inescapable trace of their particular historical origins. These sounds and images come to function as signs; they bear meaning, though the meaning is not really inherent in them but rather conferred upon them by their function within the text as a whole. We may think we hear history or reality speaking to us through a film, but what we actually hear is the voice of the text, even when that voice tries to efface itself.

This is not only a matter of semiotics but of historical process. Those who confer meaning (individuals, social classes, the media, and other institutions) exist within history itself rather than at the periphery, looking in like gods. Hence, paradoxically, self-referentiality is an inevitable communicational category. A class cannot be a member of itself, the law of logical typing tells us, and yet in human communication this law is necessarily violated. Those who confer meaning are themselves members of the class of conferred meanings (history). For a film to fail to acknowledge this and pretend to omniscience—whether by voice-of-God commentary or by claims of "objective knowledge"—is to deny its own complicity with a production of knowledge that rests on no firmer bedrock than the very act of production. (What then become vital are the assumptions, values, and purposes motivating this production, the underpinnings that some modernist strategies attempt to make more clear.)[4]

Observational documentary appears to leave the driving to us. No one tells us about the sights we pass or what they mean. Even those obvious marks of documentary textuality—muddy sound, blurred or racked focus, the grainy, poorly lit figures of social actors caught on the run—function paradoxically. Their presence testifies to an apparently more basic absence: such films sacrifice conventional, polished artistic expression in order to bring back, as best they can, the actual texture of history in the making. If the camera gyrates wildly or ceases functioning, this is not an expression of personal style. It is a signifier of personal danger, as in *Harlan County, U.S.A.*, or even death, as in the street scene from *The Battle of Chile* when the cameraman records the moment of his own death.

This shift from artistic expressiveness to historical revelation contributes mightily to the phenomenological effect of the observational film. *Soldier Girls, They Call Us Misfits*, its sequel, *A Respectable Life*, and Fred Wiseman's most recent film, *Models*, propose revelations about the real not as a result of direct argument, but on the basis of inferences we draw from historical evidence itself. For example, Stefan Jarl's remarkable film *They Call Us Misfits* contains a purely observational scene of its two seventeen-year-old misfits—who have left home for a life of booze, drugs, and a good time in Stockholm—getting up in the morning. Kenta washes his long hair, dries it, and then meticulously combs every hair into place. Stoffe doesn't bother with his hair at all. Instead, he boils water and then makes tea by pouring it over a tea bag that is still inside its paper wrapper! We rejoin the boys in *A Respectable Life*, shot ten years later, and learn that Stoffe has nearly died on three occasions from heroin overdoses whereas Kenta has sworn off hard drugs and begun a career of sorts as a singer. At this point we may retroactively grant a denser tissue of meaning to those little morning rituals recorded a decade earlier. If so, we take them as evidence of historical determinations rather than artistic vision—even though they are only available to us as a result of textual strategies. More generally, the aural and visual evidence of what ten years of hard living do to the alert, mischievous appearance of two boys—the ruddy skin, the dark, extinguished eyes, the slurred and garbled speech, especially of Stoffe—bear meaning precisely because the films invite retroactive comparison. The films produce the structure in which "facts" themselves take on meaning precisely because they belong to a coherent series of differences. Yet, though powerful, this construction of differences remains insufficient. A simplistic line of historical progression prevails, centered as it is in *Soldier Girls* on the trope of romantic individualism. (Instead of the Great Man theory we have the Unfortunate Victim theory of history—inadequate, but compellingly presented.)

And where observational cinema shifts from an individual to an institutional focus, and from a metonymic narrative model to a metaphoric one, as in the highly innovative work of Fred Wiseman, there may still be only a weak sense of constructed meaning, of a textual voice addressing us. A vigorous, active, and retroactive reading is necessary before we can hear the voice of the textual system as a level distinct from the sounds and images of the evidence it adduces, while questions of adequacy remain. Wiseman's sense of context and of meaning as a function of the text itself remains weak, too easily engulfed by the fascination that allows us to mistake film for reality, the impression of the real for the experience of it. The risk of reading *Soldier Girls* or Wiseman's *Models* like a Rorschach test may require stronger countermeasures than the subtleties their complex editing and mise-en-scène provide.

Prompted, it would seem, by these limitations to *cinéma vérité* or observational cinema, many filmmakers during the past decade have reinstituted direct address. For the most part this has meant social actors addressing us in interviews rather than a return to the voice-of-authority evidenced by a narrator. *Rosie the Riveter*, for example, tells us about the blatant hypocrisy with which women were recruited to the factories and assembly lines during World War II. A series of five women witnesses tell us how they were denied the respect granted men, told to put up with hazardous conditions "like a man," paid less, and pitted against one another racially. *Rosie* makes short shrift of the noble icon of the woman worker as seen in forties newsreels. Those films celebrated her heroic contribution to the great effort to preserve the free world from fascist dictatorship. *Rosie* destroys this myth of deeply appreciated, fully rewarded contribution without in any way undercutting the genuine fortitude, courage, and political awareness of women who experienced continual frustration in their struggles for dignified working conditions and a permanent place in the American labor force.

Using interviews, but no commentator, together with a weave of compilation footage as images of illustration, director Connie Field tells a story many of us think we've heard, only to realize we've never heard the whole of it before.

The organization of the film depends heavily on its set of extensive interviews with former "Rosies." Their selection follows the direct-cinema tradition of filming ordinary people. But *Rosie the Riveter* broadens that tradition, as *Union Maids, The Wobblies*, and *With Babies and Banners* have also done, to retrieve the memory of an "invisible" (suppressed more than forgotten) history of labor struggle. The five interviewees remember a past the film's inserted historical images reconstruct, but in counterpoint: their recollection of adversity and struggle contrasts with old newsreels of women "doing their part" cheerfully.

This strategy complicates the voice of the film in an interesting way. It adds a contemporary, personal resonance to the historical, compilation footage without challenging the assumptions of that footage explicitly, as a voice-over commentary might do. We ourselves become engaged in determining how the women witnesses counterpoint these historical "documents" as well as how they articulate their own present and past consciousness in political, ethical, and feminist dimensions.

We are encouraged to believe that these voices carry less the authority of historical judgment than that of personal testimony—they are, after all, the words of apparently "ordinary women" remembering the past. As in many films that advance issues raised by the women's movement, there is an emphasis on individual but politically significant experience. *Rosie* demonstrates the power of the act of naming—the ability to find the words that render the personal political. This reliance on oral history to reconstruct the past places *Rosie the Riveter* within what is probably the predominant mode of documentary filmmaking today—films built around a string of interviews—where we also find *A Wife's Tale, With Babies and Banners, Controlling Interest, The Day After Trinity, The Trials of Alger Hiss, Rape, Word Is Out, Prison for Women, This Is Not a Love Story, Nuove frontieras (Looking for Better Dreams)*, and *The Wobblies*.

This reinstitution of direct address through the interview has successfully avoided some of the central problems of voice-over narration, namely, authoritative omniscience or didactic reductionism. There is no longer the dubious claim that things are as the film presents them, organized by the commentary of an all-knowing subject. Such attempts to stand above history and explain it create a paradox. Any attempt by a speaker to vouch for his or her own validity reminds us of the Cretan paradox: "Epimenides was a Cretan who said, 'Cretans always lie.' Was Epimenides telling the truth?" The nagging sense of a self-referential claim that can't be proven reaches greatest intensity with the most forceful assertions, which may be why viewers are often most suspicious of what an apparently omniscient Voice of Authority asserts most fervently. The emergence of so many recent documentaries built around strings of interviews strikes me as a strategic response to the recognition that neither can events speak for themselves nor can a single voice speak with ultimate authority. Interviews diffuse authority. A gap remains between the voice of a social actor recruited to the film and the voice of the film.

Not compelled to vouch for their own validity, the voices of interviewees may well arouse less suspicion. Yet a larger, constraining voice may remain to provide, or withhold, validation. In *The Sad Song of Yellow Skin*, *The Wilmar 8*, *Harlan County, U.S.A.*, *This Is Not a Love Story*, or *Who Killed the Fourth Ward*, among others, the literal voice of the filmmaker enters into dialogue but without the self-validating, authoritative tone of a previous tradition. (These are also voices without the self-reflexive quality found in Vertov's, Rouch's, or the MacDougalls' work.) Diarylike and uncertain in *Yellow Skin*; often directed toward the women strikers as though by a fellow participant and observer in *Wilmar 8* and *Harlan County, U.S.A.*; sharing personal reactions to pornography with a companion in *Not a Love Story*; and adopting a mock-ironic tone reminiscent of Peter Falk's Columbo in *Fourth Ward*—these voices of potentially imaginary assurance instead share doubts and emotional reactions with other characters and us. As a result, they seem to refuse a privileged position in relation to other characters. Of course, these less assertive authorial voices remain complicit with the controlling voice of the textual system itself, but the effect on a viewer is distinctly different.

Still, interviews pose problems. Their occurrence is remarkably widespread—from *The Hour of the Wolf* to "The MacNeil/Lehrer Report" and from *Housing Problems* (1935) to *Harlan County, U.S.A.* The greatest problem, at least in recent documentary, has been to retain that sense of a gap between the voice of interviewees and the voice of the text as a whole. It is most obviously a problem when the interviewees display conceptual inadequacy on the issue but remain unchallenged by the film. *The Day After Trinity*, for example, traces Robert Oppenheimer's career but restricts itself to a Great Man theory of history. The string of interviews clearly identifies Oppenheimer's role in the race to build the nuclear bomb, and his equivocations, but it never places the bomb or Oppenheimer within that larger constellation of government policies and political calculations that determined its specific use or continuing threat—

even though the interviews took place in the last few years. The text not only appears to lack a voice or perspective of its own, the perspective of its character-witnesses is patently inadequate.

In documentary, when the voice of the text disappears behind characters who speak to us, we confront a specific strategy of no less ideological importance than its equivalent in fiction films. When we no longer sense that a governing voice actively provides or withholds the imprimatur of veracity according to its own purposes and assumptions, its own canons of validation, we may also sense the return of the paradox and suspicion that interviews should help us escape: the word of witnesses, uncritically accepted, must provide its own validation. Meanwhile, the film becomes a rubber stamp. To varying degrees this diminution of a governing voice occurs through parts of *Word Is Out, The Wobblies, With Babies and Banners*, and *Prison for Women*. The sense of a hierarchy of voices becomes lost.[5] Ideally this hierarchy would uphold correct logical typing at one level (the voice of the text remains of a higher, controlling type than the voices of interviewees) without denying the inevitable collapse of logical types at another (the voice of the text is not above history but part of the very historical process on which it confers meaning). But at present a less complex and less adequate sidetracking of paradox prevails. The film says, in effect, "Interviewees never lie." Interviewees say, "What I am telling you is the truth." We then ask, "Is the interviewee telling the truth?" but find no acknowledgment in the film of the possibility, let alone the necessity, of entertaining this question as one inescapable in all communication and signification.

As much as anyone, Emile de Antonio, who pioneered the use of interviews and compilation footage to organize complex historical arguments without a narrator, has also provided clear signposts for avoiding the inherent dangers of interviews. Unfortunately, most of the filmmakers adopting his basic approach have failed to heed them.

De Antonio demonstrates a sophisticated understanding of the category of the personal. He does not invariably accept the word of witnesses, nor does he adopt rhetorical strategies (Great Man theories, for example) that limit historical understanding to the personal. Something exceeds this category, and in *Point of Order, In the Year of the Pig, Millhouse: A White Comedy*, and *Weather Underground*, among others, this excess is carried by a distinct textual voice that clearly judges the validity of what witnesses say. Just as the voice of John Huston in *The Battle of San Pietro* contests one line of argument with another (that of General Mark Clark, who claims the costs of battle were not excessive, with that of Huston, who suggests they were), so the textual voice of de Antonio contests and places the statements made by its embedded interviews, but without speaking to us directly. (In de Antonio and in his followers, there is no narrator, only the direct address of witnesses.)

This contestation is not simply the express support of some witnesses over others, for left against right. It is a systematic effect of placement that retains the gaps between levels of different logical type. De Antonio's overall expository strategy in *In the Year of the Pig*, for example, makes it clear that no one witness tells the whole truth. De Antonio's voice (unspoken but controlling) makes witnesses contend with one another to yield a point of view more distinctive to the film than to any of its witnesses (since it includes this very strategy of contention). (Similarly, the unspoken voice of *The Atomic Cafe*—evident in the extraordinarily skillful editing of government nuclear weapons propaganda films from the fifties—governs a preferred reading of the footage it compiles.) But particularly in de Antonio's work, different points of view appear. History is not a monolith, its density and outline given from the outset. On the contrary, *In the Year of the Pig*, for example, constructs perspective and historical understanding, and does so right before our eyes.

We see and hear, for example, U.S. government spokesmen explaining their strategy and conception of the "Communist menace," whereas we do not see and hear Ho Chi Minh explain his strategy and vision. Instead, an interviewee, Paul Mus, introduces us to Ho Chi Minh descriptively while de Antonio's cutaways to Vietnamese countryside evoke an affiliation between Ho and his land and people that is absent from the words and images of American spokesmen. Ho remains an uncontained figure whose full meaning must be conferred, and inferred, from available materials as they are brought together by de Antonio. Such construction is a textual, and cinematic, act evident in the choice of supporting or ironic images to accompany interviews, in the actual juxtaposition of interviews, and even in the still images that form a precredit sequence inasmuch as they unmistakably refer to the American Civil War (an analogy sharply at odds with U.S. government accounts of Communist invasion). By juxtaposing silhouettes of civil war soldiers with GIs in Vietnam, the precredit sequence obliquely but clearly offers an interpretation for the events we are about to see. De Antonio does not subordinate his own voice to the way things are, to the sounds and images that are evidence of war. He acknowledges that the meaning of these images must be conferred on them and goes about doing so in a readily understood though indirect manner.

De Antonio's hierarchy of levels and reservation of ultimate validation to the highest level (the textual system or film as a whole) differs radically from other approaches. John Lowenthal's *The Trials of Alger Hiss*, for example, is a totally subservient endorsement of Hiss's legalistic strategies. Similarly, *Hollywood on Trial* shows no independence from the perhaps politically expedient but disingenuous line adopted by the Hollywood 10 over thirty years ago—that HUAC's pattern of subpoenas to friendly and unfriendly witnesses primarily threatened the civil liberties of ordinary citizens (though it certainly did so) rather than posing a more specific threat to the CPUSA and American left (where it clearly did the greatest damage). By contrast, even in *Painters Painting* and *Weather Underground*, where de Antonio seems unusually close to validating uncritically what interviewees say, the subtle voice of his mise-en-scène preserves the gap, conveying a strong sense of the distance between the sensibilities or politics of those interviewed and those of the larger public to whom they speak.

De Antonio's films produce a world of dense complexity: they embody a sense of constraint and overdetermination. Not everyone can be believed. Not everything is true. Characters do not emerge as the autonomous shapers of a personal destiny. De Antonio proposes ways and means by which to reconstruct the past dialectically, as Fred Wiseman reconstructs the present dialectically.[6] Rather than appearing to collapse itself into the consciousness of character witnesses, the film retains an independent consciousness, a voice of its own. The film's own consciousness (surrogate for ours) probes, remembers, substantiates, doubts. It questions and believes, including itself. It assumes the voice of personal consciousness at the same time as it examines the very category of the personal. Neither omniscient deity nor obedient mouthpiece, de Antonio's rhetorical voice seduces us by embodying those qualities of insight, skepticism, judgment, and independence we would like to appropriate for our own. Nonetheless, though he is closer to a modernist, self-reflexive strategy than any other documentary filmmaker in America—with the possible exception of the more experimental feminist filmmaker JoAnn Elam—de Antonio remains clearly apart from this tendency. He is more a Newtonian than an Einsteinian observer of events; he insists on the activity of fixing meaning, but it is meaning that does, finally, appear to reside "out there" rather than insisting on the activity of producing that "fix" from which meaning itself derives.

There are lessons here we would think de Antonio's successors would be quick to learn. But, most frequently, they have not. The interview remains a problem. Subjectivity, consciousness, argumentative form, and voice remain unquestioned in documentary theory and practice. Often, filmmakers simply choose to interview characters with whom they agree. A weaker sense of skepticism, a diminished self-awareness of the filmmaker as producer of meaning or history prevails, yielding a flatter, less dialectical sense of history and a simpler, more idealized sense of character. Characters threaten to emerge as stars—flashpoints of inspiring, and imaginary, coherence contradictory to their ostensible status as ordinary people.[7]

These problems emerge in three of the best history films we have (and in the pioneering gay film *Word Is Out*), undermining their great importance on other levels. *Union Maids*, *With Babies and Banners*, and *The Wobblies* flounder on the axis of personal respect and historical recall. The films simply suppose that things were as the participant-witnesses recall them, and lest we doubt, the filmmakers respectfully find images of illustration to substantiate the claim.

(The resonance set up in *Rosie the Riveter* between interviews and compilation footage establishes a perceptible sense of a textual voice that makes this film a more sophisticated, though not self-reflexive, version of the interview-based documentary.) What characters omit to say, so do these films, most noticeably regarding the role of the CPUSA in *Union Maids* and *With Babies and Banners*. *Banners*, for example, contains one instance when a witness mentions the helpful knowledge she gained from Communist party members. Immediately, though, the film cuts to unrelated footage of a violent attack on workers by a goon squad. It is as if the textual voice, rather than provide independent assessment, must go so far as to find diversionary material to offset presumably harmful comments by witnesses themselves!

These films naively endorse limited, selective recall. The tactic flattens witnesses into a series of imaginary puppets conforming to a line. Their recall becomes distinguishable more by differences in force of personality than by differences in perspective. Backgrounds loaded with iconographic meanings transform witnesses further into stereotypes (shipyards, farms, union halls abound, or for the gays and lesbians in *Word Is Out*, bedrooms and the bucolic out-of-doors). We sense a great relief when characters step out of these closed, iconographic frames and into more open-ended ones, but such "release" usually occurs only at the end of the films where it also signals the achievement of expository closure—another kind of frame. We return to the simple claim, "Things were as these witnesses describe them, why contest them?"—a claim that is a dissimulation and a disservice to both film theory and political praxis. On the contrary, as de Antonio and Wiseman demonstrate quite differently, Things signify, but only if we make them comprehensible.[8]

Documentaries with a more sophisticated grasp of the historical realm establish a preferred reading by a textual system that asserts its own voice in contrast to the voices it recruits or observes. Such films confront us with an alternative to our own hypotheses about what kinds of things populate the world, what relations they sustain, and what meanings they bear for us. The film operates as an autonomous whole, as we do. It is greater than its parts, and it orchestrates them: (1) the recruited voices, the recruited sounds and images; (2) the textual "voice" spoken by the style of the film as a whole (how its multiplicity of codes, including those pertaining to recruited voices, are orchestrated into a singular, controlling pattern); and (3) the surrounding historical context, including the viewing event itself, which the textual voice cannot successfully rise above or fully control. The film is thus a simulacrum or external trace of the production of meaning we undertake ourselves every day, every moment. We see not an image of imaginary unchanging coherence, magically represented on a screen, but the evidence of a historically rooted act of making things meaningful comparable to our own historically situated acts of comprehension.

With de Antonio's films, *The Atomic Cafe, Rape,* or *Rosie the Riveter* the active counterpointing of the text reminds us that its meaning is produced.

This foregrounding of an active production of meaning by a textual system may also heighten our conscious sense of self as something also produced by codes that extend beyond ourselves. An exaggerated claim, perhaps, but still suggestive of the difference in effect of different documentary strategies and an indication of the importance of the self-reflexive strategy itself.

Self-reflexiveness can easily lead to an endless regression. It can prove highly appealing to an intelligentsia more interested in "good form" than in social change. Yet interest in self-reflexive forms is not purely an academic question. *Cinéma vérité* and its variants sought to address certain limitations of the voice-of-God tradition. The interview-oriented film sought to address limitations apparent in the bulk of *cinéma vérité*, and the self-reflexive documentary addresses the limitations of assuming that subjectivity and both the social and textual positioning of the self (as filmmaker or viewer) are ultimately not problematic.

Modernist thought in general challenges this assumption. A few documentary filmmakers, going as far back as Dziga Vertov and certainly including Jean Rouch and the hard-to-categorize Jean-Luc Godard, adopt in their work the basic epistemological assumption that knowledge and the position of the self in relation to the mediator of knowledge, a given text, are socially and formally constructed and should be shown to be so. Rather than inviting paralysis before a centerless labyrinth, however, such a perspective restores the dialectic between self and other: neither the "out there" nor the "in here" contains its own inherent meaning. The *process* of constructing meaning overshadows constructed meanings. And at a time when modernist experimentation is old hat within the avant-garde and a fair amount of fiction filmmaking, it remains almost totally unheard of among documentary filmmakers, especially in North America. It is not political documentarists who have been the leading innovators. Instead it is a handful of ethnographic filmmakers like Timothy Asch (*The Ax Fight*), John Marshall (*Nai!*), and David and Judith MacDougall who, in their meditations on scientific method and visual communication, have done the most provocative experimentation.

Take the MacDougalls' *Wedding Camels* (part of the Turkana trilogy), for example. The film, set in northern Kenya, explores the preparations for a Turkana wedding in day-to-day detail. It mixes direct and indirect address to form a complex whole made up of two levels of historical reference—evidence and argument—and two levels of textual structure—observation and exposition.

Though *Wedding Camels* is frequently observational and very strongly rooted in the texture of everyday life, the filmmakers' presence receives far more frequent acknowledgment than it does in *Soldier Girls* or Wiseman's films, or most other observational work. Lorang, the bride's father and central figure in the dowry negotiations, says at one point, with clear acknowledgment of the filmmakers' presence, "They [Europeans] never marry our daughters. They always hold back their animals." At other moments we hear David

MacDougall ask questions of Lorang or others off-camera, much as we do in *The Wilmar 8* or *In the Year of the Pig*. (This contrasts with *The Wobblies*, *Union Maids*, and *With Babies and Banners*, where the questions to which participant-witnesses respond are not heard.) Sometimes these queries invite characters to reflect on events we observe in detail, like the dowry arrangements themselves. On these occasions they introduce a vivid level of self-reflexiveness into the characters' performance as well as into the film's structure, something that is impossible in interview-based films that give us no sense of a character's present but only use his or her words as testimony about the past.

Wedding Camels also makes frequent use of intertitles, which mark off one scene from another, to develop a mosaic structure that necessarily admits to its own lack of completeness even as individual facets appear to exhaust a given encounter. This sense of both incompleteness and exhaustion, as well as the radical shift of perceptual space involved in going from apparently three-dimensional images to two-dimensional graphics that comment on or frame the image, generates a strong sense of a hierarchical and self-referential ordering.

For example, in one scene Naingoro, sister to the bride's mother, says, "Our daughters are not our own. They are born to be given out." The implicit lack of completeness to individual identity apart from social exchange then receives elaboration through an interview sequence with Akai, the bride. The film poses questions by means of intertitles and sandwiches Akai's responses, briefly, between them. One intertitle, for example, phrases its question more or less as follows: "We asked Akai whether a Turkana woman chooses her husband or if her parents choose for her." Such phrasing brings the filmmaker's intervention strongly into the foreground.

The structure of this passage suggests some of the virtues of a hybrid style: the titles serve as another indicator of a textual voice apart from that of the characters represented. They also differ from most documentary titles, which since the silent days of *Nanook* have worked like a graphic "voice" of authority. In *Wedding Camels* the titles, in their mock-interactive structure, remain closely aligned with the particulars of person and place rather than appearing to issue from an omniscient consciousness. They show clear awareness of how a particular meaning is being produced by a particular act of intervention. This is not presented as a grand revelation but as a simple truth that is only remarkable for its rarity in documentary film. These particular titles also display both a wry sense of humor and a clear perception of the meaning an individual's marriage has for him or her as well as for others (a vital means of countering, among other things, the temptation of an ethnocentric reading or judgment). By "violating" the coherence of a social actor's diegetic space, intertitles also lessen the tendency for the interviewee to inflate to the proportions of a star witness. By acting self-reflexively, such strategies call the status of the interview itself into question and diminish its tacit claim to tell the whole truth. Other signifying choices, which function like Brechtian distancing devices, would include the separate "spaces" of image and intertitle for question/response; the highly structured and abbreviated question/answer format; the close-up, portraitlike framing of a social actor that pries her away from a matrix of ongoing activities or a stereotypical background, and the clear acknowledgment that such fabrications exist to serve the purposes of the film rather than to capture an unaffected reality.

Though modest in tone, *Wedding Camels* demonstrates a structural sophistication well beyond that of almost any other documentary film work today. Whether its modernist strategies can be yoked to a more explicitly political perspective (without restricting itself to the small avant-garde audience that exists for the Godards and Chantal Akermans) is less a question than a challenge still haunting us, considering the limitations of most interview-based films.

Changes in documentary strategy bear a complex relation to history. Self-reflexive strategies seem to have a particularly complex historical relation to documentary form, since they are far less peculiar to it than the voice-of-God, *cinéma vérité*, or interview-based strategies. Although they have been available to documentary (as to narrative) since the 1910s, they have never been as popular in North America as in Europe or in other regions (save among an avant-garde). Why they have recently made an effective appearance within the documentary domain is a matter requiring further exploration. I suspect we are dealing with more than a reaction to the limitations of the currently dominant interview-based form. Large cultural preferences concerning the voicing of dramatic as well as documentary material seem to be changing. In any event, the most recent appearances of self-reflexive strategies correspond very clearly to deficiencies in attempts to translate highly ideological, written anthropological practices into a proscriptive agenda for a visual anthropology (neutrality, descriptiveness, objectivity, "just the facts," and so on). It is very heartening to see that the realm of the possible for documentary film has now expanded to include strategies of reflexivity that may eventually serve political as well as scientific ends.

NOTES

1. Many of the distinctive characteristics of documentary are examined broadly in Nichols, *Ideology and the Image: Social Representation in the Cinema and Other Media* (Bloomington: Indiana University Press, 1981), pp. 170–284. Here I shall concentrate on more recent films and some of the particular problems they pose.

2. Films referred to in this article or instrumental in formulating the issues of self-reflexive documentary form include: *The Atomic Cafe* (USA, Kevin Rafferty, Jayne Loader, Pierce Rafferty, 1982), *Controlling Interest* (USA, SF Newsreel, 1978), *The Day After Trinity* (USA, Jon Else, 1980), *Harlan County, U.S.A.* (USA, Barbara Kopple, 1976), *Hollywood on Trial* (USA, David Halpern, Jr., 1976), *Models* (USA, Fred Wiseman, 1981), *Nuove frontieras* (*Looking for Better*

Dreams) (Switzerland, Remo Legnazzi, 1981), *On Company Business* (USA, Allan Francovich, 1981), *Prison for Women* (Canada, Janice Cole, Holly Dale, 1981), *Rape* (USA, JoAnn Elam, 1977), *A Respectable Life* (Sweden, Stefan Jarl, 1980), *Rosie the Riveter* (USA, Connie Field, 1980), *The Sad Song of Yellow Skin* (Canada, NFB—Michael Rubbo, 1970), *Soldier Girls* (USA, Nick Broomfield, Joan Churchill, 1981), *They Call Us Misfits* (Sweden, Jan Lindquist, Stefan Jarl, c. 1969), *Not a Love Story!* (Canada, NFB—Bonnie Klein, 1981), *The Trials of Alger Hiss* (USA, John Lowenthal, 1980), *Union Maids* (USA, Jim Klein, Julia Reichert, Miles Mogulescu, 1976), *Who Killed the Fourth Ward?* (USA, James Blue, 1978), *The Wilmar 8* (USA, Lee Grant, 1980), *With Babies and Banners* (USA, Women's Labor History Film Project, 1978), *A Wife's Tale* (Canada, Sophie Bissonnette, Martin Duckworth, Joyce Rock, 1980), *The Wobblies* (USA, Stuart Bird, Deborah Shaffer, 1979), *Word Is Out* (USA, Mariposa Collective, 1977).

3. Perhaps the farthest extremes of evidence and argument occur with pornography and propaganda: what would pornography be without its evidence, what would propaganda be without its arguments?

4. Without models of documentary strategy that invite us to reflect on the construction of social reality, we have only a corrective act of negation ("this is not reality, it is neither omniscient nor objective") rather than an affirmative act of comprehension ("this is a text, these are its assumptions, this is the meaning it produces"). The lack of an invitation to assume a positive stance handicaps us in our efforts to understand the position we occupy; refusing a position proffered to us is far from affirming a position we actively construct. It is similar to the difference between refusing to "buy" the messages conveyed by advertising, at least entirely, while still lacking any alternative nonfetishistic presentation of commodities that can help us gain a different "purchase" on their relative use- and exchange-value. In many ways, this problem of moving from refusal to affirmation, from protest at the way things are to the construction of durable alternatives, is precisely the problem of the American left. Modernist strategies have something to contribute to the resolution of this problem.

5. After completing this article, I read Jeffrey Youdelman's "Narration, Invention, and History" (*Cineaste* 12 [Spring 1982]: 8–15), which makes a similar point with a somewhat different set of examples. His discussion of imaginative, lyrical uses of commentary in the 1930s and 1940s is particularly instructive.

6. Details of de Antonio's approach are explored in Tom Waugh's "Emile de Antonio and the New Documentary of the Seventies," *Jump Cut*, no. 10/11 (1976): 33–39, and of Wiseman's in Nichols, *Ideology and the Image*, pp. 208–36.

7. An informative discussion of the contradiction between character witnesses with unusual abilities and the rhetorical attempt to make them signifiers of ordinary workers, particularly in *Union Maids*, occurs in Noel King's "Recent 'Political' Documentary—Notes on *Union Maids* and *Harlan County, U.S.A.*," *Screen* 22, no. 2 (1981): 7–18.

8. In this vein, Noel King comments, "So in the case of these documentaries [*Union Maids, With Babies and Banners, Harlan County, U.S.A.*] we might notice the way a discourse of morals or ethics suppresses one of politics and the way a discourse of a subject's individual responsibility suppresses any notion of a discourse on the social and linguistic formation of subjects" (ibid., p. 11). But we might also say, as the filmmakers seem to, "This is how the participants saw their struggle and it is well worth preserving," even though we may wish they did not do so slavishly. There is a difference between criticizing films because they fail to demonstrate the theoretical sophistication of certain analytic methodologies and criticizing them because their textual organization is inadequate to the phenomena they describe.

The Image Mirrored: Reflexivity and the Documentary Film

Jay Ruby

Anyone who recognizes that self-reflection, as mediated linguistically, is integral to the characterization of human social conduct, must acknowledge that such holds also for his own activities as a social "analyst," "researcher," etc.

Anthony Giddens,
New Rules of Sociological Method

My topic is the concept of reflexivity as it applies to the documentary film. Before I can approach this subject, I must first briefly examine the parameters of reflexivity, situate it in a historical-cultural context, and discuss my own relationship to the concept.

To be ideologically consistent, I should and will now situate my thoughts within my own history, in other words, be reflexive about my ideas of reflexivity. In the process of organizing the 1974 Conference on Visual Anthropology, I organized a series of screenings and discussions entitled "Exposing Yourself." The panelists—Sol Worth, Gerry O'Grady, Bob Scholte, Richard Chalfen, and myself—discussed a group of autobiographical, self-referential, and self-consciously made films in terms of a variety of concerns within visual communication and anthropology. Some of those films and ideas have formed the basis for my discussion here.

While I do not intend to proselytize, I should point out that I am partisan. I am convinced that filmmakers along with anthropologists have the ethical, political, aesthetic, and scientific obligations to be reflexive and self-critical about their work. Indeed, I would expand that mandate to include everyone who manipulates a symbolic system for any reason. You will find little direct empirical support for such sweeping statements in this paper. Instead, my focus is more modest. I intend to concentrate on a discussion of the manifestations of reflexivity in documentary films.

As a means of delineating the concept, let us examine the following diagram borrowed from Johannes Fabian's article, "Language, History, and Anthropology":[1] PRODUCER–PROCESS–PRODUCT. I am deliberately using general terms because they serve to remind us that the issues raised are not confined to the cinema even though this paper is.

While one can find exceptions, I think that it is reasonable to say that most filmmakers present us with the product and exclude the other two components. According to popular rhetoric as used in our culture by some people to explain the documentary, these films are produced by people striving to be unbiased, neutral, and objective. They employ fair and accurate means to obtain the true facts about reality. Given that point of view, and I realize that I am oversimplifying, not only is it unnecessary to reveal the producer and the process, such revelation is counterproductive. To reveal the producer is thought to be narcissistic, overly personal, and subjective. The revelation of process is deemed to be untidy, ugly, and confusing to the audience. To borrow a concept from the sociologist Erving Goffman,[2] audiences are not supposed to see backstage. It destroys illusions and causes them to break their suspension of disbelief.

On the other hand, assuming a reflexive stance would be to reveal all three components—to see things this way: PRODUCER–PROCESS–PRODUCT and to suggest that unless audiences have knowledge of all three, a sophisticated and critical understanding of the product is virtually impossible.

To be reflexive is to structure a product in such a way that the audience assumes that the producer, the process of making, and the product are a coherent whole. Not only is an audience made aware of these relationships, but it is made to realize the necessity of that knowledge. To be more formal about it, I would argue that being reflexive means that the producer deliberately and intentionally reveals to his audience the underlying epistemological assumptions that caused him to formulate a set of questions in a particular way, to seek answers to those questions in a particular way, and finally to present his findings in a particular way.

There may be some confusion between *reflexivity* and terms which are sometimes used as synonyms: *autobiography, self-reference*, and *self-consciousness*. In an *autobiographical* work, while the producer—the self—is the center of the work, he can be unself-conscious in his presentation. The author clearly has had to be self-aware in the process of making the product (i.e., the autobiography), but it is possible for him to keep that knowledge private and simply follow the established conventions of that genre. To be *reflexive* is not only to be self-aware, but to be sufficiently self-aware to know what aspects of self are necessary to reveal so that an audience is able to understand both the process employed and the resultant product and to know that the revelation itself is purposive, intentional, and not merely narcissistic or accidentally revealing.[3]

Self-reference, on the other hand, is not autobiographical or reflexive. It is the allegorical or metaphorical use of self—for example, Truffaut's films *400 Blows* and *Day for Night*. The maker's life in this work becomes symbolic of some sort of collective—*all* filmmakers, and perhaps *everyman*. It is popularly assumed that *self-reference* occurs in all art forms: as the cliché goes, an artist uses his personal experience as the basis of his art. The devotees of an art form try to ferret out biographical tidbits so that they can discover the "hidden meaning" behind the artist's work. Again, there is the cultural fact that we believe it is quite common for producers to be self-referential. What I wish to stress is that this self-reference is distinct from reflexivity—one does not necessarily lead to the other.

To be *self-conscious* in the turgid pseudo-Freudian sense of a Fellini, for example, has become a full-time preoccupation particularly among the upper-middle class. However, it is possible and indeed common for this kind of awareness to remain private knowledge for the producer, or at least to be so detached from the product that all but the most devoted are discouraged from exploring the relationship between the maker and his work; and furthermore, the producer does nothing to encourage that exploration. In other words, one can be *reflective* without being *reflexive*. That is, one can become self-conscious without being conscious of that self-consciousness.[4] Only if a producer decides to make his awareness of self a public matter and conveys that knowledge to his audience is it possible to regard the product as reflexive.

I have just suggested that it is possible to produce autobiographical, self-referential, or self-conscious works without being reflexive. Let me clarify. I am simply saying that if the work does not contain sufficient indications that the producer intends his product to be regarded as reflexive, the audience will be uncertain as to whether they are reading into the product more or other than what was meant.[5]

While I am primarily concerned with reflexivity in the documentary film, it is necessary to mention at least some of the general cultural manifestations of reflexiveness. I believe they are to be found in the growing popular realization that the world, and in particular the symbolic world—things, events, and people, as well as news, television, books, and stories—are not what they appear to be. People want to know exactly what the ingredients are before they buy anything—aspirin, cars, television news, or education. We no longer trust the producers: Ralph Nader, the consumer protection movement, truth in lending and advertising laws are the results of this felt need.

On a more profound level, we are moving away from the positivist notion that meaning resides in the world and human beings should strive to discover the inherent, objectively true reality of things.[6] This philosophy of positivism has caused many social scientists as well as documentary filmmakers and journalists to hide themselves and their methods under the guise of objectivity. This point of view is challenged by both Marxists and structuralists.

We are beginning to recognize that human beings construct and impose meaning on the world. We create order. We don't discover it. We organize a reality that is meaningful for us. It is around these organizations of reality that filmmakers construct films. Some filmmakers, like other symbol producers in our culture, are beginning to feel the need to inform their audiences about who they are and how their identities may affect their films. They also wish to instruct their audiences about the process of articulation from the economic, political, and cultural structures and ideologies surrounding the documentary to the mechanics of production.

Reflexive elements in documentaries are undoubtedly a reflection of a general cultural concern with self-awareness. They are also the continuation of a tradition in visual forms of communication. It has been suggested that reflexivity in the visual arts begins with the cave paintings where people drew the outline of their hands on the wall. It is the first sign of authorship. It reminds us of the process and even tells us something about the maker—most of the hands reveal missing finger joints.

In painting we have early examples of reflexivity in Jan van Eyck's *Giovanni Arnolfini and His Bride* (1434), where we find a mirror in the center of what appears to be merely a portrait. In the mirror are the reflections of two people, one of them assumed to be van Eyck. So that the viewer will know for certain, the painter has written around the top of the mirror, "van Eyck was here." I could trace the development of such genres as the self-portrait and other evidences of this kind of sensibility, but it would take us too far astray. It is sufficient to say that by the time movies were invented there was already established a minor tradition of reflexiveness within most pictorial communicative forms.

Turning to the cinema, we discover that reflexivity is to be found more frequently in fiction film than in the documentary. From their beginnings films have been an imperfect illusion. That is, the suspension of disbelief has been broken through either accident or design. Audiences have been reminded that they are spectators having technologically generated vicarious and illusionary experiences. In one sense, every time the camera moves one is reminded of its presence and the construct of the image. Also, there is an early tradition in film of actors making direct contact with the audience. These "theatrical asides" (undoubtedly having a theatrical origin) of Groucho Marx and other comedians, like Woody Allen in *Annie Hall*, momentarily alienate the audience.[7] However, the overall effect of both camera movements and asides is probably not significant and is hardly constructed in a manner that could be called reflexive.

There are three places where one finds sustained reflexive elements in fiction films: (1) comedies in the form of satires and parodies about movies and moviemakers; (2) dramatic films in which the subject matter is movies and moviemakers; and (3) some modernist films which are concerned with exploring the parameters of form, and in that exploration disturb conventions such as the distinction between fiction and nonfiction.[8]

From Edison to Mel Brooks, fiction-filmmakers have been able to mock themselves and their work more easily than have documentarians. Documentary parodies are uncommon and recent in origin. For example, Jim McBride's *David Holzman's Diary*, Mitchell Block's *No Lies*, and Jim Cox's *Eat the Sun*.

In fact, documentary parody is so rare and out of keeping with the sensibilities of people who make these films that when a parody may exist it is regarded as confusing. In Basil Wright's review of Buñuel's *Land Without Bread*, Wright assumed that the narration and music score were errors and not a deliberate attempt on Buñuel's part to be ironic. "Unfortunately, someone (presumably not Buñuel) has added to the film a wearisome American commentary, plus the better part of a Brahms symphony. As a result, picture and sound never coalesce, and it is only the starkness of the presented facts which counts."[9]

Whether Buñuel is, in fact, responsible for the text of the narration and the music score is unclear.[10] It is sufficient for our purposes to realize that it apparently never occurred to Wright that some audiences might regard the juxtaposition of music, narration, and images as ironic, perhaps even as a parody of travelogues and information films.

It is not difficult to see why the possibility of parody did not occur to Wright. Because parody mocks or ridicules communicative forms, conventions, and codes, it can be said that parody has reflexive qualities. Both reflexivity and parody draw attention to the formal qualities of film as film. Most documentarians wish to make their films transparent, that is, to appear to be merely records. Calling attention to the film *as* film frustrates that purpose.[11]

It is interesting to note that the tradition of parody in fiction films commences at the beginning of cinema and continues to the present. The ironic messages in Mel Brooks's *Blazing Saddles* and in *Uncle Josh Jumps*, a silent one-reeler produced in Edison's studio, are amazingly similar. In *Uncle Josh Jumps* we see a man sitting in a theater balcony watching a movie. He ducks and cringes when a train appears on the screen. As each new scene appears he behaves as if the action were live and not on the screen. When a fight appears he jumps onstage and punches the screen fighters, thereby knocking down the screen, exposing the projector and projectionist. The film ends with the moviegoer and projectionist fighting.

Both *Blazing Saddles* and *Uncle Josh Jumps* are comedies. Because they are parodies they serve an additional function. They cause audiences to become alienated from the suspension of disbelief and to become self-conscious about their assumptions concerning film conventions. As stated earlier, parody can have a reflexive function.

Hollywood has produced many films that deal with movies and the lives of the moviemakers: *A Star Is Born* and *Sunset Boulevard* are two examples. However, these films serve not to reveal but to perpetuate popular cultural myths about the glamor of the stars and the industry. As William Siska suggests, "Traditional cinema does not expose the process of production to alienate us from the story that's being told; rather, the camera, lights, and technicians are used as icons to authenticate the notion that we are enjoying a behind the scenes look at how the industry 'really works.'"[12]

Some modernist films, such as Godard's *La Chinoise*, Haskell Wexler's *Medium Cool*, and Agnes Varda's *Lion's Love*, tend to blur conventional distinctions between fiction and nonfiction. For example, in *La Chinoise*, Godard (from behind the camera) interrupts Jean Léaud's monologue on the role of the theater in the revolution and asks him if he is an actor. Léaud responds, "Yes, but I believe this anyway," and returns to his speech. The audience is unable to decide whether they are hearing the sentiments of the director spoken by a character, or the actor spontaneously expressing his personal feelings, or an actor who shares certain ideas with the director and is speaking written lines.

Documentary parodies that purport to be actual footage but are staged, scripted, and acted are similar to those films that mix fictional and nonfictional elements. Both cause audiences to question or at least become confused about their assumptions concerning fiction and documentary and ultimately, I suppose, their assumptions about reality. In that sense, they produce audience self-consciousness and have reflexive qualities. Examining the history of the documentary, we discover that it is to the Russians in the twenties and thirties and the French in the fifties and sixties that we must look for the true origins of documentary reflexivity.[13] Taken together, Jean Rouch's film *Chronicle of a Summer* (*Chronique d'un été*) and Dziga Vertov's *The Man with a Movie Camera* raise most of the significant issues.

In the 1920s Vertov, an artist and founder of the Russian documentary, developed a theory of film in opposition to that of Eisenstein. Vertov argued that the role of film in a revolutionary society should be to raise the consciousness of the audience by creating a film form which caused them to see the world in terms of a dialectical materialism. The Kino Eye (the camera eye) would produce Kino Pravda—Cine Truth.

For Vertov the artifices of fiction produced entertainment—escape and fantasies. Revolutionary filmmakers should take pictures of actuality—the everyday events of ordinary people. This raw stuff of life could then be transformed into meaningful statements. In his film *The Man with a Movie Camera*, Vertov attempted to explicate his theory.[14]

He was more concerned with revealing process than with revealing self. Vertov wished the audience to understand how film works, in mechanical, technical, and methodological as well as conceptual ways, thereby demystifying the creative process. He also wanted audiences to know that filmmaking is work and the filmmaker a worker, a very important justification for art in Leninist Russia. We see the filmmaker, but he is more a part of the process than anything else. One of Vertov's major goals was to aid the audience in their understanding of the process of construction in film so that they could develop a sophisticated and critical attitude. Vertov saw this raising of the visual consciousness of audiences as the way to bring Marxist truth to the masses. Like Godard (who at one point founded a Dziga Vertov film collective), Vertov wished to make revolutionary films which intentionally taught audiences how to see the world in a different way. To locate it in modern terminology,[15] Vertov is suggesting that in order to be able to make the assumption of intention and then to make inferences, viewers must have structural competence; that is, they must have knowledge of the sociocultural conventions related to making inferences of meaning in filmic sign-events.

Rouch, a French anthropologist engaged in field work in West Africa since World War II, is one of the few anthropologists concerned with creating a cinematic form which is peculiarly appropriate for anthropological expression.[16] His film *Chronicle of a Summer* represents an experiment to find that form. Rouch is primarily concerned with the personal: the philosophical problems of doing research and the possible effects of filming research. He is also interested in form. But questions about the formal aspects of structure come from his concern with the self more than from Vertov's concern with the process.

Both films were ahead of their time. Vertov's pioneering work had to wait almost a quarter of a century for Rouch to come along before someone would pursue the questions raised with *A Man with a Movie Camera*. Rouch has said that he sees his own films as being an attempt to combine the personal and participatory concerns of Robert Flaherty with an interest in process derived from Vertov. As we know, Morin described *Chronicle of a Summer* as being *cinéma vérité* in emulation of Vertov's Kino Pravda. Rouch's influence in France has been extensive. In the United States, however, his films are seldom seen, and his work is confused with that of such American direct-cinema people as Leacock, Pennebaker, and the Maysles brothers.

Rouch's films signaled the beginning of a technological revolution that caused some documentarians to face several fundamental issues. Prior to the mid-1960s, film technology was obtrusive, and it limited the type of filming possible. The advent of lightweight, portable sync sound equipment made it feasible for filmmakers to follow people around and film virtually anywhere, to intrude on people's lives—observe them and participate in their activities. Documentarians found themselves confronted with problems similar to those of ethnographers and other fieldworkers.[17] For some it became necessary to rethink the epistemological, moral, and political structures that made the documentary possible. They began to grapple with such questions as:

1. If documentarians claimed that they were trying to film people as they would have behaved if they were not being filmed, how could they account for the presence of the camera and crew and the modifications it caused?

2. On what basis can filmmakers justify their intrusion into the lives of the people they film?

3. Given the mandate of objectivity, how could the filmmaker convey his feelings as well as his understanding of the people he filmed and about the subject of the film?

4. What are the ideological implications of documentary film?

5. What obligations does the filmmaker have to his audience?[18]

While these questions are obviously not new—the social documentarians of the 1930s grappled with many of them—they have been raised again in the last ten years with a new urgency because of several factors: (1) the potential created by the new technology; (2) a general shift in our society toward self-awareness; (3) the influence of university education on young filmmakers (i.e., more documentarians received social science training); and (4) the effect of television news and documentary.

The desire to explore the capacities of this equipment and the self-awareness it produced created a need for new methods and forms of expression. Feeling equally uncomfortable with self-referentiality (where the self becomes submerged into metaphor) and with the apparent impersonality of traditional documentary (where the expression of self is deemed improper), some filmmakers found new ways to explore themselves, their world, and in a very real sense, cinema itself. They have confronted these questions by exposing themselves in the same way they expose others. One particular manifestation—the development of nonfiction films dealing with the filmmaker's own family and their immediate world—seems to represent a nonfiction genre which fits neither the traditional definition of the documentary nor the personal art film. In fact, these films violate canons of both genres.

The documentary film was founded on the Western middle-class need to explore, document, explain, understand, and hence symbolically control the world. It has been what "we" do to "them." "They" in this case are usually the poor, the powerless, the disadvantaged, and the politically suppressed and oppressed. Documentary films dealing with the rich and powerful or even the middle class are as sparse as are social science studies of these people. The documentary film has not been a place where people explored themselves or their own culture.

To find this subject matter one must look at the experimental, avant-garde filmmakers or at the home movie. In fact, film artists like Jonas Mekas in the treatment of his life entitled *Notes, Diaries, and Sketches* and Stan Brakhage in *Window Water Baby Moving* have developed a deliberate aesthetic from the conventions of the home movie in much the same way as Lee Friedlander and Diane Arbus created a snapshot aesthetic in art photography.

Until recently the division was relatively clear. If you wanted to make films about people exotic to your own experience you made documentaries, and if you wished to explore yourself, your feelings, and the known world around you, you made personal art films. Recently a number of films have appeared which confuse this taxonomy. They are films that deal with the filmmaker's family and culture. In subject matter they violate the norms of traditional documentary in that they overtly deal in an involved way with a personal interest of the filmmaker. Because many of these filmmakers come from a documentary tradition, they do not employ the conventions of the personal art film; rather, they use a documentary style. In other words, they have the look of a documentary even though the subject matter is exotic to the genre. Examples of these films would include Jerome Hill's autobiography *Portrait*, Miriam Weinstein's *Living with Peter*, Amalie Rothschild's *Nana, Mom, and Me*, and Jeff Kreines's *The Plaint of Steve Kreines as Told by His Younger Brother Jeff*.

These filmmakers have created an autobiographical and family genre which cannot be comfortably fit into either the art film or the documentary. This creation, which employs elements from both genres, has the effect of making us self-conscious about our expectations. In addition, these films are clearly self-consciously produced and often quite overtly reflexive.

While it is obviously impossible to reveal the producer and not the process, it is possible to concentrate on one and only incidentally deal with the other. Most of these filmmakers share with Rouch a primary concern with self as maker and person and make that quest dominate their films.

It is in other types of films that we see a concern with the revelation of process emerge. This interest seems to come from two main sources: (1) politically committed filmmakers who, like Vertov and Godard, are interested in the ideological implications of film form—for example, David Rothberg's *My Friend Vince*; and (2) filmmakers who seek validation for their work within social science and who, consequently, feel the need to articulate and justify their methodologies—for example, Tim Asch's *Ax Fight*.

Finally, there are a number of documentaries which contain reflexive elements which appear to be present through accident rather than design. Direct-cinema films, such as Pennebaker's *Don't Look Back* and the Canadian Film Board's *Lonely Boy*, are filled with what were considered at the time to be "accidents"—

that is, shots which were out of focus, shots where the mike and/or sound person appeared in the frame, etc. Very soon these "accidents" became signs of direct-cinema style, an indication that the director did not control the event he was recording. Audiences appeared to believe in them so much as a validating device that fiction-filmmakers who wished to increase verisimilitude in their films began to employ such direct-cinema signs as camera jiggle, graininess, and bad focus—for example, John Cassavetes's *Faces* or the battle scenes in Kubrick's *Dr. Strangelove*. In addition to verifying the "uncontrolled" aesthetic of direct cinema as a recorder of actuality these elements served to remind audiences of the process of filmmaking and, of course, the presence of the film crew.[19]

Other films such as Mike Rubbo's *Sad Song of Yellow Skin* and *Waiting for Fidel* and the Maysles brothers' *Grey Gardens* contain interactions between the subject and crew and other "backstage" behaviors which provide audiences with information about the producers and process.

It would appear that these apparently reflexive elements are again an accident of the moment: an unexpected turn of events during the shooting rather than the result of deliberate pre-production planning. What is interesting and does represent a departure from documentary conventions is that these "accidents" are allowed to remain in the final version of the film. It seems that these filmmakers acquired footage which had a particular "look" and which could not be cut in traditional ways. I would argue that it was primarily a professional need for a finished product rather than an interest in the question of reflexivity that motivated them to include those elements which cause these films to appear reflexive. For example, "big" Edie and "little" Edie Beale would not ignore the presence of the camera and crew, that is, learn to behave as "proper" subjects of a documentary film. In spite of this situation (or possibly because of it), the Maysles brothers decided to continue and make *Grey Gardens* even though it has a "look" which is different from their other films. In one sense, the filmmakers were allowing the circumstances of the shooting to dictate the form of the film, which consequently revealed the process and producer.

In contrast to these films of "accidental" reflexivity, there does exist a project which was designed at the outset to explore the consequences of documentary and ethnographic reflexivity. To my knowledge it is the first American film to continue the explorations of Rouch and Vertov. Hubert Smith, a filmmaker, and Malcolm Shuman, an anthropologist, are presently in the field filming an ethnography of some Mexican Indians. According to their proposal, "The principal strategy to be undertaken by this project is to invest ethnographic material in film with additional self-conscious components—the field investigators, their actions, personalities, methods, and their dealings with an advisory panel of colleagues."[20] They intend to accomplish this task by: (1) filming the Indians in a context that includes the observers; (2) filming the field team and the Indians in mutual socialization; and (3) filming the field team as they interact with each other and with the advisory panel.[21]

In addition to the films they produce, they will provide "a written body of field-related methods for investing nonfiction films with internal self-conscious statements of procedure."[22] I mention Smith's project now, even though it is incomplete and its significance is difficult to assess, because it represents a step toward a truly reflexive documentary cinema. Whatever else these films may be, they will have been intentionally reflexive from their inception. They will provide us with a chance to compare "accidental" and "deliberate" documentary reflexivity.

One could argue that the idea of "accidental" reflexiveness is a contradiction in terms and that reflexivity depends on intentionality and deliberateness. In fact, a number of the arguments presented here appear contradictory.

On the one hand, I have generated a definition of reflexiveness which situates some recent documentary films within a tradition in the visual arts, a tradition in which the producer is publicly concerned with the relationship among self, process, and product. In addition, I have tried to show how these concerns have been transformed by a general increase in public self-awareness and by the technological changes that occurred in filmmaking in the 1960s.

At the same time I have said that most documentary reflexiveness has been more accidental than deliberate. In effect, I have been arguing that some documentary filmmakers have used reflexive elements in their films (or at least have been regarded by some audiences as being reflexive) without really intending to do so, or at least without examining the implications. Further, I would argue that based on my examination of these films, on published interviews with the filmmakers, and on personal conversations and correspondence, these filmmakers appear to lack a sufficiently sophisticated philosophical, moral, aesthetic, or scientific motivation for a rigorous exploration of the consequences of reflexivity for documentary cinema. They seem oblivious to the fact that reflexivity has been explored by social scientists and other scholars for some time and that there is an extensive literature.[23] As a consequence, some of the films mentioned above which contain these "accidentally" reflexive elements are regarded as narcissistic, superficial, self-indulgent, or appealing to an elite in-group.

The contradiction can be phrased in the form of a question: Why haven't more documentary filmmakers explored the implications of reflexivity, when reflexive elements crop up in their films? To adequately explore this question would require a lengthy discussion of complicated issues such as the cultural role of the documentary or the adequacy of the concepts of objectivity and subjectivity for the documentary, and so forth. However, I would like to present what I believe to be the kernel of the issue.

To be reflexive is to reveal that films—all films, whether they are labeled fiction, documentary, or art—are created, structured articulations of the filmmaker and not authentic, truthful, objective records. Sooner or later the do-cumentarian is going to have to face the possibility of assuming the socially diminished role of interpreter of the world, of no longer being regarded as an objective recorder of reality. If this is the case, then it is not too difficult to see why these filmmakers are reluctant to explore the idea.

My intention here was to restrain my obvious partisanship. Clearly, I have failed to do so. I should now like to conclude by suggesting that documentary filmmakers have a social obligation to *not* be objective. The concept of objectivity, inappropriately borrowed from the natural sciences, has little support from the social sciences: both social scientists and documentary filmmakers are interpreters of the world. As Sue Ellen Jacobs has put it, "Perhaps the best thing we can learn from anthropological writings [and I would add films and photographs] is how people who call themselves 'anthropologists' see the world of others."[24] To present ourselves and our products as anything else is to foster a dangerous false consciousness on the part of our audiences.

Reflexivity offers us a means whereby we can instruct our audiences to understand the process of producing statements about the world. "We study man, that is, we reflect on ourselves studying others, because we must, because man in civilization is the problem."[25]

NOTES

1. Johannes Fabian, "Language, History, and Anthropology," *Journal of the Philosophy of the Social Sciences* 1 (1971): 1947.

2. Erving Goffman, *The Presentation of Self in Everyday Life* (Garden City, N.Y.: Doubleday, 1959).

3. In commenting on the manuscript of this paper, Gaye Tuchman made the following observation, which I believe to be both relevant and important to the distinction that I am trying to make between autobiography and reflexivity: "Autobiography may also be naively self-conscious. That is, autobiography is one's purposive ordering of one's life to create coherence. It assumes coherence and so necessarily eliminates that which cannot be ordered and of which the autobiographer might not even be aware. For, perhaps, we can only perceive those amorphous phenomena which we are ultimately capable of classifying and ordering. Perhaps, then, reflexive self-consciousness is not merely autobiography, but the ability to see ourselves as others see us—as co-present subject and object, as perceiving subject and the simultaneous object of others' perceptions. Such self-consciousness necessarily entails a simultaneous self-involvedness and self-estrangement; a standing outside of oneself in a way that is foreign to the non-reflexive everyday self."

4. See Barbara Babcock, "Reflexivity: Definitions and Discriminations," unpublished paper delivered at the annual meeting of the American Anthropological Association, Washington, D.C., 1977.

5. Sol Worth and Larry Gross, "Symbolic Strategies," *Journal of Communication* 24 (Winter 1974): 27–39.

6. Gunther Stent, "Limits to the Scientific Understanding of Man," *Science* 187 (1975): 1052–57.

7. I am using the term *alienate* here in the sense that Brecht used it—that is, as the breaking of the suspension of disbelief during a performance. See *Brecht on Theatre*, trans. John Willet (New York: Hill and Wang, 1964).

8. It is curious that the concern with form and structure which has dominated the works of some modernist writers, painters, musicians, and filmmakers, and of scientists from physicists to anthropologists, has not interested many documentarians. For example, I know of no documentary filmmakers who deliberately choose uninteresting and trivial subject matter in order to be able to concentrate on the significance of formal and structural elements in the documentary.

9. Basil Wright, "Land Without Bread and Spanish Earth," in *The Documentary Tradition*, ed. Lewis Jacobs (New York: Hopkinson and Blake, 1971), p. 146.

10. Roy Armes thinks that it was Buñuel (see Armes, *Film and Reality* [New York: Pelican, 1974], p. 189): "*Land Without Bread* is also remarkable in the way it anticipates later modernist cinema by its triple impact. It combines devastating images of poverty, starvation and idiocy with a dry matter of fact commentary and a musical score filled with romantic idealism." Barsam, however, seems to disagree (see his *Non-Fiction Film* [New York: Dutton, 1973], p. 83): "As an information film, even a travel film (but hardly one designed to promote tourism), *Las hurdes* is an effective and disturbing record of poverty and neglect; but as a social document it is awkward and as mute as a faded poster despite its tragic theme."

11. Jeanne Allen, "Self-Reflexivity and the Documentary Film," *Ciné-Tracts* 1 (Summer 1977): 37–43.

12. William Siska, "Metacinema: A Modern Necessity," unpublished paper delivered at the annual meeting of the Society for Cinema Studies, Evanston, Illinois, 1977. The quote is from p. 3.

13. I am excluding from consideration illustrated-lecture and adventurer/travelogue films. These cinematic forms predate the documentary. In fact, the illustrated-lecture film finds its origins in the lantern-slide lecture of the early nineteenth century. They constitute an unstudied form of the cinema and have been overlooked by most historians of documentary film. However, they do contain the earliest evidence of reflexive elements in nonfiction film. The makers frequently employ first-person narration to describe themselves as authors and the process they used to make the film. In many cases, these films are primarily about the making of the film and thereby cause the films themselves to become the object of the audience's attention. However, like the traditional fiction films about movies and moviemakers, the apparent reflexiveness of these films is partially based on the assumed difficulties of production and the heroic acts performed by the makers in the process of getting the footage. These films do not lead viewers to a sophisticated understanding of film as communication; rather, they cause them to continue to marvel at the mysterious wonders of the intrepid adventurer-filmmakers.

14. See "The Vertov Papers," *Film Comment* 8 (Spring 1972): 46–51.

15. See Worth and Gross, "Symbolic Strategies."

16. See Jean Rouch, "The Camera and the Man," *Studies in the Anthropology of Visual Communication* 1 (1974): 37–44.

17. "With the development of lightweight equipment and the growth of an aesthetic of direct cinema, the ethical problem of the relationship of filmmakers to the people in their films became more amorphous. . . . Regardless of whether consent is flawed on such grounds as intimidation or deceit, a fundamental ethical difficulty in direct cinema is that when we use people in a sequence we put them at risk without sufficiently informing them of potential hazards" (Calvin Pryluck, "Ultimately We Are All Outsiders: The Ethics of Documentary Filming," *Journal of the University Film Association* 28 [Winter 1976]: 21–29; the quotations are from pp. 21 and 29).

18. James M. Linton, "The Moral Dimension in Documentary," *Journal of the University Film Association* 28 (Spring 1976): 17–22.

19. See Stephen Mamber, *Cinéma Vérité in America: Studies in Uncontrolled Documentary* (Cambridge, Mass.: MIT Press, 1974).

20. Hubert Smith, "Contemporary Yucatec Maya Allegory Through a Self-conscious Approach to Ethnography and Ethnographic Film," a proposal submitted to the National Endowment for the Humanities.

21 The advising panel consists of four specialists in Indian anthropology (one member is Indian by birth and an anthropologist by profession), three visual anthropologists, and a philosopher of social science.

22. Smith proposal, cited n. 20.

23. For example, see Bob Scholte, "Toward a Reflexive and Critical Anthropology," in Dell Hymes, ed., *Reinventing Anthropology* (New York: Random House, 1972), pp. 430–58.

24. Quoted in Simeon W. Chilungi, "Issues in the Ethics of Research Method: An Interpretation of the Anglo-American Perspective," *Current Anthropology* 17 (1976): 469.

25. Stanley Diamond, "Anthropology in Question," in Hymes, ed., *Reinventing Anthropology*, pp. 401–29; the quotation is from p. 408.

Theories and Strategies
of the Feminist
Documentary

E. Ann Kaplan

E. Ann Kaplan teaches at Rutgers University. Her article on feminist documentary first appeared in Millennium Film Journal *in the fall of 1982. I thought the article was very good, but it was also very long, so once more there was that painful decision to reprint only the last half of the article.*

In the missing section Kaplan begins by exploring recent theories about the documentary, particularly as these have been developed in Screen. *The critique of documentary arises from realist strategies being seen as embodying the old consciousness and thus as unable to represent new ways of seeing.*

For Noel King, the documentary strategies in films like Union Maids *or* Harlan County, U.S.A. *work to suppress any discourse on the social construction of the subjects being interviewed. Rather, the films assert the individual's responsibility for bringing about change through a moral insight into justice. Like Hollywood films, realist devices in documentaries smooth over possible contradiction, incoherencies, and eruptions that might reflect a reality far less ordered and continuous than is in fact the case.*

Kaplan proceeds to survey briefly the main theoretical influences underpinning this concept of realism, showing origins in Saussurian linguistics, Barthes's study of the rhetoric of the image and of classical realist codes, Lacanian psychoanalytic theories of the construction of the subject, and finally Foucault's concept of history as discourse. The following analysis of specific feminist documentaries aims to test the validity of the theory of documentary realism and to show that issues are more complex than has been recognized.

Over the past decade, a large number of women's independent films have been produced internationally; they reflect a wide variety of styles and genres (from realism to animation, from the nonnarrative abstract film to fiction films), a broad range of subjects, and a wide spectrum of ideological perspectives. Women interested in bringing about change, however (I reserve the word "feminist" for such women), have been involved in the question of strategies in two important ways: first, ever since the publication in 1973 of Claire Johnston's essay "Women's Cinema as Counter Cinema" filmmakers and critics have been involved in an often heated debate about the most effective strategies to be used *within* film texts; second, and more recently, they have been concerned with the question of strategies of production, exhibition, and distribution of independent feminist films. Both of these involve the positioning of the spectator, but in the first, focus is on how a *text* positions the spectator (if, indeed, we agree that texts monolithically do this); while in the second, the focus is on how the *institutional context* of a film's production and reception affect the way the spectator "reads" the film.

In structuring my discussion around the issues of strategies for bringing about change, I realize that I am entering the slippery terrain where theory and practice overlap. This is dangerous on two levels: there is first the danger of alienating both theorists and those involved in practice; and second, there is the danger of slippage of terms as one moves from one discourse to another.

But in the case of feminism in particular the bridging of discourses seems crucial: feminism, as it has always defined itself historically, is a social and political movement; it has risen out of the realm of the social, that is, out of women's dissatisfaction with their political and social positioning. It is thus particularly inappropriate for feminist thought to remain locked into a theoretical discourse unrelated to practice. This is not to say that feminists should not develop theory—far from it. For if theory needs a practice to which it relates, practice without theory is equally empty.

In this first part of the essay, concerned with the debate about the most effective cinematic strategies, I will, first, demonstrate that the attack on women's realist documentary was part of an attack on realism in general and that it involved a related attack on "essentialism," or the assumption that there existed a special female power in the body of individual women. Second, I will discuss two well-known early women's documentaries in order to show that these criticisms have a certain validity while at the same time exploring some of the problems with the theory out of which the criticisms emerge. And finally, I will analyze and evaluate some alternative cinematic strategies that arose specifically out of the theoretical problems with realism.

In the second (shorter) part of the essay, I will deal with the strategies of production, exhibition, and reception, and raise a number of questions about work that needs to be done as we look back at the enterprise of the last decade—an enterprise that reveals a shift from the essentially didactic and propagandistic strategies of early activists and bourgeois feminists, to the focus on signifying practices, that is, on representation and the cinematic apparatus, which are now seen as crucial concerns in any effort to bring about change.

Part I

First, the objection against realism and *cinéma vérité*: In her essay, Claire Johnston argued that *cinéma vérité*, or the "cinema of nonintervention," was dangerous for feminists since it used a realist aesthetic developed specifically out of capitalist notions of representation. *Vérité* films do not break the illusion of realism. Since the "truth" of our oppression cannot be captured on celluloid by means of an innocent camera, for feminist cinema to be effective, she argued, it must be a countercinema. "Any revolutionary must challenge the depiction of reality; it is not enough to discuss the oppression of women within the text of the film: the language of the cinema/depiction of reality must also be interrogated, so that a break between ideology and text is effected."[1] Feminist filmmakers, that is, must confront within their films the accepted representations of reality so as to expose their falseness. Realism as a style is unable to change consciousness because it does not depart from the forms that embody the old consciousness. Thus, prevailing realist codes—of camera, lighting, sound, editing, mise-en-scène—must be abandoned and the cinematic apparatus used in a new way so as to challenge audiences' expectations and assumptions about life.

Noel King argues something very similar in a recent *Screen* article on two political feminist documentaries—*Union Maids* and *Harlan County, U.S.A.* (which belong in the category of historical/retrospective films). He elaborates on points that Johnston, given her brief essay, was unable to develop, and attempts to "read these documentaries against the grain, to refuse the reading it is the work of their textual systems to secure."[2] In doing this, he is applying the same critical categories that have been used to decode Hollywood films, making essentially no distinction between the realist techniques used in the classical Hollywood tradition and those being used in the new feminist documentary. (He is here building on work done by Stephen Neale on the thirties populist films and Nazi propaganda films.)[3] King points, for example, to the way the films' strategies work to suppress any discourse on the social construction of the subjects being interviewed in the interests of asserting the individual's responsibility for bringing about change through a moral insight into injustice: "In this sense, the politics in *Union Maids* might be termed a 'redemptive politics'; that is to say . . . a system where questions of individual responsibility are paramount. It is a politics articulated by textual mechanisms which fix the individual subject as responsible, as either fulfilling or not fulfilling a morally given imperative, and this in turn results in a notion of triumph or guilt."[4]

Second, he talks of the films' strategies as essentially narrative ones; they use, he says, "a series of sub-forms of narratives: biography, autobiography and popular narrative history." These, King shows, all follow a cause-effect relationship, the origin always containing the end. Through the linking of archival footage, the anecdotal reminiscences constructed in the interviews, and the bridging voice-over narration (spoken by the three women) talking about America in the 1930s, *Union Maids* produces a " 'discourse of continuity' which results not in 'the past' but in the effect of the past."[5] What King is ultimately objecting to is the way the narrative in *Union Maids* and *Harlan County, U.S.A.* produces a "syntagmatic flow of events, an easy diachronic progression which ensures a working out of all problems, guarantees an increase in knowledge on the reader's part, promises containment and completion."[6] This kind of suturing is, of course, the traditional device of the classic Hollywood film in its aim to smooth over possible contradictions, incoherences, and eruptions that might reflect a reality far less ordered, coherent, or continuous than Hollywood wants to admit or to know. Like Claire Johnston, King concludes by asserting the necessity of creating a different type of text, one that resists the rhetorical conventions of populist cultural history that "depicts its own strategies and practices, and which does not provide a complete, unified representation of class and collectivity."[7]

The second overall objection to women's realist films is summarized by the charge of essentialism. In their discussion of several textual strategies employed by women artists, Sandy Flitterman and Judith Barry argue that female creators of all kinds must avoid claiming a specific female power which could find expression if allowed to be explored freely. They realize that the impulse toward this notion is understandable for the way it seeks "to reinforce satisfaction in being a woman in a culture that does the opposite"[8] and to encourage solidarity among women through emotional appeal. But, they argue, this form of feminist art harbors a danger by not taking into account "the social contradictions involved in 'femininity.' " They suggest that "a more theoretically informed art can contribute to enduring changes by addressing itself to structural and deep-seated causes of women's oppression rather than its effects. A radical feminist art would include an understanding of how women are constructed through social practices in culture."[9] They argue ultimately for "an aesthetic designed to subvert the production of 'woman' as commodity," much as Claire Johnston had earlier stated that to be feminist, a cinema had to be a countercinema.

Before analyzing the validity of these positions on realist women's documentaries, it is important to understand the theoretical sources for such arguments. Although Russian formalism and Brecht had some place in their development, by far the most important influence on new film criticism generally came from the fields of semiology, structuralism, and psychoanalysis as they were developed in France in the fifties and sixties by writers such as Lévi-Strauss, Lacan,

Metz, Barthes, Kristeva, and Althusser. They found their way into British film criticism in the seventies, and shortly afterwards into the work of American graduate students who studied at the French Cinema School organized in part by Metz and Bellour. The combined influence of the French and British film theory produced a new body of theory in America that has far-reaching implications in relation to the underlying view of the human subject and of women in society, as is evident from the attack on realism.

The first crucial concept implied in the criticism of realism is that of language as a signifying system. Saussure, the French linguist, is credited with "discovering" semiology, or the science of signs. He believed that the meaning of language was to be found not within the words themselves or the thoughts of the individual speaker, but in the relation of elements within the sign system. Signifier and signified, that is, together comprise the sign, but have no meaning outside of this relation. As Saussure says: "Signs function, then, not through their intrinsic value but through their relative position. . . . In language there are only differences *without positive terms*. Whether we take the signified or the signifier, language has neither ideas nor sounds that existed before the linguistic system, but only conceptual and phonic differences that have issued from the system."[10]

As Frank Lentricchia points out, such an idea of difference "punctures the mystifying notion of a transcendental signified . . . and it punctures the persistent notion of a Cartesian subject (the key modernist version of the transcendental signified) which as pretemporal phenomenological voice could direct the play of difference without, in turn, being directed by such play."[11]

Important here is the decentering of a hitherto unquestioned autonomous and indvidualistic Cartesian "I." "I" is now simply the subject in a subject-predicate linguistic system. Far from being at the center, the producer of language, the subject is controlled and decentered by the laws that govern the language system.

Such a position clearly undermines the whole tradition of thought introduced by Descartes. This tradition was first questioned by the international Romantic and post-Romantic movement, through the thinkers who most influenced the early twentieth century: Rousseau, Darwin, Nietzsche, Marx, and Freud. These thinkers represent a variety of discourses which all, in one way or another, began to question the unproblematic self; but the full force of their work was not generally felt until the impact of the First World War made many of their theories suddenly relevant.

Semiology can be considered, then, as a reaction against nineteenth-century humanist habits of thought that remained despite the inroads produced by the thinkers outlined. But semiology takes the argument one step further by positing a subject who is constructed *in discourse* rather than preexisting and merely *using* discourse. The earlier thinkers did not question their own ability (methodologically) to analyze their subject matter "objectively," and it is this examination of the very tools of analysis (signification) that characterizes semiology and that puts the nails in the coffin of the unified self.

Influenced by semiology, Lacan contributed further to the concept of the decentered self through his adaptation of Freud's theories. For Lacan, sexual difference is constructed psychoanalytically through the Oedipal process, which is now linked to the acquisition of language; the Mirror Phase marks the creation of an alienated subject replacing the unity with the Mother that characterizes the prelinguistic stage of the Imaginary. The constitution of subjectivity, in this theory, is particularly problematic for women, who, on leaving the pre-Oedipal world of the Imaginary, enter a Symbolic world dominated by the Law of the Father. In patriarchal structures, thus, woman is located as Other (enigma, mystery) and is thereby viewed as outside of (male) language.

A third important influence was the work of Christian Metz and Roland Barthes. Metz extended Saussure's theories of language into film, while Barthes applied them to our entire cultural system. Whereas Metz articulated a semiotics of the cinema, Barthes revealed that we live in a world that comprises a whole series of signifying systems, of which language, although dominant, is only one. Sign systems range from clothing, eating, and sexual habits to photography, advertisements, and, importantly, film images. Like languages, film is a sign system that, for Barthes, functions largely on the level of myth and has lost its connection to any tangible referent. The arbitrariness of language and image signifying systems allows this to happen: we live largely in a world of connotation that is culturally produced. Images, thus, reflect not lived experience (actuality, the referent) but the dominant codes through which a culture "apprehends reality."[12]

The "reality" that our particular culture (at this historical moment) has by and large accepted is that developed through the powerful art forms which emerged at the time of the Industrial Revolution: nineteenth-century painting, music, and literature which reflected a bourgeois realism and were divorced from any historical specificity. According to Barthes, the world defined through these art forms was seen as *the* natural and unchanging "reality," outside of which there was nothing. Thus, a class-bound, limited construction of society was imposed on the culture at large, excluding other possible "realities," i.e., other conceptions of society, class, gender, and racial concerns. Although the modernist movement undermined and critiqued bourgeois realism, nineteenth-century realist conventions continued to dominate the powerful forms of mass entertainment (made possible by the Industrial Revolution and the new technologies): that is, film, radio, popular music, popular literature, television.

For Barthes, so hegemonic are the codes of the various signifying systems that it makes little sense to talk any longer of an "author" of a novel or a film; it is language or the cinematic apparatus that speaks, not the author. The reader/spectator is instead the place where the meaning of the text comes together. Theory is thus focused on how a text is "read," on the way a text constructs a certain position for the spectator by establishing certain modes of address; this, as we will see, is particularly important when thinking about feminist strategies of documentary films.

A fourth direction of research, exemplified by the work of Foucault, that has had a strong influence (it is evident in Noel King's comments on *Union Maids* and *Harlan County*) is the reading of traditional history as the "desire to make human consciousness the originating subject of all learning."[13] Historians, in this view, falsely adopt a notion of events as the actions of historical people. For Foucault, history is simply one discourse among others, a particular construction of events, usually for the benefit of those in power. This theory shows the futility of women's attempts to recreate "their own" histories in documentary, since all minority discourse has already been constructed by the dominant one. Such a history, in this view, could only be the discourse of the powerless and the excluded, as they have been positioned historically in patriarchy.

Finally, one must consider the work examining the relation between ideology and text, which echoes that between ideology and the social formation. This work is initiated with Althusser's revision of Marx's idea of consciousness shaped by the social formation (i.e., by man's experience of certain economic relations, principally the division of labor and a hierarchical class structure). For Althusser, ideology is a series of representations and images: the term no longer refers to the conscious ideological components of all bourgeois institutions and modes of production, but to the representations of reality that any society assumes, i.e., "the images, myths, ideas or concepts rather than . . . beliefs people consciously hold."[14] These myths can only be accounted for in terms of the mechanisms of the unconscious. It was in this way that feminist film critics originally committed to traditional Marxism began to turn to psychoanalysis (especially as read by Lacan) and to attempt to integrate a theory of the unconscious with Marxist concepts.[15] What in fact happened, as we will see, is that the whole theoretical base moved away from concern with social institutions themselves to preoccupation with the signifying practices through which we derive our knowledge of "reality," including that of the social structures we inhabit.

The stress on signifying practices followed logically from the theory that, given their hegemonic shaping function, these practices are in fact all we can ever "know." Yet, as Derrida has noted, people cling to the belief that there is "some final, objective, unmediated 'real world' . . . about which we can have knowledge."[16] The conventions of traditional art commit us to the voice of the primary means of communication, and this involves what Derrida calls "a falsifying 'metaphysics of presence' based on the illusion that we are ultimately able to 'come face to face' once and for all with objects." There will always be kinds of art that "appear to involve an apparently straightforward and stable commitment to an unchanging world 'beyond' themselves."[17]

Realism as an artistic style is designed to perpetuate this illusion of a stable world; and within realism it is of course the *vérité* documentary that seems most confidently "a window through which . . . [the] world is clearly visible" and "where the signifiers appear to point directly and confidently to the signifieds."[18] The realist aesthetic semiologists were in opposiiton to was developed in the postwar period, stimulated in part by the Italian neorealist movement. Theorists Kracauer and Bazin argued for the cinema "as the redemption of physical reality" and for the belief that realist techniques allowed us to perceive actuality for ourselves, unmediated by the distortions produced through other cinematic techniques. The realism outside of the commercial cinema stimulated by World War II, whether documentary or fiction, took as its aim the capturing on film of the daily experiences of ordinary people. Directors saw their closer relationship to lived experience as arising from (a) their use of working class people and issues for their subjects (i.e., this class, and its concerns, are somehow more "real" than the middle classes); (b) their basing of their films on real-life rather than fictional events; (c) their use of on-location shooting rather than artificial studio sets; (d) finally, their use of cinematic techniques, such as the long take, which were assumed to prevent the meddling with actuality that was characteristic, in their view, of montage.

The first independent women's films that I will discuss situated themselves essentially in the kind of realist tradition which is anathema to the semiologists. The immediate influence was primarily the British Free Cinema movement and the work of the National Film Board of Canada, but the French New Wave was also important. Particularly influential for women's documentaries, in the midst of this complex interaction affecting film generally, was the work of the American Newsreel Collective, started in 1962 and largely inspired by Norm Fruchter after working in England. Newsreel's aims (partly influenced by Vertov's weekly newsreel of events from the war front) were explicitly propagandistic; i.e., to publicize the many political events that sixties radicals were involved in, including civil rights, community organizing, black power, the Vietnam movement, strikes and sit-ins, the takeover of educational institutions, and finally, the women's movement. They used the, by this time familiar, *vérité* techniques (that originated in the French New Wave) of fast film stock (with its grey, grainy tones), handheld camera, interviews, voiceover (not necessarily commentary), editing both for shock effect and to develop a specific interpretation of political events. Made on a very low budget, and in a collective mode, the films are necessarily rough, often sloppy; but this reflects merely the overriding aim not to produce aesthetic objects but to create powerful organizing tools. It is precisely their validity as organizing tools that the new theory questions. For according to the theory, the films draw on codes that cannot change consciousness.

This is expressed most strongly by Eileen McGarry in her article "Documentary, Realism and Women's Cinema." She points out that long before the filmmakers arrive at the scene, reality itself is coded "first in the infrastructure of the social formation (human economic practice) and secondly by the superstructure of politics and ideology."[19] The filmmaker, then, is "not dealing with reality, but with that which has become the pro-filmic event: that which exists and happens in front of the camera."[20] She argues that to ignore the "manner in which the dominant ideology and cinematic traditions encode the pro-filmic event is to hide the fact that reality is selected and altered by the presence of the film workers, and the demands of the equipment."[21]

While this is true to a certain extent (obviously any screen image is the result of a great deal of selection, in terms of what footage to show, which shot to place next to which, the angle and distance from the subject, what words to use, etc.), as we will see, the documentarist neither has total control over the referent nor is she totally controlled by signifying practices. Paradoxically, what she does have more control over is precisely ideology. For I cannot even begin a discussion of the films without differentiating them according to ideological perspective—i.e., their feminist politics—and this is a distinction that the theory does not allow for, given its high level of abstraction. All the early films used the same cinematic strategies, but the ends to which these strategies were directed fell into two broad camps: there were, first, films like the pioneering Newsreel's *Woman's Films* that exhibited a clear leftist-activist politics; and, second, films like Reichert/Klein's *Growing Up Female* that reflected a more liberal-bourgeois stance, showing how sex roles in our society were clearly demarcated so as to privilege men, but not analyzing the underlying reasons for gender-typing or dealing with class and economic relations. The Newsreel film aimed to raise consciousness explicitly and exclusively on the matter of exploitation of working-class women by a capitalist system geared to support private enterprise and the accumulation of individual wealth, while the second film urged women to try to free themselves from the sex roles that limited their opportunities for a rich, fulfilling, challenging, individual life. Yet, the cinematic devices in the two films were identical.

Let us now look at two early films, *Joyce at 34* and *Janie's Janie* (made shortly after those already mentioned) in order to assess the degree to which some of the semiological theoretical criticisms are indeed valid, and the degree to which they are clearly inadequate: to explain concrete differences between the films (a) in terms of their ideology; (b) in terms of the conception of the cinematic apparatus, so that fiction and documentary are seen as essentially the same; and (c) in terms of the conception of the positioning of the spectator as "fixed" by the codes of the signifying practices.

First, let me summarize the degree to which this criticism of realism is valid for aspects of both *Joyce at 34* and *Janie's Janie*. To begin with, the cinematic strategies of both films are indeed such as to establish an unwelcome imbalance between author and spectator. The authors in each case assume the position of the one in possession of knowledge, while the spectators are forced into the position of passive consumers of this knowledge. The filmic processes leave us with no work to do, so that we sit passively and receive the message in the first film about how marriage, family, and career can together function harmoniously, and in the second about how, with some determination, a woman on welfare can organize her community for needed changes. There is a classic resolution in each case, since both heroines arrive at some destination, leaving us with a sense of completion, as though there were nothing left for us to do.

Second, the direct mode of address in both films encourages us to relate to the images of Joyce and Janie as "real" women, as if we could know them. Yet, in fact, both figures are constructed in the film by the processes of camera, lighting, sound, editing. They have no other ontological status than that of representations.

Third, the reason we do not realize that each female figure is a representation is that neither film draws attention to itself as film, or makes us aware that we are watching a film. Neither film, thus, breaks our usual habits of passive viewing in the commercial cinema.

Fourth, underlying all of the above is the key notion of the unified self that characterizes presemiological thought. Both Joyce and Janie, as subjects, are seen in the autobiographical mode, as having essences that have persisted through time and whose personal growth or change is autonomous, outside the influence of social structures, economic relations, or psychoanalytic laws. The use of both home movies and old photographs is crucial as a device that establishes continuity through time and that reflects the fiction-making urge that, as Metz and Heath have shown, pervades even the documentary. Used as unproblematic representations, the past images function to seal individual change instead of providing evidence of the way women and their bodies are constructed by the signifying practices of both the social and psychological institutions in which they are embedded. (Interestingly enough, this construction makes a main theme in Michelle Citron's *Daughter Rite* [1978], where the slowing down of home movies enables us to see that the representations are far from an "innocent recording," that the process of making the movies in itself functions to construct the place for the female children.)

But this is as far as the similarities in the realist mode go; the differences rise out of the different relationship to class issues on the part of the filmmakers. In *Joyce at 34*, all mention of class and of economic relations is suppressed, so that we are never allowed to focus on the privileged situation that Joyce enjoys with her freelance writer-husband (he can be at home much of the time) or on the support of her comfortably middle-class parents. The cinematic strategies here work to suture over conflicts and contradictions as in a Hollywood film. Joyce's voice-over, with its "metaphysic of presence," keeps the spectator believing in Joyce as a person. It guides us and makes coherent what would otherwise be a disoriented, disconnected, chaotic world, a series of shots with no necessary connection. Her voice alone makes a comfortably reassuring world where the signifiers respond to an apparently solid signified. And as representation, Joyce does not in herself threaten accepted norms, while her unusually handsome husband adds a gloss to Joyce's environment which, in any case, fits the bourgeois model of commercial representations.

The structure of *Joyce at 34*, thus, perpetuates the bourgeois illusions of the possibility of the individual to effect change and of the individual's transcendence of the symbolic and other social institutions in which he or she lives. In fact, reading the film against the grain, one can see how Joyce is very much at the mercy of the structures that shaped her! *Janie's Janie*, on the other hand, shows a woman who is aware of the economic and class structures that formed her and who has made a deliberate, and decisive, break with those structures. She speaks of her awareness of her position as Other to the two men in her life—father and husband—without blaming them personally for the oppression she suffered at their hands. They are also victims of the symbolic organization of things.

Second, Janie's image itself violates normal codes. As a working-class figure (one that is rarely treated with condescension in visual representation or without being seen as co-optable by reform or charity—as are the figures in Grierson's and Jennings's work) who speaks roughly and is not elegantly turned out, Janie's image is subversive. As an unabashedly militant, determined woman who is ready to fight, Janie resists dominant female placing.

Third, in contrast to *Joyce at 34*, the traditional apparatus of the "gaze" does not come into play in *Janie's Janie*. Janie is not placed as object of the male look (although she cannot avoid the look of the camera or of the male audience). Within the diegesis, she is never looked upon by men or set up for their gaze as in commercial cinema.

Finally, the cinematic strategies are not as boringly realist as are those in *Joyce at 34*. There are soft superimpositions (Janie's face in the kitchen window superimposed on the street and house outside), darkly lit shots (to suggest Janie's loneliness before starting community organizing), a poignant music track, odd angles of filming, and suggestive shots of washing blowing in the wind. There is, thus, a nice "before" and "after" division. This is a realist film which, given its parameters, manages to achieve much both ideologically and visually.

This comparison of *Joyce at 34* and *Janie's Janie* has, I think, shown that while criticisms of the realist *vérité* film are to a degree entirely valid, their monolithic abstract formulation is a problem. When one looks closely at individual realist films, one realizes the weakness of the large generalizations. Realist films, that is, are far more heterogeneous and complex in their strategies than the theoretical critique can allow for. We need a theory that will permit/ accept different positionings toward class and economic issues in the realist mode and that, while not mitigating any of the semiological problems, especially around the overall positioning of the spectator as passive recipient of knowledge, at least grants a limited area of resistance to hegemonic codes in certain examples of the form.

It is at this point important to explore the implications of the position from which the critique of realism emerged, particularly in relation, first, to the concept of the human subject in society as well as in film (i.e., is the theory of knowledge underlying the objection to realism valid?); and second, in relation to the theory of the cinematic apparatus, and the way that it functions.

First, realism is objected to because semiology denies that there is any knowable reality outside discourse, that is, outside signifying practices. If the eighteenth-century, neoclassical critics went wrong in demanding that the discrepancy between poetry and reality be eliminated (i.e., in asking that poetry imitate the external world as it is, keeping to "the *kinds* of objects that we know to exist, and the *kinds* of events that we know to be possible, on the basis of an empirical knowledge of nature and nature's laws");[22] and if the Romantic critics who followed went wrong in asserting a privileged poetic discourse that reflected not external reality but the spontaneous overflow of feelings (i.e., the poet's mind as it transformed, by intense emotional excitement, external nature and put forth images that corresponded to nothing outside of the poet);[23] then semiology goes wrong (in some applications) in conceiving of art and life as equally "constructed" by the signifying practices that define and limit each sphere.

The documentary filmmakers were misguided in returning to the eighteenth-century notion of art as capable of simply imitating life, as if through a transparent glass, and in believing that representation could affect behavior directly (i.e., that an image of a poor woman would immediately bring political awareness of the need to distribute wealth more fairly). But there are problems also in making the signifier material in the sense that it is all there is to know. Discussing semiology in relation to Marxism, Terry Eagleton points out the dangers of this way of seeing for a Marxist view of history. History evaporates in the new scheme; since the signified can never be grasped, we cannot talk about our reality as human subjects. But, as he goes on to show, more than the signified is at stake: "It is also," he says, "a question of the referent (i.e., social actuality), which we all long ago bracketed out of being. In rematerializing the sign, we are in imminent danger of dematerializing its referent; a linguistic materialism gradually reverts itself into a linguistic idealism."[24]

Eagleton no doubt overstates the case when he talks about "sliding away from the referent," since neither Saussure nor Althusser denied that there *was* a referent. But it is true that while semiologists talk about the eruption of "the real" (i.e., accidents, death, revolution), on a daily basis they see life as dominated by the prevailing signifying practices of a culture, i.e., as refracted through those discourses which define "reality" for people. While I have no quarrel with this concern with the discourses which define and limit our notions of "reality" and agree that these discourses are essentially controlled by the classes that are in power, it seems important to allow for a level of experience that differs from discourse, or that is not *only* discourse. Where semiology and poststructuralism are most useful is in finally ridding us of the notion of a privileged aesthetic discourse—a notion that has only perpetuated a hampering dualism between art and science (broadly conceived). But if we want to create art that will bring about change in the quality of people's daily lives in the social formation, we need a theory that takes account of the level now usually referred to scornfully as "naively materialistic."[25]

But before leaving the attack on realism as a cinematic strategy, I want to deal briefly with two assumptions about the cinematic apparatus that appear in the theory. First, how valid is it to apply the same criticism to realist practices used in the commercial, narrative cinema and to those used in the independent documentary form? I would rather loosen up the theory, and argue that the same realist signifying practices can indeed be used for different ends, as we have already seen in comparing *Janie's Janie* and *Joyce at 34*. Realism in the commercial cinema may indeed be a form analogous to the nineteenth-century novel, in which a class-bound, bourgeois notion of the world is made to seem "natural" and "unproblematic." But *Janie's Janie* is not *An Unmarried Woman*, while *Joyce at 34* does come close to the form as used in Mazursky's work.

Johnston's and King's attack on realism is confused by their assumption that the realist cinematic mode in *itself* raises problems about the relation of representation to lived experience. The problems reside rather in either the filmmaker's or the audience's assumptions about this relation. But taken simply as a cinematic style that can be used in different genres (i.e., documentary or fictional), realism does not insist on any special relation to the social formation.[26] As Metz has noted, it is "the *impression of reality* experienced by the spectator . . . the feeling that we are witnessing an almost real spectacle" that causes the problems.[27] It is, Metz continues, the fact "that films have the *appeal* of presence and of a proximity that strikes the masses and fills the movie theaters."[28]

In fact, as Metz goes on to show, the crucial difference is not between cinematic modes (illusion of realism versus anti-illusionism), but between an event in the here-and-now and a *narrated* event. As soon as we have the process of telling, the real is unrealized (or the unreal is realized, as he sometimes puts it).[29] Thus, even the documentary or the live television coverage, in *narrating* the event, creates the distance that affects unrealization. "Realism," Metz notes, "is not reality. . . . [It] affects the organization of the contents, not narration as a status."[30]

Thus, despite the fact that documentary and fiction films begin with different material (the one, actors in a studio; the other, actual people in their environment), once this material becomes a strip of film to be edited as the author wishes, to be constructed in whatever way he or she wishes, the difference almost evaporates. Both fiction and nonfiction tend to create fiction, as we've seen—

often in the family romance mode. And indeed, if we go along with McGarry, we have seen that even before the filming starts, the pro-filmic event is heavily coded by the cultural assumptions people bring to the process of making a film. So the documentary ends up as much a "narrative," in a certain sense, as an explicitly fictional film. Working from the opposite direction, in addition, one can argue (as has Michael Ryan) that all fiction films are really "documentaries" in that all of us watching know, on one level, that everything has been enacted, that we are watching a star playing at being someone, actions manipulated in a studio to look like real events.[31]

Yet, on two fundamental levels, one that affects the filmmakers and one that involves the spectator, documentary and fiction are different. As regards the filmmakers, there is clearly a degree more control in the fiction film than in the documentary. Documentary filmmaking may permit more or less control depending on the project (i.e., a retrospective film, relying on real footage, allows more reconstruction of actual events through montage in the manner of narrative films than, say, does a documentary about a demonstration when the filmmakers on the scene had little idea of how things will work out). But what happens in fiction is only controlled if one is working within certain genres, or within institutions, like Hollywood, that permit only certain things to happen. Otherwise, fiction has the potential for representing imaginative possibility (e.g., models for change) once the Oedipal mode is broken.

My aim in asserting a difference between fiction and documentary from the perspective of the filmmakers is to avoid the unsatisfactory alternatives of (1) a fixed, binary opposition between fiction and documentary and (2) annihilating *all* difference through the assertion that all cinematic discourse is controlled by the same signifying practices that define and limit what can be represented. While Metz's broad distinction between an event and a *narrated* event obviously holds, it works only on a very abstract and general level. In fact, we need to make distinctions between different genres in the "narrated" category, recognizing that there is a broad spectrum of film types—from narrations limited by their reliance (to a degree) on the physical world, to those that use everyday logic but construct their environments, to those that use the supernatural (what Metz calls a "non-human logic"). The problems that the filmmakers face in each case are different, and each film type has certain dangers, certain advantages.

Second, as regards the spectator: audiences are clearly positioned differently in fictional and in documentary films, as may be seen from the betrayal spectators experience in films like Mitchell Block's *No Lies* or Michelle Citron's more recent *Daughter Rite*. In both cases, the directors use *vérité* techniques, deluding us into thinking we are watching nonactors while in fact at the end we learn that everything was scripted, with actors playing the roles. The anger that audiences experience must mean that a different identification process takes place in the two situations, and this may well have implications for calculating the ultimate effect on the spectator.

Any discussion of these effects must, unfortunately, be entirely speculative, given the lack of reliable research into this area. If I may descend into totally nonscientific evidence for a moment: some responses by students lead me to believe that it's true (as Mulvey has argued) that the identification with stars in a fiction film involves a return to the world of the Imaginary (i.e., some evocation of an ego-ideal that, in Lacan's system, predated the entry into the Symbolic); whereas the documentary involves a relating to images that is *analogous* to—i.e., *not* the same as (this was the error of the neoclassical movement)—the way we respond to people in our daily lives. Although on one level the documentary realist strategies do indeed construct the spectator as passive recipient of the "knowledge" the authors hold, on another level the spectator may be making judgments about the screen-image woman that indeed have to do with the codes of signifying practice, but which result from the sociological and political positioning of the spectator, i.e., his or her class, race, gender, educational background, as this affects experiences with signification.[32] For instance, some students react quite hostilely to Janie, criticizing the way she treats her children (she is too rough on them, she does not dress them well, she does not love them enough, she does not educate them properly); some may object to the way she looks, to the fact that she wears a wig or dyes her hair different colors, etc.

Two things may be happening here: a Barthesian answer is that the spectator is applying to the screen image the codes through which we learn to perceive reality in the outside world; but in addition, the spectator may be resisting being presented with an unconventional image, one which violates his or her expectations, given commercial representations. In other words, much more may be taking place as people watch such documentaries than we know about (the representations may bore, shock, please, or inform, depending on the class, race, and background of the spectator), but an *active* response is being evoked, one that has potential for (a) challenging assumptions about what we expect from cinema and (b) adding to what we know about the world.

However, as specific organizing strategies, the films may very well not work. If semiologists were wrong in denying that realism can produce an effect leading to change, then leftist-activists were wrong in assuming that merely showing something is an argument in its own right. The authors of *Janie's Janie* evidently assumed that any spectator would automatically side with Janie because they had set her up as a figure to be admired, presented her change as an exemplary one. They did not seem aware of the possibility that Janie as *image* would appear in another light than Janie as the real woman they knew, and thus they would be shocked by the kinds of readings my students gave.

The attack on realism outlined above arose precisely out of the perception that the women's realist documentaries, in the prevailing forms, did not work strategically.[33] One possibility might have been to attempt to modify the dominant realist form, but instead the critics posited the need for a countercinema. The very women (like Claire Johnston) active in the critique of realism took it upon themselves to make some of the first avant-garde theory films. In the mid-seventies, Johnston, Cook, Mulvey, and Wollen in Britain began to develop a new feminist avant-garde that, while it drew on earlier avant-gardes (Russian formalism, Brecht, surrealism [Dulac], and the recent countercinema directors like Godard and Duras), was new in its particular combination of semiology, structuralism, Marxism, and psychoanalysis. Given their complex cinematic strategies and the dense theoretical underpinning, the films require individual and in-depth analysis. Here I can only sketch in some of the alternative film practices that various directors employed in a deliberate attempt to avoid the theoretical problems that they believed afflicted realism.

These theory films do not reflect the danger outlined by Terry Eagleton, where the referent has been "bracketed out of existence." They stand rather in a relation of tension to the links between the social formation, subjectivity, and representation. All break with the notion of a simple connection between any two of the three areas, and show the complexity of establishing relationships. The directors are concerned with demystifying representation so as to make women aware that texts are producers of ideology, and that we live in a world of constructions rather than of solid essences.

The films have the following aspects in common:

1. A focus on the cinematic apparatus as a signifying practice, on cinema, that is, as an illusion-making machine; they draw attention to the cinematic process and use techniques to break the illusion that we are watching not a film, but "reality."

2. They refuse to construct a fixed spectator, but position the spectator so that he or she has to be involved in the processes of the film, rather than be passively captured by it. Distanciation techniques insure the divorce of spectator from text.

3. The films rather deliberately refuse the pleasure that usually comes from the manipulation of our emotions (particularly around the Oedipal complex in the case of the commercial cinema—the reliance of narratives on the form of the family romance). They try to replace pleasure in recognition with pleasure in learning—with cognitive processes, as against emotional ones.

4. All mix documentary and fiction (a) as part of the belief that the two cannot ultimately be distinguished as filmic models, or (b) to create a certain tension between the social formation, subjectivity, and representation.

There are roughly three broad types of theory films:

1. Films (like those by Mulvey and Wollen that have had a lot of influence) that deal with the problem of female subjectivity, the problem of woman finding the voice and a position from which to speak. Using Lacanian psychoanalysis, these films reveal women's position as silent, absent, or marginal in a phallocentric language system.

2. Films linked to the first in their reliance on Lacan, which take as their aim the deconstruction of classical patriarchal texts, exposing how woman has been "spoken" rather than asserted as speaking subject, made to function as an empty signifier to satisfy the male hero. Sally Potter's *Thriller* and the McCall/Tindall/Pacajowska/Weinstock *Sigmund Freud's Dora* are good examples.

3. Films concerned with women's history and with the whole problem of writing history. Filmmakers in this category would agree with Noel King's criticism of *Union Maids* and *Harlan County, U.S.A.* for not presenting any problem with history. Following Foucault, these directors show that no history is possible outside of a shaping, distorting point of view, usually that of the ruling classes. Clayton/Curling's *Song of the Shirt* (about nineteenth-century seamstresses) is perhaps the best example of this kind of film. As Sylvia Harvey has shown, the directors reveal that history is a series of interlocking discourses which involve very specific constructions.[34] The film plays off against one another a variety of documents, including different accounts of the position of women who sewed and of their historical context. In addition, as Harvey notes, the *Song of the Shirt* draws attention to the means of representation within the film itself by moving the camera across various boards and TV monitors, showing the filmed reconstruction of history scenes but also presenting prints, documents, etc.[35] The alternation between documentary footage, documentary "reconstructions," fictional enactments of real events, dramatizations of fictional accounts, and so on, makes us realize that images are reproductions of reality, not reality itself. The constantly interrupted narrations provide a frustration that forces us to understand the seductive power of narrative. This strategy is repeated on the brilliant sound track, where a lyrical classical tune is repeatedly drowned out by atonal, concrete music representing the dissonances and contradictions of historical discourses which the establishment continually strives to smooth over. The effect of all these mediations, Harvey concludes, is to make us ask the important political question: "Who is representing? And for whom?"[36]

I will leave for the final section of my article discussion of problems that emerge from these theory films regarding audience response, accessibility, and relativism. In concluding my discussion of the attack on realism, I want to evaluate the social and political implications of the change from what I have called the essentially didactic and "propagandistic" strategies of leftist-activist and bourgeois-liberal women filmmakers to the strategies of the new feminist theorists (still identified with leftism) that focus on signifying practices, on the problems of female subjectivity, and on representation itself.

I have tried to show that the debate about realism is in some sense a false debate, premised first on an unnecessarily rigid theory about the relationship between form and content; and second on a theory of knowledge which, while it illuminates our contemporary system of relationships (particularly the relationship of the individual to language and the other social structures in which he or she lives) is nevertheless inadequate when applied to a practice intent upon bringing about concrete change in the daily lives of women.[37]

Let me say a bit more about the inadequacy of the theory of knowledge from which the critique of realism emerged, and which in turn has conditioned the shape of the anti-illusionist films. The danger of semiology has been the sliding away from the referent that I mentioned earlier; this is problematic because if all "reality," all external lived experience, is mediated through signifying practice, we can never "know" outside of whatever signifying system we are in. In attempting to get rid of an unwelcome dualism, inherent in Western thought at least since Plato, and rearticulated by Kant on the brink of the modern period, semiologists run the danger of collapsing levels of things that need to remain distinct if we are to work effectively in the political arena to bring about change.[38]

As I noted, the best theory films do not abandon the referent, and exist in a deliberate tension (created through the combining of documentary and fictional modes) with the social formation. The problem with the new theories is that they lead paradoxically to a focus on the subject in their very attempt to counter notions of bourgeois individualism. As Christine Gledhill points out, the linking of Althusser's and Lacan's theories has explained (a) the way that individuals have become detached from their consciousness and (b) the different positioning of the sexes within the Symbolic order. But the theories do not accommodate the categories of either class or race: economic language as the primary shaping force replaces social/economic relations and institutions as the dominant influences. Sexual difference becomes the driving force of history in place of the Marxist one of class contradictions. Thus, we learn about the construction of the subject as individual, but learn nothing about individuals in social groups.[39]

The exposing of the decentered, problematic self through semiology and psychoanalysis (I am not now questioning its validity) has not been followed by sufficient study of its political and social implications. So much concern has been given to undermining bourgeois modes of thought and perception that we have failed to consider the problem of where this leaves us. Women critics and filmmakers have been placed in a position of negativity—in strategies subverting rather than positing. The dangers of undermining the notion of the unified self and of a world of essences are relativism and despair.

At this point, then, we must use what we have learned in the past ten years to move theoretically beyond deconstruction to reconstruction. While it is essential for feminist film critics to examine signifying processes carefully in order to understand the way in which women have been constructed in language and in film, it is equally important not to lose sight of the material world in which we live, and in which our oppression takes concrete, often painful, forms. We need films that will show us how, having once mastered (i.e., understood fully) the existing discourses that oppress us, we stand in a different position in relation to those discourses. Knowledge is, in that sense, power. We need to know how to manipulate the recognized, dominating, discourses so as to begin to free ourselves *through* rather than beyond them (for what is there "beyond"?).

It should be clear that I am far from advocating a return to realism as the best or only viable cinematic strategy for bringing about change, and it should also be clear that I am excited by (and have in fact been one of the main promoters of) the new theory films. On the level of theory, I am arguing for a less dogmatic approach to cinematic practice, one that would allow directors to see realism as a possible mode given that we now know more about the way it operates, are aware of its limitations, and understand it as a system of representation, not truth. And meanwhile, theorists should continue to push the limits of cinematic practice, to see what different techniques can yield.

Part II

I want to turn, finally, to the strategies of reception, the importance of which has become increasingly evident. The problem is that the debate that I have followed has taken place mainly on an abstract, theoretical level, divorced from the concrete situation of production, exhibition, and reception. We have been so concerned with figuring out the "correct" theoretical position, the "correct" strategies *theoretically*, that we have forgotten to pay attention, first, to the way subjects "receive" (read) films; and second, to the contexts of production and reception, particularly as these affect what films can be made and how films are read.[40]

That criticism is finally turning to this area may be seen from a reading of recent articles in *Screen* and elsewhere,[41] as well as Willemen/McPherson in *British Independence*, which looks back to the thirties in order to discover how production, exhibition, and distribution practices shaped, or influenced, certain documentary forms.[42] Although it is hard to grasp the implications of practices as one is living them, the Willemen/McPherson book shows the importance of attempting to understand the ways in which *apparently* independent practice is in fact formed by the social institutions in which it is inevitably embedded. Total independent cinematic practice is a utopian myth.

Let me substantiate this last statement by looking briefly at some of the contradictions which have dominated alternate practices of all kinds during the very years when critics have been debating cinematic strategy.

1. Filmmakers have had to rely for funding on the very system they oppose.
2. In the case of the anti-illusionist films, directors have been using cinematic strategies that are difficult for the majority of people raised on narrative and commercial films.
3. Having made the films, directors have not had any mechanism for the distribution and exhibition of their films on a large scale. (Screenings have been by necessity limited to small art cinemas in a few large cities and to college campuses. It is important to note that things are rather different, and slightly better, in Europe.)
4. The culminating contradiction is that filmmakers whose whole purpose was to change people's ways of seeing, believing, and behaving have only been able to reach an audience already committed to their values.

Thus, critics (hopefully increasingly together with independent filmmakers) need to discuss cinematic strategies not only in terms of the most correct theory, but also in relation to the contradictions outlined above. We have to reexamine together (as a unit, that is) our theory, our cinematic strategies and the strategies of reception as they affect the way a film is "read." But even before doing this, we need to look carefully at the economic base for film production and at the possible influence that funding agencies have had on the very shape of alternate practice.

Much of the recent independent filmmaking was made possible by the new government funding agencies (nationally, NEH, NEA; locally, various state agencies) and by the interest that private funding agencies began to show in film projects in the seventies. But the question is, To what extent did funding sources condition the shape of the films produced? To what extent, that is, did funding agencies refuse projects that did not fit their ideologies or their notions of cinematic practice? And to what extent have filmmakers begun to gear their cinematic strategies to please funding agencies, now that they have realized the kinds of things that did receive money?

A full study along these lines would reveal the degree to which the history of independent cinema, as we can now reconstruct it, is itself a construction of funding agencies. We would see how the history of independent cinema, as of commercial cinema, is governed by the economic relations in which the practices are embedded. The study would no doubt reveal a host of projects reflecting various kinds of innovations that did not get funded and that therefore never materialized. Other films may be discovered that were indeed made through independent means but which were never widely shown for the same reasons that they were not funded in the first place. For, at least in America, the films that were officially funded were also the ones shown in film festivals, that won awards, and that reached the attention of librarians who would then buy the films, thus providing the film with a college or community audience. (A cross-cultural study would be very useful in illuminating our particular political and cultural constraints in contrast to the different European situations. The differences in alternate cinematic practice between Europe and America would in part be explained by the different cultural discourses and operations.)

If a study such as the one outlined would tell us a lot about how "history" gets made, it would also reveal the way in which alternate practice is never independent of the society in which it is embedded. Alternate cinema, that is, cannot stand outside of the dominant discourses that construct it through its very position as of opposition to mainstream cinema. We can begin to see that alternate practices are to an extent bound by the very signifying practices they aim to subvert. Perhaps it is necessary for feminist film practice to move through a series of stages analogous to those that Frantz Fanon has described for primitive cultures in their relation to colonialism. We may currently be at the stage where the only strategies available to us are those conditioned by our being in opposition to dominant forms. We need to think about how to move beyond merely reversing established codes of cinema to creating truly alternative films, but this involves the basic problems of how to move beyond discourses that are dominant. As I mentioned earlier, it may well be that we can only free ourselves by moving *through* dominant discourse.

Once we understand the situation we are in, it is possible to phrase, and then to choose between, a number of alternatives in relation, first, to producing films and, second, to the exhibition and reception of independent films. In terms of the first question, filmmakers will have to choose between (a) continuing to make theoretical, experimental films precisely as they choose, raising their own money and reaching only a small, already committed audience; (b) obtaining government or private corporation funding, paying, in this case, the price of compromise on form and content—although there is often more latitude than might be expected and there are some nonestablishment backers interested in unconventional texts; and (c) moving into dominant cinema practice and waging the struggle there. In this case, there are real dangers of co-optation or of a far higher degree of compromise on ideology and form than in the other options (cf. Claudia Weill, Lina Wertmuller, Gillian Armstrong).

Each of the three alternatives presents its own problems and challenges for the filmmakers who will have to examine ways of avoiding being overwhelmed by dominant discourses. It is through precisely this kind of tension, this sort of enlightened struggle, that we can begin to alter the modes through which we apprehend reality.

The second question involves appropriate and useful strategies for reception and exhibition. Those of us who teach, for example, are well aware of the difficulties that the avant-garde theory films pose for an average student audience. A great deal of work is demanded of the spectator, and it is work of a very special kind. A level of sophisticated knowledge, not only of cinema but also of philosophy, psychoanalysis, linguistics, and Marxist theory, is needed in ʃr to understand many of the films. For people brought up on Hollywood fⱢms, totally new cinema-viewing expectations are required, especially in relation to pleasure.

Traditional forms of pleasure, as we know, are linked to a particular kind of narrative structure that binds the spectator to the screen (mainly through the form of the family romance and recognition/identification mechanisms it reinforces), and that keeps us fixed in the established positions patriarchal culture assigns. Many of the new films quite deliberately deny spectators the pleasure they are used to. We need now to consider whether it is possible to use a narrative form that is pleasurable and that does not produce the retrogressive effects of the commercial cinema, or whether we do not have to reeducate people to different pleasure, the cognitive pleasure of learning as opposed to the pleasure of recognition/identification (an emotional one).[43]

In order to answer these questions adequately, we need to know more about how change takes place: does it happen through consciousness-raising (including the unconscious), through example (imitation of models), or through manipulating emotions? We also need to know more about how actual, concrete individuals "read" films, aside from theoretical generalizations. Helpful here, for instance, would be comparative information about how both realist and theory films have been received. In which contexts did the theory films seem to work? How were the realist films "read" in different contexts?[44] Films receive quite different responses in, for example, a Lincoln Center Film Festival showing, a classroom, and a union hall: what precisely are these differences? How can we account for them?[45]

In terms of strategies for reception of independent films, we need to think about new viewing contexts that would produce better results, particularly with the theory films. Many directors of these latter films have been experimenting with changing the viewing situation. They prepare and hand out notes explaining the film's aims and intellectual context, are present throughout the screenings, and follow them with a discussion.[46] Another tactic has been to make films for specifically targeted audiences so that the filmmakers and spectators share a common framework of concerns and the audience can thus immediately comprehend the film's intervention in a specific area.[47] This is a useful strategy for both theoretical and realist films; for perhaps the most useful realist films are those about specific political actions in specific historical moments (e.g., a strike, abortion, child care) when immediate and accessible information is needed to develop support and to clarify strategies.

Larger problems of exhibition of independent films would remain, however, even after we were able to expand our audiences beyond the small, specialized ones we already have. We will never have, under American capitalism, the kind of access to mass audiences that we ideally desire. As I noted, the situation is slightly better in Europe, where television has become a viable outlet for radical films of all kinds (especially in Germany and England)[48] and some of the independent films get theatrical release with a regularity that is rare here.[49] Obviously, the way dominant discourses function varies from culture to culture, and a look at these variations might tell us a lot about America and about what strategies might work here to achieve greater access to larger audiences without severely compromising what we want to say and how we want to say it.

It is essential for both feminist film theorists and feminist filmmakers to focus on these central questions if we are to move beyond the impasse that I think we have reached after ten years of intensive, varied, and exciting work. We must begin to create institutions in which feminist theorists and filmmakers can work together for the mutual benefit of both groups. As I've shown, at least in Britain an apparently beneficial collaboration between filmmakers and theorists has resulted in a group of interesting and innovative films. Such a collaboration is just beginning over here (cf., for example, Michelle Citron's *Daughter Rite*, which shows the influence of the new theories on her filmmaking practice in her attempt to bridge the gap between the early realist-*vérité* films and the new anti-illusionist ones). Such collaboration will, I think, produce some interesting work in the near future. Let us use what we have learned from the work of the past decade to overcome divisions between filmmakers and film theorists, and between people with differing theoretical conceptions in each group, so that we can challenge and change dominant discourses and secure ourselves a powerful and permanent voice.

Notes

1. Claire Johnston, "Women's Cinema as Counter-Cinema," in *Notes on Women's Cinema*, ed. Claire Johnston (SEFT: London, 1973), p. 28.

2. Noel King, "Recent 'Political' Documentary: Notes on *Union Maids* and *Harlan County, U.S.A.*," *Screen* 22, no. 2 (1981): 9.

3. Cf. Steve Neale, "Propaganda," *Screen* 18, no. 3 (1977): 25.

4. King, "Recent 'Political' Documentary," p. 12.

5. Ibid., p. 5.

6. Ibid., p. 17.

7. Ibid., p. 18.

8. Sandy Flitterman and Judith Barry, "Textual Strategies: The Politics of Art Making," *Screen* 21, no. 2 (1980): 37.

9. Ibid., p. 36.

10. Ferdinand de Saussure, *Course in General Linguistics*, ed. Charles Bally and Albert Sechehaye, in collaboration with Albert Riedlinger, trans. Wade Baskin (New York: McGraw-

Hill, 1966), quoted in Frank Lentricchia, *After the New Criticism* (Chicago: University of Chicago Press, 1980), p. 123.

11. Lentricchia, *After the New Criticism*, p. 123.

12. For references to relevant work by the authors mentioned, see my *Women and the Film* (London: Methuen, 1983), chap. 1, nn. 2, 6, 21.

13. Michel Foucault, "A Reply to the Cercle d'Epistemologie," *Theoretical Practice*, no. 3/4, p. 112, quoted by Noel King, "Recent 'Political' Documentary."

14. Cf. Althusser's *For Marx* and his "Marxism and Humanism" essay especially. For a brief synopsis of Althusser's impact on feminist film theory, see Christine Gledhill, "Recent Developments in Feminist Film Criticism," *Quarterly Review of Film Studies* 3, no. 4 (1978): 469–71.

15. Theorists before have tried to link Marxism and psychoanalysis (particularly the Frankfurt School), but what is new in this case is the influence of semiology with its transformation of traditional Marxist notions of the social formation.

16. Terence Hawkes, *Structuralism and Semiotics* (London: Methuen, 1977), pp. 145–46. Hawkes is paraphrasing Derrida from *L'écriture et la différence* (Paris: Seuil, 1967), pp. 41–44, 409–11.

17. Hawkes, *Structuralism and Semiotics*, p. 143.

18. Ibid.

19. Eileen McGarry, "Documentary Realism and Women's Cinema," *Women in Film* 2, no. 7 (1975): 50.

20. Ibid.

21. Ibid., p. 51.

22. M. H. Abrams, *The Mirror and the Lamp: Romantic Theory and the Critical Tradition* (London: Oxford University Press, 1953), p. 267. The whole of chapter 10 explores the issues of "truth to nature."

23. Ibid., chaps. 5 and 6, on the development of the Romantic theory of poetry.

24. Terry Eagleton, "Aesthetics and Politics," *New Left Review*, no. 107 (Jan.–Feb. 1978): 22.

25. What I have in mind here is the danger of a theory that ignores the need for emotional identification with people suffering oppression. We may be able to explain the situation of a strike, for example, in terms of dominant versus minority discourses; the dominant discourse in the factory is that of the owners who construct the position of the workers to suit their (the bosses') own interests. One of the few reactions to domination available to the oppressed group is that of striking, although it is clear that this position is very much a defensive one, constructed by the dominant discourse and causing the workers themselves a lot of hardship. The workers, thus, are on a basic material level in need of support (food, clothing), and on the psychological level in need of emotional support. The level of abstraction on which the theory functions often makes it seem as if these other levels are unimportant or not worth mentioning. That Metz is one of the few critics who retains constant awareness of the level of the social formation is evident not only in his discussion of realism in *Film Language* (see n. 27), but also in an interview in *Discourse* (paradoxically, his statements here prompted Noel King's article referred to above; see n. 2) where he supports the "naively" realist documentary, like *Harlan County, U.S.A.* Asked if he thinks a documentary of a strike could be misleading "insofar as it assumes that knowledge is unproblematic, and on the surface," replies Metz: "If the film has a very precise, political and immediate aim; if the filmmakers shoot a film in order to support given strike . . . what could I say? Of course, it's o.k." Talking specifically about *Harlan County*, Metz continues: "It is the kind of film that has nothing really new on the level of primary/secondary identification, but it's a very good film. . . . It is unfair, in a sense, to call a film into question on terms which are not within the filmmaker's purpose. She intended to . . . support the strike and she did it. It's a marvelous film and I support it" ("The Cinematic Apparatus as Social Institution: An Interview with Christian Metz," *Discourse*, no.1 [Fall 1979]: 30).

26. Cf. Dana Polan, "Discourses of Rationality and the Rationality of Discourse in Avant-Garde Political Film Culture," Ohio University Film Conference, April 1982.

27. Christian Metz, *Film Language: A Semiotics of the Cinema*, trans. Michael Taylor (New York: Oxford University Press, 1974), p. 4.

28. Ibid., p. 5.

29. Ibid., p. 22.

30. Ibid., pp. 21–22.

31. Cf. Michael Ryan, "Militant Documentary: Mai 68 par lui," *Ciné-Tracts*, no. 7/8 (1979).

32. For further discussion of this problem, see Gledhill, "Recent Developments," pp. 469–73.

33. Many women, of course, continued to make realist films, especially in America. Two recent and interesting examples are Connie Field's *Rosie the Riveter* and *Quilts*.

34. Sylvia Harvey, "An Introduction to *Song of the Shirt*," *Undercut*, no. 1 (March–April 1982): 46.

35. Ibid.

36. Ibid., p. 47.

37. For a full discussion of realist theories of knowledge and society, together with a critique of Althusserian theories, see Terry Lovell, *Pictures of Reality* (London: British Film Institute, 1980).

38. See n. 25.

39. Gledhill, "Recent Developments," pp. 482–83.

40. Julia Lesage began to think about problems of production, exhibition, and distribution in a 1974 article, "Feminist Film Criticism: Theory and Practice," *Women and Film* 1, no. 5–6 (1974): 12–20; and in general the journal *Jump Cut* focused more than others on matters of the social and political context for feminist films. Julia Lesage's article is reprinted in a slightly revised version in *Sexual Stratagems: The World of Women in Film*, ed., Patricia Erens (New York: Horizon Press, 1979), pp. 156–67.

41. Cf., for example, Marc Karlin et al., "Problems of Independent Cinema," *Screen* 21, no. 4 (1980/81): 19–43; John Hill, "Ideology, Economy and British Cinema," in *Ideology and Cultural Production*, ed. Michael Barrett et al. (London: Billings and Sons, 1979); Anthony McCall and Andrew Tyndall, "Sixteen Working Statements," *Millennium Film Journal* 1, no. 2 (1978): 29–37; Steve Neale, "Oppositional Exhibition: Notes and Problems," *Screen* 21, no. 3 (1980): 45–56; Michael O'Pray, "Authorship and Independent Film Exhibition," *Screen* 21, no. 2 (1980): 73–78; Susan Clayton and Jonathan Curling, "Feminist History and *The Song of the Shirt*," *Camera Obscura*, no. 7 (Spring 1981): 111–27, and "On Authorship," *Screen* 20, no. 1 (1979): 35–61; John Caughie, "*Because I Am King* and Independent Cinema," *Screen* 21, no. 4 (1980/81): 9–18; Steve Neale, "Art Cinema as Institution," *Screen* 22, no. 1 (1981): 11–41.

42. Don Macpherson, ed., *Traditions of Independence* (London: British Film Institute, 1980): see especially, Claire Johnston, " 'Independence' and the Thirties—Ideologies in History: An Introduction," pp. 9–23, and Annette Kuhn, "British Documentary in the 1930s and 'Independence'—Recontextualizing a Film Movement," pp. 24–35.

43. Interestingly enough, Christian Metz discusses these very issues in some detail in the interview in *Discourse*, no. 1 (Fall 1979): 20–30.

44. Cf. here Anthony McCall and Andrew Tyndall, "Sixteen Working Statements," *Millennium Film Journal* 1, no. 2 (1978), where they argue that realist films often have no lasting impact on audiences.

45. *Quilts*, for instance, evoked laughter when shown to the Lincoln Center Film Festival audience (it is a significant criticism of this kind of *vérité*-realism that its cinematic strategies did not protect its subjects from such a response), while in a women's studies classroom, the film is a moving and illuminating experience.

46. Peter Wollen and Laura Mulvey have made a practice of being present at film viewings, as have Sally Potter, Susan Clayton, Jonathan Curling, and Michelle Citron, among others. It would be interesting to compile evidence from such filmmakers about their experiences with audiences.

47. See McCall and Tyndall, "Sixteen Working Statements."

48. In England the Fourth Channel has just opened, providing an outlet for independent filmmakers. It will be interesting to see what the results are and what the filmmakers' experience is in working for the channel.

49. For instance, Sally Potter's film was shown commercially; in America, an independent film occasionally gets released, as did, for example, Kopple's *Harlan County, U.S.A.*, but it is then always in the realist mode.

Truth Claims

Jerry Kuehl

Is there anything left to say about drama documentaries? It hardly seems possible, after so many years. The form, after all, came into being as soon as the cinema turned its attention away from observing life as it passed in front of the camera, or from presenting fantastic or fictional personages, to try to tell stories which were true. Turn-of-the-century films of the trial of Captain Dreyfus or the mutiny on the battleship *Potemkin* exhibited the characteristics of the form: they dealt with real events; they showed what cameras had not recorded at the time the events occurred, and they dramatized the episodes with which they dealt.

The form has flourished for generations—and each generation of filmmakers seem to discover it anew. GPO and Crown Film Unit productions of the 1930s and '40s like *Night Mail, Target for Tonight*, and *Western Approaches* were all, in their way, as much drama documentaries as are more recent celebrated examples like *Cathy Come Home, The Missiles of October*, or *Invasion*. Yet there has always been an alternative strategy available to filmmakers: to make films which could lay claim to being truthful without telling stories—which they could do by using commentary, images, and direct statements by participants without employing actors. This technique, a natural development of the illustrated lectures of Victorian times, evolved into the traditional mainstream documentary style which is familiar to us today in the form of television series like "The World at War," or single documentaries like *Jump Jet*.

So why does the dispute between these two forms persist? Much attention has been directed to the fact that although drama documentaries invite audiences to accept their portrayals as being truthful accounts of actions rather than simply lifelike, plausible, or true to life, they rely on dramatic devices and procedures to persuade audiences. Critics have found this procedure illicit, since it obliges audiences to judge matters of truth and falsity by aesthetic criteria. Drama documentary enthusiasts are unimpressed by this argument. In their view, "traditional" documentaries suffer from the same defects (if that is what they are) as do "drama" documentaries: their producers select and manipulate participants; their camera operators film events and people deliberately and selectively; and their editors use all the tricks of their trade to dazzle and persuade their audiences. Believing that the two kinds of filmmaking are fundamentally the same, some drama documentary enthusiasts, critics and filmmakers alike, regard traditional documentaries as crippled in three distinct ways.

The first is that, even in their own terms, they can never deliver what they promise. They claim to present the "truth," yet they can never present anything other than one man's or one woman's selective version of reality. Moreover, such selective versions are necessarily impoverished both visually and dramatically. Rupert Murdoch might allow a documentary filmmaker to film him negotiating to refill his glass at a cocktail party, but hardly negotiating to buy a national newspaper. And to those who claim that access to such behavior is precisely what is secured by filmmakers like Frederick Wiseman and Roger Graef, the reply is that such filmmakers deceive themselves. The real negotiations always take place when the cameras aren't present—as Roger Graef's film on decision making at British Steel made clear by demonstrating that the decision on the Korf process had been taken before he ever began to shoot.

The second is that the methods of traditional documentary condemn its practitioners to present only the surface of people or events. By excluding reenactments, reconstructions, and invented dialogue, traditional documentaries abandon the possibilities of ever penetrating beyond appearances to the three-dimensional reality. They thereby make genuine understanding of real persons and events impossible.

Finally, if traditional documentary filmmakers are faithful to their own self-imposed limitations, they must accept that vast areas of human experience are closed to them. Moving pictures as we know them were not developed until the 1890s. Does this mean that no subjects from before that time may be treated? Only a few meters of film of Lenin survive: does that mean that his life must remain forever a barely opened book? Closer to our own time, no filmed record of Nazi extermination camps has survived (if indeed any was ever made). Does that mean that the Holocaust is forever off-limits? To the rigorous, the answer must be "yes."

Drama documentary makers have always been quick to fill the vacuum left by their traditionally minded colleagues. This is not simply a question of opportunism. The drama documentary impulse is fueled by two powerful ideas: the belief that its methods find particular favor with audiences, and the conviction that those same methods make it possible for audiences to understand far more than they would by viewing films made by the traditionally minded. Both these ideas have stood unchallenged long enough to have become part of the received wisdom of television. Neither stands up to serious examination.

Audience Response

In general, viewing figures for documentaries and factual programs are lower than for drama, sports, and light entertainment. But from this it does not follow that documentaries are inherently less popular than other forms of television entertainment. Their place in the schedule, the time at which they are transmitted, the amount of money spent on promoting them, the kind of publicity they receive, and the skill with which they are made, all affect the fortunes of documentary programs. Though one episode of Thames Television's "Botanic Man" was the most popular program in the London area the week it was transmitted, not even its most enthusiastic admirers believe it would have achieved such success had it been transmitted after the 10:00 P.M. news (as adult education programs normally are) rather than in the early evening. "The World at War," heavily promoted and transmitted at 9:00 P.M., was consistently ranked in the JICTAR top twenty. The same contractor's "Palestine" and "The Troubles," shown at 10:30 P.M. and accompanied by more modest advertising campaigns, were seen by only 2.75 million viewers.

There is, in fact, no convincing evidence for the assumption that audiences always prefer dramatized presentations. *Holocaust* was immensely popular in the United States. In the absence of any network-produced documentaries on the subject, it is unrewarding to speculate on how popular they might have been, had they been made with similar resources, promoted on the same scale, and benefited from the same position in the broadcast schedules. However, some comparison is possible for Britain. When transmitted in 1978, *Holocaust*'s much advertised episodes were viewed on average by 16.75 million people. The *Genocide* episode of "The World at War," which benefited from no special publicity, was seen by 15 million. West German experience was even more striking. Episodes of *Holocaust* were seen by between 32 and 41 percent of the available audience. But the documentary programs which accompanied them, and the studio phone-ins which followed them, were also viewed by up to 32 percent of the potential West German audience.

Clearly, no one could conclude that audiences would welcome documentary and factual programming to the exclusion of everything else. What does seem obvious is that skillfully made, adequately publicized, and sympathetically scheduled documentaries can be as popular as dramatized accounts of the same subjects.

Understanding

The most persistent claim made on behalf of drama documentaries is that audiences who watch them achieve an understanding of persons and events which they would achieve less well, or not at all, by watching other kinds of programs. The argument derives its force from the commonplace belief that most viewers prefer programs made within the conventions of naturalistic drama; that they identify with dramatic personae, and that such identification can be used by producers to get across points which elude viewers of traditional documentaries. Dramatizations can do this—so the argument continues—because they exploit the skills of writers and directors, actors and actresses, to get beneath the surface of characters remote in time and place.

Holocaust illustrates this claim well. (Those who deny that *Holocaust* is a drama documentary should note that the choice of example does not affect the substance of the argument, which applies equally to such fastidious productions as *Invasion, Dummy*, and the BBC's biography of J. Robert Oppenheimer.) *Holocaust* was seen by many people who had not previously viewed documentary treatments of the same subject. Some said that watching the series gave them, for the first time, an understanding of the Holocaust. This understanding evidently came about because characters were played by actors and actresses familiar to the audience, because the dialogue was written in colloquial language and the story unfolded according to the conventions of ordinary television dramas. In other words, however horrific the substance of what was shown and told, the manner of the showing and telling made it possible for the audience to identify with persons from that remote, ghastly epoch.

An extreme form of this argument claims that drama is not simply a more comprehensive and satisfying way of exploring characters and events than is traditional documentary, but that it is the only proper way. This view is held by those who see the multidimensionality which is the hallmark of dramatic representation as indispensable to historical understanding. But before deciding whether to accept the argument, it is important to see just what is being claimed.

Understanding is an ambiguous concept, and it may be helpful to distinguish between two of its uses: first, "understanding" in the sense of coming to know what someone did or what was done to him or her; and second, "understanding" in the sense of coming to appreciate the motives and intentions of persons who acted or were acted upon. In the first case we are looking for a causal account of actions (X told Y to do Z), while in the second case we are looking for an account of intentions (X wanted Y to do Z). Much confusion arises when filmmakers fail to distinguish clearly what is involved.

Sometimes drama documentaries claim to promote understanding in the causal sense. No film records exist of Hitler's last days in the Führerbunker, nor of the ordeal of the Czech delegation to Moscow after the Prague spring of 1968. Those chronicles must either go forever unshown, or be shown as *Hitler, the Last Ten Days* or *Invasion*. Sometimes drama documentaries undertake the equally difficult yet rewarding task of showing motive. What were the French and British delegates trying to do when they negotiated an armistice with the Germans in the Forest of Compiègne in 1918? Why was Fania Fenélon able to help some inmates of Auschwitz and not others? Why did John Foster Dulles refuse to support the Anglo-French invasion of Egypt in 1956? Since there is no film of the negotiations in the Compiègne railway carriage, or of the Auschwitz women's orchestra, or of the inside of John Foster Dulles's mind, part of the answer is *Gossip from the Forest, Playing for Time,* and *Suez*.

Not that any given drama documentary sets out to provide only one kind of account. So when a drama marries an account of what happened to the Jews of central Europe with an account of why middle-class Germans helped it to happen, viewers all over the Federal Republic are liable to call their local television stations to exclaim. "Now I understand."

The reality is that, far from being uniquely qualified to provide causal or intentional accounts of persons and events in the real world, dramas, and especially drama documentaries, are incapable of adequately doing either. What drama documentary regards as its special strengths are just those features which disqualify it from providing satisfactory accounts of either causes or motives. It is not too difficult to demonstrate why this is so. Once an episode has been recorded on film, there is no way in which a dramatic simulation can significantly add to our understanding of the original. Either the reconstruction mimics the original exactly, in which case the simulation is superfluous, or it departs from the original and thereby deforms what we know to be the case— in which event there can be no reasonable grounds for preferring the reconstruction. Episodes of which no filmed records exist are equally inaccessible to dramatic artists. The language used by performers may be "authentic" because derived from court records or other stenographic reports; but the inflections, accent, volume, and pace of what performers utter, as well as their gestures, expression, and stance, will not be those of the persons they represent. It's hard to see how the bricks of uniquely insightful portraits can be made from the straw of performances known to be inauthentic before they even begin. This inauthenticity is inescapable. It is endemic in all dramatic representations, including those in which individuals "play" themselves. For persons asked to play themselves are performers, just as much as are members of Actors' Equity. What destroys their credibility is not so much that the audience mistrusts their physical appearance, but that it mistrusts their memory (did they really say that?) and their acting skills (did they really hold the knife like that?).

But do not traditional documentaries suffer from the same defects? General MacArthur steps ashore again from the landing craft so that the cameraman can film the fulfillment of his promise to return to the Philippines from two angles. Is that not a performance? Hardly, unless the meaning of the word is to be extended to encompass all forms of flamboyant behavior. MacArthur on the beach at Leyte certainly behaved theatrically, but it would make no more sense to call him a performer than it would to so describe a marksman who demonstrates how to assemble a rifle for a training film, and who goes through the motions several times to allow for close-ups, cutaways, and different angles.

So far as providing causal accounts is concerned, makers of traditional documentaries have an unassailable advantage: they can ask real people questions, and record real answers. The real X can say, in reply to an inquiry, "In 1975 I told Y to do Z." There is no need for X to dress up in a six-year-old suit (which was of course new when the conversation in question took place) or in a new suit furnished by the wardrobe department (which wasn't yet made when the conversation took place) to speak words spoken on that occasion— or even to call upon an actor or actress to speak them on his or her behalf.

And what is true of causal accounts must be true of accounts of intention and motive as well. This is not only because of the difficulty of displaying the life of the mind in dialogue and gesture (though the difficulties of doing that are formidable enough). The defect common to all dramatic solutions to the problem of exhibiting intention is that the performer is obliged to pursue two incompatible goals: to be dramatically convincing in terms of the audience's expectations, yet provide a faithful account of the protagonist's motives and intentions. No performer can be known to have done both, unless the audience is familiar with the motives in advance—in which case any performance is superfluous.

If the subject of the film is not a real person (like the heroine of *Cathy Come Home*), the audience has no option. It must accept the account of events and motive offered by the filmmaker. But it does so only by denying to the film any status other than that of fiction. Here again, audiences can only be expected to judge the truth or otherwise of a dramatic portrayal of what people did and why, if they know independently the answers to the questions which the dramatic presentation itself purports to answer. So once again, dramatic portrayals can be seen to be either superfluous or false. Drama documentaries about persons whose native language is not English are particularly vulnerable in this respect. An American-speaking Himmler, an English-speaking Dubček, or a Khrushchev speaking American with a Russian accent does not provide audiences with a path to understanding the motives of those difficult personalities. They can provide nothing but doubly and trebly false trails, because they lead, not to the historical figures, but to the writers who wrote the lines, the actors who spoke them, and the directors who orchestrated their performances. So here, too, it should be evident that the best way to clarify intention is to ask questions of people who are in a position to give answers.

We are now, I think, in a position to judge the persuasiveness of the claim that drama documentaries lead to an "understanding" of persons and events. When someone watches *Holocaust* and says, "I understand the how and why of the Holocaust," *Suez* and says, "I understand the how and why of Eden and Suez," or *Gossip from the Forest* and says, "I understand the how and why of the 1918 armistice," that person is mistaken. He or she understands the argument of the films, but not their subjects. *Holocaust* may provoke a national debate which leads to the abolition of the statute of limitations on the prosecution of war criminals, but that does not mean that *Holocaust*'s account either of the course of events or of the motives of the participants commands attention as anything other than fiction.

Once again it may be asked whether this is not true of traditional documentaries. Are they not fictions as well, which tell us no more than what their makers want us to know, and thereby open themselves to those charges of special pleading which are at the root of all that I have said about drama documentaries? The answer is "no": at the heart of documentaries lie truth claims, and these claims are based on arguments and evidence. Did Khrushchev ever lose his temper in public? Film of him banging his shoe on the desk at the U.N. may not convince everyone; film of Telly Savalas wearing the Order of Lenin and banging a desk on the set at Universal City will convince no one. Did Eden think Nasser was another Hitler? Lord Avon can speak on the subject with some claim on our attention; but Michael Gough utters with all the authority of a member of Equity.

Drama documentaries, of course, rely on argument and evidence, just as do traditional documentaries. Both *Genocide* and *Holocaust* have a common origin in the same historical reality—survivors' stories, documents, photographs, trial records—but the uses they make of the sources are as different as can be. Nothing stands between the traditional documentary and the truth claims which it makes. (Its claims may be justified, dubious, or perfectly outrageous, but that is a different matter.) The drama documentary can make *no* legitimate truth claims, because whatever claims it makes are filtered through the artifices of actors' performances and writers' lines. And claims made through such channels are neither true nor false. They are fictions. So Ena Sharples, Basil Fawlty, and Donald Duck are siblings under the skin to Marvin J. Chomsky's Dr. Weiss, Michael Darlow's Anthony Eden, and John MacKenzie's Jimmy Boyle. Their stories may make us laugh or weep, but they are unreliable guides to the world in which we live.

Getting It Right

Elizabeth Sussex

The six-week filming schedule in and around Manchester for Granada Television's drama documentary *Strike* was due to begin on 21 September 1981. The producer/director is Leslie Woodhead, who pioneered development of the drama documentary at Granada and, with David Boulton in 1978, set up a special drama-documentary unit there. The week before filming he and writer Boleslaw Sulik (Bolek) are rehearsing the script in London with the actors: a concentrated course in Polish politics and culture as well as in the origins of Solidarity (the subject of the film). It occurs to me that quite a research effort will be needed if my planned article about all this is going to match up to the pursuit of authenticity that is the basis of any film by Leslie Woodhead, who has been described as guardian of the drama-documentary conscience. I start out by recording interview material with him.

"The project swam into view," he says, "as a result of an approach by Solidarity itself through Boleslaw Sulik, who had made it plain that there was a mass of previously undisclosed material that might be available. Their approach was because of our previous work on *Three Days in Szczecin*, which they were aware of. We heard that Walesa himself was aware of that and wanted to see it. All of that came together in a decision to go to Rome in January 1981 to contact a Solidarity delegation who were coming to see the Pope . . . So we went to Rome, stayed in the hotel they were staying in, met a number of people including Walesa and Anna Walentynowicz, and began to explore the possibility of making a program . . . We found that there was a mass of tape-recorded verbatim material about the whole period of the strike, and that right from Day One a really detailed record had been kept by many hands on home cassette recorders of everything that took place."

More than one hundred hours of taped evidence was acquired over a period of months through contacts in London, Paris, and Poland. Apart from tapes of the original meetings, Woodhead and Bolek were able to talk to many of the Solidarity people who passed through London during the year, among them Bogdan Lis, Jadwiga Staniszkis, and Anna Walentynowicz, who appears in the film. In addition, interviews were specially recorded in Poland with Andrzej Gwiazda, Bogdan Borusewicz, Alina Pienkowska, Lis, Walentynowicz, and others.

"All these people were quizzed at length about exactly what they did, what they said to whom, in whose company they were, even what they were wearing and what the room looked like. It's been the most thorough crosscheck of sources that we've been able to do for one of these drama documentaries. Bolek has also of course got extensive contacts in the dissident loyal opposition community, so he has been able to communicate with people like Mazowiecki and Gieremek and all of the Expert people. Normally we've been limited to a couple of sources, half a dozen at the outside, who crosscheck with one another."

Woodhead started making drama documentaries in 1970 because, quite simply, the form allowed him to do things he couldn't do in any other way. "As a television journalist working on 'World in Action,' " he recalled in a recent *Guardian* lecture at the National Film Theatre, "I came across an important story but found there was no way to tell it. The story was about a Soviet dissident imprisoned in a mental hospital. By its very nature, it was totally inaccessible by conventional documentary methods. But the dissident, General Grigorenko, had managed to smuggle out of mental prison a detailed diary of his experiences. As a result, it was possible to produce a valid dramatic reconstruction of what happened to Grigorenko." (Woodhead's coeditor on "World in Action" in the late sixties was Jeremy Wallington, whose "preoccupation with standards of evidence and journalistic rigor, his obsession with trying to get it right, was really," he says, "the starting point and the most important part of the Grigorenko exercise.")

His second drama documentary, *A Subject of Struggle*, Woodhead regards as "a classic case of the legitimacy of the form." This was about a senior Chinese lady put on trial by the Red Guards at the height of the Cultural Revolution: "The Cultural Revolution has always been (but particularly when we made this film in 1972) an absolutely unguessable puzzle . . . and of course no film of any duration has come out of China about it. We got hold of the trial transcript, and I vividly remember reading it on a train journey and thinking, 'This is absolutely incomprehensible. It's like material from Mars.' But then we set about months of research, talking to sinologists here and trying to decode all these references and understand what it was about. By the end I felt in a position to use dramatization to illuminate and articulate some of the most elusive material in a serious way. I can't imagine any other form which would allow us to make available to a mass television audience those themes, about something quite crucially important going on in a society which is completely closed to us."

In the case of *Strike*, the thing that cannot be shown any other way is the development of a local economic grievance and a strike for the reinstatement of an individual (crane driver and former Heroine of Labor Anna Walentynowicz) into one of the most pivotal events in East/West politics since World War II. Until the government negotiators moved in (nine days after the beginning of the strike), nothing was being filmed because nobody could guess what a momentous thing was being born. The Polish documentary *Workers '80* was known about from the beginning of the project. Some of the actors are studying it, not for the first time, while Woodhead talks to me. "Obviously there's no point," he says, "in simply redramatizing something which is unforgettably done for real by the existing documentary record. The dramatization allows us to look at the period before that, when that political evolution was being thrashed out in a fairly painful fashion. For me, it's the most interesting and precise demonstration of what the limits of the viability of dramatization actually are . . . It's particularly fascinating for Bolek and me because of having done the Szczecin film, which was concerned with an oddly parallel event in 1970, like a dry run for these events. At every step you can feel the workers being informed by what went wrong in 1970, and taking that into consideration in working out how they're going to act this time."

Tuesday, 6 October 1981.   I join the film crew, 16 actors, and 112 extras swarming round an excavator in the anonymous wasteland of the Manchester docks. The people are dwarfed by empty hulks of warehouses in the near distance and the silhouettes of huge, immobile cranes against the sky. The scene they are setting up will replicate an event that took place in the Lenin shipyard at Gdansk on the morning of 14 August 1980—the first day of the strike. The instigators, calling for more support, are interrupted by Klemens Gniech (Jon Laurimore), managing director of the shipyard, who climbs up beside them on the top of the excavator and tells the crowd they must be sensible. The scene, recorded with streamlined efficiency in long shot, mid shot, and close-up from behind the workers and from the reverse angle, is in the can in time for a quick rehearsal of the next scene before an early lunch break. I can watch it on a video viewer beside the sound recordist. Leslie Woodhead has his own portable version of this. The next scene will be Ian Holm's first appearance in the role of Lech Walesa. Woodhead is shooting the script as closely as possible in chronological order, and so far nothing has interfered with this.

It starts to rain. Covers are placed over the excavator. No problem for an hour, but by the end of the lunch break the rain is teeming down. Everyone stares out at it from the draughty shelter of the nearest warehouse. Woodhead, alone with the responsibility, paces about the hideously bleak terrain. His right arm is in a sling as a result of breaking it in a fall through the set of the gatehouse of the Lenin shipyard some ten days earlier. "Sad, yes," says Bolek, "like a broken wing. It was quite dramatic the way he did it. When he landed there was a sort of puff of dust." At 2:10 P.M. Woodhead says he will start shooting in 50 minutes whether the rain has stopped or not: "The only things that prevent shooting in the rain are puddles which you don't get here, and long lenses against a dark background which you don't get here." The ground is gravelly but so persistent is the downpour that serious puddles start to form. At 3:00 P.M. it's raining too hard to ask anyone to take the risk of climbing on top of the slippery excavator. Jon Laurimore wishes he could have solved the problem by simply saying, "Let's be sensible and continue this meeting over there, out of the rain." But it wasn't raining in Gdansk that morning, so everyone just waits until it's too late to film the scene that day. The last thing that happens: Sue Pritchard photographs the set-up for continuity purposes. "She's a perfectionist," someone says. "Who's going to notice if the excavator has been moved a little?"

In the evening I record an interview with Boleslaw Sulik, who is present in an advisory capacity during most of the filming. He tells me that at first they considered using a mixture of archive film and staged material—archive for the exteriors and reconstruction for the interiors. Their main reason for not doing so was the opposite of the superficially held view about such matters: "It was almost impossible to devise a structure that would absorb a large amount of archive material without creating really a culture shock. You have to translate it into English idiom. You can have a documentary introduction and perhaps epilogue, but the body of the film has to be consistent." He felt too that films like *Workers '80* were "a kind of political theater which hid to some extent the real political struggle behind the scenes." What they could reconstruct was a very different matter: "We are quite sure what the political process inside the shipyard was, and we became excited about how much was crammed into these seventeen days, how much of the actual political development and education, the shifting relationships, the changing political perspective all the time. I was excited by this as a political story, not *only* because I'm a Pole and of course very responsive to the imagery as well as to the political content."

Bolek hopes they are going to be able to articulate something of that specifically Polish response—the fact, for instance, that the Communist regime's use of the rhetoric of revolution has completely failed with the workers, who still respond to traditional images associated with past oppression. "Nobody would dream in the Gdansk shipyard, or now in Solidarity, of addressing another worker as 'comrade.' They actually address each other as 'pan,' which means 'sir' or 'mister.' There's an incongruity, a sort of absurdity about the fact that they've taken over the heritage of the former Polish ruling class.

That's the significance, to me, of the fact that the polonaise, the most courtly music imaginable, was actually played in the shipyard, and the workers felt moved by it . . . There are some incongruous things about Solidarity, and that dimension is difficult to communicate to an English audience, but I would like at least to refer to it."

Wednesday, 7 October. We assemble at 8:30 A.M. in designer Roy Stonehouse's impressive replica of the BHP ("Safety and Hygiene") conference hall. Built inside a huge rehearsal room across the road from the Granada offices, this is the biggest set that Woodhead has so far worked on. Like the original, the hall has no supporting pillars—something hard to find in such an enormous public space. Perhaps the most arresting "detail" is an eight-foot statue of Lenin, sculpted in polystyrene, which dominates one end of the elevated platform.

In order to get the sets right, Woodhead and Stonehouse went to Gdansk in the spring of 1981 and, describing themselves as a two-man trade union delegation from Liverpool, managed to gain entry to the Lenin shipyard. "Solidarity met us inside the yard," says Woodhead, "and in fact we had a long talk with a very charismatic young man who turned out to be Jurek Borowczak, the man who actually started the strike on the first morning. Then he and half a dozen other Solidarity officials showed us the site where the excavator was where Walesa made his first speech to the workers, showed us the administration building where the shipyard manager kept the broadcasting system to himself, the big negotiating hall where the delegates met, the BHP clubroom where the negotiations with the government took place, and, most interesting, the little room which was called the Experts' room, where some of the behind-closed-doors negotiations went on. It's a difficult thing to get into, and we were able to peep round the door of that as well. Stonehouse sort of flicked his eyes over all that and managed to draw sketches in his pocket, God knows how, but that's one of his acquired skills. Then when we got out of the yard he sat down in the car and for about half an hour simply sketched out everything he could remember of what he had seen—color references, scale, materials of wood, or whatever."

"We have a kind of shorthand going," says Stonehouse, who first worked with Woodhead in 1968 and has accompanied him on most of his research trips into eastern Europe. "When we go into places we don't actually talk to one another. He collects the information he needs, and I collect the information I need, and we come back and put it together." Their adventures on these journeys would make a lovely film. On *Three Days in Szczecin* in 1976 they narrowly escaped arrest when Woodhead was stopped by the police for exceeding the speed limit while driving round the then heavily guarded dockyards. Stonehouse, concealed under a coat, was filming the scene with an 8mm camera from the back seat. Researching *Invasion* in Czechoslovakia in 1979, the pair walked boldly into the Central Committee Presidium building, where Stonehouse bamboozled the guards with incessant chatter about finding someone who spoke English and being shown round the "Czech House of Commons."

On *Strike* several hundred still photographs taken at the time also provide invaluable reference not only for design, wardrobe, and makeup, but for the actors who, as always in Woodhead's films, aim to convey as strong a physical resemblance to their real-life counterparts as possible. Granada's head of casting, Doreen Jones, has worked on all Woodhead's drama documentaries and, in his words, "become very sensitive to the kind of underplaying which is crucial to the feel of these things." Actors' attitudes vary enormously to the peculiar responsibility imposed on them by this form. Woodhead recalls that one of the actors in *Three Days in Szczecin* "had a wretched, sleepless night imprisoned in his dilemma about the impossible obligations of representing a living person" but came out of it deciding "that there was a legitimate role for him in the terms stated by the program itself . . . Some of my leading actors have met the people they were eventually to impersonate. Others have gone out of their way not to do that. I think Ian feels that, having done the work he has done, reading about, watching, thinking about Walesa, his task now is to try to articulate that, and it wouldn't be at this stage helped by an encounter with the man himself."

The scene being reconstructed began at 1.30 P.M. on 14 August 1980. The management team arrive late for the meeting. Gniech agrees to reemploy Anna Walentynowicz providing she accepts a job in the cooperation department, but hedges about a written undertaking to reemploy Walesa himself. Walesa gives up the argument quite suddenly. As Woodhead put it, "Round one to Gniech."

There is a mixture of exits and entrances to be choreographed like a ballet and big close-ups that hang on the movement of an eyebrow. The lighting is dim by conventional filming standards: little more than the fluorescent lights already in the hall. Cameraman Mike Whittaker, who shot Woodhead's last two drama documentaries and worked with him on many a "World in Action" in far-flung places years before (another shorthand going here), is using the Zeiss Distagon fixed lenses initially developed to cope with low-light situations on news and actuality programs. These lenses allow a larger aperture than any other in the armory ($f1.3$ as opposed to the usual maximum of around $f2$) with a consequently minuscule depth of field. The nose can be in focus and the eyeballs out. For the entry of the management team, the assistant cameraman lays white boxes along the table and runs a tape measure out to each. These are physical checkpoints that enable him to see exactly when to pull focus—something that cannot be seen simply by looking through the viewfinder.

"One thing that I've been very intrigued to try to understand," says Woodhead, "is why medium telephoto shots seem to have a smack of reality about them. Once you get up to around 70 or 80 mm there's something about the texture of the picture which feels curiously real. It can only be to do with the fact that so much newsreel and documentary, simply because the cameraman can't get very close to it often, is on that medium telephoto lens."

Thursday, 8 October.   The reconstruction of the meeting on the first day of the strike continues. Walesa makes a sudden, outright demand for a monument to be erected outside the shipyard gate in memory of the workers who died there in clashes with the police in December 1970. The monument becomes a crucial issue in an atmosphere of mounting tension: an impassioned speech by Anna Walentynowicz (Frances Cox) and a reference by one of the workers to the still-taboo subject of the massacre of Polish officers by the Soviet authorities at Katyn during World War II. Gniech is forced to refer the matter to a higher authority and, in the next scene filmed, announces an agreement in principle for the monument to be erected. Now the meeting has been augmented by a crowd of interested spectators, and a smoke machine comes into play. I notice that "Lenin," who from any angle other than the camera's seems remote, in fact in some shots looms right over the heads of the leading members of the management team. Holm's performance is gathering momentum as Walesa's did, and at the end of the scene Woodhead gives a start of pleasure at what he sees in his small viewer.

Another scene: the meeting continues on 15 August 1980. "People are looking tired and droopy, which may not be too hard to simulate," says Woodhead, who chose to overlook the fact that one or two of the extras actually fell asleep the previous day. Because he long since discovered the advantage of getting synchronized reactions to real speeches rather than fabricating them, the full complement of extras is always on the set even when not reacting and not appearing in the shots. Six people representing the Young Poland Movement are handed over to Boleslaw Sulik to tell them who and what they are. The smoke is disappearing as soon as it is manufactured. Can the ventilators be sucking it away? It seems the negotiations are going badly. Life is like that. Or is it?

The more you probe, the more metaphysical the question becomes, because Woodhead's films now draw on so much unpublished and unassessed material as to make them not just authentic but authoritative documents. For example, *Collision Course*, which he made in 1979 and which contains a second-by-second reconstruction of the last ten minutes before the world's worst midair collision, over Zagreb in 1976, is being examined at the time of writing as material evidence in a reopened inquiry into the events of 1976 and the standards of safety at Zagreb air traffic control. Beyond this, we seem to be in the area of Absolute Truth. "Well, the superiority of Absolute Truth over mere accuracy doesn't need my recommendation," said Woodhead in his *Guardian* lecture. "But that's surely more valuable as a corrective against arrogance than as a prescription invalidating notions of journalistic accuracy. 'Getting it right' does have validity in journalistic terms, not against the standards of an elusive absolute 'Truth' but against standards of evidence as they might be understood in a court of law."

In *Strike*, what we are getting is as accurate as possible a rendering, or paraphrasing, of speeches and conversations that actually took place, even to a worker's extraordinary exclamation, "We are haggling here over the dead heroes like blind beggars under a lamppost"—a simile indeed to wonder at! Its inclusion in the screenplay is as good an example as any of the myriad of choices still open to a drama-documentarist who never once diverges from the evidence of over one hundred hours of tape. Every camera set-up is in the same subjective category, every performance, every decision in the cutting room. What does this tell us about the end product? To quote the Woodhead lecture for the last time: "If we accept that dramatized documentary can only be a subjective construct, we must allow that the same is inevitably true to some degree of current-affairs documentary and of news itself." He went further to point out that drama documentary at least allows clear signposting: "When I make an observational documentary with many of the same editorial interventions, it's much more difficult both for the audience to locate the subjective content, and for me to find a way to tell them about it."

In this context Woodhead particularly admires Robert Vas's drama documentary about the Katyn Forest massacre (. . . *The Issue Should Be Avoided*) for the bold way in which it states its credentials from the outset. (A group of actors approach a forest clearing, and the commentary is telling us, "This is not the Katyn Forest in the Soviet Union. It would not be possible to film this investigation there. It is a forest near London, in autumn 1970. And these men are not survivors or eyewitnesses, but actors." As the actors sit down at a long table, the commentary gives us their names and tells us what they represent: "the Polish standpoint, the viewpoint of the Soviet Union," etc.)

"At that time and to this day," says Woodhead, "it remains an enormously courageous and frank way of revealing to the audience exactly what your film is doing and how it plans to do it—quite apart from the fact that the format he had chosen, a sort of tribunal of inquiry, gave him a totally organic means of bringing in extraneous evidence. Instead of having to use archive material and books and quotations in the stuck-on arbitrary way that compilation documentary often has to do, he was able, inside that court-of-inquiry format, to call it in as evidence. The whole thing had so much structural coherence that it was a delight to look at, apart from being an immensely powerful piece of television.

"I think that no two drama documentaries actually are alike. They constantly reinvent the form. I'm aware of that about my own things. Although they try to apply certain basic guide rules, no two of them are formally quite alike. There are always new difficulties . . . And I just felt that that film, more I think than any other I've seen, brilliantly solved all those problems at one swoop. The astonishing thing was that, despite the apparent colossal alienation of having actors declare themselves in that way, it was so moving, so much more moving than it would have been to have people pretending to be the roles they were playing . . . So I found the signposting in that case in a curious way upped the emotional impact, which is an extraordinary sort of paradox, not what you would expect at all."

I must here declare a powerful interest—the continuing, constructive influence on me of having worked with Robert Vas. In his political films Robert was often trying to get it right in opposition to amazing pressures to keep it wrong, but that is certainly another story. He rarely made a film that could be called a drama documentary, but on the inventive front it seems relevant to mention the way he sometimes summoned the aid of poets to speak for those condemned to silence. In his huge film *Stalin*, quotations from Anna Akhmatova are integral to the action, and a few lines of hers, about a tiny incident in a prison queue in Leningrad, rang through that whole year-long production, echoing the director's case so poignantly that everyone, including Robert, had to laugh: "Then a woman with lips blue with cold who was standing behind me, and of course never heard of my name, came out of the numbness which affected us all and whispered in my ear (we all spoke in whispers there): 'Can you describe this?' I said, 'I can!' "

Poetry signposts itself and automatically commands greater respect in the truth stakes than prose. It might be worth considering why that is, especially when the creative treatment of actuality in terms of images instead of words arouses such profound suspicion that the problem is how to convince without taking positively counterproductive measures. When Robert made (in 1974) the first documentary film ever to reconstruct the experience of the vast majority of the British population during and after the General Strike of 1926, the few people not immensely moved by it objected on essentially two counts: that he failed to signpost certain film excerpts (notably shots made in the Depression years and not during the strike itself), and that he got the details about a cricket match wrong. The latter (although heinous) fault hardly seems to invalidate the whole exercise. The former is in that area of peculiar challenge that confronts the documentarist as opposed to the compiler. Can you describe this? Well, not by strewing captions over every shot and distracting attention from the narrative flow in order to provide constant reference to information irrelevant to all but academics. In fact, however many footnotes you append about source material, you are still interpreting that material, and the validity of your interpretation still has to be taken on trust.

The risks incurred by too obtrusive signposting seem to me demonstrated in Leslie Woodhead's enormously sincere *Three Days in Szczecin*. The initial emphasis here on defining the evidence and indicating its differing status (primarily a smuggled tape, and secondarily eyewitness accounts that enabled Boleslaw Sulik to write imaginative reconstructions of certain scenes) made the subject itself quite hard to come to grips with. The complex structure of flashbacks (fine to go into but increasingly disorienting to come out of) added to the feeling of participating in an intellectual exercise and being emotionally distanced from the real experience the film was trying to show. My reaction is certainly not shared by everyone, because these very alienating factors have been particularly praised for serving, as indeed they do, as a constant reminder of the artifice of the whole operation. *Three Days in Szczecin* is certainly important in establishing the method of signposting, through the commentary, that is the hallmark of Woodhead's later, much more involving films.

In *Collision Course* (written by Martin Thompson) and *Invasion* (1980, written by David Boulton and reconstructing the events surrounding the Soviet occupation of Prague in 1968), the same strict rules about the clarification of sources are applied, but this is no longer detracting from the inherent drama of the subjects which is increasingly, I think, coming out of the performances. Now Woodhead and the actors are using the mounds of documentation, all the source material that in his philosophy commands the maximum respect, in order to explore quite openly the underlying psychology of what occurred. So the stories are acquiring new dimensions, spreading outwards, connecting with us all. Antony Sher (in *Collision Course*) is more than a young air traffic controller who falls victim to the Yugoslav government's search for a scapegoat; he is any imperfect individual luckless enough to make one wrong move in any of our faulty systems. The nuances of behavior (in *Invasion*) between Czech party secretary Zdenek Mlynar (Paul Chapman) and the young Russian officers who hold him prisoner, or between Dubček (Julian Glover) and the Russian colonel whom he once met at a dinner party in Moscow, turn apparently unfamiliar political territory into a place we really knew of all along.

Ian Holm (in *Strike*) seems to be going even further. As Boleslaw Sulik puts it, "Walesa, who is a demagogue and a manipulator and the leader, in a sense invites speculation . . . and Ian very brilliantly in his performance gives a range of options, of interpretations of this character. We are still not interested in the purely private features of this personality, but what he is as a man in fact has a public dimension, and the film to some extent is a speculation about what it takes to become a leader of such a movement."

What exactly has been happening between Woodhead's first dramatic reconstruction and this? "The Grigorenko film is stylistically rather curious," he says, "because it's full of filmic invention and very baroque camera movement which I guess, looking at it now, really is a cover for my own insecurities about what to do with the camera while the information was chugging along. I've felt an increasing drive since then to simplify and to do less and less in terms of self-regarding or noticeable things with the camera. I suppose for anybody who's interested in that low-key, overheard photography, the person who's shown us all the right direction is Ken Loach. I've always loved the way his films look, and the astonishing visual and aesthetic self-confidence that allows him so boldly to put cameras in positions and stay with them even when it makes images which are, in any conventional terms, the very opposite of engaging. Just the power of the performances he then generates legitimizes that . . . I've certainly spent years trying to screw up my own courage to the point of that degree of self-effacement."

Woodhead, unlike Loach, never uses improvisation. He is, as he puts it, "imprisoned by definition in text," but the style of his shooting (always now on fixed lenses with no zooms, and always with practically no lighting apart from that already existing in the locations) is increasingly geared to a similarly searching amalgam of documentary and drama: "One could certainly set up the sort of scenes we're doing, and I could say to an amazingly talented cameraman like Mike Whittaker (who's spent most of his filming life with the camera on his shoulder shooting "World in Action"s and many another thing on a completely handheld documentary basis), 'OK, Mike, it's happening over there. Go in and do the best you can with it,' which is what one would have done with "World in Action." I feel that's a sort of blind alley and a dishonesty in a sense, to try to pretend to the audience that you *don't* have control. But having accepted that, I'm interested, as I say, in disappearing as far as possible in terms of the conventions of dramatic photography."

Sunday, 25 October.   I interview Boleslaw Sulik again in London. He tells me that, at the end of five weeks' filming, the excavator scene I went to see is not yet in the can and has become the joke problem of the production.

"We returned to it the week before last. It was cold but very sunny and with a beautiful light. But it turned out that the excavator was quite different. The excavator that we shot was somewhere in the center of Liverpool, and in fact it was not only different but the roof was not safe to stand on. After many deliberations we decided to shoot it not on the roof but on the base of the excavator. We didn't have time to reshoot the whole scene, so the question was, Would that cut with the previous stuff? Having looked at the rushes we decided not only that it *won't*, but Leslie said we can't compromise in such a way . . . So he decided to go there once again, to get the original excavator from Liverpool and reshoot the whole scene. Now our problem is that one of the original actors is no longer available on that day."

Curiously, such insuperable odds are always overcome. Meanwhile, marvelous things seem to have been happening the previous week: "Four out of five days were on the main set, the BHP hall, culminating in the scenes which were both the crucial point of the strike and the first time we had as many as 220 extras, who themselves generate a lot of excitement . . . I think we've been talking about it before, that the strike in Gdansk was as much a cultural event as a political event, that it was a kind of freedom festival which could only be expressed in those traditional cultural terms which are, after all, very exotic to the Western audience. I've realized more than ever during the last two weeks that there is very little one can do to translate it into the British cultural structures, that what one needed was a kind of emotional charge to bridge that gap. I am pretty convinced that this has happened—partly through Ian Holm's performance, but mainly because a relationship between him and the crowd suddenly materialized. I'm no longer worried about making this cultural transition. I think it's going to work."

Woodhead's films never stop at themselves: "They inevitably spill into the world that they're depicting, and they've nearly all gone on ringing through my professional life in curious and unexpected ways." When the Grigorenko film was first transmitted, the general was in a psychiatric prison where he seemed likely to end his days. Not so. Some eight years later, Woodhead actually met him in New York and showed him the film. Grigorenko thought the film very accurate and spoke highly of the late Hamilton Dyce's impersonation of him. His only stricture was that the conditions in his KGB cell were really much worse than the filmmakers' worst imaginings had shown. Woodhead's story goes on: "He was there with his wife, who is immensely impressive, and they both cried, and he told me that he thought that, extraordinarily, the fact of the film materially shortened his sentence . . . The KGB said to him that a bourgeois activist had made a film about him, and then he smiled and he said, 'But I never dreamed I would meet that same bourgeois activist face to face.' "

So they made a postscript, a "World in Action" program in which a long interview with General Grigorenko and his wife was crosscut with extracts from Woodhead's first drama documentary, *The Man Who Wouldn't Keep Quiet.*

As I write, events in Poland change almost every day. Press cuttings and cartoons showing Solidarity as a tiny group of moonstruck revelers ringed round by tiers and tiers of tanks or, alternately, a great dragon restrained only by the flimsiest leash proliferate about the room. It all seems very close now, very urgent. Whatever the postscript to this is, it affects us all.

Part II

Enter the Filmmaker

Introduction

This section shifts the emphasis from text to creator, in particular to some of those filmmakers who have been particularly influential in pioneering forms or changing objectives in documentary in recent years. The seven essays collected here deal with the filmmaker's purpose, belief, style, and method—in short, what to say and how to say it. The discussion ranges over objectives, targets, practicalities, finance, political problems and pressures, all the 101 difficulties that face the filmmaker in translating dream into reality.[1]

In their quest to bring the vision into being, filmmakers have trodden many varied paths, from the lone solitary trail of Flaherty to the collective endeavors of groups like Newsreel and the Kartemquin collective. I have always been fascinated by the way groups interact on a creative project and give each other strength, purpose, and energy. It is this group interaction which makes the study of the Grierson years with the Empire Marketing Board and the GPO so fascinating and which, among other things, draws us to the study of U.S. filmmakers such as Pare Lorentz, Leo Hurwitz, Paul Strand, Willard Van Dyke, and Frontier Films.

In regard to the influence of group creation on documentary history, the work of the National Film Board of Canada (NFB) is clearly outstanding. In the 1940s the NFB set professional standards, and the pioneering work continued at an even greater pace in the late 1950s and early 1960s. It was during this later phase that filmmakers such as Wolf Koenig, Roman Kroitor, Tom Daly, Colin Low, and Terence Macartney-Filgate did as much in Canada to lay the ground rules for *vérité* as Jean Rouch and Chris Marker did in France, or Ricky Leacock, Robert Drew, Don Pennebaker, and the Maysles brothers in the United States.

There have been various studies of the NFB. Among the best are Peter Harcourt's article "The Innocent Eye,"[2] about the "Candid Eye" series, and Dorothy Todd Hénaut's analysis of the "Challenge for Change" program in *Films for Social Change*.[3] In 1981, D. B. Jones published *Movies and Memoranda*, an excellent comprehensive and in-depth study of the work of the NFB from its beginnings to the present day.[4] I open the debate on filmmakers at work with two extracts from his chapter on the NFB's Unit B, which included some of the pioneers of *vérité* and the creators of the "Candid Eye" series.

Jones's piece is followed by studies of three strong documentarists, Joris Ivens, Emile de Antonio, and Fred Wiseman, all of whom combine individual styles with strong political and social drives. Joris Ivens has been famous for years in documentary circles in Europe but is less well known in the United States. He was one of the earliest pioneers of the art documentary, with films such as *Rain* and *The Bridge*. Later he came to be regarded as one of the fathers of modern left-wing filmmaking, producing such works as *Spanish Earth* and *The Four Hundred Million*. Most of his early work is described in his autobiography, *The Camera and I*,[5] a book that unfortunately achieved only a small circulation in the American edition. His work is, however, extremely important for a proper understanding of the evolution of the European political documentary scene.

After a number of films about the Vietnam war, in 1972 Ivens and his co-filmmaker, Marceline Loridan, went to China at the invitation of Chou En-lai to make what ultimately would be twelve films on modern Chinese society. These films, together with a general background survey of Ivens's career, are the subject of Thomas Waugh's "Filming the Cultural Revolution."[6] Waugh presents the working methods of Ivens and Loridan well, and one gets a full understanding of their approach to filmmaking. However, the article seems to me at fault in its slightly naive and overly laudatory treatment of both Ivens and the Cultural Revolution. Waugh makes clear his political sympathy, which is fine, but one senses that neither the critic nor Ivens himself asked the difficult questions about the Mao regime. On Waugh's part, the picture presented is too praiseworthy and rosy (a fault that in a similar way undermined Shirley MacLaine and Claudia Weill's *The Other Half of the Sky*. On Ivens's part, one must remember that he was filming during the Cultural Revolution and that he apparently was a ready follower of the line of the Gang of Four. As critic Henry Breitrose put it, "Ivens's films are curious historical artifacts about a China that existed mostly in his mind."[7]

Whereas Ivens is the man of the barricades, de Antonio is more the intellectual revolutionary, and has cut an immensely influential swath through American documentary filmmaking since the early 1960s. A pioneer—perhaps *the* pioneer—of the political archive–based film, he has had a profound effect on young political filmmakers.

Though much has been written about de Antonio,[8] he tends to be his own best publicist, even going so far as to interview *himself* in a 1982 issue of *Film Quarterly*.[9] I have selected for this section a discussion between him and Gary Crowdus and Dan Georgakas, which shows de Antonio going at top speed. As usual, he is articulate, funny, driven, provocative, and deliberately outrageous—so many of his comments have to be taken with a grain of salt.

The article mentions *In the King of Prussia*—at the time of writing, de Antonio's latest work. This film deals with the activities and trial of eight people, including Daniel and Phillip Berrigan, who damaged two thermonuclear nosecones and poured blood over defense documents at a military establishment. The film illustrates a strong commitment to nuclear disarmament; but more important, it reflects a movement beyond de Antonio's usual actuality-plus-archive film method into a style that includes dramatic reconstructions and the use of actors such as Martin Sheen.

Fred Wiseman is the third filmmaker chosen, as a knowledge of his work seems absolutely vital to understanding the evolution of modern documentary in the United States. After Drew, Leacock, Pennebaker, and the Maysles brothers pioneered the crisis and personality biography approach to *vérité* in the 1960s, it was left to Wiseman to indicate how *vérité* could be used more broadly in social investigation.

Over the years he has studied some of the key cultural patterns and social institutions in America, ranging from the mental institution in *Titicut Follies* to the Neiman-Marcus organization in *The Store*. Much has been written about him—from discussions of his use of the open text to analyses of his editing methods.[10] Stephen Mamber's study of Wiseman in *Cinéma Vérité in America* is a useful introductory text to both Wiseman and the American *vérité* practitioners in general, but it only goes up to 1974.[11] Dan Armstrong's article from *Film Quarterly*, which I include in this section, provides a more up-to-date view of Wiseman, with a close look at his methods and political approach.[12]

Armstrong embraces a leftist view, and he sees Wiseman's approach as a role model for many political filmmakers: "The self-reflexivity and Althusserian critique of ideology which *Model* displays indicates that Wiseman is a political filmmaker who must be carefully studied by Marxists and others who would develop a radical film practice in this country."[13] My own view of Wiseman is somewhat more qualified. In recent years I have found his persistent use of a pure direct-cinema form wearying, and the open-text method unsatisfactory for complex subjects, which need a certain measure of voice-over background information and explanation to place them in an understandable context.

Whereas Ivens, de Antonio, and Wiseman deal with broad aspects of culture and politics, Craig Gilbert brings us back to the *individual* as the focus for documentary study. *Vérité* always held promise for close human observation, but the American *vérité* films of the 1960s tended to present show business portraits rather than a real understanding of ordinary human beings.[14] This situation changed with *Salesman* and *Grey Gardens* and the plethora of films in the early 1970s on families, roots, and men-women relations, including series such as "Six American Families." Craig Gilbert's work in this area of family film is central to the study of documentary, and his reflections provide a vivid insight into the trials and tribulations of this kind of filmmaking.

In the 1960s Gilbert established a solid reputation as an excellent producer-director, working independently for more than ten years for CBS, NBC, and ABC television. Then in 1971, inspired by a relationship crisis in his own life, Gilbert persuaded WNET-TV New York to let him film the daily life of one family over the course of a year.[15] The idea fascinated WNET and seemed highly original (though the seeds of the idea can in fact be found in Allan King's film *A Married Couple*, which traces the course of a marital crisis over two months).[16] After half a year of research, Gilbert finally persuaded the Loud family of Santa Barbara, California, to be the subject of his film. Shooting commenced in 1971; eventually twelve films were made, under the title *An American Family*, and were screened in 1973.

The series was greeted by both praise and a great deal of criticism aimed at Gilbert's methods, practices, and ethics. "Reflections," which is extracted from a long article that originally appeared in *Studies in Visual Communication*, is Gilbert's reply to his critics; it is a frank and full explanation of his attitude, motives, and approach in making the series.[17] Personally, I consider it the most interesting and honest article on the documentary process to appear in the past ten years. Unfortunately, limitations of space forced me to omit Gilbert's opening account of his relations with WNET and of his search for a suitable family. Thus, the reprinted excerpt (in two parts—one in this section; the second in Part III, on ethics) takes off from the establishment of the ground rules for filming and Gilbert's relations with his camera team and then covers the problems of budget, actual shooting, and final editing. In the continuation in the next section, Gilbert discusses the controversies that arose after the films were shown as well as the Loud family's own reactions.

An American Family is, in a way, an ethnographic series. Not only do the films reveal the Loud family in depth, but they also say a great deal about broad cultural patterns in upper-class California society. In a sense, a clear line exists between, for instance, *Nanook of the North* and *An American Family*. The relationship between documentary film and ethnographic film has, of course, been widely discussed since the days of Flaherty. Before his untimely death, Sol Worth was a patient explorer in this field, and more recently Jay Ruby, Bill Nichols, and David McDougall, among others, have written perceptively about the challenges and difficulties of ethnographic documentary filmmaking.[18]

I wanted to say something about ethnographic filmmaking in this section, and James Roy MacBean's article *"Two Laws* from Australia, One White, One Black" finally seemed the best choice. I was attracted to it because it includes a survey of current debates in the field and then focuses on the work of both well-known filmmakers such as the McDougalls and newcomers such as Alessandro Cavadini and Caroline Strachan. The comparison of the two groups is most interesting in that it points out the different means that can be used to achieve the same objective.

To conclude the section I selected "The Politics of Documentary," which was based on a symposium held under the auspices of *Cineaste* magazine. This article gives voice to a large number of contemporary filmmakers—de Antonio, Josh Hanig, Jon Else, and others—allowing them to express their concerns about the methods and purposes of documentary in the 1980s. The sheer variety of responses to many of the questions raised in previous articles, such as how the documentary works and what it should be doing, is remarkable.

One point raised, either directly or tangentially, by most of the filmmakers in the symposium has to do with voice and authority. This perennial stalking horse is not exactly a new topic, but it continually itches the filmmaker. One senses a search for a middle path, somewhere between the voice of God in "Victory at Sea" and the absence of all commentary in the Wiseman films. David McDougall suggests that the filmmaker's voice be clearly heard and identified.[19] Bill Nichols supports this position in "The Voice of Documentary," reprinted in the previous section.[20] Such an identification of viewpoint would, of course, be very different from the neutral front-man voice of network news documentaries, and closer to the style of Bill Moyers in "Bill Moyers's Journal"—more individual, more subjective, an interjection of the filmmaker's own personality into the film.

This personal-voice method informs most of the new "family" and "diary" documentaries, but it becomes particularly interesting when it is used on a wider societal and political level. In practice it is a plea for filmmakers to present themselves as holders of opinions, as more than mere conduits for other people's attitudes. It is also a strong admission of the personal element in filmmaking. Among current filmmakers, Mike Rubbo is the strongest advocate of this personal voice being used in political films, and good examples of the practice are seen in two of his films, *Waiting for Fidel* and *Sad Song of Yellowskin*.

Another subject running beneath the surface of the *Cineaste* symposium concerns the relative weights of the filmmaker's various obligations. In one sense, documentary filmmaking is a triangular relationship and system of duties: the filmmaker's duty to personal integrity and beliefs—the filmmaker's obligations to the subject and to the people being filmed—the filmmaker's duty to the viewer. Some of the articles in this section seem to suggest that the second element in this triangular relationship should in most cases take precedence over the other two, that is, control of the subject ought to be vested in the people being filmed. This idea is, however, fraught with dangers unless tightly controlled.

The idea is certainly valuable when the purpose of the exercise is to make a film for use by the film subjects themselves, or to tell a strange audience how the subjects see themselves. The work of the NFB's "Challenge for Change" films presents a good example of the first objective, and *Two Laws* of the second. However, Waugh's article on Ivens shows clearly where the approach runs into difficulties.

Waugh applauds Ivens for his sympathy and concern for his subjects but then takes Antonioni to task for filming a Chinese gunboat and a free-enterprise peasant market *against* the wishes of his Chinese hosts. I disagree with this position. Such restrictions are fine if the film is to remain in China to be seen by the Chinese; but if the purpose of the film is to give some overall picture of China to those unfamiliar with the society, then the restrictions reek of censorship. It seems to me that in the good political and societal film the power of choice must lie with the filmmaker rather than with the subject.

Clearly, we must return finally to the audience, to the viewer. Is the viewer fully aware of what is being said, what is being shown, under what conditions the film was made, what is deliberately inserted or omitted, and so on? In short, does the viewer have all the information necessary to judge a film? This ideal situation is a nice idea, but a little removed from reality. Regardless, it is important to stress that in the triangular relationship of filmmaker-subject-audience, audience and subject must generally receive equal consideration. If that is done, the documentary filmmaker will have discharged his or her obligations.

Notes

1. See also Alan Rosenthal, *The Documentary Conscience* (Berkeley and Los Angeles: University of California Press, 1980).

2. Peter Harcourt, "The Innocent Eye," *Sight and Sound* 34 (Winter 1964/65): 19–23.

3. Dorothy Todd Hénaut, *Film for Social Change*, McGill University Studies in Canadian Communications, 1976.

4. D. B. Jones, *Movies and Memoranda* (Ottawa: Canadian Film Institute, 1981).

5. Joris Ivens, *The Camera and I* (New York: International Publishers, 1969).

6. Thomas Waugh, "Filming the Cultural Revolution," *Jump Cut*, no. 12/13 (1976): 3–6.

7. Henry Breitrose to Alan Rosenthal, Jan. 12, 1985.

8. See Susan Lindfield, "De Antonio's Day in Court," *Village Voice*, Feb. 8, 1983, pp. 36–37, and Alan Rosenthal, "In the Year of the Pig," in Rosenthal, *The Documentary Conscience*, pp. 205–27.

9. Emile de Antonio, "The Self and the Other," *Film Quarterly* 36 (Fall 1982): 28–32.

10. Bill Nichols, "Frederick Wiseman's Documentaries: Theory and Structure," in Nichols, *Ideology and the Image: Social Representation in the Cinema and Other Media* (Bloomington: Indiana University Press, 1981), pp. 208–36.

11. Stephen Mamber, *Cinéma Vérité in America* (Cambridge, Mass.: MIT Press, 1974).

12. Dan Armstrong, "Wiseman's *Model* and the Documentary Project," *Film Quarterly* 37 (Winter 1983/84): 2–9.

13. Ibid., p. 9.

14. See *Jane, Showman, Don't Look Back, Will the Real Norman Mailer Please Stand Up*, and *Ladies and Gentlemen, Introducing Leonard Cohen*.

15. In 1974 Paul Watson copied Craig Gilbert's idea for the series "The Family," which he produced and directed for the BBC.

16. For an extended discussion of this neglected film, see the interviews with the director, cameraperson, and editor in Alan Rosenthal, "A Married Couple," *The New Documentary in Action* (Berkeley and Los Angeles: University of California Press, 1971), pp. 21–55.

17. Craig Gilbert, "Reflections on *An American Family*," *Studies in Visual Communication* 8 (Winter 1982): 24–54.

18. See Jay Ruby, "Is an Ethnographic Film a Film Ethnography?" *Studies in the Anthropology of Visual Communication* 2, no. 2 (1975); Bill Nichols, "Documentary, Criticism, and the Ethnographic Film," in Nichols, *Ideology and the Image* (Bloomington: Indiana University Press, 1981); and David McDougall, "Beyond Observational Cinema," in *Principles of Visual Anthropology*, ed. Paul Hockins (The Hague: Mouton, 1975).

19. Cited in James Roy MacBean, "*Two Laws* from Australia, One White, One Black," *Film Quarterly* 36 (Winter 1982/83): 37–38.

20. Bill Nichols, "The Voice of Documentary," *Film Quarterly* 36 (Winter 1982/83): 17–36.

The Canadian Film Board Unit B

D. B. Jones

David Jones studied communications at Stanford University, teaches at Drexel University, and is a director-producer of documentaries. He also writes a great deal, and in 1981 published Movies and Memoranda, *a fine and long overdue interpretative history of the National Film Board of Canada.*

I have selected two extracts from chapter 5 of Jones's work, which deal with the Film Board's Unit B. By 1950 the board was eleven years old and consisted of four units, A, B, C, and D, each with its own staff of writers, producers, directors, and editors. The aim of the board at that time, as characterized by Jones, was to produce good solid films on specific problems, usually identified by sponsoring government departments. What emerged were rather dull films, lacking in quality, variety, and any distinguishing character.

At that point, Unit A was mainly responsible for agricultural films; Unit C produced theatrical films and the "Canada Carries On" series; and Unit D dealt with international affairs and special projects. Unit B's franchise included sponsored, scientific, cultural, and animated films. According to Jones, however, the most important distinction among the units was a difference in values. Unit B was more willing to take risks, and in the first extract included here he describes the growing individuality and experimentation of Unit B after the making of their first two distinctive films, Corral *(1954) and* Paul Tomkowicz *(1954).*

Another prototype that emerged from Unit B was *City of Gold* (1957). Colin Low had discovered in the Dominion Archives a collection of old photographs of Dawson City, the Klondike gold rush town of 1898. With Roman Kroitor and Wolf Koenig, Low planned a film about Dawson City using these still photographs. The team then came up with the idea of using actuality footage of present-day Dawson City to bracket the still-photograph content. In Dawson City—where they discovered even more photographs—they filmed quiet scenes of old men sitting in front of dilapidated stores and young boys playing baseball. For filming the still photographs, Kroitor invented a camera-plotting device that enhanced the filming by alleviating the appearance of "flatness" normally associated with filmed still photographs.

Two years after the filming of the live-action footage in Dawson City, the editing of *City of Gold* was almost complete. The music was being composed. All that remained was to write and record a commentary. Unlike *Corral*, this was a film which absolutely needed commentary. But it needed an *outstanding* commentary, one that would work together with the pictures and the music to evoke the nostalgic mood that the filmmakers were after. Wolf Koenig came up with the idea of using the Canadian author Pierre Berton, who had grown up in the Yukon. Low and Kroitor agreed to try out Berton, but they feared that he would want to change everything around. To their surprise, Berton loved the film. Berton set to work on a commentary, with Stanley Jackson helping him adapt it to the needs of film time and pacing. Berton also spoke the commentary. Despite one or two lapses into forced spontaneity, the commentary as a whole was unpretentious, informative, personal, and elegant. It enhanced the film's nostalgic effect immensely. *City of Gold* won seventeen international awards and remains today the best film of its kind, and much imitated.

As the ability of Unit B—particularly the informal group composed of Kroitor, Koenig, Low, Jackson, and the unit's executive producer, Tom Daly—became recognized by the management of the Film Board, the unit achieved a status that would allow them, occasionally, to break the rules beforehand, i.e, with permission, instead of having to quietly exceed the budget or projected completion date and then justify the transgression with an outstanding film. An example is another prototype, *Universe* (1960), one of the Film Board's most famous and successful films.

Low and Kroitor had had a long-time fascination with cosmology. The project began as a proposed classroom film about five years before Sputnik. Discussions about the project drew in several other interested persons, and the scope of the film grew. The aim of the film, they agreed, would be not so much to convey facts about the universe as to invoke a sense of wonder about it. The film would be an adventuresome project, because there was insufficient knowledge of the techniques that would be required in order to create the images that were desired. As one member of the team remembers, "We couldn't say, 'To shoot these solar prominences we'll have to do this and this and this'; we just didn't know yet how to achieve the images we wanted." Because so much technical experimentation would be required, the team knew that they would need a lot of money to make the film they had in mind.

The team prepared an outline, a rough storyboard, and a budget estimate of about $60,000, which in the 1950s was an enormous sum for a single Film Board film. Tom Daly remembers that Donald Mulholland, the director of production, suggested that the film be divided into three parts, three classroom films. That would make it easier for him to defend the cost of the project. The team argued persuasively that the film should remain a single film, a unity, for among other reasons "unity" was in a large part the very theme that they wanted the film to suggest. Jackson recalls that Mulholland said something like:

> "As a responsible director of production, I absolutely cannot authorize putting that much money into a single production. It would knock out other worthy projects. However, I am not the ultimate authority. The commissioner is the ultimate authority. Go see him and tell him your story, and ask him to phone me."

The commissioner, Albert Trueman, responded enthusiastically. He called Mulholland and told him that some way should be found to proceed with the project. Mulholland was, Jackson remembers, delighted, but still concerned about the costs.

> "But," he said, "there's no deadline, no hurry. If I give you $60,000 and say 'go ahead,' that isn't fair [to you or to other filmmakers]. So we'll do it this way: I'll give you $20,000 this year. Get going. When you've spent it, put the film on the shelf until the next fiscal year." This meant that the next time Low and Kroitor could get at the money, they'd be more sure of where they were going.

After the end of the third fiscal year, the film was still not done. More money was required. The money was provided, but with the stipulation that the film must be finished by the end of that—the fourth—fiscal year. The team finished the film on March 31, the last day of the fiscal year.

The film had taken four years, but not four whole years, because after the first few months of each fiscal year the $20,000 allocated for the year had been spent and the film had to be placed on the shelf. This on-again-off-again process may have worked to the film's advantage. William James once remarked that "we learn to swim in the winter and skate in the summer." With *Universe*, this principle was incorporated, intentionally or not, into the Film Board's battery of production strategies.

A filmmaker from outside Unit B remembers that when *Universe* was finished, and test screened, its general reception was summed up in the reaction of one filmmaker, who exclaimed, "You spent $60,000 for . . . *that*!?" But

Universe became one of the most widely distributed educational films ever made, earning much more than its total production costs in revenues. NASA ordered at least 300 prints of the film, which they used for training and for public information. By 1976, the Film Board had sold over 3,100 prints of *Universe*. Stanley Kubrick, when he started work on his *2001: A Space Odyssey*, discussed the project with Colin Low and hired Wally Gentleman, the wizard who had achieved the optical effects for *Universe*, to do the same for Kubrick's film. And Kubrick used the voice of Douglas Rain, who spoke the commentary (which Stanley Jackson had written) for *Universe*, as the voice of Hal, the computer.

The culmination of the documentary work of Unit B was a series called "Candid Eye," half-hour documentaries made for television. The series began in 1958 and ran for about three years. Koenig and Kroitor, the series's main instigators, believed that television, with its voracious appetite for material, offered far greater opportunities for experimentation than had been recognized. Most of the documentaries on television—many of them, in Canada, Film Board documentaries—were boring, shallow, and unimaginative. Kroitor and Koenig had seen *Thursday's Children*, a documentary by Lindsay Anderson and the British "Free Cinema" group of the mid-1950s, and believed that the scriptless approach of films like *Thursday's Children* could be adapted favorably to a series of Canadian documentaries. The two filmmakers were equally enchanted by the work of the photographer Henri Cartier-Bresson, who seemed capable of combining the spontaneity of candid photography with an acute sensitivity to form.

When the Unit B team proposed a series of films for which there would be no script at all, the Board's management, and many filmmakers within the Board, were puzzled. They didn't think films could be made without a script and without rehearsals of the action. Management was hesitant to approve the project, because it had no way of knowing what the results might be. Daly has summarized both the problem of getting the project approved and the solution:

> The most you could give for each film in the series was a subject, and perhaps a list of sequences you were likely to cover. It was known that the shaping and structuring would occur in the editing room. In order to get the proposal accepted— and to be able to drop a subject that later proved unsatisfactory—we gave the program committee [about] thirty-two subjects, and asked them to agree on a priority fifteen, from which we would do seven. So they had an input.

The cost of the films would not be any more than the cost of the typical Film Board documentary. Although the lack of scripts meant that more footage would have to be shot, and that editing would take a lot longer, money would be saved by skipping the script stage and by using small crews, with new lightweight equipment.

Terence Macartney-Filgate joined Koenig and Kroitor for "Candid Eye," Stanley Jackson wrote the commentaries, and Tom Daly served as executive producer. Several French-Canadians also worked on the series. They included Georges Dufaux, Gilles Gascon, Michel Brault, Claude Pelletier, and Marcel Carrière. Roles interchanged considerably. Stanley Jackson directed one of the films. Tom Daly edited sequences of at least one film. Several of the French-Canadians did some directing.

Among the more remembered titles in the "Candid Eye" series are *The Days Before Christmas* (1958), *The Back-Breaking Leaf* (1959), and *Blood and Fire* (1958). *The Days Before Christmas*, a survey of the rush of activities that precede the holiday, was the pilot film for the series, and at least six filmmakers directed sequences of it: Roman Kroitor, Wolf Koenig, Stanley Jackson, Terence Macartney-Filgate, John Feeney, and Michel Brault. Macartney-Filgate directed *The Back-Breaking Leaf*, a film about the grueling work of tobacco pickers in the annual southern Ontario harvest, and *Blood and Fire*, a film about the Salvation Army.

These films did not solve fully the formal problem presented by the scriptless, high-ratio approach to reality: how to fashion this wider and less contrived range of actuality into some meaningful, aesthetically satisfying whole. But *Lonely Boy* (1962), filmed after the end of the regular "Candid Eye" series as a kind of grand finale, did. More money was spent on *Lonely Boy*, and more editing time, than on any of the regular "Candid Eye" films. More effort, too. Koenig and Kroitor shot and codirected the film; John Spotton and Guy Coté worked on it as editors.

A totally engrossing portrait of Paul Anka, the popular Canadian entertainer who excited tears and screams in worshiping North American teenage girls in the early 1960s, *Lonely Boy* was, for the Film Board and for documentary in general, an advance in "the creative treatment of actuality." The film is a fascinating mixture of the formal and the formless. Raw, vigorous, often spontaneous content is organized into a rigorous structure.

On the one hand, much of the material in the film seems to consist of random shots—snaps, almost—of the Atlantic City environment in which much of the film is set. In one tracking shot, the camera and crew follow Anka hurriedly as he moves down a street. In another scene, the crew surprises Anka by waiting in his dressing room. In some ways, the film is almost arrogantly—for its time—sloppy-*looking*. The microphone appears in the tracking shot of Anka walking down the street. As Anka bursts into the dressing room, he stares at the camera in a brief moment of surprise. Jumpcuts abound in the interview sequences. A question from the filmmaker is heard in one scene. In one of the film's most engrossing scenes, in which Anka presents a gift to the owner of the Copacabana nightclub in New York, the filmmaking team becomes involved in the action. The owner rather insincerely kisses Anka to thank him for the gift. We hear a voice asking him to do the kiss again. Anka and the manager break into laughter. "The camera moved," the filmmaker, off-camera, explains. They kiss again, and then Anka, still laughing, asks if the film crew wants them to do it *again*. The filmmaker tells them no, just keep talking. The entire uncut sequence appears in the film.

On the other hand, *Lonely Boy* is tightly structured. The film opens with Anka singing the song of that title. "I'm just a lonely boy," he intones, as we see billboards (with Anka's name on them in huge letters), the center of the highway, etc., from the point of view of the car in which Anka is riding. The loneliness of an entertainer who has become an idol, worshiped by hordes of silly young girls, is the theme, and this theme is relentlessly held to. At a concert, a human barrier of policemen and security guards protects Anka from the screaming mob. When Anka presents his gift—a huge portrait of himself—to the nightclub owner, the gift is received with no real warmth. Rehearsing a new composition on the piano, Anka looks scared and insecure. He is surrounded by sycophants. At one point near the end, the film becomes highly stylized for a documentary. The shrieking audience, which in an earlier scene had drowned out the words of the singer, is now faded out *in the editing*, so that we hear the song, and only the song, over a series of silent shots of agonized, idolatrous fans. The film ends with more shots down the highway. Anka, inside the car, appears bored with, and alienated from, his crew of managers and agents. A woman in a passing car stares at him. On the soundtrack, we hear, again, "I'm just a lonely boy. . . . "

Paul Tomkowicz, Corral, City of Gold, Universe, and the "Candid Eye" series, each a prototype in its own right, could be taken as benchmarks in the evolution of a distinct Unit B style of *working* that was to affect the Film Board deeply, if not universally or unambiguously. With *Paul Tomkowicz* and *Corral*, perfection became regarded as a criterion far more important than the budget, the schedule, or the norm, i.e., professionalism. Grierson had urged that films must "achieve distinction or they're not worth doing at all," and, for their time, the wartime films were distinctive, or at least technically well made. But there had always been the urgencies of the war, the theatrical release date, and Grierson's Calvinistic strain to keep rein on any one project's pursuit of its full potential. It took several years of peace, and the introduction of a measure of routine, before the board began to free itself from wartime constraints. The beginning does not seem to have been a planned or conscious one. The concept of what *Paul Tomkowicz* should be, and the means to make it that, were both discovered largely by trial and error. The discovery that *Corral* did not need a commentary, and that it would be a far better film without one, occurred while struggling with the material itself, and did not follow from some theory.

With *City of Gold*, the notion of using Pierre Berton as the narrator arose from difficulty with the commentary, but in the filming of the still photos there had been an image of what the film ought to look like and then a problem-solving effort—Kroitor's camera-plotting device—to achieve the image. With *Universe*, there was the imagination and the planned-for exploration and experimentation, and even the budget and scheduling problems were anticipated, so that if the manner of the production departed radically from the professional norm, it did so purposely, with management's prior approval. In the case of "Candid Eye," the right to experiment on a grand documentary scale was negotiated beforehand, with a minimum of compromise, with management. The Film Board professional norm was no longer the rule—if you belonged to Unit B, and if you could convince management by the merit of your proposal and your track record.

This striving for perfection, which invariably involved the odious (to Grierson) "cuddling to sweet smotheroo," was nevertheless associated with characteristics Grierson had promoted. The team approach to filmmaking was one such characteristic. The names Kroitor, Koenig, Low, Daly, and Jackson occur again and again in the best Unit B films, although others were involved, too— especially Eldon Rathburn, who did the music for *Corral, Universe,* and other Unit B films, and Terence Macartney-Filgate in "Candid Eye." In several ways, the group's style of working recalled the old Empire Marketing Board in England, and aspects of the early, wartime Film Board. There was in this team and in Unit B as a whole a degree of "role freedom." A filmmaker might produce one film, direct the next, and edit a third. John Spotton, trained as a cameraman, took a pay cut to work as an editor on *The Back-Breaking Leaf* and *Lonely Boy*. Tom Daly, the unit's executive producer, would sometimes edit a film. And in any one production, the roles of producer, director, cameraman, and editor would often overlap. As a film critic wrote in the mid-1960s, the Unit B films "are so thoroughly the product of a group that their names do not matter."[1] Unlike the early EMB and early Film Board films, the Unit B films, like all contemporary NFB films, did carry credits, but the credits did not reflect clearly defined roles. Credits, Tom Daly recalls, were "apportioned at the end of the filming according to where we felt the center of gravity lay." Pay raises—another kind of reward—were also somewhat communally awarded. When there were pay raises, everyone in the unit deserving one got one, whether he had asked for it or not.

The cooperative approach of the Unit B team of Kroitor, Koenig, Low, Jackson, and Daly did not involve simple self-effacement, but something quite different. Tom Daly remembers Unit B as a group which, at its best, combined aspects of communality and individuality:

> There was a desire not to be separate. Each person, confident of his ability in one or two areas, would recognize his lacks in other areas, and other persons' abilities in those areas. Each person had a sense that his own fulfillment could not be fully achieved on his own, but only in connection with a project to which he and others contributed where they could . . . to achieve something greater

than the sum of the various contributions. . . . To achieve this harmony, filmmakers don't have to be geniuses, but they do have to be first-rate in *some*thing. And if they are, they will also be aware of not being first-rate in other things, and will therefore *enjoy* cooperating with people who *are* first-rate in those things.

But the day-to-day process by which such creative collaboration was achieved was anything but harmonious. Wolf Koenig remembers that

for all the rosy light cast on old Unit B by the haze of memory and nostalgia, it should be remembered that it had a very tough strand running through it. It's this strand, in my opinion, which made it functional (like the wires inside Michelins). And what it consisted of was opposition and conflict! What made the unit function under such apparently self-destructive impulses was that Tom Daly, our executive producer, accepted this conflict and, intuitively, used it as a source of energy for the group.

The polarities within Unit B were best expressed by the two major personalities within it: Tom Daly and Roman Kroitor. The personalities of these two men were almost diametrically opposed to each other. Tom, the conservative, pragmatic, technically and artistically accomplished, apparently unemotional administrator; raised in the traditions of Upper Canada College; apprenticed to film aristocrats like Grierson and Legg; always conscious of his obligations to pass on tradition and to serve the public's needs. In other words, truly Anglo and the nearest thing we have in Canada to an aristocrat.

Roman, on the other hand, was a rebel (in his way); an accurate but devastating critic; a Saskatchewan Ukrainian—therefore highly emotional; a brilliant student at university (a gold medal winner); a highly creative filmmaker without (at that time) a full technical knowledge, but learning fast; very nervy and, at times, disrespectful of the opinions of "older and wiser" heads; with long hair when it was unfashionable and a life style which bordered on the "bohemian." He was the object of envious ridicule by some, but, like Tom Daly, he was dedicated to the public good (although he saw it from another angle).

Well, these two personalities clashed, mostly in discreet ways, sometimes not so discreetly. Tom certainly could have gotten rid of this Kroitor guy in about five minutes and he would have been applauded for doing so. But he didn't. Instead he helped to train him and supported him in films which were, to many, very far out. At times he fought against management even though this went entirely against his own traditional upbringing. . . . So . . . it was between the polarities of these two men that the strand I mentioned earlier was stretched, and to such fine tautness that all the rest of us could balance on it.

The group dynamics of this team resembled that of the smaller two-person and thus simpler team that discovered the structure of DNA. Both James Watson and Francis Crick were expert in something—Watson in biology, Crick in crystallography—but, as in Unit B, there was a "role freedom" in the relationship that encouraged each to probe the other's area of expertise. Watson and Crick had a similar generosity toward credits; they decided senior authorship by the toss of a coin. And finally, they could criticize each other, bluntly.[2]

The work of the Unit B team and the work of the DNA scientists resembled each other in one more respect. A sociologist has noted that the motivation of scientists cannot be explained solely by desire for fame or reward, and has argued that there is a "charisma" in science which must be adduced as a complementary motivation. Among scientists, "charismatic things are those which bring order out of chaos and which guide, direct, and make meaningful human action."[3] Although there were the usual egoistic motivations in the race for the structure of the double helix, awe of the elusive structure itself was a motivation, as is evident, if not explicit, in Watson's account of the discovery.[4]

But to colleagues of Watson and Crick their pursuit of the structure seemed at times zealous or obsessive. Similarly, to many NFB employees outside of Unit B, there seemed to be a touch of messianic zeal in the team's pursuit of aesthetic perfection. Sometimes it seemed to others that Unit B filmmakers lived only to make brilliant films, subjugating all other aspects of life and living to that single purpose. For Unit B, the pursuit of perfection had apparently become "the sacred commitment" that the theatrical release date had been during the war. It was as if it were holy to seek perfection and sinful to compromise.

On this point, Stanley Jackson comments that

> it did *look* like, at times, a kind of crazy dedication . . . but it was an attitude toward the craft. There was a filmmaker who had produced a number of mediocre films, and if you asked him how the film was, he would say, and I quote, "We got away with it." For *us*, though, it had to be as good as you could make it. You had to get as much out of the material, through structuring, through the use of sound, the orchestration of all the materials, so that it would be as good as possible. It wasn't a holy crusade. It was an attitude toward the craft.

If it wasn't a holy crusade, the "attitude toward the craft" certainly had charismatic aspects. But there was now no war, and no Grierson, to inspire this charismatic devotion. Its sole source was an ideal of aesthetic fulfillment.

Unit B's aesthetic ideal involved an idea of *wholeness*. A similar idea had pervaded the wartime NFB work. But Grierson's idea of wholeness was such that each film, insignificant in itself, contributed to the "whole" picture of Canada that the Film Board was attempting to produce. An individual film might contain a *thematic* wholeness, in the sense that a "World in Action" or a "Canada Carries On" film would show single events or local situations in relation to world events. Wholeness also referred, for Grierson, to the overall *system* of production and distribution which established a dynamic relationship between production and constituency.

Unit B modified this "wholeness" in a significant way. Unit B emphasized wholeness in the *individual* films, but in none of the Unit B prototypes is the subject related, in an explicit or thematic way, to the rest of the world. The "wholeness" of *Paul Tomkowicz, Corral, City of Gold, Universe*, and *Lonely Boy* lies in the coherent fullness with which the subject is presented. The films contain an organic wholeness, a certain aesthetic integrity that avoids the imposition of forced connections to some larger issue, some greater relevance. But the avoidance of explicit relevance does not mean that these films were esoteric or trivial. Their popularity was enormous, and still is. These films did not *refer* to a wider world, but *spoke to* the wider world through their integrity of structure and material, or style and content. Perhaps their aim and effect were to find the universal in the particular—the lyricism of ranchhands rounding up horses, the occasionally tremulous inflection in Berton's nostalgic commentary, the moment at the piano when Paul Anka looks so tentative and alone—and to communicate with their audience not intellectually but emotionally. With reference to the "Candid Eye" films, Wolf Koenig wrote that the aim was to "show them on television to millions of people and make them see that life is true, fine, and full of meaning."[5]

Although in part a modification of Grierson's sense of the whole, the aesthetic "wholeness" in the Unit B films was rooted in the work of the Grierson-led wartime Film Board. Two members of the team, Jackson and Daly, had joined the board very early. Daly had developed the stock-shot library. Partly because he was the one "who knew where everything was," he became the editor of the "World in Action" series. This meant that Legg and Daly, between them, had to edit a film a month. Jackson directed and edited films, but increasingly he was called on to write commentaries.

From working in these capacities and under Grierson, Daly and Jackson developed a keen sense of structure. In the 1950s, Daly would often edit a film, but his structural sense was expressed mainly in a kind of informal teaching that was part of his approach to producing. Jackson's structural sense was brought into the work of the unit mainly through writing commentaries, an art which in documentary requires a sense of structure as much as a facility with words. Once, however, it was brought in by *not* writing a commentary, for it was precisely this structural capacity that allowed Jackson to recognize, finally, that *Corral* did not *need* a commentary. A less confident talent might have tried to force a commentary onto the film.

[Again, because of space pressures, I had to omit a section from the middle of the chapter in which Jones deals with Unit B's tendency to report *success* and the achievement of unity in its films. Thus, many of Unit B's films deliberately avoided themes that included the sick, the horrible, and the ugly. A few people, including Norman McLaren, struggled against that tendency and tried not to ignore the more difficult aspects of contemporary life. The second extract I have chosen picks up a discussion of the work of the unit's more socially critical filmmakers.—A.R.]

One such filmmaker was Terence Macartney-Filgate. His "Candid Eye" films were concerned more with the unsuccessful than with the celebrated. And just as the "Candid Eye" films made primarily by the Inner Circle team tended to select individuals as subjects, Macartney-Filgate, an individualist, tended to make films about groups. In *The Back-Breaking Leaf* (1960), Macartney-Filgate, working with several French-Canadians, explored the harsh life of tobacco pickers in southern Ontario. In his *Blood and Fire*, which examined the work of the Salvation Army, there is one scene in which a weeping, deeply troubled person, a genuine down-and-out, responds to the Call to the Mercy Seat. This scene was, during the editing, the subject of heated debates. Some believed that because the scene showed a recognizable man in a state of emotional nakedness, it should be cut out. It seemed raw and—worse—unethical. *Cinéma vérité* was in its early stages, and some filmmakers had qualms about using such material. But because there had been no attempt to hide the camera, and because the scene was so dramatic, it was kept.

Neither of these films had the coherent richness or energy of *Lonely Boy*. They were aesthetically flat. But neither of them was made under the special conditions and with the grand-finale purpose and license of *Lonely Boy*. And if they failed to achieve a tone of "praise," i.e., a life-enhancing structure or perspective, they dealt in an area that the Inner Circle team generally avoided—unsuccess.

Arthur Lipsett was another member of Unit B who tried to deal in his work with the less cheery side of life. In 1962, he made *Very Nice, Very Nice*, an eight-minute film containing perhaps as many individual shots as an average hour-long documentary. Many of the shots were stills. The sound track was composed from pieces of sound tape discarded from other films. This was several years before Jean-Luc Godard made *Weekend*, a film introduced by the title, "A Film Found on the Scrap Heap." The vision in *Very Nice, Very Nice* was as dour as that of *Weekend* and a lot more succinctly (if far less richly) expressed. The bomb, international politics, materialism, pollution, noise, and alienation are among the pathologies covered in the film.

If the Unit B classics leaned toward an easy praise, in *Very Nice, Very Nice* there was no praise at all. It was a completely sour list of complaints against society as it existed at the time. *Very Nice, Very Nice* was to the Unit B aesthetic as Dostoyevski's underground man was to the optimistic, rational positivism of Dostoyevski's time. Even the title could be taken as a sarcastic comment on the Unit B aesthetic, a sardonic response to the easy optimism that saw life as "true, fine, and full of meaning" by seeing only half of life.

Unfortunately, Lipsett saw only that other half. *Very Nice, Very Nice* was like the underground man, but it was not like *Notes from the Underground*. It was the phenomenon without the form. It stands as a rather gross example of what in literary criticism is sometimes called "the expressive fallacy," the notion that the effect of an artwork should reproduce its subject—e.g., that a novel about boredom should itself be boring. *Very Nice, Very Nice* was a disordered film about disorder, a confused film on confusion. Its effect was accomplished by chopping up random pieces of actuality footage and sound tape found in the Film Board's waste baskets. Almost any pieces would do. With *Very Nice, Very Nice*, the filmmaker was like a poet who attempts to show the decline of language and culture by writing an incomprehensible poem out of bifurcated, misspelled cusswords randomly strung together.

Very Nice, Very Nice was, however, something of a *tour de force*, and was very popular among underground film persons and members of the counterculture in North America. The film achieved an influential niche in the history of experimental film. It became a prototype. The film was influential at the Film Board, too. Several filmmakers regarded Lipsett as the board's first resident genius since McLaren. The extreme positive response to Lipsett's extreme negativism suggests that there was, within the Film Board and outside it, a severe hunger for recognition of the negative side of contemporary life. If the film fails to survive aesthetically, perhaps it was at the time a refreshing challenge to the easy optimism that dominated the screens of the early sixties. *Very Nice, Very Nice* was a filmic restatement of McLaren's milder suggestion that perhaps creative artists shouldn't be frittering their talent away on pretty things when the world was menaced with the possibility of total destruction.

Lipsett, Macartney-Filgate, Bairstow, and McLaren were at various degrees removed from the Inner Circle, the Unit B team responsible for the Board's first classic documentaries. Bairstow belonged to another unit and had little to do with Unit B. McLaren was part of Unit B for a while, but only technically. In Daly's words, McLaren was always "an original, special person, available to all, and ready to help all." Macartney-Filgate joined the Unit B team for "Candid Eye," but he did not get along well with them. The Inner Circle encouraged Lipsett at first, and actually supported and defended his work on *Very Nice, Very Nice*. Only later, as Lipsett continued to dwell on the same theme, was there a falling out.

It was as if Unit B had a group personality which could not absorb the negative into its aesthetic vision, even though it tried. Unit B's best films were made by the Inner Circle and avoided the negative: the unit's socially critical films were made by others and weren't so good. Unit B did, however, make one outstanding documentary that did not ignore the unsettling aspects of its subject. This film was *Circle of the Sun* (1961), directed by Colin Low. The film's specific subject is the Blood Indian Sun Dance, performed at a gathering in Alberta (Low's home province). This was the first time that the Indians had allowed the Sun Dance to be filmed; the reason for allowing it was that the Indians feared that the tradition might be dying. This possibility suggested the film's larger theme—the possible demise of the whole Blood Indian culture. The Sun Dance and its larger subject are explored through a portrait (and voice-over) of a young Blood Indian, who moves between two worlds, modern industrial civilization (he works as an oil rigger) and what's left of the Blood culture. This theme was not a new one, and the film did not develop new techniques, but it is a reasonably sensitive, honest, and beautiful film, its "praise" consisting in the aesthetic intensity with which the theme is rendered.

But *Circle of the Sun* does not necessarily belie the characterization of the Unit B aesthetic as overly positive. For one thing, as good as the film was, it was not a prototype. For another, it was perhaps aesthetically *too* intense. The film tends to aesthet*icize* its subject. As if the Sun Dance weren't itself sufficiently engrossing, a heavy-handed, overbearing musical score dominates the film in its most dramatic moments.

Additionally, *Circle of the Sun* was less of a team effort than the prototypal documentaries, and more the work of an individual. And its director, Colin Low, would eventually, when the team disbanded, pursue socially relevant filmmaking with a vengeance.

In sum, it does appear that the aesthetic ideal's difficulty with the negative was in some important way related to the personality of the group, a personality not reducible to those of the individual members of the group. The team had an aversion to rawness. It liked its reality precooked. It preferred to make films about subjects already somewhat coherent, somewhat whole, rather than to create that wholeness entirely itself.

The team's inability to absorb the raw into its aesthetic triumphs was a limitation to its "attitude toward the craft," but perhaps it was also an indication of aesthetic integrity. To expand the range of the aesthetic may have meant destroying it. For the Film Board of the time, the aesthetic was an indisputable advance in the art of documentary. Unit B represented the apex of the development of certain Film Board values and characteristics. It was the height of combining one's living with one's calling. It was the epitome of group filmmaking. And it was the strongest expression of a consciously considered, home-grown film aesthetic.

The unit system came to an end less than two years after *Very Nice, Very Nice*. Therefore, it is hazardous to speculate upon the possibility that the Unit B aesthetic eventually might have widened its scope. But after *Lonely Boy*, the Unit B Inner Circle (and Unit B as a whole) produced no further existent documentaries of note. Possibly the Unit B aesthetic had spent itself with *Lonely Boy*.

But possibly it hadn't. In 1963, the group's attention turned toward planning a multiscreen extravaganza, *Labyrinth*, for Expo '67, Canada's centennial celebration. One of the requirements of Expo '67 was that whatever was shown had to be something that could not be seen anywhere else. It is impossible to see the original *Labyrinth* now[6]—which is unfortunate, because in Daly's view, *Labyrinth* "was perhaps the most complete embodiment of the Unit B philosophy." Daly recalls that

> the theme was the whole development of life, dark and light sides, through innocent childhood, confident youth, disillusion and depression, the search for something more, the meeting with the Minotaur (the dark side of oneself), new directions of life, the facing of death, and the mysteries beyond. This theme was embodied in architecture, in personal movement of the audience through a "structure" of events and experiences including films as *part* of it.

If the Unit B aesthetic hadn't exhausted itself with *Lonely Boy*, it surely had with *Labyrinth*. This single project held most of the team together after the unit system's demise, but by the time *Labyrinth* was over, Koenig had returned to animation, Kroitor had left the Film Board, and Low had begun to pursue a different kind of filmmaking in Challenge for Change. And some of their younger disciples had tired of documentary and become interested in dramatic features.

But the contribution of Unit B to the Film Board documentary did not lie solely in the classics that it put into the Board's catalogue. That Unit B *had* an aesthetic ideal, that they made films which did not compromise the ideal, and that their commitment to achieving it was unswerving influenced filmmakers of various sensibilities. In addition, the success of Unit B earned for all Film Board filmmakers a greater authority over the purpose and process of filmmaking; the unusual freedoms that Unit B won for itself were transmitted to all the filmmakers in the form of structural changes that would occur in 1964. And three members of the Inner Circle—Tom Daly, Colin Low, and Stanley Jackson—would, as individuals, give generously to the Film Board documentary even into the eighties. Most of the board's later achievements in documentary owed much to the work of Unit B.

Even now, Unit B is remembered vividly. Some of its severest critics remember it with nostalgia or at least respect. One who had been an unhappy fringe member of the unit laments that

> the *discipline* of the unit system—and in its own informal way Unit B was the most disciplined—was a good thing. Everything I know now is because of the discipline I learned in Unit B. I'm trying to develop discipline in these new guys, but it's not possible. Young filmmakers nowadays want to do just what they want. They don't listen.

A filmmaker who had belonged to a different unit remarks:

> They were snobs . . . I couldn't stand them . . . And yet, you've got to be a bit of a snob to do something of quality. If you're not a snob, you might be sloppy.

And a sound mixer remembers:

> It was . . . *trying* to work with them. Quite often they'd work by committee, in endless sessions, in the mixing studio. They were very meticulous. But they were always after a *good film*. It was a challenge and a joy to mix their films.

Notes

1. Peter Harcourt, "The Innocent Eye," *Sight and Sound*, 34 (Winter 1964/65): 19–23.

2. Public Broadcasting Service, "Nova: The Race for the Double Helix," documentary aired Feb. 24, 1976.

3. Bernard H. Gustin, "Charisma, Recognition, and the Motivation of Scientists," *American Journal of Sociology* 78 (March 1973): 1123–24.

4. James Watson, *The Double Helix: A Personal Account of the Discovery of the Structure of DNA* (New York: New American Library, 1969).

5. Louis Marcorelles, *Living Cinema: New Directions in Contemporary Filmmaking* (New York: Praeger, 1968), p. 7.

6. The Film Board has prepared a single screen version of *Labyrinth*.

Filming the Cultural Revolution

Thomas Waugh

The glimpses of China we have had on American screens over the last few years have been scattered and tantalizingly superficial. Of those films made by the Chinese themselves, only the occasional documentary offers any useful insight into the shape of their revolution-in-progress; the feature films are usually based on ballet and operatic modes too deeply rooted in Chinese tradition to serve as much more than exotica to audiences on this side of the world. The Western documentarists who have visited China have brought us back fascinating films, to be sure, but they are films which remain unhappily distant from their subject, never succeeding in probing more deeply than the impressionism of any short-term traveler's notebook. Among such recent China films are Antonioni's *China*, Shirley MacLaine and Claudia Weill's *The Other Half of the Sky*, Marcel Carrière's *Glimpses of China* (from the National Film Board of Canada), and Don McWilliams's *Impressions of China*, a short compilation of slides and Super 8 footage taken by a group of Canadian high school students. Of these, MacLaine's and McWilliams's films seem to have come off the best because of their simplicity and unpretentiousness, their acceptance of their own limited focus. Unlike the larger, more ambitious films of Antonioni and Carrière, they refuse to make any sweeping assessment of a culture and a society of which they have necessarily received only random surface impressions, but have concentrated on the personal dimensions of interaction between travelers and hosts.

The Chinese themselves say that those who come to China for the shortest time write the longest books. This may have been true up to this point, but now such wisdom has been challenged by a very long film indeed, in fact twelve films, by two filmmakers who have spent a very long time in China.

In fact, a whole new era in China films has now been opened up by the appearance of *Comment Yukong déplaça les montagnes* (How Yukong Moved the Mountains), a long, intensive study of the Cultural Revolution by Joris Ivens and Marceline Loridan. *Yukong* has not yet made it to this side of the Atlantic, but in Paris, where it opened last March, it has created quite a stir.

Joris Ivens's name is no doubt familiar to American audiences because of his seminal contribution to the American documentary during the late thirties and early forties. His three most famous works of that period are *Spanish Earth* (1937), about the Spanish civil war, *The Four Hundred Million* (1938), based on Chinese resistance to Japanese aggression (both landmarks in the antifascist activism of the American left during those years), and *The Power and the Land* (1940), a rural-electrification agitprop film set on an Ohio farm, the most classical and aesthetically controlled of the films of the New Deal.

Many students of film history will also be familiar with Ivens's work before he came to America from his native Holland. His name was an important one in the international avant-garde of the late silent period: *The Bridge* (1928) has proven to be one of the most durable of the experimental films of the epoch, and *Rain* (1929), a study of Amsterdam during an afternoon shower, is the most lyrical of the "city films." But in the early thirties several trips to the Soviet Union occasioned an abrupt shift in his filmic interests, and he thereafter made some of the finest militant films of the period, including *Borinage* (1933) and *The New Earth* (1934).

Only the most exceptional of documentary buffs, however, will have been able to keep in touch with Ivens's career since he left the United States in 1944, never to return until this day. After his support of the Indonesian republican cause against the colonialist forces of his own country in 1945–46 (an advocacy resulting in the astonishingly prescient Third World consciousness of *Indonesia Calling* in 1946), the United States joined the Dutch in considering him anathema, despite the selfless service he had rendered the Allied cause during the war.

After the Indonesian adventure, Ivens returned to Europe and became a kind of roving cineaste laureate for the other side in the cold war, for the next ten years making films and teaching in the young socialist republics of eastern Europe. Among the films made during those years, he is remembered chiefly for the mammoth compilation film *Song of the Rivers* (1954), whose contributors included Bertolt Brecht, Hanns Eisler, Dmitry Shostakovich, Vladimir Pozner, and Paul Robeson. (Robeson, denied a passport by the U.S. State Department, had to record the film's title songs without musical accompaniment in his brother's Harlem parsonage and send the tapes by mail to Berlin for the mix. The film was of course never shown in the United States, and Robeson had to make a trip to Montreal for a union screening there of the finished product.) Generously praised by Jay Leyda in *Films Beget Films*, *Song of the Rivers* is virtually unknown here, although it was distributed in twenty-eight languages and was seen around the globe by 250 million spectators (half a billion according to another account). Commissioned by the Soviet-sponsored World Federation of Trade Unions, the film linked workers from around the world, by means of editorial finesse, in a common struggle against oppression, using six of the world's major rivers as a unifying theme. Today it still looks good, infused with a typical Ivensian lyrical detail and epic grandeur, as well as, once more, a remarkably prophetic solidarity with the Third World. Predictably, when the Museum of Modern Art mounted a half-hearted Ivens retrospective in 1966, they conveniently omitted this whole period, in fact jumping from 1937 to 1957 and omitting the sixteen films he made in those years.

Although Ivens has said that the documentary can only achieve its fullest potential under socialism, in 1957 he moved to Paris, his home base ever since. There he made *La Seine a rencontré Paris* (The Seine Comes to Paris) that same year, based on an idea of Georges Sadoul's and a commentary by Jacques Prevert, the only film of his since the war to have reached a significant audience in the United States. As a film, it has the distinction of being that Ivens work which is admired most by those critics who see Ivens as an artist who wasted his potential by going political (*Rain* is the other favorite of this crowd). Whether *Seine* is nonpolitical is another question (who else but Ivens could have spotted real live workers among the artists, strolling lovers, and Balmain mannequins on the banks of the Seine in the fifties); whatever, it undeniably holds up well among the other French essay films of the decade (those by Resnais, Marker, and Franju, for example). It's a powerful document, brimming with the warmth and certitude of Ivens's socialist humanism and Parisian sunshine. *La Seine* was the first of a whole series of similar lyrical essays he turned out over the next eight years, which took the Flying Dutchman, as he was often called, to every corner of the globe, including China, Chile, Sicily, Holland, and Cuba, where he taught in the fledgling national film institute and made two jubilant films depicting Cuban life in the tense days before the Bay of Pigs.

In 1965, outraged by the escalation of the Vietnamese war and greatly disturbed by the lack of Soviet aid to the freedom fighters, Ivens proceeded to intervene in yet another liberation struggle. Over the next five years, he made two features and three shorts in Indochina, most in collaboration with Marceline Loridan, who by this time was his full-time partner. (Loridan is also familiar to documentary buffs as the woman in Jean Rouch's *Chronique d'un été* who wanders around Paris with a Nagra in her handbag and a cameraman in tow, meditating aloud on her memories of her wartime deportation and internment in Nazi concentration camps.) The best known here of Ivens's work in Indochina is probably his contribution to *Loin du Vietnam*, the *nouvelle vague*'s collective contribution to the antiwar movement ("zero as art," according to Andrew Sarris). Ivens's admiring footage of Hanoi's civil defense prompted Sarris to single him out in a tirade for his "romanticization" of the peasants which the B-52s were trying to bomb back into the Stone Age.[1] The best film from this period, however, is Ivens's epic treatment of peasant defense in the heavily bombed part of North Vietnam just north of the DMZ, *The Seventeenth Parallel* (1967). A feature film shot the following year in Laos, *The People and Its Guns*, although distributed in the United States by Impact Films, has had very little exposure here, much less than it deserves, since its experimentation with a kind of Brechtian didacticism (over seventy intertitles!) compares well with the wave of similar films from post-1968 France which are seen more often here, namely those of Godard and Gorin's Vertov group.

Throughout Ivens's entire career, it has been a customary, no doubt instinctual, reflex for him to pause after a cycle of films on liberation struggles and turn to the subject of economic and social struggles in a new peacetime setting. So it was inevitable that Ivens, the anti-imperialist combatant in Southeast Asia, would shift gears and sooner or later show up in China as Ivens, the poet of socialist construction.

Ivens and Loridan's partnership was almost a decade old in 1971 when the pair visited Peking. When Ivens's old friend Chou En-lai half-seriously asked the seventy-three-year-old militant why he hadn't brought his camera with him, he had good reason to: Ivens had visited China twice before with his camera, as we have seen: once in 1938 during the war against Japan, when his film *The Four Hundred Million* had endeavored to enlist world support of the Chinese resistance; and again during the Great Leap Forward in 1958, when as a teacher at the documentary studio in Peking Ivens had supervised two films. One of these, released in Europe as *Letters from China*, is a stunning experiment in color and documentary lyricism, incorporating many of the color techniques of ancient Chinese painting; it is virtually an anomaly in Chinese film history.

In any case, Ivens and Loridan began to think seriously when Chou suggested a new China film. They gradually abandoned the few film ideas they were considering in Europe at the time, including a version of Erasmus's *In Praise of Folly* (surely the most ambitious adaptation idea since Eisenstein's *Capital*), and moved to China in late 1972.

Their topic was to be the Cultural Revolution. Although the Chinese offered valuable technical and personnel support, the film was not to be a coproduction: financing was to be entirely the responsibility of the filmmakers. Ivens and Loridan themselves produced the film with an advance from the French Centre National de Cinématographie and with additional personal loans.

Although their original conception called for a three- or four-hour work, they gradually decided that such an approach could only result in the generalized, superficial result they wanted to avoid. Their projected three-month stay was first stretched to five months and finally to eighteen to allow for the extended, leisurely immersion within Chinese society which could permit the kind of intimate, authoritative perspective they wanted. Over the next year and a half Ivens and Loridan proceeded leisurely, in a manner more reminiscent of Flaherty than of the customary urgency that had resulted in almost fifty Ivens films since 1928. They set up camp for lengthy periods in a wide range of different locations—four months in a Shanghai generator factory, two months in an experimental pharmacy in the same city, one month in a military barracks near Nanking, and similar stretches in a Shantung fishing village, a petroleum field in the remote Taking area, and a number of Peking educational institutions. The only major gap in their itinerary was the peasant milieu—no small omission, it is true, in a society that is still largely agricultural; but this gap is partly compensated for by close attention to the rapport with agricultural communities which was a feature of all the groups they observed. A thorough exploration of the agrarian application of the Cultural Revolution, they decided, would have demanded a full year of exposure to the seasonal cycle, etc. And in any case, the film's Western audience was expected to be largely urban and able to identify more closely with the problems examined by the filmmakers in urban settings. For the filmmakers were hardly interested in a travelogue which would have no application to the lives of their audience.

On returning to France in mid-1974, the pair set about editing the 150 hours of synchronized rushes they had accumulated. Eighteen months later they had realized eleven hours and fifty minutes of finished film: twelve films in all, four features, four medium-length films, and four shorts. This prodigious collection of documents was subdivided into four programs of digestible length which opened simultaneously in four Left Bank art houses in early March and settled in for a long run, basking in almost unanimous critical acclaim.

The working title of the film had been *The Second Long March*, but the release title finally chosen had an appeal with considerably more mystery about it. *How Yukong Moved the Mountains* is the title of an old Chinese fable which appears in the writings of Chairman Mao:

> We are told that once upon a time there was an old man called Yukong. . . . He decided to carry away, with the help of his sons, two great mountains which blocked the access to his house, by means of a pick. Another old man . . . burst out laughing and said to them: "You will never be able to move those mountains all by yourself."
>
> Yukong answered him, "When I die, there will be my sons. . . . In this way the generations will come after each without end. . . . With each blow of the pick, they will get that much smaller. . . . Why then won't we be able to flatten them?"
>
> Heaven was moved by this and sent down to earth two celestial genies who carried away the mountains on their backs. Our heaven is none other than the masses of the Chinese people.[2]

Ivens and Loridan's answer to our curiosity about China contains the same devastating logic that is in Yukong's response to his questioner, and the same infectious confidence that is at the root of Mao's revision of its moral.

The new China films are particularly important for those of us whose engagement on the cultural front as film scholars has been animated by the kind of idealism which draws us to film for two reasons—for its potential as an instrument of social change and for its ability to reflect the vitality and resistance of ordinary people, especially where it serves as their means of expression when they are in the process of developing a revolutionary awareness or are caught in the flux of revolutionary change. As Walter Benjamin put it, it is a question of "modern man's legitimate claim to being reproduced."[3]

From such a perspective, the last fifteen years or so have been an era of disappointed promise. If the new technology of *cinéma vérité* at first suggested special possibilities in this direction, it ultimately failed to focus consistently on potentially radical topics or to be exploited systematically for radical ends. Little-known currents of a politically motivated *cinéma vérité* in Canada and France, and better-known but isolated and sporadic movements of similar orientation in the United States and Latin America, were never seriously built up into a continuous tradition with a wide base, a genuinely radical content, or a significant impact.

With *Yukong*, we finally have a film that represents that convergence of technical potential and revolutionary subject matter which has been so long in coming. *Yukong* provides a brilliantly detailed reflection of a people involved in the process of radical change, and it is a reflection conveyed in a technology and a style finely tuned to capture the dynamism and intricacy of the revolutionary process, in terms of both the images and the voices of the people carrying it forward.

The Cultural Revolution is by no means presented as a *fait accompli*. Rather than fall into that trap into which Soviet socialist realism plummeted headfirst after its initial moment of inspiration in the mid-thirties, Ivens and Loridan and the Chinese themselves present their revolution as a constantly ongoing process in the lives of flesh-and-blood individuals, a process constantly in need of self-criticism and renewal, and one transforming not only political and economic structures but personal ones as well. Ivens and Loridan have not written an exhaustive book of the methods and effects of the revolution. What they have done instead is taken the time and energy to really observe and listen to Chinese people taking control over their own lives, and they have done this with an amazing degree of intimacy, the sense of which they have succeeded in passing on to us.

The finest compliment that has been paid the film in the French press is that of Louis Marcorelles, the high priest of *cinéma vérité*[4] in France, who has referred to Ivens and Loridan's achievement as "cinematic Maoism."[5] And the term is apt, with all of its connotations of a populist-based inspiration and authority and a self-renewing dynamic rooted in that popular base. Direct cinema previously "let the people speak," to use Marceline Loridan's expression for the goal of the China films,[6] with many important successes to its credit.

But when the resources of direct cinema were finally applied to a society which itself "lets the people speak," the result is staggering.

In technical terms, Ivens and Loridan have let the people speak in a variety of ways. Often the camera confronts a subject head-on, usually in close-up, and the subject talks directly to it in response to provocatively worded questions thrown out from behind the camera by Loridan. The subjects respond with a candor and spontaneity that easily matches the finest achievements of direct cinema in the West over the past fifteen years, and in a way that effectively challenges whatever myths of Chinese reserve or Red Guard cant an audience might hold before seeing such a film. Loridan gradually learned the language, that is, the Peking dialect, over the period of her stay: that she and Ivens should have achieved such intimacy with their subjects despite the language barrier is all the more amazing. In any case, Loridan's talent for putting her subjects at ease has been amply demonstrated before, in those films made with Ivans about postindependence Algeria and about Indochina. (Could anyone who has seen *The Seventeenth Parallel* forget the nine-year-old Pham Cong Duc's loquacious charm as he told the cameraperson of his adventures tracking down American helipads in the jungle and how he might be afraid if he met a tiger but never of an American?) In China, two full-time interpreters functioned as an integrated part of the crew, but the refreshing naturalness of the discourse in the film ultimately comes from the dedication of the filmmakers and the openness and humility with which they were able to relate to their subjects and receive their trust.

More often the camera and recorder simply sit in on an ongoing event, which always continues with remarkable spontaneity in spite of their presence. Ivens and Loridan's success in so unobtrusively witnessing an ongoing criticism session among the staff of the pharmacy, for example, derives from their applying a principle well known to practitioners of direct cinema in the West, from Jean Rouch to Allan King, Michel Brault, and Frederick Wiseman— that is, the patient and gradual immersion of the crew within an environment and the slow building up of mutual confidence with the people to be filmed. Admittedly, an afficionado of direct cinema could justifiably approach the film with apprehension. After all, for the last fifty years Ivens has obstinately insisted on the documentarist's right to "reconstruct" the event to be filmed, and that the look and feeling of authenticity are more important than actual authenticity. What is more, in their less inspired moments his films occasionally reveal a trace of the socialist-realist penchant for static, declamatory mise-en-scène, assimilated no doubt from Ivens's constant exchange with that camp over the years. As late as 1967 he had been scolded by Marcorelles for falling back into the classical cinema in *The Seventeenth Parallel* because of that film's intercutting of sound and visual explosions with antiaircraft firing to signify on-target hits.[7] But such apprehension is unnecessary. Ivens has gradually perfected his mastery of direct cinema, begun during the Indochina period, wherever budgets and bombing lulls permitted, and there is not a trace of pretense, self-consciousness, or crypto mise-en-scène in this work.[8]

As we have seen, a principal visual coefficient of the film's extraordinary intimacy with its subjects is the close-up. Indeed, the succession of long contemplative close-ups of the Chinese people is itself a source of genuine fascination. But there is a categorical distinction to be made between this technique as used by Ivens and Loridan and that used by Antonioni in his China film, which is also in many respects a physiognomical treatise or, as he says in his burdensome narration, "a survey of faces." There are worlds of difference between Ivens and Loridan's open trusting portraits, based on the mutual trust of filmmaker and subject, and the close-up telephoto zooms which Antonioni inflicts, for example, on reticent subjects in a remote village who have never seen a Westerner, or close-ups taken in a market with a hidden camera filming shoppers among the vegetable and poultry stalls[9]—shots in principle hardly different from the close-up zooms of the chickens and hogs which also compose the sequence. And of course there is also a qualitative difference between silent faces captured by a camera and close-ups of subjects in dialogue with the filmmakers behind the camera. In the one case, the artist seems to impose him/herself upon the subjects; they become mystified, exoticized, colonialized, if you will. In the latter case, the artists have subjected themselves to the people filmed in a kind of cinematic democracy in which people have had control over their images through the exercise of their capacity for self-expression. The central principle of Ivens and Loridan's film is that in order to get close to people one must listen as well as observe. The filmmakers have extended the Maoist emphasis on people's control of their own lives and social situation to the realm of the image.

Antonioni in his film repeatedly violated the right of the subject (in progressive filmmaking, at least) to control his or her own image. He seems perversely to have insisted on filming whatever his hosts requested him not to: for example, a gunboat in Shanghai harbor, a free-enterprise peasant market on a rural road, even a burial caught in telephoto when his hosts suggested that the filming of a burial would offend the Chinese sense of privacy. As he and Ivens/Loridan have demonstrated, it is easy to shoot film in China; it is far more difficult and a far greater achievement to receive and honor the people's trust. For Ivens and Loridan, their first responsibility was to their subjects, and Antonioni would have done well to be so motivated.

Ivens and Loridan's success in letting the people speak is particularly praiseworthy, for traditional cultural barriers to self-expression have always operated in Chinese society, against which not only the filmmaker but also the revolutionary has had to struggle.

The other visual coefficient of Ivens and Loridan's "cinematic Maoism" is the sequence shot. The cinematic approach based on long takes and a spontaneous, mobile camera is completely foreign to the Chinese tradition, yet Li Tse-hsiang wielded the camera (an Eclair 16) with flexibility and sensitive control throughout the film. It is hard to believe that Ivens and Loridan trained him in this technique, it is so accomplished.

It would hardly seem necessary for Ivens and Loridan to have chosen the sequence shot as a means of guaranteeing the integrity of their subject matter, but the graceful long takes with which Li has circled about an event and moved dexterously from one participant to another do have that happy effect. They confirm the sense of authenticity and spontaneity which is already richly connoted by other visual and behavioral cues. Political cinema confronts the skepticism of some Western audiences who have long had reservations about the staginess of traditional socialist realism, not to mention audiences totally dominated by those hostile attitudes inherent in liberalism toward agitational art in any form. If such attitudes need to be countered, then the brilliant use of sequence shots in this film will certainly provide the solid phenomenological evidence necessary to do so. More important, the sequence shot preserves a sense of the pace and the structure of the political discourse which is so much a part of the Cultural Revolution, of the perpetual self-questioning and self-awareness which impels that revolution forward at its roots. The sequence shot is also the structural embodiment of the commitment of the artist to the event, that is, the artist's self-effacement before the natural shape of an event instead of the imposition of his or her own ideologically determined shape upon it.

It would of course be absurd to make exaggerated claims for the abstract virtues of the synchronous close-up and the sequence shot. Direct cinema, like any other art form, is shaped inevitably by the selectivity and subjectivity of the artist. But here a real dialectic is in effect. Ivens and Loridan have found a cinematic form which has minimized their own subjectivity, retaining to be sure whatever elements of personal structuring are demanded by the dynamics of their interaction with their Western audience. This form is especially open to and dependent on the subjectivity of the people being filmed and respects the integrity of the events before the camera, which are transmitted to us as free of the filmmakers' subjective mediation as is perhaps possible. The Chinese people are speaking to us more directly than they ever have before.[10]

Regretfully, this cinematic Maoism has not yet entered the cinematic lexicon of the Chinese themselves. As Ivens is eager to explain, drawing from that profound intercultural respect which comes from his forty years of Marxist practice in exile, there are too many superstructural interventions in the area of the film form for us to demand this of the Chinese at present:

> The Chinese cinema is different from ours. It is more contemplative, more static. The camera doesn't take part in the action; the camera records, it observes it. According to ancient Chinese philosophy, man, standing between heaven and earth, looks at the ten thousand things of the universe. The result is that the

camera doesn't move. For a cameraperson, to understand that he or she can move with the camera, it's quite an upheaval. And most often, when this is undertaken a Chinese cameraperson falls into the opposite extreme and moves it too much. It is necessary to explain to him or her the role and the function of each camera movement. Another important point is that in the Chinese cinema, in general, there are fewer close-ups than in ours. That's also tied to a cultural tradition. In the body of their visual art, you don't see portraits brought up close to people, except in the Buddhist tradition. It was necessary for me then to explain the role I was giving to the close-up, why compact framings were useful. That took a long time, because in China you have to have the patience to convince people. It is not a question of persuading them with arguments on the basis of authority, as you can often do elsewhere. That also is the Cultural Revolution.[11]

In China, you know, man [*sic*] is not the center of the universe, like in the West. Look at Chinese paintings: man is represented there as very small, his relationship with the world is thus of another sort.[12]

Li Tse-hsiang's achievement, when regarded in these terms, takes on a different aspect. Ivens and Loridan chose this talented man by screening a great number of Chinese films upon their arrival and deciding upon one where the camera style showed the promise of the flexibility they wanted. One wonders how the cultural cross-fertilization set off by this cooperative undertaking will affect the future course of the Chinese documentary. It would not be the first time that Ivens's roving camera had had a stimulating effect on the cinematic practice of another society in this way.

There is only room in this short article to look at a few specific instances of the general observations which have been made thus far.

Of the films I have seen, *The Pharmacy* is the most fully achieved. The inspiration to film such an establishment came quite spontaneously. Although the filmmakers tended toward the ideal of dealing with some kind of commercial setting in Shanghai, they felt that any of the large department stores would have resulted in too diffuse a film. When Ivens became ill during their visit to Shanghai, it happened that the workers in a small neighborhood pharmacy took a special interest in his care and recovery; Ivens and Loridan developed a special friendship with them. Impressed with the workers' experimentation with a program of community outreach beyond the usual merchandising notion of pharmacy, Ivens and Loridan decided to make a film on it. They spent the next two months constantly at the store and in the neighborhood, following the staff in the course of their duties. During the film we see the interaction between the pharmacists and the local community as they provide all sorts of clinical consultation and care as well as drugs (free if dispensed from a prescription). They even engage in on-the-spot acupuncture for a variety of minor ailments. We also witness endless meetings among the staff themselves as they conduct evaluations of their work and their own personal roles. (With

Antonioni, the content of those one or two such meetings which he presents is not relayed directly or literally to the audience but is either summarized in voice-over narration or omitted altogether.) The members of the pharmacy staff each become live and identifiable characters. One young man gets impatient and nervous with clients whom he considers "idiots" and conducts perpetual self-criticism of this failure without ever offering the audience any convincing hope that he will improve; a young woman had once wanted to be a doctor but after the Cultural Revolution decided that service to the people was more important; an elderly clerk is ultimately revealed to have been the former owner of the pharmacy and is now an employee of his one-time enterprise. This last character is charmingly candid before the camera and jokingly admits to nonrevolutionary feelings, namely an unquenchable taste for profit, but his admission is contradicted by the evidence of his rapport with his fellow employees and his conscientious work behind the counter.

Here again we can make a telling comparison with Antonioni's treatment of a similar subject. Ivens and Loridan treat the role of acupuncture as part of the pharmacy's clinical practice almost matter-of-factly. They emphasize the sociopolitical and personal relations among the characters, whom we know on other terms than as agents of acupuncture, and also the totality of the pharmacy's social role, of which acupuncture is only a small part. Antonioni, on the other hand, chose to observe the use of acupuncture techniques in major surgery (a childbirth) as conducted by gowned functionaries to whom we are scarcely introduced; in general the observation seems detached from any systematic view of Chinese sociomedical practice. Antonioni's interest in the scene is twofold; it's in the exotic significance of the needles and the "human" drama of the woman giving birth, specific and concrete to be sure, but abstract in its divorce from any societal context. In *The Pharmacy* the acupunctural ministrations of the young pharmacists have a political as well as a dramatic and visual meaning.

In contrast, the filmmakers deliberately decided to focus another of the feature films on a generator factory. Ivens and Loridan could film any topic they wished, except a nuclear installation; they even would have been permitted to go to Tibet had not Ivens's asthma prevented it. In any case, even with a collection of twelve films to be made, the initial choice of individual areas of concentration had profound political and aesthetic implications. The pharmacy the team focused on in Shanghai was admittedly a model one; it was a sort of pilot project experimenting with the idea of extended community service. If the team had dwelt exclusively on such experiments, and they were certainly dazzled by the diversity and the scale of experimentation of this kind, the resulting films would have had a certain utopian relevance without reflecting the exact reality of contemporary China. Accordingly, they decided to find a factory suitable for filming; they made a firm commitment to focus on an ordinary, typical work situation to balance the utopian aspect of films such as those on the pharmacy:

> We visited fourteen other factories, tractor factories, watch factories, pilot factories, exemplary for their management, for their relations between cadres and workers, for their role in the Cultural Revolution. But we wanted at any price to film something average. It would not have been interesting to film the watch factory which gave rise to the most important *dazibao* movement [wall posters]. We would have described a perfect democratic situation, at a given moment, and would not have touched at the heart of the difficulties. Whereas with choosing an average factory, that involved hoping that something would happen. . . . In any case, if we had filmed in the watch factory, with these people working on microscopic pieces, that would have been less spectacular. You have to create a strong visual impression as well. [13]

It was their good fortune and ours that something did indeed happen in the generator factory that the team filmed. Another *dazibao* movement took place during their four-month stay, during which event they could even work alongside their subjects. In this film, we witness a spontaneous movement of criticism by workers against the management, expressed first in the huge, strikingly cinematic banners which have long dominated the Western media's visual impressions of Chinese politics. The workers directed criticisms against administrators who always stay in their office, against favoritism seen in such matters as the distribution of cinema tickets, and against general ineptitude in the running of the factory. Eventually we sit in on workers' meetings, study sessions on Engels's *Anti-Dühring* and the general problem of revisionism, meetings with the bosses, and joint efforts to arrive at a new antihierarchical and nonbureaucratic organization of the factory in revolutionary committees. We hear the voices of the workers as they design their *dazibao*s:

> You should draw it like this . . . The truck is stuck in sand in the desert and its wheels are turning round and round . . . You can hear the noise of the motor but the truck is not moving . . . That's how we should represent management.

The film gives an overwhelming sense of being present at a particularly important moment of history. [14]

One of the shorts from *Yukong, Story of the Ball*, covers a single incident which Ivens and Loridan happened upon quite by accident during the course of a routine visit to a high school. The film has an entirely different sort of dramatic interest than in those films with a larger scope. As the filmmakers arrived in the schoolyard, they noticed a sense of excitement in the air. Students and teachers hastened to give the filmmakers their own versions of a student-teacher dispute which had just taken place. A woman teacher had rung a bell signifying the start of class, and a teenaged boy, engrossed in his play, had kicked a ball in her direction which had struck her in the face. She then confiscated the ball. When the crew arrived, a meeting of the class had just been called to discuss the affair, and the filmmakers were invited to record the session. After an initial recap of the incident by playground bystanders, the camera proceeds inside and the rest of the film follows the analysis by teachers and students of what happened. At first both sides are evasive, self-righteous, and accusatory, the boy providing alibis for his behavior and freely charging the teacher with not respecting his ideas, and the teacher remaining adamant. This remarkably spontaneous discussion moves through various stages, each freely commented upon by those present, the girl students sometimes siding with the teacher and sometimes with the boy and his allies. The meeting finally arrives at a moment of reconciliation which is curiously ritualistic but affecting and authentic all the same. The teacher finally admits to having underestimated the boy's political consciousness in confiscating his ball, and the boy admits to having tried to avoid loss of face in constructing his excuses. An awkward handshake and exchange of grins concludes the episode. This eleven-minute film provides a thoroughly absorbing vignette of a revolution-in-progress.

One of the most significant aspects of the Cultural Revolution for many Western viewers of the film will be the specifically feminist dimension of that revolution. It has long been a commonplace of the "China film" to point out how Chinese women used to have their feet bound. Neither Antonioni nor Ivens and Loridan depart from this tradition, but again a comparison points out important differences. Once more there is a qualitative distinction between Antonioni's gratuitous and crude close-up of the feet of a nameless old woman passing by, and the manner with which Ivens and Loridan's reference to the old custom comes almost incidentally from a character whom we have come to know naturally, as a person, within the framework of the film rather than as an exotic specimen of *chinoiserie*.

No doubt, it is partly Loridan's influence that the film's response to feminist problems is such a progressive one. Certainly since Ivens's association with Loridan he has perceptibly modulated his perspective on women. For instance, in his iconic repertory, woman-mother is now given secondary emphasis in relation to woman-soldier and woman-worker. (To be fair, Ivens has always been more sensitive than most of his contemporaries to the importance of women's labor and the drudgery involved in housework. He presents the farmwife in *The Power and the Land* as an equal partner in the Ohio dairy farm with such fairness that we can almost forgive him for the beatific smile which he has her bestow upon her husband as the husband eats his roast beef in the film's electrically powered climax.) History, as well as Loridan, has also played a role in Ivens's shift in emphasis: the role of women in the Spanish civil war, for example, hardly compares to that in the Indochinese struggles in which, according to Ivens and Loridan's filmic testimony, their heroism and perseverance were crucial to the final military (and economic) victory.

Of the twelve *Yukong* films, two are wholly directed to feminist issues—*A Woman, A Family* studies the working and home life of a woman welder and union official from Peking; and *The Fishing Village* is about a collective of young women in Shantung province who have undertaken the group livelihood of high-seas fishing. In addition to these two films, there is in general throughout the twelve hours a rigorous commitment on the part of the filmmakers to balance the role of women in the ongoing revolution to that of the men, even and especially where a certain form of the sexual division of labor still exists. This is true, for example, in the oil fields, where the manual work and most of the engineering jobs seem to be assigned to men, and, as usual, this work is often more cinematic than that of the women. In this and other such cases, there is special attention to the feminist issue in the film's monitoring of political discussion among workers, and especially among women workers. The women in the oil fields say, for instance, that formerly their husbands never talked of anything serious with them, but that now they discuss economics and politics; that formerly their husbands' permission was necessary in their allotment of the family income, but that now there is no such hierarchization of family responsibility. The women hoeing vegetables in the shadow of the derricks reject the possible status implications of such a division of labor, taking pride instead in their contribution to the oil project and claiming equal importance in their roles with the men. Elsewhere, an animated discussion by women sewing-machine workers of Marxist theory and economic policy is interrupted by one of the film's rare interpretative voice-over interventions— this voice-over updates Lenin's famous remark that revolution consists in a woman kitchen-worker participating in the state, with the corollary that revolution must also mean seamstresses talking of philosophy. At one point, the anti-Confucius campaign which intrigued Western correspondents a few years ago is given a feminist slant when Confucius is referred to as the "woman-eater" and is quoted as saying that "a door opening on a courtyard is not a real door; a woman is not a real human being."

The film does not whitewash the situation of women in China, as feminists in the West who have serious reservations about the Chinese achievement in this area will be glad to hear (not to mention those who choked on the word "seamstress" in the previous paragraph). Although there seem to be women on the research and administrative bodies of the oil project, as we have already seen, the film does not hide the residual existence of what seems to be an unnecessarily rigid sexual division of labor. Even more, the implication of the twelve films seen as a whole is that the liberation struggle of women has advanced much further in the vocational area than on the home front. During a weekend visit to the young woman pharmacist's home in *The Pharmacy*, the husband is carefully shown doing his duty at the washboard, but he is also clearly disgruntled at being filmed doing so. Kao Chou Lan, whose professional duties as welder and union official are the focus of *A Woman, A Family*, seems clearly more outspoken in the exercise of her job than in relation to her husband, whom she sees only on the weekend. Moreover, the film, and by extension Chinese feminist discourse in general, is unhappily reticent in its probing of the areas of sexual mores and family structures (although it is to the Chinese credit that the openness of the discussion of birth control carried on in public in the crowded pharmacy puts our society to shame). Kao's discussion of her decision not to expand her family and the revelation of a number of situations in which husband and wife live apart seem the only tentative probes of alternatives to the traditional heterosexual-familial framework which is otherwise taken for granted.[15]

But this open admission of the miles still to go adds enormously to the credibility of the film. The feminist achievement in China is not seen as an Amazon utopia, whose veracity we would have to doubt, but as a slow, constant process involving everyone, men and women, in a process of analysis and critique like the larger Cultural Revolution itself. And it is this process revealed in all its dynamism and promise which makes the film so encouraging. Significantly, the best feminist films in Western society have relied, like Ivens and Loridan, on various incarnations of direct cinema in their endeavor to capture the process of perpetual analysis, consciousness-raising, and ideological offensive which are the preliminary requisites and continuing support for the feminist struggle.

Certainly American radical filmmakers, not only those with a specific feminist orientation, will have much to learn from *Yukong* when it finally becomes available in this country; and those who have already experimented in the same direction as Ivens and Loridan will probably receive a much-needed reinforcement. As to when U.S. audiences will see it, there is still no word on negotiations with American distributors, although possibly ultimately public television will bring *Yukong* to its American audience. Until that happens, the foregoing assortment of critical responses, tentative, perhaps random, and admittedly euphoric, can only be seen as a provisional assessment of these films' importance.

Notes

1. Andrew Sarris, "The New York Film Festival," *Village Voice*, Oct. 12, 1967. Reprinted in *Confessions of a Cultist* (New York, 1971).

2. Mao Tse-tung, *Oeuvres complètes*, vol. 3, p. 290. My translation from the French.

3. Walter Benjamin, "The Work of Art in the Age of Mechanical Reproduction," in Benjamin, *Illuminations*, trans. Harry Zohn (New York, 1969), p. 232.

4. Or direct cinema, as the French more precisely call that form of *cinéma vérité* prevalent in France and elsewhere that places more emphasis on the auditory, or more precisely, on the

focal component of the medium than is customary in the United States, at least in its traditional form. I will rely on this terminology from this point on.

5. Louis Marcorelles, "Pélérinage et voyage de deux cinéastes occidentaux en Chine." *Le Monde*, March 11, 1976, p. 16.

6. That is, "donner la parole au peuple," which more literally means "giving speech to the people." Marceline Loridan, interviewed by Waugh in Paris, Feb. 1976.

7. Louis Marcorelles, "Sans peur et sans reproches," *Cahiers du cinéma*, no. 200/201 (April–March 1967): 122.

8. I have seen only about four hours of *Yukong*, and I hope I can be forgiven for this and other similar instances of rather reckless extrapolation.

9. To be fair, one of *Yukong*'s twelve parts, *Impressions of a City*, a medium-length study of Shanghai, does suggest the travelogue vein of the Antonioni film, and as such contains hidden-camera material taken from a truck in the streets of the city. The problem is of course the tendency of Chinese crowds to stare at foreigners, especially filmmakers, in public places. However, Ivens's use of a hidden camera is more the exception than the rule in *Yukong*, entering into only one out of twelve films, whereas it characterizes Antonioni's (in my opinion) voyeuristic approach in general.

10. Ivens and Loridan chose to transcend the traditional linguistic limits of direct cinema not by subtitles but by that form of dubbed translation in a voice over the original-language soundtrack, somewhat lowered in volume, which is much more common in Europe than here. "I believe that the option—subtitling or dubbing—is one of the fundamental choices: you have to give a film to be read or to be seen," says Ivens in an interview in *Le nouvel observateur*, March 8, 1976. It is to the filmmakers' credit that the dubbing is done very smoothly and sensitively.

11. From an unpublished interview with Ivens and Loridan by Jean-Marie Doublet and Jean-Pierre Sergent, distributed by Capi-Film, Paris. My translation.

12. "Rencontre avec Joris Ivens et Marceline Loridan," *Le Monde*, March 11, 1976, p. 17.

13. Ibid.

14. I am indebted to Maria-Antonietta Macciocchi for this and one or two other impressions of parts of *Yukong* which I have not seen; "Chaque fois que passe la politique," *Le Monde*, March 11, 1976, p. 16.

15. Ibid.

Filmography

How Yukong Moved the Mountains

About Petroleum (81 minutes). A survey of the oil fields at Taking, crucial in the development of China's self-sufficiency in terms of energy resources, with emphasis on the community of workers, men and women, that has sprung up about the project.

The Pharmacy (74 minutes). An experimental Shanghai pharmacy and the efforts of its staff to reach out into its community with a higher level of service and constantly to evaluate their own role and performance.

A Woman, A Family (101 minutes). The working and family life of Kao Chou Lan, welder and union official. A film on her everyday life, the locomotive factory where she works, and her views on marriage, love, education, and women's liberation.

The Generator Factory (120 minutes). A factory employing 8,000 workers near Shanghai. A criticism movement directed against the administration. The concept of a factory as a social and political institution as well as an economic one. The factory as an open place, not walled in, where families of workers are part of a living and working community.

The Fishing Village (95 minutes). The village of Da Yu Dao, where a collective of young women have become sailors and fishers. Everyday life in the village and the application there of the Cultural Revolution.

A Barracks (54 minutes). A view of army life where officers eat with the men, soldiers help peasants with agriculture, soldiers' wives and officers work alongside the soldiers in neighboring factories, and the military helps the civilian community in road upkeep, cultural activity, and militia training.

Story of the Ball (11 minutes). A playground confrontation between teacher and student which reveals the working of the Cultural Revolution in microcosm.

Professor Tsien (12 minutes). A university teacher who had been the favorite target of the Red Guard during the Cultural Revolution tells his story.

A Performance at the Peking Opera (30 minutes). The training of opera performers in acrobatics and dance and a performance of a new work.

Training at the Peking Circus (14 minutes). More training of performers and another performance, of acrobatics this time.

Craftsmen (13 minutes). The transmission of traditional arts from the old generation to the young.

Impressions of a City (55 minutes). Shanghai.

History Is the Theme of All My Films: An Interview with Emile de Antonio

Gary Crowdus and Dan Georgakas

Cineaste: *How do you go about making a compilation documentary such as* In the Year of the Pig? *Do you start from a predetermined political thesis that you want to illustrate, or do you do film research first and work out a narrative line from the material available?*

Emile de Antonio: I approach all my work from a consciously left viewpoint. It's very hard to articulate what it means to be a Marxist today, but it was a little bit clearer in 1967 when I began *Pig*. The film originally grew out of anger, outrage, and passion, but I knew that all of these, estimable as they are as motivations, are wrong if unchecked in a film, because you end up with only a screed, a poster that shouts, "Out of Vietnam!" It seemed to me that the most passionate statement that could be made was to make a film that would treat the history of Vietnam as far back as the footage would take it, to cover the whole history of the war, from its earliest days to the Tet Offensive in 1968, which was the year I completed the film. Compilation filmmaking lends itself best to history, which is, frankly, the theme of all my films.

The first thing I did was read about two hundred books in French and English on Vietnam, because I figured that was one way I could find the images. Many who do compilation documentaries today come from an anti-intellectual generation, or have no historical sense, and they're motivated primarily by flashy images or simple prejudices, when what they should be looking for are historical resonances which are filmic.

In other words, you're really interested in finding images for a general schema that you've gotten after all your reading, whereas some filmmakers feel that they can just rummage through a lot of archival footage and find a film there.

Yes, that's right. I think you've got to do a hell of a lot of homework. I then proceed to assemble a chaotic draft of the subject. I knew that I was going to pursue a historical line, although not necessarily a chronological line. I had a friend who owned a box factory, and he used to give me corrugated paper in rolls nine feet high, and I'd tack them up on my office walls. I'd start out by writing, "Han dynasty"—even though I knew I'd never put anything about the Han dynasty in the film—because the Chinese experience begins there. I would obviously write down, "Dien Bien Phu, 1954, May 8th," and abstract concepts like "torture," "inhumanity," and other things that interested me. Sometimes I would also paste a picture into it, so I would have visual images as well as words on the walls.

Once this huge outline was done, I started to do extensive film research. I went to Prague, for instance, where the NLF had a main office, and they gave me tremendous footage. I went to East Germany and there I met the Soviets who gave me Roman Karmen's restaging of the battle of Dien Bien Phu. Sometimes it's very sad, by the way, when good research pays off, because most of the people who saw *In the Year of the Pig* thought that really *was* the battle of Dien Bien Phu. When I lecture with the film today, I tell audiences, "You should look more carefully, because if you look at those Vietminh troops, you know they're not actually in combat. They're all so neatly dressed and running at port arms, as if some major were in the back giving orders." Still, it was beautiful footage, and I think I used it well, because I cut from that to the real footage of all those white faces surrendering to yellow faces, which is one of the symbols of that war.

I met with the Hanoi people in Paris, and I was the first Westerner to get an extraordinary film called *The Life of Ho Chi Minh*, which is their view of Ho, with early stills of Ho and his family and great material of Ho joining the French Communist party in 1922. I love that kind of material. I also got access to the French army's film library, the greatest collection of Vietnam footage that exists—it goes back to 1902. While there, I saw Pierre Schoendoerffer's great footage that nobody's ever seen. He was a sergeant in Vietnam, the head of a camera crew, and got some of the greatest shots of tanks in battle in the jungle that I've ever seen. He later made several documentaries, including *La 317ème section* and *The Anderson Platoon*. I had acquired a whole bunch of this stuff when one of the two young French sergeants assigned to me said, "Listen, they're going to pull it out from under you, because now they know who you are, and you're not going to get one frame of this stuff." There's this beautiful shot in *Pig* of something you can't get in this country. It's Ho Chi Minh with Admiral d'Argenlieu, the French commissioner of Vietnam, aboard the battlecruiser *Richelieu*. It's the end of talking, a really symbolic scene, because the war's really going to go now, and as Ho leaves the ship, with the French saluting, he takes a cigarette out of his mouth and, in that casual way of his, flips it over the side. I had to have that shot, so I said to the kid, "Listen, I'm going to steal this. Would you mind going out, because I don't want you to be implicated in all this." So I just cut that shot out of the roll of 35mm negative and stuck it in the pocket of my raincoat. I realized that since they knew who I was now, there was a good chance that the guys with the guns at the gate would stop me, and I could have gotten five years for that in France, but I thought it was worth it. Making films is risk taking.

The thing that staggered me was that even though the TV networks were going on and on about Vietnam, and other people were making films about Vietnam, no one found the footage I did for *Pig*. I located several great scenes no one ever picked up, including one of the film's best scenes from the 1930s, which is of these absolutely arrogant Frenchmen in their colonial hats and white suits being pulled in rickshaws by Vietnamese. They arrive in front of a cafe where there is a tall Moroccan with a fez—the scene encapsulates the whole French colonial empire—and when the Vietnamese put their hands out for payment, the Moroccan sends them away like trash. To me, that said everything you could say about colonialism without ever saying the word. If anything shows the primacy of the image over the word, what the image can reveal, it's the image of those rickshaws. It's the equivalent of a couple of chapters of dense writing about the meaning of colonialism.

Of course, *Pig* is only partly compilation; it includes a tremendous amount of interview material. I sought out the major left French historians, for instance. Not Communists, because the problem with most French Communists is that they talk like *L'Humanité*, it's a dead language. I filmed people such as Jean Lacouture, who had written a biography of Ho Chi Minh, and Phillippe Devillers, the editor of a French intellectual journal about Southeast Asia who had served in Vietnam. I used them as voice-overs for that early Vietnamese footage of the rickshaws—not talking about colonialism, because the image explained colonialism—but explaining what was behind colonialism, what the *corvée* meant, what the French were trying to do, the white face/yellow face thing, and all the rest of it. At the same time I was weaving the life of Ho Chi Minh in and out of the whole film right down to the end where I film Dan Berrigan, who had just come back from Hanoi where he saw Pham Van Dong at the end of 1967.

The old footage I found went back to the thirties, so the film covers some thirty to thirty-five years of history, from the early colonial experience through the thirties into the imperial experience under us, down to the Tet Offensive, including World War II, the French cooperation with the Japanese, the rise of Ho Chi Minh and the Vietminh, the American intervention in 1949 and 1954, and so on.

How do you respond to those who dismiss the film as propaganda?

There is out-and-out propaganda in the film, obviously, although sometimes I don't know what the distinction is between propaganda and passion, and propaganda and politics. I wanted to make Ho look as good as he could be made to look. It wasn't very hard. Ho was a patriot and a Marxist. There's a lovely sequence of Ho surrounded by a bunch of children, and Dan Berrigan says in a voice-over, "The Vietnamese know what it is to have a leader who leads a simple life." I used another shot they gave me of where Ho lived, which was a small space with a tiny typewriter and one extra Vietnamese suit hanging there, and you knew it wasn't bullshit.

An interesting thing happened when I spoke with the film on May Day in 1969 at Columbia University. It was still tumultuous there, even though it was after the '68 riots. In the film I have scenes of Sam 3 missiles shooting down American planes, and when the first American plane flew over, with its insignia clearly visible, and it was shot down, the whole audience clapped. I thought, "Jesus, that's weird, isn't it? What have I done?" I mean, I was in the Air Force, I flew, and, looking at that scene on the editing table, I wouldn't have clapped. They were right, of course, except that my reaction was a little more complex.

What is your approach to editing?

I'm very slow. I mean, I could cut my new film in two weeks, and it would be OK, but it wouldn't be my film. I work very hard at editing. I'm never satisfied. I always edit with the whole picture in mind. When I finish a sequence, I run the entire film from the beginning to see how it plays. I'll continue working on a scene until I'm satisfied. Finding a suitable ending to *Pig*, for example, proved a real problem. Originally, the ending I was going to use was some footage that the Hanoi people had given me. I had been playing with it for weeks. It was a very quiet scene of a road in North Vietnam, and suddenly the brush around the road gets up, it's the Vietminh, and they come charging out. But I thought, "Shit, I'm an American. I mean, I hope the Vietnamese win this war, I think our position is immoral, and I'm a Marxist, but I'm not Vietnamese. That would be a suitable ending for a Vietnamese film, but I'm an American." I decided to show that, even though we're Americans, the Vietnamese can punish us, so I got all this footage of dead and wounded Americans with bandages around their eyes, blinded, being evacuated. Then I took a shot of a Civil War statue—a young man who died at Gettysburg—and reversed it, put it into negative, to show, in my mind anyway, that our cause in Vietnam was not the one that boy had died for in 1863, and then added a kind of scratchy version of *The Battle Hymn of the Republic*. For me that was a suitable ending, a politically coherent ending.

The temptation of the compilation film, though, is the high, jazzy moment, that plateau moment that you want in there even though maybe it doesn't belong.

In other words, you try to avoid the easy things that would play well for an audience.

The dream, of course, is to find something that's good, that plays to the audience and that's absolutely supportive of what you're trying to do. For example, I had completed *Pig*, the mix date was a day and a half away, when I received a phone call from a young woman at the Sherman Grinberg Film Library. She said, "Mr. de Antonio, I've noticed you here looking for film. I know and support what you're doing, and we've just had come into the shop this extraordinary piece of film featuring Colonel Patton." It's that sequence, of course, in which Patton gives a little speech after some American troops have been killed, and, at the end, he gives that maniacal smile and talks about his men being "a bloody good bunch of killers." Well, no matter what, that just had to go in, and I made room for that at once. Sure, it was one of those plateau moments, the kind of thing you dream about, but it was so quintessentially the position of so much of our brass, that butch, phony-Hemingway sentimentality of the tough guy who's practically in tears about the men in his own company who were killed, but for whom, on the other hand, killing gooks didn't make any difference.

Those plateaus are the temptations. Nixon gives you a lot of those. Making a film such as *Millhouse* or *Point of Order*, where you have so much good material, it takes a lot of discipline to throw some stuff out that's absolutely brilliant, that you know people will laugh and clap about, but that has no meaning.

Speaking about Point of Order, *you took a big artistic chance in making what at that time was a form that hadn't been seen before.*

You're right, but it was the only way it could have been done. There were many mistakes in *Point of Order*—it was the first film I ever did, and it was done over and over. It took almost three years; that's a long time to do a compilation film. It was all there, though, there was no research at all. I had 188 hours of material. It took a month to look at it all, and the first cut I made reduced it to 20 hours. The trick with that film was structural.

I was fascinated with the idea of making a film about a historical event with a theme that would never be mentioned. The theme is the fall of a demagogue—the greatest demagogue of our time—and the idea was to begin somewhere near the beginning and not tell what the issues are, but to let them evolve, to let the struggle evolve between the issues as well as among the different personalities, and conclude with the ending—an artificial ending which I imposed—of the empty, silent committee room.

I had no idea how an audience would respond to it, and when the film was completed and the Museum of Modern Art asked to screen it, it was my virgin experience with an audience. I had a seat in the back row, but I was very fidgety so I finally stood up in the back of the auditorium. Then, the first time I hoped someone would laugh or respond, the whole house did, and it was just amazing. I think it was one of the high points of my life, and then, when people clapped at the end, it surely was. It later opened at the Beekman and ran for a long time. It was during the winter, and cold as hell, but I used to drive by at night just to see people standing in line to see a movie that was hard to look at. I mean, it's a dry, intellectual film—no sex—and yet I still find it exciting. A lot of people have imitated it since, but, as it turns out, I was unknowingly imitating somebody long since dead whose work I had then never seen—Esther Schub.

You've said that you were disappointed with the critical reaction to Point of Order *and the way that audiences tend to see Welch as the hero of the film.*

I saw how effective Welch was, but I thought that people, particularly the critics, would see through it. My point was that there were no heroes in the film, but the press and many people tried to make a hero out of Welch. For instance, a lot of people I know who are gay are disturbed by that sequence in *Point of Order* with the word "fairy." The point I was making, of course, was that Welch was perhaps not as unscrupulous as McCarthy, but nevertheless unscrupulous. Welch was badgering this McCarthy aide, just the way McCarthy badgered people, saying, "Now, where did that picture come from that hung on Schine's wall?" And the guy said, "I don't know where that picture came from," and Welch said, "Well, sir, did you think it came from a pixie?" And McCarthy—then at the end of his career, with that absolutely unerring instinct to destroy himself—interrupts and says, "Let Mr. Welch define pixie for us. I think he might be an expert on that." It was as if Welch had baited a trap. Nobody could have done it better. Welch, who was so quick, looked at him and said, "Sir, a pixie is a close relative of a fairy. Have I enlightened you, sir?" And the camera turns on Schine and Cohn and McCarthy, and the whole audience burst into laughter. There was that rather meaningless rumor that two or three of McCarthy's people were gay, and Welch knew it. But when the film was released, a lot of people asked, "What did you bring up that fag thing for?" My feeling was that it belonged, not because of the allegations against them, but because that was Welch's technique.

What bothered me most about the critics was the political judgment that made them dwell on how funny the film was. All those critics, however, almost without exception, were silent during the McCarthy days, so what they were doing was enjoying a kind of vicarious solidarity with history. Those people had all been intimidated by that monster and demagogue Joseph R. McCarthy, the junior senator from Wisconsin, and some ten years after the events they all had a chance to dump on McCarthy. Critics such as Brendan Gill at the *New Yorker*, Bosley Crowther at the *New York Times*, and Archer Winsten and Jimmy Wechsler at the *New York Post* all wrote things that made me puke, particularly Wechsler who called the film "a love letter to Miss Liberty."

How did your film Charge and Countercharge *come about?*

In attempting to reach a larger audience with *Point of Order*, a major publishing company came to me and said, "We love your film, but it could never be used in a classroom." I asked, "Why not?" They said, "A classroom hour is like a Freudian hour, it's about fifty minutes. Your film is ninety-seven minutes. That's two entire classes, and it almost makes the teacher an unnecessary appendage. We'd like something about forty-three minutes. That will allow the teacher time to talk." So, in putting together *Charge and Countercharge*, the subtlety had to go, because subtlety depends on time; but all the great moments are kept.

Your "negative" films which attack the establishment, such as In the Year of the Pig *or* Millhouse, *tend to be better, more accomplished works than what might be categorized as your "positive" films about the left, such as* Underground *or* America Is Hard to See. *How do you account for the surprising lack of critical edge in those latter films? Is it a fear of criticizing or undermining the left?*

I don't share that perception entirely. I think *America Is Hard to See* is a film which was not understood. Basically, the subject of that film is the failure of the liberal left. Liberalism came down the pike with its most articulate spokesman, Eugene McCarthy, a genuinely intellectual man, and there was a brief moment when something of a normal democratic process might have worked here if McCarthy had had a little bit more courage, if he had played hard in the convention and attacked Humphrey instead of rolling over like some obscure monk who didn't want to get into a brawl.

As for *Underground*, its weaknesses are many, and among them—speaking only for myself now, since more than one person was involved in that film— was a generation gap. I've never shared all the Weather Underground's politics, although I supported large assumptions they made. They were the last gasp of a movement I had been following, from the early days of SDS on, of an entire generation younger than me. It's a film about endings, not about where life is going, it's the end of that generation's most important political organization.

Do you think that's the way audiences perceived that film?

No, maybe not. It's not downbeat, because I did admire those people personally. It's a very confused film, and, since the truth has to come out on this sometime, collectives of two are impossible. This was basically a collective between Mary [Lampson] and myself. Mary had always worked for me, had been my employee, and then suddenly we were equals. It was a very hard thing, and we struggled over it. I think Mary was much more deeply moved by them than I was. I had to give way a good many places in that film where I would not have given way previously. I was working very hard to be collective and self-effacing, which is something I'm not by temperament. I was trying very hard to be a superfeminist. I mean, I don't have a hard time being profeminist, but being a superfeminist is very hard because it's a false position. The Weather people had that same problem, and it shows in the film.

In fact, I thought the Weather people were incredibly arrogant. I can't remember if we left this in the film or not, but at one point I said, "Look, if you don't want to talk about who you are, why don't we just get a fucking copy of *Prairie Fire* and you can read it?" And they said, "OK, that would be good, that might be better." I said, "No, that wouldn't be better. It's not well written, it's a boring magazine in many places."

I wanted them—and they had originally agreed to do this—to tell how they got to where they were. In other words, how did essentially middle-class people—and some of them came from the upper class—become revolutionaries carrying on an underground war against the government. That was the story I always thought we were going to do, and it was only when we got underground that they pulled their own gig. We argued, and I wanted to put that argument into the film. Mary and I had a lot of problems about that, and I think the reason Mary didn't want it in the film is because I'm the one who did the arguing and it would have made it much more my film. Mary didn't argue with them, Haskell did somewhat, and I argued a lot.

My feeling was that nobody gives a shit about all this abstract political terminology. American political people, especially SDS types, have almost no theoretical formulation to fall back on. Every time I heard them talk about Lenin or Mao, my heart skipped a beat, because it was never anything different from what they wrote in *Prairie Fire*, whereas I thought the human stuff would have been fascinating.

Afterwards, I realized we didn't have enough to make a film, because much of what we shot didn't work, they didn't want to say very much, and the jargon didn't appeal to me. So I thought, "Well, I'll make an anthology of the left. I'll talk to people I know and get excerpts from their films to put in." So there's a great sequence of Malcolm X, there's something from Saul Landau's *Fidel*, something from Chris Marker's film about the Pentagon, and so on. Those are the roots that the Weather people came from. They're the roots, for that matter, of anybody who was in SDS or for most young people in the American left, and I wanted to confer on them a kind of historical authenticity by tying them up to all that. I mean, I found Malcolm X more interesting than they were.

Now, I don't want it to seem as if I'm running down the Weather people. It was my idea to make the film. I was the one who approached them: I was the one who got Mary and Haskell into it. I did it because I found what they were doing exciting. That does not necessarily mean that I shared their politics, but there was something in their desperation that I felt myself. Ford was in office, it was all going to be the same thing over and over again, the whole left seemed shattered, all those great demonstrations, all those forces that seemed to be alive were dying, and these people were the last spark that was left of all that. There was something that appealed to me, almost in an avant-garde sense, about what they were doing. I mean, to put a bomb in the lavatory of the Capitol, to put a bomb in a police station, in Gulf Oil, in Rockefeller Center, and to get away with it every time. There was a Robin Hood quality about that.

Someone at the time said that the Weather Underground's strategy was to destroy capitalism, bathroom by bathroom. It's ironic, but perhaps the most significant aspect about Underground *was how the Hollywood filmmaking community came to your defense when the FBI subpoenaed you to turn over your film and tapes.*

We were supported because our stand was so aggressive and so rational. We kept saying, "Our crime is that we made a film, not that we belong to any organization." Even Peter Bogdanovich, who is a fairly apolitical person, signed the petition in support of us, and Robert Wise, then the head of the Directors Guild of America, spoke out officially in our favor.

You've had a long history of harassment by the FBI, the CIA, and the government in general. You're perhaps the only filmmaker who was on Nixon's Enemies List. Has any of that ever seriously hindered your work?

Sure, I've had a lot of fucking over. Many times I would set up an interview to be filmed and then, at the last minute, it would be short-circuited. I think the government also goes out of its way, directly and indirectly—and the indirect way is the more potent way—to prevent certain films from getting the kind of exposure they might get. *In the Year of the Pig*, for instance, was booked to open in a good house in Los Angeles, and someone broke into the theater in the middle of the night and painted on the screen a hammer and sickle and the words "Communist traitor." News of this spread to other theaters, and that was the end of the film theatrically.

Something strange also happened with *Millhouse*. The film grossed $36,000 in its first week at the New Yorker, which was a house record. It was in the *Variety* charts, so all the other theaters wanted it. Louis Sher of the Art Theater Guild, who owns seventy theaters out West in cities such as Denver and Albuquerque, booked *Millhouse* in his theaters. Then, just like that, they were all canceled. But who knows the real reason why? I got a letter from a theater manager in Denver who said, "My company canceled your film, which I was looking forward to, here at the Bluebird Theater in Denver, and to this day I don't know why it was canceled." I know the kind of muscle the White House exerted, because I have copies of all these memoranda on White House letterhead about the film. I don't moan or complain about it, because if you attack the reigning president of the U.S., if you attack the government, you can't expect them to treat you with a light hand. It comes with the territory. *Millhouse* did show theatrically in twenty cities, but it could have been shown in seventy other cities where documentaries ordinarily don't play.

When *Millhouse* opened in Washington, D.C., Larry O'Brien's assistant at the National Democratic Committee called me at my hotel and invited me to come by for a drink. He asked me, "Mr. de Antonio, how can we use your film?" I told him, "You can't. You'd be tarred with my reputation. But I'll tell you how you could use it. Buy a hundred prints, let me give a week-long course on Nixon to about three hundred young people. Then let them take the prints to all the territories you're sure to lose—the South, the Midwest—and have people look at that life." He said, "Gee, that's a good idea, but you're right, there's no way we could do that."

Millhouse did have a wide distribution for a documentary. Of course, audiences were laughing at Nixon, which I wasn't doing. Basically, I use him as a comic figure, but I wasn't laughing at him. There's a difference. I'm not unsympathetic to that poor, wretched, clumsy, mixed-up man. I wouldn't want him for a friend, but I understand the drive that must have made him from the first moment of his life. What I wanted people to understand in that film is that the souring of the Horatio Alger myth is almost a necessity in our kind of culture. Nixon, the glib opportunist who trampled over Helen Gahagan Douglas and Alger Hiss and everyone else, that is the way you became a Horatio Algerish mythic hero—you know, pluck and luck turned out to be something quite different. He paid the price right along the line, although more of us paid the price in a bigger way than he did.

How do you account for your fascination with history and politics?

I come from a long line of intellectuals, there's no other word for it. My grandfather was a philosophy professor who translated Lucretius, and my father was also an intellectual. I was raised in a home with five thousand books in it. The stories I heard as a little boy were Homer, Dickens, or my father's versions of European history. I knew the French Revolution fairly well, as well as the Italian movement to create a unified Italy.

Was your father a teacher?

No, he was a sort of upper-class gentleman, a doctor who owned a hospital and who had money and time.

How were you politically radicalized?

I was very early confronted with the reality of class. We lived in a big house in Scranton, Pennsylvania, with a chauffeur, cook, and maid. When I was five or six years old, I can remember, every Thanksgiving we collected money for the poor children in Scranton who lived only a mile or so from us. I used to ask why that was. I entered Harvard when I was sixteen and immediately joined the Young Communist League, the John Reed Society, and the American Student Union. I knew that's where I wanted to be. I've never deviated from those ideas, although I left all formal groups long ago.

When did you become interested in film?

I disliked most films. I had very strange, perverse tastes. I thought Louis Jouvet, the thirties French actor, was absolutely fantastic. I loved Renoir's films, and Chaplin and Keaton. I didn't care for John Ford's films at all. I mean, I saw that the images were beautiful, but I quickly got tired of Monument Valley and those tacky songs.

The one movie that turned me on—because I knew all the people in it and the guy who wrote it—was *Pull My Daisy*. It's a movie that doesn't hold up today, by the way, but it was so much of that time, and it made me want to make a movie, that's another reason why it's important to me. I saw that an interesting film could be made for very little money.

We understand that Andy Warhol made a film about you. What was that like?

Andy and I have been friends for a long time, since long before he was a painter. One day he said to me, "De, I think we should make a film together." I said, "Come on, Andy, we're friends, but I like to make political films and you make these frou-frou films." Then one night I saw him at a bar, when I was drunk, and I said, "OK, Andy, let's do it!" He said, "What shall we film?" and I said, "I'll drink a quart of whiskey in twenty minutes." I knew that twenty-two-year-old Marines had died doing it, but I knew what I was doing. I'm a very good drinker.

I showed up at his studio with my wife and a drinking companion. They turned the lights on, and I sat there cross-legged against a wall and drank a quart of J&B whiskey in twenty minutes. It was boring, nothing happened. I didn't want the glass, so I broke it. I had some ice and I threw that away. Andy was filming with a twelve-hundred-foot 16mm magazine which runs for thirty-five minutes. When it came time to change the magazine, he was so untrained in the use of the camera that it took him about fifteen minutes to change it. So by the time the second roll went on, I was on the floor. I mean, I couldn't even get up. My hand goes up the wall, trying to pull myself up, I'm singing Spanish civil war songs and shouting, "Fuck you!" It was unspeakably degrading. I finally walked out with the help of my wife and friend and went home and slept it off. The next day I was sharp enough to call my lawyer and have him call Andy and tell him, "De never signed a release, so if the film is ever shown, we'll sue." It appears in Andy's published filmography—it's called *Drink*—but it's never been shown.

How does Painters Painting *fit in with your political films?*

I think *Painters Painting* is a political film, too, except it's political in another, more complex sense. In my lifetime, the most significant cultural event, which took place in an absolutely closed circle, was called New York painting. It addresses itself to a few thousand people. I mean, maybe a few million people go to museums, but only two or three thousand people—the painters, the collectors, the owners, and the dealers—actually comprise the scene. That was a scene I knew intimately. Nobody was as well qualified by experience as I was with those people. They would say things to me that nobody else could even ask them. I knew the answers to the questions in advance. I was fascinated by these people. They were amazingly articulate, I loved their work, they were my friends, so I made a film about them.

Their work was the highest commodity we produced. It became something that every sophisticated millionaire had to have. I mean, any asshole could buy a Rolls Royce or a $2 million house, but it took exquisite taste to have a painting by Frank Stella or Robert Rauschenberg. *Painters Painting* is a film largely enthusiastic about American art, and I'm aware of all the political contradictions. The history of the West is replete with similar examples. The great art of the nineteenth century was the art of imperial France when they had African colonies. But for a moment after World War II, all this stuff exploded and New York became the art capital of the world. One of the reasons it happened, of course, is that many European artists fled Hitler, and many of them—particularly Hans Hofmann, Marcel Duchamp, and Max Ernst—came here to New York where their work was immediately shown by Peggy Guggenheim. Jackson Pollock was painting like an American romantic realist when, suddenly, he became acquainted with the unconscious through these people and, boom, developed a genuinely native American art nonetheless. Nothing has happened since then like that explosion between 1945 and 1970.

Would you tell us a bit about your new film? We understand that for the first time you will be utilizing actors and fictional sequences.

The heart of the film is the trial of the Plowshares Eight. Originally I went down to Pennsylvania, hired a very good lawyer, and petitioned the court to film the trial. I was denied the right to film, even after an appeal to the Supreme Court of Pennsylvania. At first I tried to film all around the trial—meetings between the defendants and their lawyers, demonstrations, prayer vigils—but I knew I didn't have a film, so I said, "Fuck 'em, I'll write my own screenplay." I got all the trial transcripts and from thirteen hundred pages of transcript I made a seventy-page screenplay.

Did you elaborate on the trial transcripts?

Well, I changed things. This is not a documentary. For example, all throughout the trial the defendants kept asking to produce expert witnesses, and the judge said, "The only thing that's pertinent here is your crime, not nuclear war." The defendants were going to call witnesses like Robert Aldridge, who'd designed five generations of nuclear warheads for Lockheed then one day realized that what he was doing was wrong, and he became a leader in the antinuclear movement. Daniel Ellsberg, Dave Dellinger, and others were going to be called. The judge refused to allow any of them to testify, but since I'm making my own trial, I've put the witnesses in.

So you're filming the trial they were not allowed to have.

Yes, I've reconstructed the whole trial, with the Berrigans and the other defendants playing themselves, and everyone else is an actor, including Martin Sheen, who plays the judge. I had met Martin in the days of the *Underground* fracas, and he impressed me as being not only a very fine actor, but also a fantastic human being, a person of commitment. I asked him if he'd be in the film, and he said, "Absolutely. I'll give you a week's shooting time for free." Then he asked, "Don't you need some money?" I said, "Yes," and he gave it.

I videotaped every actor who tried out, and ended up with as many as forty actors trying out for one role. So I had very good actors working for scale.

The film has a real interaction between real people and actors. The tension began to build during the shooting, you could see it in the defendants. I mean, there was Martin Sheen, acting the way the judge was supposed to act, and George Crowley plays the prosecuting attorney who knows that this is his last chance, that if he's ever going to be anything other than an assistant prosecuting attorney in this small, right-wing town, he *has* to win. So all those other forces and struggles are in there. The actors were wonderful, and the Plowshares Eight really got angry. In fact, Dan Berrigan gave the greatest performance I've ever seen in a courtroom. He did it better than Welch, better even than he did it in the real courtroom. Dan Berrigan is a brilliant guy, a Jesuit priest who also happens to be a great actor, among other things. One of the things I learned on this film is that the Catholic left is a very real left. I was raised in an anticlerical household and was never very sympathetic to the Catholic church, but they are really a committed left, their bodies are out there.

I'll be integrating documentary material with the fictional sequences. I've already filmed two members of the jury, and in two weeks I'll be filming the real judge, Judge Salus, and the district attorney. They're going to talk about the trial.

Do you know how all of this is going to cut together?

Nope. I've never done this before. But isn't that part of the fun of art? You take those chances, and you can come out looking like a fool or you can come out feeling that you've done something good. Both possibilities are there.

We understand that you used tape instead of film.

Yes, we shot on videotape. I knew that I didn't want to have a tape person shoot it for me, though, so instead I chose Judy Irola, a woman whose work I liked and who had never, ever done anything on videotape. It was the most intelligent thing I did in making the film. We shot on one inch, which is professional gauge, and the technicians in the video truck said, "Wow, we've never seen stuff like this," because Judy shot it like a film.

Why was it shot on tape?

Because I started out shooting the documentary stuff on tape. When you shoot three-quarter inch for documentary, it's incredibly cheap. Later we'll take it up to one inch, and it'll look not quite as good as film, but I don't want it to. The real part will look slightly tacky and the trial part will look highly professional, but that difference between the documentary and fictional scenes is quite intentional.

Where do you find money to finance your films?

Rich liberals. I don't use foundations. I ask people I know who have money and who have been supportive of left projects in the past. It was always easy, I never had any trouble raising money. But I've noticed an enormous difference in my fundraising ability today as opposed to eight or nine years ago. You become unclean after a while, and the times have changed. A friend of mine told me about a fundraising party last night where they screened Diego de la

Texera's new film on El Salvador. A lot of theater and film people were there, and ten years ago, during the Vietnam war, the checkbooks would have flashed out at the end of that film, but last night nobody gave, they were all afraid. Some people said, "Here's a hundred dollars in cash," but nobody would put their name on anything. They were afraid that something might happen to their careers. That's reflected in raising money right now to complete my new film. I mean, I never thought that I'd have trouble raising money for Catholic activists, but I'm having a harder time with that than anything I've ever done.

When you receive money, is it an outright gift?

No, rarely. I've a moderately good record of making my own high-handed rules, which is that I pay people back but they get no profit, because I figure they have more money than they need anyway. But they're entitled to be paid back, and they get a tax benefit.

Some of your readers may be interested in a ploy that I think more left-wing filmmakers—particularly compilation filmmakers, and particularly if you're as thorough as I am—should use. When I was done with *In the Year of the Pig*, for example, I had the most complete film library on Vietnam in existence in this country, tens of thousands of feet that I couldn't use. The law says that the artist can't take a tax write-off on such material, so what I would do was to find the person I was going to ask to put money into my next film—*Millhouse*, say—and explain, "Look, this footage is worth $100,000. If you put X amount of money into *Millhouse*, (a) I'll guarantee to repay you, (b) you can claim a loss this year because the film is being made and you obviously can't make a profit on it, and (c) two years hence, as an inducement for getting you to invest in the film, I will sell you these Vietnam outtakes for the money that you're putting into the film, and you can donate them to the University of Wisconsin and claim a tax write-off on their declared value." The film then becomes part of the university's archive—and I'm lucky, of course, because there's an archive about me at the University of Wisconsin—and they make it available for study by scholars, film historians, and the like. If you're in a high tax bracket, you make a fairly good profit just getting your money back, plus that later tax write-off. It's a very good inducement and should be used by young filmmakers who know rich people.

How do you perceive your audience? Who are you making films for, and what sort of political impact can your films have?

A great American, Walt Whitman, said that to have great poetry, you must have great audiences. Since I'm interested in history, I'm obviously interested in what happens to my films over the long haul. Anyone who makes films wants them to be seen, and I would do anything except change my films to reach a larger audience. But in America and most Western capitalist countries, film—from its earliest, nickelodeon days up to the most sophisticated mind control today through television—has been seen as an opiate, as entertainment. As the old Hollywood saw has it, "If you have a message, use Western

Union." Well, all my films have messages, but I don't want to send them by Western Union.

I have never looked upon documentary as an apprenticeship for the making of Hollywood films. That's bullshit. I've always chosen to make documentaries. I love documentary film, I love the political tradition of documentary film, and I love the subjects that documentary film can treat. I never saw making documentaries as preparing me to do a *Gidget* film or even a fake serious film like *Coming Home*.

My bet's with history. I'm an American who believes in history. That's a very rare thing, because most Americans live by seconds, they try to live outside of history. But I live in history, and I think that people will be looking at *Pig* and *Point of Order* long after I'm dead. I don't think it will be millions, but there will be audiences who will know that *Pig* is a history of the war in Vietnam as good as any book on the subject. Those images that you have to struggle to find and to make effective will endure, because history endures. That's an optimistic view of the human race, and I realize it's almost kind of silly to be optimistic about the human race today at the rate we're going.

But, to answer your question more directly, I get the audience I know I'm going to get. I suffer from small audiences, I know that. It's too bad that those gorgeous color spectaculars are the things that reach masses of people, and that films like mine are customarily seen by college graduates, intellectuals, East Side audiences, or public television audiences. What kind of audience, theoretically, would I have wanted for *In the Year of the Pig*? I would have liked police and working class, blue-collar guys who were for the war to have seen it. I would have liked them to have seen that the Vietnamese were fighting for their country, even though they might have hated the film.

Does it always have to be a question of reaching massive numbers of people? Is it possible to be politically effective reaching a smaller audience?

I lecture at universities a lot, and I can't tell you how many times I've been absolutely *bouleversé* by having some young woman come up to me and say, "You know, I was radicalized by seeing your film *In the Year of the Pig*. I was going to the University of Kansas when I saw it, and it made me see the war in a different way and I joined SDS." Or a young person will come up to me and say, "I just saw *Point of Order*, and I think I understand something about McCarthy now." That has happened many times.

Your films are also very popular overseas.

They do well in countries such as Sweden, England, West Germany, and France—the French in particular like our mad president, our mad demagogue, and our unsuccessful war, which was just as unsuccessful as their war, because they think I'm anti-American, which I'm not. I like this country, and if I didn't, I'd go somewhere else. I'm an American. This is my space, and that's why I want to change it.

Wiseman's *Model* and the Documentary Project: Toward a Radical Film Practice

Dan Armstrong

While Frederick Wiseman's films bear out the claim that he is free of any fixed ideological position, including Marxism, there is no other American filmmaker today whose work is more relevant to historical materialism. His fourteen documentaries produced between 1967 and 1980 offer a comprehensive analysis of American society. In the context of antagonistic class relations, these films examine the coercive and ideological apparatuses of the state (the bulk of his documentaries), commodity production and the modern assembly line (*Meat*), and, most recently, cultural production (*Model*). Particularly useful for their insights into the class struggle at the level of ideology and cultural hegemony, these films offer an unparalleled social history and critique of daily life in America during the sixties and seventies. Furthermore, the ensemble of Wiseman's film practices, the distinctive set of formal devices and strategies he employs, has useful implications for the development of a politically effective materialist cinema in America. The typical Wiseman film is an open text which creates audience distance and critical reflection, committing the spectator to a (not Puritanical) work of coproducing meaning. Despite important differences, the aesthetic is Brechtian, working against the grain of the culinary cinema produced by the dominant apparatus in America—both the Hollywood narrative feature film and the standard documentary. Of particular relevance to Wiseman's development of a radical film practice, *Model* (1980) self-reflexively examines the codes and conventions of cinematic and photographic representation. This film represents the fullest development of Wiseman's art and politics, and we shall take a closer look at it later.

A small but growing body of commentary on Wiseman recognizes his place within the traditions of Marxist social criticism and the aesthetics of a materialist cinema. Placing Wiseman's films in the tradition of *cinéma vérité* founded by the revolutionary Soviet filmmaker Dziga Vertov, Michael Arlen has written cogently of the affinity between the two in cinematic impulse and method, calling Wiseman "Our Man with the Movie Camera."[1] Roland Tuch, working from the theoretical basis of the writings of Marxist aesthetician George Lukács, contrasts Vertov's affirmative socialist analysis of labor in *Man with a Movie Camera* with Wiseman's chilling study of the alienation of labor on the modern assembly (disassembly) line in *Meat* (1976), a film which presents a process of alienation and reification so total that the workers themselves "have been reduced, in effect, to mere bodies, to meat."[2] Finally, Bill Nichols—combining the semiotics of Christian Metz, to offer a careful theory of structure, and the Marxism of Louis Althusser, to describe the "dialectic of individual and institution" which the films embody—identifies the characteristic features of Wiseman's distinctive style of *cinéma vérité*. Nichols is particularly useful in his description of Wiseman's films as "mosaics," in which the "facets" or "tesserae" (sequences) express distinct aspects of the total design without merging into a single impression or narrative. And he goes on to suggest that each film is "a facet in a mosaic constituted by his overall oeuvre."[3]

A major element in the unity of Wiseman's oeuvre that helps to define the relationships among the films as "facets" within the overall "mosaic" has not been described in the existing criticism. While everyone recognizes that Wiseman's films are studies of the fundamental institutions in American society, no one fully recognizes the extent of his analysis of the class struggle within this institutional context. Even Nichols, certainly the most sophisticated of Wiseman critics, asserts that Wiseman does not place the encounters between institutions and their clients in his films into the context of class differences and class struggle. In fact, however, Wiseman's films, both individually and collectively, examine contemporary American class struggle from the perspective of the ideological and cultural hegemony of the Professional-Managerial Class (PMC) over the subordinate working class. Unlike most other progressive documentaries about contemporary America that address "bread and butter" issues (Barbara Kopple's *Harlan County, U.S.A.*, for example), Wiseman's films emphasize the "cultural" issues. The class struggle in Wiseman is fought over the issues of authority, skill, and knowledge—all of which are at the center of the PMC/working class interface in America today. Ultimately, his films examine the reproduction of capitalist culture and capitalist class relations through the work performed by the PMC within the various dominant institutions which his films observe. Wiseman's cinema can therefore be better understood in light of the three-class model of capitalism presented by Barbara and John Ehrenreich in the mid-seventies.[4]

Until the current two-year pause in his career, Wiseman produced one documentary each year in his comprehensive study of social production and cultural hegemony in America: *Titicut Follies* (1967), *High School* (1968),

Law and Order (1969), *Hospital* (1970), *Basic Training* (1971), *Essene* (1972), *Juvenile Court* (1973), *Primate* (1974), *Welfare* (1975), *Meat* (1976), *Canal Zone* (1977), *Sinai Field Mission* (1978), *Manoeuvre* (1979), and *Model* (1980). The mere listing of film titles, indicating the general nature of each facet in the total mosaic, suggests the scope of the project and the range of institutions (social, military, and corporate) treated. What is not immediately apparent are the intricate relationships among the various facets in the design. Generally, the films can usefully be seen in pairs or trios. Thus, *High School* and *Basic Training* are to be seen together as a study of the relationships between education and the military. As the final "summing up" sequence in *High School* makes perfectly clear, schooling in America is in the service of the military, producing "parts" for the war machine. Similarly, the soldiers in boot camp in *Basic Training* are gradually transformed into proper fighting instruments through a program of classroom and field instruction that parodies the conventional educational process—complete with "orientation," "flunky" (Private Hickman), and, for the successful students, "graduation" ceremonies.[5] What are generally conceived as separate spheres of society, Wiseman shows to be intimately connected, reciprocal and mutually sustaining. The mosaic of Wiseman's oeuvre is intricately bound together, facet to facet, by a network of cross-references, mirror images, continuations, and reversals of pattern too rich and complex to detail in a brief paper. But the critique of American civilization implicit in the total design is devastating.

The mosaic as a metaphor for Wiseman's documentary series is in one respect misleading: it suggests a fixed, static quality, which when considering the tone of his social criticism and the cast of his political thought is not really accurate. As Wiseman goes even deeper into the institutional matrix of the American social formation in the course of his documentary project, his politics evolve from liberal reformism in the early films, through an increasing disillusionment in the middle films, and finally to a considerably more radical vision, essentially in harmony with the perspectives of historical materialism, by 1976 when *Meat* was produced. The usual critical view of Wiseman's later films as somehow less hard-hitting fails to recognize, I think, the subtler and more detached forms of social criticism in such films as *Model*. Where the early films, like *Titicut Follies* and *High School*, more directly express Wiseman's personal outrage, at times heavily underlining meaning and directing our emotional and moral allegiances, *Meat* and *Model* observe their respective subjects more analytically and dispassionately, inviting the viewer more fully and freely to participate in the process of constructing meaning. So while nothing in the later films seems as trenchant, for example, as the remarkable sequence in *Titicut Follies* in which Wiseman intercuts images showing the preparation of a dead inmate for burial with images of his being force-fed through the nose while still alive, there is merely nothing as heavy-handed. And the gain in formal subtlety and open-endedness in the later films is accompanied by changes of emphasis—away from specific institutional abuses and individual villainy or professional ineptness (e.g., the Viennese psychiatrist) and toward the broader, more impersonal mechanisms of the marketplace and the division of labor in a class-divided society. The genuinely hard-hitting insight of these later films is that the "system" is often most pernicious when it works the way it is supposed to, not when there is a gap between institutional ideology and practice or a breach of professional ethics. To what extent and in what ways major historical events "outside" Wiseman's films shaped these changes of political perspective "inside" them is difficult to gauge with any precision. But some relation to changing prospects for rapid and positive social change is clear: as the antiwar movement and black rebellion of the sixties and the emergence of the women's movement in the early seventies gave way in the mid and late seventies to Watergate, economic and imperial decline, and the emergence of Reaganism and the New Right, Wiseman (like many on the American left) lost a great deal of his innocence. And that "loss of innocence" can be traced in his oeuvre.

Model begins and ends on a musical note familiar to students of his cinema. It opens, puzzlingly, with a band in Central Park striking up the elegant rondo from Mauret's "Symphonic Fanfares," the musical theme of public television's "Masterpiece Theater," and closes with a spectacular fashion-buyer's show, in which elegantly dressed models pirouette down a runway to a recorded medley of slick and snappy show tunes, most notably "Strike Up the Band." Wiseman's allusion to his very first documentary, *Titicut Follies*, is unmistakable: that film began, memorably, with a surreal, zombie-like rendition of "Strike Up the Band" as part of an inmate-staff variety show at the Bridgewater, Massachusetts, State Hospital for the criminally insane. With this musical allusion Wiseman brackets his documentary series, first to last, and couples apparently unrelated worlds, while neatly suggesting the substantial unity of his films. While Wiseman's political vision changes and grows within the oeuvre, the fourteen documentaries from 1967 to 1980 are essentially one long film, one continuous political discourse. And *Model* in many ways is the film toward which the documentary project has been moving from the beginning. In subject matter, point of view, and means of representation, it is the culmination of Wiseman's cinema. However, through its dazzling analysis of photographic and cinematic production, *Model* reflects on all the earlier films in the documentary project, insofar as they exist on the level of cultural reproduction that is examined in the film. *Model* thus articulates the level of the social formation on which Wiseman has been working since 1967.

More successfully than any other film by Wiseman, *Model* immerses the spectator in the market society, a world of commodities where social relations are most clearly reduced to relations of purchase and sale. Zoli's agency, a kind of fashion model's meat market to which Wiseman returns throughout the film, is the central marketplace, offering to buy the labor (and good looks) of hopeful young models and to sell the services of the few it hires to customers in advertising, television, and films. In effect, Zoli's is the nexus in the film of a vast apparatus of cultural production which makes use of the camera to promote the goods and values of the marketplace. And while fixing the steady gaze of his camera eye on various facets of this apparatus, particularly advertising, Wiseman reveals much about the dominant means of social control and reproduction in the consumer society. Hegemony, the complex orchestration of consent, is guided by an omnipresent ideology of possessive and competitive individualism that celebrates the "good life" supposedly always within reach through purchases: beauty, glamor, youth, "freedom," leisure, wealth, sexuality, and "personality." It is precisely this imaginary realm, which promises personal transformation, that we see so carefully constructed in sequence after sequence in the film. *Model* shows us the highly organized production of what John Berger calls "glamor" and what, in a broader sense, Stuart Ewen calls "the political ideology of consumption."[6]

As Wiseman alternates between studio sets and street scenes in *Model* he reveals an aspect of contemporary American culture which is represented in its camera-produced "public images" and reflected in myriad social practices in the course of daily life. In a recent essay on modern American culture, Warren Susman describes precisely what I think Wiseman shows us in *Model*: a culture of "personality." Among other things, this culture of personality involves the terrible need to make an impression on others, to be seen as Somebody: "The problem is clear. We live now constantly in a crowd: how can we distinguish ourselves from others in that crowd? While the term is never used, the question is clearly one of life in a mass society ('crowd' is the most commonly used word)."[7] "Personality," as Susman has defined it, is precisely what the advertisers in *Model* purport to sell, and what the models posing try to portray. Furthermore, the pursuit of personality, with its attendant emphasis on performance, is what Wiseman shows us in a number of street scenes. Toward the end of the film, for example, a young black man dances, transistor radio in hand, in front of a department store window, a star watching himself in his own movie. By this continual alternation and intermingling of the realms of "the imaginary" and "the real," Wiseman reveals an omnipresent ideology of a distinctly Althusserian kind: largely unconscious, widely diffused (like air) in society, a process or operation negotiated in a variety of ways.

Throughout *Model*, Wiseman plays with notions of the imaginary and the real—and their interdependence. In sequence after sequence he shows us models at work, presenting themselves to the camera after being suitably dressed, painted, combed, brushed, placed into a context, and moved about. They are, in effect, so many props, inanimate objects, mannequins to display the clothing and project "personality." In one revealing sequence, three French models get the pose "right" only after following directions to "ignore one another.

Pretend you're mannequins in a Bloomingdale window." Later in the film, at a party of the "beautiful people," where male models line the walls in frozen poses, Wiseman moves his camera and sound recorder around the room to capture a highly artificial social event in which suddenly, in the final shot, a mannequin stands in profile amid clusters of "beautiful people" in conversation. And throughout the film, Wiseman returns, over and over again, to beautifully clothed mannequins in department store windows, employing them as symbols of the commodified self, the individual as object and product of the market. And always, as we are shown the mannequins, we see the reflections in the glass of passersby, the prospective consumers of the goods, whose coexistence with the mannequins seems ontologically equivalent. The two realms, "real" and "imaginary," are fused. Momentarily, Wiseman is able to freeze the process or operation of the marketplace ideology as it is lived in the consumer society.

Model is Wiseman's *Man with a Movie Camera*, in which he investigates our contemporary "Camera Age" and the performances of the main actor in that age, the camera itself. Like Vertov before him, Wiseman simultaneously provides a critique of daily life (though a narrower slice of it) and of the illusionary nature of photographic and cinematic representation. While documenting the world of high-fashion modeling at various distances and proximities to life on the streets of New York City, *Model* turns back on itself, self-reflexively examining the methods and means of creating meaning within camera-produced texts, its own as well as those of the cultural producers whose work Wiseman observes in the film. And Wiseman leads us to see how these texts—*Model* itself, the numerous ads and fashion photos, the thirty-second Evan Picone television commercial, and the documentary being filmed within Wiseman's larger documentary—can have such different political messages while speaking in the same language, using the same grammar.

Putting Wiseman's use of the camera temporarily aside, *Model* shows us the various ways in which the camera is employed, to conceal reality in the service of the marketplace. Presenting the images and sounds of "the good life," these fashion photographs and television commercials (and in a different way also the documentary-within-the-documentary) deny the process by which they were constructed and came to be imprinted on film stock. The tedious, variously trained and paid, highly technical, infinitely specialized, alienated labor which we have seen go into the final product is always denied. And while denying its own process, the final product suppresses any notions of labor whatsoever, creating the impression of a world of leisure, freedom, and pleasure, where no one needs to work. Nowhere in the film is this gap between process and product more evident than in the extended sequence which shows the making of a television commercial for Evan Picone hosiery. For nearly half an hour we watch an immense production unfold, culminating in a slow, mechanical process whereby a four-second "peacock effect" is to be produced by filming a model's leg in eight different positions. The labor of many is carefully documented, from the production crewman who sweeps the sidewalk to the directors who alternately browbeat and cajole the models, who really *are* reduced to mere props. Particularly memorable in this respect are the labors of the female model whose leg is photographed over seventy-nine takes and who is, by the end, nearly exhausted from kicking and holding her leg in place before the screen. The resulting commercial, which Wiseman shows us, is stunning for the suppressions that are revealed and for the mystified impression of reality created: a world of instant happiness and beauty where the only work suggested is the dazzling unfolding of a peacock's tail feathers.

Not merely human labor but all the various mechanical and chemical processes of photography and cinematography are being suppressed, as we see, in cultural products like the Evan Picone commercial. Walter Benjamin's remark about film in general applies here: "The equipment-free aspect of reality here has become the height of artifice; the sight of immediate reality has become an orchid in the land of technology."[8] And the resulting texts all convey the same message, a highly depoliticized impression of reality that denies the class-based and class-divided work system in order to reproduce it. Commodities, the collective product of that class system, must seem to float in a world apart, though capable of being entered through "magical" purchases. Whatever might interfere with the smooth and automatic transport of the spectator-consumer into this world, this Fantasy Island, must be carefully avoided. Particularly through the use of the close-up, by detaching the beautiful faces of these models and the aura of personality which they project, the camera renders reality from a point of view designed to enchant the viewer with visions of personal transformation.

Wiseman uses his own camera differently in *Model*, not to conceal but to reveal. By continually altering the length, angle, distance, and point of view of his shots, he shows us the larger context and restores the "production" suppressed by the others. Like Vertov's Kino Eye, Wiseman's camera is used to unmask reality, "to strip us bare, so that he may build us anew." It is not that Wiseman is technically incapable of the slick and ideologically determined use of the camera in order to promote the status quo of the consumer society. Several times, but particularly in one long sequence involving a female model posing in several disguises or costumes, Wiseman uses his portapack camera in precisely the same way that the many fashion photographers have used their cameras throughout *Model*—to celebrate the commodity-model, to caress the model almost sexually through close-ups from various angles. Wiseman's success at catching the look and feel of a 35mm fashion photograph can be gauged by the close similarity between Wiseman's images in that sequence and those still photographs of the same model which are inspected under magnifying glass by some Zoli employees in a sequence near the end of the film. Wiseman's art here is the height of self-reflexivity: as he shows us these still photographs near the end, he refers us back to the success of his own camera, his parody of 35mm fashion photography in the earlier sequence, bringing into relief his own very different use of the camera.

The place that Wiseman's camera creates for the viewer is not at all the place created for the spectator-consumer by the other camera users in *Model*: we are not passively to consume a mystified image or text which seals us into the place of consuming subjject. Instead, we are installed into a place much like that occupied by the numerous residents of New York City who are several times in the film shown observing the Evan Picone commercial and other advertisements made on the street—standing outside, watching the "enchanted world" as it is being so obviously and heavily produced, and (temporarily?) immune to its enchantment. But Wiseman gives us the added perspective of watching *them* watch the spectacle being made, giving us (the mass or crowd in a mass society) the opportunity to inspect ourselves as the mass. And in frequent close-ups of the faces of these ordinary people (so different from the "beautiful people" within the spectacle) we see something approaching disgust, or perhaps disenchantment. In quite a different (and much less obvious) way than earlier films by Wiseman, *Model* violates a taboo, revealing images which are generally concealed in our culture. While *Titicut Follies* may show us naked madmen dancing in their cells, *Model* shows us the making of our public images, the various liftings and adjustments whereby the mask is so carefully put into place. The looks on the very ordinary faces of the pedestrian-spectators suggest—not unlike our response to *Model* as a whole—the shock of an exposure to the forbidden. That "crowd" is us.

The self-reflexivity of *Model*, inherent in many of the film's strategies that I have discussed, is signaled directly by the frequent glimpses in the second half of the film of documentary film crews at work: at the party of beautiful people where the mannequin suddenly appears, which I discussed before; at interview sessions with two professional male models and later with Zoli himself; and particularly at a shower scene involving a male model, which has apparently been staged by a documentary film crew whose work Wiseman documents. In all these sequences we are shown the cameras, sound equipment, and crew at work—reminding us of the very similar process Wiseman is using to produce *Model*, the larger documentary as it were. By referring us to the devices and methods of the documentary, however different from his own, Wiseman reminds us of his own sleights of hand, by which he too creates an illusion giving the impression of reality. In this way Wiseman moves us from the position of passive consumers of an imaginary reality to the position of distanced, demystified coproducers of the film's meaning, invited to observe and puzzle out the paradoxes and contradictions of the text. By exposing the transparencies and self-effacements of the traditional realist text, which are everywhere else in the film seen to define the limits of cultural production by the dominant apparatus, Wiseman offers a critique of the way in which the media employ the camera in the service of the dominant ideology. This dominant ideology of the marketplace and bourgeois social arrangements, we come to see, is given free passage in the other texts within the film—and is reinforced by the camera's own ideology, the ideology of the mirror.

Wiseman's critique of the ideology of the mirror, the ideology whereby the camera creates the impression of reality in order to promote an imaginary relationship of opposition-identity, is suggested in the many sequences in *Model* in which Wiseman teasingly plays with mirrors, shooting into them to document negative film space. Early in the film, for example, production crewmen on location hold up a giant mirror to create light effects from the reflected sun in a sequence involving a male and a female model posing in and around an automobile while a helicopter hovers overhead. Wiseman shoots the sequence alternately in positive and negative film space, frequently shooting into the mirror to show us the models, crew, and equipment as they are reflected there. The spectator effect is one of purposeful confusion: the viewer is not always sure in this sequence where he or she is, where the "real" (positive) and the "imaginary" (negative) space begin and end. Similarly, late in the film, during the sequence in the shower, Wiseman shoots nearly the entire sequence into the vanity mirror opposite the shower where the male model is showering. But we are made aware that Wiseman is shooting this sequence in negative space (into the mirror) only near the end of it, when Wiseman's cameraman turns the angle of his camera just enough to reveal himself (or is it the cameraman from the *other* documentary crew?) in the mirror. Momentarily, we see the model finishing his shower and the cameraman in front of him shooting the scene from the reflection in the vanity mirror. Again, we as spectators are not really sure where we stand in relation to "reality." Through his self-reflexive exploration of negative film space, Wiseman defeats the ideology of the camera, the impression of reality created to enchant the viewer into accepting the imaginary, illusory world as the "real" one. And in the process Wiseman blocks passage to the spectator of the dominant ideology of "personality" and competitive individualism in which the commodity-model in the shower is bathed and which the documentary within Wiseman's documentary is attempting to celebrate.

Model thus brings to a halt the documentary project which began fourteen films earlier with *Titicut Follies* in 1967. With the emergence of this latest film by Wiseman, we can see more clearly his contribution toward the development of a materialist cinema in America. The self-reflexivity and the Althusserian critique of ideology which *Model* displays indicate that Wiseman is a political filmmaker who must be carefully studied by Marxists and others who would develop a radical film practice in this country. The typical Wiseman film, and *Model* above all, is a politically motivated, modernist, open text, running thoroughly counter to the culinary cinema generally produced in

America. As in the theater of Brecht, Wiseman's cinema offers not the pleasures of identification and catharsis within an imaginary relationship to the real, but the pleasures that arise out of instruction, satisfying our need to understand the nature of social reality. His cinema fulfills the prescription which Fredric Jameson has given for a revolutionary aesthetic in Brechtian tradition: Wiseman "transforms the process of 'knowing the world' into a source of delight or pleasure in its own right; and this is the fundamental step in the construction of a properly Brechtian aesthetic."[9] In Wiseman's documentary project, as in Brecht, pleasure is a function of coming to know the world in order to change it.

There is simply no other filmmaker in America today who has illuminated so well as much of our collective experience during the past decade and a half. I am continually struck when teaching Wiseman in the classroom how well his films are able to create connections among those of us who watch and discuss them, drawing on our shared experience and moving to the center of those tensions and contradictions that inform it. The impact is huge, partly for the temporary community they create, but also because of the range and variety of pleasures they offer. Inured as we are to the pandered dreams and formulas of Hollywood and television, Wiseman's documentaries explode our ingrained expectations and temporarily repair the cleavage between work and play that defines ordinary daily life and cultural experience. As we watch these films, the realm of the quotidian is rescued from the obfuscations of "the obvious." By making the familiar strange and the strange familiar, Wiseman helps to restore our capacity to take back the control of our lives.

Notes

1. Michael Arlen, "Fred Wiseman's Kino Pravda," in Arlen, *The Camera Age* (Toronto: McGraw-Hill, 1976), p. 120.

2. Roland Tuch, "Frederick Wiseman's Cinema of Alienation: A Vision of Work on the Assembly Line," *Film Library Quarterly* 2 (1978): 14.

3. Bill Nichols, *Ideology and the Image: Social Representation in the Cinema and Other Media* (Bloomington: Indiana University Press, 1981), p. 211. Nichols makes no claims to resolve the problematic nature of the place of the viewer in the Wiseman text but argues that the recent materialist critique of the realist text cannot be applied simply to dismiss the films because of their self-effacing style: "Although Wiseman's films are not self-reflexive in a formalist or political (Brechtian) sense, neither are they simple transparencies of a bourgeois world that we, as spectators, passively contemplate" (p. 235). As I shall argue later in this paper, *Model*, which appeared after Nichols wrote the above passage, takes up the project of resolving these structural tensions through a self-reflexive text which places the viewer unambiguously beyond the imaginary relationship and the realm of the "merely enjoyable" or pleasurable.

4. See Barbara Ehrenreich and John Ehrenreich, "The Professional-Managerial Class," in *Between Labor and Capital*, ed. Pat Walker, pp. 5–45 (Boston: South End Press, 1979). Rejecting the traditional Marxist two-class model of capitalism as inadequate for an understanding of late capitalism, the Ehrenreichs define the place and function of the PMC in the social formation in precisely the ways that Wiseman captures in his cinema: to reproduce capitalist culture and

capitalist class relations. For example, Wiseman's most Marxist works—the Lukácsian *Meat* and the Althusserian *Model*—neatly "cover" the two major divisions within the PMC that the Ehrenreichs describe, suggesting much about the complex nature of social control through ideological consent in the interrelated processes of production and consumption.

5. For a full discussion of *Basic Training* as a sequel to *High School* and a parody of the educational process, see Richard Fuller, "*Basic Training*," in *Frederick Wiseman*, ed. Thomas R. Atkin, pp. 103–12 (New York: Monarch Press, 1976).

6. See John Berger, *Ways of Seeing* (New York: Viking Press, 1973), and the film by the same title, particularly part 4, "Painting and Advertising"; and Stuart Ewen, *Captains of Consciousness: Advertising and the Social Roots of the Consumer Culture* (New York: McGraw-Hill, 1976).

7. Warren I. Susman, " 'Personality' and the Making of Twentieth-Century Culture," in *New Direction in American Intellectual History*, ed. J. Highman and P. K. Conklin (Baltimore: Johns Hopkins University Press, 1979), pp. 217–18.

8. Walter Benjamin, "The Work of Art in the Age of Mechanical Reproduction," in Benjamin, *Illuminations*, trans. Harry Zohn (New York: Harcourt, Brace and World, 1955), p. 235.

9. Fredric Jameson, "Reflections in Conclusion," in Jameson, *Aesthetics and Politics* (London: New Left Books, 1978), pp. 204–5, quoted in Sylvia Harvey, *May '68 and Film Culture* (London: British Film Institute, 1980), p. 81.

Reflections on
An American Family, I
Craig Gilbert

Finding the Louds

On that first night at 35 Woodale Lane, there were drinks and pleasant conversation. I met all the children with the exception of Lance, who had gone to New York to work on a new underground magazine. We talked about television and the series and the practical considerations of how it would all work. After about an hour the family agreed to participate. As a matter of fact, my private feelings were that they had agreed a little too rapidly, that they did not fully realize what they were letting themselves in for. I thought it would be good for them to experience being followed around for a day by a camera crew. On the following day there was to be a runoff election between Kevin Loud and another student for the office of president of the student body at Santa Barbara High School. In anticipation of Kevin's winning the election, a party was planned at the Loud home. This sounded like an ideal situation in which to introduce the family to the conditions of *cinéma vérité* filming. They agreed, and I returned to the motel to make the arrangements.

After several phone calls I contacted a Los Angeles film crew (unknown to me) who were willing to come to Santa Barbara the following day. Once the shooting started it became quickly apparent that the crew was not very skilled at *cinéma vérité* filmmaking, a highly specialized technique which demands a kind of sixth-sense understanding between the person who is doing the shooting and the person who is doing the sound. Much of what was interesting that night was missed, and most of what was shot was badly framed and included not only the microphone but the man holding it. However, I really didn't care. I had no intention of using the footage; I just wanted the family to know what it felt like to be followed by a camera, lights, and a microphone.

My suspicion that the Louds had agreed to the project without really knowing what they were getting into proved to be correct. Around midnight, Pat and Bill asked if we could talk for a while. Their first question was whether they could have final approval of what was included in the series. It was clear what they were concerned about. Liquor was flowing quite freely at the party, and I had noticed the cameraman getting quite a few shots of both Pat and Bill serving drinks to kids who were both underage and already quite obviously drunk. Two years later, when the Louds were claiming publicly, on television talk shows and in newspaper interviews, that we had shown only the bad times in their lives and none of the good times, they always mentioned this party as an example of the happy life that we had excluded from the series. I allayed their fears about the party footage by explaining that none of it was going to be used. But I made clear that in the future, when the shooting got started in earnest, I would have to retain the right to make that decision. However, I agreed that before any of the episodes were "locked up," the family or any member of the family would be allowed to see it and raise objections, which I promised would be listened to seriously and discussed fully, and changes would be made if they were warranted.

There were other problems, but the party was still going on and I wanted the children to be involved in any further discussions. So I dismissed the camera crew and suggested we all get some rest on Saturday and I come back on Sunday to discuss the matter thoroughly. When that was agreed on, I went back to the motel and slept for almost thirty-six hours. It had been a little more than two months since I had started the search for the family, but I still did not feel secure enough to call Curt Davis and tell him the search had been successful. With a day's rest and plenty of time to think over the pressure of Friday night, I had no idea whether the Louds would change their minds.

Setting Ground Rules

The discussion on Sunday centered around three main points. The first had to do with privacy: where would the camera go and where would it not go? In this respect I promised the camera would never go through a closed door. If the family or any member of the family wanted to be alone, all they had to do was go into a room and close the door. In addition to this, I explained that a normal shooting day would begin around eight in the morning and end around ten at night. There might, of course, be exceptions to this, but generally that would be the schedule. If the family wanted to talk over anything they didn't want us to see or hear, it should be before or after those hours.

The second point had to do with what would happen if the family collectively came to the decision that they had made a mistake, that the whole thing was too much for them and they wanted to quit. I said that if this happened I would of course want to talk it over with them to find out what was bothering them. If possible, whatever it was would be eliminated. If that could not be done, I said, the family would have the right to call it quits, and that would be it.

The final point revolved around how much the filming would interfere with their lives. This was a difficult thing to talk about, since there were so many imponderables. Obviously, it is not normal to have a camera crew following you around all day. For a while at least, I explained, it was going to feel strange and awkward. But my hunch was it wouldn't take long for the new circumstances of their life to feel reasonably comfortable. How quickly and how easily this happened would depend on the skill of the camera crew and the ability of the members of the family to get used to their presence and go on about their lives without feeling self-conscious.

My instructions were that they were to live their lives as if there were no camera present. They were to do nothing differently than they would ordinarily. This would be hard at first but would, I promised, become increasingly easier. We would never ask them to do anything just for the camera. In other words, we would never stage anything and we would never ask them to do or say something over again if we happened to miss it. To the best of our ability we would not become involved in the family's problems. By that I meant that as far as was humanly possible we would not intrude our feelings, opinions, or personalities into family disputes, discussions, or relationships. This last restriction became, as the filming progressed, the hardest restriction to live up to.

I wish to make it clear that at no time did I bring up the subject of payment, nor did any of the Louds ever ask for any compensation for participating in the project.

After we had talked about all these problems, the unanimous decision of the family was that they would participate in the project. We now had to set a date for when the filming would get started in earnest. Pat Loud said she would be flying to New York the following Saturday to spend a week or so with Lance in New York. We decided to start the shooting officially then. Pat said she would call Lance at the Chelsea Hotel and tell him what was happening, and I said I would go back to New York and get in touch with him sometime before Saturday.

I spent the rest of the day with the family, eating and talking and just getting acquainted. The next morning, I called Curt Davis at NET and told him I had found the family. He said it was a good thing I had, because he had decided to give me only one more week and then was going to call a halt to the whole undertaking. I told him I was going to fly back to New York on Tuesday and asked if he could set up a meeting with the appropriate production executives for Wednesday morning. He said he would.

Establishing a Budget

Back in New York, the major production problems were the budget and the fact that I wanted to start shooting in two days' time. Most of the production people took the position that this was impossible. They were adamant that there would be no shooting until a firm budget had been established. I was just as adamant in maintaining that Pat Loud's visit to New York to see Lance had to be covered.

As I mentioned earlier, before I left on my search for a family, $600,000 had been found somewhere to fund the project. I now discovered the money had come from canceling a series called "Priorities for Change," a public affairs series scheduled for production in the new season.[1] Without my knowing about it, "Priorities for Change" had been dropped from the schedule, its budget had been made available to my project, and its six producers had been given their notice. Needless to say, this did not make me very popular with the Public Affairs Department or with Bill Kobin, the vice-president in charge of programming, whose background was hard news and whose relationship with Cultural Affairs had been strained over the years.

In preliminary conversations with the production people it soon became clear that $600,000 would not be enough to cover the cost of *An American Family*. To find out just how much more would be needed, I was told to sit down with a production manager and figure out a realistic budget. One of the barriers that stood in the way of doing this quickly was the question of the camera crew and what their individual salaries would be. On the last film I had made I had used the camera and sound team of Alan and Susan Raymond. When that film was completed, I had promised the Raymonds that they would work on my next project.

After *The Triumph of Christy Brown*, and to a certain extent on the strength of that film, Alan Raymond and his wife had gotten several assignments from other producers at NET, in the course of which they had dealings (most of them fraught with antagonism and anger) with several of NET's production managers. In fact, on one of those films Alan had managed to antagonize the very man he would now be negotiating with about his salary and the salaries of his crew. It was a very delicate situation, and I told Alan as much when we met in my office prior to our first budget meeting. That meeting proved to be a disaster whose ramifications continued to be felt for the first two months of shooting. Alan's initial request (or, more accurately, demand) caused the meeting to end almost before it started, just short of a fistfight, and generated so much anger that no progress of any kind could be made for almost a week.

What Alan wanted, before the specific question of salaries even came up, was an advance from NET so he could buy his own camera and thus eliminate the expense of renting one. On the face of it this did not seem an unusual request; in fact, it made sense, inasmuch as NET would ultimately have to pay the rental fee anyway. The problem was the way Alan demanded this concession. Something in his voice and attitude touched off a lingering dislike of him, and within minutes the two men were glaring at each other, all pretense at maintaining the ordinary amenities out the window. When Alan called the production manager every obscene name he could think of, the meeting ended abruptly. The result of all this was that Alan Raymond wasn't close to having an agreement with NET, and Pat Loud was scheduled to arrive in New York in two days.

Some NET production people took the position that there would be no filming until an agreement was reached with the Raymonds, no matter how long it took. This, of course, was totally unacceptable to me. It was finally agreed that the Raymonds would be allowed to shoot for the length of time Pat Loud was in New York at a rate that, it was understood, was for that week and that week only and would have no bearing on the long-term agreement if and when it was ever worked out.

With this first problem at least temporarily solved, we turned our attention to the coverage of Pat Loud's visit; this meant contacting Lance at the Chelsea Hotel. Numerous phone calls by Alan Raymond and myself had been unsuccessful—Lance was never in, and he never returned our calls. About three hours before Pat was due to arrive, Alan reached Lance, who said yes, he had been told what was going on by his mother, and sure, the camera crew could come down to the Chelsea to meet him and to see what problems might be encountered in shooting in Lance's room.

At this meeting it became clear for the first time that Lance was a homosexual and was not in the slightest way ashamed of the fact. One of the more idiotic charges leveled against *An American Family* was that, through some strange alchemy, the process of shooting the series induced Lance to reveal his hitherto hidden sexual preference to the American public. This is pure nonsense. Lance was a homosexual before the shooting, during the shooting, and after the shooting. The fact that we didn't find out about it until we did neither excited nor depressed me. In my original talks with Bill and Pat in Santa Barbara it had been agreed that whatever happened would happen, whatever came up in the course of the filming should not be considered a good thing or a bad thing but simply another thing that occurred in their daily lives.

Pat's visit to New York ended up as episode 2 in *An American Family*—an episode I have always considered one of the best in the series. From New York, Pat went to Baltimore to take care of some business for her husband, and the Raymonds and their assistant were allowed to follow and film her at the same temporary weekly rate which had been agreed to for the shooting at the Chelsea Hotel.

As I write this I have my notes from that period in front of me, and as if it were happening all over again I can feel the incredible frustration of trying to mediate the salary dispute between the Raymonds and the people at NET responsible for agreeing to a final budget. The NET position was that the Raymonds could continue to shoot on a weekly basis but I could not leave New York until the dispute was settled. This meant that when Pat Loud flew back to Santa Barbara on June 9 accompanied by the Raymonds, I was not on the plane. For the first crucial week of shooting with the entire family I was three thousand miles away.

My absence, of course, naturally disturbed the Louds. I had entered their lives out of the blue, asked them to take part in this crazy undertaking, and then disappeared. Why? What had happened? Could they really trust someone who acted this irrationally? The Raymonds did nothing to help the situation. Although they knew perfectly well I was being kept in New York to try to write a budget that could include their salary demands, they never volunteered this information. To questions from the Louds about why I wasn't there, they would shrug their shoulders and claim they had no idea.

After long hours of pleading with NET executives and several quick weekend trips to the coast to reassure the family that I was not a figment of their imaginations, I was finally allowed to conduct the endless budget negotiations from Santa Barbara. I say "endless" advisedly. According to my notes, the first meeting at NET about the Raymonds' salary (the one in which Alan Raymond and the production manager almost came to blows) was held on May 27. A deal was finally made with the Raymonds around the middle of July.

Much has been written about how unnatural it must have been for the Louds to have a camera crew following them for twelve or thirteen or fourteen hours a day and how difficult, if not downright impossible, it must have been under these conditions to lead a normal life.[2] Citing the Heisenberg principle became a favorite gambit for all manner of critics, columnists, and feature writers who felt the need for scientific justification to question the worth of the series.

Shooting

In point of fact, on a normal day the crew (Alan and Susan Raymond and an assistant) would arrive at the Loud home at about eight in the morning and would leave at about ten at night. Sometimes they would get there earlier or leave later, but not often. While they were at the Louds', the Raymonds obviously would not shoot continuously. When, in their view, something interesting was going on, they would shoot; the rest of the time they would put their camera and sound recorder down and, in effect, become two more members of the family, talking, listening to music, or watching television. And some days they did not shoot at all.

When actual shooting was going on, the Raymonds were the only outsiders present in the house. The assistant remained outside loading fresh magazines with film, and I was hardly ever present, having decided at the beginning of the project that the fewer people standing between the camera and the Louds, the better. A director or a producer or anybody else on the production staff, for that matter, would have been merely a distraction to the crew and to the family.

After the crew departed at night I would try to spend an hour or so chatting with the family to keep in touch with what its various members were up to and to try to get some idea of what might be happening in the next few days. I also tried, in this way, to stay in touch with the emotional state of the family, without, as I have said earlier, becoming involved in its affairs. On those days when the crew was filming Bill Loud at his office or at a business meeting, I sometimes spent the whole day at the house.

When the Raymonds were not shooting, I would talk to them in person or on the phone about what was happening in the family, what we felt was going on, and what kinds of things to pay particular attention to. Despite this day-to-day communication with the Raymonds and despite their apparent understanding of my basic premise for the series, Alan's perceptions about the family and its individual members were not always my perceptions, his view of what was important was not always my view.

Since the moment-to-moment decisions as to what to shoot and what not to shoot were up to the crew, the arrangement was not always a happy one. Indeed, from time to time it was the cause for some serious and painful disagreements. But there was no viable alternative, and in the long run I think the Raymonds did a remarkable job. Because life has a tendency to repeat itself—which meant that if Alan missed something I wanted the first time, he could get it the next time it happened—I think that over the seven-month period he and Susan recorded an extraordinarily accurate picture of how the Louds lived.

As for lights, whenever possible the Raymonds relied on natural light and sensitive film. For night shooting, they substituted photo flood bulbs for the regular bulbs in all the lamps and overhead fixtures in rooms where shooting was likely to take place. These photo floods stayed in place for all seven months, so as a matter of course there was enough light for evening shooting in the house without any frantic last-minute preparations. This also meant the Louds soon got used to living in a house that was somewhat more brightly lit than usual. There were no reflectors and no yards of black cable winding sinuously through the living quarters.[3]

I do not want to imply that having their daily lives recorded for seven months was easy or normal for the Louds, or without problems. It wasn't. I am simply trying to point out that it was not as disruptive as many people, including the critics, believed.

For the production staff, the period from the end of May 1971 to January 1, 1972, was hardly problem-free. Almost every day there was a new crisis—

personal, emotional, logistical, technical. Some of them—those that shed light on the filmmaking process—are worth mentioning.

Crises During Shooting

One of the early crises was caused by Lance's announcement that he was going to spend the summer in Europe. It was imperative to cover his trip, but the budget, in its final, approved state, did not allow for a second 16mm crew to wander around Europe for a couple of months. Our problem was finally solved through the good graces of Richard Leacock, a pioneer *cinéma vérité* filmmaker in the fifties and early sixties, who had started an 8mm film department at MIT. He and his students had spent a good deal of time trying to develop a Super 8mm recorder and camera rig that could shoot acceptable *cinéma vérité* film with synchronous sound in the field. He agreed that Lance's trip would provide an ideal test for the equipment. I do not remember what the exact financial arrangement was, but I do know it was reasonable enough to pass the careful scrutiny of the zealous guardians of the budget. The result was some marvelous footage (shot by John Terry) which, when blown up to 16mm, added immensely to the overall interest of the series.

Pat Loud's trip to Taos, New Mexico, with her daughters Michelle and Delilah triggered a whole series of problems. Pat and the girls had not been gone for more than an hour before Bill was quite openly making arrangements to fly to Hawaii with his current girlfriend, the manager of a boutique in Santa Barbara. The fact that he made no attempt to hide these shenanigans put an enormous burden on all of us. As I mentioned earlier, I had tried to impress on the entire production staff the importance of not getting involved in the family's affairs. This was, of course, an extremely difficult ideal to live up to, and none of us was totally successful at it. The very fact of living as close to the Louds as we did for seven months made it humanly impossible to remain completely detached and unaffected by what was happening in their lives.

Like most of us, Bill Loud was a complicated man: he could be devious, irritating, and breathtakingly obtuse; he could also be astonishingly sensitive and quite perceptive. And when he wanted to, he could be irresistibly charming. So when he went out of his way to introduce his girlfriend to me, as if to do so was the most natural thing in the world, it was very difficult to know exactly how to act. I didn't want him to think I approved of what he was doing (which is what he wanted), nor did I feel in a position to lecture him on the subject of infidelity.

Bill's flaunting of his relationship with the boutique manager also created filmmaking problems. Once the shooting of the series got underway, it didn't take long to realize that Bill was a compulsive woman-chaser; from time to time he would allude to the affairs he had been involved in over the past several years. But to be faced with his current girlfriend in the flesh was quite different from hearing about his conquests of the past.

In the days following Pat's departure for Taos and preceding Bill's departure for Hawaii with his girlfriend, the question arose as to whether we would shoot them together having drinks at her house and dining at various restaurants in Santa Barbara. I made the decision not to. God knows, I was tempted. But in the final analysis it seemed to me that doing so would put us in an impossible position with Pat and seriously endanger the completion of the series. From time to time Bill and Pat and the kids would ask to look at various pieces of film, and I didn't want to have to lie about what we had shot while she was away. After Bill and Pat separated, there was no need to continue this self-imposed limitation.

The Raymonds and Susan Lester, the production assistant, flew to Taos to cover what was called Pat's "vacation," but which, in fact, turned out to be an intense period of soul-searching during which she made up her mind to ask Bill for a divorce. This decision was reinforced by a phone call from a well-meaning friend in Santa Barbara informing Pat that Bill had flown to Hawaii with the boutique manager.

One night three or four days after the crew arrived in Taos, I received a phone call from Alan Raymond. He complained that he was getting very little on film. For one thing, Michelle and Delilah hated Taos and sat around all day complaining about what a dull town it was. And for another, Pat seemed very uptight and nervous and spent most of her time talking to Susan Lester, thereby making it impossible for him to do any shooting. Alan ended by asking me to get Lester out of Taos so Pat would not be venting all her emotions in conversations which could not be filmed. I told him to do the best he could and said I would speak to Susan when the crew returned to Santa Barbara. (Incidentally, the best Alan could do, in this instance, was very good indeed. Somehow or other he managed to get on film a portrait of a woman at the end of her rope, trying to divert herself by attending art classes, engaging in aimless chitchat at dinner parties given by people she hardly knew, and wandering, under threatening skies, through Indian ruins with a sullen and alienated Michelle.)

When the crew returned to Santa Barbara I had a long talk with Susan Lester. Susan is a bright, talented, ambitious young woman. *An American Family* was the first major film project she had ever worked on. Her reaction to Alan Raymond's criticism of her conduct was not unexpected. As she reminded me, she was one of the members of the production staff who felt my early admonition not to get involved in the affairs of the Loud family was not only unworkable but inhuman. From the very beginning of shooting, Susan had developed a close relationship with Pat which I attributed to their both having an offbeat sense of humor and a sharp eye for the ironies of life and the pomposities of people. Evidently, Pat had slowly but surely opened up to

Susan about the dark side of her life, and Susan had proved a willing and intelligent listener. In Taos, while Pat was wrestling with the painful question of divorce, she depended heavily on Susan for advice, support, and the understanding of a trusted friend.

Susan readily admitted to all this. She also agreed that, very likely, her long conversations with Pat had made it difficult for Alan Raymond to do his job. She added that if there had to be a choice (as there appeared to be in Taos) between maintaining a friendship and the integrity of a film, she would opt for the friendship every time.

We talked for many hours. I sympathized with her point of view; indeed, there were times during our discussion when I felt that her point of view was the only sensible and decent one. But in the end I held to my commitment to make *An American Family*, as far as possible, a series of films about the Louds, and not about how the Louds interrelated with a film crew from NET. I knew damn well that no matter how we conducted ourselves we could not avoid having some effect on the family. But I was adamant about trying to keep that effect to an absolute minimum.

There was no question about firing Susan; she was much too valuable a member of the staff. We worked out a reassignment which was mutually acceptable, and in the final credits for the series Susan Lester's name appears as associate producer. Today Susan is a producer in her own right, and though we are still friends, I have no idea what her position would be now if faced with the same problem.

One evening early in September, while Bill Loud was away on a business trip, the Raymonds returned to the motel and told me that Pat had announced she was going to file for a divorce. They added that the following day she was going to drive to Glendale, a suburb of Los Angeles, to inform her brother and sister-in-law of her decision. I asked the Raymonds if they had made any plans to go along. They had not talked to Pat about it, they said.

I phoned the house and told Pat I had just heard about her decision, and we discussed it for a couple of minutes. I tried to be as noncommittal as possible. After a while I mentioned her planned trip to Glendale and asked if we could film it. She said it was all right with her but it was really up to her brother and his wife, since any shooting would have to take place at their house.

Pat planned to reach Glendale late the next afternoon. I told her that I would get there earlier to talk to her brother and his wife. If they didn't want their talk with Pat filmed, I would be gone by the time she got there. If it was all right with them, I would meet her at the house with the crew. Pat agreed to the arrangement.

Her brother and sister-in-law not only agreed to the filming, they were enthusiastically in favor of it. Although they were against the divorce and planned to tell Pat as much, they felt the series should include Pat's side of the story if the divorce actually took place. When Pat arrived, however, she had a change of heart; she no longer wanted the discussion to be filmed.

This was a moment I had dreaded; it was the first and last time anyone in the family objected to our shooting a sequence which I felt was absolutely necessary for the series. I asked Pat if we could talk privately. She agreed and requested that her sister-in-law be present. Now, almost nine years later, I cannot possibly recreate that conversation. But at the end of half an hour Pat consented to have the film crew present.

In interviews after the series was on the air, Pat sometimes said I had talked her into letting us film her explanation of why she was getting a divorce. And sometimes she said it was her "best scene." Because of these apparently conflicting statements, I could never figure out whether she was condemning me or thanking me, whether she was angry or happy that the scene had been filmed. I'm not sure she knew herself.

When Pat actually confronted Bill with a request for a divorce and asked him to pack his clothes and leave the house, one family became, in effect, two families, and I had serious doubts about whether the Raymonds could cover both of them. It did not take long for my doubts to crystallize into a conviction; I decided to hire another camera crew. First I had to convince NET that this was an absolute necessity and that the expense could be accommodated with a certain amount of budgetary juggling. As hard as this was, it was nothing compared to the problems which arose when I broached the idea to Alan Raymond. He hit the roof and didn't come down for a couple of days. When he did, he threatened to leave the series. (He did in fact disappear for several days, after which I received a phone call from him in which he said if I wanted to talk he would meet me in a Hollywood restaurant. I met him, we talked, and he returned to Santa Barbara.)

I had been through a less intense version of this dispute with Alan during the making of *The Triumph of Christy Brown* in Dublin. Then, I had let him have his way, and I had lived to regret it. He had badly botched the shooting of a key scene simply because he could not be everywhere at once. I had learned my lesson the hard way and was not about to let it happen again. His position, of course, was that he could cover Bill's life and the lives of Pat and the kids perfectly adequately by himself. I was convinced there was no way he could possibly pull this off. I knew what was going on in his mind. He simply didn't want to share his credit with anyone. And there was nothing I could say that would get him to budge one inch. He knew he had me over a barrel; after almost four months of shooting, he was indispensable to the series. There was no way I could fire him (I considered this option through many sleepless nights) without seriously jeopardizing the delicate personal and professional balance that had been established with the Louds.

Finally I had no choice but to ignore his objections and hire another crew and try my best to keep the whole undertaking from falling apart. And it almost did. Faced with another crew on what he considered his territory, Alan submitted an ultimatum that included the following points: (1) under no circumstances was the new crew to be allowed to shoot in the Loud house; (2) he would not consent to communicate with the new crew in any way whatsoever; and (3) he would not attend any screening at which "dailies" shot by the new crew were shown.

Luckily, the cameraperson of the new crew was an understanding, intelligent, easygoing woman named Joan Churchill who, though she thought Alan Raymond was crazy, agreed to go along with the restrictions. In fact, Bill's social activities increased to such an extent once he was on his own that there was more than enough to keep her and her crew busy. And from time to time, when Alan was busy elsewhere, she even shot in the house.

Finally, there was one more production crisis that should be mentioned, not because it is of any earthshaking importance, but because it graphically illustrates how convictions, deeply held in theory, can evaporate in a minute under the pressure of actual shooting conditions.

It occurred on Thanksgiving day. Alan and Susan Raymond were at the house filming, and I was at the motel feeling sorry for myself. It was the first Thanksgiving I had been alone in sixteen years (in my life, as a matter of fact); memory and desire were giving me a hard time. Suddenly the phone rang; it was Alan complaining that Thanksgiving dinner at the house was turning into a disaster. It was the first major holiday without Bill, and although nobody was actually saying as much, it was clear, according to Alan, that he was sorely missed. There was nothing to film; everyone was sitting around looking gloomy. He and Pat had talked and agreed it would be a good idea if I rounded up as many production people as I could find at the motel and brought them up to the house for some turkey. Alan said he would not get the production people on camera, and that it might make Pat and the kids more animated.

This was a total reversal of the position Alan had taken in Taos (I thought this but didn't mention it). For reasons which even now I cannot quite be sure of, I agreed, thereby also completely contradicting the position I had taken in my discussion with Susan Lester.

I rounded up five or six members of the production staff, and we went to the house. It was clear from the minute we got there that it wasn't going to work. Everything was strained and artificial. After a while—if I remember correctly, before the turkey was actually served—I told Alan that it wasn't going to work and that I was going to leave and take the production people with me. He didn't object strenuously.

It was a sad day all around. It was a sad Thanksgiving for us at the motel, and it was a sad Thanksgiving for Pat without her husband and for the kids without their father. But at least it was an honest sadness and not a phony gaiety.

Editing

The filming of *An American Family* ended in the early morning hours of January 1, 1972. On or about February 1, the editing of *An American Family* began, a process that lasted a full twelve months and strained the patience and taxed the talents of almost twenty people.

In the seven months of shooting we had accumulated 300 hours of film. The first thing we had to do was look at every hour of that film in chronological order (i.e., the order in which it had been shot). When I say "we," I mean the two editors, David Hanser and Eleanor Hamerow; their two assistants; Susan Lester; Jacqueline Donnet, the coordinating producer; and myself. Of the seven people in the screening room, only two, Susan Lester and I, had been involved in the shooting and had any day-to-day relationship with the Louds. This was purposeful; I wanted to guard against the possibility of reading anything into the film that wasn't there. The five pairs of fresh eyes were a guarantee that this would not happen. The possessors of those eyes had never met the Louds and knew next to nothing about them. Unlike Susan and me, they could view what was happening on the screen with something approaching reasonable objectivity.

For almost three months—five days a week, six hours a day (more than six hours was intolerable)—we sat in a darkened screening room and watched as the Louds lived their lives from the end of May 1971 to January 1, 1972. To put it mildly, it was a strange and unsettling experience. Slowly but surely, the lives of the people on the screen started becoming more real than our own; without even being aware of it, we found ourselves using words and phrases common to the Louds and talking about family situations as if we had actually participated in them.

Finally that particular purgatory was over, and then for a week, in a bright, sunlit room, we discussed at length what we had seen, our individual reactions to the footage, and the best way of turning that footage into a series people would find interesting. In the discussions that arose I tried to make one point over and over again: what we were dealing with was a record (not complete by a long shot, but certainly representative of the major events) of how the Louds had lived their lives for a period of seven months. Whether we liked or disliked the individual members of the family, or whether we approved or disapproved of how they lived those lives or how they dealt with those events, was irrelevant. Our job was to put this film record together in such a way that it would not violate the characters of the individuals, the lives they led, or the events they participated in.

To put it simply—in practice it turned out to be a very hard thing to do— I was asking the editors to let the material speak for itself rather than, as editors are trained and paid to do, create something out of the material. A couple of examples: if, for reasons of clarity or for some other reason, we decided to use a sequence that was filmically dull, we should not, through tricks of editing, try to make it less so; if a family member had a certain speech habit, we should not, simply because we were tired of hearing it and thought it repetitive, try to minimize it through editing; if we decided to deal with a particular event, we should deal with it (as far as humanly possible) in its entirety and not compress it, through editing, to a more manageable length. During the week, we discussed all these things and much, much more. We also agreed that each episode would be one hour long and that the episodes would run chronologically.

Then I went home and faced the problem of breaking down the 300 hours into episodes. I worked with a log, listing the contents of every roll of film that had been shot—a log, incidentally, as thick as those enormous dictionaries in libraries that have special stands of their own. As I remember, the first breakdown I came up with had about thirty episodes. This was obviously an unworkable number, and I enlisted the aid of Susan Lester to sweat the total down to twenty-four.[4]

The problem of how many episodes there would be in the completed version of *An American Family* continued to plague me and the editors and the management of WNET/13 even after the series had started to appear on the air.[5]

Now, seven years later and under no constraint to be scrupulously fair (at least in interviews) to my employer, I can also say it is a classic illustration of the penny-wise, pound-foolish attitude that continues to prevail in public television. The final budget for *An American Family* was $1.2 million. In other words, each one-hour episode cost $100,000, which was dirt cheap when you remember that, even in those days, it was not unusual for a single one-hour documentary to cost anywhere from $150,000 to $200,000.

The three extra episodes (13, 14, and 15) would have fulfilled the artistic unity implied in the structure of the series.[6] The cost for all three of the extra episodes, the total cost of three more hours, would have been somewhere between $40,000 and $80,000—a small price, it seemed to me then and still seems to me now, to make a logical and aesthetic whole out of something that had already cost $1.2 million. After the final decision was made to spend no more than was necessary to finish episode 12, I asked management if I could try to raise the money outside the station for the last three shows. They gave me permission.

Bob Shanks, who at that time was in charge of the late-night 11:30 to 1:00 A.M. time period at ABC, was very interested. We started to talk after the series had been on the air for two or three weeks, and he was intrigued about the possibility of getting some cheap shows that would cash in on all the publicity being generated by *An American Family*. What he wanted was four shows. The first would be a recap of the highlights of episodes 1 through 12, and the others, of course, would be episodes 13, 14, and 15. He was very excited about the possibilities of this arrangement. I wasn't very happy about the recap idea, but I did want the money to complete the series properly.

Our talks proceeded smoothly—so smoothly, as a matter of fact, that one day Shanks announced that the next step was to get top management at ABC and WNET/13 involved in the discussions. (I should point out that I did not own the rights to *An American Family*; I was functioning as a salaried staff producer. I had been given permission to look for money, but any deal had to be signed by Mr. Iselin and his lawyers.) Shanks said he would call me in a couple of days to let me know how negotiations were progressing.

He was as good as his word. But when he called me, the news was bad. It seems that when he had contacted the proper executives at ABC to get them involved in the project, he was told that they were not interested. They gave him two reasons for this decision, and I set those reasons down here exactly as Shanks repeated them to me: (1) if the programs were successful, they (the executives) would be asked why they hadn't done them in the first place, and thereby been able to avoid having to buy them from public television; and (2) if the programs were successful, they would be asked to do more of the same, which they (the executives) agreed unanimously they did not want to do. In other words, from the executives' point of view, it was a no-win situation. It seemed to me then, and even more so now, that the reasons they gave are a pretty good indication of the kind of thinking that prevails in commercial television.

In addition to the dispute over the number of episodes, there were other disagreements with the management of WNET/13 during the editing period. Any fairly frequent viewer of public television cannot help but be aware of how often a host is used at the beginning of a program to tell you what you are about to see, and at the end of a program to tell you what you have just seen. One day I was called to a meeting in the office of Jay Iselin, president of WNET, to discuss the advisability of having such a host for *An American Family*. When I asked why such a person was needed, I was told it would help to set the programs "in context." At the time I honestly didn't have the slightest notion of what "in context" meant, and I objected to the idea strenuously. It was finally abandoned.

I have thought quite a lot about "in context" since then, and I think today I have a better idea of what it means. It is a euphemism for blunting whatever uncomfortable impact the program may have on the viewer; relieving viewers of the necessity to think for themselves about the contents of the program; and getting the station management off the hook if the program should turn out to be socially, politically, or historically unpopular.

Although I argued successfully against the use of a host on *An American Family*, I lost my battle to prevent an hour-long discussion by assorted "experts" from being aired immediately following the broadcast of the final episode. I watched this discussion at home and then had drinks with several of the participants. One of them, an anthropologist, asked whether I had heard his perceptive remark about the credits in the last episode. It seems that he alone had noticed that the credits seemed to be dissolving, a subtle and telling commentary on the breakup of the family. He congratulated me on this deft touch. When I told him this "deft touch" was wholly unintended, that it was simply the result of a technical problem called "tearing," he was taken aback for a minute and then quickly recovered, giving the opinion that, intended or not, the effect was the same. Until then I had never been overly fond of panel discussions by experts; at that point my opinion of those television mutations reached a new low.

Perhaps the most violent argument I had during the editing period with the men who ran WNET/13 was over the question of an Executive Producer credit for Curt Davis. When the credit list was submitted as a matter of course to the proper executive, the uproar was such that you would have thought I was suggesting the series acknowledge its indebtedness to Adolph Hitler and Joseph Stalin, with perhaps a bow in the direction of Jack the Ripper.

As I pointed out earlier in this account, *An American Family* would never have been made had it not been for Curt Davis. In addition to prodding me into coming up with the concept and having the faith to pursue the possibility of what, in the beginning, seemed to me like a pipe dream, Curt had been enormously supportive of the project through all the shooting and the early months of editing. At that point, as part of the phasing out of NET, he had been fired.

We had never discussed what his credit would be, but there never was any question in my mind that the one he deserved and the one he would get was Executive Producer. When I was told that this was out of the question, I exploded. There were extremely heated words, and at one point I said that if Curt's name did not appear as Executive Producer, I would destroy the series and the station would be left with the task of explaining why it did not appear on the air. The battle continued for over a week; in the end, Curt got his credit.

You may well be asking why the station had such strong feelings about what seemed, on the surface at least, to be such an insignificant issue. The answer, which has been confirmed many times since then, has to do with the politics of public television. By the time *An American Family* appeared on the air, NET, which had been responsible for the series, had disappeared without a trace. Its functions, on a national level, had been taken over by the Corporation for Public Broadcasting and, on a local level, by WNET/13. Jim Day, the president of NET, and Curt Davis, the head of the Cultural Affairs Department of NET, were no longer on the scene. A revisionist history of public television, in which the dirty word, NET, would never appear, was in the process of being written. Three years later, while I was sitting in the waiting room of the corporation in Washington before an appointment, I leafed through the coffee-table literature that told the history of public television and listed its triumphs.

Nowhere was there any mention of NET or *An American Family*. Quite simply, the intensity of the fight over Curt's credit had to do with the issue of whether, for those who cared and remembered, there would be a lasting reminder that before the Corporation for Public Broadcasting, before PBS, and before WNET/13, there had been another organization which, for all its faults, had represented courage, freedom, and a tentative, but growing, integrity.

The actual ending of the series was a long and laborious process, but it went well except for a difficult problem which arose quite early in the process. That problem had to do with the inability of one of the editors, Eleanor Hamerow, to live with the editing guidelines I had tried to establish.

I liked Ellie very much; she was an interesting, intelligent, warm woman. From the very beginning we got along well together. For many years she had been employed as an editor on issue-oriented documentaries—what recently have come to be known as "investigative reports." These documentaries are put together by shooting as much material as possible on both sides of the issue being examined within the time allotted by the budget and then bringing the footage back to the cutting room where it is given its shape by the editor. In other words, Ellie had spent a great deal of time creating interest, tension, conflict, and drama from footage which, in its original state, was essentially devoid of these qualities. She was an expert at "making something" out of interviews, silent footage, stills, stock material, and other random film.

Her first assignment on the series was to cut episode 1. After a reasonable length of time, I asked her how it was going. She said she was having some trouble but thought she knew how to solve it. Days and weeks went by, but still there was no rough cut of the episode. I began to get frightened and went to the cutting room to talk to her. To my horror, she said she was having trouble "making something" out of the material. When I asked her what she meant, she explained that she was trying to make Pat Loud a little more acceptable as a human being. In the next few days we talked at length about the problem, and slowly but surely it became clear that Ellie not only didn't like Pat but that she didn't like the entire family and was trying to make them less objectionable through her editing. Finally, regrettably, I had to let Ellie go. It was difficult for both of us.

Ultimately, the series employed three editors: David Hanser, Pat Cook, and Ken Werner. A large part of whatever distinction the series has is due to their skill as editors and to their decency and compassion as human beings.

Notes

1. There were two departments at NET: the Cultural Affairs Department, headed by Curt Davis, which produced shows having to do with the arts, history, literature, music, etc.; and the Public Affairs Department, headed by Don Dixon, which produced shows on politics, social

issues, and topical news subjects. "Priorities for Change" was to have been produced by the Public Affairs Department, which several months earlier had been responsible for an NET Journal called *Banks and the Poor* and an installment of "The Great American Dream Machine," in which there was a segment on the FBI. Both these shows had brought the full fury of the Nixon administration down on NET. I have a hunch that one of the reasons, but certainly not the only one, that Jim Day had given the go-ahead to *An American Family* and that the Corporation for Public Broadcasting had agreed so rapidly was a desire to shy away from any programming that could in any way be considered controversial. I am sure no one expected any trouble from what promised to be an innocuous series about an American family.

2. In an article entitled "Spy Drama," an unnamed writer in the March 5, 1973, issue of *The Nation* had this to say: "Further, anthropologists have long known that even the most tactful and unobtrusive intervention in the life of a social microcosm significantly changes the phenomena under observation; so that if one wished to generalize from the behavior of the peculiarly uncritical Louds, it would be necessary to ask first how natural was the presence of Gilbert, his camera crew, microphones, lights, reflectors and yards of black cable curling sinuously through the living quarters?"

3. For those whose ideas of how a *cinéma vérité* team works have been formed by movies and television, it should be noted that the new 16mm technology has eliminated the old slate/clapsticks method of identifying the shot and providing a sync mark for the editor. To start shooting, the sound person simply flashes a light, which is recorded as a beep when the tape is rolling; the cameraperson photographs this light and continues shooting. All the editor has to do is line up the beep on the sound tape with the light on the film and he is "in sync." This effectively eliminates the necessity of an assistant's standing up in front of the camera with a small blackboard and announcing, "*An American Family*, scene 10, take 1," and then clapping the sticks; it can be done so unobtrusively that it is sometimes hard to tell when shooting is actually taking place.

4. In a memo dated June 10, 1972, to a WNET/13 executive, which accompanied our list of episodes, I wrote ". . . this does not mean, by any stretch of the imagination, that this is the correct structure or the proper breakdown of the material. All it represents is our best guess as to how to solve the problem. I know that you are aware of this, but I am still reacting to the knowledge that—for a long time around here—guesses tended, in a remarkably short time, to be regarded as positive statements of opinion. . . . The only positive statements I or anyone else will be able to make about the structure will come out of working with the material in the cutting room."

5. In an article which appeared in the *New York Times* on January 22, 1973, John J. O'Connor, the television critic, succinctly explained the background and nature of the problem:

> *An American Family* began as a project of NET. Curtis W. Davis, no longer with public television, receives credit as executive producer. Last year, however, the New York operation was given a new executive regime headed by John Jay Iselin, now acting president of WNET/13, and Robert Kotlowitz, senior executive editor.
>
> As the programming focus switched from national to local levels, the nationally oriented NET was absorbed into WNET. Mr. Iselin and Mr. Kotlowitz were then faced with a decision on what to do about the 300 hours of material already filmed but not yet edited for *An American Family*. At one point it was thought 8 hours might be enough. Mr. Gilbert objected strongly, and the 12-hour format was accepted by all parties.
>
> Now Mr. Gilbert says that as the editing evolved, it became apparent that 12 hours would be inadequate for his creative purposes. Under the old NET regime, in which the film maker frequently prevailed, the producer may have had his way. But the current WNET management, acutely more concerned about costs and limited funds, insists it is not about to be swayed.
>
> The result is a classic illustration of the broadcaster versus the film maker, the editor versus the creator.

6. The first half of episode 1 covered New Year's Eve at the Louds' house at 35 Woodale Lane. The kids are having a party and at one point Lance calls from New York to wish his brothers and sister Happy New Year. We hear his voice but don't see him. We briefly see Bill, who has been living in a motel for three months. Halfway through episode 1 (as the kids and their guest are singing "Auld Lang Syne" to Pat) there is a slow dissolve to the entire family having breakfast seven months earlier. The narration says, "Our story begins on a bright spring day in late May."

From that point on we planned to move chronologically from the end of May to New Year's Eve again. The New Year's Eve footage in the final episode would have been some of the same that was used in episode 1. But there would have been new footage of how Lance spent his New Year's Eve in New York, including the circumstances under which he made the call to his family. And although there was a little footage in episode 1 of how Bill was spending his New Year's Eve, there would have been a lot more in the final episode, including a phone call which he received from Lance while having drinks at the home of the boutique manager.

Two Laws from Australia, One White, One Black

James Roy MacBean

The Recent Past and the Challenging Future of Ethnographic Film

Recently, a new documentary film dealing with Australian Aboriginal peoples and their historical struggles to preserve (or win back) their traditional lands has been screened in the United States, mostly on the West Coast but also in New York City, where it was presented in October at the 1982 Margaret Mead Film Festival. Completed in 1981, *Two Laws* is a feature-length documentary that succeeds both in being informative and in undercutting many of our expectations regarding ethnographic films in particular, and documentary films in general.

Already hailed in Australia, where its subject matter—Aboriginal land rights— is considered politically controversial, *Two Laws* was nominated for (although it did not win) the Australian Film Institute's 1982 award for best documentary. At a running time of two hours and ten minutes, *Two Laws* is an ambitious, complex, problematic film that was made *collectively* (and I mean this word quite literally and rigorously) by two white Australian filmmakers, Alessandro Cavadini and Caroline Strachan, and the Borroloola Aboriginal community from the remote Gulf of Carpentaria region of Australia's Northern Territory.

The questions raised by *Two Laws* will have to be taken seriously in ethnographic film circles, and elsewhere as well, if for no other reason (but there are others) than the fact that this is a film, unlike 99.9 percent of ethnographic films,[1] in which the traditional (or tribal) peoples themselves collectively controlled the decision-making processes of what to film and how to film it—

even down to what lens to use on the camera. That the results, cinematically, look so different from what we are accustomed to seeing in even the "best" ethnographic films up to now certainly causes us to sit up and take notice, and to raise questions (and doubts) about how ethnographic filmmakers have been proceeding.

International Ethnographic Film Conference, 1978, Canberra, Australia

In addition to raising important questions, *Two Laws* may also provide at least a tentative answer to a question posed in 1978 at the International Ethnographic Film Conference, which I attended, in Canberra, Australia. This conference was a major event in ethnographic film circles: it had strong participation from—and reverberations among—Australia's Aboriginal peoples; and several of the individuals who subsequently went on to collaborate on the film *Two Laws* participated in this conference; so it seems important to offer, by way of background, a summary of the way various issues in ethnographic film were discussed at this lively and seminal conference.

One conference participant, Roger Sandall (himself an ethnographic filmmaker in Australia) reported in *Sight and Sound* (Autumn 1978) on the remarkable and volatile mix of people gathered from around the globe at this conference— a mix that included not only ethnographic filmmakers and anthropologists but also, for a change, various representatives of the traditional peoples the ethnographers usually study. Of course, most conferences, as Colin Young (who featured prominently in this one) has recently pointed out, are really about *power*. Young, head of Britain's National Film School, puts the issues this way:

> Go to most conferences, and the subject, no matter what is on the agenda, is power. Which methodology is going to win out? People invest in their methods to the exclusion of others. The method defines you, and you it. If I criticize your method I harm you. It's a way of saying that I don't like you. . . . Supporters of a methodology are racist with respect to all others.[2]

At the 1978 conference, *power* was certainly very much at issue. Indeed, it was even placed on the official agenda by the conference conveners, David and Judith MacDougall—eminent ethnographic filmmakers themselves, and resident directors of the Film Unit of the Australian Institute of Aboriginal Studies, which hosted the conference. Sympathetic with Aboriginal peoples' increasingly vociferous demands to be provided access to the media and to the means of film and television *production*, the MacDougalls had scheduled a session in the conference agenda to explore these issues. However, the amount of time allotted was not considered sufficient by many invited participants, who requested, and were granted, a session on these issues, which was scheduled for the final day of the conference.

Before that final day, the struggle for power was carried out in the territory staked out by Colin Young—that of rival documentary film methodologies. As the conference's senior statesman, Young presented the opening salvo, offering his own summary of documentary film history. Young spoke of the accomplishments but mainly of the dangers and limitations of the Grierson approach ("too polemical and didactic"); of the virtues of the Flaherty approach ("he got close to his subjects"); of the fundamental flaws in Robert Gardner's filmic strategies in *Dead Birds* ("he *tells* us on the sound track information not substantiated by the image"); and of the refreshingly participatory filmic strategies of Jean Rouch ("in *Turou et Bitti* the filmmaker almost functions as the combustion element in a ritual leading to trance").

In addition, Young turned over the podium briefly to Timothy Asch, who delivered homage to John Marshall for his longstanding dedication to filming the Kung Bushmen of the Kalahari. (Asch, a former associate of Marshall's, has gone on to make a number of important films on the Yanomamo of the Orinoco Basin in collaboration with anthropologist Napoleon Chagnon.) Finally, Young also spoke of the breakthroughs made in the early sixties by the practitioners, mostly French, Canadian, and American, of *cinéma vérité*.

All this could be taken as uncontroversial documentary film "history"; but there was also a tendentious side to Young's presentation. As he totted up the assets and liabilities of each documentary approach, Young wove a clearly discernible thread of apparent historical "progress" into the chaotic fabric of documentary film history, in such a way that, in his account, it would seem to reach some at-least-for-the-present optimum realization of its potential (and, implicitly, of its "realist vocation") in the contemporary methodology of what Young calls "observational cinema."

This approach consists of a refined version of *cinéma vérité*'s ability to use lightweight, unobtrusive equipment and a minimal crew (often only two persons) to film long takes in synchronous sound of the ordinary interactions and conversations of people going about their regular daily lives. It is demonstrated, Young asserted, in the films of David and Judith MacDougall as well as in the "Vermont Conversations" series by Hancock and DiGioia (and in their film *Naim and Jabar* for the "Faces of Change" project), and in Roger Graef's studies of decision making for the two British television series "The Space Between Words" and "Decisions."

As Colin Young would be the first to admit, there is a decidedly "incestuous" cast to the lineup he proposes under the rubric of "observational cinema." The MacDougalls, Hancock, and DiGioia all got their starts in film as students in the ethnographic film program started by Young (and Walter Goldschmidt) at UCLA in the late sixties. Of course, the community of filmmakers, anthropologists, and other scholars involved in the world of ethnographic film is a fairly small one in any case. We have all known one another from way back. I have known the MacDougalls as close friends for about twenty years, and I have known Colin Young (through the MacDougalls) nearly as long. Friendship notwithstanding, I would have no hesitation in picking the MacDougalls' films (from their first, *To Live with Herds*, right up to their latest films dealing with Australian Aboriginal peoples) as representing the best of contemporary tendencies in ethnographic film. However, I must take issue with Colin Young on one point, because I am not convinced (nor was I at the 1978 conference) that the complex filmic strategies employed by the MacDougalls are done justice by the term *observational cinema*. (I shall deal with these issues in the following section of this essay.)

Where Young's historical survey of documentary film at the conference is concerned, Bill Nichols pointed out in his remarks to the conference that while Young's presentation had been interesting as a personal account of how he, Young, and presumably others had found their own paths through the thicket of documentary methodologies, the thicket itself had not really been cleared for cultivation on solid theoretical ground; and the discussions were strangely devoid of recourse to recent developments in film theory, communications theory, or anthropology itself.

Indeed, it became clear in ensuing days that what was being presented was a low-keyed, disarmingly attractive yet tendentious version of both the history and the present situation of ethnographic film—as seen by proponents of one particular school of documentary methodology. The morning after Young's opening presentation, the mantle was passed to James Blue, a longtime friend and associate of both Young and the MacDougalls, who announced that his contribution would be to demonstrate in more detail, and with specific illustrations, the general line set out by Young's opening talk. Blue's presentation emphasized the virtues of Robert Flaherty's filmic strategies, exemplified by a seal hunting sequence from Flaherty's *Nanook*, which was projected side-by-side with a sequence (also showing seal hunting) from Asen Balikci's Netsilik Eskimo series of films.

Blue's argument was that Balikci, although one of our contemporary ethnographic filmmakers, had reverted to an older, anachronistic, and more "didactic" style of shooting and editing ethnographic film. Blue's comparison of the two sequences was all to the favor of Flaherty, who was credited with simply letting the action unfold in front of the camera instead of breaking the action up into different edited pieces shot from different camera angles.

The only trouble—and Blue, sensing this, got off to an awkward and somewhat nervous start—was that the morning's audience wasn't ready to buy this praise of Flaherty, at least partly because the previous evening's conference event had turned into a tumultuous debate, touched off by a screening of Flaherty's

1934 film *Man of Aran*, followed by George Stoney's just-completed documentary exploration, *Robert Flaherty's "Man of Aran": How the Myth Was Made*. Stoney's film, while appreciative of Flaherty's genius for poetic imagery, had popped the lid off all the distortions and omissions in Flaherty's highly romanticized depiction of life on the Aran Islands off Ireland.

Many in the audience at the conference's premiere screening of Stoney's revelatory documentary had been incensed at what they now saw to be Flaherty's falsification of the life he had purported to be documenting. Particularly troublesome was Flaherty's total lack of interest in the actual sociopolitical affairs of the Islanders, who, in his film, are represented by only three people—significantly, a nuclear family of man, wife, and son—whose highly romanticized struggle for survival in an awesomely inhospitable Nature becomes the "whole" picture.

On this issue Stoney's film effectively documents how distorted—and *politically* skewed—is Flaherty's depiction of the allegedly arid and inhospitable soil of the Aran Islands. Showing us the very same rugged, rocky terrain that Flaherty had filmed, Stoney then makes a small pan with his camera to show that with this simple camera movement one can see the lush, fertile agricultural landholdings that were in Flaherty's day and still are in the hands of a few absentee landlords. The richest of these, Stoney observes, had in fact turned over his baronial house, the largest on the islands, to the Flahertys, where the filmmaker and his wife, Frances, had enjoyed a quasi-feudal relationship to the impoverished islanders during their stay.

Such revelations as these had made their points with the conference audience. In Flaherty's retreat from the realities of the contemporary situation in favor of a highly romanticized vision of ways of life no longer practiced, many conference participants saw a betrayal of documentary film's mission to "show it like it is." Small wonder, then, that James Blue (whose death in 1980 is a loss to us all) met with such resistance when he valiantly went ahead with his presentation of the virtues of Flaherty's filmic strategies. He prefaced his remarks with an account of how he too, like others in the audience, had been influenced by his years studying film in the heady political milieu of Paris; how he too had gone through a phase of politicization during which he sought to root out all traces of "fascist" film style from his filmmaking repertory; and how he too had wanted, indeed still wanted, to make films that were politically constructive. But gradually he had discovered, he told us, that Flaherty's way of letting the camera simply observe what was happening had seemed to him the most honest and direct way to get at the larger truth and complexity of a situation.

It was all very affably, albeit defensively, put by Blue, and there was much to consider in what he said. And yet, to many in the audience, Blue's championing of Flaherty, and his treatment of his own "politicized phase" as if it were merely a childhood stage one outgrew, smacked of an attempt to take the edge off any politically activist approach to documentary filmmaking. At least this is how it was "read" by many of the young Australian documentary filmmakers present, who also construed it as a pitch to tone down the political element in their films to make them more acceptable to the potential television market, which, according to both Young and Blue, was ready to open its doors to ethnographic film.

The possibility of television distribution, however, was perceived by the Australians to be the proverbial carrot held out in front of the horse who allows himself to be fitted with blinders. The modest success in Great Britain of Brian Moser's "Disappearing World" series of ethnographic films for Granada Television was hardly persuasive, especially when Granada's representatives to the Canberra conference acknowledged that very few of the "Disappearing World" films had taken up in any way the vital *political* issues of why so many (but not all) tribal or traditional societies are in danger of "disappearing" in today's world.

To many conference participants, the single-minded emphasis on an "observational" camera style (coupled with an apparent insensitivity to the political dynamics of ethnographic filmmaking) began to wear very thin, and a current of reaction set in against the "house style" proposed by Young and Blue. Filmmakers Cavadini and Strachan, for example, later expressed their frustration with the apolitical approach that dominated the early days of the conference.

> We've been amazed at the way ethnographic filmmakers deny that their films are political. This denial is enforced by a claim that the camera in particular is neutral and observational; but what is in fact produced are visions of the exotic or the romantic. This came out very strongly at the Canberra conference. There is an explicit lack of theorising about the politics of going into and disrupting a community, or taking information and images from one society to be exploited by another.[3]

Moreover, there were problems, many of us at the conference felt, with the argument James Blue developed in his comparison of the Flaherty and Balikci footage. To present an alternative view, I pointed out that one could argue that Balikci's way of breaking a complicated process (of seal hunting) into different shots taken from different camera angles at least had the merits of (1) revealing details of the action that might not be visible or noticed from one single camera position and (2) openly acknowledging the filmmaking process—of selecting camera angles, of shooting, of editing, etc.—at the same time as it explored the Eskimo's process of seal hunting. In short, Balikci's filmic strategies (including his avoidance of omniscient narration on the sound track) could be credited with being both *process-oriented* and *self-reflexive*.

By contrast, I observed, Flaherty's filmic strategies in the seal hunting sequence from *Nanook* could be seen as mystifying the processes both of seal hunting and of filming. Flaherty sets up his camera in advance at a small hole in the ice, toward which Nanook is seen to make his way from the distant background, as if searching the ice floe for telltale signs of the presence of a seal's airhole. Thus, in effect, Flaherty gives the camera the classic privileged narrator's point of view that implies—but does not openly acknowledge—the godlike omniscience of the filmmaker while reinforcing the seemingly un-impeachable authority of the information provided by the image. Such an "impression of reality" was especially problematic, I argued, in the case of Flaherty. After all, in *Nanook*, as in *Man of Aran*, the apparent "reality" being filmed is an extremely contrived reenactment of ways of life that were never quite as romantic as Flaherty makes them out to be, and which are *not*, in any case, the ways of life of the contemporary people he is actually filming.

Moreover, even if the viewer does not notice that Flaherty's camera has been set up in advance at the very spot Nanook eventually "discovers," there is ample evidence to tip off the fact that this entire sequence is staged for the camera. At Flaherty's urging, no doubt, Nanook hams up his demonstration of the process of spearing a seal through the breathing-hole in the ice. In fact, the scene is turned into slapstick comedy, with Nanook ostensibly being tugged this way and that by the not yet visible seal beneath the ice. Finally, when the seal is ultimately hauled up through the ice, it is so obviously long dead—and apparently frozen solid—that the entire sequence becomes ridiculous.

At the Canberra conference, the appearance of the dead seal was greeted with great hoots of laughter. Jokes were made of "the observational style of filming a frozen-seal hunt." Soon nearly everyone was taking pot shots at observational cinema and at Flaherty—with Blue and Young still valiantly attempting to defend their position. Finally, the session was adjourned, but many participants kept right on arguing the issues, moving in for the kill, wielding their small personal tape recorders like weapons as they endeavored to pin down, for the record, their respective antagonists. At this point, the event was laughingly dubbed "the battle of the tape recorders"—a battle of ritual warfare enacted by a strange and exotic tribe of academics and media professionals. In a verbal play on the title of James Blue's own latest film, *Who Killed Third Ward?* (about redevelopment in Houston, Texas), it was jocularly suggested that a sequel to the conference be planned, under the prospective title "Who Killed Observational Cinema?"

This is the question I alluded to at the beginning of this article—the question to which the 1981 film *Two Laws* provides at least a tentative answer. Of course, one film, even such a probing and forceful film as *Two Laws*, does not by itself bring about the imminent demise of observational cinema. Nor would I wish for its demise. I am confident that there will continue to be a place (or, rather, certain types of ethnographic and documentary situations) where the filmic strategies associated with observational cinema will still be fruitfully employed. However, what *Two Laws* may be instrumental in laying to rest is a notion of observational cinema as a panacea that could cure all the infirmities of ethnographic or documentary filmmaking.

Unfortunately, it was this more ambitious and hegemonic view that seemed to be promulgated at the 1978 conference. Doubtless sobered by that conference, and looking even further back at the formative years of observational cinema, Young now offers what amounts to his own *mea culpa*: "Without knowing it very specifically at the time, we were preparing our methodology, which we would develop, refine and then practice—to the exclusion of others."[4]

Even in his *mea culpa*, however, Young may be drastically overstating things when he implies that observational cinema was practiced, by *filmmakers*, to the exclusion of all other methodologies. Fortunately, filmmakers—even those touted by Young as leading practitioners of observational cinema, such as the MacDougalls—have been more sanguine and open-minded about what they were doing. As far back as 1971, when Colin Young was writing a manifesto-like essay entitled "Observational Cinema" for Paul Hockings's anthology *Principles of Visual Anthropology*, David MacDougall was writing for the same anthology a more probing and exploratory essay entitled "Beyond Observational Cinema." More important, the *films* of the MacDougalls have always manifested a healthy multiplicity of filmic strategies.

Beyond Observational Cinema: The Films of David and Judith MacDougall

Much attention has been given (in print as well as at the 1978 conference) to the MacDougalls' innovative decision to dispense with the old documentary crutch of a running voice-over commentary and to rely instead on subtitled translations of native-language dialogue filmed in sync sound as normal tribal life unfolds. It has often been overlooked, however, that a MacDougall film typically presents a great variety of different kinds of filmic material, by no means all of which is "observational." In fact, the observational cinema label has always seemed to me too constricting a term to apply to the complex filmic strategies of the MacDougalls.

Their earliest film, *To Live with Herds* (1968–69), for example, offers, in addition to "observed" sequences involving interaction between two or more Jie tribespeople, other sequences in which only one tribal subject is present and the interaction involves a dialogue between him or her and the filmmakers. Sometimes this dialogue is clearly instigated by the filmmakers, who are heard on the sound track asking specific questions. At other times, a Jie man or woman will talk nonchalantly while doing some chore, "addressing" the filmmakers in an informal way, as if picking up the thread of some ongoing conversation. Moreover, *To Live with Herds* makes liberal use of informational intertitles. To purists of observational cienma these would be considered didactic and anachronistic. But the MacDougalls prefer to acknowledge that there are limits to the observational approach and that certain kinds of information simply cannot be "caught" by observational means. And while they dispense with the running voice-over commentary of the sort that used to guide us through so many documentary films, the MacDougalls, in *To Live with Herds*, purposely utilize occasional bits and pieces of voice-over commentary in which David speaks in the first person, acknowledging the filmmakers' presence and their active role in certain interactions with their tribal subjects.

In the MacDougalls' now-completed "Turkana Conversations" trilogy (*The Wedding Camels, Lorang's Way*, and *A Wife Among Wives*—which they filmed in Kenya during 1973–74 and edited between 1978 and 1981), a similarly rich variety of filmic strategies is employed. In *A Wife Among Wives* the MacDougalls actually utilize quite a lot of voice-over commentary. It is not, however, the old Olympian "voice of authority" commentary. Rather, it is the commentary of someone there on the spot, incorporating bits of fieldnotes and journals into the film (sometimes visually as well as aurally), and yet undercutting any claims to omniscience, as the filmmakers openly communicate to us some of the dilemmas, doubts, hesitations, and false steps they encountered in their fieldwork and filming.

There is in fact a crucial difference between this occasional first-person commentary and the old-style commentary of the "omniscient narrator"; and, incidentally, it is a difference Colin Young seems to ignore when, writing in 1982, he asks disparagingly, "Is it because documentary fell into the hands of the teachers, propagandists and 'communicators' that the first-person narrator rules supreme?"[5] *Pace*, Colin, but isn't this the pot calling the kettle black? Moreover, it has *not* been first-person commentary that has ruled supreme in documentary films. In fact, it still doesn't.[6] What did rule supreme in older documentaries was the omniscient narrator, the studio voice (often that of a professional actor) which told us everything we needed to know [*sic*], which somehow got into every character's head and told us what they were thinking— the voice which, in John Marshall's *The Hunters*, not only knows what the Bushmen are thinking as they try to deduce from the tracks where the giraffe they have wounded might be, but knows also where the giraffe is and what is going through the giraffe's head at the same moment!

In summary, what is innovative about the MacDougalls' films is precisely that they get away from the "voice of authority" of the omniscient narrator and establish instead the direct, open acknowledgment of their presence and their active first-person presentation of the different sorts of filmic material that comprise their films. To put it another way, it seems to me that the MacDougalls are not practicing a documentary cinema that is primarily ob-servational and narrative in nature, as has been touted, but rather that they are combining elements (some observational, some not) in a *collage* or mosaic pattern whose overall logic is less that of the narrative than that of the *audiovisual first-person essay*. In point of fact, their films usually have only a weak narrative (*To Live with Herds, Kenya Boran, Lorang's Way*, and *A Wife Among Wives*); but even where there is a strong narrative, as in *The Wedding Camels*, the MacDougalls constantly remind us of their own interactions with people during the events being filmed and of their own structuring of the material in the editing.

The point about ethnographic filmmakers acknowledging their own interactions with the people being filmed is a crucial one—and in this respect the MacDougalls' work is so exemplary that I think it could even be said to pave the way for the kind of collective creation (across cultures) represented by *Two Laws*. For example, in *A Wife Among Wives* the MacDougalls openly discuss with the Turkana such questions as "If you were making a film about Turkana life, what would you film?" And when this tack gets nowhere (the Turkana answer, "I don't know anything about that. You're the filmmakers."), the MacDougalls turn the tables on themselves and ask the Turkana what they would film of white or "European" society if they had a chance—to which the Turkana reply, "We would not know what to film about you if we had the cameras. We would not understand properly." But a moment later, the same Turkana woman, after some reflection, says, "I would film your things, your boxes, your cups and saucers, your clothes, beads as beautiful as ours; I'd film your Land Rover." And a bit later, given a Super 8 camera to use, she does just that, filming the interior of the MacDougalls' temporary house while David films her filming—the two cameras shooting simultaneously, and their respective footages intercut in the editing to give us a feel and a visual record of this particular interaction between two cultures.

While in *A Wife Among Wives* (and filming among the Turkana generally) this approach may not go very far, this should not, I think, be taken as mere "tokenism" on the MacDougalls' part. Rather, it demonstrates, I believe, their openness to explore the ethnographic filmmaking situation beyond the narrow paths set out by any one methodology which might make claims to exclusivity. In this respect, the MacDougalls don't even want to claim exclusivity for the views presented in their films—which views could come, if the tribal or "traditional" subjects were willing, as much if not more from *them* as from the MacDougalls.

Interestingly, this latter is exactly what seems to be happening in the films the MacDougalls have been making recently in Australia. Working with Australian Aboriginal people, the MacDougalls have made a number of films that bear little resemblance to their films from African pastoralist societies. In three films completed in 1980 (*Takeover, Familiar Places,* and *The House-Opening*), the MacDougalls rely less and less on "observational" material of the everyday life of their ethnographic subjects, and they concentrate increasingly on aspects of the Australian Aboriginal people's ongoing struggle to retain their culture and to regain their lands. In these films, as in several others, the MacDougalls are in fact devoting themselves to subjects which the Aboriginal people themselves have requested that they film. Often these films explore controversial issues. *Takeover*, for example, functions almost as a piece of hard-hitting investigative journalism, exposing the hypocritical double-dealing of the Australian federal government in its handling of jurisdictional disputes with the state of Queensland over the Aboriginal community at Aurukun.

When I asked the MacDougalls, in a public discussion of their films at the Margaret Mead Film Festival, how they would account for the striking differences in style between their African films and their Australian films, they replied that the Australian Aboriginal people, unlike the Turkana or Jie or Boran of East Africa, are already quite acculturated to Western ways. The East African pastoralists paid little heed to the filming process precisely because the prospect of having a film made about their way of life meant little to them; they foresaw no *use*, to themselves, for such a film. On the other hand, the Australian Aboriginal people, acutely aware of the potential uses (to them or to others) of film and the media in general, assert themselves quite actively in delineating what they want filmed.

This, of course, was one of the things that came out at the 1978 conference in Canberra, when Aboriginal people emphasized quite militantly that they want to gain access to equipment and to instruction that will enable them to start making films themselves about their own struggles and the cultural issues that concern them. Which brings us, at long last, up to the making of the film *Two Laws*.

Two Laws: The Theory and Practice of Ethnographic Film

Having voiced their demands loud and clear at the 1978 Canberra conference, and having obtained from the Institute of Aboriginal Studies a strengthened commitment to proceed faster in providing Aboriginal people access to equipment and to filmmaking instruction, Australia's Aboriginal people also intensified their efforts to enlist some of Australia's white documentary filmmakers to work with the black communities in making films that would *express* rather than merely *observe* Aboriginal culture. Many Aboriginal communities initiated requests for films to be made, and many of these requests were directed to David and Judith MacDougall in their roles as director and assistant director of the Film Unit of the Institute of Aboriginal Studies.

Already heavily involved in making a series of films requested by the Aurukun Aboriginal community (which has been in the center of Australia's most controversial political struggles over land rights, mining rights, and conflicts of federal and state jurisdiction), the MacDougalls and their staff simply couldn't handle all the requests for films coming from various Aboriginal communities.

However, the Borroloola people were determined that they wanted to make a film dealing with the history of their community. Leo Finlay had seen *Protected*, a film on the Palm Island Aboriginal community made collectively by two white Australian filmmakers, Alessandro Cavadini and Caroline Strachan, in collaboration with the Palm Island community. *Protected* was a very impressive film; so Leo Finlay paid a visit to Cavadini and Strachan in Sydney and asked them to help in making a film on the Borroloola community. Cavadini and Strachan accepted the invitation, went to Borroloola, and spent the first two months traveling from one Aboriginal settlement or camp to another, learning their proper "skin" or kinship relation within the Borroloola Aboriginal society, and discussing what sort of film the Aboriginal people wanted to make.

From the beginning, it was clear what the general outline of the film was to be. The Borroloola community wanted to provide a historical background to their insistence that their Aboriginal system of law was, in fact, just that— a system of law which regulated their interactions with one another and with land and property. This was important, they felt, because preliminary hearings in land rights cases during the seventies had demonstrated that white judges tended to discount Aboriginal land claims based on Aboriginal tradition whenever they were in conflict with land claims based on leases, titles, and contracts recognized by white law.

Even before commencing filming, Cavadini and Strachan found that the Aboriginal sense of "law" pervaded everything the Borroloola community did. When Cavadini and Strachan arranged evening screenings of films dealing with land rights issues, the next morning there would be a formal meeting, according to Aboriginal law, where the community would collectively discuss the previous night's films, debate their strengths and weaknesses, and explore their potential use, to them and to their film, of this or that stylistic approach. Gradually, in this way, the community collectively planned what it wanted to film and how it wanted to film it.

Cavadini and Strachan gradually realized that this traditional collective decision-making process was itself a fundamental feature of Aboriginal law, that "leaders" were only ceremonial figures, and that, correlatively, the formal community meeting could provide the structural base of the film. Once this was decided, it became obvious how these formal meetings were to be filmed. As Cavadini and Strachan explain it,

> Because there isn't any television and few films had been seen, the people were unfamiliar with the whole of Western film culture, so their ideas came largely from Aboriginal structure. For instance, when we got down to filming there was automatically only one position for the camera and one position for the sound recordist—because everyone has their place in a highly structured spatial ar-

rangement. Men sit in one position, women in another, and each individual sits with particular relatives. So the determinations had to do with the tribal structure in which the film fitted as opposed to being outside it.[7]

Moreover, as Cavadini and Strachan point out, not only camera and sound positions were engendered by Aboriginal sense of law and structure, but also even the choice of what lens to use on the camera was engendered this way.

> During those first two months we did do a number of tests to try out different ideas, and the choice was made to shoot the entire film with a wide-angle lens. It was the one that people responded to and liked. With a wide-angle lens you can include much more in the shot than with a standard lens, but it's not so appropriate for close-ups. If someone wants to make a statement, others have to be present to make that statement possible—to confirm or contradict it. Sometimes there was disagreement between people, but it's presented as a group discussion as opposed to one individual being the authority.[8]

The title, it was decided, should be *Two Laws*, and the film should begin with a shot of a formal meeting where Leo Finlay introduces Cavadini and Strachan by saying simply, "I think you know these two, Alessandro and Caroline; they're going to help us make a film, and it's our film so let's make a good film." The camera, with its wide-angle lens, pans right to left across the seated community at the formal meeting, men on one side, women on the other; and as the camera completes its pan we even see the sound recordist— a woman, Caroline—in her designated place alongside the Borroloola women.

The film overall is divided into four parts, arranged chronologically (although with some overlaps) into sections called "Police Times," "Welfare Times," "Struggle for Our Land," and "Living with Two Laws." "Police Times" deals with the situation in the thirties, a period still vividly remembered by a few older members of the Borroloola community but largely unknown to most younger community members, who only learned of these times and events in the process of making the film.

Although "Police Times" focuses on one particular event that happened in 1933, especially as this event is recalled—and reenacted—by people who participated in it, there is a sense in which the present community's effort to grasp an understanding of its past is far more important than a reconstituting of the past. As Cavadini and Strachan explain it,

> The way Aboriginal people approach history is very different from the way we see history as located firmly in the past. People talk about history in the present tense, use the first person, employ dialogue, reenact events. In everyday life people tell stories that happened yesterday or happened one hundred years ago.[9]

The task of retelling the past—specifically, the events of 1933, as characteristic of those times—is carried out in a complex, sophisticated combination of oral history (storytelling) and reenactment *plus analytical commentary* on both the telling and the acting-out of history. Moreover, the reenactment includes its own *self-reflexive* component of *analysis*, for the reenactment is presented in a way that emphasizes the group process of playacting. Aboriginal community members sit in rows on the ground as the camera pans or tracks to pause as each one introduces himself by saying, "My name is X, and I'm playing the part of Dolly," or Doris, and so on.

Furthermore, although they filmed enough reenactment footage to comprise a ninety-minute drama film, the Borroloola community decided not to go that route, preferring, for political reasons, to emphasize the overall *context* of events rather than the events themselves. Finally, the 1933 events—a forced march of Aboriginal people who were rounded up by one Constable Stott, who beat them into a forced confession of killing and eating a bullock owned by a white rancher—were judged too brutal in their depiction of violence to be used in the finished film. So it was decided instead to emphasize the acting-out strategy, to film stylized and symbolic expressions of the violence enacted upon Aboriginal people. Thus, there are scenes where the white actor "playing" Constable Stott symbolically lowers his stick slowly across the back of an Aboriginal man instead of bashing him with it, or slowly applies his stick first to one side of an Aboriginal woman, then to the other, to indicate the brutal beating which resulted in her death. And in another scene, an old Aboriginal man describes how he was beaten across the back, first one way, then the other; then he grabs a stick and proceeds to demonstrate how he was beaten by bashing a tree first this way, then the other. "Finally," he says, "I was forced to confess. 'Yep,' I told him, 'I ate that bullock, ate the whole thing!' "

The Aboriginal people's sense of humor is evident in many moments of *Two Laws*, as they laugh in retrospect about what they had to endure in the past, and as they revel in the chance now to recall and act out what they have experienced. This is most evident in the second part, "Welfare Times," where a group of Aboriginal women discuss with a white woman how the latter should play her part as a welfare administrator. Rehearsing a scene where the Aboriginal women have to present themselves for inspection, they coach the white woman on the lines the welfare administrator should speak. Running through the scene, the welfare woman speaks her lines in an impressively convincing way, and the Aboriginal women remark, "Yes, that's just the way they would talk to us; and we would just stand there and look down at our feet, not daring to speak a word."

But immediately after this remark there is a cut to another take of this same scene, with the Aboriginal women presenting themselves for inspection and the white woman saying, "Good morning, have you all washed today? If you're nice and clean and if your children are nice and clean then you'll get a pretty dress for being good girls. And you'll get clothes for the children too. But if you're not clean or if your hair is untidy, then you'll not get anything until you've fixed yourself up properly." And here, in this take, the Aboriginal women are shown laughing at the whole scene, dramatizing, in effect, both what used to happen to them and the distance they have come in asserting themselves.

The welfare system, as they see it, was blatantly assimilationist. By way of introducing "Welfare Times," one Aboriginal woman reads a passage from the government's submission to the Land Claims Court, which reads as follows: "The year 1953 was the beginning of the Welfare Ordinance. Its aim was to direct and encourage the re-establishment of the Aborigines, that they would eventually be assimilated as an integral part of the Australian community"— to which the Aboriginal woman adds, looking directly into the camera, "Which means that they wanted us to be like white people."

While assimilation was certainly the Australian government's long-term plan for the Aboriginal population (paralleling the U.S. government's position on native Americans), at least as important was the short-term urgency of getting the Aboriginal people out of the way of the white mining interests that wanted access to the country's vast mineral deposits. In *Two Laws*, the Borroloola Aboriginal community recounts—and reenacts—how they were suddenly told that their welfare station and the entire Aboriginal community would have to move to Robinson River, several hours away by truck. There was no consultation involved; they were just told to pack their things, and a government truck was provided to carry them and their possessions. Only later did they find out that large mining interests had obtained a lease on huge tracts of land around Borroloola and had insisted on the Aboriginal community's removal to make way for the vast Mt. Isa Mines operations.

The notion of two different legal concepts of land tenure (one black, one white) is best brought out by the third part of the film, "Struggle for Our Land." Interestingly, there is one sequence in this section which is filmed utilizing what might be called an observational approach. It involves a conversation between a white Australian laborer (a recent immigrant from Yugoslavia) and an Aboriginal man who is protesting that the white laborer, by razing hundreds of trees along a dirt roadway, has both diminished the Aboriginal food supply (they eat the fruit of this particular tree) and, more important, desecrated a sacred site which had been entrusted, ceremonially, to his particular custodianship, or *djunkai*.

The conversation is filmed in sync sound and long takes, and since both men are speaking English, there is no need for subtitling of dialogue. The white laborer questions the black man's ability to prove his "ownership" of the land. "Do you have a title to the land?" he asks. The Aboriginal man responds that when the white men came, they just took the land and didn't bother with titles. The white laborer then retorts that land wasn't always just taken, that sometimes blacks actually sold land to the whites. "Can you prove," he asks, "that your father, or his father, didn't sell that land to the whites?"

Pausing for a moment, the white laborer then continues, "And if that land was sold to the whites, then what would happen now if the government or the land claims court decided to give that land back to the blacks? Who would pay back the money to the whites that they had originally paid the blacks for that land?" The Aboriginal man reflects on these questions for several minutes, then shakes his head stoically, observing that "you're still just thinking in white people's terms about all this."

The point is well taken, although it would be nice if the Aboriginal terms of communal land tenure—as opposed to private property—had been spelled out more explicitly. Apparently, this is exactly what happens when the finished film is shown to audiences of other Aboriginal communities throughout Australia: they actually leap to their feet at this moment in the film and start discussing loudly exactly what *they* would have said to that white laborer. And even within the film we see the way the filmmaking process offers material for further work and reflection, as we later see several Aboriginal women activists listening, with ear phones, to the sound tape of that particular conversation— which stirs them to compose a letter offering *their* response to the white laborer. In short, even the observational sequence is clearly and firmly placed in the overall context of a process initiated and carried through by the Aboriginal community itself—a process that involves the members in making a film in the first place, because they are above all involved in a political struggle to retain—or to regain—their traditional land.

Keeping the political context in mind, the Aboriginal community is able to incorporate into *Two Laws* some footage of traditional rituals and ceremonial dances, but in such a way that does not allow this material to fall into the trap of the exotic—where the Aboriginal is depicted as the mysterious "other." Instead, by delaying any treatment of ritual until the fourth and final part of *Two Laws*, and by including footage of rituals involving some of the men, and especially some of the women we have come to know somewhat through the first three parts of the film, the Aboriginal community is able to provide the audience with a sense of the interrelatedness of all these activities and of their articulation within the overall context of their ongoing lives and struggles.

All in all, the film *Two Laws* is a breakthrough of major significance in ethnographic film. It may not provide the kind of drama and action we are used to in the cinema, even in the "observational cinema," but it provides much more important things. Above all, *Two Laws* provides the ethnographic "subjects"—in this case, the Australian Aboriginal community of Borroloola— the opportunity to express what they want to express about their lives and their culture and their struggles, and to express all this in filmic terms of their own choosing. In doing so, they may have made that "disappearing world" a bit more visible and audible again, to the benefit of all of us.

Notes

1. There have been a few experiments set up by white American academics to investigate whether minority subcultures (Navajo Indians, lower-class urban black children), given some rudimentary training with film equipment, might be able to express, in original and indigenous imagery, certain essential characteristics of their cultures. The work with Navajos by Sol Worth and John Adair resulted in a number of short pieces (of several minutes duration) of "subject-generated" film imagery, only one example of which was thought to express genuinely "Navajo" imagery. Similar results were obtained in work with lower-class urban black children by Richard Chalfen.

2. Colin Young, "MacDougall Conversations," *Royal Anthropological Institute News*, June 1982.

3. Quoted from an interview with Cavadini and Strachan conducted by Charles Merewether and Lesley Stern, published in *Filmnews*, Sydney Filmmakers' Cooperative, April 1982, p. 8.

4. Colin Young, "MacDougall Conversations," p. 5.

5. Ibid., p. 7.

6. Except perhaps in such television blockbuster series as David Attenborough's "Life on Earth," Carl Sagan's "Cosmos," or Kenneth Clark's "Civilisation," where the documentary material is "personalized" for us by a luminary who is whisked magically about the globe from shot to shot, but who is always "on the spot," no matter how remote, to offer us a first-person commentary which, however, by virtue of the apparent immensity of the luminary's erudition, also functions simultaneously as the voice of authority in the style of the old "omniscient narrator."

7. Quoted from Cavadini and Strachan interview (see n. 3), p. 9.

8. Ibid.

9. Ibid.

The Politics of Documentary: A Symposium

Barbara Zheutlin

Several of America's leading social documentarians discuss esthetic and political issues involved in producing documentary films, including the effectiveness of narration, ways of creating drama, the ethics of interviewing, scripting, and preplanning, the use or avoidance of "buzzwords," and the influence of cinéma vérité.

The documentary film in this country has still not been granted the serious attention it deserves. It's not surprising, therefore, that documentary film-makers—especially those whose work reflects a social and political commitment—are not often asked to describe their creative process. Part of the problem is that the new wave of political filmmakers that has been emerging throughout the past decade has been more concerned with what it has to say than with how it says it. As a whole, these documentarians prefer to talk about the subjects they've filmed rather than about their craft. They are interested in reality, truth, showing life as it is actually lived, or exposing hidden aspects of our society. It has seemed almost a luxury to them to have time to think and talk about how they do what they do. Questions of art, esthetics, and the craft of communicating have too often been ignored or belittled by politically motivated filmmakers. The results, too frequently, are impassioned and politically well-intentioned but unimaginative and poorly crafted films that are incapable of communicating successfully with the audiences for which they are intended.

In an attempt to initiate a discussion of some of these esthetic and political issues, Cineaste *associate Barbara Zheutlin sent a questionnaire to a number of independent filmmakers whose films have played an important role in educating and inspiring people. Those groups and individuals who responded include Emile de Antonio (director of* Point of Order, In the Year of the Pig, Millhouse:

227

A White Comedy, *and* Underground, *among other films), Pacific Street Films* (Free Voice of Labor: The Jewish Anarchists, Frame-Up!: The Imprisonment of Martin Sostre, Red Squad, The Grand Jury: An Institution Under Fire, *and others), Josh Hanig (codirector of* Men's Lives *and* Song of the Canary*), Dave Davis (codirector of* Song of the Canary, Year of the Tiger, DC III*), Jon Else (*The Day After Trinity, Stepping Out: The De Bolts Grow Up, You Don't Live Here, *and* Arthur & Lillie*), Connie Field (*Rosie the Riveter*), and the Kartemquin Collective (*The Chicago Maternity Center Story, Taylor Chain, All of Us Stronger, Trick Bag, Now We Live on Clifton, *and* Winnie Wright, Age 11*).

Many other filmmakers invited were unable to respond due to the pressure of busy production schedules, but we hope the responses published below will encourage other filmmakers—as well as everyone concerned with the development of socially committed documentaries—to a greater appreciation of what is involved in creating better films.

How conscious are you when you are shooting and editing your films about the problem of creating drama and involving the audience? Do you think about casting your documentary? Have you made choices to edit parts of your films to make them more entertaining?

Josh Hanig: Too many leftist films are too long, too intellectual, and don't have enough music. Most of these films are full of interviews, and because people like to talk when being interviewed and like to make points, they often repeat themselves in subtle ways. I always listen carefully and cut, cut, cut. Better to have cutaways than to be repetitive, thereby throwing off your focus, as well as your flow and pacing.

We Americans like to have fun, to be entertained. We also respect humor. I frequently hear expressions like, "Why go pay to see problems when you've got enough of your own for free?" Somehow, the moviegoing public will pay to be horrified by blood-and-gore movies, but they shy away from being horrified by daily reality shown in documentaries. However, they don't seem to have so much trouble laughing at those same horrors. We need more of a *Strangelove* mentality in our films—more irreverence toward authority.

Dave Davis: You think about all these things, but you really succeed or fail in the editing room. You try to prepare for editing by providing yourself with the right raw material—good interviews, beautiful images for montage cutting, dramatic sound and images, cutaways for every scene where dialogue will have to be condensed, personal and emotionally rich expressions of people's experiences, good camera work and sound recording. You plan to film people to some extent based on how they will come across in front of the camera. Some people freeze up in front of a camera, some don't. This is very important

and can often be determined by doing preliminary interviews during prepro-
duction.

I think a storyline, a dramatic unfolding of events, helps a film tremendously.
Sometimes this can't be done, and the unfolding is the development of certain
themes or ideas or information. The more entertaining films, though, have
some suspense, conflict, storyline, and drama to them that holds our interest.
I'm personally trying to develop more in this direction—I think I've been
prone to a thematic, linear, informative style, rather than in telling a story or
building into a film some conflict and tension that holds suspense for the
audience.

Jon Else: The most important thing about *Trinity* is that we tried to make
it work like a feature film and in that sense tried, I suppose, to invent a weird
new genre. The key, the nut, the *sine qua non*, the very heart of what we are
about is storytelling. Half the battle in making documentaries is finding subjects
which embody an emotionally charged drama, lived by people worth caring
about.

The other half is finding the money.

Connie Field: One thing I learned from the makers of *Word Is Out* is to
videotape before selecting people for the film. I wanted to find people who
could express themselves emotionally as well as intellectually, and videotaping
was an excellent tool to use in making an accurate judgment toward this end.

Through the influence of Lorraine Kahn, who was an associate producer
on the project and who felt strongly about the importance of locations, and
the influence of Veronica Selver from *Word Is Out*, who explained how they
"dressed the set," I was very careful about locations. I don't believe you
should shoot an interview with a white wall behind it—the background has to
say something. Remember, people are looking at an image, and you don't
want the interview to be visually boring. So all of our interviews were shot
in different locations that revealed something about each woman.

Two of the women were filmed where they used to work, Lynn on an old
victory ship that was built in the Second World War, and Lola in front of a
factory where she used to work, with the New York skyline in the background.
I flew Margaret from Los Angeles to my offices in the Bay Area because I
couldn't afford to fly my crew down. I then created a clinic-type atmosphere
for her in one of our offices because she then worked in a clinic, and I wanted
her surroundings to say something about her life now. With Juanita, I rented
a Winnebago and drove her out to the Ford River rouge plant so we could see
the factory in the background with the smoke rising out the window, because,
in my mind, that image says Detroit. And Gladys was filmed inside her house
because it rained. We were going to shoot it outside her house, but it still
works well for her because the house is decorated in a way that is characteristic
of homes in the southern mountains, which is where she grew up.

Another thing that I consciously went for was a dramatic curve to the film, and I used that concept to structure the film. I was very conscious of wanting the audience to feel the experience, for it to have an emotional impact. First there is the initial excitement of entering new jobs. Then the emotion dips down as we get into the issues of the double day and of occupational health and safety; then it builds up with Lynn's torch story and the thrill of seeing the ship launched, and with Lola's "Work makes life sweet" to the excitement of the war ending. Then, bam!—the disappointment of losing your job and having to go back to lower-paying work.

We also wanted the audience to gain a greater understanding of the propagandistic nature of the newsreels and to learn how to read them *as* the film progresses. In other words, the contradiction between the propaganda and the women's experiences gets more and more obvious as the film goes on.

The simplest way to get your viewpoint across to an audience is to use narration. But there's been a generally shared assumption among political filmmakers that narration is boring, can't be trusted, is not filmic. What has influenced your decision to use or not use a narrator? How did you select the person to narrate?

Emile de Antonio: Among the angelic orders, films are made by purple butterflies with cameras screwed into their gossamer wings, catching every iridescent jagger and flicker. For me, film is tug, pull, conflict, process. Will there be narration? Who will write it? Who will speak it? Dan Talbot and I produced *Point of Order*. I raised the money. In the beginning, all was one. We agreed there would be no narration, only the material itself speaking for itself. Time produced tugs. Our experienced editor did not believe people could understand without explanation. Dan finally agreed with him. I had never made a film. I caved in. I hired Richard Rovere, who was author of the *New Yorker*'s weekly "Washington Letter" and of a book on Joe McCarthy, to write the narration. Mike Wallace lived near me in the country; I knew him; I hired him to read Rovere's narration. I was unhappy. We all met in a sound studio, and Mike read. I knew it was wrong. *New Yorker* prose is cadenced harmoniously enough, but not for film; Mike was too blustery.

I listened and listened to that tape of narration. I killed it. I fired the experienced editor. I said to Dan (paraphrase), "Okay, now we'll do it your way or my way. I'll match you." Dan: "Come on, De, be realistic. I've got the theater to run, family responsibility, neither one of us has ever done this before." Me: "Okay, I'll do it. No one else will see except those working with me until we have an answer print." A year later we screened it in the Movielab building. It was 1963. There was no narration. It was my film.

Pacific Street Films: Well, the question of narration is a good one; it's something we've struggled with. The problem with any narration is that if it's a disembodied voice, it always comes out seeming like the disembodied voice of authority. We've tried to stay away from that, although there are times, like in *Frame-Up!*, where information has to be conveyed and there's no way to do it other than with narration. It was the same thing with the grand jury film; we tried to use a male voice and a female voice. However, we basically don't like the use of narration if the characters themselves or the people who are interviewed can get across that information. Somewhere in the middle there is a compromise: to establish the voice in the beginning as belonging to some person, and then continuing it throughout as a voice-over. In *Red Squad*, for instance, we used an interview with ourselves which we had on-screen, and then selected sections as voice-overs. In our current film, *Anarchism in the United States*, we're doing the same thing. We've conducted an interview with ourselves which we'll use on-screen and then, we hope, as voice-over to tie together the rest of the sections.

Josh Hanig: Our documentary ancestors used narration as an integral part of their films. It was considered an art; people such as Archibald MacLeish utilized it with great effectiveness. Our generation seems to shy away from it. It is more mysterious and artful not to use it. Certainly the mass audience is used to it and accepts it all the time on TV documentaries. They, in fact, feel comfortable with it, to be guided along through the film, so to speak. If you have a strong storyline, and don't need it, why use it? But if you want to get across information and be analytical, it can be both effective and unobtrusive in the feel of the film—it can, in fact, enhance it.

On both films we tried to avoid it, but in the cutting realized it was too complicated to tell the story without it. I like to think it was because the films were so complex. What we got on film was not in the design, but had to be added with meticulous writing and rewriting at the rough-cut stage. My preference, even in a political film, is first-person narration. It can be involving.

I like to think my films are for a mass audience, and I don't think a mass audience gives a damn about whether or not there's a narrator. If it works for that particular film, it works. The only people who look down on narration are effete film theoreticians and people who think their film is not art if it's narrated.

Dave Davis: Necessity. Sometimes there is just no other way to get certain information into the film. Subtitles are very expensive, so often verbal identification of the subject is most economical. I also like it better. Narration can also work extremely well if it's well written and dramatic, as in Jon Else's film *Day After Trinity*.

Jon Else: A word on narration: I get terribly frustrated by the feeling among filmmakers, particularly on the left, that narration is, per se, a bad thing. Bad narration is a bad thing, and we grew up, for the most part, on bad narration. There are, however, as many kinds of narration as there are kinds of films, and a well-written, evocative ten seconds of narration can often do a better job than two minutes of tortured film. In dealing with the overwhelmingly complex subjects which so often attract us, narration should be thought of as a friend and ally, not as a necessary evil. Every documentarian should sit down and really listen to *Night and Fog* or *Day After Day* or *Volcano* or *Night Mail* or *The River*. Narration might also be the key to accessibility for a mass audience. If an audience can't trust the narration, why should it trust anything else in the film? Is there any less potential for manipulation in editing, music, composition?

Connie Field: It obviously depends on the type of film one is making, but I lean toward the nonnarrated documentary. In *Rosie*, I thought the vitality would come across better without narration. Because I was dealing with a controversial issue, I thought it would be better to let the material speak for itself, and I think the choice was correct because it's hard to argue with people's experiences combined with historical documents, and this gives the film a lot of credibility.

I think the disembodied voice of a narrator distances people from the material. And I don't mean Brechtian distance, which is a whole other thing. I mean the kind of distancing that can minimize the impact of the material. I believe that audiences are intelligent enough to get the point, even subtle points. I believe in presenting the material in an analytical structure that's accomplished in the editing room, if possible, and in letting people deduce for themselves— aided by an analysis you give in the way you structure the material.

Kartemquin: Questions of style are also affected by considerations of use. *Taylor Chain*, for example, has no narration. When information was needed that wasn't present in the scenes, we wrote a title card. This was extremely difficult. We must have gone through $50 of Pilot Fine Points rewriting those title cards to achieve the correct tone—conveying the necessary information, but also indicating what was important about that information. We had decided that narration would be wrong because we had no authentic voice from within the story that could say all that needed saying. An anonymous narrator would have been distracting and might have diluted the film's reality and credibility. Possibly another reason for the decision, in hindsight, is that a story about democracy can be "acted out" much more persuasively than it can be "narrated." In any case, it's obvious that often the questions of effectiveness, or usefulness, and questions of stylistic coherence are closely related.

The Chicago Maternity Center Story had to have narration. There was no other way to guide the viewer through such complex historical and analytical material. In this film we were lucky enough to have an acceptable voice close at hand, one that could speak with authority and feeling and had no need of objective pretense. For us, a narrative voice that comes from the subject is the most honest and persuasive. We also feel that letting the narrative bias show, instead of hiding it, lets the audience know that we respect them, that we are not trying to manipulate them with subtle narrative tricks. We like to state our case openly, whether by narration or by the way we structure the scene in the editing room.

To what extent have you scripted your films before shooting? To what extent have you filmed first and shaped your film later in the editing? What are the advantages and disadvantages of the two approaches?

Pacific Street Films: We try to get our point of view across in the editing. Our films have usually not been scripted before we've begun them, but lately we have tried to give them a little more form. In the past, we've filmed first and shaped the film later in the editing, and that's created quite a few problems— being faced with a massive editing job is like trying to piece together a huge jigsaw puzzle. The advantage to a scripted film, of course, is that the editing becomes a way to piece things together simply, according to the paper-cut.

Josh Hanig: With *Men's Lives*, we produced a twenty-five minute prototype slide show which we showed for fund-raising. Surprisingly, we followed the style and format of the slide show fairly closely in the film. With *Song of the Canary*, I wrote a treatment for PBS (again, in order to raise the money), and upon recently rereading it I was surprised to see how closely the finished film resembles the treatment, not in specifics, but in style, pacing, and effect. The problem, of course, is that in documentary, what you film is what you get, not necessarily what you want or intend to get. So the cutting becomes the process of carving out the original intentions from actuality.

In shaping both *Men's Lives* and *Canary*, we had the problem of writing narration toward the end of the process in order to tie together loose ends, clarify hazy points, and make transitions. In both of those films, that kind of thinking could have been done a little bit more beforehand. In both cases, I'd hoped we wouldn't have to use narration, and in both cases it became clearly necessary only after months of cutting.

Dave Davis: I don't script films. I outline the content I want to cover—the issues, the themes, the types of sequences I want to include in the film and what they will hopefully convey in terms of the issues. The rest is done in the editing room and in writing narration. Often things emerge in the editing that you hadn't anticipated and couldn't have scripted.

Jon Else: Trinity was not scripted. We did several years of research, an extensive story outline (not of the film, but of the history involved), and, most importantly, a "toy movie," which David W. Peoples wrote and which was a hypothetical full-blown screenplay for a finished film. We never intended to actually produce the toy movie, but it was the foundation for getting at the meat of our story. In the end, the film was shaped about 50 percent before shooting and 50 percent during editing, and it would have been shaped 85 percent before shooting had we not cut it down from four hours to forty minutes during the last month of postproduction. Here again, the overriding reason for truncating *Trinity* was that American television does not acknowledge four-hour programs.

Connie Field: In *Rosie*, the point of view was grounded in historical reality and based on extensive research. I let the government films and the women express themselves.

Although *Rosie* was not scripted, it was carefully planned before shooting. I outlined the history, all the issues. The women I had chosen for the film—five of them—I had interviewed quite extensively before filming, and then, in filming, I asked specific questions which would elicit certain stories I knew they could talk about.

What was set in the editing was the pacing and, of course, final content selection. I went very broad in terms of the stock footage I collected and in the scope of the interviews. Obviously, in the editing certain of the stories fit and others didn't. When a woman would use abstractions, it would never work. If she spoke of *the* "black experience," it didn't work as well as when she gave a specific experience from her life. Some stories I particularly wanted—for example, Juanita actually broke down the color bar at Murray Bodies; she was the only black woman courageous enough to do that. But the story was not told clearly enough to communicate its dramatic impact to an audience. We must have worked on that story for a month, trying it over and over again in the editing. It was a very hard story to lose, because it was so important.

What this shows is that the form that I chose to use also limited the content, even though I would never have chosen any other way for this particular film. I feel very strongly that interview documentaries can be extremely powerful if people are revealed in such a way that you can care and feel for them and can receive their stories as drama. If I was using people *just* for information, I could have used some of these stories which, for whatever reason, didn't carry the emotional weight that matched up to the events they were describing.

How familiar are you with the history of documentary films? Have you been influenced by them? What role do you think cinéma vérité *has played in shaping the political documentary?*

Emile de Antonio: I was familiar—when I began making documentaries—with Flaherty, Lorentz, and a few Europeans. I did not see the work of Esther Schub until 1972, when Anna-Lena Wibom of the Swedish Film Institute gave me a retrospective. I was overwhelmed.

I realize now, after years of work, how uncomfortable I am with the myth of Flaherty and why. The charm and power of his camera are marred by distortions, lies, and inaccuracies which pander to a fake romantic, fake nature-boy view of society. The struggles of modern man are not between man and economic and social models inimical to life and growth. *Louisiana Story* was financed by Humble Oil. The oil riggers, their rigs, the crocodiles, the boy, the bayou are romanticized to the point where one understands very clearly why Humble Oil gave away prints to any theater in the country which would play them. *Nanook* is a masterpiece of cinematography, and grossly wrong. The Eskimo did not live apart from Western influence. Nanook was not self-indulgent and romantic; he was an actor in a film by a self-indulgent romantic.

I have not been influenced by the work of any documentary filmmaker. *Cinéma vérité* is two halves of an apple, half rotten and half rather decent eating. The decent part is the technical improvement of light sync-sound camera equipment that came from Leacock, the Maysles, Pennebaker. The rotten half is most of the work, the pretentiousness behind it. There lies behind *cinéma vérité* the implication of a truth arrived at by a scientific instrument, called the camera, which faithfully records the world. Nothing could be more false. The assumption of objectivity is false. Filmmakers edit what they see, edit as they film what they see, weight people, moments, and scenes by giving them different looks and values. As soon as one points a camera, objectivity is romantic hype. With any cut at all, objectivity fades away. It is why so many *soi-disant vérité* filmers made rock-docs. The least appetizing of all *cinéma vérité* is Wiseman's watery stew, made up of his debt to light cameras and my use of nonnarration structure. Suitable pap for PBS. Bland, floury stuff offensive to no one, only to the art of films.

Pacific Street Films: We're very familiar with the history of documentary film, and we've seen quite a number of historical documentary productions. We all grew up on those kinds of films and were influenced by them, particularly by the compilation films that were produced by the networks in the fifties and sixties, like "The 20th Century" and "Victory at Sea."

Cinéma vérité has, of course, been an extremely crucial part of political documentary, but not so much in our films; we've done some *vérité*, but we haven't structured our films totally around the use of *vérité* footage. We don't think that works. You have to have some kind of historical context or dramatic style that supersedes the use of a totally *vérité* approach.

Josh Hanig: I wish we Americans were seeing more European and Japanese documentaries. I really have very little idea what they're up to, but I know there's some interesting work being done. I love looking at other documentaries, especially when they break the mold. I was very influenced by the Murrow documentaries of the fifties, and, of course, the early *vérité* work. Lately, I find myself very influenced by filmmakers who take some personal risks, like Mike Rubbo's Canadian Film Board films. He puts himself in the middle of a social milieu and tries to tell the story from the point of view of the outsider who's been thrown inside trying to figure it out. He can be your guide, and if it doesn't all make sense, well, we people on the left have a hard time accepting that everything doesn't make sense. A hard thing to accept with a materialist training. But I think it's much more human and accessible to an audience to perhaps once in a while admit this or acknowledge it.

Jon Else: I am very familiar with the documentary tradition and feel influenced by it, although certainly not by political *cinéma vérité*. When I think of political documentaries which have made some difference to me and, perhaps, to audiences, I think of *Night and Fog, The Sorrow and the Pity, Memorandum, Hearts and Minds,* and only secondarily of *Harlan County*, which I loved, or the Maysles and Wiseman films. Joris Ivens falls somewhere in between, I guess. It is ironic, I suppose, that nearly all of my own filmmaking prior to *Trinity* has been hybrid *cinéma vérité*, and that is what I most love doing.

How consciously have you sought out interviewees to express your views? Do you interview people before selecting them to appear in your film? To what extent do you try to make your arguments by providing facts and logic, and to what extent do you try to appeal more to the audience's emotions—to arouse their sympathy or anger, rather than to convince them through information? How do you balance the two?

Pacific Street Films: Before we start a film we try to do as many preinterviews as possible, both with people who express our viewpoint and with people who are antagonistic to it. Usually, one of the ways we try to give form to our films is by finding people who are not necessarily sympathetic to our position and then utilize them to draw attention to some of the key themes. In *Frame-Up!* we gave a lot of play to the county sheriff who was instrumental in framing Martin Sostre; he came off so ridiculously that there was no question in anybody's mind that he had been part of that frame-up. So it often pays to give that kind of antagonist a fair amount of publicity.

Josh Hanig: I usually like to interview people first, unless I know there will be an urgency to them spilling out a particular story. Then you want it fresh. I, myself, like to look for "the common wisdom" in normal nonanalytical people—the simple truth. If that can't be found and there are gaps, or things are misleading, then it's often necessary to find that person with a point of view you want represented. Of course, now that our point of view is less and less visible, maybe I'll stack my next film with gadflies.

Dave Davis: I often do preinterviews in order to select people for a film. Usually one character or speaker in the film will not represent the filmmaker exactly, but partially. A part of the truth, as I see it, when combined with many other parts, creates the whole of the film which does represent my perception of what was going on at the time, as I saw it at the time—all of this is very subjective, of course.

Jon Else: We sought out people, not for their views but for their credibility as characters, their storytelling charm, and their depth of knowledge. I preinterviewed about seventy-five people and filmed sixteen, of whom fourteen ended up in the film. I was always forthright (and I feel that a filmmaker must always be forthright) about the film we were making, and about our point of view—which was not, in fact, a point of view, but a genuine curiosity about where the atomic bomb came from.

I always tell subjects that I am filming: it is dirty pool not to tell them. As Bertolt Brecht put it, "Alas, we who would teach others kindness could not ourselves be kind."

Connie Field: I chose women whose stories and job histories were typical of the times and who could also reveal important historical events such as the black struggle for employment and union organizing drives. We did extensive preinterviews—seven hundred women were interviewed over the phone, two hundred in person on audio tape; thirty-five were videotaped; and we filmed five. We interviewed so many for two reasons. First, the response to our press releases was overwhelming. Second, the oral histories were a crucial part of the original research necessary for the film.

Many of the women do express our point of view, but some of that came as a surprise when filming. For instance, Lola Weixel, who makes that incredible statement at the end of *Rosie* about how society prepares women psychologically for whatever role it wants women to play—after losing so many men, America wanted babies and we wanted babies, but we gave up everything for that— had never expressed that thought to me until the day I filmed her. I had no idea she felt that. And someone asked me if I wrote that for her.

None of my questions was ever that direct. Sometimes they were like, "Tell me what happened when you went to Murray Bodies . . ."; or if it was a specific story, I'd say, "Oh, tell me that story again," or, "What happened with your union?" They were broad questions, but not leading questions. One thing that I did seek out consciously was a couple of women who were conscious of what happened to them in the larger historical framework. To that end I chose someone like Margaret, who talked about the propaganda and the media after the war.

Another interesting thing that happened with the film is that I didn't consciously set out to have two white women and three black women. It was a matter of just having certain issues and certain stories covered, and these five women were the ones to do it, and three of them happened to be black. Though I'm immensely pleased with the effect because all too many times blacks are used in films just to elicit the black experience, and therefore become tokens, and I think that the effect of this film is the opposite. The black women aren't tokens, they are integral to the whole concept of the entire film.

How do you decide whether or not to use the words socialism *or* communism *or* capitalism *in your interviews? In your narration? Do you think these words should be avoided because of their impact on an audience?*

Pacific Street Films: Words like *socialist* or *communist* or *capitalist* are not necessarily evil in themselves, only in terms of their context. With certain people, who are going to react in a certain way to those buzzwords, perhaps it's better to substitute something else. It depends on what kind of a reaction you want and what the situation is. They shouldn't be avoided in general just because they might have a negative effect on the audience. If the situation is appropriate and the best description is in terms of communism or capitalism, then that's the way to phrase it.

Dave Davis: In most cases, I avoid them, although I think in certain key spots it's good to use words like *capitalism* or *socialism*. That has to be done very carefully, so that the use of these words seems very natural, nonrhetorical, and is fully justified and explained by the development of the film. The audience must be convinced, by what they've seen and experienced in the film, that these terms are totally appropriate and nonrhetorical. And here I mean audiences that are not already sympathetic or oriented toward the left.

Connie Field: This is a very difficult question. We live in a very oppressive society. Ideas that oppose the status quo are not looked upon very favorably. And most Americans do not understand what socialism and communism mean. What people do understand—some of which I feel is true—is that some of the realities of communism as it is lived out in the Soviet Union today are bad. It's true that there isn't freedom of the press there. It is true that there isn't the same production of consumer goods in socialist societies as we have in the U.S. But people in socialist societies take for granted things that we do not have, such as full employment, day care, and virtually free medical care. But because the meaning of socialism and communism is not understood by Americans, we need to be careful about our use of these terms.

I think when a person's experience of belonging to the CP or the Socialist Workers' Party is integral to the experience that you're filming, then it definitely should be said. It's doing an injustice to the true history of America by not saying it. I think it's obviously much better to let the people in the film say this, and to avoid it in the narration. But I don't think *capitalism* is a dirty word in this country. It's our system.

The word *communism* is used in *Rosie*. I didn't avoid it or delete the story that Lynn tells. I also feel that her story puts the issue in the most uncannily accurate perspective when she talks about being accused of being a communist. This is something labor audiences all over the country have had a hearty laugh over, because anyone who has organized or been involved in standing up knows that they are going to be called "communist," whether they are or not.

At the time, Lynn did not know what it meant. Her response to it at that point was to say, "Well, if communists object to the kind of treatment that officer was giving the Filipinos, then I'm the biggest communist you ever saw in your life." At that point the colonel wants her to shut up, which is also typical of a certain American who thinks it's too dangerous to go around saying those words.

How do you decide what subject to make a film about? In picking your subjects, do you think about what kinds of films the left should be making today?

Jon Else: On the matter of esthetics and choosing subjects, I do try very consciously to choose subjects that "the left should be making," but I do not try to make them for the left. The left doesn't need them. With *Trinity*, we very deliberately tried to make a film that would be accessible to and even enjoyed by people who would not ordinarily choose to sit down for ninety minutes and hear about "some left-wing pinhead who got himself involved with Faust."

We tried to make *Trinity* as simple as possible on one level (story, drama, humor, suspense, narration) so that it would have as wide an audience as possible. I feel very strongly that if one is going to make these films, they have to be made and distributed in such a way that millions of people will see them and be moved by them. For better or worse, this means prime-time television, and I take great pleasure in the fact that *Trinity* was scheduled for nationwide broadcast in prime time.

The thorn in all of this, of course, is the potential betrayal of your own politics and esthetics. The only solution I've been able to come up with is one that involves using fairly conventional stylistic devices on the surface level and avoiding the exposition of specific ideology or doctrine. Hand in hand with this is the notion that documentaries are best at evoking feeling and raising questions, and worst at listing facts and answering questions.

If I did not care about a mass audience, *Trinity* probably would have been a different film, and probably would not have had structural elements such as an extensive expository narration and a linear chronological structure. On the other hand, the feeling that *Trinity* generates is exactly what I sought, regardless of form.

Emile de Antonio: The documentary film artist lives in opposition. He or she is nurtured best on revolutionary soil: Ivens, Grierson, Rotha, Schub. My films come from the life and times of my country. Our government provides us with subjects daily: General Plague; thermonuclear war; El Salvador; declaration of war on the poor at home, and on the Third World everywhere. Let PBS and the networks sell news. Let the documentarians' world be full of surprises. Let the form, the film, grow organically, so that the maker doesn't know its look until it's finished.

Pacific Street Films: There are many different reasons why we pick a particular subject. Sometimes it's circumstances, like when we were involved with an anarchist group that became subject to governmental surveillance (*Red Squad*). Or it could be because someone has called us up and told us that there are certain things that ought to be investigated, like in *Frame-Up!* Or, currently, we've always had an interest in anarchism, and we've wanted to make a film that would really bring to light what we think is an overlooked movement.

Josh Hanig: I have three criteria. The subject has to be one that I care about deeply; there has to be a need for the film—in other words, there cannot be a glut of films on the same subject; and it has to be an issue of strong concern to a broad group of people. In the mid-seventies there were several films on Chile. Now, I felt a burning desire to do something on Chile, but there were so many films being done on the subject it seemed absurd for me to do a film on Chile, even though I very much wanted to. I look for subjects that I know need some exposition but have little exposure, even though large numbers of people are affected by the issue. After I became interested in the issue of occupational health and safety, I made a review of the films made on the subject and couldn't believe how little had been done, considering the scope of the issue and the tremendous potential for showing some of the more raw and brutal effect of capitalist economics. That's when *Canary* started to become a reality.

If you pick a subject which hasn't been covered extensively, and one for which there is a need, your film will be seen by many more people. On the other hand, there are some subjects that translate well into film and others that don't. I have asked myself the question, "Could this issue be better served by using the thousands of dollars of film budget to print up a flier and hire a lawyer to pressure government or file a lawsuit?" For me, the subject has to have some strong emotion to it.

Dave Davis: A number of factors come into play: my own interests, my own political judgment, the judgment of others I work with and trust, my perception of where there is an audience that can use the film, where there is a political movement that would benefit from having a film, whether or not money can be raised for the film, and whether or not the film has a broad enough or politically important enough audience to merit the tremendous expense.

Connie Field: I do think about what films the left should be making, and political relevance is therefore my first criterion. I also ask myself, Is the subject something that will help people understand the social conditions under which they live in a way that can help them change those conditions? Also, will the subject lend itself to film so that the impact of the information can be both emotional and dramatic? I also consider how the film can be used as an organizing tool and whether there are active groups which will actually use it.

Kartemquin: We always attempt, whenever possible, to base our ideas for films in the use the films will have. What is it for? How will they use it? Beginning with these questions can do a lot to answer broader political questions, such as, "What kinds of films should the left be making today?"—not to mention eliminating exercises in self-indulgence. But certainly, if politics are in command, the use of a film will control most of your basic decisions, no matter how many surprises the subject might have in store for you along the way.

In *Trick Bag*, an interview film about the changing attitudes toward racism among white working-class youths in Chicago neighborhoods, we worked directly with a community organization, Rising Up Angry, which, in effect, gave us the idea for the film, gave us assurance of its use, and also provided a lot of the people we interviewed. This was close to being a "sponsored" political film, except for the fact that no money changed hands between us and the community group.

In contrast, two films about younger city kids, *Now We Live on Clifton* and *Winnie Wright, Age 11*, were at first just ideas we had that grew out of our dissatisfaction with existing images of kids that age on film. When grant money came along, we got more disciplined and went back to the problems of "audience" and how we could present positive but provocative images of working-class city kids, their neighborhoods, their everyday lives—and make films that would be used in the public schools. When the films were finished, we were so involved in those questions that we took the films to dozens of schools, ourselves, to test the results.

Sometimes the outcome of a project is impossible to foresee. *Taylor Chain* started out to be a film that would teach workers how to bargain for health and safety language in their contracts, but it ended up telling a story about the dynamics of democracy in a union local during a strike. As the situation in which we were filming changed, so did our ideas of what it was most important and useful to make the movie about.

The Chicago Maternity Center Story was supposed to be a short descriptive film about the struggle to save a model institution. It ended as an hour-long film which provides an analysis of the politics of health care in America, and at the same time documents a year-long struggle to save the center. Through all the changes in these latter two projects, we continued to be guided by the use the two films would have. We saw how the story at Taylor Chain would be important to unions and labor educators, and how the expanded Maternity Center material would cut across many layers of economics and history for a number of audiences.

Do you see your role as calling attention to a problem or issue, or as suggesting solutions and/or plans of action?

Pacific Street Films: Our films can be seen in two ways—they call attention to a problem, as in *Frame-Up!*, and they also suggest a solution or plan of action, as in *The Grand Jury: An Institution Under Fire*, where we had a number of different people at the end provide the alternatives to the current grand jury system.

Josh Hanig: In *Canary* we clearly are trying to show and warn against a widespread problem. We are also trying to dissect the reasons for the problem, and therefore are attempting to point toward broad-reaching solutions. On that film, several union officials said they couldn't use our film much because it didn't show workers how to file a health-and-safety grievance or to file a complaint with OSHA. So it doesn't try to solve problems in a nuts-and-bolts way, as many sponsored or educational films do.

Why do you make documentaries instead of fiction films?

Pacific Street Films: We make documentaries primarily because our background has been in that genre, and we consider ourselves political filmmakers. Documentaries currently provide the only real framework to make a political statement.

Dave Davis: Because, personally, I have always been more interested in looking at real people as they are affected by the social or political process than in constructing a fiction treatment of the same. Also, the process of making documentaries is to me much more satisfying—less cumbersome, there's more control, more direct contact with people and issues and institutions, less film technology, and less expense. The frustrations are that documentaries have a much smaller audience and are taken less seriously in most cases.

Connie Field: Rosie was made as a documentary because the story could not have been told as a fiction film. One of the main concepts was myth versus reality. The film is as much a statement about the effect of media propaganda on our lives as it is a history of women workers. Therefore, the documentary form, which allows for the juxtaposition of real experiences as told by the women themselves with the actual newsreels of the day, creates a stronger impact.

Emile de Antonio: Because I choose to. The documentary is not a step to fiction film but a step to freedom. Commercial fiction film is only real estate. When real *auteurs*, the Harvard Business School graduates, produce films, their concern is neither art nor ideas, but money. Maximize rents for a space called a seat. In documentaries, I confront our history on my own terms. Brecht said that only boots can be made to measure. He was right.

Part III

Documentary Ethics

Introduction

The relationship of ethical considerations to film practice is one of the most important yet at the same time one of the most neglected topics in the documentary field. Although public discussion has proliferated on questions of theory, style, and method, until the mid-1970s there was almost complete silence on the subject of ethics. Erik Barnouw's otherwise excellent history of documentary virtually ignores the issue, and neither the 1971 edition of Lewis Jacobs's *The Documentary Tradition* nor Richard Barsam's 1976 *Nonfiction Film: Theory and Criticism* makes any reference to ethics.[1] These authors are not necessarily to be critized for this neglect of ethics; the issue was simply not at the forefront of discussion in the early 1970s. Nevertheless, the omission of the subject in standard texts is unfortunate, to say the least, as the question of ethics is at the root of any consideration of how documentary works and what it should be doing. The essence of the question is how the filmmaker should treat people in films so as to avoid exploiting them and causing them unnecessary suffering. The ramifications of this issue provide the subject for this section.

The main pioneer in the modern discussion of ethics is Calvin Pryluck. Pryluck sensed accurately that the search for "ultimate truth" through *cinéma vérité* techniques was raising many serious problems, and in his 1976 article "Ultimately We Are All Outsiders" he blazed a new trail.[2] The issue, as he put it, was to define the proper relationship between the public's right to know about a subject and an individual's right to be free of the shame, indignity, and humiliation that might be inflicted as a result of the filmmaking process. Pryluck's article brought the subject to the fore and has since been followed by articles, books, and conferences, such as that on Image Ethics held at the

Annenberg School of Communication in 1984—all explaining and elaborating on this crucial topic.

The problem can be fairly simply framed: Filmmakers use and expose people's lives. This exploitation is often done for the best of motives, but it occasionally brings unforeseen and dire consequences into the lives of filmed subjects. So the basic question is, What is the duty of care, or responsibility, owed by filmmakers to those they film?

Many questions lead from the main issue of how far a filmmaker should exploit a subject in the name of the general truth or the general good. To what extent does the subject realize what is really going on, what the implications and possible consequences of being portrayed on the screen, or of being interviewed, are? When consent was given for filming, what did the filmmaker really intend, and what did the subject understand him or her to mean? When should the filmmaker shut off the camera or destroy footage? Should the subject be allowed to view, or even censor, the edited footage?

As mentioned above, critical writing on documentary has until recently rarely considered the topic of ethics. The treatment of *Nanook of the North* is a good example. Although hundreds of articles have been written on the film, about Flaherty's artistry, techniques, reconstructions, and so on, few explore Flaherty's treatment of Nanook or Nanook's subsequent death a mere few years later. The same is true of *Man of Aran*, where Flaherty's endangering of the fishermen's lives while filming and his exploitation and then neglect of the lives of his stars afterward are shamefully ignored. *Triumph of the Will* is another notorious example—for too long, Riefenstahl's aesthetics were praised to the heavens, while her ethics in filming Hitler's gangsters were completely ignored.[3]

The problem of what to do with people's lives has always been present in documentary filming, from *Nanook* through the Grierson years to the present. It is quite clear, however, that a totally new dimension was added to the issue with the coming of *vérité*. Here was a technique that allowed a closer, more personal and probing view of people's lives, as well as less time for reflection and consideration of one's reactions, than anything that had gone before. In the beginning, the excitement aroused by the method swamped a tentative awareness of its dangers, as films such as *Primary, Jane, Titicut Follies, Warrendale, A Married Couple*, and *The Things I Cannot Change* explored new and exciting areas of intimacy and revelation.

The question of ethics was not ignored by the early *vérité* filmmakers; rather, such questions simply weren't taken seriously. Often the question of ethics was reposed to ask who holds ultimate authority in the filmmaking process. When I interviewed Fred Wiseman many years ago, for instance, he told me he could never make a film that gave somebody else the right to control the final print.[4] In another case, the British filmmaker David Elstein described to me the pressure he had to put on somebody to stop him withdrawing from a film: "He had been a witness to the bribery. Just about a week before transmission he got anxious. Would we indemnify him against a possible libel suit? We said no. Would we pay him an increased fee to cover his legal expenses? We said no, we wouldn't. 'Well, I want to withdraw from the film.' 'Well, you committed us this far, you can't withdraw.' 'What if I'm prosecuted for bribery?' 'That's a risk you will have to take.' He finally decided to go ahead."[5] In due course the man was prosecuted and got a two-year jail sentence on the basis of what he told Elstein. The important words obviously were Elstein's "You are committed to us," and the man submitted to the strong pressure to put the television company's interests before his own.

I use Calvin Pryluck's article "Ultimately We Are All Outsiders" to introduce the ethics discussion, because it was this article that finally placed ethics on the agenda of serious debate. It surveys the work of *vérité* filmmakers such as Leacock, Pennebaker, Allan King, the Maysles brothers, and Craig Gilbert to illustrate the problems they confronted, and it is very good at defining the perimeters of the subject. "We Are All Outsiders" opened the floodgates and was quickly followed by other articles, such as James Linton's "The Moral Decision in Documentary" and Pryluck's "Seeking to Take the Longest Journey," in which Pryluck talks with Albert Maysles about the ethical issues raised in *Grey Gardens*.[6]

Pryluck and Linton discuss the questions raised when the filmmaker confronts a stranger as film subject. In an important paper written in 1984, John Katz and Judith Katz take the matter a stage further by discussing the filmmaker's duty of care to friends or family who become involved in film projects.[7] They center their discussion on films of the 1970s, such as *Nana, Mom and Me, Joe and Maxi*, and *Best Boy*, and argue that the obligation of the filmmaker to the subject may be even higher in the "family" film than in the "stranger" film because the sheer closeness and familiarity of the relationships in the former may lower the subject's usual guards and defenses.

Brian Winston's article "The Tradition of the Victim in Griersonian Documentary" provides a historic overview of the subject before concentrating on the implications of the phrase "the public's right to know."[8] He traces the attention of British filmmakers from Grierson and Rotha onward—on social problems such as poverty, housing, and education—but argues that the people involved in the films, "society's victims," rarely had a voice in the films and so became in due course media victims, simple subjects for fashionable documentaries. Among other things, Winston maintains that too many documentaries run away from social meaning, substituting empathy for analysis and paying more attention to effect than to cause. In the end, society's deviants become a fascinating subject for the middle class, without the films in any way ameliorating the problems they are supposed to be discussing. Like Jay Ruby,[9] Winston thinks that the money spent on many social documentaries would be far better used if it went into practical schemes to help the poor and under-privileged.

Winston is always interesting, scholarly, stimulating, and provocative, but I find some of his conclusions debatable. The analysis of root causes in social problems is an admirable activity, and I suspect it is done far more often than Winston admits. For instance, *No Harvest for the Reaper*, which Winston cites, analyzed the underlying problems of migrant work, and Jack Willis's *Hard Times in the Country* did a similarly thorough job of investigating economic problems in American farming. However, may it not be sufficient for the documentary simply to *witness*, to bring a neglected subject to the attention of the public, leaving the analysis to others?

I would argue further that Winston is a shade unfair in his discussion of the results brought about by documentary. I agree that it is difficult to prove a direct cause-and-effect relationship in film—to show where films have directly helped to improve social conditions—but it is possible. *No Harvest for the Reaper* was successful in bringing about legislation beneficial to American migrant workers. *Cathy Come Home*, about conditions of the homeless in England, was the right film at the right time, serving to catalyze action in a social issue that had been simmering just below the surface for years. Most critics of documentary concur with Winston and are wary of attributing direct social change to documentary. They may be right, but I still believe that films can change attitudes, setting up a climate for improvement—which helps in the long run. In the worst case, many films at least focus attention on a problem, probably preventing further deterioration of conditions in that arena.

Although I am not in total agreement with Winston's comments on the victim and the amelioration of conditions, I think that his remarks on the duty of care are very much to the point. He provides an extremely thorough analysis of the meaning of legally acquired consent and the issues of privacy and the law, as well as of the relationship between film and the other media in regard to these issues. His sympathy lies almost entirely with the subject, not with the filmmaker, who he argues should work within greater legal restraints that will ensure the preservation of the filmed subject's dignity. More of Winston's remarks on ethics can be found in his article "Direct Cinema: Third Decade" in the last section of this book.

While researching this book I discussed the implications of the "right to know" with critic and film teacher Henry Breitrose, who pointed out some other aspects of the problem. In essence, Breitrose argues that we don't pay enough attention to what he calls "political exploitation." The filmmaker is in the business of *using* his or her subjects—most often to make a substantive point, to achieve a strategic objective. or to fit into a pattern of argument or exposition that transcends individual lives. Film subjects are thus a means to an end, but it is generally the filmmaker's end, not the subjects'. Here Breitrose is obviously extending MacBean's comments on anthropological filming to cover a much wider ground.

Breitrose further argues that part of the problem, at least in the United States, derives from a confusion between news and documentary and from their inclusion under the same roof in commercial television. The journalistic enterprise in the United States has a very special constitutional status because of the importance attached to the public's "right to know" and the precedence accorded it in interpretations of the Constitution when this right to know comes into conflict with the individual's right to privacy. But documentary is different from news reporting, and according to Breitrose it may well be that the right to privacy is being abused by documentarians who think they are journalists or who are all too willing to partake of the journalist's special status.

After discussing the "right to know," the second excerpt from Craig Gilbert's "Reflections" focuses attention on filmmaker-subject relations as seen from the documentarist's point of view.[10] His article, using *An American Family* as the case in point, provides a useful meeting ground for theory and reality. After its broadcast, many critics blasted *An American Family* as being unethical and unfair to the Loud family. Pat Loud, a main subject of the series, herself published a book denouncing the filmmaker.[11] This section of "Reflections" is Gilbert's answer to his critics and his attempt to come to grips with some of the more far-reaching questions of documentary responsibility.

One key ethical issue has to do with the disclosure of objective or purpose on the part of the filmmaker, and with the understanding of this objective, leading ultimately to consent to filming, on the part of the subject. Seeing how this topic was perceived by both sides becomes crucial to an understanding of the violent arguments surrounding *An American Family*. Gilbert's and Pat Loud's views of the matter are illuminating and fascinating in their misperceptions of one another. For instance, on the matter of disclosure Gilbert writes:

> [Pat Loud asked] "Craig, what the hell is this series supposed to be about?" She has asked the question several times; the first time, of course, had been when I went to visit her and her family and told them what I was planning to do. This time I said, "You know what the series is about, Pat. It's about how you and everyone in this room and everyone in this country is fumbling and trying to make sense of their lives." Pat's response was immediate and understandable. "I'm not fumbling, for Christ's sake. That's a lot of shit . . . " Pat's answer wasn't entirely honest, but then neither was my answer to her question."[12]

Discussing the same incident, Pat Loud says:

> Craig came back and sat for two hours talking about educational TV, living anthropology, how candor leads to truth, public TV . . . its considerable problems. After it was all over none of us understood what he was talking about. That set the tone for many future talks we had with Craig; *what did the nice man really say?*[13]

One of the virtues of Gilbert's article is a complete openness in the discussion of motive and drives, even when the actions of the filmmaker are seen in a problematic light. He makes one comment which is devastatingly true—it goes to the very heart of the problem and has nowhere else been stated with such frankness and clarity:

> More often than not, and certainly more often than has been admitted, documentary filmmakers are unable to tell the whole truth of what they are up to without running the risk of being told to peddle their papers elsewhere. It is not that one is a liar or more dishonest than anyone else; it is simply that the nature of the business we are in makes it impossible, a good deal of the time, to be absolutely candid. . . . We are using human beings to make a point, . . . we are "exploiting" them to make our films, . . . and the fact is that our incomes and our careers often depend on our ability to conceal the truth of this exploitation from our subjects.[14]

My sympathies in this discussion go out to Gilbert. He seems to face up to the deceptions of the craft with a certain forthrightness and shame, unlike, for instance, the makers of *Marjoe*, who seem to me to have been much more dishonest in their filmmaking. However, Gilbert leaves out one important element in his comments: that is, that film subjects come from widely different backgrounds and have very different levels of intelligence and sophistication. At some point this consideration must affect the filmmakers' responsibility and duty of care. Without pushing the argument too far, I would maintain that the Louds' ability to comprehend the nuances and effects of *Family*, and the Bealeses' in *Grey Gardens*, was far higher than that of the unfortunate housewife in the NFB's *The Things I Cannot Change*. Accordingly, the resulting duty of care was fractionally less on the part of makers of *Grey Gardens*.

Gilbert's comments on income and career touch on another neglected aspect of ethics, that of economic exploitation. As Gilbert points out, filmmakers make a living from their work, and build reputations that are convertible into economic advantage. Their subjects, in contrast, generally acquire no direct economic gain from the enterprise. Since documentary filmmakers do not, for the most part, pay their subjects, they must gain cooperation by friendship and dissimulation, as in Gilbert's case, or by sheer bullying, as in the case of Elstein and the bribery witness. Where does everyone stand at the end? Gilbert achieved a certain degree of fame. I doubt, however, that Pat Loud profited much, and the poor man who cooperated with Elstein ended up in jail. Obviously the subject is worth more discussion; indeed, I would have included an article about it in this book if more had been written on the topic.

Jay Ruby's article "The Ethics of Imagemaking" (condensed from a larger paper) discusses the third side of the relationship triangle, the filmmaker's duty to the audience. Ruby argues that the audience must be made aware of methods, biases, deceptions, artifices, and the like in order to understand where the film is coming from. His discussion elaborates on many of the points raised in the section on documentary theory, but I felt the proper context for the article was the ethics chapter, as a means of amplifying the main issues.

One important question related to ethics is, Why bother to make the film at all? To state and publicize a problem is one answer, to further one's career another. The third and most familiar response is that the public has a right to be informed about a matter of public concern. This line quickly leads to the area of television documentary and investigatory journalism, a subject I explored in *The New Documentary in Action* and *The Documentary Conscience*.[15] Unlike independent documentaries, the network television documentary deals much of the time with public and semi-public figures. The gloss on the ethical question then comes to whether the duty of care owed the public personality is different from that owed the public as a whole.

This question has been widely debated with regard to print journalism and libel. The view has generally been that since public figures are more open to comment than are private ones, a public persona would have to prove malicious intent to win a libel suit, whereas the private individual would not.[16] This position implies a lesser duty of care. It is thus worrying in regard to network documentary that even given the broad boundaries outlined above, one senses in recent years the violation of ethical standards and a distinct abuse of power by the networks.

This feeling led me to include Michael Arlen's article "The Prosecutor," about the work of the "60 Minutes" team.[17] Arlen argues that the networks too often jump into the accusatorial role, with little evidence to support their actions and with dire consequences to the subjects of their films. To illustrate his thesis, he covers the "60 Minutes" investigation of suspected corruption among state officials in Wyoming. What he finds is the pursuit of drama for the sake of television action itself, a situation with no clear indictment, no jury, no judge, no defense counsel—merely the insidious blackening of the names of a few people who have no clear charge to answer.

Part of the ethical stance of the parties to the discussion may depend on the relative powers of each. Winston criticizes Wiseman's ethics in *Titicut Follies* because, among other things, the inmates of the institution could not protect their position.[18] The other side of the coin can be seen in *Millhouse*, in which de Antonio presented a devastating satirical portrait of President Nixon and his pre-1970 career. It can be argued that de Antonio's methods were unfair, with scenes taken out of context and editing used to present Nixon in the most stupid and unappealing way. However, given Nixon's immense power at the time to answer such a film with his own justifications and to counterattack, de Antonio's work cannot be considered truly unethical.

The Ed Murrow and Fred Friendly film on Senator McCarthy for CBS (1954), which is discussed more fully in the next chapter, raises further interesting points on this issue. The film was an hour-long exposé of McCarthy, then at the height of his power and influence. Most reviewers praised the film for its courage, and McCarthy himself was given an hour of airtime to reply to the Murrow attack. The situation would appear to be fair to both sides. However, Gilbert Seldes, a noted media critic, took Murrow and Friendly to task for a lack of ethics, arguing that McCarthy and his advisers totally lacked their attackers' skills to use the medium and that therefore the talk of balance and fairness was a sham.

The power of the television medium and the fairness (or otherwise) of its attacks continue to make headlines. *Death of a Princess*, mentioned earlier in this book, was one center of controversy in England in 1982. Later, in 1984, *The Uncounted Enemy: A Vietnam Deception* (made in 1982) became the focus of one of the most famous libel trials since the end of World War II.

In *The Uncounted Enemy*, CBS alleged that General Westmoreland had, in 1967, led a top-level military conspiracy to sustain public support for the Vietnam war by deliberately giving the White House a gross underestimate of the size of enemy forces. General Westmoreland vociferously denied the allegation. Later in 1982, Sally Bedell and Don Kowet wrote an article entitled "Anatomy of a Smear," alleging that there had been extreme bias in the collection and preparation of materials for the program.[19] They also challenged the basic integrity of the network's reporting procedures. In an internal memo, CBS News Division president Van Gordon Sauter conceded that CBS had let almost every judgment go against General Westmoreland in order to prove the point of the program. Although Westmoreland eventually withdrew the case, the ethical standards of CBS seem clearly in need of review.

Vivian Sobchack's article "*No Lies*: Direct Cinema as Rape" is included to bring the reader a little closer to the workings of *vérité* and to the problems it raises.[20] *No Lies* is a short 16mm fiction film made by Mitchell Block, in which a woman discusses her rape with a *cinéma vérité* reporter. The viewer follows the relentless, unfeeling pursuit of the woman by the cameraman as he probes for answers to his questions about the rape. Slowly, the film processes itself as a form of rape in its own right, thus confronting the viewer with uneasy questions about *cinéma vérité*'s violation of privacy, trust, and sensibilities. It is to Sobchack's credit that she outlines the ethical issues raised very clearly, so that they can be grasped by those who have not seen the film.

Where does all this discussion lead? The explorer of ethical issues is confronted by two challenges—first to map the territory; and then, to explain how that territory can be crossed in safety. Pryluck, Winston, Linton, Ruby, Katz, Gilbert, and others have all done an excellent job with regard to mapping and exploration. They have also occasionally suggested ways to pursue the journey and avoid the main dangers. Winston, for example, pleads for an extension of legal rules regarding rights and privacy. That is one answer. Personally, I think the main answer lies in fostering a new sensibility among filmmakers, by means of articles and discussions, as to the results and implications of their work, and in encouraging in them greater compassion, sensibility, and concern for the people whose lives they use. When this is done, I think the balance of duties and concerns will come into equilibrium, instead of being weighted in favor of the filmmakers' concern for targets and self, as seems to be the situation at the present.

Notes

1. Erik Barnouw, *Documentary* (New York: Oxford University Press, 1974); Lewis Jacobs, *The Documentary Tradition* (New York: Hopkinson and Blake, 1971); and Richard Meran Barsam, *Nonfiction Film: Theory and Criticism* (New York: E. P. Dutton, 1976).

2. Calvin Pryluck, "Ultimately We Are All Outsiders: The Ethics of Documentary Filming," *Journal of the University Film Association* 28 (Winter 1976): 21–29.

3. Leni Riefenstahl's ethics and her relationship to the Nazi party are discussed in depth in Susan Sontag's "Fascinating Fascism," in *Movies and Methods*, ed. Bill Nichols (Berkeley and Los Angeles: University of California Press, 1976).

4. Alan Rosenthal, *The New Documentary in Action* (Berkeley and Los Angeles: University of California Press, 1971), p. 71.

5. Alan Rosenthal, *The Documentary Conscience* (Berkeley and Los Angeles: University of California Press, 1980), p. 119.

6. James Linton, "The Moral Decision in Documentary," *Journal of the University Film Association* 28 (Spring 1976): 17–22; and Calvin Pryluck, "Seeking to Take the Longest Journey: A Conversation with Albert Maysles," *Journal of the University Film Association* 28 (Spring 1976): 9–16.

7. John Katz and Judith Katz, "Ethics and the Perception of Ethics in Autobiographic Film," in *Image Ethics: The Moral and Legal Rights of Subjects in Documentary Film and Television*, ed. Larry Gross, John Katz, and Jay Ruby, Annenberg Communication Series (1985).

8. Brian Winston, "The Tradition of the Victim in Griersonian Documentary," in Larry Gross, John Katz, and Jay Ruby, eds., *Image Ethics: The Moral and Legal Rights of Subjects in Film and Television* (in press).

9. Jay Ruby, "Image Ethics," in *The Documentary Today* (working papers) (Minneapolis: Film in the Cities, 1983).

10. Craig Gilbert, "Reflections on *An American Family*," *Studies in Visual Communications* 8 (Winter 1982): 40–51. For further discussion on *An American Family*, see Eric Krueger, "An American Film," Melinda Ward, "The Making of an American Family," and Melinda Ward, "An Interview with Pat Loud," all in *Film Comment* 9 (Nov.–Dec. 1973): 17–31. For further general discussion of the ethics issue from the filmmaker's point of view, see the interviews with Susan McConnachy, David Elstein, and Richard Cohen in Rosenthal, *The Documentary Conscience*.

11. Pat Loud, *A Woman's Story* (New York: Bantam, 1974).

12. Gilbert, "Reflections," p. 43.

13. Loud, *A Woman's Story*, p. 85.

14. Gilbert, "Reflections," p. 44.

15. See nn. 6 and 7.

16. The 1984–85 Arik Sharon libel case against *Time* magazine failed in the end because malice could not be proved against *Time*.

17. Michael Arlen, "The Prosecutor," in Arlen, *The Camera Age* (New York: Penguin, 1981), pp. 158–79.

18. Winston, "The Tradition of the Victim," p. 16.

19. Sally Bedell and Don Kowet, "Anatomy of a Smear," *TV Guide*, May 29, 1982.

20. Vivian Sobchack, "*No Lies*: Direct Cinema as Rape," *Journal of the University Film Association* 29 (Fall 1977): 13–18.

Ultimately We Are All Outsiders: The Ethics of Documentary Filming

Calvin Pryluck

In one of the Ten Commandments, God enjoins us against making graven images. Some contemporary sects, like the Amish, take this injunction literally and consider it sinful to be photographed. There are primitive peoples who have never heard of our God and who feel the same way: the taking of a picture is the taking of a soul. On the other hand, it is less than a hundred years since George Eastman told us: "You push the button, we do the rest." A photograph—perhaps the ultimate graven image—is imbued with a kind of magic that leads children in the street to accost anyone with a camera and raucously cry: "Take my picture!" Perhaps more revealing is the latter-day greeting: "Smile! You're on Candid Camera."

So long as motion picture equipment remained cumbersome and created logistical problems, photographing and being photographed were calculated acts. Immortality lost and immortality gained were matters for theological and aesthetic speculation; the legal, ethical, and moral problems surrounding the two kinds of magic remained manageable. The problems remained almost containable when somebody figured out how to make money from actuality photographs of people making fools of themselves. It was easy to condemn "Candid Camera," with its cheap comedy based on the humiliation of ordinary human beings going about their private business.

With the development of lightweight equipment and the growth of an aesthetic of direct cinema, the ethical problem of the relationship of filmmakers to the people in their films became more amorphous. It is not quite so easy to condemn the work of men like Leacock, the Maysles brothers, and Wiseman. They have shown us aspects of our world that in other times would have been obscured from view; in this there is a gain. In the gain there is perhaps a loss.

Leacock summed up one goal of direct cinema: "To me, it's to find out some important aspect of our society by watching our society, by watching how things really happen as opposed to the social image that people hold about the way things are supposed to happen." While one can argue about whether we can ever know what *really* happens, inevitably in filming actuality, moments are recorded that the people being photographed might not wish to make widely public: adult citizens riding in a public bus are provoked into making hostile responses to high school students; a long unemployed worker gets rowdy drunk and has an altercation with the local police; a teacher who happens to wear thick corrective lenses is shown in an extreme close-up that emphasizes her heavy eyeglasses.

Many of the best-known people dealing with contemporary documentary film recognize the ethical problem as a perplexing one. These expressions of concern appear occasionally in film reviews and published interviews; rarely are remarks extended beyond the topic immediately at hand—a particular film or a particular filmmaker. Only occasionally is it pointed out that the apparent ethical lapses are recurrent, not isolated. More than morality is involved; ethical assumptions have aesthetic consequences, and aesthetic assumptions have ethical consequences.

These appear to be simple matters. So simple that to Mamber, in *Cinéma Vérité in America*, the whole issue of privacy in *cinéma vérité* "seems like a manufactured problem"; the solution is easy: "Provided that those being filmed give their consent, where is the immorality?" It may be that there is none. But it cannot be settled by fiat. Or by possibly inappropriate assumptions. Consent and privacy are too complex to be dismissed in a dozen words.

Consider the following: You are an old man, a clinic patient in a municipal hospital, terrifed that you may have cancer. While you are being examined there are strangers in the room with strange-looking equipment. Another stranger—a woman, a physician—is questioning you about the sores on your genitals and the condition of your urine. How valid would your consent be, even if one of the strangers tells you, as Wiseman does, "We just took your picture and it's going to be for a movie, it's going to be shown on television and maybe in theaters. . . . Do you have any objections?" Wiseman finds— as did Allen Funt of "Candid Camera"—that few people do object.

This is not surprising. The method of obtaining consent is stacked in the filmmaker's favor. The ethical problem raised by such approaches is that they give the potential subject no real choice: the initiative and momentum of the situation favor the filmmaker. The presence of the film crew with official sanction is subtly coercive. So is the form of the question, "Do you have any objections?"

The filming and the question are like the numerous rituals that are a prelude to receiving treatment in a clinic. There is duress in placing the onus of affirmative refusal on those who do not wish to participate in an activity that has nothing to do with medical treatment. So the picture gets taken, and damn the consequences.

Coercion takes many forms. For *Salesman*, the Maysles brothers followed salesmen on their rounds. All three of the visitors—the salesman carrying his sample case, Albert Maysles with his camera gear, David Maysles with microphone and recorder—would approach a door. A brief explanation would be offered. "That took me maybe thirty seconds," Albert said. "Most people at that point would then say they understood, even though perhaps they didn't. . . . Then when the filming was over . . . they would say, 'Tell me once more what this is all about,' and then we would explain and give them a release form which they would sign." In exchange, the subject would be given a dollar, "to make it legal."

In such situations, the film gear serves to intimidate the wary. Even government officials can be intimidated by something so simple as portable video equipment. A community organizer explained why she takes video equipment into meetings with officials: "The head of the welfare office is not going to be so quick to tell ten ladies to fuck off if they have all that shiny hardware along." If a bureaucrat is reluctant to make an ill-mannered response to ladies with all that shiny hardware, how likely is it that a householder will tell Al Maysles with his gear to get lost?

In actuality filming, the emphasis is on getting a legal release consenting to filming. Even Allen Funt can boast, "We get 997 out of every thousand releases without pressure." Other filmmakers recognize an ethical problem but are candidly cynical about an adversary relationship between themselves and their subjects. Some deny that there is a problem.

Al Maysles reported a conversation where Arthur Barron said, "Jesus, don't you sometimes get awfully disturbed that you might hurt somebody when you film, and don't you sometimes question the morality of what you're doing?" Maysles's response reveals his own stance: "I almost never feel that fear myself. . . . Arthur was saying, 'Aren't you afraid that you're exploiting people when you film them?' and that has never occurred to me as something to be afraid of."[1]

Despite his private fears, Barron has been outspokenly hostile to subjects; he has referred repeatedly to several cities that he "can forget about going back to." Barron described his approach in making arrangements for the production of *Sixteen in Webster Groves*: "I must say I wasn't totally honest in persuading the school board to let me do the film. There was, as in many films, a certain amount of conning and manipulation involved."

Marcel Ophuls is aware of the ethical problem: "As a filmmaker, you're always . . . exploiting. It's part of modern life." Ophuls finds personal "problems and depressions" in the professional exploitation of people's "great urge to communicate because of loneliness, because of insecurity, because of bottled-up complexes." Nevertheless, he explained, "my biggest problem was con-

vincing people to be interviewed. . . . If you have moderate gifts as a fast
talker or diplomat, or if you appear moderately sincere, you should be able
to get cooperation. . . . It's a con game to a certain extent."

The con during the shooting of *Marjoe* sounds like an excerpt from the life
of Yellow Kid Weil or other confidence men. "There was no problem getting
permission from the local ministers to shoot. Marjoe convinced them of the
filmmakers' integrity. When questioned of their intent, the filmmakers replied
that they were making a film about Marjoe and his experiences in the Pentacostal
revival movement." This is the pattern of the classic con game. A confederate
ingratiates himself with the mark, introduces other operators, and both use
partial truths. At no time was it said that the film would show "Pentacostalist
crowds who are exploited, demeaned, and manipulated." From the producer's
viewpoint, "it was essential that Marjoe not blow his cover before the shooting
was completed."

Regardless of whether consent is flawed on such grounds as intimidation
or deceit, a fundamental ethical difficulty in direct cinema is that when we use
people in a sequence we put them at risk without sufficiently informing them
of potential hazards. We may not even know the hazards ourselves. Filmmakers
cannot know which of their actions are apt to hurt other people; it is presumptuous
of them to act as if they did.

With the best intentions in the world, filmmakers can only guess how the
scenes they use will affect the lives of the people they have photographed;
even a seemingly innocuous image may have meaning for the people involved
that is obscure to the filmmaker.

In the sixties, the National Film Board of Canada made films that were
intended as sympathetic portrayals of what it was like to be poor. *The Things
I Cannot Change* and *September 5 at Saint-Henri* were both direct-cinema
documentaries, and both turned out badly for the people depicted. They felt
debased and humiliated; they were mocked by their neighbors; one family felt
forced to remove its children from the local schools.

Cultures other than our own are not the only ones that pose problems for
filmmakers and their subjects. Even renditions of cultures and life-styles we
think we know something about are filled with pitfalls for the people involved.

Ultimately, we are all outsiders in the lives of others. We can take our gear
and go home; they have to continue their lives where they are. The criticism—
deserved or not—directed toward the Loud family following their appearance
as *An American Family* is too well known to bear repeating. Earlier, CBS
featured one particular family in a study of an upper-middle-class suburb of
Detroit. Whatever the family's faults and virtues, they were used—exploited,
if you will—for purposes not their own. As a result of their participation they
became the center of a community controversy that included letters to the
editor describing the family as "shallow, materialistic social climbers." I don't

know how long this kind of thing continued, but can their lives be the same as before they allowed CBS to use them in a film?

These kinds of family misfortunes are notorious examples of the consequences of appearing in a documentary. The results of sequences in other documentaries are less widely publicized, yet one can speculate about them. One can wonder how the teacher in *High School* feels about herself since seeing her bottle-thick eyeglass lenses larger than life on the screen.

The climax of Leacock's film *Happy Mother's Day* is a community celebration in honor of quintuplets born in Aberdeen, South Dakota. In the film there is a scene of the mayor making a speech that one critic has described as "incredibly ludicrous" and another termed "an extraordinarily inflated speech." One can wonder how the mayor felt when he saw himself saying, "Never in the history of the United States has a city official had such a great responsibility." How did his friends and neighbors feel? We already know how some critics felt. Is the good opinion of strangers to be less valued?

The mayor's speech was a public event; in direct cinema, the private scenes are perhaps more problematic. Mamber has described as the more revealing moments in Drew Associates films those where "the subject is stripped of his defenses as a result of failing in some way." He cites as "truly a fulfilling moment" the scene in *On the Pole* when, after losing the Indianapolis 500, Eddie Sachs "shows himself being afraid to show disappointment, trying to act 'natural' but not being sure what natural means in terms of the image he wants to present of himself."

The Maysles brothers' film *Salesman* follows the experiences of Paul Brennan and three colleagues as they travel around selling Bibles. In the last scene, according to Mamber, "the presence of the camera appears to make Paul even more acutely aware of his failure, threatening to expose feelings he might prefer to keep hidden."

Mamber's judgment on these two sequences highlights a central ethical problem in direct cinema as currently practiced. In both scenes we are dealing not with the relationship of men with others, but with themselves. They may have agreed to serve as subjects for the films, but a waiver of privacy is not absolute.

The right to privacy is the right to decide how much, to whom, and when disclosures about one's self are to be made. There are some topics that one discusses with confidants; other thoughts are not disclosed to anyone; finally, there are those private things that one is unwilling to consider even in the most private moments. When we break down the defenses of a Paul Brennan or an Eddie Sachs and force them to disclose feelings they might prefer to keep hidden, we are tampering with a fundamental human right. And making the disclosures widely public only compounds the difficulty. The coerced public revelations of private moments is one of the things that make "Candid Camera" so clearly objectionable.

If this week, or next week, or the week after were all there was, the privacy problem might be balanced by the greater good done by the increase in society's understanding. But actuality footage harbors dormant potential for mischief. Pat Loud, speaking of the effect on the children, speculated: "Twenty years from now, somebody will be knocking on their door saying, 'How [*sic*] was it like to be a member of *An American Family*?' They may never be able to live it down, or get away from it."

A homey example that has touched just about everyone past a certain age is the pictures of naked babies on bearskin rugs that parents used to have taken. To others the snapshot might be cute, charming, and delightful; to the now grown-up subject the picture might be something else. Does the adult who grew from the infant child have no rights, simply because the image exists?

Thanks to *Marjoe*, the ticking-bomb effect can be seen as more than just speculation. In the film there is a newsreel sequence of four-year-old Marjoe performing a marriage ceremony for a couple, described by one critic as "a nervous red-faced sailor and his heartbreakingly ugly bride." This was a questionable sequence twenty-five years ago; something other than the right to know is involved today. What Marjoe does to himself is his business. But do he and his associates have a right to implicate others in their affairs by resurrecting for selfish purposes tasteless footage? How far into the future may an individual waiver of privacy reach? What are the ethics of once again exposing to public scrutiny the now middle-aged "heartbreakingly ugly bride" in a perhaps aberrant moment?

The known and unknown hazards posed by direct cinema suggest the necessity for extreme caution on the part of filmmakers in dealing with potential infringements on the rights of subjects. While assenting to the serious intention of an aesthetic of direct cinema, one can wonder about the dignity, respect, and pride of the people in the films. Even a partial list of films that have been criticized on ethical grounds reads like a list of the important documentaries of the recent past. Are we asking sacrifices on one side for a positive good on the other? What is the boundary between society's right to know and the individual's right to be free of humiliation, shame, and indignity?

This is not completely uncharted ground; while the problems may be unique to our era, they are not unique to documentary filming or sound recording. The ethical problems of the conjunction of the search for knowledge, new technology, and individual integrity have been extensively considered in the fields of medicine and the social sciences. In many ways, scientists are distinct from filmmakers, yet in their own way they all search for their version of truth. In one important respect the ethical problems of actuality-filmmakers are identical to those faced by research physicians, sociologists, psychologists, and so on: scientific experiments and direct cinema depend for their success on subjects who have little or nothing to gain from participation.

The use of people for our advantage is an ethically questionable undertaking; in its extreme it is exploitation in the literal sense. In documentary filming as in scientific research such exploitation is justified through claims of society's interest in advancing knowledge. This is Wiseman's explicit rationale. Because the films he has made "are about public, tax-supported institutions," Wiseman said, "they are protected under the First Amendment, and the right of the public to know supersedes any right to privacy in a legal sense."

This kind of argument is based on ethical assumptions of an earlier era. If the aesthetic assumptions of documentary have changed, can it be merely stipulated that the ethical relationships remain unchanged? Is there no difference in ethical relationships when the camera is free to peer into every obscure corner in contrast to an earlier time when events had to be consciously performed in front of the camera? Or when the only means of reporting was through word pictures?

Privacy is only part of the counterclaim to society's right to knowledge. In our society there is a profound social respect for the right to decide for oneself how to live one's life.

The right of privacy is part of this broader right of personality, which includes the right to be free of harassment, humiliation, shame, and indignity. For reasons that reach to its core, actuality filming poses a threat of more serious infringement on the rights of personality, than does either traditional documentary production or verbal reports. Staged performances are no threat at all, since the right of self-expression is one of the personality rights. However, lightweight equipment makes endemic the kind of hidden camera and grabshots that were questionable even in traditional documentary.

When using words, private matters can be kept private unless there is an overriding social interest in making the information public. Private information is typically disguised to the largest extent possible to preclude identification of individuals. The confidentiality that can be maintained when using words obviously contradicts the whole idea of direct cinema. And the impossibility of anonymity renders questionable any print-based assumption about the balance between privacy and the right to know.

Society's dual interest in further knowledge and in protection of personality can be seen as complementary; neither means much without the other. An attempt needs to be made to balance these two equally important claims; one mechanism through which balance is maintained is the requirement for consent.

Consent is far from a simple matter; consent, privacy, and related issues have generated extensive discussions in medicine and social science. There is no reason to think that consent is any less complex in film than in science, since both depend on the collaboration of individuals who are not otherwise involved in the enterprise.

In the scientific literature, there is wide consensus that consent is not valid unless it was made (1) under conditions that were free of coercion and deception,

(2) with full knowledge of the procedure and anticipated effects, (3) by someone competent to consent. The requirement that consent be truly voluntary is a recognition of the fact that there is typically an unequal power relationship between investigators and subjects; the disproportion of status and sophistication is subtly coercive. It is probably not by accident that large numbers of participants in medical experiments are prisoners and otherwise indigent. In the first place, they are available in prisons and charity wards. As dependents of the state they are (or think they are—which amounts to the same thing) in a weak position to refuse to cooperate. Margaret Mead stated the case bluntly: "The more powerless the subject is, per se, the more the question of ethics—and power—is raised."

The act of volunteering presumes that one knows what is being volunteered for; subjects must be informed about the procedures and possible effects. Considerable argument has developed over what constitutes "informed consent," but one point is clear. *Consent is flawed when obtained by the omission of any fact that might influence the giving or withholding of permission.* The decision to participate is the subject's absolute right; no one may take it away by the manner in which the question is asked or the circumstances explained or not explained.

A third component of voluntary informed consent—competency to consent—is also shrouded in complexity. By law, a child is not competent to consent; approval must be given by a parent or guardian. Where the child has an interest in the contemplated procedure, this is a reasonable requirement. Presumably, the adult will consider the child's best interest in making important decisions. There are, however, sometimes conflicts between the interests of parents and those of minor children; in these cases an impartial decision may be sought from the courts.

The ethical status of responsible consent becomes obscure where what is being agreed to is only marginally for the benefit of the minor child—as is the case in nontherapeutic research. It can be argued that a child's integrity is infringed when a parent or guardian makes these decisions without considering the child's wishes. A minor has rights, the argument goes, and these rights cannot be waived by anyone else.

A similar kind of argument in an ethically even more murky area involves the question of who is competent to give consent for institutionalized subjects such as prisoners or mental retardates. The officials of the institutions are in many cases the legal guardians of their charges. Yet it is clear that in some situations there could be a conflict between the interests of the guardians and the interests of the individuals they are responsible for. This ethical dilemma underlies the difficulties of *Titicut Follies* in the courts of Massachusetts.

The officials of the hospital where the film was made may have had selfish reasons to prevent their practices from becoming public knowledge. At the same time, Wiseman was not exactly a disinterested party when he sought to make the film. Caught between these two interests, the legitimate interests of the patients were lost.

The basic point of the restrictions around voluntary informed consent in medical and social research is the protection of the physical and psychic well-being of the subjects. Extending the general ideas around consent, there are specific propositions and practices that are particularly germane to actuality filming. A basic postulate in social research is that subjects should not be humiliated by the experience; they should not leave the experiment with lowered self-esteem and social respect. The ethical sense of this postulate is violated with regularity in actuality filming, sometimes consciously, sometimes innocently.

A Vietnamese peasant understood this when he said, "First they bomb as much as they please, then they film it." Peter Davis, director of *Hearts and Minds*, understood when he commented, "The second confrontation of Vietnamese with American technology is only slightly less humiliating than the first."

On the assumption that no one can know a culture as well as its members, it is a practice in the social sciences for investigators to state their understanding in their own words and check these formulations with members of the culture. The information-gathering process thus becomes a collaborative seeking after knowledge on the part of scientists and their subjects. It is not unusual for this process to continue through to the final draft to permit subjects second thoughts about the propriety of disclosing certain private information.

If all of this sounds familiar, it should. It stretches back to Flaherty and the Eskimos: "My work," Flaherty said later, "had been built up along with them. I couldn't have done anything without them. In the end it is all a question of human relationships."

The idea of the subject participating in the creative process past the actual shooting stage is not completely unknown in direct cinema. Often, however, this follows from a simple dictum: Respect flows to power. Levine had veto right over *Showman*, as did John Lennon over *Sweet Toronto*, as did Queen Elizabeth over *Royal Family*.

On the evidence, I am forced to wonder whether less-powerful personages than Joe Levine, John Lennon, and Queen Elizabeth would have been given the same assurances. The more common stance seems to be an extension of the adversary approach that emphasizes the filmmaker's exclusive control over the film.

Barron is on record that he would never show rushes to subjects "unless I wanted to incorporate them into the film." The production group of *An American Family* was willing to eliminate some objectionable material, yet Pat Loud has a long list of alleged distortions. "The thrust of the film was their decision, and they were adamant about that."

In his defense, Craig Gilbert, producer of *An American Family*, made the point that "eight reasonably intelligent, compassionate, caring people reviewed the footage to make the film an accurate, compassionate, and unbiased portrayal of the family." Maybe. A skeptic can ask, though, what happened to the seven reasonably intelligent, compassionate, caring people who were the most important collaborators—the subjects of the film.

Marcel Ophuls mocks the whole idea of collaboration. "During these discussions [of ethics], the idea seems to come up that in documentary films there's some sort of participatory democracy—that the fair thing to do, the only really decent thing to do, is to have the people you have used look at the rushes and then decide collectively what should be used."

It is a charming vision—all those people seated around a Steenbeck trying to decide what shot comes next. But that's not the way it works. Typically, the filmmaker starts the cut and carries it through. In the traditional approach, the people in the film are presented with a completed film.

In a collaborative approach to editing, the participants have an opportunity to offer their interpretations of the material before the form of the film is irrevocably set. George Stoney has done this for years. At various stages in his editing, Stoney shows a copy of his workprint to the people in the film and anyone else who might be able to contribute some insight. All of this feeds back into subsequent editing.

Perhaps because he is a social scientist, Jean Rouch follows the social science practice of showing his material to the people he is working with. Sometimes, as in *Chronique d'un été*, these showings serve as impetus for further filming, but unlike Barron, this is not why Rouch shows his films. Rouch is emphatic on this point: "The great lesson of Flaherty and *Nanook* is to always show your films to the people who were in it. That's the exact opposite of the ideas of Maysles and Leacock."

Other filmmakers have used variations of the collaborative approach. In the making of *Asylum*, a film about an R. D. Laing therapeutic community, provisional consent was obtained before filming. The original twenty hours of rushes were cut to a four-hour version. Final consent was obtained on the basis of this version of what would be included in the final ninety-minute film. It was perhaps Laing's influence, but the schizophrenics in his care were accorded the dignity of deciding for themselves how they wanted to be presented on the screen.

Canadian critic Patrick Watson summed up the filmmaker's antipathy to collaboration in editing: "Ceding authority over the edit is revolutionary; it requires a curious submission of the director's ego." Yet, established filmmakers like Colin Low and Fernand Dansereau do not feel threatened by the collaboration of their subjects in the editing process.

Dansereau has described how the process worked in the National Film Board of Canada production of one of "his" films. *Saint-Jerome* is a study of the way in which people and institutions in the small town of that name behave in periods of rapid change. At the outset, in contrast to current practice for many filmmakers, Dansereau made a pledge to the less powerful that was not extended to the more powerful. Ordinary citizens—but not politicians—received assurance that they would have control over the final product.

In the process of successive screenings of rushes and workprint, there was an interplay between filmmaker and participants—each trying to put meaning to the experience. After "considerable stirring up of ideas and emotions . . . the two approaches coincided and grew together, and the film was accepted without difficulty." When the local Chamber of Commerce tried to restrict showings of *Saint-Jerome*, the major community organizations defended the film.

Dansereau was not degraded by the collaboration; quite the opposite: "I can feel within me, infinitely stronger and more durable than that from either critics or any anonymous public, the recognition of the people with whom we lived. It is they, finally, who assure me of my functions as an artist."

Filmmakers who insist on sole control of a film overlook a crucial point about the nature of actuality filming. They are using assumptions that are only questionably appropriate to the situation. Although actuality may be used as inspiration in other art forms, such as painting and writing, these creations are solely the result of the artist's activity. No one mistakes *Moby Dick* for anything but an interpretation by Melville. No one criticizes the behavior of the people in a painting by Hieronymous Bosch. The words of Tom Wolfe (either one) are inevitably and uniquely his, regardless of the source of inspiration.

The situation in fiction film and old-style documentaries is not exactly the same as in other art forms, but the characters are instrumentalities of the creators. They would not exist except for the lines written for them, the actions prescribed for them by the writer and the director. The romantic assumptions about artistic control and self-expression are appropriate to these conditions.

None of this is true for direct cinema. It would not exist without the uniquely personal speech and lines made available by the people being depicted. A direct-cinema film is irreducibly the product of the personalities of the subjects as refracted through the personality of the filmmaker; this strength of direct cinema is vitiated when filmmakers insist instead on imposing their own personalities. Since filmmaker and subject are embarked on a collaboration from the moment of conception, romantic aesthetic assumptions are inappropriate.

The logic of complete collaboration is the logic of direct cinema. If one is serious about using direct cinema to make valid statements about people, then collaboration should be welcome. The subjects know more than any outsider can about what is on the screen. Without the insider's understanding, the material could be distorted in the editing process by the outsider.

It makes a difference, for instance, in the scene with Eddie Sachs whether he is struggling to maintain his self-image or whether, as Leacock claims, "Eddie is just damn well pleased to be alive." If Leacock is right, but the audience is led by the editing to believe otherwise, then the audience is being deceived just as if the scene were staged altogether.

It turns out that the ethical problem is also an aesthetic one. The tension between filmmaker and subject can be creative or destructive. It is likely to be destructive when filmmakers try to make new ethical facts conform to inappropriate aesthetic assumptions. We are then all demeaned: filmmakers, subject, and the audience. The new assumptions that have begun to be sketched, notably by Marcorelles in *Living Cinema*, recognize that both filmmaker and subject have unique contributions to make to the creative process of direct cinema.

Collaboration obviously discharges one ethical responsibility. When others supply themselves as characters telling their own story, filmmakers incur an obligation not to deform the subject's persona for selfish motives. Collaboration fulfills the basic ethical requirement for control of one's own personality. If the mayor has no objection to showing his speech, I can have none.

Things get complicated if the mayor changes his mind after the film is in release. Obviously, a filmmaker's commitment to a subject cannot be open-ended. It need not be. There is less basis for grievance if subjects actually collaborate in the editing while the film is still being worked on than if they had merely been offered a final print for approval. However, some subjects do not realize that they make easy targets, or during the editorial screenings they become so entranced with their images that they are unable to consider the implications of the persona on the screen.

The filmmaker's best guess on the potential effects of the film and particular scenes must be part of truly informed consent. A simple human principle can be invoked here: Those least able to protect themselves require the greatest protection. In the extreme, utter helplessness demands utter protection.

When Dansereau yielded control over the final print to ordinary citizens but not to politicians, he was following a general policy at the National Film Board of Canada. The tendency there in recent years has been to give more power over a film to those who were vulnerable and could suffer as a result of being filmed. Those who can defend themselves—whether politicians or celebrities—are offered little or no control over the final product.

Such a practice, of course, makes it more difficult to obtain permission to film celebrities, but it might result in more revealing portrayals. Otherwise the agreement of celebrities to appear in a film becomes one more business enterprise like any other personal appearance; when such a venture suffers a reverse, filmmakers have no special claim to attention.

If subjects by their own actions have abrogated a claim to humane consideration, then filmmakers have little ethical responsibility toward them. It is not always easy to know when deceit is ethically acceptable. "Candid Camera" is probably indefensible even if permission is subsequently sought and granted; World War II resistance cameramen had no ethical obligations toward those who had placed themselves outside of the filmmaker's moral community. Between the extremes we must each make our own judgments.

Caution is required. Unless the judgment is clearly motivated and justifiable, it is easy to slip into narrow prejudice against Pentacostalists, homosexuals, or upper-middle-class families. Perhaps as an emotional guide, filming should be considered like any other human relationship; is the filming practice something that would be done in a private social context?

Collaboration does not solve all of the ethical problems raised by the new possibilities of actuality filming. Still to be detailed on some other occasion are the implications stemming from the critical fact that different people make different interpretations of the things they see in films. What is the ethical situation where only a few people perceive an ethical violation? Does the situation change when a basically honest interpretation is possible despite a blatant ethical violation? An obvious part of the answer is that people start from different ethical premises. Beyond this the questions are even trickier than questions of ethical conduct.

My own incompletely worked out feelings tell me that once standards of conduct are accepted, their application is more or less objective; yet it is not always easy to know from a film when standards have been properly applied. Even though what appears on the screen must be the central evidence, an infringement is not mitigated because it is overlooked by some part of an audience. Any other position trivializes an ethical discussion. Where audience acceptance is the only criterion, the end justifies the means—ethical considerations are irrelevant.

We are not quite at a standoff between the subjective component of interpretation and the objective nature of violations of accepted standards. As we make explicit our ethical standards there will be a greater sensitivity to ethical violations, and determination of deviations will become more objective. We will then be able to discuss more rationally whether the social gain outweighs the individual loss.

Where there is still a split judgment on ethical violations we may have to go outside of the internal evidence of the film; suspicion of a violation might have to be resolved on the basis of external evidence. A related possibility is that scrupulously ethical productions will begin to recognize—in the filming and the film—that the production crew is in social interaction with its subjects. Wiseman, for instance, claims to record on film his request for consent. If the audience had these available, we would be better able to judge the degree to which unequal power influenced the agreement to appear in the film.

Discussion of ethical issues will not by itself solve the problems; it may remind us of their existence and perhaps lead to a more fruitful relationship between filmmaker, subject, and audience. Application of these ideas in actuality filming would not always be easy, but some guidelines are needed if we are to avoid cynical exploitation.

The acrimony surrounding a controversial film may be good for the box office; it is sometimes of questionable value for art. The hustlers among us will make increasingly bizarre films for the sake of controversy. In the whirlwind, the more thoughtful and profound films will be lost.

In the end, since the dignity of others is best protected by a well-informed conscience, sober consideration of our ethical obligations may serve to impress all of us—beginner and old pro—with the power we carry around when we pick up a camera.

Note

1. In a subsequent interview, Al explained what he meant: "It's so hard for me to imagine that what I'm doing might hurt people in any way because I'm not imposing any kind of thing on what they're doing" (Calvin Pryluck, "Seeking to Take the Longest Journey: A Conversation with Albert Maysles," *Journal of the University Film Association* 28 [Spring 1976]: 14).

Notes on Sources

The basic sources for the material on documentary practices were G. Roy Levin, *Documentary Explorations* (Garden City, N.Y.: Doubleday, 1971), and Alan Rosenthal, *The New Documentary in Action* (Berkeley and Los Angeles: University of California Press, 1971). The basic sources for the discussion of scientific practices were Paul A. Freund, ed., *Experimentation with Human Subjects* (New York: Braziller, 1970), and Freund, ed., *Experiments and Research with Humans: Values in Conflict*, Academy Forum no. 3 (Washington, D.C.: National Academy of Sciences, 1975). Material on right of personality is from O. M. Reubhausen and O. G. Brim, Jr., "Privacy and Behavioral Research," *Columbia Law Review* 65 (1965): 1184–1211; a classic, and still valuable, discussion is Roscoe Pound, "Interests of Personality," *Harvard Law Review* 28 (1915): 343–65 and 445–56.

Additional material on direct cinema and *cinéma vérité* includes: Stephen Mamber, *Cinéma Vérité in America* (Cambridge, Mass.: MIT Press, 1974); Stephen Mamber, *"Cinéma Vérité* in America," *Screen* 13 (Fall 1972); and Louis Marcorelles, *Living Cinéma* (New York: Praeger, 1973).

The material on the National Film Board of Canada and community organization is from *Challenge for Change Newsletter*, no. 7 (Winter 1971/72) and no. 1 (Winter 1968/69), and Patrick Watson, "Challenge for Change," *Artscanada*, April 1970. The second Wiseman quote is from Janet Handelman, "An Interview with Frederick Wiseman," *Film Library Quarterly* 3 (Summer 1970). The Flaherty quote is from "Robert Flaherty Talking," in *The Cinema 1950*, ed. Roger Manvell (Harmondsworth, Eng.: Penguin, 1950).

Further material about specific filmmakers came from individual interviews. Those from *Film Comment* include: Maxine Haleff, "The Maysles Brothers and 'Direct Cinema' " 2 (Spring 1964); James Blue, "One Man's Truth: An Interview with Richard Leacock" 3 (Spring 1965); Arthur Barron, "The Intensification of Reality" 6 (Spring 1970); Harrison Engle, "Hidden Cameras and Human Behavior: An Interview with Allen Funt" 3 (Fall 1965); and Melinda Ward, "Interview with Pat Loud" 9 (Nov.–Dec. 1973). See also Pat Loud, *A Woman's Story* (New York: Bantam, 1974). Interviews in *Filmmaker's Newsletter* include: Bruce Berman, "The Making of *Hearts and Minds*: An Interview with Peter Davis" 8 (April 1975); Betty Jeffries Demby, "A Discussion with Marcel Ophuls" 6 (Dec. 1972); and Steven T. Glanz, "Marjoe" 6 (Nov. 1972). See also "Hollow Holiness," *Time*, Aug. 14, 1972, p. 45, and Thomas Meehan, "Portrait of the Con Artist as a Young Man," *Saturday Review*, Aug. 26, 1972, p. 67.

The Tradition of the Victim in Griersonian Documentary

Brian Winston

> *You know, this film [*Children at School*] was made in 1937. The other thing is that this film shows up the appalling conditions in the schools in Britain in 1937, which are identical with the ones which came out on the television the night before last: overcrowded classes, schoolrooms falling down, and so on. It's the same story. That is really terrible, isn't it?*
>
> Interview with Basil Wright, 1974

I

A. J. Liebling once remarked that it was difficult for the cub reporter to remember that his or her great story was somebody else's disastrous fire. Much the same could be said of the impulse to social amelioration, which is a central element in Grierson's rhetoric and which, therefore, has become over this past half-century a major part of the great documentary tradition. Documentary found its subject in the first decade of sound, and by the late thirties the now-familiar parade of those of the disadvantaged whose deviance was sufficiently interesting to attract and hold our attention had been established. It was not yet dominant, and the war was to distract from its importance, but it was there. Each successive generation of socially concerned filmmakers since the war has found in housing and education, labor and nutrition, health and welfare, an unflagging source material. For the most prestigious publicly funded documentarist as well as the least effective of local news teams, the victim of society is ready and waiting to be the media's "victim" too.

This "victim," however, does not figure much in the theoretical or public discussion of documentary. There, an agenda has been set which concentrates on issues of transparency and narratology, on the morality of mediation and reconstruction, on the development of style and the effects of new equipment. The people whose cooperation is crucial to documentarists have as little place in that discussion as they do (usually) in the making of the films and tapes in which they star. Indeed, documentarists by and large take an aggrieved view of this issue, should it be raised. As Frederick Wiseman said: "Sometimes after films are completed people feel retrospectively that they had a right of censorship, but there are never any written documents to support that view. I couldn't make a film which gave somebody else the right to control the final print."[1] Wiseman's attitude is, I would argue, the typical one. Interference of any kind is a clear breach of the filmmaker's freedom of speech and, as such, is to be resisted. But given the "tradition of the victim," the filmmaker's freedoms often seem like nothing so much as abridgements of the rights of his or her subjects, rights which, for all that they are less well defined, are nevertheless of importance in a free society.

The persistence of the social problems that these texts are, at a fundamental level, supposed to be ameliorating is never discussed. But if it is the case that housing problems are unaffected by fifty years of documentary effort, what justification can there be for continuing to make such films and tapes? Grierson's purpose was clearly enunciated: "To command, and cumulatively command, the mind of a generation. . . . The documentary film was conceived and developed as an instrument of public use."[2] There was nothing, though, in this ambition to be the propagandists for a better and more just society (shared by the entire documentary movement) that would inevitably lead to the constant, repetitive, and ultimately pointless exposure of the same set of social problems on the televisions of the West night after night—the assumption here being that Grierson's practice directly influenced contemporary filmmakers in many countries, including the United States, and that benchmarks were thereby established for all subsequent work both in film and in television for the entire English-speaking world and beyond.

II

Between 1929 and 1937, Grierson synthesized two distinct elements. First, he focused the general social concern of his time into a program of state-supported filmmaking. Such were conditions during the Great Depression that even on the right in Britain the need for measures of state intervention in many fields was accepted. Indeed, the generation of young Conservatives whose political philosophy was formed at this time were exactly those postwar leaders who agreed to the welfare state and thereby established the consensus which is only now being destroyed. I mention this simply because it is easy to treat the group around Grierson as dilettantes. (Wright speaks of his "slight private income";[3] Rotha writes of his parents as "far from well-off," who, nevertheless, managed to send him to thirteen private schools in as many years;[4] Watt states: "I came from a normal middle-class background. My father was a member of Parliament.")[5] To modern eyes, the films they made, virtually all of them stilted and condescending, tend to reinforce the unfortunate impression that, as a group, they were nothing but poseurs, clutching their double firsts from Cambridge. There is no reason, though, to doubt the sincerity of their impulse to "get the British workmen on the screen" or indeed to help the working class in other ways.[6] "To start with we were left wing to a man. Not many of us were communists, but we were all socialists."[7] Grierson's first job, lecturing on philosophy at the Durham University outpost in Newcastle-upon-Tyne, allowed him time to work, and work seriously, in that city's slums.[8]

In its day, the social attitude of Grierson's colleagues was genuine and to be expected, and their achievement on the screen was not inconsiderable. Grierson claims that "the workers' portraits in *Industrial Britain* were cheered in the West End of London. The strange fact was that the West End had never seen workmen's portraits before—certainly not on the screen."[9] The films "were revolutionary because they were putting on the screen for the first time in British films—and very nearly in world films—a workingman's face and a workingman's hands and the way the worker lived and worked. It's very hard with television nowadays and everything, to realise how revolutionary this was, that British films, as such, were photographed plays, that any working class people in British films were the comics."[10] This emerging iconography, a contrast to the parade of Noel Coward servants that was the norm, did not, at first, concentrate on the lower classes as victims.

On the contrary, the second element influencing the movement ensured that this would not be the case. Robert Flaherty's powerful example moved the desire to document the realities of working life into the realm of the poetic. Flaherty was responsible for *Industrial Britain*, although the film was finished by Grierson (and ruined by the distributor who added the "West End" voice and overblown commentary). Grierson's group admired Flaherty's approach enormously. Their primary aesthetic influence was the Soviet silent cinema, which meshed well with their socialist rhetoric, but they were also susceptible to Flaherty's poeticism, despite the fact that it eschewed the social responsibilities they embraced. Grierson was dismissive of what he called Flaherty's emphasis of "man against the sky," preferring films "of industrial and social function, where man is more likely to be in the bowels of the earth."[11] "There wasn't any serious attempt at characterisation of the kind you find in Flaherty because we regarded this as a bit romantic. We were all pretty serious-minded chaps then, you know, and we believed, like the Russians, that you should use individuals in your film in a not exactly dehumanized way but a sort of symbolic way."[12] Edgar Anstey encapsulates the group's view; but despite this collectivist tendency, for the Grierson group Flaherty's insistence on using the individual as the centerpiece of his narratives was to prove as seductive as the poeticism of his camera style. Flaherty's contribution to the notion of the documentary (the individual as subject, and the romantic style) when mixed with Grierson's (social concern and propaganda) leads directly to privileging "victims" as subject matter. For the working class can be heroes only in the abstract sense that Anstey describes: "The early school of documentary was divorced from people. It showed people in a problem, but you never got to know them, and you never felt they were talking to each other. You never heard how they felt and thought and spoke to each other, relaxed. You were looking from a high point of view at them."[13] Examining the individual worker, given the predilections of these filmmakers, meant moving from the heroic to the alienated. Hence victims, and the emergence of a subschool of filmmakers who "wanted to lay on what the problems were for Britain so that we should see and learn and do something about it. But you don't do something unless you feel some sort of empathy and concern with the problem, and the cold commentary voice doesn't really excite you very much."[14] The competition between Grierson's line and the splinter group was short-lived. Grierson's attempt to reconstruct the landscape of industrial Britain in terms of Flaherty's exoticism (and Eisenstein's editing methods) withered on the vine.

> We worked together [explains Grierson] and produced a kind of film that gave great promise of very high development of the poetic documentary. But for some reason or another, there has been no great development of that in recent times. I think it's partly because we ourselves got caught up in social propaganda. We ourselves got caught up in the problems of housing and health, the question of pollution (we were on to that long ago). We got on to the social problems of the world, and we ourselves deviated from the poetic line.[15]

Grierson is being a little self-serving here, for the group as a whole did not get "on to the social problems of the time"; in fact, it split apart on the issue. Arthur Calder-Marshall, ever the most perceptive of Grierson's contemporary critics, summed up the problem. Commenting on the failure of the GPO film unit to document the unrest of postal workers, he wrote: "Mr. Grierson is not paid to tell the truth but to make more people use the parcel post. Mr. Grierson may like to talk about social education surpliced in self-importance and social benignity. Other people may like hearing him. But even if it sounds like a sermon, a sales talk is a sales talk."[16] Grierson's autocratic grip on documentary production in Britain was loosened, and the "serious-minded chaps" established a measure of distance and independence from him. What is more significant is that they also established the way forward, a way that the "poets" themselves came to in a few years.

Paul Rotha, partly because of personality clashes but more on principle, had quit to set up his own unit. Now Anstey and Arthur Elton, although still disciples, also left. In the films these men made in the mid-thirties can be plotted the shift from worker as hero to worker as victim.

In *Shipyard*, a typical Griersonian project about the building of a ship, Rotha (commissioned by the shipping line and working for a subsidiary of Gaumont-British) injected an understanding of how the shipbuilders would be once more idle when the work was completed. Out of material collected on his journeys to and from the yard, he also made, for the electricity-generating industry, *Face of Britain* which, inter alia, contained the first material on the slums of the industrial heartland. That same year, 1935, Elton was making *Workers and Jobs*, a film with synchronous sound about labor exchanges, for the Ministry of Labour. With Anstey he worked on the crucial *Housing Problems* for the gas industry. This too employed synchronous sound.

In *Housing Problems*, Cockney slum dwellers address the camera directly to explicate the living conditions the film depicts. This was the first time that the working class had been interviewed on film in situ. Giving them a voice by obtaining location sound with the bulky studio optical recording systems of the day was an exercise in technological audacity as great as any in the history of the cinema. Sound had come slowly. In 1934 Grierson was promising, "If we are showing workmen at work, we get the workmen to do their own commentary, with idiom and accent complete. It makes for intimacy and authenticity, and nothing we could do would be half as good."[17] Rotha had used a shipworker to do the commentary on *Shipyard*, but for synchronous sound it was necessary to go into the studio, building sets and duplicating all the procedures of the fiction film. It is no accident that the first of their synchronous-sound productions was *BBC: The Voice of Britain*, for the locations were studios, albeit designed for radio. In *Night Mail*, technological limitations meant all the train interiors being shot on a sound stage. The desire to add the worker's voice to an authentic location image was easier to announce than to achieve.

But *Housing Problems* was much more than an early solution to a major technical problem. In making the film, Elton and Anstey had rethought much of the artistic rhetoric that Grierson had imported from Flaherty. Anstey summed it up thus: "Nobody had thought of the idea which we had of letting slum dwellers simply talk for themselves, make their own film. . . . We felt that the camera must remain sort of four feet above the ground and dead on, because it wasn't our film."[18] Because Elton and Anstey eschewed the usual proprietary artistic attitude, the people in *Housing Problems* are all named and allowed the dignity of their best clothes and the luxury of their own words (albeit somewhat stiltedly expressed for the gentlemen of the production unit). Of course, this claim of nonintervention ("it wasn't our film") cannot be taken too seriously, since the interviewees were chosen and coached by the team and the results edited without consultation. But it did represent a new theme in the group's thinking about the function of the documentary director, one which was unfortunately not to be heard again for three decades.

What was immediately influential was Anstey's view of his interviewees. Instead of heroic representatives of the proletariat, he thought of them as but "poor, suffering characters"—victims. The films were moving in topic from romanticized work through unemployment to the realities of domestic conditions.

In the years to come, Anstey's view of his role—that of enabler rather than creator—and the courtesies he afforded his interviewees would disappear. The victim would stand revealed as the central subject of the documentary, anonymous and pathetic, and the director of victim documentaries would be as much of an "artist" as any other filmmaker.

In the years before the war, Anstey was to make *Enough to Eat*, about malnutrition, and for "March of Time" he was to cover a bitter strike in the Welsh coal fields—far removed from the titanic miner at work who was the earlier icon of the industry. Harry Watt was to do a number of exposés for "March of Time" on the scandal of church tithes and the riches of football pools (a soccer-based commercial lottery) promoters. Basil Wright, the most poetic of them all, made *Children at School*.

It is with some justice that these men claim that all current documentary practice can be traced back to their activities in the thirties. The most potent of their legacies, however, is this tradition of the victim.

Factual television cements the tradition into place. It affords a way of apparently dealing with the world while (as Calder-Marshall said of Grierson's *Drifters*) "running away from its social meaning." For it substitutes empathy for analysis, it privileges effect over cause, and therefore it seldom results in any spin-offs in the real world—that is, actions taken in society as a result of the program to ameliorate the conditions depicted. So although the majority of television documentaries and news features deal with victims, normally as types of deviants, such treatment scarcely diminishes the number of victims left in the world as potential subjects.

Independent documentary production is in like case. The rise of direct cinema produced, by the early sixties, the currently dominant style of "crisis structure" documentary. Robert Drew, whose position in these developments is not unlike Grierson's thirty years before, describes the goal of such work: "What makes us different from other reporting and other documentary filmmaking, is that in each of these stories there is a time when a man comes against moments of tension, and pressure, and revelation, and decision. It's these moments that interest us most. Where we differ from TV and press is that we're predicated on being there when things are happening to people that count."[19] But where the direct-cinema practitioners turned out to be the same was in their choice of the people they would witness in such situations. Of course, they could and did observe presidents and movie tycoons but, as in the thirties, the more fruitful strand turned out to be not the powerful but the powerless. And more than that, direct cinema gave the victim tradition the technology that allowed a degree of intrusion into ordinary people's lives that was not previously possible.

Direct cinema and *cinéma vérité* were the outcome of a concerted effort, culminating in the late fifties, to develop a particular technology—a lightweight, handholdable, synchronous-sound film camera. The demand for this had developed directly out of the Griersonian experience, where any sort of synchronous shooting required enormous intervention, if not reconstruction, on the part of the filmmakers. In the years after the war it seemed to many that without such portable equipment, documentary film would never deliver on its promise to offer un- (or minimally) mediated pictures of reality. It can be argued that this was entirely the wrong agenda, because reconstruction was not the real issue, since mediation occurs in far subtler and more or less unavoidable ways whatever the techniques used. The argument was nevertheless deployed and the equipment developed.

Television had already begun to use 16mm for news-gathering purposes, forcing the creation of ever more sensitive film stocks. The equipment the industry used for this work formed the basis of the direct-cinema experiments. In turn, the broadcasters took up the adaptations the direct-cinema practitioners made and thereby created a market for the manufacture of custom-designed self-blimped cameras and high-fidelity battery-driven tape recorders. The possibility of events being more important than were the processes of filming them now existed for the first time. No door, especially the door behind which the disadvantaged were to be found, need or could be closed to the filmmakers.

Aesthetic as well as technical trends also favored the victim as subject. It is received opinion that television demands close-ups, but it is no part of professionalization, in my experience, to stress any such thing. The industry tends to avoid the big scene because of the expense such shots involve rather than because they are considered unreadable by the audience, which, palpably, they are not. A number of other factors lead to the close-up—against light backgrounds, receiver tubes (for at least twenty years after the war) tended to overmodulate and reduce all darker areas to silhouette; by moving into the face this could be avoided. The very small eyepieces of 16mm reflex cameras (and, latterly, lightweight video equipment) again encourage the close-up as being more easily focused than longer shots. The prevalence of the 10:1 zoom lens, which can only be properly focused at the long (i.e., close-up) end of its range, has the same effect. All these technological constraints result in the close-up emerging as the dominant shot in the documentary.

(There was an early period when the direct-cinema style encouraged the use of a wide-angle lens to simplify focusing problems. This lens has been largely abandoned because the variable shot size possible with the zoom lens better serves the needs of transparent editing. It also avoids distortions, again serving the needs of transparency. And because it is much more difficult to use than a wide-angle, the *mysterium* of the cameraperson's craft is more effectively maintained.)

The documentary tradition begins with the individual heroic Inuit, "against the sky" in long shot. Currently it most often displays the private inadequacies of the urban under class, "in the bowels of the earth" in close-up. The line that enabled this to happen can be traced from Flaherty's exotic individuals, through Grierson's romanticized and heroic workers, to Anstey's victims caught in Drew's crisis structures. The line was an easy one to follow because technological developments, journalistic predilections, and ideological imperatives all played a role in facilitating it.

But there is one major concomitant problem involved in the emergence of the victim tradition which has never received the attention it demands. By choosing victims, documentarists abandoned the part supposedly played by those who comment publicly on society (the watchdogs of the guardians of power). Instead, in almost any documentary situation they are always the more powerful partner. The moral and ethical implications of this development are not only ignored, they are dismissed as infringements of filmmakers' freedoms.

III

A monstrous, giant, smouldering slagheap towering over a shabby street of slum houses, hovels fallen into ruin with one lavatory for fifty persons. But inhabited. Rent for a house was 25 shillings per week. All the property belonged to the company that owned the mine. Few men were in work. I watched the rent collectors at their disgusting job; wringing a few shillings from women some of whose men were bloodying hands and shoulders in the earth hundreds of feet below where they stood, or standing on the street corners. From some petty cash I had with me, I paid the rent for some families and bought beer in the pub for some of the miners. It gave me pleasure that the profits of Gaumont-British should be so used. How I justified it in my accounts when I got back to London is neither remembered nor important. So this was Britain in the 1930s.[20]

Rotha went to the village of East Shotton in Durham because J. B. Priestley had reported on it in a series of newspaper articles (which became the book *English Journey*). This fact describes perfectly the normal relationship between the print and audiovisual media, but I quote the diary because it is one of the few references to a filmmaker's relationship with a subject that I can find in the literature on documentary film. For instance, Joris Ivens, the most overtly political of the great documentarists, in his memoir of four decades of filmmaking (*The Camera and I*) details only one non-unidimensional relationship.[21] Normally, filmmakers regard contact with their subjects as too uninteresting to report.

In consequence, the literature tends to contain only references to what are considered deviant encounters, usually where the filmmaker has to resort to subterfuge to get the material needed.

> While I was waiting outside with the film crew . . . a truck pulled up in front of us and a burly guy clambered out and started yelling, "What the hell are you guys doing here? You're trespassing, and get the hell off my property." This was Chudiak, president of the farmer's co-op, but I didn't know it at the time and had to figure out, first, who is this guy; second, what do I say to prevent the whole show from disappearing then and there; third, how can I prevent him from learning what I'm really doing but still tell him a sufficient amount so that I won't feel forever guilty of having lied; and fourth, how can I keep the trust of the migrants, the crew chief, and gain the confidence of this guy, all at the same time?[22]

A filmmaker's lot is clearly not a happy one—but it is, arguably, less unhappy than that of the migrant workers, the subject of the above documentary. Filmmakers do worry about lying—to exploit farmers or the like. This sort of worry can be traced back to the thirties. Watt described conning vicars while making his "March of Time" about church tithes: "Being film people, we'd take advantage. We used to go to sweet vicars living in a twenty-room house and with a congregation of ten, mostly old women. And I'd say, 'What a beautiful house and beautiful church. May I photograph?' Of course, I was showing that he was living in this enormous house and having ten parishioners. The Church was very annoyed about the whole thing, but it was just what 'March of Time' wanted."[23] With all due respect to these filmmakers, such worries are easy. They reveal the filmmaker in a traditional journalistic role as protector of the powerless and fearless confronter of the powerful. The more vexing moral issue is raised not by the need to misrepresent oneself before the farmer but rather by the necessity to remain silent about the reality of the situation in the presence of the migrant workers. It is not the fabrication of intention for the vicar but the easy assumption that the filmmaker and the film production company know better than the Church established what the society best needs. And it is these issues that are not addressed.

The victim tradition makes it all too easy to itemize, almost at random, a wide range of problems.

First, when dealing with the powerless, what does the legally required consent mean? Since for most people the consequences of media exposure are unknown, how can one be expected to evaluate such consequences? For some people, as with the mentally ill in Wiseman's banned *Titicut Follies*, there is a question of whether or not consent can truly be given in any circumstances. The same would apply to the male child prostitutes appearing in the videotape *Third Avenue, Only the Strong Survive.*

In this same text is raised a second question, that of complicity. The crew reconstructed a car heist and then filmed one of the protagonists in prison subsequent to another robbery of the same kind. All films about deviant activities place the filmmakers in, at best, quasi-accessory positions.

Beyond the illegal there is the dangerous. Flaherty paid the men of Aran five pounds to risk their lives by taking a canoe out into a heavy sea. (There is some quite infuriatingly stupid comment about this sequence suggesting that the men were in no danger because of the peculiarities of the waters around Aran. Any who believe this have simply failed to look at the film.) Or there can be more specific danger, as in a student project which took a man recovering from compulsive gambling to the track to see how well he was doing and to provide the film with a climax.

A more unexpected problem arises when the subject desires media exposure, as in a BBC documentary about an exhibitionist transsexual shot in the most voyeuristic manner consistent with public exhibition. In another British television film, *Sixty Seconds of Hatred*, a man's murder of his wife was examined. I screened the movie, on the eve of transmission, with the murderer and the teenage son of the marriage, who was a child when the crime was committed. There was no doubt that the man was eager to relive the incident, but beyond a careful decision not to include the son in the film, nobody had further considered what such a public retelling of the tale might do to the boy.

These are not, in my view, abstract concerns affecting only the subjects of documentaries. The problems also redound to the filmmakers. In a British television documentary, *Goodbye, Longfellow Road*, the film crew documented a women's descent into pneumonia. The crew interviewed the doctor as he was rushing her stretcher to the ambulance and ascertained that it was indeed the result of living in a hovel that had caused her condition. As a television producer, I would find it extremely difficult to comfort myself with the thought that I had contributed to the public's right to know when I could have, for a pittance, provided my victim with a roof, however temporary. Of course, I would have needed another subject for my film.

Other problems arise from the fact that these texts have extended, perhaps nearly indefinite, lives. Paul, the failed salesman in the Maysles film of that name, is constantly exposed as such wherever documentary film classes are taught or Maysles retrospectives are held. The anonymous midwestern boy who spews his heart up as a result of a drug overdose in Wiseman's *Hospital*, spews away every time the film is screened. Should it be played in the community where he is now, one hopes, a stable and respectable citizen, there is nothing he can do about it. For the film is not a lie, it is not maliciously designed to bring him into either hatred, ridicule, or contempt, and therefore he has no action for libel. And the film was taken with his consent, presumably obtained subsequent to his recovery.

And this consent is, indeed, all that the law requires. The question must be asked, is it enough?

IV

In 1909 two steamships collided in Long Island Sound. On board one of them, a radio operator, John R. Binns, successfully (and for the first time anywhere) used his machine to call for help. As a result of his CDQ, only six of the seventeen hundred passengers on board drowned. Binns was a hero. The Vitagraph Company, after the fashion of the day, made a "documentary" about the incident, entirely reconstructed and using an actor to impersonate Binns. Binns the actor was shown as lounging about and winking at the passengers at the moment of the collision. Binns the hero sued—not only for libel but also for invasion of privacy. He won on both counts. But the privacy decision was to prove exceptional.[24]

The courts over the years, according to the account given by Pember in *Privacy and the Press*, were to take the basic view that any filmed event, if not reconstructed, was protected by the First Amendment.[25]

The only line of exceptions to this arose, both for films and for the press, out of a series of decisions about the unauthorized use of images in advertisements, the earliest being heard in the English Court of Chancery in 1888. By 1903, New York State had a privacy statute on the books that was specifically limited to such unauthorized uses for advertising or "trade purposes." The courts were to be very restrictive in defining "trade purposes," and again and again privacy actions failed if the commerce involved was simply the commerce of the news business, whatever the medium. In such cases the conflict is seen as being between the public's right to know and the private citizen's right to privacy—and the former normally prevails.

The courts were happy to distinguish between advertising and news, and the above exceptions were based on that distinction. For despite the terminology used, the cases turn on some sense of property, on the idea that another should not profit *directly* from the use of one's image. Other arguments have been advanced suggesting that persons should be protected from exploitation by the news media because they are private individuals. These have been, by and large, as unsuccessful as the attempts to extend the concept of commercial exploitation. The idea of the "public man" goes back to 1893 and was extended in the twenties.[26] The right to privacy was then defined as "the right to live one's life in seclusion, without being subjected to unwarranted and undesired publicity. In short, it is the right to be left alone. . . . There are times, however, when one, whether willing or not, becomes an actor in an occurrence of public or general interest. When this takes place he emerges from his seclusion, and it is not an invasion of his right of privacy to publish his photograph with an account of such occurrence."[27] One can become an "involuntary public figure" by giving birth to a child at twelve years of age, being held hostage by a gunman, or having one's skirts blown above one's head in public.[28] And becoming an "involuntary public figure" was no temporary thing. A boy prodigy could not prevent the press pursuing him and removing the cloak of obscurity he had sought.[29] Neither, since the common law has never acknowledged distress as a ground of action, could parents prevent the publication of pictures of the dead bodies of their children.[30] Nor can the victims of rape, for the same reason, keep their names from the media, unless statute orders otherwise (which it does in some states).

Images of people in public domain, even if engaged in deviant (but not illegal) activities, are protected as newsworthy too. A couple embracing in a public place claimed that a photographer—in this case Cartier Bresson—had invaded their privacy. They lost.[31] Places of public access offer limited protection. In Wisconsin, in an admittedly obscure and extreme case, a tavern owner was permitted to photograph a woman in the toilet of his premises and show the picture at the bar.[32]

Many other examples could be given of the zealousness with which the courts have guarded press rights, and the courts have not been loath to extend these protections from the press, first to newsreels and latterly to television. An innocent man filmed while being thrust against a wall in an hotel and questioned by police officers was held to have no action against the television station using those images, even though his innocence was in no way reported.[33] Newsworthiness encompassed all the previous excesses of the press. A newsreel company was entitled to film fat women in a private weight-reduction class. The judgment states: "While it may be difficult in some instances to find the point at which public interest ends, it seems reasonably clear that pictures of a group of corpulent women attempting to reduce with the aid of some rather novel and unique apparatus does not cross the border line, at least as long as a large portion of the female sex continues its present concern about any increase in poundage."[34]

All aspects of the law were transferred wholesale to the new media. In *Cohn v. Cox Broadcasting*, the Supreme Court, in 1975, refused to acknowledge any concept of media amplification. Since the name of the rape victim in that case had appeared in the public record, the company was free to broadcast it.[35]

Consent, equally, has never been developed as a concept, except that it was deemed to be unobtainable from minors. In *Commonwealth of Massachusetts v. Wiseman* it was further held that consent was not obtained from the participants in the film *Titicut Follies*. Of the sixty-two mental patients seen in the film, most were not competent to sign releases, and only twelve such forms were completed.[36] (The need for written consent had been established in a case in which CBS was successfully sued by a person who was represented in a dramatic reconstruction of a real-life incident, which had been made with consent and advice but without written permission.)[37] Wiseman's account of the *Titicut Follies* case is in rather different terms: "I had permission from the superintendent. I had permission from the commissioner of correction. I had an advisory opinion from the attorney general of Massachusetts, and I had the strong support of the then lieutenant governor. However, some of these men turned against me when the film was finished, with most of the trouble starting two or three months after the superintendent and the attorney general had seen the film."[38]

Wiseman in this interview claims that "this was the first time in American constitutional history . . . whereby publication of any sort which has not been judged to be obscene has been banned from public viewing." This is not wholly accurate; rather, it was the first time that an injunction was obtained on the grounds of failure to obtain consent *outside of advertising*. The case, although therefore important, still does not acknowledge the existence of a right of privacy in any well-defined way. It joins *Binns v. Vitagraph Co.* as one of the few precedents that go against the interests of the press, almost all of which turn on consent issues.

The fact is—as those hostile to the idea of a tort for invasion of privacy maintain—there is no basis for such an action in the common law. It was in the *Harvard Law Review* of December 15, 1890, that two young Boston lawyers, Warren and Brandeis (later to become a Supreme Court justice), first enunciated the right of privacy.[39] Arguing on the basis of mainly English precedent, they suggested that an action might lie, specifically to prevent what they saw as the gossiping excesses of the Boston press of the day. They relied on the old doctrine of ancient lights (whereby one cannot make a window to overlook one's neighbor, unless proof of a previous window could be brought) and analogy with copyright law. They suggested that the common law acknowledged a right to an "inviolate personality" and afforded as much protection of that right as it did of inviolate property. They used a range of authorities to support this contention, including a case in which the publisher of the private drawings of Queen Victoria and Prince Albert had been restrained. (The royal case, which anyway could have turned on copyright and general notions of property, is dubious, since Victoria—despite the Magna Carta and the English civil war, which took away the power of the monarchy—had a way with the courts. The logical absurdity of the verdict of "guilty but insane" arose in another case entirely because of Victoria's objections that any who tried to kill her, however deranged, had to be guilty.)

But despite the best efforts of Warren and Brandeis, the English common law will not sustain a right to privacy or the concept of an "inviolate personality." The textbook on torts I was assigned as a law student waxes positively amused at the thought.

> A much discussed point is whether the law of torts recognises a "right of privacy." There may be circumstances where invasions of privacy will not constitute defamation or any other tort already discussed. For example, the jilted lover who makes his former sweetheart a present of a bathing costume which dissolves in chlorinated water; the farmer who offends the old spinsters across the road by encouraging his beasts to mate on Sunday mornings in a paddock in full view of the old ladies; the hotel manager who rushes into the plaintiffs' bedroom and says: "Get out of here—this is a respectable hotel" (and the plaintiffs are man and wife); the newspaper which, on the eve of an election, rakes up the forgotten past of one of the candidates; . . . the newspaper reporters who, regrettably, sometimes stop at no invasion of privacy in order to "get a story." No English decision has yet recognised that infringement of privacy is a tort unless it comes within one of the existing heads of liability.[40]

It seems to me that this whole area has passed beyond the "regret" of lawyers. In Britain the right to privacy does not exist. In the United States, except against the government and in the case of unauthorized advertising, it is extremely unclear. One cannot but agree with New York Supreme Court Justice Sheintag, who stated nearly half a century ago: "A free press is so intimately bound up with fundamental democratic institutions that, if the right of privacy is to be extended to cover news items and articles of general public interest, educational and informative in character, it should be the result of clear legislative policy."[41]

The legislation has never been forthcoming, and in the intervening decades the waters have been considerably muddied. Most important, the courts have been slow to understand the implications of new technologies. In 1927, in *Olmstead v. United States*, the Supreme Court held that wiretapping by the government did not infringe the Fourth Amendment's prohibition against "the right of people to be secure in their persons, houses, papers and effects, against unreasonable searches and seizures." This was because no things were seized, only conversations overheard. It took exactly forty years for the court to reverse itself.[42]

The line from *Olmstead v. United States* to the Privacy Act of 1974 (which protects citizens from the misuse of government data about them) has important repercussions on the string of press victories documented above. For now, with the emergence of computer databases and the convergence of media, there is considerable and widespread concern about abuses to the right of privacy which the new technological configuration could entail. While tyranny has functioned all too well without the computer, most seem to feel it could function very much better with it, and throughout the West, legislation is being put in place to combat that possibility. It is likely that in democratic societies such concern might also express itself in a more aggressive establishment of the tort of invasion of privacy than has hitherto been possible. It could also be the case that such extensions would begin to breach the protections of the

First Amendment and that, in the wash of the mounting concern about information in general, important media freedoms could be jeopardized.

The situation is not unlike that of the British in Singapore in 1941. Guns facing the sea, the garrison was confident it could not be attacked from the jungle to its rear. Yet that is exactly what the Japanese did, and the British guns were captured cold, pointing the wrong way.

One understands and sympathizes with the emotions stirred by the First Amendment, but it is an eighteenth-century device addressing eighteenth-century situations. Insisting that what was conceived of as a virtual private right should attach to any legal entity in the society however large; insisting that no technological advance in communications has affected the basic essence of privacy and reputation; insisting that these freedoms are so fragile, only a domino-theory approach can protect them—all of these stands must be abandoned if the real dangers of the late twentieth century are to be faced. The point is that the media have traditionally been considered not just as representatives of the general public but as the general public itself. Such a view, while understandable in eighteenth-century terms, fails to distinguish present day realities—where the media are not at all the general public but are instead a special interest dominated by an oligopolistically arranged group of international conglomerates. The commonly held view that the freedoms of expression demanded by such entities must be protected because identical individual freedoms will be at stake if they are not is, I submit, simply false. The individual's right to free speech is now separated from the media's right to the same by an abyss of technology. They can and should be treated differently.

V

Rights are normally accompanied by duties. Press rights are accompanied by minimal duties not to blaspheme, libel, or utter sedition. Desuetude characterizes the first and last of these, and libel is a remedy available only to those with enough resources, emotional and financial, to take on the great corporation, which is, today, the commonest libeler.

For film- and videomakers caught in the Griersonian tradition of seeking social amelioration through the documentation of societies' victims, the law, given the amplification of message possible with current technologies, allows too much latitude. Documentarists, by and large, do not libel and, by and large, do not "steal" images. Yet they are working with people who, in matters of information, are normally their inferiors—who know less than they do about the ramifications of the filmmaking process. It seems appropriate that an additional "duty of care" be required of them. "In order to protect the interests of others against the risks of certain harms, the law prescribes certain standards of conduct to which persons in particular circumstances ought to conform, and if, from failure to attain those standards, such harm ensues, this is actionable."[43] The "harm" resulting from invasion of privacy is not normally considered actionable if it rises out of exercise of press freedom. Nor does an individual have an "inviolate personality" along the lines proposed by Warren and Brandeis. Were this to change, then defining the filmmaker's duty of care to his or her subject would devolve on the concept of consent. Instead of the crude "consent" we now have, more refined consideration would be needed. Such refinements already exist in the medical and social science research procedures developed, mainly without the pressure of law, by many professional bodies. Among the most comprehensive of these was the Nuremburg Code.

> The voluntary consent of the human subject is absolutely essential.
>
> This means that the person involved should have legal capacity to give consent; should be so situated as to be able to exercise the free power of choice, without the intervention of any element of force, fraud, deceit, duress, over-reaching, or other ulterior form of constraint or coercion; and should have sufficient knowledge and comprehension of the elements of the subject matter involved as to enable him to make an understanding and enlightened decision. This latter element requires that before acceptance of an affirmative decision by the experimental subject there should be made known to him the nature, duration and purpose of the experiment; the method and means by which it is to be conducted; all inconveniences and hazards reasonably to be expected; and the effects upon his health or person which may possibly come from his participation in the experiment.[44]

Substitute *film* for *experiment* and *experimental* in the above, and a fair definition of a filmmaker's duty of care results. Filmmakers will argue that this would massively reduce access to subjects. So be it. Since the fifty-year parade of the halt and the lame has patently done more good to the documentarists than it has to the victims, I see no cause to mourn a diminution of these texts. To facilitate the operation of a duty of care, I would suggest that society refine its view of film- and videomaking activities to acknowledge the following:

1. *That different channels of communication have different effects.* The decision in *Massachusetts v. Wiseman* limiting the distribution of *Titicut Follies* to professional audiences is perfectly good from this point of view. It is reasonable to suggest that social value could accrue from a film or tape in specialized circumstances, whereas social damage could result in other, more general situations. Questions of *cui bono* are not inappropriate in this setting, either. Courts should be less hesitant to examine the commerce of the media than they have been hitherto.

2. *That the law distinguishes public and private personae.* At a commonsense level, the distinction between a public figure and a private person is obvious. The law often defines far more complex social phenomena,

and there is no reason why such a distinction could not be made part of the consideration of privacy issues. Public and private personae should be afforded different degrees of protection. At the moment, ordinary people are left naked in the glare of publicity. Conversely, sometimes public figures use the scant protection the law intends for ordinary persons to inhibit or prevent what would be, in their cases, quite proper exposés. (I am conscious that this happens more in Great Britain than the United States.)

3. *That the protection afforded the private domain be extended to private personae in semipublic and public areas.* This would allow a measure of protection to the "bystander." At the moment, acts of the media are like acts of God in that one can be hit by them, as it were, in almost any circumstances. It is difficult to see why this should be considered an essential prerequisite for the freedom of information.

4. *That the effect of media exposure of otherwise permissible actions be assessed.* I have argued that social deviance is an essential element in the victim tradition. Such deviance often crucially depends on domain, so that what is permissible in private becomes deviant, even illegal, in public. The effect of *publication* of permissible actions, where because either the actions are deviant of themselves or the fact of publication renders them deviant, ought to be considered.

Any or all of the above could be fatal to the victim tradition of documentary filmmaking, but I would see that as no loss. Indeed, for the concerns expressed here and for other reasons, I would much prefer a style of documentary along the lines of Rouch's "participatory anthropology"; but the real question is not, what effect would such a proposal have on documentary, but rather, would it abolish essential media freedoms?

The concept of a duty of care in privacy is to be balanced against the established right of the public to know and of the media to publish. These rights would be constrained, just as many rights in other areas are—but not more so. Freedom of comment, the power to investigate the publicly powerful, the right to publish facts would be unimpeded by the sort of development I propose. All that would go is the unfettered media right to exploit those in society least able to defend themselves. By defining what exploitation means, how and where it takes place, and who those defenseless people are, the constraint could be delimited and the functions of the media otherwise maintained.

For many, especially in the United States, such proposals are anathema, yet the changing times demand some fresh response. It is not the case that since the thing works, it should not be fixed. The thing in this case, privacy, works none too well and looks to be getting worse. The media need to establish a distance from the most vexed of the information technology areas, where controversy is likely to result in a serious curtailment of activity. The media need to reestablish their special position. That can only be achieved by the assumption of suitable late-twentieth-century responsibilities. Otherwise,

> limited freedom for any instrumentality of society always threatens the stability of society, and society will react to protect its stability. Totally unfettered media could threaten and in the view of many already do threaten the stability of American life. Americans will react to reestablish and strengthen that stability. The lesson should not be lost on the press, radio and television. . . . The press is never really free unless it accepts a pattern which protects it from the perils of self-destruction.[45]

Notes

1. Alan Rosenthal, *The New Documentary in Action* (Berkeley and Los Angeles: University of California Press, 1971), p. 71.

2. Forsyth Hardy, ed., *Grierson on Documentary* (London: Faber, 1979), pp. 48, 188.

3. Elizabeth Sussex, *The Rise and Fall of British Documentary* (Berkeley and Los Angeles: University of California Press, 1975), p. 21.

4. Paul Rotha, *Documentary Diary* (New York: Hill and Wang, 1973), p. 1.

5. Sussex, *British Documentary*, p. 29.

6. Rotha, *Documentary Diary*, p. 49.

7. Sussex, *British Documentary*, p. 77.

8. Forsyth Hardy, *John Grierson* (London: Faber, 1979), p. 29.

9. Hardy, ed., *Grierson on Documentary*, p. 77.

10. Sussex, *British Documentary*, p. 76.

11. Hardy, ed., *Grierson on Documentary*, p. 64.

12. Sussex, *British Documentary*, p. 18.

13. Ibid., p. 76.

14. Ibid.

15. Ibid., p. 79.

16. Arthur Calder-Marshall, *The Changing Scene* (London: Chapman and Hall, 1937).

17. John Grierson, "The G.P.O. Gets Sound," *Cinema Quarterly* (Summer 1934), quoted in Sussex, *British Documentary*, p. 44.

18. Sussex, *British Documentary*, p. 62.

19. Richard Drew, quoted in Stephen Mamber, *Cinéma Vérité in America* (Cambridge, Mass.: MIT Press, 1974), p. 118.

20. Rotha, *Documentary Diary*, p. 104.

21. Joris Ivens, *The Camera and i* (New York: International Publishers, 1974), pp. 193–204.

22. Rosenthal, *The New Documentary in Action*, p. 108.

23. Sussex, *British Documentary*, p. 89.

24. *Binns v. Vitagraph Co.*, 210 N.Y. 51 (1913).

25. Don R. Pember, *Privacy and the Press* (Seattle: University of Washington Press, 1972).

26. *Corliss v. E. W. Waler and Co.*, Fed. Rep. 280 (1894).

27. *Jones v. Herald Post Co.*, 230 Ky. 227 (1929).

28. *Meetze v. AP*, 95 S.E. 2d 606 (1956).

29. *Sidis v. New Yorker*, 133 Fed. 2d 806 (1940).

30. *Kelly v. Post Publishing Co.*, 327 Mass. 275 (1951).

31. *Gill v. Hearst*, 253 Pa. 2d 441 (1953).

32. *Yoeckel v. Samonig*, 272 Wis. 430 (1956).

33. *Jacova v. Southern Radio-TV Co.*, 83 So. 2d 34 (1955).

34. *Sweenek v. Pathe News, Inc.*, 16 F. Supp. 746 (1936), Judge Moscowitz @ p. 747 et seq.

35. G. Snyder, *The Right to Be Left Alone* (New York: Messner, 1976), p. 84.

36. Pember, *Privacy and the Press*, pp. 224ff.

37. *Durgom v. CBS*, 214 N.Y. 2d 1008 (1961).

38. Rosenthal, *The New Documentary in Action*, pp. 68ff.

39. Reprinted in A. Breckenridge, *The Right to Privacy* (Lincoln: University of Nebraska Press, 1970), pp. 132ff.

40. Harry Street, *The Law of Torts* (London: Butterworth, 1959), p. 411.

41. Pember, *Privacy and the Press*, p. 112.

42. Snyder, *The Right to Be Left Alone*, pp. 148ff.

43. Street, *The Law of Torts*, p. 103.

44. Quoted in P. D. Reynolds, *Ethics and Social Science Research* (Englewood Cliffs, N.J.: Prentice-Hall, 1982), p. 143.

45. W. Marnall, *The Right to Know* (New York: Seabury Press, 1973), p. 212.

Reflections on
An American Family, II
Craig Gilbert

On the Air and the Reaction

During a twelve-month period in 1967–68 I made a documentary called *Margaret Mead's New Guinea Journal*. In the course of that experience I became a friend of that remarkable woman, and we remained friends until she died. Shortly before *An American Family* went on the air, I invited her to a screening of the first couple of episodes. Her comments were perceptive and flattering, but she also added a realistic warning: "There are going to be a lot of people, Craig, who, after they've watched the series for a little while, are going to ask themselves: what would a camera crew see if they lived with my family for seven months? This thought is going to make them very nervous, and it won't be long before that nervousness turns to anger and they turn you off."

As was usually the case, Margaret Mead was extraordinarily accurate in her prediction. But I think we were both more than somewhat shocked (I know I was) by the source of the anger she had predicted. By and large, viewers all over the country liked the series, although perhaps *liked* is not the correct word to use. In the incredible amount of mail generated by the series, the writers said they found the series "painful but true" about many aspects of their family life, that they appreciated seeing "something on television that portrays family life the way it is," that the series helped them to feel that they were "not alone." There were viewers, of course, who did not like the series. But the source of most of the anger I was aware of came from the Loud family and the critics. By critics I mean not only the reviewers of television programs, but the men and women who write articles and feature stories for newspapers and magazines.

It is hard for people to believe I did not anticipate the anger of the Louds. Perhaps I was naive, perhaps I chose to ignore that it was a very real possibility. Ultimately I understood, even sympathized, but when it first broke around my head I was puzzled and hurt. Throughout the shooting we had been good friends, and we remained so during the year it took to edit the series. As I had promised, we screened every episode for a member of the family (usually it was Pat, sometimes Pat and Bill, and occasionally one or more of the kids would be present) before it was "locked up." There were very few objections, certainly none of any substance.[1]

After one such screening, the staff of *An American Family* received a letter from Pat. I quote from her letter as a contrast to her and her family's future anger. It said, in part:

> I think you have handled the film with as much kindness as is possible and still remain honest. I think you have put it together in such a way and with such fine pacing that a vast audience, quite unknown to us, will find enough in each program to look forward to the next. I am, in short, simply astounded, enormously pleased, and very proud that your collective wits have collaborated on this venture. You have eminently justified the faith my family tacitly put in you when we started this series and, my dears, we shall keep the faith. . . . Believe me, if anyone ever wants to muck around in my life again, it has got to be you.

The lives that Pat and Bill and their children had lived during the seven months we filmed them could not be called unusual by any stretch of the imagination. Although I never regarded any of the Louds as typical or average, I did suspect that the emotions they felt, the problems they encountered, and the pressures they attempted to cope with were fairly representative of those experienced by members of millions of families all over the country. The Louds didn't see themselves as unique or in any way out of the ordinary, and neither did I.

But it was precisely this ordinariness and our faithfulness to it in the filmmaking process that caused all the trouble. Because, in the recording of it over a seven-month period, something extraordinary was revealed. It took me a long time to understand what I am now about to say, and an even longer time to face the implications of it. And I may not be able to say it very well. But I will do my best.

At the very beginning of this account, I theorized in my proposal for the series that if you could stay with a family, any family, for a long enough period of time *something interesting would be revealed about why men and women in their various roles were having such a difficult time in the America of the early seventies.*

The operative words here are *difficult time*. Yes, I am guilty. I had a point of view. My senses, my perceptions of what was happening in my life and in the lives around me led inevitably to that point of view. No, I did not think men and women were blissfully happy; no, I did not think relationships, by and large, were mature, mutually satisfying, and productive; no, I did not think family life was the endless round of happy mindlessness pictured in television commercials, or a convenient cornucopia of serious problems that could be resolved neatly and joyously in the space of an hour, as the television sitcoms and dramas would have us believe. If I had felt all this, if I had felt that "Ozzie and Harriet," "The Brady Bunch," and "Father Knows Best" were accurate portrayals of the way American women and men were living their lives, I would not have spent two years of my life making *An American Family*.

Yes, I thought that what I was proposing would reveal some unpleasant, disturbing, depressing things. Yes, what I found was unpleasant and disturbing and depressing, but not because I or anyone on the staff manipulated the Louds' lives as they lived, in actuality or on film. I found these things, and they appeared in the series because they were there.

And what I wanted to say was that, because of the very ordinariness of the Louds, the universality of the problems they faced, the emotions they felt, and the pressures they had to cope with, this is a series about all of us, you and me and every man and woman, young or old, rich or poor, white or black, who lives in the United States in the second half of the twentieth century.

I hoped that viewers would sense the universality and understand it and in the course of experiencing the "shock of recognition" begin to realize that many of the things they felt were also felt by millions of other men and women. I was not foolish enough to think that *An American Family* would solve any problems, but I did hope it might be the beginning of a small awareness. And I hoped this awareness might be the beginning of something more.

And it was. Several families on a block would get together to watch the series and talk about it afterward, schools assigned classes to watch the series and prepare for a discussion the next day, clergymen gave sermons on the series and suggested that their congregations turn it on. I know this is true from the mail the series generated and from talking to audiences in several lectures I made around the country after the series was off the air. In short, and I know I have said this already but it is important to emphasize the point, millions of viewers were pleased that *An American Family* was on the air; they found it interesting, helpful, and positive. In their letters, they found the Louds courageous, understandable, likable, and more than a little similar to themselves or someone they knew.

Some of the critics (not too many) felt the same way and said so in print. As a matter of fact, the trouble (my trouble) started with a review by a critic, Fredelle Maynard, a freelance writer whose piece "An American Family: The

Crack in the Mirror" appeared in *Image*, WNET/13's membership magazine, a couple of weeks before the first episode of the series appeared on the air. The following are some excerpts:

> They could be the Geritol couple. He's handsome, charming, sexy, a good talker. She's beautiful and elegant, with legs a twenty-year-old might envy and a kind of total calm. But he never says, "Honey, you're incredible!" In fact, he seldom speaks to her directly. From the first breakfast scene of *An American Family* you sense that . . . these two decorative people lost each other a long time ago. . . . Most viewers will experience the shock of recognition. There we are, and our friends and neighbors. . . . Flying, partying, quarreling, just talking, the Louds reveal a peculiarly American faith in simple solutions, instant cure. Unhappy? Take a trip. Lonely? Give a party, set your hair. Pat's instinct in a crisis is to reach for a drink. . . . The breakdown of communication so striking in the Loud family is perhaps a typically American disease, the result of disproportionate emphasis on maintaining surfaces, keeping cool. These people touch without meeting, meet without touching. . . . Again and again a single scene encapsulates the family tragedy. . . . Lance, after his mother leaves, climbing what seems an endless flight of stairs. Bill turning on the charm over cocktails— "Have you been in a wreck lately?"—and revealing himself more than he knows as he plays out the line. . . . What went wrong? What does it mean? As the camera searches for answers—the fault is everyone's and no one's—something remarkable happens to the viewer. He finds himself thinking not just about the Louds but about families in general—and about himself.

When I read this review I was very pleased. It was the first outside professional evaluation of the series we had received, and it said all the things I had hoped it would say. In seven months of filming this decent, ordinary family something indeed had been revealed, and Fredelle Maynard had seen what it was.

My joy was short-lived. Lance, who loved to cause trouble, got hold of the article and read it over the phone to his mother in Santa Barbara. And of course she hit the ceiling. (I say "of course" now, but it wasn't so easy to say "of course" at the time.) Pat's anger stemmed from a conviction that I had betrayed her and her family, something I had promised I would never do. And I didn't think I had, either in the seven months of shooting or in the twelve months of editing. Her letter, it seemed to me, was proof of that. Pat Loud and Fredelle Maynard had looked at the same twelve episodes; the problem was that, inevitably, they had seen them in different ways. The old cliché that we never see ourselves the way others see us had come home to roost with a vengeance.

Eighteen months earlier, during the shooting in Santa Barbara, an incident had occurred which Pat's anger now triggered in my memory. One night, Pat and I and several members of the production staff were sitting around having drinks when, out of the blue, she turned to me and asked, "Listen, Craig, what the hell is this series supposed to be about?"

She had asked the question several times; the first time, of course, had been when I met her and her family and told them about what I was planning to do. I have tried my best to remember what I told her then and on the other occasions, but I honestly can't. However, I do remember what I said this time.

Perhaps it was my mood, perhaps it was the several drinks I'd already had, perhaps it was the knowledge (always with me) that only recently I had failed in my own marriage. Whatever the reason, I blurted out, "You know what this series is about, Pat? It's about how you and I and everyone in this room and everyone in the country is fumbling around trying to make sense out of their lives." Pat's response was immediate and understandable: "I'm not fumbling, for Christ's sake. That's a lot of shit."

None of us likes to be told we are not in complete control of our own destinies, at least not in front of other people. On the other hand, sleepless, at three in the morning, most of us have felt the gnawing fear that all is not right with our lives. I had a strong suspicion that Pat Loud was currently experiencing many of those fears. In this sense, her response, though consistent with her character, was not entirely honest. But then, neither was my answer to her question.

Unless you are doing what I have referred to earlier as an "investigative report," it is hard to explain, with absolute truth, what your documentary is about. If what you are doing is concerned with an "issue," it is easy and accurate to say, "I am making a film about the dangers of nuclear energy," or "I am making a film about how nursing homes mistreat old people," or "I am making a film about the spread of terrorism in the world." But if what you are doing is concerned with more general questions of human behavior, it is a good deal more difficult to give a specific and satisfactory answer without either misleading or antagonizing the subjects of your film and in the process endangering the life of the project.

Having read thus far in this account, you are well aware of my desire, in *An American Family*, to explore the reasons why, in the early seventies in the United States, it seemed to be so difficult for adults to get along with each other in their roles as men and women, husbands and wives, fathers and mothers. However, I was well aware that the so-called *cinéma vérité* technique of following the members of the Loud family as they lived their lives for seven months could produce a series of films which would touch on many aspects of those lives *in addition to the ones I consciously set out to explore*. The *cinéma vérité* net invariably comes up with much more than the fish you are trying to catch. So for this reason, a precise, definite, conclusive answer to Pat's question would have been misleading. But there were other reasons not quite so altruistic.

Human beings do not like to be treated like guinea pigs. If you tell the subjects of a documentary that their behavior and their lives are being used to make a larger statement about human behavior and human lives in general, they are more than likely going to be highly insulted. We all tend to think of ourselves as special and unique, with problems, fears, likes, and dislikes different from those of every other person in the world. Of course, this is not true, and the discrepancy in perception between the way we see ourselves and the way others see us always comes as a distasteful shock when we are forced to confront it. Incidentally, it is also this discrepancy, if the proper subject is chosen, that makes the *cinéma vérité* technique such a powerful and exciting form of filmmaking.

Finally, people have a tendency to idealize themselves. If, for instance, I had told Pat I was trying to do a series of films about how men and women feel about themselves and their various roles, I'm sure she would have said something like, "Listen, baby, we're perfect," and considered me crazy for trying to compare her family with any other family in the country. At the very least she would have been more self-conscious, and she might even have considered backing out of the project.

If Bill had asked what the series was about (he never did and didn't seem to care), I would have been in even more trouble. After *An American Family* was on the air, he stated publicly that one of the hardest things for him to understand was why his family had not been perceived by viewers and press as the West Coast Kennedys.

At any rate, I know there were problems in responding to Pat's question with complete honesty, and I also know those problems were not limited to the special conditions under which *An American Family* was filmed. More often than not, and certainly more often than has been admitted, documentary filmmakers are unable to tell the whole truth about what they're up to without running the risk of being told to peddle their papers elsewhere. It is not that we are liars or more inherently dishonest than anyone else; it is simply that the nature of the business we are in makes it impossible, a good deal of the time, to be absolutely candid.

The bottom line, as they like to say in television, is that we are *using human beings* to make a point. To invoke the harsh but accurate word, we are "exploiting" them to make our films, and no matter how sensitive, caring, or understanding we may be, the fact is that our incomes and our careers often depend on our ability to conceal the truth of this exploitation from our subjects. That some subjects accept this exploitation, and others even revel in it, does not alter the fact that documentary filmmaking poses very real ethical and moral questions which must be dealt with carefully and compassionately.

In retrospect, it is clear that Pat would have been angry with any comment that implied less than total approval of the way she, her husband, and her children conducted their lives. Understandably, she was happiest with those reviews and feature stories which accepted her violent protestations of betrayal and manipulation as the gospel truth and went on to denigrate the series as a malicious put-down of the essential nobility and sanctity of the American family and definitive proof of the deviousness and viciousness of Craig Gilbert, the filmmaker.

This was the beginning but not the end of my disillusionment with American journalism. Faced with a difficult, complicated story that had great bearing on a number of important issues—not the least of which was television's ability or inability, willingness or unwillingness, to deal with certain kinds of reality— reporters chose to take the easier and more salable road of sensationalism. And the great majority of them, deeply dedicated to fairness and objectivity, never even bothered to pick up the phone to get my side of the story. As an example of this kind of journalism, I quote from an interview with Pat Loud by Kay Gardella in the *New York Daily News* of February 20, 1973, as follows:

> "If Craig Gilbert gets an Emmy for the *American Family* series," said a disturbed Pat Loud yesterday, "then I guess we get the brass garbage can. I feel like Joan of Arc on a jackass riding backwards! . . . " Pat, the 45-year-old divorced mother of the Loud family of Santa Barbara, feels betrayed by the series' producer and WNET and she's not sure how to react and what to do about it. . . . "I was assured by Craig that everything would be handled with great delicacy, taste and sensitivity. Instead it has been handled with enormous sensationalism and cruelty. . . . I don't understand why WNET and Gilbert permitted the printing of Fredelle Maynard's article in the station magazine when they promised there would be no editorial comment on the series. . . . " I don't know how scientific such a series can be. Anyway, the people making it aren't scientists, although Gilbert is claiming now to be an instant anthropologist. Pat has been doing television appearances and will be seen with members of her family on tonight's Dick Cavett show. If she resents exploitation and editorial comment, why, we asked her, is she going on the talk show? "I want people to see us as we are on a program that won't be edited or shaped to a concept. We've had everything said about us and have been treated with such cruelty that I think it's time we stood up and defended ourselves."

I am tempted even now, eight years after this appeared in print, to offer a rebuttal, point by point. But I think it would be a waste of time; I have already explained the state of mind Pat was in when she gave the interview. For those interested in trivia, however, I should point out that I did not get an Emmy for *An American Family*; I was not nominated for one, nor was the series, nor was any individual who worked on it. During the award ceremony, the series was dismissed with a rather snide joke in an exchange between Robert MacNeil of PBS and Walter Cronkite.

A couple of weeks before *An American Family* went on the air, a few of us who had been involved with the series for two years were sitting around the production office talking about nothing in particular. At one point someone asked, "What do you think the critics are going to say about the series?" I won't pretend the question had not occurred to me as the air date grew closer, but there were many other things to worry about and I had never given it much serious thought. Now, without even thinking, I said, "I really don't see how anyone can review the series without reviewing his own life." I cringe as I write this, because it sounds pompous and arrogant and not a little bit sanctimonious. But what I meant was this: We had filmed the Louds for seven months and had put together a twelve-part series showing what their lives had been like during that period. We had done this as honestly as possible. We (and I don't mean the editorial we—I mean everyone who worked on the series) had all been keenly aware that we had a responsibility not to play fast and loose with the trust the family had placed in us. The fact that the family had approved of each and every episode was proof enough for us that we had lived up to their trust.

Those of us who had worked on *An American Family* were not new to the documentary form. We had no illusions that we had put together a *complete* record of the family's life during the shooting period, nor did we kid ourselves that what was up there on the screen was the *total* truth of who the members of the family were and why they felt and behaved the way they did.

Within the limits of the documentary form and the time and money allotted to us we had tried to give some indication of the characters of the various members of the family. We had tried to show how the members of the family related to each other and how, singly and together, they dealt with some of the daily events of their lives.

We knew that to some extent the family had been affected by the presence of the camera despite our best efforts to minimize this effect; we admitted this in a statement that appeared at the beginning of episode 1.

Finally, we knew that *An American Family* was firmly rooted in a well-defined tradition of documentary filmmaking which had existed in the United States since the late 1950s and early 1960s. In his book *Documentary: A History of the Non-Fiction Film*, Erik Barnouw characterized this tradition, in part, by commenting:

> the special glories of the genre were its unpredictability and its ambiguity, qualities that scarcely made for comfortable relations with sponsors.[2]

Barnouw further states:

> One of the problems hanging over observer-documentarists was the extent to which the presence of the camera influenced events. Some practitioners—Leacock, Malle—worried about this. Others—Maysles, Wiseman—tended to minimize it. Some filmmakers, notably Jean Rouch, held still another view. Rouch maintained that the presence of the camera made people act in ways truer to their nature than might otherwise be the case. Thus he acknowledged the impact of the camera but, instead of considering it a liability, looked on it as a valuable catalytic agent, a revealer, of inner truth.

Because of the relatively long and much-written-about history of this kind of filmmaking technique and its general acceptance by the profession and the public, it didn't seem to me the critics would consider it worth more than a passing mention. The problems we had faced in the making of *An American Family* were the same problems that had been faced for the past twenty years by every filmmaker who made a *cinéma vérité* or direct-cinema film. By 1973 there was nothing startlingly innovative about the technique. It was employed wholly or in part in most documentaries appearing on television, and had been for some time. Except for the length of time spent with the subjects and the creation of a series rather than a single program, we had done nothing new.

Since *An American Family* had not been directed, at least not in the usual sense, direction was an aspect of the series which the critics could not evaluate. And they couldn't praise or find fault with the acting or screenwriting, since neither of these disciplines was involved in the series.

For all these reasons, I felt, naively, that the critics would have no choice but to deal with the material that was up there on the screen, and that in doing so they could not avoid dealing with their own lives. If they found anything in the series that reminded them of their own childhoods, their own relationships with men or women, their own marriages—if, in short, they found any similarities between themselves and the Louds—then, I thought, they would like the series, or at the very least treat it with respect. If, on the other hand, they could find nothing to identify with—if nothing on the screen evoked echoes or resonances in their own circumstances—then, I was afraid, they would not like the series and would dismiss it as a commendable but unsuccessful effort.

I couldn't have been more wrong. Kay Gardella's mindless and exploitive acceptance of Pat Loud's understandable and inevitable anger was the most obvious example of the use of sensationalism as a way to invalidate the content of the series.

Other journalists, though appearing to be more thoughtful than Ms. Gardella, discovered equally irrelevant reasons for avoiding any serious discussion of what they had seen on their television screens.

Newsweek: Some critics stung the Louds by identifying their central problem as an inability to communicate with each other. In at least one sense, however, they were perhaps too good at communicating. Their impromptu remarks in the film often seem improbably articulate, as though they had been scripted ahead of time.

National Observer: An American Family is a monument to Heisenberg's Principle of Indeterminacy—that the mere fact of observation has an influence on the observed. There is no pure data gathered by the motion-picture camera, and it is a slick deceit to pretend otherwise.

The Nation: An American Family was a bad idea. It is not art, because art does not use people, but rather celebrates them; and it is not fact, because man, for all his compulsive display, is essentially as secretive as the fiddler crab.

Commonweal: So, on the Cavett show for example, they [the Louds] try to fill in the gaps and reveal what the film ignored. . . . Craig Gilbert the producer is there. He is now an essential part of the drama. Not only has the *New York Times* linked him with with Pat,[3] but now the whole family angrily wants to know why he took out one sequence and left in another. He stutters and stumbles. The audience is getting a glimpse of this character who has been so much a part of the whole process.

New Republic: . . . what we have in the end is a long way from the thing-in-itself. Which means, inevitably, that the series on one level has to be judged as a work of art or artifice, and there it fails rather badly. Art enhances life. This replaces it. And something of the preciousness inherent in all experiment clings stickily to these films, partially barring sympathetic entry. It's expressed in the glib satisfaction the producer feels in the series (which the Louds, incidentally, largely hate). Craig Gilbert has patted the family in a condescending way, calling them "incredibly human" (maybe he was expecting mandrills?).

I do not mean to imply that no one had anything nice to say about *An American Family.* For example:

Time: An American Family is extraordinarily interesting to watch.

Newsweek (Shana Alexander): Their [the Louds'] candy-box ideal of "family" is something all Americans to some degree share. Why do we sacrifice so much on this altar? Why do we exhaust and consume ourselves in the struggle to create and maintain the nest? Partly we do it for the children, believing that in this way we can pass along the finest part of ourselves. But partly we do it for us, to prove to ourselves that we have worth, that we are good. . . . And so the silence of the Louds is also a scream, a scream that people matter, that they matter and we matter. I think it is a scream whose echoes will shake up all America.

Esquire (Merle Miller): I felt that the Louds emerged as very human and that the series is one of the most remarkable achievements ever. I think all kinds of important things will come out of this new way of looking at ourselves, and when the series is repeated, as surely it will be, we may even be able to set our personal discomfort aside and learn something from it.

New York Times, March 4, 1973 (John O'Connor): Whatever its faults, *An American Family* is posing serious questions. About values. About relationships. About institutions. About a constantly consuming society. About accelerating treadmills to meaningless status. About avoiding, at any cost, problems. . . . Those questions, in turn, are now being avoided as the massive publicity entertainment

mills devour the Louds. If the series and the reaction to it have been painful for
the family, let's reduce it to a joke!

The most difficult criticism for me to understand consisted of articles which
took the position that the Louds were some strange mutation of human animal,
certainly not American and very possibly not of this earth. An overwhelming
majority of the critics and columnists chose to admit no kinship whatsoever
with the Louds. As a matter of fact, they took quite the opposite view. When
they wrote about the members of the family, they described them as strange
creatures who bore little if any resemblance to any human beings the critics
had ever known. It was strange to read the daily outpourings of these writers,
in which the Louds were described as "foolish," "pathetic," "uncommuni-
cative," "spoiled," "superficial," "stupid," "insensitive," "unaware," and
embodying a long list of other qualities, none of which could possibly be
attributed to the families of the critics or to any family, in fact, residing in the
United States. In short, the Louds and the series about them could be dismissed
as having no bearing whatsoever on any aspect of life in the good old U.S.A.

On the other hand, letters by the hundreds were being sent to the series
production office by viewers describing the Louds as "courageous," "likable,"
"sympathetic," "representative," and "recognizable," and their problems as
"painful but true," "the way it is in my family," and "similar to the way it
is with our friends and the people we know."

It was strange, to say the least—the same series provoking such widely
divergent, indeed diametrically opposed, opinions. In honesty, I had trouble
seeing the Louds as anything but a normal upper-middle-class family; during
all the months of shooting and editing there were moments of intense *déjà vu*
when I had the eerie feeling that what I was seeing or hearing in Santa Barbara
I had seen or heard many years before when I was growing up in Woodmere,
Long Island.

By no stretch of the imagination, however, do I mean to imply that there
were no legitimate grounds for a critic to dislike *An American Family*. Some
considered it boring; others found it difficult to listen to because of inferior
sound. There were those who considered the series superficial and pretentious
and those who felt that, though the series conveyed a good idea of what the
Louds were *doing*, it didn't convey very much at all about what they were
thinking.

Although I did not agree with these opinions, I understood, at least during
my calmer moments, how they could be held. What I couldn't understand was
what appeared to me to be an unreasonable hostility toward the Louds and a
need, almost an obsession, to deny their membership in the human race.
Coupled with this was an equally strong need to ignore what was on the screen
in favor of the filmmaking methods involved. If any or all of these methods

could be proved invalid or sleazy, the critics seemed to be saying, then the series itself could be disqualified from any serious consideration.

Toward this end, they concentrated on five main points:

1. *The presence of lights, cameras, and microphones, etc., influenced the Louds to such an extent that their behavior on the screen had no relation to the way they would have behaved under normal conditions.* I will add only the following to what I have already said. Even if people can change their behavior or their life-style or their way of relating to people for a week or two weeks or perhaps a month, they cannot keep this up for seven months. Sooner or later, they will have to revert to living their lives the way they have always lived them. This is *one* of the reasons I insisted on such a long shooting period.

2. *Without manipulation, the Louds would not have permitted the filming of such a revealing portrait of their family life.* A corollary of this charge was that many of the scenes would not have happened without being staged. I have already said quite enough about these charges. I would add only this: there is more manipulation and staging in one twenty-minute segment of "60 Minutes" than there is in all twelve hours of *An American Family*.

3. *The invasion of the privacy of the Loud household was unethical, immoral, and outside the limits of acceptable documentary filmmaking technique.* When every night on every local news show in the country a reporter shoves a microphone in the face of a grieving mother and asks how she feels about her recently killed child, I suggest it is about time to redefine "invasion of privacy."

4. *The editing process by which some three hundred hours of film were cut down to twelve is proof positive that the series was dishonest or at the very least a highly prejudiced account of their lives.* All television critics should be required to take a crash course in documentary film-making. One of the things they would learn is that the *cinéma vérité*, or direct-cinema, technique is a very wasteful one. Since nothing is scripted and since there is a commitment *not to manipulate or stage*, a great deal of useless footage is shot. The ratio of film shot to film used on *An American Family* was twenty-five to one—a normal ratio for this kind of shooting. Unlike most of us, television critics seem to be ignorant of the fact that most of life is dull, boring, and uneventful.

5. *Heisenberg's Principle of Indeterminacy—that the mere fact of observation has an influence on the observed—undermines the validity of the entire series.* This is sheer nonsense. But let's for a moment suppose it's true. Then serious doubts would have to be entertained not only about *An American Family* but about all documentaries.

As a matter of fact, the same thing can be said about the other points on which the critics harped. If indeed they applied to *An American Family*, which they most certainly don't, then they also apply, like the Heisenberg principle, to every other documentary which has ever been made.

It seems to me that the critics' preoccupation with these points is an excuse for not dealing seriously (favorably or unfavorably) with the real context of the series, a tacit admission that there was something about it they didn't want to confront, something about their own lives they didn't want to face up to. I know that sounds self-serving, but after eight years it is the conclusion I have come to.

About six months ago I was asked to participate in a series of discussions about the documentary and television. First there was a screening of episode 2, and then there was a question-and-answer period lasting almost two hours. A week or so later I received a letter from a woman who had been in the audience that night. I did not meet her then, nor do I know whether she asked any of the questions which I tried to answer. Her letter says in part:

> I went back to a different college library this time and reread some of those 1973 articles. . . . In those articles I picked up a peculiar note of hostility, the same feeling I picked up at the Walnut [Street] Theatre [in Philadelphia, where the discussion was held] last month. What people were saying was "It's *your* fault I'm in pain." And relatively trite issues, "It's not a scientific sample," etc., are offered as evidence of the pain. Clearly nobody is asking *why* they were so bothered.

It seems to me what the woman is saying, and what I have finally come to believe, is that an awful lot of time and energy was spent trying to find scientific or moral or technical reasons for invalidating *An American Family*, for doubting its integrity, for questioning its conclusions. In short, there was a great deal of effort expended to avoid having to deal with the content of the series, and when all else failed, the last resort was to reduce it to a joke.

I said earlier that the only innovative aspect of *An American Family* was the length of time spent with the Louds. However, there is something else about the series—perhaps the most important thing—which sets it apart from most of the documentaries being made today. And that is its subject matter.

Because of considerations of time and money, most *cinéma vérité* filmmakers like to hedge their bets by picking subjects that promise, ahead of time, excitement and dramatic conflict. *Primary*, in which two men battle for the presidential nomination, *Happy Mother's Day*, in which a family fights for its dignity and survival against the onslaught of commercial exploitation, and *Salesman*, in which gullible believers are hustled into purchasing Bibles, are but a few examples of subject matter that guaranteed interesting films before shooting began.

Another way in which the *cinéma vérité* filmmaker traditionally hedges his bet is to choose as his subject a celebrity involved in a glamorous occupation. In this way, even if nothing happens in the time allotted for the shooting of the film, the inherent interest in watching the celebrity perform the routine functions of everyday life will be enough to hold the attention of most audiences.[4]

There is nothing wrong with this kind of filmmaking. Indeed, for almost twenty years I made films in exactly the same way, carefully picking subjects which had obvious interest and built-in drama. Some succeeded and some didn't. But whether they succeeded, whether they communicated to the viewer what I hoped they would communicate, their subject matter was foreign, to a greater or lesser degree, to the experience of the people who viewed them. I am proud of *Margaret Mead's New Guinea Journal*, which was a film about how people change and a portrait of a great and fascinating woman, but I don't think too many people who watched it were able to see similarities between their problems and the problems of the people in the tiny little New Guinea village of Peri. I am also proud of *The Triumph of Christy Brown*, a film about the necessity of establishing some sort of human contact and communication no matter how isolated and imprisoned we are in the cage of our own emotional fears and physical infirmities. But I have a sneaking suspicion that comparatively few viewers saw this film as anything more than a portrait of an Irish novelist with cerebral palsy who taught himself to use a typewriter with his big toe. A film about courage, yes; an inspiring film, yes; but not a film, I'm afraid, perceived by millions of Americans as being relevant to their own daily lives.

But *An American Family* was something different; it was based on the belief that there is considerable drama in the daily lives of ordinary citizens. The citizens themselves may be unaware of this, as the Louds were, but it is there just the same, waiting to be captured by the peculiar alchemy of the camera in the hands of anyone with the ability to see and the patience to wait.

Had Jim Day or Curt Davis asked me what I expected to find by filming the Louds for seven months, I would not have been able to answer with any degree of certainty. But they didn't ask that question, because they shared with me a general vision of what life is about and a specific vision about the quality of life in the United States in 1971. They were as convinced as I that if we could afford to spend the money and the time—*time to let things happen*—something fascinating would be revealed. None of us had the slightest idea what the something would be, but we gambled—based on what we knew of our own lives and what we sensed about the life of the country—that whatever it was, it would say something important and revealing about all of us.

Many critics dismissed the events in *An American Family* as "lucky breaks." In their view, it was "lucky" that Pat asked Bill for a divorce; it was "lucky" that Lance was a homosexual; and it was "lucky" that Delilah was experiencing the joys and sorrows of first love. The implication was that if none of these things had happened, particularly the divorce, there would have been no series.

My answer is that television critics, like most journalists, wear blinders, which limit their perceptions and keep them from any true understanding or identification with the people they write for and about. They tend to see themselves as slightly apart from the rest of us and better able to cope with, if not entirely immune to, the passions, fears, hopes, and disappointments motivating their readers and the subjects of their articles. By calling Bill and Pat's divorce, Lance's homosexuality, and Delilah's romance "lucky," they not only demean those individuals, they miss completely the point of the vision behind the series. That vision was that *something* would happen. If it hadn't been a divorce, it would have been something else. It might have been a serious illness or the loss of a job or a birth—or all three. *Whatever happened* would have revealed, within the context of the Louds' daily life, as much about how men and women feel about each other as those events that actually did occur.

I feel strongly that the television documentary, if it is to have any future, must go in this direction. It must be in a series form—repetition and involvement with characters is what holds viewers—and it must be concerned with the events in the daily lives of ordinary citizens.

In a proposal I wrote for another project three years after *An American Family*, I tried to explain one of the reasons why I feel this way:

> A documentary series that deals with how we Americans live our lives—how we relate to each other, how we earn our livings, what we think of our institutions, our government, the way we deal with our hopes, our fears, our disappointments— has a very special ability to break through the aching sense of being alone that most of us feel even though we are surrounded by friends, neighbors, relatives, and hundreds of fellow citizens.
>
> The cumulative effect of the events of the past thirty years, the death of the Dream and the resulting sense of hopelessness, have caused us to draw into ourselves, to feel threatened by and alienated from other human beings. There is an ever-increasing sense that we can depend on no one and no thing, a conviction that it is every man for himself.
>
> A documentary series, like the one I am proposing, can help alleviate this sense of being alone, can convey to millions of viewers an awareness that, to a remarkable degree, the great majority of us share the same hopes, the same fears, the same doubts, the same frustrations, the same insecurities. It can show us, in fact, that we are anything but alone.[5]

Despite these high-sounding words about what I think should be the future course of the television documentary, I honestly don't feel that the documentary in any form has very much of a future at all. There are numerous reasons for this; I will mention just a few.

Every year the race for ratings and the advertiser's dollar becomes more intense than the year before. In this competitive climate, airtime is perceived as being much too valuable to waste on documentaries, which traditionally rank near the bottom of the Nielsen listings. If, under these conditions, there are fewer and fewer normal one-hour documentaries on the air, it would be approaching insanity to expect that a documentary series could even be considered.

In a futile effort to improve the low ratings and prove to the powers that be that their films deserve airtime, the makers of television documentaries and the executives who employ them are taking a position diametrically opposed to the one that I feel would work. Instead of making films about ordinary people, they are making films about people who are wretchedly poor, terminally ill, or violently rebellious. They are making films about the disenfranchised, the bewildered, and the angry in such a way as to emphasize the symptoms of the problem and not the causes. They ask us to look at these horrors, but they neglect to give us any insight into how these horrors came about. I insist that it is possible to make films which are not specifically about these people but which would explore the reasons for their plight in much more interesting, understandable, and meaningful ways. Poverty, sickness, and violence are not the special preserve of the poor, the uneducated, and minorities. You and I are touched by these conditions every day; the potential for them exists in every one of us, and so does the understanding required to deal with them in our own lives and in society.

It does not take great genius to make films that will say these things, but it does take a certain amount of courage and understanding to allow them to be made and shown on the air.

Appendix

An American Family Credits

Conceived and produced by Craig Gilbert
Filmmakers:
Alan Raymond, camera
Susan Raymond, sound
Coordinating Producer: Jacqueline Donnet
Associate Producer: Susan Lester
Film Editors: David Hanser, Pat Cooke, Ken Werner, Eleanor Hamerow

Additional Photography: Joan Churchill

Additional Sound: Peter Pilafian

Super 8 Footage:
  Produced and filmed by John Terry
  Sound—Al Mecklinberg

Assistant Cameramen: Tom Goodwin, Peter Smokler, Mike Levine

Assistant Film Editors: Janet Lauretano, Joanna Alexander, Bob Alvarez, Ernie Davidson

Sound Editor: Thomas Halpin

Assistant Sound Editor: Pete Begley

Editing Assistants: Tikki Goldberg, Dan Merrill, Joe Lovett, Sue Steinberg

Editing Apprentices: Jesse Maple, Hannah Wajshonig, Harvey Rosenstock

Production Managers: Kathleen Walsh, Michael Podell, Hal Hutkoff

Assistant Production Manager: Janet Freeman

Location Unit Managers: David Burke, Bernard Katz, Peter Scarlet

Production Assistants: Kristin Glover, David Henry

Research: Will MacDonald

"Vain Victory" Sequence:
  Camera—Adam Giffard
  Assistant—James Ricky
  Gaffer—Jack Riedel
  Sound—Mark Dichter

Series Title Film: Elinor Bunin

Title Music Supervisor: John Adams

Production Secretary: Alice Carey

Engineering Supervisor: Ed Reingold

Senior Video Engineer: Art Emerson

Sound Mixer: Richard Vorisek

Sound Mixer (episode 12): Lee Dichter

Funding Provided by:
  The Ford Foundation
  Corporation for Public Broadcasting

Executive Producer: Curtis W. Davis

The Credits: A Few Notes

More than fifty people were involved in transforming *An American Family* from an idea into a series of twelve-hour-long films. For a variety of reasons (including time and space), their names have never appeared before in one coherent list. That has always bothered me. This is a chance to set the record straight—a chance to correct an omission that has nagged at my conscience for the past eight years.

Credits, while serving the purpose of designating a specific function, do not always tell the whole story of a person's contribution to a project. The credits for *An American Family* contain several such examples.

Jacqueline Donnet is listed as coordinating producer, a title which, although not unknown to films, is not all that common. What it means on *An American Family* was that while the rest of us were filming in various parts of the country and Europe, Jackie ran the series production office at NET headquarters in New York. One of her most important jobs was keeping close tabs on the budget. In this capacity she had to answer, on almost a daily basis, a neverending series of questions from NET executives about why we were spending certain sums of money. She did this with good humor, accuracy, and an understanding gained from long experience in the business. In doing so, she took the heat and allowed those of us in the field to devote our full energies to filming the daily life of the Louds. Jackie also paid the bills, saw to it that salary checks were for the right amount and mailed out on time, and on one occasion acted as producer, on the "Vain Victory" sequence which Adam Giffard and his crew shot at the La Mama theater in New York. In addition, Jackie was intimately involved in the editing process, and her spontaneous reactions of heart and mind to what was for her fresh footage guaranteed that the rest of us did not lose sight of the humanity of the Louds and the universality of their joys and sorrows.

Four film editors are listed in the credits, but David Hanser was the only one who was around for the entire year that it took to put together the twelve episodes that make up *An American Family*. In a very real sense his title should have been supervising editor. From the very beginning he understood the editing theories that I tried, not always successfully, to articulate. The other editors looked to him for advice and encouragement, and I looked to him for understanding and compassion when the problems piled up. When the editing started, I hardly knew David; today he is a close and valued friend.

There is no "directed by" in the credit list for *An American Family*. This was not an oversight. It was a conscious decision I made after giving the matter a great deal of thought. Most *cinéma vérité* films do list a director; I had taken the credit myself many times in the past. There was ample precedent for my doing so on *An American Family*. But in all honesty, I had never been totally comfortable with the custom. To say that an unstaged film about how people live their lives—whether those people be rock stars, patients at an emergency ward, or New Guinea natives—is directed in the generally accepted sense of the word always struck me as somewhat misleading. Not misleading enough to prevent me from taking the credit, but misleading nevertheless. To be sure, in any kind of film there has to be a single vision that prevails, and from time to time I had asked myself what the possessor of a *cinéma vérité* vision should be called. Needless to say, I have never come up with a satisfactory answer.

And the experience of making *An American Family* did not provide me with one. Yes, I had had the vision for the series; yes, I had picked the family; yes, I had made the large, general decisions about what to film and what not to film; yes, I had given instructions to the editors and approved their final version of each episode—but I had not directed the series in the conventional sense of that word. And I was afraid that television viewers would be hopelessly confused by seeing "directed by" in the credits for a series which claimed to be a recording of real life as it actually happened.

Two or three months before *An American Family* was to go on the air, I sat down with Jackie Donnet to make up the credit list. As we were in the process of doing this, Alan Raymond appeared in the office and objected strenuously to being designated "cinematographer." Since that was exactly the function he had filled on the series, I was somewhat perplexed. Surely he would rather have "cinematographer" than "photographed by" or "filmed by." Yes, that was true, he said, but none of these was satisfactory. Well then, what did he want? What he wanted, it turned out, was "filmmakers" for himself and Susan. We discussed the matter for some time, and finally I gave in. This argument with Alan came after a long and difficult two years, made longer and more difficult by the many nasty confrontations with him. At the time of this particular disagreement I was battling with the executives of channel 13 on several fronts, and I was simply too exhausted to engage in a long, drawn-out war of attrition with Alan Raymond.

In giving him the credit he asked for—but which he did not deserve—I made a mistake that will plague me for as long as *An American Family* lives in the public consciousness. By not taking a "directed by" credit, by giving Alan and Susan Raymond credit as filmmakers, and by retreating from the controversy generated by the series, I created a situation in which a man who had held a camera and a woman who had held a microphone could, by capitalizing on public misunderstanding and journalistic sloppiness, slowly but surely begin to take credit for being responsible for *An American Family*. They never actually came out and said as much. They simply talked in such a way as to lead whoever was interviewing them into naturally assuming that *An American Family* was their vision, their creation, their "baby."

Nothing could be further from the truth. The Raymonds had absolutely nothing to do with conceiving the series, nor were they involved in choosing the family. They did not participate in producing the series, directing the series (in the sense I have discussed above), or editing the series. In short, they were hired as a camera and sound team, and that is the function they performed.

Notes

1. As an example, in one restaurant scene Bill thought he was shown drinking too much, so we eliminated a round of drinks. A little bit later in the same scene a male friend of Bill and Pat's in Santa Barbara walked by with a woman who was not his wife. Bill made some comment like, "There goes John Doe with Jane Smith." He asked us to eliminate the name of the woman, and of course we did. There probably were other changes that were asked for, but I can't remember them. And whatever they were, they were very, very minor.

2. It might be of interest to point out here that although *An American Family* was entirely financed by public television funds, an effort was made to recoup some of this money from corporate underwriting. The series was submitted for this purpose to some of the largest corporations in the country. None of them, of course, wanted to have anything to do with it. The reaction of the representative from the Kraft Food Company is indicative of the general feeling. He said, "I think the series is, perhaps, the most important thing that has happened in television in the past twenty-five years. But having said that, I must also tell you that my company wouldn't touch the project with a ten-foot pole."

3. Not long after the series began appearing on the air I received a telephone call from the publicity office at WNET. It seems John O'Connor had called to check out the rumor that I had had an affair with Pat Loud. It was suggested I call him right away. I did and we got together for lunch. I told him that I had definitely not had an affair with Pat Loud, that I had never even considered it, and that I was sure she never had either.

4. There were many such films in the early days of *cinéma vérité*: Don Pennebaker's *Don't Look Back* (1966), a profile of singer and songwriter Bob Dylan, and *Monterey Pop* (1968), about the jazz festival in that city; and the Maysles brothers' *Showman* (1962), featuring movie producer Joseph E. Levine, *What's Happening! The Beatles in the USA* (1964), *Meet Marlon Brando* (1965), and *Gimme Shelter* (1970), following the Rolling Stones on tour. The 1981 Oscar for Best Documentary was *From Mao to Mozart*, a film record of Isaac Stern's trip to China.

5. The following quote is from a letter written by an executive at one of the networks in response to this proposal:

> I'm not quite sure how to put my finger on the problem. I think perhaps it is that you and I have been discussing ideas that are not very "journalistic," although perfectly respectable as documentary subjects and treatments. We have really been discussing a way of pushing back the frontiers of normal news documentaries and exploring more intimately ordinary human life and finding there the drama that others seek in news activities—reporting big events, disasters, or wars. This I warmly welcome as an approach. However, I think in order to sell such a notion both to [name of network] and to the American public we need to come up either with a new idea so startling that it cannot be resisted or with a proposal that is not too extravagant in terms of money and time. A lot of the work you and I have been discussing would necessarily be highly experimental in that we would have to be ready to abort if we did not get results. I write all this with some diffidence, because I greatly enjoyed your series on the family [he screened two episodes—1 and 9—and told me he looked at 9 before he looked at 1, but he didn't think it made much difference] and would dearly like to find other applications of the same technique. In short, I would be most happy to continue our dialogue (and this I would not say if I did not sincerely mean it), but I would not raise your hopes too high and prevent you from pursuing discussions elsewhere, because I'm not too sure that [name of network] is quite ready yet for the approach that you and I have been talking about.

The project we had been discussing was a series which, through the lives of eight or ten or twelve people living in a medium-sized midwestern city, would tell the story of what has happened to this country between the end of World War II and the present time.

The Ethics of Imagemaking; or, "They're Going to Put Me in the Movies. They're Going to Make a Big Star Out of Me . . ."

Jay Ruby

In this paper I will discuss the moral questions that arise when one person produces and uses a recognizable image of another. I am interested in an exploration of the ethical problems that stem from the justification of the use of human beings in the pursuit of art, science, news, or entertainment when those uses involve the production of realistic and recognizable images of people. The questions that can be raised are seemingly infinite, and many important issues will merely be touched on here. Let me cite a few of the more obvious. What does "informed consent" mean when a family is asked by a television crew to have their lives recorded and packaged into a series for national television? How does one balance the public's right to be informed with the individual's right to privacy? Are objectivity and "balance" the primary obligations of the photojournalist? Do visual artists have a moral license to use people in ways different from the ways scientists or reporters use them?

I am not a lawyer, philosopher, or theologian. I will not attempt to deal with the legal controversies or with the larger moral issues these questions imply. I am an anthropologist involved in the study of visual communication as a cultural system. For the past twenty years I have been a participant/observer in the production and consumption of documentary and ethnographic photographs and films. I speak as both native and researcher.

I am concerned about society's shifting moral expectations of the image maker and the consequent ambivalence some professionals feel about their own ethical base. This uneasiness bespeaks a deep-seated and widespread concern with the nature of images. At times we seem to be more confused than informed by them. The traditional arguments used to justify the behavior of artists, journalists, and scientists who make images are becoming increasingly inadequate, convincing neither the professionals involved nor the public as thoroughly as they once did.

As we enter an era of telecommunications where image-producing, -distributing, and -consuming technologies are becoming ever more decentralized and Andy Warhol's idea that eventually everyone will be a star for fifteen minutes is no longer futurist thinking, the urgency of these questions increases. The moral base on which image producers have relied is shaky, if not crumbling. Before every city block has its own news service and resident visual artist, we should have a better understanding of how one reaches the decision to use someone else's image and where our responsibilities lie.

Ethnic minorities, women, gays, third- and fourth-world peoples, the very rich and the very poor are telling us—the middle-class, middle-aged white males who dominate the industry—that our pictures of them are false. Some wish to produce their own representation of themselves and control or at least monitor the ways we now image them. The New World Information Order cannot be ignored any more than can the organized protests against the Metropolitan Museum's photographic exhibition *Harlem on My Mind* or the gays' rage against the film *Cruising* or, most recently, the Puerto Rican community's displeasure over *Fort Apache, The Bronx*. The list is long and grows daily.

The time when an artist could take photographs of strangers, usually poor or in some other way removed from the mainstream of America, and justify the action as the inherent right of the artist is, I believe, ending.

The time when one could reconstruct a historical event by creating composite, and therefore fictional, characters for the sake of plot and not be held legally and ethically responsible ended with the popularity of the television docudrama.

The time when a reporter could rely on the principle that the public's right to know is more important than the individual's right to privacy, when people believed that a journalist's primary ethical responsibility was to be objective, fair, and honest, is over.

The time when a scientist could depend on the public's belief in the material benefits of scientific knowledge to justify the use of double blind studies, often employing hidden cameras, ceased with Stanley Milgram's frightening explorations of people's willingness to obey authority.

Examples are endless, and they signal the demise of our naive trust that since the camera never lies, a photographer has no option but to tell the truth. We are beginning to understand the technologically produced image as a construction—as the interpretive act of someone who has a culture, an ideology, and often a conscious point of view, all of which cause the image to convey a certain kind of knowledge in a particular way. Image makers show us their view of the world whether they mean to or not. No matter how much we may feel the need for an objective witness of reality, our image-producing technologies will not provide it for us.

I believe that the maker of images has the moral obligation to reveal the covert—to never appear to produce an objective mirror by which the world can see its "true" image. For in doing so we strengthen the status quo, support the repressive forces of this world, and continue to alienate those people we claim to be concerned about. So long as our images of the world continue to be sold to others as *the* image of the world, we are being unethical.

To pursue this argument efficiently I must be specific, and so I confine myself to one variety of imaging. I will not try to separate assertion from supportable theses; I will simply state that the argument presented here is based on a combination of personal experience, research, and passionately held belief. I make no claim that all aspects of the argument are verifiable, only that all other points of view are much less convincing to me.

I use case studies from the documentary tradition—still and motion pictures—simply because I know the tradition well. A similar case could, of course, be made using fiction films or paintings, but since the documentary is such a marvelously confused genre of motion pictures, it allows me to deal with art, science, reportage, etc., in a rather inclusive way. In addition, the production of documentary images and the production of anthropological knowledge are in fundamental ways parallel pursuits. The moral and ethical concerns of one can be applied to the other. Most documentarians would agree that the following quotation from Dell Hymes could just as well apply to the documentary tradition:

> The fundamental fact that shapes the future of anthropology is that it deals in knowledge of others. Such knowledge has always implied ethical and political responsibilities, and today the "others" whom anthropologists have studied make those responsibilities explicit and unavoidable. One must consider the consequences of those among whom one works of simply being there, of learning about them, and what becomes of what is learned.[1]

For a variety of reasons, anthropologists have been conducting public discussions about their ethical responsibilities longer than documentarians have. I believe that the experience social scientists have had in grappling with these questions provides documentarians with usable insights into their own problems. I have consequently incorporated some of those findings into this paper.

The production and use of images involves three separable yet related moral issues which when combined into a professional activity becomes an ethical position. These three issues are: (1) the image maker's personal moral contract to produce an image that is somehow a true reflection of the intention in making the image in the first place—to use the cliché, it is being true to one's self; (2) the moral obligation of the producer to his or her subjects; and (3) the moral obligation of the producer to the potential audience. The solution to these questions will vary with the producer's intention, his or her sociocultural role and that of the image's subjects, and the contexts in which the image appears.

I have argued elsewhere that images are polysemic, that is, a photograph or film has a variety of potential socially generated meanings.[2] The cultural expectations producers, subjects, and audiences have about the various communication events that transpire in the production and consumption of images predispose people to employ different interpretive strategies to derive signification and meaning from images.[3] These interpretive strategies are embedded within a larger body of cultural knowledge and competencies which encompass or are supported by a moral system. That is, systems of knowledge and epistemologies are attached to moral systems. As an anthropologist I would argue that morals and ethics are only comprehensible in relation to other facets of a culture.

The particular signification or meaning that is appended to an image emerges as a consequence of a variety of factors: (1) the label attached to the image—for example, photographs that are considered to be news photos are regarded differently from art photos; (2) the context in which the image appears—for example, news photos which are made into high-quality enlargements and placed in an art museum tend to be regarded primarily as art; and (3) the socially acquired expectations of the audience toward certain types of images produced by certain types of image makers which tend to appear in certain types of settings.

An illustration will help make these abstractions less abstruse. At the beginning of the century, Lewis Hine, a sociologist turned social reformer, took a series of photographs, commissioned by the National Committee to Reform Child Labor Laws, of children working in factories. The archetypical Hine image is that of a prepubescent child, quite small, often frail, and always dirty, standing in front of an enormous piece of machinery. The child is staring into the lens of the camera, and consequently into the eyes of the viewer. The machines are black and dirty, and the factory so dark that the edges of the machine disappear into nothingness. These images were designed to appear in tracts that detailed the social and psychological abuses of child labor. They were often printed on inexpensive, porous newsprint with a cheap half-tone process. All of the subtlety of tone and detail present in the negatives disappears. These tracts were sent to legislators, the clergy, and prominent citizens and handed out at meetings. The intended message of these images in this context is a pragmatic one—they are a call to arms. One is to feel pity for the child and anger at the exploitation by the factory owner implied in the large and ominous machine. If the photographer is thought of at all, he is assumed to be on the side of truth and justice, providing irrefutable evidence of wrongdoing.

If we were to prepare a set of Hine's photographs for exhibition at the Museum of Modern Art in New York, enlargements of fine quality would be matted, framed, and hung with a brief but articulate and insightful explanatory text in a stark white room with subdued lighting. The audience in this context becomes people whose primary interest lies in art and photography, not in reforming labor laws. The photographs are now regarded chiefly for their syntactic elements, that is, formal and aesthetic qualities. The waifs are no longer pitiable examples of capitalistic exploitation, but aesthetic objects with interesting, if not haunting, faces. The machines are now examined for their texture and lines—as industrial art objects, not as symbols of oppression. A little girl's stare is now simply a sign of her willingness to be photographed, not an indictment of our economic system. It is unlikely that anyone seeing the exhibit would be motivated to do anything except admire and applaud the artistic accomplishments of Lewis Hine. I am virtually certain that no one would rush to West Virginia to see whether similar conditions might still exist.

The photographs in these two scenarios are the same, but the cultural expectations created by the two contexts cause us to regard the photographer and his works in different ways. I am not suggesting that Hine was never regarded as a photographic artist when his images were used in political tracts or that no one would ponder the political or economic implications of the photographs in the museum. I am suggesting that one interpretive strategy seems more appropriate to most people given a particular setting. It's hard to imagine people concerned with the plight of children in factories arguing about Hine's compositional style, or tuxedoed gentlemen and bejeweled ladies rushing out into the streets to picket a corporation thought to be exploiting children.

In fact, our readings of most images vacillate between these two extremes.[4] It is a case of the confusion I alluded to earlier with regard to documentary images. We are often uncertain whether the image maker is an artist who is to be critiqued for his mastery of the form or a technician who holds the mirror to the world.

This lack of clarity confronts producers with a moral dilemma that can be traced back to the beginnings of the tradition. Robert Flaherty, the American father figure of documentary film, was immediately accused by his critics of "faking" *Nanook of the North*. The film confused many film commentators— some failed to see any coherent story, since the narrative line was not obvious; others accused him of using actors and staging the entire movie. Criticism of the documentary form has not progressed far since the 1923 reviews of *Nanook*, and as a consequence, theory, criticism, and even review flounder on the question: Is the documentary art or reportage?

This cultural confusion has so limited the semantic and syntactic possibilities that some leave the documentary tradition for the apparent freedom of fiction. The moral obligations of the producers of fiction—written and visual—are certainly not clear, and some recent court decisions (particularly the 1978 decision against Gwen Davis Mitchell for apparently basing one of the characters in her novel *Touching* on a California psychologist, Paul Bindrim) appear to greatly limit the artistic license of even fiction makers—but seldom do its producers get accused of faking or criticized for staging or for misrepresenting their subject.

If documentarians choose to regard themselves as artists and are so received by the public, conventional wisdom argues that their primary ethical obligation is to be true to their personal visions of the world—to make artistically competent statements. In this way artists are thought to fulfill their moral responsibilities to the subjects of their work and to their audiences.

The artist is often regarded as being somewhat outside the moral constraints that confine other people— as having license to transform people into aesthetic objects without their knowledge and sometimes against their will. Until recently, few critics except Marxists argued that art contains and espouses the ideology of the artist, that even photography is in no way a universal language transcending cultural boundaries. Now, even Susan Sontag acknowledges that a Nazi film like *Triumph of the Will* was produced by a fascist filmmaker who must bear the moral responsibility of her art no matter how competent it might be. Some people argue that ethics should have priority over aesthetics, or perhaps more correctly, that a morally acceptable ethical position produces the foundation for a good aesthetic.

If one takes the everyday lives of people—a favorite subject matter of the documentary—and transforms them into an artistic statement, where does one draw the line between the actuality of their lives and the aesthetic needs of the artist? How much fiction or interpretation is possible before the subjects not only disagree but begin to be offended, or even fail to recognize themselves at all? These questions have recently been raised with great passion with reference to videotapes produced by video artists, people not from the documentary tradition but in the field of nonrepresentational video art. When a Juan Downey or an Edin Velez produces tapes that include images of native people such as the Yanomano Indians of Venezuela, some audiences become quite upset about the "exploitation" of the subjects for the sake of art. It would appear that documentarians who employ more subtle and less obvious techniques of construction are less likely to be criticized for being exploitive than are the video artists who employ overt techniques of aesthetic manipulation. Where does the documentary artist seek verification and justification for his or her work? Must the subject agree with the artist's interpretation? Or is it sufficient that the artist remains true to a personal vision regardless of how offensive it might be to others? I believe that we are now less certain of an easy answer to this question than we once were.

Where does the documentary artist's responsibility to the audience lie? Most audiences believe documentary images to be accurate representations of reality, unless they are overtly altered as in the case of the videotapes just mentioned. Given our belief in the image, should the documentary artist remind the audience of the interpretive and constructed nature of the documentary form—that is, demystify the construction? For example, is it important for people to know that Flaherty cast his films by looking for ideal types? "Family members" in *Nanook of the North, Man of Aran*, and *Louisiana Story* are not related to each other; they were selected because they suited Flaherty's conception of what makes a good Eskimo, Irish, or Cajun family. Is the documentary artist being more ethical if methods and techniques are revealed? Does that knowledge cause us, the audience, to regard the film differently?

Traditionally, documentarians have not revealed these things within their films, and some have never discussed the mechanics of their construction anywhere. (Obviously Flaherty has, or we would not be able to contemplate the consequences of his revelation and actions.) To remind an audience of the constructive and interpretive nature of images is regarded by some as counterproductive, if not actually destructive, to the nature of the film experience, that is, to the creation of an illusion of reality. Moreover, some people regard such revelation as self-indulgent, in that it turns the audience's attention away from the film and toward the filmmaker. For many, effective art requires a suspension of disbelief; being reminded that the images have an author disrupts the fantasy.

It is commonly assumed that art should be a little mysterious to be successful. A reflexive art has never been very popular and, at least in film, has become confused with a kind of self-indulgent autobiographical film that has recently become popular, in which young filmmakers expose themselves, exploit their families, and use the camera as therapist. Reflexivity has gotten a bad name because of its mistaken association with narcissism, self-consciousness, and other forms of self-contemplation.[5] I believe, however, that an intelligently used reflexivity is an essential part of all ethically produced documentaries. I will return to this idea later.

The confusion about which moral guidelines should be used to judge a documentary is compounded by the fact that some documentarians respond to aesthetic and moral criticism of their art by suggesting that their works are mere reflections of the reality observed and that their role as producer was to faithfully record and transmit what they experienced. They are not really the "authors" of their works, nor are they responsible for any conclusions audiences might draw. If one sees someone in a documentary image who appears stupid or disgusting, the implication is that the person so imaged is in reality stupid or disgusting, since the camera merely recorded what was in front of it without any modification. This aesthetic and moral "neutrality" is to be found in films like Frederick Wiseman's *High School*.

When the American direct-cinema movement, founded by people like Robert Drew and Richard Leacock, used television as their primary outlet, they associated the documentary with the ethical canons of broadcast journalism. Fairness, balance, and objectivity became paramount. In doing so they brought the tradition full circle. As Dan Schiller has argued, objectivity became an ideal for journalism partly as a consequence of the photograph's being introduced into newspapers.[6] As newspapers capitalized on the public's belief in the objectivity of the photograph, print journalists sought to emulate this objectivity in their writing. Fifty years later, documentary film became concerned with being objective because of its association with broadcast journalism.

Documentarians as journalists logically assume the ethical codes of the latter profession. In doing so they become virtually unassailable, for, unlike their printed-word brethren, photo and film journalists are thought to be employing a medium that when used properly is inherently objective. Thus, apart from the occasional accusation of the outright faking of a picture or the staging of a scene in a television program, documentary broadcast-journalism has not been subjected to much critical examination.

The recent arguments raised by Marxists, structuralists, and others about the relation between ideology on the one hand and the producer of images on the other have, however, caused some people to begin to critique broadcast journalism in a fashion similar to that discussed earlier for art. Stuart Hall and other British scholars of mass communication are among these analysts. Criticism of objectivity as the primary ethical responsibility of journalists is on the increase. As James Carey pointed out:

> What are lamely called the conventions of objective reporting were developed to report another century and another society. They were designed to report a secure world . . . about which there was a rather broad consensus, . . . a settled mode of life: . . . which could be rendered in the straightforward "who says what to whom" manner. . . . Today no accepted system of interpretation exists and political values and purposes are very much in contention . . . and cannot be encased within traditional forms of understanding. Consequently, "objective reporting" does little more than convey this disorder in isolated, fragmented news stories.[7]

Print journalists have responded to this criticism by acknowledging the active role of the reporter in creating, not finding, news. The so-called new journalism of Tom Wolfe and Hunter Thompson is written in the first person and employs narrative techniques of fiction. With Truman Capote and Norman Mailer writing fiction in the same style, it is often impossible to know from the text whether you are reading fiction or not, and often even then there is no easy answer. Is *The Right Stuff* by Wolfe or *The Executioner's Song* by Mailer fiction or not? Does it really matter? It is a fascinating legal and ethical question but too great a detour for now. However, I would like to point out that there has yet to be invented a visual equivalent to new journalism. When Truman Capote's nonfiction novel *In Cold Blood* was made into a movie it became straightforward fiction.

Most documentarians who consider themselves more journalist than artist are people interested in investigating rather than merely reporting. They are committed people motivated to make images of social or political concerns. Since Jacob Riis and John Grierson, many documentarians have been social reformers, and some, even radical revolutionaries who shared Lenin's belief in the power of the cinema. They produce images to inform audiences of injustices, corruption, and other societal ills, often to persuade people to act against these evils.

The ethical considerations of these image makers differ somewhat from those of the documentary artist. Since politically committed image makers have definite points of view, often prior to the production of any images, they approach the content of the images, the people imaged, and their audiences with a fairly clear agenda. Unlike the documentary as art, here the pragmatic features of the image must dominate—they must have their desired effect to be successful, and that effect is known in advance. People in these images are no longer aesthetic objects, but rather symbols of some collective force. A poor person is often used to stand for poverty, or a factory owner for all of capitalism. The question has to arise: Is it acceptable to use someone's life to illustrate a thesis? Are the considerations different when you are seeking to aid someone you regard as a victim by using that person in your film, as opposed to using a subject in order to expose him as a villain?

Let me use an example from one of the favorite themes of documentary images—housing conditions for the poor. Let us say you are making a documentary on slums for local television and you select a family who appears to have suffered directly because of an irresponsible landlord. How do you weigh the possible harm that might come to the family as a consequence of their public exposure in the film versus the possibility that the film may cause city officials to crack down on slum owners and consequently improve the living conditions for a large number of people?

Is it justifiable to try to avoid explaining your motivation and point of view to the landlord in order to be able to interview him on film? To be blunt about it, is it ethical to lie to an assumed evil person in order to perform what you regard as a positive act? For example, a film like Rogert Mugee's *Saturday Night in City Hall*, an exposé of then mayor of Philadelphia, Frank Rizzo, could not have been made if many of the people in it had known the maker's intention.

Because of the economic realities of distribution, documentary images with a political intent are usually viewed by the already committed, people who immediately comprehend the film's thesis. However, some find their way into theatrical release or public television and hence to a more diverse audience. Should the makers reveal themselves, their methods, and their goals to their audiences, or are they justified in employing the techniques of advertising and other forms of propaganda and persuasion? A recent example is to be found in Julia Reichert and Jim Klein's film *Union Maids*, a skillfully edited set of interviews of three women active in union organizing in the thirties. The makers failed to mention that the women were members of the Communist party, because they felt that some audiences would be alienated from the primary message of the film—the unsung role of women as union organizers.

Does this sort of selection taint a film to such an extent that all of it becomes suspect? Are political-documentary makers caught in the dilemma of having a responsibility to reveal methods and motives, which might lessen the impact of their message? Can political-image makers justify their sins of omission on the basis of the service they provide in helping to bring public attention to our social problems? I think not. I am skeptical of the motives and sophistication of many political-image makers. Even though thousands of films and millions of photographs have been employed in political causes in the past fifty years, there is little or no empirical evidence to suggest that they are a significant means of influencing people.

If all the money expended on all the images of the plight of migrant laborers since Edward R. Murrow and Fred Friendly's *Harvest of Shame* program had been used for day-care centers and the improvement of these workers' living conditions, their plight would be significantly improved. I doubt that the "professional sympathizers" who produced all these images can defend their work with much tangible evidence. Power comes more directly from the end of a gun than it does from the lens of a camera. Few revolutions were won in a movie house or on the six o'clock news.

I have barely touched on a large number of important questions concerning the ethical obligations of the professional image maker. Whether artist, journalist, or social documentarian, image makers need to confront their responsibilities in a more reflective and reflexive way than they have so far. I have argued elsewhere for the necessity of a reflexive documentary and anthropological cinema.[8] I would extend the argument to all image makers.

I believe that the filmic illusion of reality is an extremely dangerous one, for it gives the people who control the image industry too much power. The majority of Americans, and soon the majority of the world's population, receive information about the outside world from the images produced by film, television, and photography. If we perpetuate the lie that pictures always tell the truth, that they are objective witnesses to reality, we are supporting an industry that has the potential to symbolically recreate the world in its own image. Technology grows out of a particular ideology. The Western world created image-producing technologies out of a profound need to have an irrefutable witness—to control reality by capturing it on film.

We stand on the threshold of the telecommunications revolution—a revolution potentially as profound and far-reaching as the agricultural and industrial revolutions. The one significant difference between the present changes and past changes is that the telecommunications revolution is happening so fast, we can actually be aware of it. It took five thousand years of gradual change from the first experiments in plant domestication until people were fully sedentary farmers. Today, there are people still active in television who contributed their talents at the very beginnings of the industry. We have the opportunity to make the revolution anything we want it to be. As privileged members of that segment of the world who manage, if not control, the image empires, we have an obligation to pause and reflect on the past and to contemplate the future. We should not let the rush of the marketplace destroy our responsibility to act intelligently. We need to demystify these technologies so that we can cultivate a more critical and sophisticated audience. We need to make it possible to include a greater variety of human experience via these media—to give the many voices available access to this revolution. The human condition is too complex to be filtered through the eyes of a small group of people. We need to see the world from as many perspectives as possible. We have the means to do so now.

Notes

1. Dell Hymes, ed., *Reinventing Anthropology* (New York: Random House, 1972), p. 48.

2. Jay Ruby, "In a Pic's Eye: Interpretive Strategies for Deriving Significance and Meaning from Photographs," *Afterimage* 3, no. 9 (1976): 5–7.

3. Sol Worth and Larry Gross, "Symbolic Strategies," *Journal of Communication* 24, no. 4 (1974): 27–39.

4. Alan Sekula, "On the Invention of Meaning in Photographs," *Artforum* 13, no. 5 (1975): 36–45.

5. Barbara Myerhoff and Jay Ruby, Introduction to *A Crack in the Mirror: Reflexive Perspectives in Anthropology*, ed. Jay Ruby, pp. 1–38 (Philadelphia: University of Pennsylvania Press, 1982).

6. Dan Schiller, "Realism, Photography, and Journalistic Objectivity in Nineteenth-Century America," *Studies in the Anthropology of Visual Communication* 4, no. 2 (1977): 86–98.

7. James Carey, "The Communications Revolution and the Professional Communicator," *Sociological Review Monographs* (Jan. 1969): 35.

8. Jay Ruby, "Exposing Yourself: Reflexivity, Anthropology, and Film," *Semiotica* 3, no. 1–2 (1980): 153–590.

The Prosecutor

Michael J. Arlen

It's hard not to like "60 Minutes," at least much of the time. The general reporting is brisk and capable, neither too trivial nor too densely detailed, as in the better tradition of the general-magazine feature. And the investigative stories, for which the program has become well honored and remarkably popular, are often hard-hitting and dramatic. The show's four correspondents, Mike Wallace, Morley Safer, Dan Rather, and Harry Reasoner, are all good interviewers, and Wallace and Rather are also uncommonly tough interviewers: combative, probing, a far remove from the once typical TV newsman whose interrogatory technique consisted mainly of proffering his microphone, like an ice cream cone, to a public figure who would then, as often as not, make an election speech with it.

It's been good, at last, to see tough interviewing on the air—especially in an era when important persons so often try to hide behind imperturbable, on-camera pronouncements or else behind shields of lawyers and accountants so thick that most politely mellifluous TV reporters can scarcely make a dent in them. The pugnacious "60 Minutes" musketeers unfailingly dent such shields, and sometimes penetrate them, while awards are won and ratings climb. But there's also a danger in this approach, for clearly much of what sustains the popularity of the program is the thrill of the chase: the excitement that comes from watching a quarry being pursued and brought down by aggressive questioning on the air. As a result, the program (with its large staff of producers and researchers) is bound to be on the lookout not just for newsworthy stories but for situations that will specifically provide this drama of pursuit, and for interview subjects that can be made to serve, willingly or unwillingly, as the quarry. Thus, with the "60 Minutes" newsmen being more frequently drawn into prosecutorial scenarios, it's been inevitable that some of them would begin to assume a trial lawyer's role, or at least manner, with its emphasis on courtroom tactics and judgmental righteousness.

An example of this increasing tendency to have prosecutorial indignation do the work of actual investigative reporting—or do more of the work than it should—occurred recently when one of "60 Minutes"'s sternest musketeers, Dan Rather, galloped into Wyoming to uncover low- and high-level corruption in the state. To begin with, let me say that I have no doubt whatsoever that all manner of wickedness exists today in Wyoming, for it is a region of enormous mineral and petroleum wealth, much of which has only lately begun to be developed (or exploited), and it seems to be one of the givens of natural-resource capitalism that wherever there are grown men (or women) trying to make some money out of the ground there are usually all kinds of deals and payoffs and improper goings-on to be found in the offing. The challenge, then, was to find the story, and not so much to make the case—for that is presumably a matter for the law to undertake—but at least to ascertain the basic facts and present them to the audience. What seemed to interest "60 Minutes," however, was less the story than the *appearance* of a story: the dramatic texture of televised confrontation.

The first of the two Wyoming reports (CBS News's foray into the state was clearly no nickel-and-dime operation; two separate twenty-minute installments were prepared, to be aired on successive Sunday evenings) was titled *Our Town*, and seemed largely devoted to the prostitutes of Rock Springs, Wyoming: a historically rowdy mining town of around 25,000 inhabitants, half of whom had arrived in the last five years as a result of the energy boom. From the start, somewhat in the manner of a district attorney running for office who tries to stir up the citizenry against the local whorehouse, Rather professed to be astonished at the presence of vice in western mining communities:

Tonight, "60 Minutes" looks at charges of payoff and cover-up in one American city, where vice runs rampant and a handful of men run the city as they please. New York? Detroit? Los Angeles? Chicago? Wrong. Not this time. The corruption we're talking about is in a city far off in the hills of Wyoming.

Then he professed to be shocked at vice itself:

When the sun goes down in Rock Springs, the town becomes a western sin city. Hookers openly work the streets and the bars, each of them earning a minimum of a thousand dollars a week.

Then, as if his audience wasn't sufficiently writhing in prurient disapproval, he returned to his opening theme, which presumably had made *Winesburg, Ohio* so popular sixty years ago: Good people, can you believe that they're doing it *right here* in Winesburg? Thus:

If you're saying, "So what?"—remember this is not New York or New Orleans or Chicago. This is Rock Springs, with more working hookers than you can shake a wallet at. By conservative estimate, prostitution alone is a two-million-dollar-a-year business here in this little Wyoming town.

Notice that Rock Springs has changed from "one American city" to "a western sin city" to "this little Wyoming town." Notice also the mathematics. If each prostitute earns $1,000 a week and all of them together earn $2 million a year, then there must be a grand total of around forty hookers in Rock Springs. Which may be vice, but in a town of miners, oil workers, and construction hands, it may not be everybody's idea of vice running rampant.

Then we got to see the sinful creatures themselves. For "60 Minutes," sparing no expense, had brought "a special night lens," as Rather described it, which "enabled us to film it all in almost total darkness." Indistinct women varying in color and appearance drifted about in the murky Rock Springs night, as if moving through fog. Stoutish women, clearly of ill repute, shuffled along on a sidewalk. Others stood in a parking lot. There was a brief scene of a prostitute overhead engaging in a transaction with a man. She: "Well, what can you spend—thirty?" He: "Well, what kind of work for thirty?" This was surely pretty heady stuff for members of the urban audience, who would otherwise have had to drive several miles out of their way, wherever they lived, to witness similar transactions in their own cities.

But Rather wasn't only interested in bringing back U-2 photographs to show that prostitution existed in Rock Springs. He was after bigger game: official corruption. Thus he observed solemnly, "The local police will hurry to stop a fight but hardly ever to arrest for prostitution." A female undercover agent was produced on camera, who substantiated this grave charge.

"Were you hassled by the police?" Rather asked the woman.

"No, not at all," she replied. "The police—we've seen them several times on K Street in their cars. Never was any attempt ever made [at an arrest]."

A less determined prosecutor, one imagines, or a less pious reporter who had once worked a city beat, might have asked himself if police in most American cities (certainly including New York, where "60 Minutes" and Rather are based) even hurry to stop fights, let alone bother with arresting hookers and dumping them in the courts. But to admit the question, or the answer, would be to diminish the tone of moral outrage, and thus the story. As it was, having so far put forward a supposedly significant case against Rock Springs vice—which consisted of (a) blurry views of prostitutes on a sidewalk and in a parking lot and (b) his own shocked indignation—Rather next brought his courtroom talents to bear on an effort to involve the upper reaches of the state administration itself in the shady doings on K Street.

Now there were two undercover agents on camera, who sat facing Rather, all business in a trimly tailored suit, seated stiffly in a straight-backed chair and balancing a reporter's notebook on his knee (though it was unclear why he needed the notebook, since a sound recorder was clearly running along with the camera). One of the agents had just given it as his opinion that Rock Springs not only was a place where prostitution ran rampant but also was a transfer, or "pass through," point for narcotics. Rather then engaged the two agents in a trial lawyer's catechism that went as follows:

Rather: In your personal opinion, the police chief knows about it?

Agents: Yes.

Rather: Sheriff know about it?

Agents: Yes.

Rather: Mayor know about it?

Agents: Yes.

Rather: Members of the city council know about it?

Agents: Yes.

Rather: County attorney know about it?

Agents: Yes.

Rather: State attorney general know about it?

Agents: Yes.

Rather: Governor know about it?

Agents: Yes.

On a theatrical level, this was an obviously effective performance. In the manner of a trial lawyer, Rather had presented his allegations in the form of dramatic questions—knowing, as trial lawyers do, that the questions themselves contained the power of persuasion, regardless of the answers—and so had cleverly led his jury, or audience, in the direction he wished it to take. For, starting with little more than those blurry glimpses of prostitutes, he had next asked the audience to accept an opinion that pimps and narcotics traffic existed alongside the prostitutes, which is generally a plausible supposition though not necessarily a fact; and then, by presenting, in a deliberately courtroomlike fashion, additional opinion as to who might "know about" the situation, he had involved the attorney general as well as the governor of the state in the vice in Rock Springs. But the fact remained that, whatever the actual state of affairs in Wyoming might be, Rather's "case" before the television audience consisted almost entirely of style and texture, with little reportorial substance to back it up. After all, think of whom a reporter might *not* ensnare in a similar catechism about vice in most cities. "Sir, do not prostitutes openly parade the sidewalks of Forty-second Street?" asks the accuser sternly of his witness. "And does not the mayor know about it? Does not the police commissioner?

Do not both senators? Does not the governor? Does not the archbishop? Does not the vice-president of the United States? Does not the president himself?" In other words, if a link did exist between vice in Rock Springs and the State House in Cheyenne, it was not being shown in "60 Minutes"; it was only being implied or insinuated.

Even so, Rather, with his "special night lens," seemed on solider footing in the first week's installment, trying to press charges of sinfulness against the little Wyoming town (or "western sin city") of Rock Springs—whose mayor, on camera, inspired no greater confidence than the mayors of most American towns, and maybe less—than he did a week later, when he attempted to expose and attack corruption at higher levels in the state. This installment was titled *High Noon in Cheyenne*, and Rather began it in the briskly confident style of a successful prosecuting attorney who has already proved his point and is now going after the "big one." Thus:

> Our story last week, entitled *Our Town*, looked at the little city of Rock Springs, Wyoming, steeped in prostitution, gambling, and narcotics . . . Tonight, *High Noon in Cheyenne*, as we look at charges that Wyoming officials as high as the governor and the attorney general may be involved in covering up corruption, not just in that little city of Rock Springs but in the state as a whole, with alleged links to organized crime out-of-state. It is accusation and confrontation and it is high noon in Cheyenne!

Soon it became clear that Rather's charges were actually those of a man named Neil Compton, who until his dismissal five months before by the governor had been head of Wyoming's criminal-investigation unit. On camera, cued by Rather, Compton was an assertive and articulate witness.

Rather asked him why he had been dismissed.

Compton said, "I was fired because I went to the governor on two separate occasions and brought to his attention that the attorney general for the state of Wyoming was a crook."

Rather then backed up his own witness. "We'll return to the specific charges in a moment," he said, "but first it's important to know that the man who makes them, Neil Compton, has a long reputation for being a superb investigator. He does not have a reputation for shooting from the hip."

However, after a brief check with members of the Wyoming press and with civic officials around the state, it turns out that Neil Compton has been at the very least a highly controversial figure on the local scene, whose authority had been frequently questioned—privately and publicly—on the very grounds that Rather had mentioned: shooting from the hip. It was a fact, for example, that Compton, in the two years before his dismissal, had been the subject of two separate meetings of Wyoming sheriffs and police chiefs, who had gathered largely to criticize his investigative methods, which had sometimes involved middle-of-the-night raids on unsuspecting households in an attempt to catch college-age youths in the possession of minor quantities of marijuana. (One citizen of Worland, Wyoming, had complained to the state attorney general's office that Compton himself had arrived at her house at two o'clock in the morning, seeking to arrest her son, then away at college, for selling an ounce of marijuana.) As the sheriff of Gillette said to me on the phone when I asked him about Compton: "I think about eight percent of the law officers of this state questioned his judgment."

At any rate, Rather had three main charges of Compton's to present to the large and respectful "60 Minutes" audience. The first was that the state's Democratic party chairman, Don Anselmi, had "attempted political cover-up" in order to protect an employee of a motel he co-owns "who was caught in a major drug case." Briskly, Rather interviewed Anselmi as if he had him on the witness stand:

Rather: You know John Vase? He works for you?

Anselmi: He's my assistant beverage manager. My partner's son.

Rather: He's the son of Mike Vase. Right? Your partner here?

Anselmi: Right.

Notice that Anselmi had already told Rather, in his first reply, that John Vase was his partner's son, so Rather's second question had no point except as courtroom rhetoric—to make it sound as if the investigator were ferreting out information from a recalcitrant witness. Then Rather buttressed his charge by producing another female undercover agent, who had apparently befriended young Vase and then turned him in:

Rather: The case stood up?

Agent: The case then was transferred to be prosecuted in the federal government.

Rather: The county attorney in effect got rid of it?

Agent: Yes, sir. The attorney general got rid of it. It was taken out of his hands. And the federal government took over this case. And at this time he pled guilty. He didn't want to go to court. He pled guilty.

However, a fairly rapid check of this situation produces a somewhat different impression. In the first place, according to the easily accessible Sweetwater County records, young Vase's crime turns out to have been the delivery of "five baggies, a tie-stick [*sic*], and one branch of marijuana," which may be illegal but hardly constitutes a "major drug case." Secondly, the undercover agent seems to have got the disposition of the case upside down, for the state court hadn't "got rid of" it to the federal court. In fact, the federal government had never taken over the case at all, for the charges had originally been filed in the state court, where they had been prosecuted. And there, far from escaping justice, Vase had pleaded guilty for the reason that he was guilty, and was punished with a fine of $750, five years' probation, and the forfeiture of his car.

But, having disposed of the Vase case to his satisfaction, Rather went on to list other charges against the Democratic state chairman—for instance, "that Anselmi was party to a stolen-gun deal." He said: "Anselmi denies it. A federal grand jury looked into that case three years ago. A prosecutor told us political pressure stopped the investigation." Here a little checking turns up the fact that Compton's "stolen-gun deal" charges against Anselmi stemmed largely from accusations brought by a former convict, Michael Dansdill, whose release Compton was involved in, and who later retracted the charges. The possibility of "political pressure" always exists, but since the Dansdill affair was well known in Wyoming, having been amply covered in the local press, it was too bad that Rather's "prosecutor" didn't mention that aspect of the matter, or that Rather didn't pass the word along to the audience.

In any event, having further demonstrated Anselmi's shadiness, Rather went on to link the Democratic chairman to even bigger crime. Compton broached the charge:

> At the time [1970], I found that there were the connections between Mr. Anselmi and Arizona . . . There was a real-estate and property buy-up in Wyoming by subjects from Arizona, Colorado, that had been a subject of organized-crime investigations in those particular states.

Rather took it up:

> The Arizona connection means to Compton that Don Anselmi is doing business with the land-scandal people who have connections to mobsters, who have bilked the public out of the millions of dollars in fraudulent deals in the Southwest.

There was a brief glimpse of Anselmi flatly denying the charge. Then Compton and Rather tried to link Anselmi's "connections" with Arizona to a man called Danny O'Keefe, who, Rather said, had been indicted in Colorado on land-fraud charges. Anselmi also denied ever having talked with O'Keefe, or ever having known him.

Here it should be said that Rather had visually linked Anselmi to an "Arizona connection"—a connection as yet unproved—by showing unrelated film scenes of Arizona desert and also a brief film sequence of a man said to be Danny O'Keefe who was seen arriving on his own at an airport. Now Rather proceeded to cast his net over the top officials in the Wyoming capital. First, he asked Compton what he thought a grand jury might concentrate on. Compton replied:

I would ask that the grand jury look at the governor in relationship to land purchases with Don Anselmi.

Rather showed some exterior views of a ranch that had apparently been bought by Governor Ed Herschler, of Wyoming, and then took his camera to the governor himself:

Rather: Governor, your partner in purchasing this Yellowstone Ranch in Fremont County, nineteen hundred acres, is Mr. Don Anselmi.

Governor: It's closer to twenty thousand acres. And leases—and federal leases. I suppose there's about a million acres involved.

Rather: And your partner is Mr. Anselmi?

Governor: He's one of them, yes.

Having thus linked Governor Herschler with Anselmi, who had earlier been linked with a "connection" in Arizona and "land-scandal people who have connections to mobsters," Rather returned to Compton:

Rather: Source of the money [for the Yellowstone Ranch]?

Compton: Source of the money? It is my belief the source of money is from organized crime.

Rather: Do you think that could be proven?

Compton: I believe that could be proven with subpoena power from a grand jury.

Rather: Organized-crime connections with the governor of the state? Democratic state chairman?

Compton: That's correct.

In effect, the intrepid "60 Minutes" investigators had shown us some television views of the Yellowstone Ranch and of Governor Herschler saying that he was one of its purchasers, while darkly implying that if the real source of the purchase funds should ever be uncovered (an investigative operation that would require the assistance of a grand-jury subpoena!) it would be traceable to the coffers of organized crime. But in fact—though, for all I know, the governor of Wyoming may have been hand in glove with the Mafia or the Baader-Meinhof gang in other areas—in the matter of the purchase of the Yellowstone Ranch, a couple of modestly investigative phone calls produced the somewhat less exciting information that this particular deal was consummated through Lowham Associates, a well-known Wyoming firm specializing in ranch properties; that a major portion of the purchase price of $1.8 million was financed by loans from the Federal Land Bank Association of Wyoming and the First National Bank of Casper; that a lesser part of the purchase price was financed through a second mortgage to the sellers, Mr. William McIntosh and his niece Jennifer McIntosh; and that the relatively minor sum of $25,000 in cash was paid by each of the four partners.

The subject of Rather's final charge against the Wyoming administration was not without foundation and had already been extensively covered in the regional press, though, once again, Rather seemed more interested in prosecuting it than in reporting it. A case that involved charges that public officials were stealing from a state home for the elderly was first archly described by Rather as "a seemingly minor scandal, perhaps no bigger than that 'third-rate burglary' at Watergate" and then, more grimly, in the statement "It may become a Democratic Prairiegate here in Wyoming!" According to numerous earlier newspaper accounts, the mess in question had to do with allegations that two officials involved with the administration of Wyoming's old-age homes (both of them, in fact, *Republican* appointees from a previous state administration) between them had ripped off the Pioneer Home in Thermopolis, Wyoming, taking several thousand dollars' worth of goods presumably intended for the elderly pioneers: a half dozen or so TV sets; several stereo units; some bath towels; and generous supplies of nuts and candy. It was Compton's and Rather's accusation that Governor Herschler and his attorney general, Frank Mendicino, had engaged in a cover-up when the latter "refused to prosecute." But once again, the facts, though they hardly spoke well for the attorney general's political savvy, were decidedly more ambiguous than they were made to appear on the air. For one of the two men, Kenneth Brighton, though he had not actually been brought to trial, had indeed been charged in a state court on eleven felony counts and was awaiting trial when he died as a result of complications from heart surgery. It is true that Mendicino was laggard in prosecuting the second man, Lloyd Hovee, but his explanation (which was repeated in several press stories) was that he needed Brighton's testimony in order to build a strong case against Hovee and was plea-bargaining with Brighton when he died. Perhaps there was more than carelessness in Mendicino's delay in bringing the second Pioneer bandit to trial, but it is troubling that Rather, in his eagerness to produce a "Democratic Prairiegate," neglected to mention the charges already brought against Brighton, or the eleven counts that the state was prosecuting him on, or any of the background information (for example, that the culprits were Republican appointees anyway) that might have put the attorney general's behavior in a less sinister light.

At any rate, there rested the "60 Minutes" investigation of corruption in Wyoming: not exactly a legal prosecution, for there had been no indictment, no jury chosen, no counsel (at least for the defense), and no judge to guide the proceedings; on the other hand, not strictly speaking a reporting job, for there were few facts, and those facts that were referred to often turned out to be inaccurate or incompletely presented or ambiguous. A couple of conclusions seem worth drawing from this sorry affair. One is that since for some years now newsmen have been protected by the Supreme Court decision in the case of *New York Times Co. v. Sullivan* to the extent that "actual malice" must be proved before a public figure can be awarded damages in a libel action, it might be in the self-interest of the press—given the reporters' Sullivanian immunity—to act with less careless belligerence in its pursuit of investigative quarries. Investigative reporters, as has been observed elsewhere, are the guard dogs of society, but the trouble with guard dogs is that they sometimes attack with equal fervor the midnight burglar and the midday mailman.

The second conclusion relates more directly to television news and its conflicting attitudes toward the still different worlds of print journalism and entertainment. On the one hand, "60 Minutes" appears to imitate the surface conventions of the city room or magazine office, with its correspondents nearly always properly attired in white shirt, necktie, and suit (in the fashion of a 1950s *Time* reporter), and brandishing their little spiral notebooks as they ask the old-fashioned newsman's tough questions. On the other hand, the form in which "60 Minutes" presents its investigations has little to do with the conventions of print journalism. It's not better or worse, but it's different; a television news story is first of all part of the television process, and whatever it borrows from other media is bound to be secondary. In a standard-print investigative report, although the reporter may have experienced a variety of difficulties and surmounted numerous obstacles before bringing in the story, what is finally published usually relates directly only to the subject of the investigation; essentially, it is a relatively distanced account that depends for heat and accessibility on the stylistic flourishes of the reporter. But with "60 Minutes," the news-gathering process itself has become part of the story—sometimes a key part, with the TV newsman first shown outside, trying to get in, then inside, facing down an uncooperative or hostile subject, who in turn is shown in close-up on the screen (as were the generally cooperative Wyoming politicians), often caught by the camera in a carefully edited grimace or expression of seemingly revealed truth, which later may turn out not to have been truth at all—or truth of a quite different sort. One obvious result of this cinematic dramatization of the news interview is that the public is all too likely to follow the seductive flow of the news-gathering drama without paying very close attention to its content. An additional hazard is that when on-camera newsmen assume the mantle of prosecutors, in a quasi-trial context where they control the cameras and the editing machines and where there is no counsel for the defense, then the reports that these methods produce can sometimes drift fairly far from that orderly or reporterly presentation of information that the Founding Fathers probably had in mind when they invoked their crucial safeguards for our press. At any rate, now that "60 Minutes" has made its mark as an enterprising and interesting news program, perhaps Dan Rather and some of his colleagues will consider giving up their trial robes and courthouse righteousness and return to the kind of solid, forthright reporting they've often done so well in the past. And maybe they'll even revisit Wyoming. They don't seem to have quite got the story right the first time around.

(1977)

Postscript

A couple of notes seem worth adding to this essay, whose original appearance in the *New Yorker* evoked a surprisingly thin-skinned and belligerent response from the normally cool executives of CBS News. Over a period of several weeks after publication, a series of meticulously typed, single-spaced, quasi-legal communications (often of immoderate length as well as temper) arrived at my office, in several instances hand-carried from the elegant CBS building six blocks to the north, though not presumably by the correspondents themselves. These letters generally fell into two categories. First, there were those that sought to impugn the credibility of my observations on the grounds that I was a parochial easterner, whose surely limited acquaintance with the state of Wyoming was obviously no match for the "special familiarity" of newsman Dan Rather, who, I was briskly informed, had visited the state "no less than fourteen times." Then, when it became known that, in fact, I had actually spent quite a bit of time in Wyoming (although mostly as a summer resident, staring at the sagebrush and watching my children fall off horses), a second flurry of mail arrived, which now questioned both my candor and my motives, by suggesting that since I was reportedly a Wyoming landowner (alas, not true), I had acted doubtless "in collusion" with Wyoming "special interests" and might even have an ax to grind on behalf of the state's Democratic administration. Though I felt briefly flattered to be thought of, even inaccurately, as a power to be reckoned with in the state, it seemed to me that this latter inference was a curiously unprofessional one for a television news organization to be making in regard to a television critic going about his job, especially one who had gone to some pains to make it clear in the same essay that, far from advocating the spotless purity of Wyoming politics of either party, a person would have to be some kind of born fool to think that an energy boom might be taking place in this fine Rocky Mountain state and no one was cutting any corners there. The focus of my criticism, however, had been the particulars of the "60 Minutes" report, and this was not a focus that my distinguished correspondents seemed much interested in replying to. Indeed, when now and then some elaborately titled executive got around to considering the questions of fact that had been raised, it was invariably to state, in an alternately sanctimonious and bullying tone, that inasmuch as these matters were currently in the hands of a Wyoming grand jury, it would not be "appropriate" to make a public reply to them "at this time." I might add that one of the few "60 Minutes" luminaries who did not engage in any of this solemn tantruming was Dan Rather himself, who possibly did not have access to meticulous, single-spaced, quasi-legal typing, or else had better things to do.

Fortunately, the Wyoming grand jury has since been disbanded. This was the second such grand jury empaneled in Wyoming's history, and it is still referred to in the state, in varying tones of voice, as the "60 Minutes" grand jury. In 1977 an official investigation had been loudly sought by Neil Compton, who was nationally seconded by Dan Rather and "60 Minutes." The jury was empaneled by Governor Herschler in November 1977, and it met for a little over one year. One hundred and fifty-five witnesses were heard. Three hundred thousand dollars of taxpayers' money was spent. The results of these labors were roughly as follows. No evidence was found that warranted naming Governor Herschler (of the so-called ranch-purchase scandal) in an indictment. No evidence was found that warranted naming former Democratic party chairman Don Anselmi (of the so-called Arizona land-grab scandal) in an indictment. Former attorney general Frank Mendicino was named in an indictment, but the indictment was dismissed in district court. None of the Rock Springs officials, including Mayor Wataha, was named in an indictment. (The grand jury criticized the Rock Springs group for having been too tolerant of prostitution and gambling in their community.) A few minor malefactors were successfully indicted, such as Lloyd Hovee, the sixty-four-year-old Republican appointee who had been accused of playing fast and loose with the Pioneer Home's television sets and candy supplies. Hovee was sentenced to sixty days in jail but received a pardon on the grounds of ill health. In the aftermath of the grand-jury investigation, Governor Herschler was reelected to the governorship by a comfortable majority. Don Anselmi resigned his party chairmanship as a result of the "60 Minutes" publicity and is no longer active in public life. Frank Mendicino also resigned and now practices law in Cheyenne. Neil Compton left Wyoming, first for Colorado, where he held police jobs in Greeley and Fort Collins and ran unsuccessfully for sheriff in Larimer County; then he moved to California, where he reportedly has a "security job" in a Los Angeles suburb. Dan Rather, of course, was named to replace Walter Cronkite on the CBS Evening News.

An additional comment might be made here, though not with specific reference to the Wyoming programs. At the time of writing "The Prosecutor," I had suggested in my concluding remarks that newsmen, who then didn't seem to be at all badly protected by the *New York Times Co. v. Sullivan* decision, could probably stand to be a little more equanimous in their investigations, at least to the extent of not so determinedly playing the time-honored role of underdog newshound while at the same time laying about with telegenic accusations of persons who are handicapped by the need to prove "actual malice" in order legally to protect themselves. Even as I wrote, however, other forces were evidently at work to upset the already delicate balance between the press's right to report the news and the citizen's right to privacy—some of them, in fact, having been set in motion by an earlier "60 Minutes" program which contained a dramatically prosecutorial interview by correspondent Mike Wallace with Lt. Col. Anthony B. Herbert, a well-known critic of military police in the Vietnam war. Indeed, ten months later came the *Herbert v. Lando* decision (Barry Lando had been the producer of the Wallace interview with Lt. Col. Herbert), in which the Supreme Court, by a six-to-three margin, reversed the decision of a lower court and held that journalists henceforth could *not* use First Amendment protection to avoid answering questions about their "state of mind" when they became targets of libel suits brought by public figures. The *Herbert v. Lando* decision did not replace *New York Times Co. v. Sullivan*, but it effectively changed the balance of power between journalists and their subjects. Reporters are not exactly underdogs again, but they are less free to go about their business now than they were under *New York Times Co. v. Sullivan*, and I don't believe it would be excessive to say that to some degree it was the reporters themselves whose immodesty, as it were, coupled with the power of television journalism, brought about the unfortunate change. Clearly, *Herbert v. Lando* is a terrible decision: murkily abstract, dangerously illiberal, and radically hostile to the obvious intentions of the Constitution. But just as clearly, it is a decision that was somehow squeezed from a divided and morally uncertain court by the pressures of new behavior and new news-gathering techniques. One might go so far as to say that although fairness in reporting has been deemed in recent years to be unexciting, insufficiently dramatic, and lacking in viewer appeal, the price of prime-time advocacy journalism may turn out to have been fairly steep. Luckily, the issues involved are all continuing ones and are not likely to be decided overnight.

No Lies:
Direct Cinema as Rape
Vivian C. Sobchack

You wanta know what a rape is. You'll never know what a rape is. You'll *never know what a rape is! So how can I explain it to you? There's no way of explaining it to you.*

These are the words Shelby Leverington, the female "subject" of *No Lies*,[1] yells in a half-choked voice at Alec Hirschfeld, the male "filmmaker," at the climax of this important and very disturbing short film by Mitchell Block. Philosophically in agreement with Shelby's outburst that rape can't be "explained" to someone who has never experienced it, the film avoids explanations; rather, *No Lies* opts for action. It is not merely *about* rape. Cinematically, it also *demonstrates* and *commits* rape—and it does so in such a way as to make the experience of being the unwary, unprepared victim of an aggressive assault on one's person, on one's pride, and on one's expectations of and security in familiar activity in familiar surroundings a very real experience accessible to anyone of *either* sex who views the film.

Adroitly and manipulatively using both its subject and its style—indeed, its subject *is* its style—*No Lies* expands the meaning of rape beyond the physical and sexual violence other films about rape have found appropriately cinematic and photogenic, and upon which they have, perhaps, overemphatically focused. It is in both its enlargement of our perception of rape and in its experiential nature that *No Lies* becomes significant. Giving lie to Shelby's words, after we have seen the film we do know and feel—at least to some degree—what a rape is.

Certainly, sexual assault has been a cinematic subject since the beginnings of film. One can cite instances from a multitude of "respectable" film texts:

the racially oriented and unsuccessful attempts on both Mae Marsh and Lillian Gish in Griffith's *The Birth of a Nation* (1915), the former foiled by suicide and the latter by the unwitting intervention of the victim's father; the off-screen rape of Jennifer Jones in Vidor's *Duel in the Sun* (1947), an assault indicated by bold strokes of lightning and an abrupt change in the weather; the Academy Award–winning rape of silent Jane Wyman in *Johnny Belinda* (1948) and, in the same year, an attempted rape of Loretta Young in *The Accused* (William Dieterle). Ida Lupino directed Mala Power's rape in *Outrage* (1950), and even Esther Williams, her mermaid's chastity threatened out of water, was attacked by one of her own high school students in *The Unguarded Moment* (Harry Keller, 1956), a film scripted in part by Rosalind Russell. In 1961 there was *Something Wild* (Jack Garfein), which was indeed, positing as it did rape victim Carroll Baker falling for her would-be attacker. In 1968, Richard Fleischer gave us Hollywood's first split-screen rape in the schizo-phrenically shot *The Boston Strangler*. And 1972 offered us Hitchcock's *Frenzy*, which combined macabre humor with scenes of painful explicitness, Peckinpah's misogynistic *Straw Dogs*, in which a lascivious Susan George indulges chau-vinistic rape fantasies by strutting around "asking for it," and John Boorman's *Deliverance*, which dared to show us, albeit slightly off-screen, a mainstream male rape. Rape also made responsibly mounted appearances on television: the produced-for-TV movies *A Case of Rape* and *Cry Rape* made the act and its aftermath respectable for the family room and inspired numerous apings on the growing number of police shows, where it alternated weeks with stories about returned Vietnam veterans going murderously berserk. Most recently, of course, there's been *Lipstick* (Lamont Johnson, 1976), a film which features, for the first time, a rape victim getting her own back but good, and which— in its frighteningly grim espousal of vigilante tactics—can be best described as *Death Wish* in drag. And then, out of the mainstream although it's a feature film, there's been Martha Coolidge's *Not A Pretty Picture* (1975), which has rape acted, the actors discussing having to act rape out, and the filmmaker remembering her own rape many years before.

Superficially, this brief chronological catalogue may seem to indicate that rape on the screen (or slightly off) has fairly wide parameters when it comes to the films' stance toward the act, its perpetrators, and its victims. There is certainly an attitudinal and tonal difference between the treatment of Jane Wyman's deaf-mute, asexual farm girl and Susan George's whorish wife as rape victims, between Tony Curtis's schizophrenic angst in *The Boston Strangler* and Barry Foster's cheerfully despicable psychosis in *Frenzy*. Yet, in terms of film itself, the basic formal and structural elements which comprise a film's visual point of view and, thus, its placement of the audience who watches it, this variety of attitude and tone toward screen rape must be seen as primarily literary and merely skin deep. Indeed, the only major change in the visual treatment of rape in mainstream cinema has been in the area of explicitness. We can now see most of what used to be only suggested.

Otherwise the cinematic treatment of rape has been a constant from *The Birth of a Nation* to *Lipstick*. In all cases, the films have focused on the sexual and physical nature of rape. Even those films which have attempted to place their major emphases elsewhere have been hard put to do so successfully, a fact which has much to do with the supposed "nature" of the film medium. The movies have always had an affinity for that which moves; and, all moral and social judgements aside, one has to admit that scenes of sexual and physical assault move. They are a veritable frenzy of activity, both in the content in the frame and in the cutting. Thus, on a visual level alone, it is nearly impossible for even their brief presence in a movie not to inform and often overshadow the entire film, and particularly the relatively more quiescent and inert scenes of emotional and psychological turmoil which, though they may occupy more screen time, make much less of a mark on one's visual memory.

Besides placing their major photographic emphasis on the physical nature of rape, on rape as an *activity*, the films have another cinematic common denominator. In all cases, the audience has been placed in the position of voyeur rather than victim. This is as true of *Not A Pretty Picture* as it is of *Straw Dogs* and has finally little to do with the filmmakers' intent, prurient or not. In all cases, no matter whether the rape victim or the rapist is the protagonist of a given film, and aside from infrequent and conventional under-stood-rather-than-felt subjective camera shots, the audience watches from a safe and separate dimension. All the aforementioned films, no matter how varied they seem, are similar in the relationship they establish with their audience. They are all *about* rape; rape is object rather than subject. We watch these movies abstracted safely into narrative cinema, films which have a pre-destined beginning, middle, and end—and which ask for nothing from us but our attention, that we *watch* rather than participate. Certainly, *all* narrative film makes this request of us, not solely those films about rape. Although we have the illusion of immediacy before us, in narrative film we are also aware of the shape of a *fait accompli* in which we cannot possibly intervene. Thus one of the qualities of narrative cinema: we are relieved of having to act responsibly, socially, morally, of having to act at all.

Indeed, voyeurism is, and always has been, one of the great pleasures of film viewing. However, when rape is the object we view with such traditional passivity, the pleasure of our safety must be, to some degree, diminished by our scruples. Although we may, at selected moments, "identify" with the victim (and I would argue that such identification is available to both male and female viewers), the very shape of traditional narrative cinema forces us to become helpless passersby, thankful on the one hand that it's not we who are being assaulted, and ashamed on the other that we are so thankful and so curious and so permitted to indulge our curiosity about the act itself. As well, the films allow for an indulgence in fantasy, the very privacy of the darkness and the passivity of the viewing experience conducive to the dream state in which Siegfried Kracauer says we watch feature films.[2] Thus, art and pleasure aside, the traditional narrative film about rape has enforced a rather amoral, if unintentional, passivity upon the audience which may be in direct contradiction to the messages communicated by the film's literary structure. We end up watching even the most socially motivated movies about rape from the distance of a third person, at worst titillated by the peculiar beauties of the violence we're protected from and at best sympathetic to and moved by the shadows on the screen.

Mitchell Block's *No Lies*, however, although it is a narrative film, subverts narrative tradition and offers an alternative to the customary treatment of rape in the movies. Using unorthodox—and, to some, unethical and offensive—means, it shakes us into a first-person encounter with rape and betrayal and forces us to confront our customary voyeurism and passivity as it is evoked by our usual cinematic experience. Unlike traditional films about rape, *No Lies* shifts the emphasis from the physical and sexual nature of the assault to its intellectual and emotional nature; there is no on-screen sexual attack (suggested or explicit) to overpower and delimit the film's broader definition of rape. As well, while pretending to support and maintain the viewer's comfortable and safe role as voyeur, the film actually undermines it, so that by the end of *No Lies* the viewer is revealed not only as voyeur but also as victim. All this upheaval is accomplished in sixteen minutes and through a method which—like all things brilliant—is deceptively simple. Block has found an ideal metaphor for the physical act of rape in the methods and effects of *cinéma vérité*, what we now call direct cinema. The sexual assault discussed by the film's two characters on the screen has found an experiential analogue in the filmic assault on both the movie's female subject and its audience. Rape becomes interchangeable with an act of cinema. The film, thus, provides us with an exploration and an experience of both.

The action of *No Lies* is simple. A young woman, Shelby, is interviewed by a student filmmaker, Alec, as she is preparing to leave her apartment to see a movie. During the course of her preparation and banter with the filmmaker and as she moves around in the limited space of three rooms and a narrow hallway, she reveals that she has been raped the previous week. She seems cool about the event, almost reportorial about her doctor's magazine-article response that it happens "all the time," almost incredulously amused at her suspect treatment by the police. Alec's handheld camera wavers as he starts to question Shelby, revealing his surprise at and disapproval of the young woman's seeming nonchalance. He proceeds to verbally attack and photographically corner her until she breaks down in front of the camera. After Shelby's emotional outburst about the rape (the climax of which begins this article), Alec apologizes but continues filming until Shelby goes off to see, appropriately perhaps, *Night of the Hunter*, closing the apartment door on the filmmaker who has promised to join her as soon as his film runs out. The screen turns to blackness and credits appear, informing the audience that the entire film has been a constructed and directed fiction, a narrative and not a documentary. Thus *No Lies* occupies screen space. The psychic space it occupies, however, is of a different and much more complex order. By the film's end, the audience has been subjected to three rapes rather than one and has experienced them on increasingly threatening levels.

Paradoxically, the least immediate and affective rape is the physical rape, the sexual assault described by Shelby. Safe in our seats, we can listen to Shelby's recounting of a rape past, a rape off-screen, a rape *unseen*. Thus, ironically, the only physical rape of the film is the least physical rape *in* the film. It is communicated verbally in a fairly nonexpressive vernacular and in terms of past time; it has no palpable or visual screen presence. And, as Shelby indicates, the act cannot be effectively communicated through language alone. Although the viewer may be most sympathetic and most intellectually aware of the horror of the physical rape, the viewer is also completely physically protected and emotionally distanced from the act itself. It is told rather than committed, and one can only experience it as a story, a completed oral narrative. In retrospect, it is touching that informing all of Shelby's dialogue—used as a verbal tic but finally acting as a plaintive refrain—is the expression "You know." Because neither Alec, the filmmaker, nor the viewer does know, at least not from Shelby's verbal offerings. We are both too spatially and too temporally abstracted from her experience.

This spatial and temporal distance is mitigated, however, by the film's second rape. Whereas the first and sexual assault is rape described, the second attack is rape demonstrated. Again the victim is Shelby, but this time—to use her turn of phrase—the "friendly neighborhood rapist" is Alec, the filmmaker. Alec stalks and corners Shelby physically and emotionally. We watch him violate her privacy, her trust, her defenses, her space. He relentlessly probes and insensitively attacks, hurting and humiliating the young woman who seems unaware, caught off guard, consistently blind to Alec's betrayal of her to the camera and the audience. Alec's end goal is, of course, not a violent screw; it's a dramatic film. Casual at first, he wins Shelby's trust by kidding around, and then he proceeds to exploit her confidence and orchestrate her breakdown for his camera. He is demonstrably guilty of everything connected with rape *but* sexual assault; he does to Shelby in the present and on the screen what she describes as having been done to her off-screen and in the past by both the rapist and the police.

Like the rapist and the police, Alec intimidates her. His weapon, however, is not a knife or an official report but a camera. Shelby reveals her discomfort. Ill at ease, she laughs a lot and says: "You're making me nervous," "You're really intimidating me with that camera." When she tells Alec as she goes into her bedroom, "Okay, that's it. That's all you're gonna shoot," he responds with an ingenuous incredulity which masks a certain menace, "What do you mean, that's all I'm gonna shoot?" Shelby wants to change her clothes and says, "You can't come in here." But Alec follows her. "I can't . . . ? What are you talking about? I'm making a movie here, if you haven't realized." Shelby submits to the power of the camera by deciding not to change her clothes, only her necklace.

This begins her capitulation, her submission to Alec, the filmmaker, who is as calculating and manipulative as were the rapist and the police she describes. He not only encourages Shelby's breakdown but causes it, playing an active role by his off-screen questioning. He brutally makes her relive the rape emotionally, go through it again—in detail. After being told about the assault and recovering his equilibrium and control (for a moment the camera seems like a jaw dropped in surprise), Alec asks for "a little background on the thing." Shelby then shares her "incredible" experience. "They, they asked me, you gotta get ready, they asked me what I was wearing, like if I had, they wanted to know if I'd gone out to the garbage in my negligee . . . ," she says, only to have Alec ask, "Well, what *were* you wearing?" She foreshadows her own breakdown before Alec when she talks about how the police made her cry. And she discusses the horror of having to relive details for a nosy detective with possibly prurient motives as she relives the details for Alec who is being callous, nosy, and, if not prurient, then certainly exploitative. In her final outburst, and apropos of Alec's insensitive refusal to accept her attempts to deal with the rape in the only way she feels capable, Shelby says, "A rape is . . . is a reality of cops coming in and humiliating you and telling you it was your fault . . . because you took a shower after it happened." Her words parallel with excruciating obviousness Alec's blaming Shelby for her attempts to cleanse herself psychically. And, like the police, he cruelly questions the reality and severity of the rape as well. After asking her, "Are you sure it happened at all?" and telling her that she's got "too much of a resigned attitude" for him to believe, he attacks her for being too "willing to accept it and take it" and says that her attitude "makes it look like it wasn't really a rape . . . or it wasn't so much of a rape."

Finally, Shelby is browbeaten into tears and explicitness, her attempts to "explain" herself a painful humiliation examined in detailed close-up by Alec's avid camera. Unlike the viewer who has grown to loathe Alec's brutal insensitivity, Shelby seems only half-conscious that she is the filmmaker's victim. Her sole articulation of the possibility comes after her climactic speech. Wiping her tears while trying not to disturb her makeup, in a voice drained and feeble, she says, "But I want you to know that I didn't enjoy it. Because that's what you're intimating. And it's not true." Alec apologizes, yet the film ends with him again forcing Shelby into confession and submission as he asks her to spell out why she wants him to walk to the movies with her, and directs her exit out of her own apartment.

As viewers, our relationship with this second rape in *No Lies* is quite a bit different from our relationship with the first. Seeing a rape in action we are certainly more involved emotionally although we are still not threatened ourselves. In fact, we derive a certain immense, if unstated, pleasure at our safety and our superiority to Shelby. Certainly we grow to hate Alec and his assault and to sympathize with his victim. But we also must feel Shelby is less smart than we are. We can donate our pity for her from the largesse of our cultivated sensibilities which allow us to see right away that Alec is violating Shelby whereas the poor girl doesn't see it at all. As is traditional, we remain voyeurs of the action on the screen, distanced enough to appreciate our own perceptiveness. We can pride ourselves on our intellectual recognition of the film's central metaphor: direct cinema, documentary filmmaking, as an act of rape. And we can pride ourselves on being better than the two people in the film; we're smarter than Shelby and nicer than Alec.

During the course of the film we're either so fascinated at being privy to the relationship between the filmmaker and his subject or so intent on making intellectual connections between the form and the content that we really don't question the basic nastiness of our pleasure. Rather, this second, on-screen, rape in *No Lies* allows us to feel moral superiority. It seduces us into a sense of smugness, into a state of self-congratulation.

Which brings us to the third and most significant rape in the film. From rape described to rape demonstrated, we move off-screen again—this time into the audience—to rape experienced. The confrontation is direct. Once we have learned that the two people on the screen are characters in a fiction, they no longer separate us from the real filmmaker, Mitchell Block, and from the real victims of assault, ourselves. We find out, abruptly and shockingly, that the only real rape has happened to us. Lulled into smugness by the action on the screen and by our assumptions about it, we are humiliated into a recognition of our own gullibility, have to face our own foolish and childlike trust, our own ridiculous hubris. Immediately after "psyching out" the film and feeling superior to its victim, secure in our seats and in our conviction that the kind of rape we've seen on the screen could never happen to us, we're confronted with our own victimization. The film makes a lot of people angry.

Mitchell Block says of *No Lies*: "My goal was to make a fictional film that would convince the audience it was an actual documentary, a film that would be frankly manipulative."[3] It is to this manipulation that we respond so strongly, so unpassively. Consider the possibilities of responding as strongly if—in the manner of Pontecorvo's *The Battle of Algiers*—the film had kept its documentary style but had announced at the beginning it was a narrative. Or alternatively that, as it seemed to be, *No Lies* was, indeed, an actual piece of direct cinema. In the first case, I would guess that we would mutually congratulate ourselves and the filmmaker for appreciating each other's aesthetic intelligence and cinematic literacy. In the latter case, I would suggest a grimmer possibility: that we would leave the theater feeling smug and superior to a misguided filmmaker and an actual rape victim. In either case our passivity would have been traditionally served, our expectations met rather than violated. Why, indeed, aren't we happy and relieved at the film's revelation that Shelby and Alec are performers and that there's been no rape? The answer has little to do with the abstractions of film criticism or documentary ethics. What bothers us after seeing *No Lies* is our own violation.

We are, after all, such easy marks. Speaking of her fictional rape, Shelby says: "I was just not prepared for it. I just didn't go out of my house that night thinking to look around and some sneaky guy was going to creep up on me and . . . and grab me by the throat and stick a knife in my neck. And . . . and like rape me!" Like Shelby, we are not prepared. We don't go to movies— an activity as familiar as Shelby's taking out the garbage—expecting to be betrayed by the filmmaker. Thus, when *No Lies* begins with Shelby putting on makeup in a harshly lit bathroom and the filmmaker making his own presence known, we in the audience become comfortable and settle down for a familiar documentary experience, a *cinéma vérité* movie with real people functioning in real time and revealing real emotions in uncontrolled real situations. The very style of the film immediately authenticates its content. Through its seeming lack of control, evidenced by haphazard set-ups, handheld camera, natural lighting and sound, and apparently continuous shooting, the film confers realism on the people and events themselves. Or—*we* confer realism on the film by virtue of our past cinematic experience. *No Lies* carefully cultivates its spontaneity and ingenuousness so that Block gains our confidence, as Alec gains Shelby's.

To begin the film, Block plays up its amateurish qualities to lull us into complacency. This is no Fred Wiseman *Hospital* or *Welfare*. The filmmaker seems ineffectual at first, the subject self-conscious and giggly. We are made aware of the clumsy process of filming, of the particulars of Alec's ego and of his student status. The film seems so uncontrolled as to not have any purpose in being; it has no center, no focus. In addition, we're *told* the film is *cinéma vérité* in an interchange which subtly implies that whatever happens before the camera will be in the film, no matter how dull and usual. Shelby asks, "What are you wasting your film for . . . taking a picture of me changing my necklace." And Alec replies, "This is *cinéma vérité*." We are set up by the directionless, relatively uninteresting nature of the film's first few minutes to believe Shelby's dramatic revelation later.

Our confidence in the film's spontaneity and undirectedness established, Block then proceeds to involve the audience in a consideration of the ethical problems which are raised by the kind of direct cinema with which we are confronted. After initially invading Shelby's privacy, Alec—sniffing drama as if it were blood—becomes neither an impartial observer nor a sympathetic confidant. Shelby would rather talk about movies, perhaps, but Alec—not your ideal *cinéma vérité* filmmaker—shapes her responses looking for a "privileged moment," what Jean Rouch defines as one of those "exceptional moments when, suddenly, there is in effect no camera, no microphone. There's a revelation, a staggering revelation because it's totally sincere—and totally provoked. And totally artificial, if you like, because you asked someone to . . . talk."[4] Alec goes a step further; not merely satisfied that his filming has happily (for him) resulted in a revelation of an intensely dramatic nature, he attacks and exploits Shelby, squeezing emotion and footage from her, probing and prolonging her anguish so that it is almost completely controlled and directed by him. We contemplate how the very basis of direct cinema may be perverted, whether through its supposedly nonmanipulative recording functions or its self-reflexive admission of manipulation within acknowledged parameters. As well, Alec's calculatedly destructive assault on Shelby demonstrates that direct cinema has less of an affinity for the usual event than it has for the catastrophic. Alec dramatically builds his own crisis structure, aware that it will give his film shape.

Raising these ethical considerations, *No Lies* reveals a dimension that is extremely satisfying to an intelligent and receptive audience. To quote Block, not only is the film "about rape in both a literal and a figurative sense," but it is also "a statement on documentary films."[5] Because we in the audience have to make the connections, to acknowledge the central metaphor revealed by the film's action and method, and because this requires a bit of active effort on our part, some brief thought, we are lulled into thinking that we've plumbed the film's depths.

But *No Lies* proceeds to make fun of us, dares to show us the lack of investment we usually have in such "real-life" documents, by hitting us where we really live—in our pride. Many viewers echo Karen Horowitz who, reviewing the film, called it "offensive" and said, "By the end . . . I was totally furious at the camera operator, but even more so at the end titles which indicated that the participants were actors."[6] The fury comes, I would suggest, from an experience akin to the one Shelby, as a fictional victim of sexual assault, describes and reveals. We feel humiliated and victimized and foolish at our susceptibility to Block's attack, and we also feel horribly impotent. We're like Shelby, who says to Alec: "There's nothing that I can do, there's no one that I can take it out on. There's no man that I'm gonna go out in the street . . . and I'm gonna punch in the face and say, 'I'm taking it out on you!' " How do we punch a film in the nose? And how morally culpable is the film anyway, since it makes us aware of how casually we place our trust and faith in the cinema? The film may attack us, but it is our own expectation that makes us vulnerable. Why do we even trust the credits? The film leaves us dislocated, unsettled, challenging us to believe it when it says it's lying.

At worst, the violation of the audience by *No Lies* could be considered a cinematic gimmick, a one-time shocker. It has been suggested that the film would have no impact on an audience who knew it was staged or that it would offer little of merit upon second viewing. But the film is more than a mere "The Lady or the Tiger" short. The shock and experience of a first viewing can never be repeated, but the viewer is able to substitute another response which serves a similar function in making him confront his film experience. Upon repeated viewings, one searches for clues to the filmmaker's deceit, for those moments which seduced us; having been participants in our own violation, we look back for that moment when we could have said "no" and didn't, to that instant both before and after we lost our virginity.

No Lies presents an interesting alternative to traditional narratives about rape, and, as well, it cinematically posits some very important critical questions, not only about the often aggressive and exploitative methods of direct cinema, but also about the audience's relationship with *all* the films it sees. And finally, in making the analogy between rape and direct cinema an emotional as well as an intellectual experience accessible to persons of both sexes, *No Lies* deserves praise from those who see film as a powerful social force. Using unethical methods, sneaky tactics, and a brilliant idea, it fulfills, after all, a civic responsibility.

Notes

1. *No Lies*, 16mm, Color, 16 minutes. Producer/Director: Mitchell Block. Release date: December 1973. Distributor: Phoenix Films, New York. All quotes from the film were obtained from a personally taped transcription.

2. Siegfried Kracauer, *Theory of Film: The Redemption of Physical Reality* (New York: Oxford University Press, 1960). See chap. 9, "The Spectator."

3. Mitchell Block, "The Filming of *No Lies*," *Filmmaker's Newsletter*, Feb. 1975, p. 18.

4. Jean Rouch, interviewed in G. Roy Levin, *Documentary Explorations: Fifteen Interviews with Filmmakers* (New York: Doubleday, 1971), p. 137.

5. Block, "The Filming of *No Lies*."

6. Karen Horowitz, "Elephants, Home Movies, Senior Citizens, and Yanomano Anthropologists Go Bananas," *American Film* 1 (Sept. 1976): 66.

Leslie Woodhead, director, watches Ian Holm being made up as Lech Walesa in the docu-drama STRIKE *(Granada TV).*

SOLDIER GIRLS, *by Nick Broomfield and Joan Churchill, 1981.*

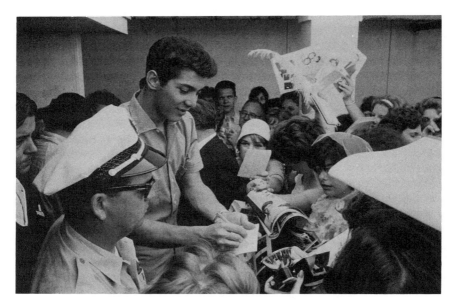

Paul Anka and his fans in LONELY BOY *(National Film Board).*

CITY OF GOLD
(National Film Board)

Martin Sheen re-enacts the federal judge's role in the trial of the Plowshares Seven: IN THE KING OF PRUSSIA, *by Emile de Antonio.*

From MODEL, *by Fred Wiseman (photo: Oliver Kool).*

From AN AMERICAN FAMILY.

Filming in progress on TWO LAWS.

Filming in progress on POLICE: *Director Roger Graef (in beard and glasses) talks to cameraman Charles Stewart.*

Firearms training in POLICE.

Frame blow-up from SEVENTEEN, *by Joel Demott and Jeff Kreines.*

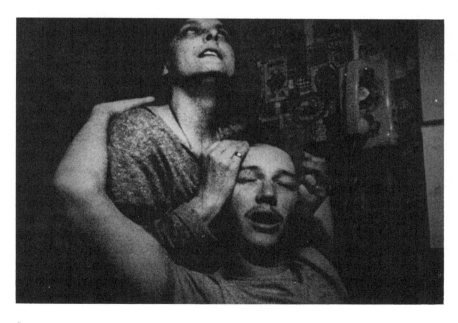

SEVENTEEN.

Tom Sigel and Pamela Yates filming in Guatemala: WHEN THE MOUNTAINS TREMBLE.

Part IV
Television

Introduction

Although there has recently been some growth in theatrical distribution, television is still—in the 1980s—the key medium for presenting documentaries to the public. This chapter looks at some of the implications and ramifications of that situation, particularly with regard to the American scene, since the British and European television documentary is a specialized subject in itself.

Whatever the medium, whether art, literature, or film, the ability to bring the finished work to an audience—in this case the mass audience—is the ultimate power. This section, then, is about the workings of that power in the United States, within both the commercial networks and the public broadcasting system; it is about the filmmaker's ability to tap into that power; and it is about the constraints that social, governmental, and commercial pressures impose on that power, leading sometimes to submission to trends in public taste or even to censorship.

Few of these themes are new to the documentary discussion. Access, funding, and the tension between independent filmmakers and the public broadcasting system are among the central topics of discussion whenever filmmakers meet and have been debated in many magazines over the years, from *American Film* to the *Independent* and the *Journal of the University Film and Video Association*.[1] Many of these subjects, however—for instance, funding—have in the past been discussed in isolation. This chapter is an attempt to show the *relationship* between a number of disparate topics: it looks at the distance between theoretical and practical expectations for bringing documentary to wide audiences via the television medium and tentatively explains why, given the realities of the system, hopes for documentary expansion may be too high.

From its early days after World War II as a mass-audience medium, television was a prime documentary showcase, providing filmmakers with the three essentials of sustained existence: a demand for their films, an audience for their message, and the money needed to go out and shoot. Although filmmakers were slow to see this potential, eventually television documentary blossomed in both England and the United States, and by the mid-1950s and early 1960s it was enjoying a "golden age," with regular weekly series such as NBC's "White Paper" and "Panorama" and the BBC documentaries under the leadership of Richard Cawston.

The history of American and British television documentary is outside the scope of this book, however, and in any case the subject has been amply covered by William Bluem and Norman Swallow.[2] What interests me is the situation as seen in the 1980s. Four points in particular seem worth making in regard to the commercial networks: first, it is clear that the network documentary is still a closed system, barred almost entirely to outside access; second, there has been a drastic decline in the number of documentaries made by the networks, and I doubt whether that trend is reversible; third, there has been little decrease in the pressure to play it safe in terms of subject selection; and finally (and on a slightly more positive note), after years of rigidity it looks as if style and manner are loosening and opening out into freer forms of expression.

For decades independent filmmakers have complained that the commercial network system and its audience are closed to them.[3] The networks have answered that their requirements for objectivity, professionalism, and top journalistic skills limit them to use of their own staffs. In the late 1970s the work of a few independents, such as Marcel Ophuls and Susan and Alan Raymond, did occasionally appear on network television, but such instances have been the exceptions that prove the rule.

Despite the clamor for access and the threat of litigation against the networks, there seems to be little sign of change. This situation is due in large part to the second, and the most important, point raised above, that is, the tremendous decline in the number of network documentaries made and screened between 1975 and 1984. If the 1960s were the golden years, then the 1970s into the 1980s have been the years of drought and famine. Indeed, it might not be going too far to say that the one-hour in-depth documentary is an endangered species within the networks, having been supplemented by the magazine-format series such as "60 Minutes" and "20-20"—and even these magazines sometimes lead a precarious existence.

A survey of two average years provides a good picture of the scene. In 1975 CBS aired twenty-eight one-hour documentaries, ABC eighteen, and NBC fifteen. In the following year CBS put on fifteen (almost a 50 percent reduction in filming), ABC eight, and NBC 13.[4] In a 1978 article for *American Film*, Robert Sklar, welcoming Pam Hill to her position as executive producer for "ABC Close-Up," expressed positive hopes for the future of television documentary.[5] However, during the period in which his article was being prepared, September to December 1978, only *one* prime-time news documentary, *Terror in the Promised Land*, was aired by the networks' news departments. Sklar's optimism was clearly not well founded. In the following year the number of documentaries aired decreased still further, with "ABC Close-Up" appearing most irregularly, and then sometimes at 11:30 at night.[6]

What accounts for this decline? Certainly not a deterioration in the quality of the films submitted for broadcast, since the 1970s were marked by some outstanding work, including Peter Davis's *The Selling of the Pentagon*, Helen Whitney's *Youth Terror*, and Irv Drasnin's *The Guns of Autumn*. One answer lies in the growing competition within the video entertainment market in general. Between 1976 and 1983, the nighttime network audience fell by 12 percent thanks to cable-TV competitors and movie channels such as HBO and Showtime—not to mention the booming VCR business.[7] This sharp decline sent the networks scurrying for surefire programs that would boost their ratings— and the documentary was definitely not seen as an audience grabber.

Unfortunately, the network perception of audience interest seems to be absolutely correct. Public interest in documentary is not high, except it seems, for films based on sex or violence, such as NBC's *Violence in America*, the highest-rated news documentary ever broadcast. In a commercial world where ratings are the name of the game, it is depressing to see documentaries like *Justice on Trial* or *The Second Battle of Britain*, both highly creditable efforts, finish up with small audiences. But this is a general trend. In a *Variety* listing of seven hundred programs broadcast between September 1977 and September 1978, thirty-two out of the thirty-nine documentaries screened fell into the bottom hundred programs in the ratings. A low rating may, of course, correspond to an audience of eight million, no mean figure, but for advertising purposes programs that earn low ratings are not considered worthy of network consideration. The fact that documentaries made in the public interest are almost non-profit items is nothing new. In short, the pressure of increased competition on all sides, coupled with the necessity of high ratings, has made the documentary the most easily expendable item on the network list.

Market and profit considerations affect not only how many documentaries are made but also what subjects are deemed appropriate. In a 1978 article for the *New York Times*, John Culhane listed a number of subjects which he considered taboo for the networks.[8] They included the investigation of big business, unions, the military industrial complex, the networks themselves, and nuclear power. His regret at network timidity is certainly understandable, but it would be naive to sound too surprised. After all, sponsors and advertisers are generally more interested in profit than in prestige. Controversy can offend, even enrage, both the audience and the politicians, who in turn can create immense trouble for both network and sponsor. The lesson is clear: in the interests of peace and commercial profitability, stay away from anything too tough-minded, divisive, or problematic.

Within the networks themselves there tends to be a running battle between the filmmakers on one side, who believe the networks should say something about the issues of the day, and play-it-safe sponsors and network executives on the other, who fear the results of controversy. Examples of this conflict litter the history of documentary filmmaking. In 1954, Edward R. Murrow screened a controversial exposé of Sen. Joseph McCarthy on CBS. The reaction of a fearful and timid CBS was "Great program—but sorry you made it." In 1965, a CBS documentary took a slightly critical look at the Vietnam war. When CBS phones were jammed with calls accusing the network of being "commies," the network obediently clammed up and, like other networks, made few long documentaries on the Vietnam war in the succeeding years. *The Guns of Autumn*, a powerful documentary by Irv Drasnin on hunting in America, was seen by CBS affiliates as commercially dangerous, and a great many commercials were in fact dropped following loud protests from prohunt organizations.[9]

Although between 1975 and 1985 the number of network documentaries declined relative to the previous ten years, accepted network style appears to be changing as well—and for the better. Dispassionate journalistic objectivity with its cool analytical commentary, the cornerstone of network style since 1948,[10] is no longer the rule in the 1980s—the guidelines are fractionally bending. This loosening-up has come about to a certain extent because of the courage of some of the ABC executives. When Pam Hill commissioned *Youth Terror* for "ABC Close-Up," she sanctioned—for almost the first time since Robert Drew worked for ABC in the early 1960s—a *vérité* documentary that excluded commentary and depended for its force solely on images and sync sound. The purchase and screening of Susan and Alan Raymond's *Police Tapes* took this process still further.

Meanwhile, in a series of documentaries for "CBS Reports" Bill Moyers injected his own viewpoint, allowing it to take precedence over a distancing objectivity. Largely through his influence, the network documentary of the late 1970s and early 1980s has edged ever closer toward private committed opinion. As Moyers said of *Born Again*, "My stance is not that of a neutral observer. It is of a narrator who experiences the story and brings the viewer along."[11]

The reasons for the stagnation of network documentary are clear enough. In a field dominated by the profit motive and experiencing increasing competition for audience, any increase in the number of documentaries made, much less in risk-taking regarding controversial subjects, is unlikely. And given this decline, the chances that the networks will open their gates to independents are lower than ever. But what about educational television? Is the situation any better there?

Public television is the second major showcase for documentary presentation, after commercial network television. Since it broadcasts in and for the public interest rather than for profit, its limitations and problems tend to be different (though not always) from those of the commercial networks.

The basic structure for public broadcasting in the 1970s and 1980s was suggested by the Carnegie Commission on Educational Television in 1967. The Corporation for Public Broadcasting (CPB) was to receive federal funds and then allocate them in the best interests of public programming. In turn, the Public Broadcasting Service (PBS) would oversee film distribution among the member stations of the system. This suggestion was viewed favorably by independent filmmakers, who foresaw a great future for themselves under the wings of the CPB/PBS unit, with the possibility of increased funds for their films; greater access to the system for presentation of their work; and the freedom to indulge in stylistic experimentation and to cover more extensively minority cultures and interests.

In the 1970s, independently produced work by filmmakers such as Fred Wiseman, Susan and Alan Raymond, and Allan Francovich did indeed provide some of the most thought-provoking and innovative programming seen on public television. Yet at the time of writing—mid-1985—only a fraction of the independents' hopes have been fulfilled.

Adequate funding is the basis for all the aspirations and dreams of public television. For fifteen years, however, funding has not been sufficient to realize even half the plans originally put forward, and the independent filmmakers have fared very poorly vis-à-vis the educational member stations in the struggle for financing. The allocation of the CPB Program Fund illustrates the problem. Set up in 1978 with a budget of $20 million, the fund's aim was to encourage innovation and exciting programming in public broadcasting. In practice, most of the fund went to support "American Playhouse," "Great Performances," and the WGBH documentary series "Frontline," whereas the two series that were supposed to support and energize independent documentary, "A Matter of Life and Death" and "Crisis," received only 8 percent and 3 percent of the fund, respectively.[12]

At the same time that the independents have felt increasingly neglected and cut out of the system, internal station productions have thrived. Since 1975 documentary on public television has been dominated by the blockbuster superseries, with WGBH-Boston and WNET-New York leading the way. Thus WGBH has supported "Enterprise," "Nova," "Frontline," and the Vietnam war series, and WNET has brought in "The MacNeil-Lehrer Report," "The Brain," "Heritage: Civilization and the Jews," and *An American Family*. On the other coast, in Los Angeles, the most notable success has been KCET's "Cosmos" with astronomer Carl Sagan.

Most of these series are well intentioned and competently made, and they have helped keep the documentary idea alive in the mind of the audience. Here and there individual films within the series have been brilliant. For the most part, however, the series have taken safe subjects and executed them in a fairly conventional style, meanwhile siphoning off most of the available funds. And so the independents have struggled on with grants from the NEH, the NEA, and various arts councils, knowing that when their films were completed they stood a fair chance of being screened on public television if they were of any quality. Unfortunately, the returns for such local screenings are at best minimal, ranging from $200 to $1,000 per broadcast hour,[13] which is unlikely to make the independent jump for joy—especially in view of the millions spent on "Cosmos," "Heritage," and "The Brain."

Like commercial television, public broadcasting in the United States is subject to pressures, mostly from the federal government or sponsors and relating to subtle and not so subtle threats to cut funding when controversial matters are raised. Thus the hoped-for freedom to investigate all and sundry is still more dream than reality.

The case of *Death of a Princess* provides a good example of how pressure is applied. This documentary drama based on the 1977 execution of a Saudi Arabian princess and her lover—and presenting an extremely negative picture of the way the Saudi aristocracy and elite behave—was scheduled to be aired on public television in 1980. Before its American screening, Lawrence Grossman, then president of PBS, was told by the State Department that the film would offend Saudi Arabia and its presentation should be reconsidered. Clement Zablocki, chair of the House Foreign Affairs Committee, was blunter: he spoke of a substandard film wasting public money—a scarcely veiled hint to CPB to avoid antagonizing its funding source.

This pressure from the federal government was then supplemented by pressure from Mobil Oil, a coproducer of Saudi oil and a major contributor to public television. Mobil's strategy was to run advertisements in a dozen newspapers asking PBS to renounce its screening decision and to "exercise judgment in the best interests of the United States."[14] To the credit of PBS, most stations went on with the broadcast; a mere six declined to air the show, of which five were in North Carolina.

With *Death of a Princess*, fear of offending a sponsor was subordinated to the wish to broadcast an interesting and gripping story. Sometimes the issue goes the other way, though. This was particularly true with *Seventeen*, one of Peter Davis's six "Middletown" films, which because of sponsorship displeasure was never used in the series.

Broadcasting in Great Britain is also subject to pressures, though these often have less to do with funding than with politics. Although this book does not delve into the complexities and constraints of British broadcasting, one fascinating example of the interrelated pressures across the ocean must be mentioned, and that is the furor surrounding the nonbroadcast of the film *At the Edge of the Union*, originally scheduled for screening by the BBC in the summer of 1985.

The program, one in a series called "Real Lives," featured interviews with Martin McGuiness, a man accused of being chief-of-staff of the Provisional IRA (Irish Republican Army), an organization generally considered to be devoted to anti-British and anti-Protestant terrorism. The interviewing on British television of Irish terrorists or terrorist sympathizers had, of course, been a controversial subject for years. The issue split between those who believed the public had a right to know about *all* political matters and that no one should be banned from the screen and those who objected vehemently to giving publicity to murderers and terrorists on television.

Although controversies about the suitability of particular programs for broadcast on the BBC or on Independent Television had been frequent since the late 1960s, they were usually resolved internally by the managements of the television systems themselves. What made *At the Edge of the Union* different was the intervention of Home Secretary Leon Brittan, the government's main minister in charge of public order. In a letter to the Chairman of the BBC, Brittan stated that it would be contrary to the national interest to show a television documentary featuring an interview with an alleged leader of the IRA, a criticism that was later supported by Prime Minister Margaret Thatcher. At the time of their remarks neither Mrs. Thatcher nor Brittan had seen the film in question.

Over the years the BBC had always maintained that it was politically independent of the government, yet here the most blatant political pressure was being exerted to stop a broadcast. In the end, the BBC governors decided that it would be unwise to show the documentary, at least in its then-current form. They argued, moreover, that they had reached this decision independent of government pressure, but few believed this statement—it definitely was not accepted by British TV journalists, who staged an unprecedented one-day strike to protest the censorship action.

Quite clearly, the coverage of political violence does pose a dilemma for a free society and its press. In this case, although the government had the legal right to compel the BBC to suppress information against the national interest, it did not in fact invoke that right. Instead, the government simply requested suppression of a program, controversial to be sure, but prepared under established rules for dealing with political violence. When the BBC gave in to the home secretary's plea there were two main casualties: first, the BBC's credibility; second, its admirable tradition of independence.

At the time I made the selections for this part of the book there was no good article available that commented in depth on the *Union* affair. However, the seven articles that are included here amplify or refer to most of the other issues raised above. The only exception is the first article, Stuart Hall's "Media

Power: The Double Bind," which raises a number of new questions. Hall, a noted British critic and expert on mass communications, provides in this article a theoretical analysis of the assumptions made about television-audience relations, particularly with regard to news and documentary. This analysis, by examining broadcasting's relationship to the power structure of society and its accommodation to social forces, helps clarify some of the complex reasons and motivations behind the actions of people involved in television, both in production and in managment. Hall's arguments touch on many of the points raised by Dai Vaughan in Part I regarding coding and societal norms, and he shows why television must, on the whole, sustain the political and social status quo rather than challenge it.

Hall's arguments are amplified in an interesting way in an article by Anthony Smith on the television coverage of the troubles of Northern Ireland, which unfortunately was too long to be included here.[15] Smith, focusing on the tension between government authorities and the broadcasters, starts out by accepting the premise that broadcasters, may wish merely to comment on a volatile situation, but he then goes on to show how difficult it is to maintain this benign neutrality when the broadcast *itself* may change the status quo against the interests of the government. Smith thus clearly shows how the complex interpretation of "impartiality" and "objectivity"—two of Hall's "mediation techniques" between broadcaster and society—now serves as a source of disagreement between documentary filmmakers and makers of broadcasting policy.

> The tension emerging between the broadcasters and their employers was a tension between an old feeling about broadcasting and a new one; between the view that broadcasting should invariably create and transmit a simulated balanced model of the prevailing political scene, and the view that broadcasting should now exist as a reporting tool pure and simple. The doctrine of impartiality had forced on broadcasting organizations a social role that now made them extremely vulnerable. Since objectivity did not flow naturally out of the material being presented, it had to be imposed by hierarchy.[16]

After Hall's theoretical discussion, the vaunted tenets of "objectivity" and "balance" seemed worth exploring within a given situation. Since war provides such a staple diet for television news and documentary, I decided that that would be an interesting area to investigate. The articles by Larry Lichty and Pam Yates in Parts V and VI cover some of this ground, but both look at coverage of *specific* wars. Mark Crispin Miller's article in this section provides us rather with a view of the general practice of television coverage, whatever the conflict zone. (His focus is on news coverage, but most of his thesis is applicable to war-documentary techniques as well.)[17]

Miller argues that though fairness, objectivity, and balanced and informed analytical reporting are supposed to provide the bases for television war coverage, this is often far from the case. He sees television methods as shoddy, uninformed, superficial, and biased: in order to make a good program, television demands a victim and gross simplification of the issues. The goal ultimately seems to have less to do with reporting the war fairly than with adapting war to advertising requirements so that it can be marketed to attract maximum audiences and satisfy commercial needs.[18]

The general tendency—and I include myself here—is to criticize the commercial networks for their avoidance of difficult issues. Occasionally, however, controversial subjects are dealt with forthrightly, seemingly with little regard to the possible consequences, and Edward R. Murrow's 1954 broadcast attacking the methods of Senator Joseph McCarthy must rank as one of the most courageous of these moments in documentary history. Unfortunately, his accomplishment has largely receded from memory, so my use of Fred Friendly's discussion of the McCarthy documentary is an attempt to reclaim that memory for a later generation.

During the 1950s Ed Murrow was probably the most esteemed and trusted broadcast journalist in the United States. For some years he and Fred Friendly had worked as partners putting on a weekly investigation series, "See It Now," for CBS, and in 1954 they decided to tackle Senator McCarthy, then at the height of his malign influence. Initiating such a documentary, with the aim of standing up publicly to the junior senator from Wisconsin and showing the extent of his lies and distortions, not only took immense personal courage, it marked the first real challenge to McCarthyism.[19]

The sections I have excerpted from Fred Friendly's book *Due to Circumstances Beyond Our Control*[20] do two things: the first extract establishes the general mood of the time and shows the prevalence of McCarthy-inspired blacklisting within the networks themselves; the second gives a sense of the mood and technique of the broadcast itself. Both sections reveal the integrity, tenacity, and courage of Murrow and his crew. They also illustrate points discussed earlier: the tension between the filmmaker and the executive branch, the one wishing to expose a subject for the public good, the other fearful of negative public and sponsor reaction and loss of profit. Hence the sadness behind the final words of the extract, when Friendly, having just participated in one of the most significant documentary broadcasts in history, encounters a network executive who, unable to refer to the subject and congratulate him, merely engages him uncomfortably in smalltalk.

Robert Drew is possibly less of a forgotten figure than Murrow. His article, "An Independent with the Networks," is included for various reasons, not the least being the detailed account he gives of his own participation in the birth of *cinéma vérité* in the United States. His remarks in the second half of the article are just as interesting, however, as they provide very detailed information on the fragile and tenuous relationship between at least one major independent and the networks and sponsors. His notes on the film *Storm Signal* are particularly fascinating, since it was one case of networks rejecting a film that the sponsor, Xerox, particularly wanted shown.

Peter Biskind's article on *Blacks Britannica* shows some of public television's limits. Although generally public television is somewhat more accommodating than the commercial networks to the private or passionate voice, *Blacks Britannica* shows the problems that arise when the ideal of freedom for the individual voice conflicts with executive caution on a controversial subject. The makers of *Blacks Britannica*, a film on black-white race relations in England, claim that the film was censored by WGBH-Boston. The article states their point of view, but it is unconvincing.

In any case, two points are worth making with regard to *Blacks Britannica*. First, one can almost definitely assume that the contract David Koff, the director, had with WGBH gave the station the right of final cut, as it is legally liable for anything that goes out over its airwaves. Second, as an Englishman myself, fairly well acquainted with the British scene, I get the feeling that Koff might have been co-opted by the Paddington Trotskyites and that his version of the film, while possibly correct from their point of view, was factually inaccurate.

The radical viewpoint is obviously handled with caution by PBS, and one suspects that minority views are heard less often than they should be. A great deal of controversy is obviously hushed up behind the scenes, but now and then disputes do flare up and catch the public eye: the Kartemquin Collective's *Chicago Maternity Center Story* for instance, which was taken off one PBS station because its narration was thought to be too partisan;[21] or, in 1979, Don Widener's *Plutonium—Element of Risk*, which Chloe Aaron, then PBS vice-president in charge of programming, asked stations not to air, ostensibly because she felt that the film did not conform to PBS standards of journalism.[22]

Between 1980 and 1985, the most notorious PBS refusal to broadcast a film was the case of *Seventeen*, one of the six original films in Peter Davis's "Middletown" series. "Middletown" took its title from an academic study published in 1929 by sociologists Robert and Helen Lynd about Muncie, Indiana. The Lynds analyzed social behavior and attitudes in what they claimed was a typical American community, and Davis maintains that his film series followed a similar sociological thrust. (In Part VI of this book Brian Winston, too, discusses the series' merits, including how much material of genuine sociological interest found its way into the project.) The films were finally broadcast on public television in April 1982—all, that is, except *Seventeen*. Commenting on the omission, PBS claimed that the film was substandard and offensive in its use of language. The filmmakers themselves, Joel DeMott and Jeff Kreines, argued that the failure to screen *Seventeen* was the result of pressure on PBS executives by Xerox, the series sponsor, who objected not just to the language, but also to the interracial dating shown in the film.

Ironically, it is possibly the sociologically most interesting and illuminating of all the films in the series.

To complete this section I decided to use "New Boy," which covers my own experiences as a freelance director for Israel Television. My object was to describe how the television documentary process works under a totally different system, where some of the pressures and constraints differ from those in America and where others remain exactly the same.

Notes

1. See, for example, Pat Aufderheide, "Public Television's Prime Time Politics," *American Film* 8 (April 1983): 53–58, and Patricia Zimmerman, "Public Television, Independent Documentary Producers, and Public Policy," *Journal of the University Film Association* 34, no. 3 (1982): 9–23.

2. William Bluem, *Documentary in American Television* (New York: Hastings House, 1965), and Norman Swallow, *Factual Television* (London: Focal Press, 1968).

3. See also the interviews with Abe Osheroff and Jill Godmilow in Alan Rosenthal, *The Documentary Conscience* (Berkeley and Los Angeles: University of California Press, 1980).

4. John Culhane, "Where TV Documentaries Don't Dare to Tread," *New York Times*, Feb. 20, 1977, pp. 1, 13.

5. Robert Sklar, "Network Vérité," *American Film* 5 (Dec.–Jan. 1979/80): 19–23.

6. Marvin Barret, "TV Diplomacy and Other Broadcast Quandaries," *Columbia Journalism Review*, May–June 1979, p. 72.

7. Erik Mink, "Why the Networks Will Survive Cable," *Atlantic Monthly*, Dec. 1983, p. 63.

8. Culhane, "Where TV Documentaries Don't Tread," p. 1.

9. Ibid., p. 13.

10. For further discussion of the network's attitude toward style, see the interview with Arthur Barron in Alan Rosenthal, *The New Documentary in Action* (Berkeley and Los Angeles: University of California Press, 1971).

11. Laurence Bergreen, "The Moyers Style," *American Film* 5 (Feb. 1980): 53.

12. For full discussion of this subject, see Aufderheide, "Public Television's Prime Time Politics," and Zimmerman, "Public Television, Independent Documentary."

13. Zimmerman, "Public Television, Independent Documentary," p. 15.

14. *Newsweek*, May 19, 1980, p. 58.

15. Anthony Smith, "Television Coverage of Northern Ireland," in Smith, *The Politics of Information* (London: MacMillan Press, 1978), pp. 106–128.

16. Ibid., p. 124.

17. See, in particular, NBC's *Terror in the Promised Land* (1979) and ABC's *"Close-Up"* on *Sabra and Shatilla* (1982).

18. I saw this myself, very extensively, while I was filming the 1982 Israeli incursion into Lebanon. I watched a number of British, French, and American crews at work and then saw how material was selected for broadcast in Tel Aviv editing rooms. There seemed to be tremendous distortion of facts, particularly with regard to casualties, and little background analysis of the events portrayed. The Israeli-Lebanese war was clearly very marketable, unlike the earlier Lebanese civil war, which produced higher casualties but was almost totally ignored by American news and documentary filmmakers.

19. For further discussion about McCarthy and television coverage, see the interview with Emile de Antonio in Rosenthal, *The Documentary Conscience*.

20. Fred Friendly, *Due to Circumstances Beyond Our Control* (New York: Vintage Books, 1968).

21. Aufderheide, "Public Television's Prime Time Politics," p. 57.

22. Barret, "TV Diplomacy," p. 72.

Media Power:
The Double Bind

Stuart Hall

British broadcasting institutions have a great deal of formal autonomy from the state and government, but their authority to broadcast derives from the state, and, ultimately, it is to the state that they are responsible. What are usually understood as "external influences on broadcasting" are in fact the everyday working context for broadcasting.

The study of such specific "influences," therefore, is an inadequate model for examining the mediation between broadcasting and power. It is predicated on a model of broadcasting which takes at face value its formal and editorial autonomy; external influences are seen as encroaching upon this area of freedom.

I do not mean to deny specific instances of pressure, influence, and censorship to which broadcasters have been subject. Nor do I mean to deny the relative autonomy of broadcasting in its day-to-day practice. Nevertheless, the real relationship between broadcasting, power, and ideology is thoroughly mystified by such a model. One difficulty is that we have few ways of understanding how power and influence flow, how relative institutional integration is accomplished, in societies which are of the formal democratic type. Institutions are conceived of as either state-controlled and dominated, in which case they belong within the complex of state power, or as free and autonomous. We cannot, from an "external influences" model, predict or comprehend the specific areas of conjecture and disjuncture which arise between different institutions in civil society. Thus, we would find it impossible to account for the fact that on some specific occasions broadcasters assert their editorial independence against clear political pressure, and at the same time account for the mutual adjustments, the reciprocity of interests and definitions, occurring from day to day between broadcasters and the institutions of power.

The coverage of recent events in Northern Ireland has been subject to massive internal watchfulness and external constraint. Specifically, this has operated with respect to the broadcasters' right to interview representative spokesmen of the IRA. Here, clearly, the broadcasters have been subject *both* to "external influence and pressure" *and* to internal institutional self-censorship. But even had no specific representations on the issue been made to the broadcasters, can one envisage a situation in which, systematically, the broadcasters of their own accord gave precedence in their current-affairs coverage to the definition of the Northern Ireland situation proposed by the IRA and its sympathizers? There seems to me only one, distant but just conceivable, contingency in which such a practice could ever become widespread within the broadcast organizations: if opinion were to crystallize so powerfully against government policies that the broadcasters could refer to an external authority alternative to that of the state itself—"public opinion." Otherwise, whether the state intervenes directly to censor broadcasting's coverage of Ulster or not, the prevailing tendency of the organizations has been to orient themselves within the dominant definition of the situation. The broadcasters' decision not to interview IRA spokesmen is the "free" reproduction, within the symbolic content of their programs, of the state's definition of the IRA as an "illegal organization": it is a mirror reflection and amplification of the decision, to which both political parties subscribe, that the IRA does not constitute a legitimate political agency in the Ulster situation.

Simpler, but more misleading, models are frequently advanced by both the political right and the political left. On the right, spokesmen try to account for what they call a "taste for agitprop" in the media by what they see as the leftist tendencies of the people who are recruited for work in broadcast institutions. Much the same proposition, in reverse, is advanced by those on the left.

Television certainly recruits from an extremely narrow social band, and those who work in television are powerfully socialized into the ethos and morale of the broadcasting institutions. But I do not believe that television's built-in biases can be accounted for in terms of the overt political inclinations— to left or right—of its individual practitioners. What is far more significant is the way quite different kinds and conditions of individuals are systematically constrained to handle the variety of news and accounts which they process daily within the framework of a limited set of interpretations. Nor do I believe that the broadcasters are systematically censored and pressured from extrinsic sources except in limited and largely exceptional cases. Just as it is impossible to "net" the influence of advertising in the press in terms of the number of times advertisers have explicitly threatened editors with the withdrawal of their custom, so it is impossible to "net" the real structure of interests in television or radio in terms of direct representations by government officials to broadcast institutions. Certainly there are issues and areas where the system of scrutiny is very precise—and it is important to identify where and what these are. But the relative autonomy of the broadcasting institutions is *not* a mere cover: it is, I believe, central to the way power and ideology are mediated in societies like ours.

Broadcasting accommodates itself to the power-ideology nexus by way of a number of crucial intervening concepts. These concepts mediate the relationship of the broadcasters to power. They provide the structure of legitimations which permit the broadcasters to exercise a substantial measure of editorial and day-to-day control without contravening the overall hegemony. At the same time, it is essential to recognize that this orientation of broadcasting within the hegemonic ideology is *not* a perfectly regulated, fully integrated one-dimensional system.

The central concepts which mediate broadcasting's relationship to the power-ideology complex are balance, impartiality, objectivity, professionalism, and consensus.

Broadcasting institutions are required to operate a system of balance between conflicting interests and viewpoints. Until recently, producers were expected to provide balance within single programs, and whenever a topic is controversial, this ground rule is more strictly applied. Elsewhere, it has come to be more liberally interpreted: balance "over a reasonable period of time." The broadcasters are thus *required to recognize* that conflicts of interest and opinion exist. Indeed, because controversy is topical and makes good, lively broadcasting, controversial programs flood the screen.

Thus broadcasting appears as the very reverse of monolithic or univocal—as precisely open, democratic, and controversial. Yet balance is crucially exercised within an overall framework of assumptions about the distribution of political power: the conflict here is scrupulously regulated. A debate between Labor and Conservative party spokesmen—an area subject to both executive and informal sanctions—is itself *framed* by agreements, set elsewhere but reproduced in the studio, on television's presentational devices and in its very discourse.

Political balance operates essentially between the legitimate mass parties in the parliamentary system. Balance becomes trickier when groups outside the consensus participate, since the grounds of conflict then become the terrain of political legitimacy itself—an issue on which Labor and Conservative spokesmen stand together, against the others. In this way television does not favor one point of view, but it does favor—and reproduce—one definition of politics and excludes, represses, or neutralizes other definitions. By operating balance *within a given structure*, television tacitly maintains the prevailing definition of the political order. In one and the same moment, it expresses and contains conflict. It reproduces unwittingly the structure of institutionalized class conflicts on which the system depends. It thereby legitimates the prevailing structure of interests, while scrupulously observing "balance between the parties." It also, incidentally, offers a favorable image of the system as a system, as open to conflict and to alternative points of view. It is this last twist which keeps the structure flexible and credible.

Impartiality defines the way broadcasters negotiate situations of conflict from within. Broadcasters are not supposed to express personal opinions on controversial issues: they are committed to a rigorous impartiality between the conflicting parties. In practice, of course, all broadcasters have views. The working compromise is to insist that the broadcasters must be the last person, if at all, to express a view. But as all good producers know, there is more than one way of cutting a program. Producers have become extremely skilled at producing "balanced" studio teams; the infinite calculation of how many Bernadette Devlins make an Ian Paisley is one of those editorial acts which all producers are skilled at intuiting.

Yet the practice of impartiality has several inescapable consequences. It leads broadcasting into the impasse of a false symmetry of issue. All controversial questions *must* have two sides, and the two sides are usually given a rough equality in weight. Responsibility is shared between the parties; each side receives a measure of praise or censure. This symmetry of oppositions is a *formal balance*: it has little or no relevance to the quite unequal relative weights of the case for each side in the real world. If the workman asserts that he is being poisoned by the effluence from a noxious plant, the chairman must be wheeled in to say that all possible precautions are now being taken. This symmetrical alignment of arguments may ensure the broadcaster's impartiality, but it hardly advances the truth.

Impartiality as a practice gives the broadcaster/presenter a built-in interest in compromise, in conflict resolution. It commits him to the pragmatic view of politics. His only way of intervening actively in a controversy is to act, in the studio, the shadow-role of the compromiser, the middleman. His only legitimate interventions can be to salvage some "lowest common denominator" from the deeply held but opposing positions before him. All conflicts thus become translated into the language of compromise: all failures to compromise are signs of intransigence, extremism, or failures in communication. The other way of neutralizing conflict is to assert some overriding interest which subordinates the conflicting parties. Thus all broadcasters are safe in asserting that Britain's perilous economic position overrides all industrial conflict, even if the strikers have "a good case."

This stake of the broadcaster in conflict resolution has the function of legitimating those elements in a conflict which are "realistic"—which can be abstracted from a general case and built into a "package." The case which is intrinsically not amenable to this process is "unrealistic" and "unreasonable."

Broadcasting is thus raised above the conflicts that it treats. It seems to stand outside the real play of interests on which it reports and comments. The men and women who produce programs are real social individuals in the midst of the conflicts they report. But this subjective dimension is repressed in the "objectivity" of the program. The programs they produce are outside these conflicts; they reflect on and judge them, but they do not participate in them. This tendency of broadcasting to stand above conflict is especially damaging for the viewer, who is encouraged to identify with the presenter and who thus comes to see himself as a neutral and dispassionate party to a partisan and impassioned struggle: the disinvolved spectator before the spectacle of conflict.

If the broadcaster is required to be impartial between witnesses, he is also enjoined to be objective before "the facts." Objectivity, like impartiality, is an operational fiction. All filming and editing is the manipulation of raw data—selectively perceived, interpreted, signified. Television cannot capture the whole of any event; the idea that it offers a pure transcription of reality, a neutrality of the camera before the facts, is an illusion, a utopia. All filmed accounts of reality are selective. All edited or manipulated symbolic reality is impregnated with values, viewpoints, implicit theorizings, commonsense assumptions. The choice to film *this* aspect of an event rather than *that* is subject to criteria other than those embedded in the material itself: *this* aspect rather than *that* is significant, shows something special, out-of-the-ordinary, unexpected, typical. Each of those notions is operating against a taken-for-granted set of under-standings and only has meaning within that context. Each decision to link this piece of film with that, to create a discourse out of the disparate fragments of edited material, makes sense only within a *logic of exposition*. The identification of social actors, their projects in the world, is accomplished against the prevailing schemes of interpretation which we regularly but tacitly employ for the rec-ognition and decoding of social scenes: it partakes of the stock of social knowledge at hand which men employ to make sense of their world and events in it. Such a stock of knowledge is not a neutral structure; it is shot through with previously sedimented social meanings.

The illusion of "reality" *depends* on such contexts of meaning, such back-ground schemes of recognition and interpretation, for its construction. How "objective" is a clip from a miner's picket line used in a news or current-affairs documentary program? The images we see are real enough; no one doubts that the cameraman and reporter were there, saw it happen, are trying to show it "as it is." Yet the brief extract of this denoted foreground event is an enormously compressed item of information, rich in connotations. It only has meaning for us within its multiple contexts: the picket (from the viewpoint of the strikers) as an index of the union's power to hold the line while the strike continues; the picket (from the viewpoint of the Coal Board) as an index of the strength and effectiveness of rank-and-file resistance; the picket (from the viewpoint of the government) as an element which might contribute to the defeat of the government's wages policy; the picket (from the political viewpoint) as an index of escalating class conflict; the picket (from the viewpoint of the police) as a problem in the policing of class conflict; and so on. Whether the item is accompanied by commentary or not, whether it provides the "actuality" basis for a studio discussion or not, its meaning lies in its *indexical* significance within the relevant context of meanings; we *decode* its significance—it cannot literally be "read off" the denoted images themselves—in terms of these contexts of awareness, in terms of the connotative power of the message. The different logics of interpretation within which this objectively presented item makes sense in a public discourse are not neutral networks of meaning, and no broadcast program can offer such an item without situating it within one or another of those logics.

All professionals generate their own distinctive ideologies and routines. Professionalism in broadcasting seems to serve as a defensive barrier which insulates the broadcaster from the contending forces which play across any program making in a sensitive area. It is often a species of professional retreatism, a technique of neutralization. By converting issues of substance into a technical idiom, and by making himself responsible primarily for the technical competence with which the program is executed, the producer raises himself above the problematic content of the issues he presents. What concerns him is identifying the elements of "good television": cutting and editing with professional finish; the smooth management of transitions within the studio or between the program elements; "good pictures," full of incident and drama.

The most pervasive of these semitechnical structures is that of *news value* itself. The media journalist, like his counterpart in the press, "knows a good news story when he smells one"; but few can define what criteria are integrated within this notion. News values are, however, a man-made, value-loaded system of relevancies. Such a system has great practical use, since it enables the editor to get his work done, under the condition of heavily pressured schedules, without reference back to first principles. But the idea that such sedimented social knowledge is neutral—a set of technical protocols only—is an illusion.

Consensus may be defined as the "lowest common denominator" in the values and beliefs which are widely shared among the population of a society. Consensus provides the basis of continuity and fundamental agreement in common social life. "The consensus" is the structure of commonsense ideology and beliefs in the public at large. In formal democracies, a great deal of what holds the social order together consists of those tacit, shared agreements about fundamental issues embedded at the level of "commonsense ideology," rather than what is formally written down in constitutional protocols and documents.

"The consensus" on any specific issue is, however, extremely fluid and difficult to define. The opinions of very few individuals will coincide exactly with it. Yet, without the notion that *some* shared bargain or compromise has been reached "on fundamentals," it would be difficult either to govern or to broadcast in formal democratic societies.

In modern, complex bureaucratic class societies, consensus plays the role which "public opinion" was cast for in ideal democratic theory. In practice, since the majority of people have little real, day-to-day access to decisions and information, commonsense ideologies are usually a composite reflection of the dominant ideologies, operating at a passive and diffused level in society.

Though "the consensus" is extremely difficult to locate, its existence also underwrites and guarantees the broadcaster in his day-to-day functions. His sense of the "state of play" in public opinion provides a sort of warrant for his performance. It offers a rough-and-ready way of referring to "what people in general are thinking and feeling about an issue." It is my impression that in their everyday professional practice, broadcasters are *more consistently* regulated by their sense of their audience than by any single other source.

But, as we have noted, the consensus is in fact an extremely fluid and ambivalent structure, at best. In practice, the agencies of government and control, while responsible in some formal sense to the people (the electorate, public opinion, the audience) are for that very reason driven to treat the area of consensus as an arena in which they *win* consent for or assent to their actions and policies, their definitions and outlooks.

The elites are in a powerful position to win assent (a) because they play a dominant role in crystallizing issues, (b) because they provide the material and information which support their preferred interpretations, and (c) because they can rely on the disorganized state of public knowledge and feeling to provide, by inertia, a sort of tacit agreement to let the existing state of affairs continue. We are thus in the highly paradoxical situation whereby the elites of power constantly *invoke*, as a legitimation for their actions, a consensus which they themselves have powerfully prestructured. Thus the process of opinion formation and attitude crystallization is, like so many of the other processes we have been discussing, a process "structured in dominance."

We can now understand why broadcasting itself stands in such a pivotal and ambiguous position: for the media and the dominant institutions of communication and consciousness formation are themselves the primary *source* of attitudes and knowledge within which public opinion crystallizes, and the primary *channels* between the dominant classes and the audience.

At the same time, as the rift in the moral-political consensus in the society widens, the consensus ceases to provide the broadcaster with a built-in ideological compass. The ruling elites thus have a direct interest in monopolizing the channels for consensus formation for their preferred accounts and interpretations, thereby extending their hegemony: they also have a vested interest in insuring that, when left to their own devices, the media will themselves reproduce, on their behalf, the tentative structure of agreement which favors their hegemony. In such moments, the media themselves become the *site* for the elaboration of hegemonic and counterhegemonic ideologies and the *terrain* of societal and class conflict at the ideological level.

Both the television's functions are locked into this process: those occasions when it elaborates interpretations and accounts of the world on its own behalf, and those many occasions when, via the skewed structures of access, it is obliged to reproduce and validate the status of accredited witnesses, whose views it is obliged to attend and defer to and whose statements "in other places" (in Parliament, in conferences, in boardrooms, in the courts) it is required to transmit. The media cannot long retain their credibility with the public without giving some access to witnesses and accounts which lie outside the consensus. But the moment television does so, it immediately endangers itself with its critics, who attack broadcasting for unwittingly tipping the balance of public feeling against the political order. It opens itself to the strategies of both sides, which are struggling to win a hearing for their interpretations in order to redefine the situations in which they are acting in a more favorable way. This is broadcasting's double bind.

How TV Covers War

Mark Crispin Miller

Technology, which has made war both invisible and all-consuming, has also blessed us, many think, with the means to remember what's at stake, by giving us television.

Is TV in fact a potent force for peace? It would appear to rediscover precisely what those long-range weapons do, what those euphemisms actually refer to. It reminds the man who's dropped the bomb just what that bomb is meant to do to men and women, children, neighborhoods; and it deftly undercuts the pose of objectivity implicit in a government's bureaucratese: "incursion," "protective reaction strike," "limited nuclear exchange," "political infra-structure," etc. When such unsuggestive language fills the newspapers, George Orwell wrote in 1946, "a mass of Latin words fall upon the facts like soft snow"; that snow doesn't stick on television, which always homes in on the dead, allowing no excuses.

Modern war clearly demands this kind of plainness, as we learn from the recent history of literary style: our machinery has helped us to commit atrocities, yet has simultaneously enforced the sort of diction needed to describe them. The Civil War and the "mechanical age," Edmund Wilson points out, combined to simplify American prose, demanding "lucidity, precision, terseness"; and the later, larger wars honed down still more the language of those many writers—journalists as well as novelists and poets—who have struggled to convey the horror, paradoxically, by understating it, rendering it with photo-graphic coolness and exactitude. Through such unflinching reporting, it might be argued, the best war correspondents, and writers like Hemingway, Remarque, Céline, and Mailer, have aspired, *avant l'image*, to replicate in words the bleak and graphic vision of TV.

The TV coverage of the war in Lebanon seems to have persuaded some that the medium, with its direct and unadorned depictions, may someday usher in an Age of Peace. Confronted with the image of the dead, the viewer can only see and sorrow, and never stand for war again. That, at any rate, is the conclusion drawn by some well-known commentators, who agree about the fact, but differ on the question of its value. A war usually has a purpose, writes George F. Will, of greater moment than the suffering of its victims. Will therefore distrusts TV's inherent pacifism, suggesting that "had there been television at Antietam on America's bloodiest day (September 17, 1862), this would be two nations," since Americans "might have preferred disunion to the price of union, had they seen the price, in color in their homes in the evening." Ellen Goodman, on the other hand, sees this "price" as all-important, and so asserts that TV, "intrinsically antiwar," "brings home what war is all about: killing, wounding, destroying. It doesn't film ideas, but realities," and "this is our greatest hope."

Both of these responses take for granted the idea that television does indeed, as the cliché has it, "bring war into our living rooms." We often hear the same assertion from the figureheads of television, who venerate their medium for having pulled us out of Vietnam. "For the first time," writes Dan Rather, "war was coming into our homes"; and William S. Paley too recalls that "television news brought the war into American living rooms almost every night." These observers are only speaking metaphorically, but they present the metaphor as fact: they identify war footage with war itself, as if, after watching each night's newscast in the 1960s, the average viewer had to count his dead, and vacuum the shrapnel out of his couch.

It is, in fact, the great myth of television that the medium somehow gives us an immediate impression, conveying not images, but actualities; and its coverage of war is supposedly the most compelling example of such supreme truthfulness. This pretense of objectivity makes TV's many actual distortions—whether inherent or imposed—all the more insidious, because their camouflage is perfect, fooling not only the viewer, but even most of those who work within the medium, naively claiming to reveal "the way it is."

But what do we see when we sit at home and watch a war? Do we experience an actual event? In fact, that "experience" is fundamentally absurd. Most obviously there is the incongruity of scale, the radical disjunction of locations. While a war is among the biggest things that can ever happen to a nation or people, devastating families, blasting away the roofs and walls, we see it compressed and miniaturized on a sturdy little piece of furniture, which stands and shines at the very center of our household. And TV contains warfare in subtler ways. While it may confront us with the facts of death, bereavement, mutilation, it immediately cancels out the memory of that suffering, replacing its own pictures of despair with a commercial, upbeat and inexhaustibly bright.

While it thus surrounds its painful images with buffers, TV also mitigates them from within. The medium may pose as the purveyor of raw history, but if war weren't suitably processed for the domestic market, if each disaster didn't have its anchorman and correspondent to introduce it, gloss it, and pronounce its simple moral, we wouldn't stand for it, any more than we could take last year's football games without the usual commentary. The TV newsman comforts us as John Wayne comforted our grandparents, by seeming to have the whole affair in hand. This hero functions as the guardian of our enclosed spectatorship. Therefore, when we see a newsman shot to death, as happened in Guyana and El Salvador, we react with an especial horror, because we realize that TV is not, in fact, immune to the events which it observes, but that the protective apparatus can be shattered; and if the medium does not confer invincibility on those who manage it, it surely can't safeguard its helpless viewers.

It is only this kind of violence—extraordinary, unexpected, fully visible, and inflicted on the viewer's alter ego—which can make a strong (if brief) impression on TV. For, despite all we have heard about the harrowing plainness of the footage, we simply can't and don't respond to televised violence as intensely as we would if we were right there on the scene. If we did away with all the ads and newsmen, in other words, the experience would still, necessarily, be mediated, and its impact ultimately slight. Even in extreme close-up, the medium maintains a subtle distance between viewer and victim, presenting every pang and ruin with an ineradicable coolness. Over the years we have seen not only wars, but assassinations, executions, drownings, beatings, shoot-outs, fatal brawls, and nearly every other kind of cruelty—but how much of this do we remember vividly? If we had actually been present at the many horrible events that we have seen take place on television, we would all be as hard and wise as the Wandering Jew, or a nation of quivering shut-ins.

Because the TV image is intrinsically restrained, then, it is not the newsman's purpose to take the edge off an unbearable confrontation. His illusory control performs a different function, necessitated not by the nastiness of actual events, but by TV itself. What upsets us most about those images of aftermath is not so much their painfulness as their apparent randomness; we suddenly arrive upon this unexpected scene and ask ourselves, *"Why this?"* Watching the news, we come to feel not only that the world is blowing up, but that it does so for no reason, that its ongoing history is nothing more than a series of eruptions, each without cause or context. The news creates this vision of mere anarchy through its erasure of the past and its simultaneous tendency to atomize the present into so many unrelated happenings, each recounted through a sequence of dramatic, unintelligible pictures.

In short, the TV news adapts the world to its own commercial needs, translating history into several mad occurrences, just the sort of "story" that might pique the viewer's morbid curiosity. Thus political events appear as lurid crimes: the wars in Lebanon, El Salvador, Guatemala, come to seem as chilling and mysterious as the Manson killings, Patty Hearst's kidnapping, and the Tylenol affair. *Everything* begins to seem the work of chance, so that "chance" begins to lose its meaning; and the news itself, while fostering this impression, at the same time purports to comprehend the chaos. And so we have the correspondent, solemnly nattering among the ruins, offering crude "analysis" and "background," as if to compensate us for the deep bewilderment that his medium created in the first place.

While TV confuses us precisely through its efforts to inform us, so it only numbs us through its mechanical attempts to work us up. If it can't convey some sense of a war's origins or purposes, then perhaps, as Ellen Goodman thinks, it must at least enable us to apprehend war's personal results—"killing, wounding, destroying." But the medium's immanent remoteness won't permit such revelation; and so TV's custodians struggle desperately to overcome this reserve, trying to find a technical method of arousing the very sympathy that their technology inhibits to begin with. They invariably zoom in tight on the mourner's face, as if we can feel more intensely for another by looking deep inside his nose; and they cut hectically from one appalling image to another, seeking to force revulsion through a sort of photographic overkill.

Even the newsman himself has become an affective device, sending us clear signals about how we must respond. Dan Rather, entirely the creature of his medium, introduces each story on the evening news with a broad display of the appropriate emotions, each charged with his particular air of bursting mania. Before a report on some apparent upset or coincidence, he looks perfectly astonished; before an account of some atrocity, he switches on an outraged glower; before the inevitable heart-warmer, his mouth snaps into a frozen grin, and both eyes twinkle like a pair of distant headlights. Although this strained emotiveness is supposed to "humanize" the newscast, it only mechanizes all response. It is too clearly calculated to suggest or foster any genuine reaction; and it even absolves the viewers of the need to do their feeling for themselves, since they have that high-strung face to do it for them. Worked into this inept performance, war becomes the routine occasion for an automatic lamentation, and so disappears among TV's countless other momentary stimuli.

And while television keeps us unenlightened and unmoved, it fails to evoke the conflicts that it covers. As a means of conveying the realities of war, TV is all but useless, precisely because of that very quality which, some think, makes TV the perfect instrument for just such communication: its uninflected vision. For war is, above all, intense, whereas television is too detached to convey intensities. Passion, for instance, rarely registers on television except as something comical or suspect. The medium therefore undercuts the warrior's ardor: crusaders, patriots, and revolutionaries all seem equally insane on television, and the will to power seems nothing but an aberration, a recrudescence of "machismo" or a burst of "deviance." This, according to the liberal argument, is all to the good, since all "aggression" is unnatural and ought to be exposed as such. But TV also strains out the intensity of suffering, flattening the martyr as it ridicules the persecutor, trivializing both victim and tormentor. "Television especially is supposed to reveal the real tragedy of war," Peter Jennings complained from West Beirut last August, "but the camera has not adequately captured the misery this battle between ideologies has produced."

But that camera can't record "real tragedy," because death has no finality, no poignancy, on television. Because the medium cancels out the living presence of its figures, homogenizing all identity, whether individual or collective, it can't restore the impact of a single loss, or express the decimation of a people. Since no one seems to live on television, no one seems to die there. And the medium's temporal facility deprives all terminal moments of their weight.

The uniformity of TV's view includes not just war's victims, but wars themselves. As the medium subverts all overpowering commitment, all keen belief and pain, so it equates jihad, class struggle, imperialist assault, blood feud, and border strife, never capturing whatever is peculiar to specific conflicts, and thereby reducing all wars to a vague abstraction known as War. The medium gave us a "keyhole view" of Vietnam, writes Michael Arlen, reducing that war to a mere handful of unilluminating images, rarely gruesome, never evocative. Similarly, the war in Lebanon was nothing but a lot of sunny rubble, explosions amid tall white buildings, dark women railing at the camera; the wars in Central America nothing more than rumpled guerrillas doing push-ups in the woods. In short, TV expresses War largely through a few aesthetic images; and even these impressions are unsuggestive. The medium's eye is too jaundiced, its on-the-scene equipment much too cumbrous, its scope too limited, to permit the full delivery of the particular atmosphere—frightening, unique, and fatally arresting—of a given war at a certain time and place.

While the writer or filmmaker can recreate the ambience of a war long finished, the correspondent can't evoke the war that's going on around him. Here again, some presumed advantages of television turn out to be mere hindrances. TV's celebrated presence-on-the-scene only prevents its commentators from arriving at a larger sense, a more informed impression, the sort of grasp that viewers need in order to be moved themselves. Perhaps we can't expect a working journalist thus to transcend his own assignment when he has a daily deadline; but there is one kind of detachment that doesn't necessitate long reflection, and that is the *ex post facto* reconstruction that the writing journalist must perform. However, even this achievement is beyond the TV newsman, whose expressive faculties have been supplanted by his footage: if he can show you what he sees, then he needn't labor to express it, and so his eloquence recedes, his perceptions coarsen, as all he has to do is make authoritative noises for the soundtrack and stand there for the visual cadence, mike in hand. In covering modern war, the newsman is no less reduced by his equipment than are the soldiers flying overhead or rumbling past in tanks. Thus diminished, the newsman is not only incapable of sounding like Hemingway, but he can't even reach the descriptive level of earlier war correspondents like Philip Gibbs, Herbert Matthews, Webb Miller, or Edward R. Murrow.

Unable to evoke or analyze, the TV newsman, we would think, ought at least to live up to the claims of his medium and tell us what he knows (if anything) objectively. But TV may be the least objective medium, because it makes its loaded points from an apparently neutral mask: "The camera doesn't lie." While the news report is more or less devoid of atmosphere or telling information, that seeming vacuum is in fact filled with expressions of the televisual world view, which is the intellectual equivalent of the broadest, coarsest visual image. This world view is a heavy distillation of our general ideological assumptions, which are often dangerously simple to begin with. Further simplified to make a bold impression on the little screen, our ideology comes back to us in especially crude, delusive hunks, disguised, of course, as straightforward reportage.

According to this televisual reality, in a war there are no issues, and only two sides: the bullies and the little guys. Since TV brings us conflicts ahistorically, an attack must necessarily be unjustified and unexpected, its victims innocent, its authors brutal. The purpose of this melodrama is not so much to "awaken public opinion"—TV can't properly be said to awaken anything—as to treat the viewer to an easy dose of rage and pity. This kind of manipulation may seem quite noble, a cry of honest indignation meant to halt a heinous crime, but it is actually expressive of the subtlest bigotry, the most self-serving moralism.

For the TV news loves a good victim; and while this attitude suggests a most enlightened, charitable impulse, it is not conducive to an activist response, because this love is fatally possessive of its broken object: "Stay as you are!" it tells the oppressed. "Your battered face has earned you our esteem!" Within this schema, the worst thing that can happen to the underdog is not to die or go on suffering, but to become unpitiable, to stand up strong. Because the news allows no categories between those of the noble weakling and the ugly victor, any group that does attempt to shed its lowly status zips straight from subjugation into villainy. Whenever this occurs, the journalists turn indignant; yet they wouldn't have it otherwise, as long as the new configuration yields fresh victims for the sympathetic camera.

This sentimental strategy relies on and perpetuates the oldest stereotypes, and is therefore the expression of mere bigotry, largely unconscious, frequently well meaning, and therefore worse than any overt hatred. Blacks and Jews, the most despised of peoples, have been the major objects in this scheme, shifting from handsome victim to pariah, from one debased status to the other, according to how autonomous they seem to those who work on television. As long as blacks abided by the principles of King and Gandhi, they were aestheticized as Eternal Losers, eyes soulfully pitched upward; but as soon as they acted on their anger, whether as rioters or Black Panthers, the news took back that holy glow and cast them as an unexpected menace, only to reinstate their wings and halos in these quiescent times. And now the Jews of Israel have forfeited their saintliness by acting as Americans used to, expropriating land that isn't theirs, teaching their enemies a cruel lesson, and doing some harm to innocents as well.

According to the news, the real crime of the Israelis was not their invasion per se, but their willful abandonment of the Jew's historic role as martyr. This was the dominant theme of TV's coverage of the war in Lebanon. "Israel," said Richard Threlkeld from Beirut, "has confounded its enemies and . . . commanded fear and respect, but it is not the Israel that its first prime minister, Ben-Gurion, always imagined it would be: that Israel, that light unto the nations." Despite the denials of the networks' presidents, it was indeed the case that the coverage of that war was heavily biased against Israel, although not in a way that ought to comfort the Palestinians. The news did consistently inflate the casualty figures, dwell on atrocities, stress heavily the fact of censorship, and otherwise depict Israel as the only guilty party. The Palestinians have also suffered at others' hands—for example, King Hussein's—but the TV news never trumpeted that outrage.

This is hardly meant to justify what Israel did in Lebanon, but merely to define the real animus behind TV's characterization of that war. For the Palestinians, too, have been diminished by the coverage. As Israel was excoriated for having shed her crown of thorns, the Palestinians were suddenly ennobled, playing the erstwhile Jewish role of victim. As such, they were translated into total helplessness, mere bleeding figures with no grievance, no threatening aims, no voice other than the networks' voices. "In the news," writes Ellen Goodman in approval of the TV coverage, "the sides are not divided into good guys and bad guys, but aggressors and victims." This nondistinction actually equates the "victims" with the "good guys," and thereby cancels out the complicated history in Lebanon, along with the PLO, which doesn't really fit in either TV category.

This omission preserves the simple-minded opposition that the medium imposed upon that conflict. And which side benefits from this reduction? Certainly not the Israelis, who, once the PLO has been erased, appear to have invaded Lebanon simply for the fun of killing Lebanese civilians; and the Palestinians too have been distorted by the TV fiction, which presents them as disorganized, unrepresented, politically unconscious, and therefore fit for pity, in dire need of the medium's own illusory protection. As in El Salvador and Northern Ireland, so here TV created a beleaguered and pathetic mass, "caught in the middle," completely apolitical, and therefore in no shape to strike back later: TV, in short, will only champion those groups whom it can sentimentalize. It has no interest in a stoic people, or in a population that takes careful steps toward self-possession. For when the Palestinians fight again, their belligerence will, as usual, appear as unexpected; and if they eventually find that they too "command fear and respect," they may also find themselves portrayed, therefore, as evil.

What can television tell us, then, about a war? Here is a rich example of the medium's expressiveness, chosen at random from last summer's [1982] coverage. On the NBC Nightly News on August 2, Roger Mudd delivered the following introduction: "Watching the shelling and the panic and the smoke and the death in Beirut on television night after night can have a powerful impact. But, as John Chancellor's commentary tonight reveals, seeing it in person is of quite a different magnitude." Chancellor then appeared from overseas, and gave us this:

> What will stick in the mind about yesterday's savage Israeli attack on Beirut is its size and its scope. This is one of the world's big cities. The area under attack is the length of Manhattan Island below Central Park. Five hundred thousand people live here. One in a hundred is a PLO fighter. And it went on for such a long time: before dawn [sic] until five in the afternoon. Systematic, sophisticated warfare. The Israeli planes just never stopped coming. For an entire day, Beirut rocked and swayed to the rhythm of the Israeli attack. The Israelis say they were going after military targets with precision. There was also the stench of terror all across the city.
> Nothing like it has ever happened in this part of the world. I kept thinking yesterday of the bombing of Madrid during the Spanish civil war. What in the world is going on? Israel's security problem on its border is fifty miles to the south. What's an Israeli army doing here in Beirut? The answer is that we are now dealing with an imperial Israel which is solving its problems in someone else's country, world opinion be damned. Nobody knows how the battle of Beirut is going to end. But we do know one thing. The Israel we saw here yesterday is not the Israel we have seen in the past.

Chancellor clearly wanted to convey his own experience of bombardment, but his language is dead, its function having long since been usurped by the videotape. What was it like? Well, "it went on for such a long time," the "planes just never stopped coming"; and these colorless phrases culminate in an image both impersonal and feebly aesthetic: "Beirut rocked and swayed to the rhythm of the Israeli attack." This image, which reduces the bombardment to a sort of urban jitterbug, does not convey a strong impression of the citizens' fear, as Murrow's London broadcasts did so well. All that the clause does, in fact, is reproduce the viewer's detached perspective; Chancellor might just as well have watched the bombing on TV, which is equally incapable of expressing others' fears and sorrows. The report's one reference to the vivid human presence is a mere cliché, thrown in as an afterthought: "There was also the stench of terror all across the city."

"What in the world is going on?" Chancellor asks. "What's an Israeli army doing here in Beirut?" These are good questions, but he's supposed to answer them, not pose them. Rather than provide some history, he merely bolsters our incomprehension with his own, thereby turning the event into a mystery, which, like a priest, he can seem to grasp and solve by uttering a well-known moral formula: "The Israel we saw here yesterday is not the Israel we have seen in the past."

Thus, into the descriptive void of the report comes the familiar cloud of ideology, disguised as an objective fact: "But we do know one thing." At once "savage" and "imperial," Chancellor's Israel has undergone a sudden, terrifying metamorphosis. "I kept thinking of the bombing of Madrid during the Spanish civil war." Why? Was little Johnny Chancellor, age 9, in Madrid when it was bombed in 1936? Probably not. Then is the Spanish civil war in any way comparable to "the battle of Beirut"? Not noticeably. What Chancellor actually means by comparing this war to one he's only read about is that Israel has indeed become its opposite, has jumped straight into that other category, since Madrid was bombed, for Franco's sake, by the Junkers 52 of Hitler's Condor Legion.

As this report is typical of television, we must conclude that the medium brings home not "what war is all about," but rather what TV is all about. Television's seeming transparency is in fact the medium's cleverest fiction, offering what seems a clear view of the world, yet in a way that only makes us more familiar with, more dependent on, TV.

But let's set aside all these distortions—the shrinkage, the implicit distancing, the illusory containment, the imperceptible cloud of ideology—and grant that TV does tend to present, as Goodman puts it, "less glory and more gore." Does this also mean that TV is "intrinsically antiwar"? There is no reason to think so; and this belief in television's salutary bias is not only unfounded, but intolerant, positing only one morally acceptable response. To assert, with Ellen Goodman, that on TV "the sides are not divided into good guys and bad guys, but into aggressors and victims," is to say that the viewer, when he sits down to watch TV, is suddenly cleansed of all personal identity, all preconception, and can now apprehend the conflicts of the world from an exalted, unimpeachable standpoint, seeing reality through God's own eyes, or Ellen Goodman's. Far from conducing to a world of peace, such "objective" certainty is probably more dangerous than any archaic faith, because it reflects, and has at its disposal, the most enormous system of technology that has ever choked the world.

For not even the most sophisticated Sony has a perfect moral faculty built into it. We usually see what we want to see on television—and TV complicates this tendency by helping to determine that original desire. If it thinks that we want war, it sells us war. The medium can easily circumvent the pacific influence (if any) of its graphic images. Like radio or the yellow press, TV, too, can beat the drum. "Granted, television helped get us out of Vietnam," writes Michael Arlen, "but it also helped march us in."

And even if the medium weren't influential, the images per se dictate no automatic pacifism. Confronted with those pictures of the slaughtered Palestinians, a Phalangist viewer would surely smile at seeing all those dead "aggressors"; nor would the televised corpses of Israelis draw tears from any fervent anti-Zionist. And it isn't only foreigners who take sides. Had there been television at Antietam on America's bloodiest day, this country might indeed still be two nations—not necessarily, as George Will supposes, two nations frightened into peace, but two nations still at war, each side still watching every battle and still finding, on the screen, excuses for refusing to negotiate.

And had the Civil War been thus prolonged by television, the newsmen would, of course, continue to lament it, crying automatically for peace while shooting everything in sight. Truth is indeed the first casualty in any war, and our journalists have never been less honest than in this sentimental era. In his memoirs, published in 1946, Herbert Matthews wrote this sentence:

> The urge to go out and fight, to pit one's strength and wits against the forces of nature, to seek adventure, risk life, and take joy in comradeship and danger— these are deep feelings, so deep that even I who love life and family and luxury and books have yielded to them.

And, of course, that stirring list of hard inducements implies another, which Matthews took for granted: "the urge for a terrific story." No TV newsman would make such a frank avowal: Matthews's "deep feelings" have been not only very difficult to gratify, but entirely taboo; and the old craving for a scoop now comes concealed in journalistic pieties about "the public's right to know." In a recent *TV Guide*, Dan Rather, asked what event he'd most like to report in the year 2000, came up with this: "Good evening, from CBS News. Peace and good will toward all living things prevails [*sic*] everywhere on earth and throughout the cosmos."

Now what would Dan Rather do, deprived of war and ill will in the cosmos? His utopian pronouncement, as frightening as it is disingenuous, does not reflect the sentiments of a living human being, but rather the contradictory longings of the medium that has consumed him. TV has us automatically deplore or ridicule all anger, fear, political commitment, deep belief, keen pleasure, exalted self-esteem, tremendous love; and yet, while making all these passions seem unnatural, the medium persistently dwells on their darkest consequences, teasing the house-bound spectator with hints of that intensity that it has helped to kill. In fact, despite its pleas for universal calm, what TV depends upon is something else: brutal wars abroad, and an anxious peace in every living room.

The McCarthy Broadcast

Fred W. Friendly

Fred Friendly's Due to Circumstances Beyond Our Control *was published in 1968. At the time, it received excellent reviews, but it seems to be all but forgotten in the 1980s. This is a pity, because Friendly's book contains not only a detailed account of the birth of "CBS Reports," but also a fascinating inside look at the tensions between a documentary unit and a broadcasting organization (CBS). It is, indeed, a seminal work for any serious student of the history of broadcasting.*

"The McCarthy Broadcast" is taken from chapter 2 and deals with the circumstances of the broadcast. Unfortunately, space limitations necessitated my omitting the second half of the chapter, in which Friendly discusses the mixed reactions to the broadcast, the attacks on Murrow's patriotism, the answering broadcast of McCarthy himself, and the comments of media critic Gilbert Seldes.

Seldes, although a longtime friend of Murrow and a foe of McCarthy, nevertheless severely criticized the broadcast. He thought it was unfair for only showing McCarthy at his worst and damned it for pretending to be a report when it was actually an attack. His most biting comment came early in the review, with the words "In the long run, it is more important to use our communications system fairly than to destroy McCarthy."

Interestingly, Broadcasting Magazine, *which generally reflects the sentiments of station owners—many of whom objected to the McCarthy broadcast—went against type and praised the program. Its publisher, Sol Taishoff, called it the "greatest feat of journalistic enterprise in modern times."*

After listing many of the comments both for and against the program, Friendly closes off the chapter by setting out Murrow's own reactions, which were mixed. Murrow told Seldes personally, and the press generally, that he felt uncomfortable about the broadcast and hoped that so drastic a use of the medium would not be required again. However, he also stated that he would never regret having done the program. It is a verdict which time has endorsed.

"When the record is finally written, as it will be one day, it will answer the question, Who has helped the Communist cause and who has served his country better, Senator McCarthy or I? I would like to be remembered by the answer to that question."
Edward R. Murrow, April 6, 1954

To say that the Murrow broadcast of March 9, 1954, was the decisive blow against Senator McCarthy's power is as inaccurate as it is to say that Joseph R. McCarthy, Republican, Wisconsin, single-handedly gave birth to Mc-Carthyism. The disease was here long before he exploited it. Elmer Davis compared it to malaria and prescribed courage as the only antidote. What Murrow did was administer a strong dose of that medicine, then in such short supply, and it was fitting that he did it on television, where the disease had reached epidemic proportions long before McCarthy became its chief carrier.

By the early fifties the central nervous system of the vast broadcast industry was so conditioned that it responded to self-appointed policemen and blacklists as though they were part of the constitutional process. For me, one scene, enacted in an office on the fourteenth floor of CBS, still retains all the noxious atmosphere of the period.

Murrow and I never believed in background or mood music for documentaries, but we did want to commission an original composition for the opening and closing titles and credits of our broadcasts. I had gone to see the vice-president in charge of programs, who at that time had administrative control over "Hear It Now," and later "See It Now," to explain the project and request special funds for it. When the vice-president asked me what composer we had in mind, I handed him the names of three well-known modern composers listed in order of our preference. He glanced at the top name and asked, "Is he in the book?"

"I don't know," I said, "but I'm sure Music Clearance has his number."

"I know," said the vice-president, "but is he in the book?"

I started to ask a secretary for a telephone directory when the vice-president pulled open a drawer in his desk and said, "This is the book we live by." It was a pamphlet called *Red Channels*.

Even today I can recall every item in that desk drawer: the *Red Channels* blacklist, a rating book beside it, some paper clips, pencils, an eraser, an extra set of cuff links, a small Civil War memento. Luckily, "the book" did not contain the name of our first choice, though both of the other composers were listed.

Red Channels and its weekly companion piece, *Counterattack*, the bible for broadcast companies, sponsors, advertising agencies, and motion picture studios, among others, was a catalogue of quarter-truths, gossip, and confessions of ex-Communists and other informers of questionable credentials. In the fifties it was the death warrant for the careers of hundreds of talented actors, playwrights, directors, composers, authors, and editors. Some of the most valued and loyal news broadcasters were rendered unemployable by *Red Channels*. Raymond Swing, one of the innovators of radio journalism in serious interpretation of foreign affairs, chose to fight *Red Channels* publicly by debating its publisher and suffered grievous personal loss because of his stand. His career was never the same again, and for a time his employment with Voice of America was jeopardized. Called before the McCarthy committee, which of course could not prove any of its allegations, Swing stayed with Voice of America until he was reconfirmed, and then resigned in protest at the State Department's failure to defend its own agency. Later Swing joined CBS in a nonbroadcast capacity to assist Murrow with his nightly radio series. Even the great Elmer Davis, who even earlier than Winston Churchill had alerted Americans to the Cold War and warned of Stalin's aggression, was attacked by *Counterattack* as a "smearer of anti-Communists."

Red Channels was not the only blacklister at that time, however. Sponsors, who in those days exerted much more control over program content than they do today, had their own little dark books. When I was at NBC in 1949 producing a news quiz broadcast called *Who Said That?*, the sponsor, an oil company, dictated a blacklist of its own, which NBC accepted. The list of objectionable guests included Norman Thomas, Al Capp, Oscar Levant, Henry Morgan, and several prominent congressmen—not because they were necessarily part of the Communist conspiracy, which they weren't, but because in a live, ad-lib broadcast "they just might say something." Perhaps the classic example of this kind of dreaded spontaneity occurred at Christmas of 1952 when on a CBS broadcast, *This Is Show Business*, George S. Kaufman said, "Let's make this one program on which no one sings 'Silent Night.' " Though this was a wish shared by others, the advertising agency decided to banish Kaufman from the show even before the program was over.

The case of Jean Muir, the actress barred from playing the mother of Henry Aldrich on an NBC situation comedy because of a *Red Channels* blacklisting which disturbed the sponsor, was to have its echo as late as 1966 when ABC deleted a reference to the incident during an interview with Miss Muir.

The flat Indiana twang of Elmer Davis kept pleading, "Don't let them scare you," but the industry *was* scared, and by winter of 1954 much of Washington was so terrorized by McCarthy that national policy was often made in reaction to his tirades. Dean Acheson, whom the *New York Daily News*, a McCarthy supporter, later called a strong secretary of state, was dubbed the "Red Dean" by the senator, and his last years in office were ineffective partly because of this monstrous slander. General Marshall, whom Harry Truman called the "greatest living American," was denounced in the Senate as virtually a traitor by the junior senator from Wisconsin: "A man steeped in falsehood [and part of] a conspiracy so immense and an infamy so black as to dwarf any previous venture in the history of man." The Eisenhower administration fared little better. By 1953 it was "twenty years of treason," and the guilt included the Republicans, the State Department, the U.S. High Commissioner for Germany James Conant, the ambassador to the USSR Charles Bohlen, and Mutual Security Administrator Harold Stassen.

. . . .

On Thursday, March 4, we informed the company that next week's "See It Now" would deal with McCarthy. Whether the news ever reached the twentieth floor I am not certain. We did ask Bill Golden to run an advertisement on the morning of March 9, and when he said that the management had turned down his request, Murrow and I came up with some money of our own—part of it award money we had put aside for just a purpose. The ad was scheduled to appear in the *Times* on Tuesday, but we still had not made a final decision on whether to run the program. The point of no return, a decision to go or scrub, would be made on Sunday night.

We had made a veiled reference to the McCarthy project on our previous broadcast on March 2, and this was fortunate because of a strange series of events that clouded the weekend. In a Miami speech, Adlai Stevenson made a strong political attack on the Republican party, including several critical references to McCarthy. CBS and NBC televised the speech, and McCarthy demanded equal time to answer, which was denied. McCarthy supporters protested vehemently, and when the Murrow broadcast was officially announced a few days later, the cry was heard that this was CBS's way of getting even with its critics. Nothing could have been further from the truth, and our mention of the program on March 2 was evidence. (The networks finally did provide the Republican party with time, and Vice-President Nixon answered Stevenson.)

At nine o'clock that Sunday evening we viewed the next-to-the-last edit of the film. It was still seven minutes longer than the hour allowed us, and Ed and I had our usual tug of war over the cuts. We had to drop four minutes from the McCarthy–Reed Harris inquisition, but even when cut it still held much of its original impact. No network or newsreel service had had cameras running during McCarthy's castigation of Zwicker because it was a closed session, but by rare good luck Mack and Wershba, two of our personnel, had been present in Philadelphia when the senator restaged the entire episode— including the verbatim reading of the transcript—for a Washington's Birthday celebration. The scene, enacted under a huge mural of the first president, took on additional terror because of McCarthy's obvious delight in reliving it all—

the unbridled bravado and rage were interspersed with the famous McCarthy giggle.

We had also extracted from the Philadelphia speech the senator's savage attack on Secretary of the Army Robert T. Stevens, the bland, naive defender of the army's position. Of Secretary Stevens, McCarthy intoned: " 'On what meat does this our Caesar feed . . .' "

We moved the Philadelphia re-enactment up near the beginning of the show in order to establish the senator's violent streaks early, and placed the Reed Harris sequence toward the end as a lead-in to Ed's final comments. In between there was a variety of the McCarthy techniques; after each one, Murrow would point out the misuse of the facts. There was also a glowing tribute to the senator by one of his ardent supporters at a testimonial banquet, and McCarthy's emotion-choked reply. There were some McCarthy quotes on Eisenhower, on the Democratic party's twenty years of treason, and on the Republicans' share of the guilt from another West Virginia speech.

After the cutters had taken the reels back to their editing tables, we sent out for coffee and ran a final critique on our footage. I had sensed a certain uneasiness on the part of some members in the unit. I was not sure whether this was timidity over our confrontation with the senator or whether there was something in their own background which might make us vulnerable. Looking back on it now, I suppose it was my own uncertainty and fear that made me decide that it would not be fair to Ed or CBS to enter into this battle if we had an Achilles heel. Also, I wanted all hands to share in a decision that would obviously involve everyone's future.

Ed agreed, and so a meeting of the unit was called. We asked each member, first, whether he thought our analysis of the senator's technique was effective enough to make the points we were striving for; and second, whether anyone knew of any reason why we should not do the broadcast. Was there, in other words, anything in their own backgrounds that would give the senator a club to beat us with, because if this broadcast was successful, he and his supporters would certainly be looking for one. Although this was a team effort, we all knew from the aftermath of the Radulovich show that Murrow would be the target of all the attacks.[1] But if there was anything in any of our lives that might make us vulnerable, we had to know now. Ed reminded everyone that we were not referring to *Red Channels* or any other such blacklist.

We moved around the room from editor to cameraman to reporter to field producer, and each indicated his position. Two or three of our colleagues were unhappy that we did not have the Wheeling speech and that the material was not as dramatic or cohesive as the Radulovich and Indianapolis programs. Perhaps we should wait another few weeks and assemble more McCarthy material; the senator had some speeches scheduled for the following week, and there would undoubtedly be more hearings in Washington. I said that I disagreed; if we were going to do the program at all, this was the time, and I was convinced that if we could sustain the proper mood for the first twenty-five minutes, Ed's ending would more than justify our stand.

Then each person talked for a few minutes about himself; no one had any personal reservation or indicated any vulnerability. One man told us that his first wife had been a Communist party member but that their marriage had been dissolved years before.

At the end we all turned to Ed. In a characteristic pose, his elbows on his knees, his eyes on the floor, he was silent for about ten seconds. At last he said, "We, like everyone in this business, are going to be judged by what we put on the air; but we also shall be judged by what we don't broadcast. If we pull back on this we'll have it with us always." He snuffed out what was probably his sixtieth cigarette of the day and said he would have his summation on my desk by morning.

When I got up on Monday and went to work, it was the beginning of a grueling but stimulating weekly routine; few of us would see a bed or get home until early Wednesday morning. In the meantime, the life of the broadcast took over. We told Bill Golden to give final confirmation to the advertisement in the *Times*. The copy read simply: "Tonight at 10:30 on 'See It Now,' a report on Senator Joseph R. McCarthy over Channel 2"; there was no CBS eye or any other trademark, and it was signed "Fred W. Friendly and Edward R. Murrow, Co-producers."

We were tempted to tell Alcoa that because of the importance and nature of the broadcast we wanted to run their commercials at the beginning and end, thus eliminating a middle break, but decided that rather than involve them in any of the decision making we would simply exercise our prerogative and do it on our own. We tried to persuade CBS to do some air promotion, but there was little interest. Shortly before noon, Murrow showed me his closing piece, and I asked him to rewrite the opening I had drafted. He changed a few words and inserted the sentence "If the senator believes we have done violence to his words or pictures and desires to speak, to answer himself, an opportunity will be afforded him on this program."

Ed's conclusion, the product of six or seven rewrites, was tight and forceful. There was no doubt in his mind that this ending crossed the line into editorial comment, but we both knew that that line had to be crossed. To do a half-hour on so volatile and important a matter and then end with a balanced "on the other hand" summation would be to dilute and destroy the effect of the broadcast.

We briefly debated sending a copy of the ending to Sig Mickelson [director of news and public affairs], but again decided against it. It would be unfair to him to involve him in the editing process in this isolated instance, when we were not inclined to accept any major changes. Of course, if Michelson asked to see the script, it was available.

On Tuesday morning [CBS chairman of the board] Paley called Ed, as he occasionally did on the day of an important broadcast, and wished us well. "I'll be with you tonight, Ed, and I'll be with you tomorrow as well." Murrow was moved by the implication and tone of the message.

This was one broadcast we wanted time to rehearse so that there would be no chance of being run over by the stopwatch. We determined to go into triple-pay overtime in the cutting room and Studio 41 in order to start our final run-throughs by 8:30. Ed could have a quick sandwich after his 7:45 radio program and we would still have time for two complete rehearsals. But we ran late in the cutting room with the mix, though we had started early on Tuesday afternoon, and it was almost nine o'clock before Murrow and I and all the film and tape were in the studio.

Because the control room was also our studio, we had standing orders that there were to be no visitors, no company brass or sponsors. But on this night I asked the security department of CBS to furnish uniformed guards at the Grand Central elevator and just outside the studio. By this time Murrow was getting crank telephone calls, and emotions on the senator ran so high that conceivably some fanatic would try to crash the studio while we were on the air.

Fifteen minutes before broadcast time we finished the final run-through. Don Hewitt, our control-room director, told us that it was thirty seconds long, and we decided to kill the closing credits if we needed the time. The test-pattern easel was pulled away from camera 1 as Ed settled into his chair. At 10:28 the assistant director whispered that we had one minute. Hewitt picked up the private line to Master Control and asked them not to cut us off if we ran long: there might not be time for credits, and we needed every second we could squeeze. "Give us till 10:59:26," he pleaded. One of the outside lines rang and Don smothered it. "No, this is not the eleven o'clock news. Try 44. Operator, I tell you every week to shut off these phones. Now, *please*, no calls until eleven o'clock."

Murrow was usually "unflappable," but as broadcasters go he was a much more tense performer than Walter Cronkite or Robert Trout. When he was emotionally involved in a story it usually showed. At the close of one of our Korean reports about a wounded GI fighting for his life, Ed's voice broke ever so slightly. It was because he always cared so much, and also because he had a trace of camera fright which he never completely lost. But this was one night when he wanted a steady hand, when he did not want to be accused of an emotional attack.

The preceding program ended; it was followed by what is known as "system"—thirty seconds of blackout, when local stations identify themselves and insert their local commercials. During this seemingly endless void, I leaned over to Ed and whispered, "This is going to be a tough one." His answer was, "Yes, and after this one they're all going to be tough."

Suddenly the hands on the clock pointed straight up and the red light came on. Ed leaned into the camera. "Good evening. Tonight 'See It Now' devotes its entire half-hour to a report on Senator Joseph R. McCarthy, told mainly in his own words and pictures." Looking up at the long bank of monitors, I knew that Murrow was in complete control of the air and of himself; in contrast, my right hand was shaking so that when I tried to start my stopwatch I missed the button completely and had to compensate by two seconds all through the half-hour.

For the next thirty minutes that control room was like a submarine during an emergency dive; fourteen technicians and a director were all responding to Murrow's cues, and he to theirs. Murrow into a 1952 film of McCarthy . . . Murrow to radio tape of the senator . . . Murrow to Eisenhower . . . Murrow live in the studio reading from a stack of American newspapers, most of them critical of the senator's attack on the army . . . Murrow introducing film of the senator laughing and scoffing at Eisenhower . . . the Zwicker affair . . . the senator attacking "Alger, I mean Adlai," which was how McCarthy referred to Stevenson.

Finally we came to the Reed Harris hearing. Somebody in the control room started to talk while the mikes were closed during this footage. Murrow shut him up quickly; he wanted to hear every word of the questioning, almost as though he were listening to it for the first time instead of the tenth. I suspect that subconsciously he wanted no one in the entire nation to miss a single word or nuance of the questioning.

> *Murrow:* Now a sample investigation. The witness was Reed Harris, for many years a civil servant in the State Department directing the Information Service. Harris was accused of helping the Communistic cause by curtailing some broadcasts to Israel. Senator McCarthy summoned him and questioned him about a book he had written in 1932.
>
> *McCarthy:* Mr. Reed Harris, your name is Reed Harris?
>
> *Harris:* That's right.
>
> *McCarthy:* You wrote a book in '32, is that correct?
>
> *Harris:* Yes, I wrote a book, and as I testified in executive session—
>
> *McCarthy:* At the time you wrote the book—pardon me, go ahead. I'm sorry, proceed.
>
> *Harris:* —at the time I wrote the book the atmosphere in the universities of the United States was greatly affected by the Great Depression then in existence. The attitudes of students, the attitudes of the general public were considerably different than they are at this moment, and for one thing there certainly was no awareness to the degree that there is today of the way the Communist party works.

McCarthy:	You attended Columbia University in the early thirties, is that right?
Harris:	I did, Mr. Chairman.
McCarthy:	Will you speak a little louder, sir?
Harris:	I did, Mr. Chairman.
McCarthy:	And you were expelled from Columbia?
Harris:	I was suspended from classes on April 1, 1932. I was later reinstated and I resigned from the university.
McCarthy:	You resigned from the university. Did the Civil Liberties Union provide you with an attorney at that time?
Harris:	I had many offers of attorneys, and one of those was from the American Civil Liberties Union, yes.
McCarthy:	The question is, did the Civil Liberties Union supply you with an attorney?
Harris:	They did supply an attorney.
McCarthy:	The answer is yes?
Harris:	The answer is yes.
McCarthy:	You know the Civil Liberties Union has been listed as a front for and doing the work of the Communist party?
Harris:	Mr. Chairman, this was 1932.
McCarthy:	I know it was 1932. Do you know they since have been listed as a front for and doing the work of the Communist party?
Harris:	I do not know that they have been listed so, sir.
McCarthy:	You don't know they have been listed?
Harris:	I have heard that mentioned or read that mentioned.
McCarthy:	You wrote a book in 1932. I'm going to ask you again: At the time you wrote this book, did you feel that professors should be given the right to teach sophomores that marriage "should be cast off of our civilization as antiquated and stupid religious phenomena"? Was that your feeling at that time?
Harris:	My feeling was that professors should have the right to express their considered opinions on any subject, whatever they were, sir.
McCarthy:	I'm going to ask you this question again.
Harris:	That includes that quotation, they should have the right to teach anything that came to their mind as being a proper thing to teach.
McCarthy:	I'm going to make you answer this.

Harris: I'll answer yes, but you put an implication on it and you feature this particular point out of the book, which of course is quite out of context [and] does not give a proper impression of the book as a whole. The American public doesn't get an honest impression of even that book, bad as it is, from what you are quoting from it.

McCarthy: Then let's continue to read your own writings.

Harris: Twenty-one years ago, again.

McCarthy: Yes, we shall try and bring you down to date if we can.

Harris: Mr. Chairman, two weeks ago Senator Taft took the position that I taught—twenty-one years ago—that Communists and socialists should be allowed to teach in the schools. It so happens, nowadays I don't agree with Senator Taft as far as Communist teachers in the schools is concerned, because I think Communists are in effect a plainclothes auxiliary of the Red Army, the Soviet Red Army, and I don't want to see them in any of our schools teaching.

McCarthy: I don't recall Senator Taft ever having any of the background that you have got.

Harris: I resent the tone of this inquiry very much, Mr. Chairman. I resent it not only because it is my neck, my public neck that you are, I think, very skillfully trying to wring, but I say it because there are thousands of able and loyal employees in the federal government of the United States who have been properly cleared according to the laws and the security practices of their agencies, as I was, unless the new regime says no. I was before.

Senator McClellan: Do you think this book you wrote then did considerable harm? Its publication might have had adverse influence on the public by an expression of views contained in it.

Harris: The sale of that book was so abysmally small, it was so unsuccessful that a question of its influence . . . Really, you can go back to the publisher, you'll see it was one of the most unsuccessful books he ever put out. He's still sorry about it, just as I am.

McClellan: Well I think that's a compliment to American intelligence, I will say that.

Murrow: Senator McCarthy succeeded only in proving that Reed Harris had once written a bad book, which the American people had proved twenty-two years ago by not buying it, which is what they eventually do with all bad ideas. As for Reed Harris, his resignation was accepted a month later with a letter of commendation. McCarthy claimed it was a victory.

The Reed Harris hearing demonstrates one of the senator's techniques. Twice he said the American Civil Liberties Union was listed as a subversive front. The attorney general's list does not and has never listed the ACLU as subversive, nor does the FBI or any other federal government agency. And the American Civil Liberties Union holds in its files letters of commendation from President Eisenhower, President Truman, and General MacArthur.

That was the technique of the entire broadcast. The viewer was seeing a series of typical attacks by the senator, which they had seen many times before, but for the first time on television there was a direct refutation—Murrow's correction of McCarthy's "facts." Each time the senator was his own worst witness; each time the facts countered his distortions.

At 10:54:30 the film portions of the program were over, and Murrow went into his ending right on schedule. I think I knew then for the first time that we were home.

> *Murrow:*   Earlier the senator asked, " 'Upon what meat does this our Caesar feed.' " Had he looked three lines earlier in Shakespeare's *Caesar* he would found this line, which is not altogether inappropriate: "The fault, dear Brutus, is not in our stars but in ourselves."
>
> No one familiar with the history of this country can deny that congressional committees are useful. It is necessary to investigate before legislating, but the line between investigation and persecuting is a very fine one, and the junior senator from Wisconsin has stepped over it repeatedly. His primary achievement has been in confusing the public mind as between [the] internal and . . . external threat of Communism. We must not confuse dissent with disloyalty. We must remember always that accusation is not proof, and that conviction depends upon evidence and due process of law. We will not walk in fear, one of another. We will not be driven by fear into an age of unreason if we dig deep in our history and our doctrine, and remember that we are not descended from fearful men, not from men who feared to write, to speak, to associate with, and to defend causes which were for the moment unpopular.
>
> This is no time for men who oppose Senator McCarthy's methods to keep silent, or for those who approve. We can deny our heritage and our history, but we cannot escape responsibility for the result. There is no way for a citizen of a republic to abdicate his responsibilities. As a nation we have come into our full inheritance at a tender age. We proclaim ourselves—as indeed we are— the defenders of freedom, what's left of it, but we cannot

defend freedom abroad by deserting it at home. The
actions of the junior senator from Wisconsin have caused
alarm and dismay amongst our allies abroad and given
considerable comfort to our enemies, and whose fault is
that? Not really his. He didn't create this situation of
fear; he merely exploited it, and rather successfully. Cas-
sius was right: "The fault, dear Brutus, is not in our stars
but in ourselves."

Good night, and good luck.

Then it was over. Ed slumped in his chair, head down. I thanked everyone
for a perfect show; it had gone off without a hitch and we had not run out of
time. A few seconds later Don Hollenbeck was on Channel 2 with the local
news. He was our first contact with the outside world, and he was obviously
exhilarated: "I don't know whether all of you have seen what I just saw, but
I want to associate myself and this program with what Ed Murrow has just
said, and I have never been prouder of CBS."

Still, at 11:03 the phones remained quiet, until finally a messenger came
in with a note from the operators: "We are swamped. Could we now put
through some calls to Studio 41?" We all roared with laughter, and in a
moment the greatest flood of calls in television history—at least up until that
time—swamped the control room, the switchboard, and the affiliates. CBS
Press Information had set up a bank of receptionists, but they could handle
only a fraction of the traffic. Some of the messages were vicious and obscene;
many were against Murrow and the broadcast; but the majority, by a ratio
estimated at ten to one, were favorable.

The scene at the Pentagon bar was much more sober than after the Radulovich
program. We knew that we had dropped a bomb, and now we were all awaiting
the resulting shock wave. The reports from Press Information and the switchboard
kept pouring in. Most callers were getting a busy signal, but it was obvious
that the contagion of courage had been infectious. Many people were calling
because, as they said, "I just had to do something."

By 12:30 I had dropped Ed off at his apartment. He told me later that the
doorman and the elevator attendant shook hands with him. At two o'clock
New York time, the switchboard at KNXT–Los Angeles reported hundreds of
calls, all but a handful congratulating Murrow. The Washington switchboard
said that it received over five hundred calls, all but forty of them favorable to
the broadcast. Milwaukee registered four hundred phone calls and told the
New York Times that not one was anti-Murrow—a claim difficult to believe
from McCarthy's home state. Chicago reported more than twelve hundred
calls, with a ratio of two to one for Murrow. San Francisco said they'd had
more messages than on any broadcast since Vice-President Nixon's "Checkers"
speech and that the balance was favorable to "See It Now."

So it went all night, and by morning there were thousands of telegrams as well. By noon, more than ten thousand phone calls and telegrams had been counted. In the next few days the letters swelled the total to something between seventy-five and one hundred thousand; we never really knew the exact count, and unfortunately we did not have the machinery to acknowledge more than a few of them. At best, the count ran about ten to one in favor of Ed, though there were places where the tally was far less favorable.

The Wednesday morning papers in the East carried little about the broadcast; eleven o'clock was past the deadline for many, and there were only a few news stories. In the Wednesday afternoon *New York World Telegram*, Harriet Van Horne called the program an autopsy: "distilled culture of McCarthyism. . . . Those who regard the senator as the scourge . . . went to bed feeling that Mr. Murrow had permitted . . . McCarthy to hang himself." His supporters, she said, "may feel it was a splendid thing." The *New York Journal American* quoted the CBS figures but reported that the paper itself had been flooded by calls hostile to the broadcast, as had "other papers." The *Journal*'s television critic, Jack O'Brian, had a long piece about Murrow's "hate McCarthy telecast" in which he reported—falsely—that CBS board chairman William S. Paley had "personally ordered the pompous portsider to take a more middle ground," and that Murrow had refused. He also berated Hollenbeck for praising the broadcast, which O'Brian later called part of the Murrow-Machiavellian-leftists propaganda.

As for the management's general reaction, one innocuous conversation that occurred the next afternoon said it all. I had kept a promise made to my wife, Dorothy, to take Wednesdays off. These were particularly important Wednesdays because we had recently bought a house in Riverdale and were planning to move in March. Each Wednesday was spent visiting the house with painters, carpenters, and electricians and ratifying the plans that Dorothy had set in motion. But by noon of March 10, feeling sure that the foundations of broadcasting must be quaking, I could stay in Riverdale no longer. Shortly after two o'clock I entered the CBS building on Madison Avenue; as I did, Jack Van Volkenburg, then president of the television network, got out of a taxi. It was my first encounter with any member of the management since the broadcast.

" 'Afternoon, Jack," I said.

"How are you, Fred?" Our elevator door closed. Jack said, "How's your family?"

"Fine, Jack. We're getting ready to move, you know."

"Really? Where to?"

"Riverdale. We found a nice house. How's your family, Jack?"

"Fine. How's Ed?"

"Good. A little tired. Well, here's where I get off, Jack."

"So long, Fred."
"So long, Jack."

Note

1. Before the McCarthy show, Murrow had done an earlier broadcast presenting the case of Lt. Milo Radulovich, who was threatened with dismissal from the Air Force because of anonymous charges that his father and sister had procommunist sympathies.

An Independent with the Networks

Robert L. Drew

I have been asked to write about myself and two questions: How do I happen to make documentary films the networks seem willing to broadcast? What role do I play as executive producer of Drew Associates films?

An Independent

About myself, I was a high school student in Fort Thomas, Kentucky, when I ran into a kind of music man. He stomped on the floor to beat time, smoked powerful cigars, and taught music by shouting into your face. His name was McKenna and he had a temper. He drove me to practice the trumpet a lot over a period of years. He also led the band and made good music. What that got me when I left for the Army Air Corps was an appreciation of fresh air and a lot of bugle playing. I graduated from flying school on my nineteenth birthday. On my twentieth I was taking a long walk through occupied Italy after my last mission as a fighter pilot.

Back in California, I flew the first U.S. jet fighters and wrote a story about that for *Life* magazine. I spent the next ten years as a *Life* correspondent and editor in Los Angeles, Detroit, New York, and Chicago.

As for my role as an executive producer, it began in 1954, the year I had an idea about television. Television was reaching more and more people, but its documentary films were not reaching me. However interesting I might find the subject matter, I dozed off in the middle of documentary programs. Why that had to be I could not imagine. My job was covering the real world, and I found it exciting. Every few days I would go out with the likes of Alfred

Eisenstaedt, Leonard McCombe, or Eugene Smith to bring back still pictures of reality that captured the excitement, spontaneity, and, sometimes, even emotion.

The idea was no very great leap. It simply occurred to me to go after some of the qualities in motion pictures that we were already getting in still pictures. But it was an idea that could grow on you. For instance, if one made a more interesting documentary, one might interest larger audiences and inform viewers on levels that journalism had not reached before. Such storytelling might pay for itself, develop its own independence, and improve the lot of journalism, television, and the public.

Because the changes I had in mind were so simple and the steps to make them so obvious, I decided to take a few months off and do them myself. *Life* gave me leave. NBC gave me the money to make a magazine of the air. I put *Life* photographer Alan Grant behind the main camera and set off to cover a half-dozen stories.

The crew was not immediately enthusiastic, I think because wrestling with the big, blimped camera, the oak-hewn tripod, a table-sized 16mm tape recorder, movie lights, and trunks full of cables had diverted their attention from the finer things in filmmaking. Spontaneity didn't wait around for all this stuff to be set up, and the only real surprises that took place in front of the camera were the shock of the clap-sticks and outbursts of the sound man shouting "Cut!"

I found that an operation like this had to be planned and directed, and I directed it. I edited the film, wrote a narration, and delivered to NBC a magazine show under two different titles—*Key Picture* and, naturally, *Magazine X*. NBC professed to like the program and set off to try to sell a series based on it. I retreated to *Life* to try to figure out what had gone wrong.

After a few months I thought I had figured out most of the answers. Yes, we could get more talent into the process. Yes, we could reduce the size and complexity of the equipment, given money and time—maybe a million dollars and three or four years. Add a year or so at the front end to raise the money and a couple of years at the tail to make some breakthrough films and my simple fix had grown from a project of a few months to maybe six or eight years.

That's how you get hooked. I was pretty committed by now, and I had a terrible feeling that one problem remained for which there might not be a solution. Grant and I had done some good things. But the film we turned out was not measurably better than some other documentary films. The things we had done were really not that important to the overall power of the film. Something was wrong that photography and writing did not remedy. As we tracked it down, the problem appeared to be the editing, the way we put the pictures together. On one level they made perfect sense, but on another they didn't build power. Until we got a line on that problem I feared that other improvements might not make the big difference I was after.

For clues I looked to Walter Lippmann, William Allen White, John Grierson, Henry Adams, Robert Flaherty, Josiah Royce, George Bernard Shaw. Josiah Royce? Yes, he was a philosopher, a contemporary of William James, and he wrote one book for laymen, *The Philosophy of Loyalty*. Royce had an inflammatory impact on me, not because he offered an answer, but because he offered an injunction: "Plunge ahead!"

I went off to Harvard on a Neiman Fellowship and spent the year on basic storytelling—the short story, modern stage play, novel. I wish I could tell you just how the answer grew on me over the course of that year, the realization of exactly what was wrong with the editorial thinking behind *Key Picture* and much other documentary filmmaking. The hints came from many sides and built up slowly until the answer seemed to me convincing and, yes, simple. It was so simple that I was embarrassed at the time it had cost me to realize it.

I am sure it is all perfectly clear to you today, but here is what I finally saw. Most documentary films were in fact lectures. They were then, and most remain today, lectures with picture illustrations. It was as clear as the lectures I was attending every day at Harvard and thrown into relief by the novels and plays I was reading every night. In television documentaries the logic was in the words, the narration, the lecture.

I tuned in to watch Murrow's "See It Now." As the program progressed, I turned off the sound and watched the picture. The progression disintegrated. What power had been there turned to confusion. The logic left. When I turned the picture off and listened to the sound, the program tracked perfectly. Later that year, Murrow's television programs were printed in book form. They read very well.

Obvious as all this must seem to you, it was staggering news to me. It made many things clear. A lecture on the living medium of television must be dull. The apparent exception is when the lecture contains news, but then it is the news that sustains, not the lecture. A lecture can promise a great deal. But the level of excitement it can deliver over a television hour cannot build. At best it remains flat. Even in a very good lecture, the curve of interest will generally droop.

The kind of logic that does build interest and feeling on television is the logic of drama. Dramatic logic works because the viewer is seeing for himself and there is suspense. The viewer can become interested in characters. Characters develop. Things happen. Whether the drama is a movie or a football game or a well-made play, the viewer is allowed to use his senses as well as his thoughts, his emotions as well as his mind. Dramatic logic may build power on a curve that has the possibility at least of going right through the roof.

When this works, it puts viewers more in touch with the world, in touch with themselves and revelations about events, people, and ideas.

By this time, later in the Neiman year, the storytelling problem was beginning to sort itself out. Candid photography would capture the spontaneous character and drama that make the real world exciting. Editing would use dramatic logic to convey the excitement of the natural drama captured by the camera.

The other Neiman Fellows, all of them newspaper people, were not shy about offering me a challenge now and then, usually an alcoholic challenge as well as an intellectual one. I wondered what would give first, my liver or my brain, as we debated over martinis into the night the question of what, if anything, all this stuff about storytelling had to do with journalism. Whatever the damage, I came out of the experience having considered some questions about knowledge, journalism, and storytelling.

Henry Adams lived through perhaps the most dramatic of the knowledge explosions. When he went off to college in the mid-1800s, it was expected that he would learn all there was to know. By the time he finished *The Education of Henry Adams* in 1904, diversities in knowledge were so great that he believed any sense of unity to be impossible. But, he said, I am old, and it may be that as I die, a baby will be born who will grow up to believe that he can see the unity of it all. Unity, like beauty, may be in the mind of the beholder.

By 1955 Walter Lippmann had applied Henry Adams's pessimism to American politics. Democracy cannot continue to function, said Lippmann, because the electorate can no longer know enough facts to vote rationally. Newspapers are declining. Television is leading us down the path of diversion and escapism. Knowledge is exploding, and nothing can make up for our not being able to keep up with it.

Such pessimism did not impress John Grierson at all. He agreed that no voter could know enough to vote rationally, but, he said, we've never made our decisions that way anyhow. It is "commonly shared experience" that has allowed us to make decisions together in the past.

But Grierson agreed with Lippmann that we do have a problem. Nations have become too large and complex to function as tribes, towns, or courts, or what the founding fathers had in the past. Grierson had a plan to fix all that. All we need to do, he said, is build multitudes of theaters across the landscape, put films about the real world into them, and persuade whole populations to go to those theaters. Thus would Grierson use technology and filmmaking to give the millions the commonly shared experience necessary to the workings of their democracies.

I couldn't help taking Grierson's side because I recognized a certain kindred megalomania there and also because I had seen his improbable theaters actually materialize. I had one in my living room. Television had gone Grierson one better, and now what were we going to do about it?

Journalists have problems deciding what to do with television because most good ones are captive of the medium in which they learned their trade. Thus an Indian smoke signaler might fail to appreciate the possibilities of the telegraph key. A radio reporter might have trouble showing things instead of telling them. A lecturer might have trouble allowing a drama to unfold.

But journalism is not one medium or another. It is a function that combines what is going on (news) with the means to communicate it. Each means of communication survives by doing what it can do uniquely and best. Thus the *New York Times* does not try to print *Life* pictures. Nor does *Life* try to print all the facts. Try to do what some other medium does uniquely better, and you are misusing your medium.

In television the nightly newscast is its own medium. What it does uniquely and best is summarize the news. Thus it calls for talkers to tell you many things quickly—a lecture with picture illustration that works because of its timeliness. The prime-time documentary is a different medium altogether. What it can add to the journalistic spectrum is something absolutely unique—strong experience of what it is like to be somewhere else, seeing for yourself into dramatic developments in the lives of people caught up in stories of importance.

To address the question raised by my fellow Neimans, all this storytelling stuff has to do with creating a new television journalism that will bring the documentary into action doing what it can do uniquely and best. This means leaving to other media what they best can do. So don't look for facts. Do be ready for some illuminating, high-voltage experience. And the print media should also be ready for floods of new and interested readers. The right kind of documentary programming will raise more interest than it can satisfy, more questions than it should try to answer. It should create interests to fuel a multimedia engine for informing, a system for knowing that leads from television to newspapers to books.

That is how the year went. At the end I wrote a piece on some of these things for Neiman Reports called "See It Then."

I went back to *Life* hoping to quickly assemble my teams and engineer the lightweight equipment. But I found myself running in place to try to keep up with writing and editing chores. The managers of Time Inc.—Henry Luce, Roy Larsen—had looked at *Key Picture* and passed. Networks kept offering me jobs. I already had one of those. I was making $13,000 a year, and I needed a million dollars.

I was getting inspiration and sometimes help from a number of talented people: Richard Leacock, cameraman and filmmaker on a remarkable film for "Omnibus," *Toby in the Tall Corn*; Arthur Zegart, a producer of CBS documentaries; Bill McClure, a cameraman for "CBS Reports"; Morris Engel and Fons Ianelli, experimenters with mobile equipment and filmmaking.

It took me five more years before I had the team, the lightweight equipment, and the story for a breakthrough film. In the meantime I had made a number of short films financed by Andrew Heiskell, the publisher of *Life*. Bullfighters in Spain, experiments with weightless men, a balloon flight to look at Mars through a telescope above most of the atmosphere, a college football game—each of these was the subject of a *Life* story and also of a short film by me. The films were picked up and broadcast on network television by the "Today" and "Tonight" shows, between variety acts on the "Ed Sullivan Show," and on network news programs. *Life* got its money back in promotion. I got to exercise my teams and develop techniques. But we did not yet have our lightweight equipment, and the films were only preparation for making the candid dramas.

In 1960 I was invited to move from *Life* to Time's broadcast division. It owned television stations and had a terrific capital equipment budget. Wes Tullen, vice-president in charge of Time Inc.'s real estate and television operations, welcomed me aboard and asked me to teach the people in his stations "to make your kind of film." In return he would provide funds to buy and modify equipment and make my candid films.

To carry out my side of the bargain I commissioned a West Coast equipment maker, Loren Rider, to build a new machine that would allow us to edit complex films while mixing many sound tracks in any hotel room. It would be completely portable, and we could take it to any Time Inc. TV station, set up, and make our kind of films. To engineer our lightweight cameras I asked Leacock to lay out the specifications, and we assigned Don Alan Pennebaker, a filmmaker who once managed an electronics company, to translate these specifications to our equipment modifier, Mitch Bogdanovich. By March 1960 I felt I was ready to make the first really candid film in which the camera-recorder would live intimately with characters involved in a real story.

I settled on a young senator, John F. Kennedy, running for president in a Wisconsin primary against another senator, Hubert Humphrey. I told both senators that for this new form of reporting to work we would have to live with them from morning to night, shooting anything we wanted to shoot, day after day. They could not know or care when we were shooting, and that was the only way we could capture a true picture of the story. When Kennedy raised an eyebrow I said, "Trust us or it cannot be done." Kennedy agreed. Humphrey agreed.

To shoot the film *Primary* I assembled three teams in Minneapolis. Each was composed of a photographer and a correspondent who also took sound. I assigned Leacock with myself as correspondent to Kennedy and photographers Al Maysles and Terrence Macartney-Filgate to swing between coverage of Humphrey and political gatherings. Pennebaker was there on his way to set up the new, portable editing machine in a Minneapolis hotel room.

It was six years since *Key Picture*, five years since Leacock and I had met, four years since we had begun preparing, and now we felt the excitement of a beginning about to begin.

On our first day with Kennedy, Leacock and I were riding in the candidate's car when it stopped in a small town. Kennedy bounded out, down a sidewalk, into a doorway, through a hall, and into a photographer's studio. The photographer posed Kennedy and took his picture, and Kennedy walked back out to his car. Leacock had never stopped shooting; I had never stopped recording. Now we looked at each other. It was a thrilling moment—the first time we had ever exercised such mobility in sync sound—maybe the first time anyone had.

We shot for most of a week. I gathered the teams every night to trade notes on what we had shot and make assignments for the next day. Two dramatic lines unfolded—Kennedy fighting to overcome the prejudices against a Catholic candidate, Humphrey warning the farmers against "easterners who laugh at you." We followed those lines down to the night of the election. Kennedy was holed up in his hotel suite, and he had agreed that one of us would be there shooting. But Leacock was down in the coffee shop, reluctant to intrude on Kennedy's privacy. A laudable, decent fellow, this Leacock, I thought, as I walked him to the door and saw him into Kennedy's room. Leacock dropped midgetape recorders in a few ashtrays and shot what happened as Kennedy first appeared to be losing, then came from behind to win.

We arrived in Minneapolis with forty thousand feet of film. The door opened to the hotel room in which Pennebaker and Ryder had set up our new portable editing machine. It was the size of a ballroom and full of machines and cables. "Don't worry," Pennebaker said, "we've wired the fuses." The thing was a monster. We worked around the clock to get it working and to synchronize the sound and tape. There had been an invisible break in the wire Leacock and I had struggled so hard to maintain between the camera and my recorder. There was no sync signal. The film and tape would not match up. But Ryder had included a new gadget in his system. He called it a resolver, and all we had to do was turn the crank at the right rate in the right direction and we could transfer the sound in sync. The rates and directions changed constantly, and each piece took hours to bring into sync. Pretty soon we did not know whether it was day or night.

The people from the Time Inc. station would look in on us as they arrived for work in the morning and again as they left after work in the evening. They never showed the slightest interest in learning to make films our way.

This was the year I decided that photographers and correspondents must also edit. This would give them responsibility for paying off on what they shot and help each one of them develop as a "filmmaker"—a person capable of going beyond his or her specialty to also produce and manage the editing of films.

In this hotel room my theory ran into the first of the considerable problems it was to trigger over the next few years. Al Maysles was a brilliant cameraman, but there was something about sitting at an editing table hour after hour that immobilized him. Filgate, notorious for a corrosive wit, became positively ferocious after a few days and nights staring into a viewer.

The editing soon boiled down to Leacock, Pennebaker, and me. We schemed out sequences together. They cut them long. I cut them down. In the end I called in an editor from New York, Bob Farren, who combined the sequences. I gave the film a final pacing and wrote a spare narration. The film ran fifty-two minutes. Later Leacock reduced this to thirty minutes for air.

Primary seemed at that moment like a culmination. It was only a beginning. One thing it began was a period of furious production by an independent who was about to encounter the networks.

With the Networks

Independent documentary filmmakers have tended to regard the networks as huge, hostile, and indestructible. Yet the networks' actual output of documentaries has been limited in number and style, and many independents will probably survive the networks very nicely.

Not all networks have been hostile all the time. ABC has used or accepted outsiders from time to time—myself, David Wolper, the Raymonds. NBC has accepted some documentary making when it came through the entertainment side (the "Life Line" series), and it has employed or bought from independents for particular jobs (John Alpert's forays into Afghanistan and Cambodia). CBS has been more consistently closed to independents, though the entertainment division has been able to float documentary series such as "National Geographic" and "The Body Human." But some tough reasons for hostility have remained—reasons of pride, style, and overhead.

When *Primary* was ready to be screened in mid-1960, nearly all network documentaries were based strictly on the written word. Narration carpeted almost every film, with spots left open for interview, all edited so that the word flow never ceased. *Primary* contained less than three minutes of narration. It showed characters in action, and it was meant to be looked at as one would look at a theatrical film. The reaction of network executives to *Primary* was summed up by my friend Elmer Lower, then an NBC News VP and later to become president of ABC News. "You've got some nice footage there, Bob."

The program was broadcast by station groups (Time Inc., RKO) and syndicated to local stations. It was never broadcast by a network.

Primary won the Flaherty Award for best documentary and the blue ribbon at the American Film Festival. In Europe, *Primary* was received as a kind of documentary second-coming. It was broadcast on the television networks, won prizes, and made its way into theaters. Film critics in Paris rated it above the top fiction films of the year. My colleagues were lionized by the Europeans, and new wave directors paid us the compliment of sending back our camera style in fiction films such as *Breathless* and *Tom Jones*.

After *Primary* things began to happen on the network front. I made a film on Indianapolis race driver Eddie Sachs, *On the Pole*. The vice-president in charge of programming at ABC, Tom Moore, had been watching the evolution of our films. He showed *On the Pole* to his chairman, Leonard Goldenson, and came back to me with our first network proposition. Edward R. Murrow had just gathered a lot of credit for several documentaries on Africa. Moore wanted me to make a program for ABC on Latin America.

I protested that television journalism should be making films on people. I suggested we let Murrow have the continents and that we do something else.

"What else?" asked Moore.

I took a week to puzzle out what else in regard to Latin America and came up with a story that could be seen through people in conflict who represented the nations, factions, and ideas that were clashing there. Moore commissioned it, I shot and edited it with my team in a hurry, and the program, *Yanki No!*, was broadcast in the fall of 1960. It made a splash with critics and the public. ABC News's vice-president quit because his management had made the film with an independent. The sponsor, Bell and Howell, asked for more.

So the first network deal I made was for a single program on Latin America. It came about on the network's initiative because its chairman had a need his organization could not fulfill. We were selected because we were there at the right time with something promising to show. What we made for the network attracted commercial demand from a sponsor. That cemented a major agreement between this independent and that network with Time Inc. as a profit-taking financial partner.

The arrangement called for me to produce programs in volume. I had never done that, but it fitted my theories. To build audiences big enough to pay for our programs and develop our independence we would have to broadcast the programming in a regular pattern. To do that we would have to produce in volume—perhaps two or three dozen hours a year. My theory called for most of those hours to be multisubject programs (magazine shows). I believed that we were selling "an experience," not "subject matter." But the network, sponsor, and Time Inc. wanted hours devoted to particular subjects, and that is what we were assigned to produce.

So far I had pretty much hand-made the programs one by one. But my theories called for training specialists who showed talent for producing— cameramen, journalists, editors, writers—to conceive the films, manage the shooting, and "make" them in the editing. I called them "filmmakers" and began crediting at least one person as filmmaker on every production.

With Time Inc.'s help, I formed Drew Associates and saw that it was owned by the key, creative "associates." I set up a research staff to find stories. I developed the concept of each program with a filmmaker and sent him or her off to shoot the story.

When the film came back, the whole production team would screen it, the filmmaker would present his "scheme" for editing it, and usually a free-for-all would ensue among the team members. Out of this I would adjudicate or, if necessary, compose a final scheme for editing. The filmmaker would go off with the scheme, the raw film, and a half-dozen or so editors to make the first cut. A month or two later, I would see that cut and either approve it or recut it. Once or twice I was able to approve a cut. Mainly I found myself deep in the editing business. This was hurtful to filmmakers' pride, and I regretted it, but I conceived it to be part of a necessary training process. In later years I have come to believe that the theory was wrong. It is true that a number of fine filmmakers have emerged. The first generation included Richard Leacock, Gregory Shuker, Don Alan Pennebaker, Hope Ryden, and James Lipscomb. Mike Jackson, Nick Proferes, Tom Bywaters, and Anne Drew rose from the ranks of editors. From the correspondents came Tom Johnson and Harry Moses. From the production side came Peter Powell, Phil Burton, and Sidney Reichman. I am now persuaded, however, that a great photographer does not have to be a total filmmaker and that anyone who sets himself up to make himself one may be defying the laws of art and nature.

Thus, in the first season with ABC, Drew Associates produced a half-dozen "Close-Ups" for Bell and Howell, broadcast at irregular intervals by ABC.

But Time Inc. and ABC were giants who competed. They both owned television stations. ABC "stole" a Time Inc. station. A Time Inc. executive insulted ABC's president. Time Inc. lost its access to ABC air time. Against my feverish advice, Time Inc. placed a multimillion-dollar order with Drew Associates for a dozen new programs. I could see disaster for Time Inc.'s pocketbook and my whole editorial idea if I produced a revolution on film that could not find its way to the public via regular scheduling on a network.

Time Inc. ordered the programs. I produced them. They were syndicated at odd times in odd places. The film festivals loved our programs, but they built no television audience. Time Inc. finally had to release Drew Associates from what had been an exclusive contract.

This move set up Drew Associates' first direct network deal. We were shooting on speculation a film on President John Kennedy in the White House, working with his brother, Attorney General Robert Kennedy, to counter the governor of the state of Alabama, who was trying to prevent black students from attending the state university. Tom Moore called to say that ABC would like to buy the program. That was nice because we had just run out of money and I was about to call back our team, call off the film, and, in fact, call off the company.

ABC sold the film, *Crisis: Behind a Presidential Commitment*, to Xerox, and we negotiated a two-year arrangement by which Drew Associates would produce six documentary specials for ABC News. The day after the deal was signed, a new ABC News president arrived to take over his duties—it was Elmer Lower. We had a nice lunch at Tavern-on-the-Green. He made me an offer. "Tear up the contract," he said. "Bring your people aboard as a unit of ABC News and you can make films as long as you like." There was a pause. "If you insist on remaining independent, these will be the last films you make for us."

For two years it was quite clear that we were "independent." We made films on Vietnam and Malaya and the death of President Kennedy, but Elmer and I didn't see too much of each other. The end of that period, 1964, was the end of our production for ABC News.

In 1965, Xerox asked me what subjects were too tough for networks to assign. I gave them a two-page list. They assigned an hour on drug addiction. The film, *Storm Signal*, won a first prize at Venice, but it was rejected by every network. Xerox bought time on stations in the top fifty markets, ran the film several times in each, and got back figures proving that it was the most looked-at documentary of the year and ranked among the top ten specials of any kind.

In 1967, the Bell Telephone Company decided to commission a series of documentaries on the arts. The first year I produced three specials: Gian Carlo Menotti's "Festivals of Two Worlds," the opening of the new Metropolitan Opera House, and a jazz festival in Belgium with Benny Goodman. The programs were broadcast as specials on NBC and won all kinds of prizes, including a Peabody Award.

The next year, Bell Telephone asked me to produce all their specials—an even dozen. For the first time in my life I turned down business. I agreed to produce half of the hours, six, and suggested they stick with their original producer, Henry Jaffee, for the other six. I felt I owed Jaffee something because he had brought me together with Bell, but also I wanted more time for hand-making the films. One of the programs, *Man Who Dances*, on ballet dancer Edward Villella, won an Emmy.

It was now 1969. Looking back, some interesting things had happened that had influenced relations between this independent and the networks. The one network that had known it could use independents now had a news president who felt that he didn't want any. This closed down our access to public-affairs subject matter for network broadcast.

The sponsors who had influenced networks to go after special qualities in documentaries were fading. Bell and Howell and Xerox and other companies had shifted into a less active and more conservative mode of broadcasting. As the costs of network hours increased, fewer sponsors could afford to buy whole programs. The networks gained strength as a buyer's market became a seller's market. They became less responsive to sponsors' wishes. As network competition for audiences increased, culture disappeared as a regular commodity in prime time. The Bell Telephone Company was denied airtime for a continuation of its series. At the same time, a kind of program that appeared to be a documentary but entailed none of the risk of dealing with the current real world was becoming fashionable—the "Cousteau Undersea" series and the "National Geographic" series. Finally, the cost of film increased, making it so costly to shoot real life uncontrolled that for me it became nearly impossible to continue to make really candid films. A lot of imitations appeared that tarnished the name that had been applied to our films in Europe, *cinéma vérité*.

Thus came about, simultaneously, a network freeze and an economic hold on development of the ideas on which we had been making some progress. For me, the 1970s became what the 1980s seem to be becoming for television in general, a move to more specialized audiences. This was a bit hair-raising and exciting, and demanded new combinations of filmmaking and technology. In science, we made a series of films for NASA on planets, Mars, astronauts, and extraterrestrial life. In the arts, we made films on dance, opera, mime, and the struggles of young artists as they tried to make careers. In government, we made a series of films on how a state, Pennsylvania, tried to manage its most pressing problems. For corporations (LTV, IBM, Portec, Westinghouse, Mutual Benefit Life), we made films on corporate mergers, computers, Tall Ships, the Bicentennial, and Einstein. For a number of these corporations, we also made commercials—our major representation on network television being minidocumentaries running thirty seconds to three minutes. We also made political films for Nelson Rockefeller and a feature-length film for theaters on soaring.

Our network relations were at a standstill as the '70s brought on the blossoming of a multisubject hour, in the form of CBS's "60 Minutes" and later magazine shows at NBC and ABC. These shows frustrated me because I was not producing them, because they were still relying mostly on word logic, and because I thought I knew how they could be better done.

In 1979 I proposed a one-hour special to NBC that wound up as an assignment to produce a shorter film for the "NBC Magazine" show. As he was beginning to make the assignment, Paul Friedman, executive producer of the show, said, "Wait a minute, I'm not sure I can do this." He disappeared down the hall and came back; "Yep, I can do it," he said. This magazine show, it appeared, could do what it wanted with independents.

Over the next two years I produced a half-dozen pieces for the "NBC Magazine" show, half of them on videotape. This gave me a view on videotape and on some of the problems and prospects of the current "Magazine" shows.

I believe "Magazine" shows should provide opportunities for independents to work with networks. Those opportunities will entail some frustration because the magazine-show styles that are working with audiences provide an odd pattern for any broad-ranging or deeply felt journalism. "60 Minutes" entrapment journalism is no way to try to look at the world in general. Nor is "20/20"'s talky consorting with show business celebrities. NBC I regard as not frozen into a pattern because it has not yet been successful in attracting an audience.

On the subject of videotape, I expect to see a more powerful, experience-based journalism appear when we marry the journalistic ideas on which we have been working to tape. By removing the cost barrier posed by film, tape is freeing us to shoot candidly in ways that we have never been able to do before. I am determined that we will produce the new material in volume, program it regularly, and engage larger audiences with a true, broad-ranging form of real-life reporting.

I hope the networks, the public television network included, remain intact. We need ways of assembling audiences. The many alternative ways of broadcasting that seem headed our way promise to fragment audiences. I think our purposes could be more allied with than against the networks. But if I am wrong, one thing appears clear: the networks will be outlasted by independents who have learned to flourish in other environments.

Blacks Britannica:
A Clear Case
of Censorship
Peter Biskind

When is censorship not censorship?

When the liberal management of a local Public Broadcasting affiliate (WGBH-Boston) with a reputation for progressive and innovative programming recuts a film for reasons of "editorial integrity." At least, that is how WGBH executives and a U.S. district court judge see the matter. The latter recently refused to issue a restraining order preventing the station from showing its version of an hour-long documentary on blacks in Britain, called *Blacks Britannica*.

The film's producers, David Koff and Musindo Mwinyipembe, see it somewhat differently: "It's a clear case of censorship," said Koff. "They simply don't like the politics of the film."

The recut version, prepared by executive producer David Fanning, was aired nationwide on August 10, 1978, and the original version was shown a few days later, in the Boston area only, after pressure was brought to bear on WGBH by a coalition of local groups called the Ad Hoc Committee to Defend *Blacks Britannica*.

There the matter stands, except that WGBH has filed a lawsuit against producer-director Koff aimed at preventing him from distributing his version of the film. Meanwhile, the British government has gotten into the act. Conservative Mr. Dudley Smith reportedly complained about the film to the U.S. ambassador in London. The deputy director of the British Information Service in the United States called *Blacks Britannica* "dangerous," and the BIS has asked WGBH for a program showing race relations in Britain in a better light. The British Commission on Racial Equality has initiated a campaign to counter the film by placing prepared statements on the editorial pages of friendly newspapers.

Do the changes in *Blacks Britannica* amount to censorship? Or is this just another chorus in the perennial lament of filmmakers deprived of final cut?

It is easy to see why *Blacks Britannica* raised hackles at WGBH. It is no comfortable exercise in class nostalgia like *Upstairs/Downstairs*. This documentary breaks every rule in the book. Instead of being "balanced" and "objective," it is a harsh, relentless, and passionate indictment of the British ruling class for manipulating and exploiting British blacks in the interest of profit.

Through skillful use of interviews, *verité*, and stock footage, Koff and the film's editor, Tom Scott Robson, draw a bleak picture of British blacks trapped at the bottom of the heap, dual victims of race and class oppression. The film doesn't only present blacks as victims, however. It shows them as articulate, intelligent, and militant. The film justifies street crime in the name of class warfare; it attacks traditional liberal nostrums like urban renewal and integration as no more than disguised methods of social control. Worse, it omits the voices and images of moderation. It doesn't show bobbies helping little black children across the street; there are no prosperous black doctors telling us how fast and how far they have come. Unlike most films you're likely to see on TV, *Blacks Britannica* is not content to identify "the problem" and wring its hands. Rather, it sees British racism from an uncompromising Marxist perspective, showing how it is used to create a permanent underclass and to set the working class at war with itself. ("The danger of *Blacks Britannica*," according to Stephen Wright, deputy director of the British Information Service, "is that it is not merely an emotional approach to the problem of racism, but it is a highly scientific one in the Marxist sense.") Finally, *Blacks Britannica* builds logically and inexorably to a call for violent revolution as the only solution.

Blacks first came to England in great numbers at the end of World War II. They filled the dirty and difficult jobs nobody else wanted. Forty years later, with the disintegration of the British empire and the downhill slide of the British economy, many of those jobs don't exist anymore (unemployment reaches 80 percent among black youth in some industrial centers), but blacks are still expected to fill those that do, no matter how menial. For both reasons— because they can't get work and they don't like the kind of work they can get—they are in a state of permanent unrest.

The film regards government policies toward blacks as aimed more at controlling potential violence than at meliorating endemic unemployment, discrimination, and so on. *Blacks Britannica* opens with the destruction of black ghettos like Moss Side in Manchester and "Brown Town" in London. Demolition balls crash through brick walls; the camera tracks past shells of what once were homes and now are condemned, abandoned, or just rubble. "I was born here," one woman tells the camera. "It's not an ideal community, but it is a community where people know one another, and they don't want to move out." The government bulldozed the area anyway and relocated the population into huge, fortresslike cement buildings like one the camera shows in Hulme. Ron Philips, an educator, observes that the building just happens to have only two entrances, easy to monitor in case of riots.

Britain's political parties are part of the problem, not the solution. One brilliant scene collapses England's electoral spectrum into one color: white. Enoch Powell, Margaret Thatcher, John Kingsley Read, and Harold Wilson are quoted in quick succession, all making essentially the same speech: Powell—"The picture is not that of a province, or a corner of the country occupied by a distinct and growing population—though that would be perilous enough—the picture is that of the occupation of key areas"; Thatcher—"People are afraid that this country might be swamped by people with a different culture"; Read—"We will fight you with every bone, every nerve"; Wilson—"We have reached the absorptive capacity in respect to new immigrants. . . . The strictest control is now necessary." As the director of the Institute of Race Relations observes, "What Enoch Powell says today, the Conservative party says tomorrow, and the Labour party legislates the day after." Another man underlines the message: "I don't want you to believe that . . . if we get some blacks, and put them in the exact position where those are, everything is going to be all right. . . . [You have to] understand that we are dealing with a system of exploitation of which those people are only the political organizers."

While the parties do their electoral dance, the burden of enforcing de facto racism falls on the police. For this they are admirably suited. With the aid of a law novel to the annals of Anglo-Saxon justice, called "sus" (arrest on suspicion of being *about* to commit an arrestable offense), bobbies make it virtually impossible for black youths to walk the streets unmolested. One scene shows police taking target practice at life-sized human cut-outs, unmistakably black. Cut to a procession of marching policemen—a sea of white faces.

The response of black people themselves to all this has not been to turn the other cheek. One man, discussing the case of three black youths arrested for something or other, says this: "To me, it's not a case of guilty or not guilty. We know we're engaged in a war. It's whether we win or whether we don't."

Blacks Britannica views these problems as insoluble. Black sociologist Colin Prescod sums it all up at the end of the film: "One thing we have to remember about Britain today is that it's not so great any more. Its empire has been taken away, and the economy is technically bankrupt. The predicament of blacks highlights the inability of British capitalism to deliver the goods. . . . [If] we can't get [what we want] under capitalism, well then, capitalism has to go." Shock cut to blacks trashing a police car during the last year's Notting Hill riots. The camera pulls back to reveal a full-scale street battle in progress. Cut to a recording studio where Steel Pulse, a reggae band, chants "revolution . . . revolution." Not very subtle, but there's no mistake about the film's message.

It is hardly surprising that WGBH found this a bitter pill to swallow. The trouble started when Koff, who is American, returned to the United States and showed the fine cut to station personnel. They were impressed, but they worried about the effect of the film on their audience and sponsors. Koff said that David Fanning's first reaction was, "What about the guy in the wheatfields in Kansas. He'll call us communists." They discussed ways of "framing" the film for an American audience—disclaimers, discussions—but never tampering with the film itself. Fanning told Koff to go back to England and cut the negative, which Koff understood to mean that the film had been accepted, since it would be unusual to cut the negative if changes were anticipated. Koff did so, only to find out a month later, at a second Boston screening, that the July 13 air date was to be canceled and the film was definitely to be recut. At this screening, according to Koff, Fanning's boss, program manager Peter McGhee, charged that he had handed the film over to a small group of people who shared the same ideology. "What ideology is that?" Koff asked. "It's clear from the moment when somebody mentions the word 'Engels,'" replied McGhee.

Publicly, Fanning claimed that the film would confuse American audiences. On July 13 he released a statement saying, "I strongly disagree with the arrangement of the material within the film, which, when viewed out of context by an American audience, would be confusing." WGBH officials stoutly maintained that censorship was the last thing they intended. "I never had any dispute with the central premise of the film or with its content," said Fanning. "In no way is the content or message of *Black Britannica* altered." Later, however, he told *Newsweek*, "I was concerned with the film's endorsement of a Marxist viewpoint."

When the film was finally aired, his concern was evident. The recut version provides an object lesson in the anatomy of censorship. WGBH was truthfully able to deny that much had been cut (no more than four minutes, including, however, the revealing shot of bobbies blasting away at black targets) or that the content had been altered; but it was clear that the film's *meaning* had been changed by the simple expedient of rearranging the sequence of shots. There are numerous instances of this. For example, in the original there is a remarkable quote from former commissioner of police Sir Robert Mark to the effect that crimes of violence (murder, rape, etc.) are less serious than "the tendency of people to use violence to achieve political or industrial ends." Cut to a demonstration at which police are unmistakably beating up white people. Cut to black demonstrators chanting, "The pigs, the pigs, we gotta get rid of the pigs."

There are three points made by this sequence of shots: first, that by beating demonstrators it is the police who use violence for political ends; second, that whites are beaten as well as blacks when it is in the interests of those ends; third, that black anger at the police ("We gotta get rid of the pigs") is a result of police provocations. In the Fanning version, the third shot in this sequence ("We gotta . . . ") comes first. The logic of the argument is disrupted, and it is made to seem as if black anger provokes police violence, not the other way around. Moreover, Sir Robert Marks's words are now a voice-over over the shot in which the police beat white demonstrators, so it seems like this shot is an illustration of his point of view rather than a contradiction of it. Regardless of whether or not one agrees or disagrees with Koff's analysis, to say that the rearrangement of this footage makes no difference to the meaning of the film is at best disingenuous.

The most crucial change comes at the end. The unabashed call for revolution that concludes Koff's version arises largely from the ordering of the shots. In Fanning's version, the street-fighting scene is buried somewhere in the middle of the film. It therefore ends on a softer note, a series of lyrical dissolves with a humanistic appeal for black "dignity." The song remains, but isolated from its context.

WGBH is the showcase station of the Public Broadcasting System. It is run by a collection of Boston's elite educational and cultural institutions (Harvard, MIT, Tufts, the Boston Symphony), along with board members of large corporations, like New England Telephone and Telegraph. Station president David Ives recently told a Federal Communications Commission hearing that WGBH "pours into this community programs reflecting the highest ideas of civilized society." WGBH pioneered the practice of importing British series, such as "Masterpiece Theater," *The Forsyte Saga*, and *Upstairs/Downstairs*. It developed shows like "The Advocates," "Nova," and the "World" series, of which *Blacks Britannica* was a part and which was supposed to provide a platform for "voices from within." The trouble with *Blacks Britannica* was that the voices from within were saying things that WGBH executives did not want to hear. They substituted their own voices instead.

Over the years, the station has been involved in a number of collisions with Boston's black community. First Boston's blacks blocked the cancellation of WGBH's only black program, "Say, Brother," winning the right to co-select the producer and to have ongoing input into preparation of the show. Then there was the mysterious erasure of a videotape investigation of Polaroid's role in South Africa (Cambridge-based Polaroid is a major financial backer of the station). Most recently, the local chapter of the African National Congress forced cancellation of an "Advocates" show on U.S. investment in South Africa which had been prepared without consulting the ANC.

"WGBH is a Yankee bastion," said Chuck Turner of the "Say, Brother" Community Committee. "They run WGBH in the name of the public and see themselves as the arbiters of culture. That's a fiction. They don't represent us, and the only culture they know is white Anglo-Saxon culture."

"The station has a missionary complex," said one source close to the situation. "They're caught in the classic liberal dilemma. Sure, they want to engage social issues, as they do with "The Advocates," but only within the usual on-the-one-hand, on-the-other-hand format. Programs with strong points of view, with passion or anger, are either just not shown, or they are censored, or they are buried in disclaimers, rebuttals, or roundtable discussion. They get the Eric Sevareid treatment."

Blacks Britannica was bound to collide with the liberal premises built into the concept of the "World" series. "We believe that facts are important, but that a large portion of the world's troubles are 'people problems,' " wrote Fanning in a memorandum to potential producers. "At least as important as physical facts are the ways people perceive them." This happy notion, that enormous inequities in wealth and power, runaway exploitation of people and resources, disease, hunger, and so on are largely the result of a misunderstanding, is obviously antithetical to the analysis Koff and Mwinyipembe present.

Koff is still fighting WGBH's four-part lawsuit which charges him with infringing its copyright, defaming the station, and so on. He would like to settle, retaining his right to distribute his film, but WGBH seems intent on crushing *Blacks Britannica* entirely. (WGBH lawyers in London tried to persuade the Edinburgh Film Festival to cancel the film.) Koff's attorney, Jeanne Baker, has countersued, charging WGBH with censorship and artistic mutilation. One key issue is whether the film was made on a work-for-hire basis or on a commission basis. If the former, the copyright may reside with the station; if the latter, the copyright may be Koff's. Whichever way the court rules, attorney Baker hopes the case will help establish in the United States what is known in Europe as *droit moral*, the doctrine that the artist has the moral right to control his or her own work, regardless of who owns the copyright.

If WGBH is upheld, it will be a serious setback not only for Britain's blacks, who rarely get a chance to make themselves heard, but also for American independent filmmakers, whose right to show their work on the airwaves has never been recognized by either the commercial networks or the so-called Public Broadcasting System.

New Boy:
An Independent with
Israel TV

Alan Rosenthal

Outside the graveyard the soundman was looking at me as if I was a cross between Dracula and Frankenstein. "I don't care what you're shooting . . . I can't go in." "Why not?" I asked, puzzled. "Because I'm a *cohen*, a member of the priestly cast. And under Jewish law a cohen can't go into a cemetery." The "priest" was dressed in stained levis and an old denim shirt, and carried the nagra and two gun mikes. Some priest! But because of his hesitations we shot the scene from outside the offending area.

That wasn't the first such incident. There had been one like it a few days earlier. I'd shot an innocuous ten-minute film profile of Yaakov Pins, a Jerusalem artist, and was going over the rushes with the editor. He was one of the best cutters around but had recently returned to very strict Jewish orthodoxy. So he literally edited with the Bible open next to the Steenbeck. In the middle of viewing, he'd stopped and thrown up his hands in horror. "Graven images! You've shot graven images! I'm not touching any footage that has idols in it." I looked again. In my shot the artist was admiring a head of Buddha he had acquired in Indonesia. This was the idol that had offended my editor. We argued, but the scene came out.

These two incidents were typical of the rather surrealistic, esoteric atmosphere surrounding my first few months filming in Israel. It was May 1968, and I'd been invited to Jerusalem for a year to help set up Israel TV. For ages there had been talk, now suddenly there was to be action.

Israel was in fact very late coming onto the television scene, deciding to establish a government-controlled television only after the Six Day War.[1] This was after years of dallying with the idea and years of anti-TV sentiment among the conservative and religious elements of the country. The showing of the

1967 war on the neighboring Arab screens had demonstrated the propaganda value of television, and now the government wanted TV as fast as possible.

So after a decade of hesitations, things began to move. Equipment was ordered from America. CBS experts arrived in Brooks Brothers suits carrying wondrous organizational charts. Would-be filmmakers were corralled (mainly from the radio and press). And finally, to cap the whole thing, eighteen foreign advisers, including myself, were invited to spend a year teaching Israelis the splendid art of film and television and to assist in getting the operation off the ground.

Prior to the invitation I had been working as a filmmaker and lawyer in England and the United States and had established a fairly good reputation in documentary. I'd also filmed a few times in Israel: with the Eichmann trial in 1961, and a piece on kibbutzim in 1964. I guess those two facts, added together, had occasioned the invitation—and I was looking forward to the third visit. But this time there was some trepidation. I knew that working in Israel on a long-term basis would present a completely new set of challenges, both on the practical and technical side and in terms of cultural understanding.

Nitty Gritty Practicalities

To come from the United States with its hundreds of stations to Israel with its one fledgling station[2] was to enter a weird and wonderful world—a world where very little of what one knew before counted or even made sense. But it was a stimulating and vibrant world, where talent was high and technique low, where almost anything could be tried (at least once), and where nobody paid the slightest attention to anybody else, least of all to the advisers. It was a world where the students studied directing on Monday and set up their own school for production techniques on Tuesday.

The training of TV crews started in April 1968, and by September the station was already broadcasting a few programs. In less than a year the station was in full swing and broadcasting between two and three hours a day to 80 percent of the country. In its turn, television gave a boost to Israeli filmmaking in general, so that the early years of the 1970s saw a massive growth in the production of both shorts and features in the country.

For most of 1968 and 1969 I worked full-time on the TV staff. My job consisted in the main of training film crews, trying to build a documentary department, advising on policy, and acting as producer-director on six or seven films. I then left Israel for a couple of years, and in 1971 I came back to try my hand as a freelance filmmaker. As anyone can easily guess, the story then became very different, and the work conditions much more difficult and confining.

The way a freelancer worked was fairly simple. Although Israel TV preferred to make all its films with tenured staff and on its premises, by 1971 it had begun to contract films out to private production companies. These companies in turn then contracted out the writing and directing to freelancers, and it was at this last stage that I entered the game.

Because I had been a founding father, so to speak, the work was fairly easy to come by, but the most appalling restrictions applied. For the staff of Israel TV, neither time nor materials mattered very much. One could take between three and six months making a half-hour film and not too many questions would be asked. Nine months on a film was not unusual, and one friend of mine boasted that quality demanded that he not do more than one film a year. The point is, no matter how long the film took, the TV paid a fairly good salary to the staffer every month.

Working as a freelancer you saw the other side of the coin. Israel was broke, we were told, and the TV could afford only a pittance for our films. Thus—regrettably—time, money, and materials all had to be restricted.

At that time, the total budget for a twenty-minute freelance film would probably be between $4,000 and $6,000. For such a film you were allowed four days for research, three days for filming, and, with luck and a lot of pressure, nine or ten days for editing. The film was always shot in black-and-white (Israel had no color television then) and on a strict five-to-one ratio. As often as not the research was done by the writer-director without any backup, and production help was minimal: you never went out with a production assistant, and a production manager was uncommon.

I should add that unions did not yet exist, and the private production companies took full advantage of this fact. Thus an average shooting day would run some thirteen to fourteen hours. Why didn't we complain? Because it was a classic buyer's market, with everyone dying to get into the industry no matter how lousy the conditions. You didn't want to direct? Fine, there was another director waiting outside the door.

A typical example of the situation is a film I did in 1971 called *Battle Officer*, about two lieutenants in the Israeli army stationed near the Suez Canal. For research I was allowed one day to drive from Jerusalem to the canal, tour the length of the canal, do the interviews, and then drive home the same evening. All together that involved six hundred miles of driving, by myself, mostly through desert and sandstorms.

The shooting merely repeated the story, though this time I was with a crew and didn't drive. We left Tel Aviv at noon on a Tuesday and drove across the northern Sinai desert to get to the canal in the evening, where we started shooting immediately. On Wednesday we arose at 5:00 A.M.; we shot through Wednesday and Thursday until midnight; and we traveled back through the desert early Friday morning. No one said anything—it was simply standard procedure.

Our complications came from the production companies' budget maneuvers and scrimping. Their contracts with the TV often stipulated six or seven days of shooting, budgeted, let us say, at $500 a day. The company, however, would only allow the director three days' shooting, thus quietly pocketing $1,500. Everyone knew about this practice but could do very little.[3]

Although the TV had a documentary department, films could just as well be made for the religious department or the children's department, or as a cultural special. For the most part they were in Hebrew, but occasionally they had to be in Arabic. At that stage my Hebrew was fairly fluent, since I had attended a government language course, but I had practically no Arabic. This didn't matter too much, as I could interview in Hebrew or English or through an interpreter, then write the full commentary in English and have it translated into Arabic. There was only one catch: Arabic comes out about three times as long as English. So when I wrote "I like you," which takes a second and a half in narration, I had to keep in mind that in Arabic the phrase would emerge as "Your eyes are luscious as dappled swans floating over the moonlit sea" and allow ten seconds for the commentary track.

It would be nice to say the rewards were commensurate with the effort, but they weren't. Most of my films took two to three months from start to finish. In almost every case I acted as writer-director, and occasionally I took on the job of working producer as well. In the end these Herculean labors would bring in all of $700, of which a third went to the government in taxes.

Generally speaking, these conditions had a very negative effect on film quality, but not necessarily on the filmmaker. On the downside the conditions meant hasty surface research, inability to let a situation develop over time, the abandonment of anything approaching a true *vérité* style, hesitation in the face of experiment, a hurried news style of shooting, and frantic editing. It also meant ulcers, worries, tension, and gray hair. Yet ironically, because of these very conditions, one often emerged at the end of the process a better filmmaker. Because of the sheer hunger for television in a new country, a tremendous number of films could be made under a fantastic variety of circumstances. So in my first years I found myself doing films on bedouin festivals, road safety, the Israeli Olympic team, scientific research, psychology, urban renewal, and child welfare.

As a freelancer, time was money, and once the film was thrown at you you learned to go like a bomb. First you learned the necessity of shaping your film very clearly and strongly before you began shooting; you learned very quickly what would and would not work; you learned to shoot and direct under immense pressure; you learned to work with minimum footage and against the clock; and finally, you worked the whole time with the thought in your mind, "How will this edit?" In short, you couldn't afford to go wrong.

In its own way it was fun. You could feel yourself changing. You became honed and focused. The final result was that although the films may not have been superb, you emerged from the process (if you weren't killed by it) a competent and technically proficient filmmaker, with skills you hoped to put to better use when the chance arose.

The Minefield

With perseverence and sheer bloody-mindedness, I eventually learned to cope with the practical aspects of the work—even to laugh at them. Coping with the culture and the pressures around Israel TV, however, was infinitely more tricky and complex.

For example, I was, for the first time, making films about Israel for Israelis and not for a foreign audience. That doesn't sound too hard, but it was a situation I felt quite uneasy about. Put simply, the question I had to ask myself was, did I know enough to make meaningful films about the culture and society without appearing a complete idiot in front of the natives? I just wasn't sure!

Experience would suggest that this area is a minefield, having taken the toll of many foreign filmmakers. Antonioni's film on China was blasted by the Chinese. Louis Malle's "Phantom India" series was scorned by the Indians. Both filmmakers were ostensibly condemned not because they criticized the culture (though this is certainly part of the reason for the attacks on Malle) but because they failed to understand the subject—the society—and the mores and beliefs with which they were dealing.[4]

Israel, too, has had its share of itinerant foreign filmmakers, and it has usually viewed them with suspicion. There have been too many digests of Israel based on a week's "expertise" or a three-day briefing. The irony is that many of these efforts, scorned by the Israelis as sheer misreadings of a situation or the culture, have been praised to the skies abroad. Thus Susan Sontag's *Promised Lands* (1973) was hailed by *Commentary* magazine as possibly the best short ever done on Israel.[5]

In contrast, Claude Lantzman's three-hour *Pourquoi Israel* (1975) was an incredible tour de force for a foreigner. Almost every Israeli I met agreed that for once a stranger had really understood and shown what was going on. But even then there were a few faux pas. For example, in an interview with an Ashdod port worker, the worker complains about his miserably low wage, which Lantzman obviously accepts as true. When I saw the film at the Hebrew University, the audience burst into hysterics at this juncture. It knew, only too well, that the port workers were the highest-paid workers in Israel, getting an incredible amount per day. Clearly, Lantzman had taken the image of the Marseilles port laborer and applied it to his Israeli counterpart, where it just didn't fit.

When I came to Israel in 1968, I was seen as a foreigner—my having previously spent six months in the country counted for nothing. Nor did the fact that I knew Hebrew. "You're a bloody Englishman and you don't know our ways. You're a new boy. You haven't been in a youth movement. You haven't been in the army. You haven't got a clue." My students at the TV said this to me. They were pleasant but cocky, arrogant Israelis. They *knew*, because of their birthright—I didn't. And, to my chagrin, they were largely correct. The only thing I could do was look, learn, observe, read, talk, and hope that time would bring insight.

My first problem of filmic acculturation was to understand the audience— to grasp very completely that I was making films for the locals and not for Americans, Australians, or Englishmen. Further, I had to grasp that the difference between making Zionist films and making Israeli films was like the difference between night and day.

This acculturation may sound simple, but it had an immense number of ramifications. I had to understand emotionally, and not just in my head, the sheer diversity of the audience. We were making films for a population of over three million, the majority being Jews, but a large minority were Moslem Arabs. Whereas the Arabs were fairly homogeneous, the Jewish population was divided in every way imaginable. There were the sophisticated Berliners who had arrived in the thirties; the Yemenites from Saana who came in 1949; the North Africans from Morocco and the semi-bedouin Jews from the Atlas Mountains who came in the fifties; and the Russians from Georgia, Moscow, and Leningrad who came flocking in in the seventies.

And Israel's fantastic diversity extended well beyond the population. One stumbled on Christian tour groups going over Crusader castles, Moslems celebrating Ramadan, and blue-shirted Jewish youngsters visiting the site of the Dead Sea Scrolls. Geographically, historically, and religiously it presented a painting of a thousand different colors. And to add to the fantasy, one always saw in the background a Hollywood television team shooting the story of Moses in the Sinai desert or reconstructing the Masada epic. At last I understood the expression "mind-boggling." For that first year my mind well and truly boggled.

This worked very negatively on my filming. Everything was exotic, everything was a wonder. This included the rabbi who looked as if he'd walked out of a medieval Polish village. It included the bedouins who looked to be straight from *Ben Hur*, and their disgruntled camels. And it certainly included the sexy, flamboyant Greek Orthodox priests with their majestic grey beards and hair tied behind in a bun.

But for the Israelis all this was commonplace, not worth a second glance. I was seeing a *New York Times* travel section on Israel, but what had to appear on the screen was a different Israeli reality—more subtle, more somber, more probing—a vision relevant to life as it was lived in Tel Aviv, in the Negev, and in the kibbutzim rather than to life as lived in the great beyond.

My social acculturation took time. I had thought about the problems before I came and was therefore on my guard. What I hadn't considered too seriously, though, were the areas of censorship and security—how careful you had to be, and how the possible impact of your films could never be dropped from your mind for a moment.

From its beginnings, Israel has been surrounded by countries with whom it was in a state of war, and except for Egypt, this is still the case. Yet because of proximity, nearly all Israeli broadcasts can be seen in parts of Lebanon, Syria, and Jordan. The impact of one's broadcasts on the enemy, then, while not central to one's filmmaking, is always in the background. The impact of one's films on Israel's own Arab population also warranted serious thought (more on that shortly).

Official censorship was the easiest to handle. It came up mainly in the context of films dealing with the border situation, terrorism, and the army. In nearly all these cases permission had to be sought for filming and the films had to be cleared cleared before broadcast. Though I didn't deal much with the first two subjects, I did do two films on the army, *Battle Officer* and *Letter from the Front*, and so went through most of the stages of censorship.

The first move was to apply to the army bureaucracy for approval to do the film. The outline idea was submitted, and in 80 percent of cases it was approved. Occasionally the army would get difficult. No one could be spared! The subject was under wraps! The film would undermine army morale! But these were exceptions, as in general the army was slow but helpful. Restrictions usually extended to saying you could only film in X, not Y, or only do a picture about officer A, not officer B.

Once official permission had been given, your director's credentials had to be approved by the army spokesman's office. During the actual filming itself, an officer from the same office accompanied you everywhere. His task was to tell you what you could and couldn't film. The battles consisted of the officer saying no, it couldn't be done, and myself trying to recall where I had just seen a published picture of that tank, that new artillery piece, that new carrier. If I could quote chapter and verse, I could go on filming. Buildings up to eye level could be filmed, but nothing revealing place or situation. Everything was quoted as taking place *esham bamidbar*—"somewhere in the desert." General dialogue was OK, specific battle comment and operating procedures definitely out. No names could be mentioned, no units cited.

Later the rushes were seen in toto by another censor, and the final censorship took place when the married print was ready. *Battle Officer* had featured some fortifications near the canal, tanks on maneuvers, and searches for mines and terrorists. It had good, exciting material that I was loathe to lose, and I was quite fearful that the film would be emasculated. In the end, the censors left all the visuals and merely cut out three passages of dialogue dealing with specific operations, cuts that I recognized as being totally justified.

During the Yom Kippur War, while working on *Letter from the Front*, I saw another aspect of the censorship game. What was unique about the war was the immediacy and involvement of the coverage. This was not a war being filmed a thousand miles away, to be shown to viewers who were for the most part uninvolved: it was a war being filmed a mere fifty or one hundred miles from the TV set. It was also a war that was being shown not weeks and months after the battle, but scarcely half a day later. In a country as small and as intimate as Israel, few of the faces on the screen were anonymous: all were immediately known and recognizable as sons, husbands, friends, and acquaintances.

All this implied both practical and emotional censorship rules that provoked different reactions among foreigners and among Israelis. In the early days of the war, journalists couldn't really get to the front, and when they did their copy was severely restricted. This irked many of the foreign journalists used to relatively free battle coverage from Vietnam. The Israeli attitude, with which I agreed, was that what was merely a news story for some people involved matters of life and death for others, and that security and human feeling came before world information or war as entertainment.

Letter from the Front, shot during the war, was a ragbag of film grabbed on the run everywhere from the Sinai front to the Golan Heights. Seven camerapersons participated, three directors, and a couple of editors. I shot two sequences in Safed military hospital, one at Fayid (the old British Egyptian airfield), one around the tank battles in the north, and another sequence of soldiers at a kibbutz.

The material was heartrending—just too much to bear—and I was happy to leave the film to the two other directors (which word is really a misnomer when applied to war footage) to finish. I hadn't a clue what they would do with the material or what shape they would give it. I merely knew they were up against a bind, as film had to be out within two weeks.

A few days later I got a call from the producer. The film was finished, which is to say totally edited, with picture locked and a music and effects track recorded—but somehow it wasn't working. Could I write a link commentary for it, but . . . er . . . no visuals could be changed and the commentary had to be ready by tomorrow.

I looked at the film on the editing table. It was half an hour long and went all over the place. One moment we were with the fighting, the next moment with a family, the next moment back at war again. It was a mess, but it had some marvelous sequences. And it was a challenge. Because of its confusion, an A to Z script was out (thank God), but I felt some interesting things could be done if the script was internalized and personalized and told how people *felt* rather than how wars were fought.

Everything then became simple. I looked at the film a few times, took a shot list and timing, and went home. In my bedroom I drew out copies of my recent letters to family in England, took out my diary, poured a glass of brandy, and started to work. The script was the easiest I've ever written—to use a cliché, it wrote itself and was finished in about an hour and a half. The following day we recorded the narration and then put the film into the lab. In retrospect I think it's the most personal film I have ever done, and certainly the one which has brought the most satisfaction.

War films and military films were only a small part of my life. My films had much more to do with religion, history, urban politics, and the social scene. And here the informal censorship of the system was much more subtle than that of the military censors.

Now, every TV system has its own unwritten rules. These can vary from dealing with the Irish situation with kid gloves and being polite to the queen to keeping quiet about Vietnam, not knocking the FBI, and leaving the president's family in peace. So what I am discussing is not new, but just an indication of where Israel's sensibilities lie as opposed to those of England or America.

Because the TV came into existence only in 1968, the ground rules were at first quite fluid. At least that was my sense of the situation at the time. When I came back to Jerusalem in 1971, the ground rules, though never openly stated, had crystallized very clearly. These guidelines were (a) no criticism of religion[6] and (b) no documentaries analyzing the rough house of politics, political parties, or problematic situations, social or otherwise—in short, no rocking the boat.

From the start the religious affairs department produced a lot of documentaries and was a good bread supply to freelance directors. In the main these films were fairly simple pieces, such as the profile of a young rabbi, the scientist as believer, or a righteous convert. Outside of Judaism there was always something to be done on Ramadan or Christmas at Bethlehem.

The films on Judaism, however, suffered from two peculiar problems. First, some of the small ultraorthodox groups objected vehemently to being filmed, any time, any place—the old graven-image taboo. Thus they would take refuge from photographers by covering their faces with their traditional black felt hats. This, of course, was their right, as is anyone's to privacy. However, they would often interrupt filming in accepted public places, which could be a bit much. Sometimes they did this by stoning the photographer; other times they hurled imprecations. Once while filming around a wonder worker's tomb I was told to stop, otherwise the objector would write to the Hassidic rabbi of Bessarabia to excommunicate me. Lunch was ready, so I stopped, otherwise who knows what would have happened to my immortal soul.

The second drawback to filming religious subjects was that because of the strictly interpreted ban in Jewish law regarding Sabbath work, it was forbidden to film on the Sabbath and on certain Jewish holidays. Now, this makes things a little bit tricky when so much of one's filming consists of trying to shoot a Saturday morning bar mitzvah, a New Year celebration, or a Passover seder. The answer—not totally satisfactory—was to stage most of these events and then superimpose a title reassuring the righteous that these events were not shot on the Sabbath or whatever.

All the above was in its own way quite funny and a challenge to the inventiveness of both director and cameraperson. Subject censorship was much more serious. In no way as a documentarist could you get through with a film that might offend orthodox religious susceptibilities or comment critically on the religious state of affairs.[7] You couldn't do a film debating the power of the religious courts: the subject was simply out of bounds. You knew this and wouldn't even waste time writing a proposal on the subject. The same was true if you wanted to do a piece looking at some of the slightly shady goings-on involved in conversion.

My own run-in in this area came in a film I wanted to do on marriage. In Israel there is no civil marriage, only religious. Thus, not only can a Jew not marry a Christian or a Moslem, but the marriage—even for unbelievers—has to be religiously performed. Naturally, this state of affairs has been a battle ground for years, with traditionalists opposing civil reformers. Like others, I thought this would be a good subject for a film if I could find the right approach. The best answer seemed to be to come at the general subject through the particular incident, and I chose three stories that would illustrate the dilemmas.

My first profile was to be a Jewish kibbutz girl who wanted to marry an Arab. Then I found a cohen (a "priest," like my sound man) who wanted to marry a divorced woman, a relationship forbidden by Jewish law. Finally, I wanted to film a director friend who wanted to marry a non-Jewish American girl. He had found this was impossible in Israel and was planning to marry in Cyprus.

I thought the film had tremendous potential for investigating the subject. I also thought I was the right person to do it because, though in favor of reform and not particularly religious, I was fairly sympathetic to religious traditions. So, buoyed with high hopes, I took a ten-page proposal to the head of programming at the TV.

We drank a few beers. He slapped me on the back. "Great subject. Fantastic idea. But of course we can't do it. Maybe in two years time. Just now it's . . . er . . . a bit sensitive." So the idea got dropped. Instead, the TV did a film on three ethnic wedding celebrations—what I would call a lovely moving wallpaper picture.

My film *Battle Officer* also brought up awkward moments for the TV. Here my central character, a tank officer, had made two "offending" statements. The first was that few soldiers in his unit wanted to attend morning prayers. The second, also highly personal, was that his deeply religious parents objected to his serving in the army.

The executive producer argued that these passages be cut. The impression he wanted to create was that the army was gung-ho for religion and that the religious community was right behind the army. I argued that the passages were personal and must stay. In the end we compromised. The expressions stayed in but were "balanced" by commentary supporting the executive producer's views.

Aside from the religious limitations, many of us were also troubled by the unseen political limitations. At the root of the problem was a mistaken belief on the part of the government and politicians concerning the power of television to influence opinion, something professional communicators were and are much more cautious about.

So the unstated messages filtered down through the ranks. Not so much "Don't do that subject," but rather, "If you do it, it is going to create a lot of problems for us, so why don't you try something else. Something safer, less noisy"—all complicated by the fact that you were an independent director. Thus, if your controversial films were made and created a ruckus, your chances of getting another film from the system were diminished. As I've said, I don't think it's much different elsewhere, but it is frustrating when you think your films might be able gradually to create a climate of change.

Nevertheless, and happily, people fought this situation. Early in 1968 a friend of mine, Ram Levy, did a film on two families—one Jewish, one Arab—both of whom had lost sons in the 1967 war. It was a very sensitive and human story showing that grief and tragedy know no political barriers. The film was finished in 1968 and then reviewed by committee after committee. I'd see them meeting in the editing room next door, pontificating on whether this mild, gentle film would spark riots in the Gallil or would cause Arabs in the Old City to rise in revolt. Eventually it was shown, in 1972 or 1973—a mere four years late.

Sitting in the TV cafe with friends in the early seventies I would go through the films we had suggested that had been turned down without consideration. They ranged from the obvious "naughties"—Jewish converts to Christianity and the Zionist dirty linen of the twenties and thirties—to more shaded areas such as drugs, homosexuality, poverty in Israel, and the character of the political parties. This last area really attracted me, especially after seeing a BBC film on the British Labour party called *Yesterday's Men*. But cold water was poured on the idea in the preliminary discussions. According to the pundits, such a film would either propagandize for the party or probe too many grubby secrets. Neither result was acceptable.

I must add at this juncture—in order to be fair—that all this was in the early seventies and that the mid-seventies saw an improvement in the situation. All the controversial sex subjects were discussed, poverty was admitted, and the buried pages of history were uncovered. Nor did Judgment Day follow. In fact, one of the highlights of the last few years was a drama, shot documentary style, which showed some actions of the 1948 war in a distinctly unfavorable light. The film, *Chirbat Chiza*, became a *cause célèbre*, and though there were protests galore the film was screened as scheduled. Unfortunately, at the time of writing—March 1981—the situation has again slightly deteriorated.

Sometimes the constraints of the Israeli political atmosphere made for a double-edged sword. On one cutting edge were all the forbidden subjects. The other edge, equally dangerous, represented the special-interest subjects. Here care was needed to avoid being "used" if you were to maintain some kind of integrity as a filmmaker.

In this area the biggest traps were usually encountered in attempts to show aspects of the Israeli Arab conflict on the screen. Sometimes the problem would be historical, such as dealing with the old Hebron killings by the Arabs or the Deir Yassin killings by the Jews, or it might arise out of contemporary life and problems in the administered territories.

My own turn to be involved arose out of a suggestion from the Arabic department of the TV. Could I write and direct a twenty-minute film about a village called Abu Ghosh? Nothing serious—just a short profile piece depicting its history, its current life, and featuring a few of the village personalities.

The village lies about eight miles from Jerusalem and straddles the old road to the capital. It was founded by the Abu Ghosh brothers a few hundred years ago, and its strategic situation made it a favorite bandit "tax point" for robbing pilgrims and travelers. Today the village shelters hundreds of the descendants of the original brothers. It also talks of a Crusader tradition, claims a few biblical remains, and boasts a few rather lovely churches. All in all, a dead easy film to do.

The catch lay in the motivation behind the film proposal. Abu Ghosh had been taken as a positive example of an Arab village that didn't flee in 1948 and whose inhabitants had lived ever since in prosperity and peace with their Jewish neighbors. In short, a positive, picturesque story of harmony and friendship to counter some of the propaganda about Arab refugees. So the underlying interest of the TV was fairly clear. But if the story were true, I was all in favor of telling it.

My research turned up a rather more complex situation. In the 1948 war, the Arabs had in fact been asked to leave the village so that the Jewish *haganah* forces could better defend the entrance to Jerusalem. The Arabs were reluctant to go but eventually complied with the wishes of the Jewish officers after being reassured that they could return in a few weeks. After the war, however, their return was denied them. In the end it took the forceful intervention of Yitzhak Navon—now president of Israel, then a young officer—against the authorities to ensure the villagers' return and the fulfillment of the original promise. Even then the Arabs claimed that much of their land had been forcibly requisitioned, with only a small recompense paid.

This was not quite the story the TV had hoped for. Yet any film on Abu Ghosh would be nonsense unless this history was brought out. I discussed this with the head of Arabic programs, who had proposed the film, and he was rather taken aback. To his credit, he decided the story must be told and supported me the whole way through. Given the internal pressures of the TV, this was quite courageous. The only thing he insisted on was that I interview Navon (not in my original script) to get a fuller understanding of the context of promises and counterpromises.

While making that film I also became prey to a few Arabs who wanted to use it for an anti-Israel diatribe. Did I know that conditions in the village stank? That social help was being deliberately withheld? That the youth of the village was being exploited? That village lands had once stretched from Jerusalem to Tel Aviv and had been taken and ruined?

The charges couldn't be ignored, and I spent about a week tracking down welfare grants to the village, statistics on aid it received, compensation it had been paid, and so on. I also interviewed about fifteen people from the village to try to cross-check stories as to what happened between 1948 and 1975. In the end I found most of the charges were unsubstantiated nonsense, and I didn't even refer to them in my program.

Abu Ghosh was almost the last picture I did for the TV. After it came two films on archaeology in the Sinai and a profile of a bedouin musician, but none of the films had problems. That was in 1977. Since then I have worked almost exclusively for American and foreign network television via my own production company. This has meant a better financial reward, but also some emotional loss, as my films are not going to the audience that counts: the Israelis themselves.

Looking back, between 1968 and 1977 I made over twenty films for the TV. They ranged from pieces on soldiers, academics, and workers, through films on the holocaust, politics, and Israeli history to social investigations, child welfare, and profiles of musicians. I learned scuba diving for a film on underwater archaeology, did a three-hour climb up Mount Sinai to get the desert at dawn, traipsed through almost every religious site in the country, shot factories beyond recall, and amused myself making a film about Burt Lancaster playing Moses.

In all this I count myself very privileged. I saw the country from the ground up (and underwater) and learned to understand firsthand its ways, its nuances, its peoples. At the same time I would like to think my work made a small impression on a country in a state of flux, a country in the process of defining itself and its character and institutions. Maybe. One never knows.

Recently I've had a renewed appetite to work for the TV, and I gave them a few proposals. One of them deals with the difference between the Israeli dream and reality. The head of the department liked it but had a few negative comments. "Where are the rabbis? What's happened to the Arabs? No camels. No deserts. Why can't you begin to think like a tourist?" Hearing that, I knew my time as a "new boy" was over. Graduation day had come at last.

Notes

1. Israel TV takes the BBC independent corporation idea as its model but in practice is subject to much more political pressure.

2. In fact, a small educational television station had been set up in Tel Aviv by the Rothschild Foundation in the early 1960s. In 1968 it was still broadcasting, but only to a limited audience of a few thousand pupils.

3. This practice has diminished as the Directors' Guild has grown in strength.

4. What *can* be done and shown by foreigners with a deep knowledge and understanding of an alien culture is seen in the China films of Joris Ivens and Marcelle Loridan. In contrast, Shirley MacLaine and Claudia Weill's film *China: The Other Side of the Sky* is a highly praised but superficial piece in which almost everything is accepted at face value and almost all serious questions are evaded.

5. *Commentary*, Oct. 1976, p. 78.

6. For years the religious parties, though small, have held the balance of power in the government. Their few votes have given the ruling party its majority, whether Likud or Labor. Thus, no one is willing to ruffle the feathers of the religious, particularly not on TV.

7. The news department, because it dealt with immediate events in the public eye, was a much freer department in this respect. Even then, its broadcasts on controversial issues were made only after a struggle.

Part V

Documentary and History

Introduction

History—looking back and analyzing the past—has become one of the basic themes of documentary, especially television documentary. And, with over $4.5 million going to produce the Vietnam war series and some $10 million being spent on "Heritage: Civilization and the Jews," it has also become big business.

Television histories made by the major stations have tended to use the series format. Some, such as "Ascent of Man," "Civilisation," and "Heritage," have looked at the overall progress of mankind. But many more have focused specifically on war, especially this century's wars—from "The Great War" through "Victory at Sea," "20th Century," "The Generals," "The World at War," to "The Unknown War" and "Vietnam: A Television History," to name only a few.

This prevalence of the war theme has various explanations, from the sheer availability of material through social, political, and psychological interpretations of audience needs. My own sense is that war films, by showing human conflict at its most extreme, are riveting for the audience, and they present a nationalist appeal, which is dramatic, entertaining, and good for ratings.

Independent filmmakers, too, particularly in the United States, have seized on the past as an area of investigation. Their concerns, however, have centered more on social and political analyses, with an emphasis on the history of the underprivileged—including women and blacks—or the history of the radical left and union organization. Their films are usually individual works rather than series and include such notable examples as *Union Maids* and *With Babies and Banners*.

Occasionally one person's past will serve to illustrate a whole period, as in *Kitty: A Return to Auschwitz* and Martin Scorsese's *Italian American*. Or a film's inspiration may come from the century's mass movements, for example, "Destination America," which looks at European immigration to the United States. Sometimes the filmmaker will turn to the arts and the media, as in "Let There Be a Love," which covers twentieth-century popular music; "Hollywood," which looks at the growth of the film industry; and *The Golden Age of Second Avenue*, which examines the development of the Yiddish theater in America.

Clearly, the documentary history has become a major—possibly the most important—means for learning about the past. In an age when reading is in decline, the documentary—much more than the theater, newspapers, or feature films—may well be the only serious access people have to history once they have left school.

This chapter considers the major difficulties confronting the history documentary. These difficulties are of both a practical and a theoretical-ideological nature. The practical problems include the use of archives, the framing of programs, and the use of experts, witnesses, and narrators. The theoretical-ideological problems are concerned for the most part with issues of interpretation, voice, and acceptability. Of course, the separation of issues is immensely difficult, as both kinds of problems are wrapped up in each other. And this section is necessarily limited in that it deals exclusively with the "factual" documentary based on archive or live "record" filming, rather than with the drama documentary, or dramatic reconstruction (such as "Search for the Nile" and *Strike*), whose complexities were considered briefly in Part I.

Can documentary deal seriously with history? The answer has not always been given in the affirmative. Many historians dismiss the documentary history as mere entertainment, lacking in accuracy and having no academic value whatsoever. This fundamental problem was dealt with at length in the book *The Historian and Film*, an excellent general introduction to the topic.[1] Although in recent years this hostility to the documentary history has eroded somewhat, certain key questions remain of major importance, affecting our perception and understanding of the relationship between the documentary film form and history. The most serious of these questions concern *where* and *how* the documentary history differs from academic history: What are the expectations? What are the limitations?

The first two essays in this section, "History on the Public Screen," parts I and II, by Donald Watt and Jerry Kuehl, address these questions at length. Watt, approaching the various topics from the academic point of view, distinguishes between the respective strengths and weaknesses of word-based history and visual history and succeeds in laying most of the academic doubts to rest. Kuehl, a former university professor turned filmmaker, continues the discussion by examining the practical differences between academic and film history, particularly with regard to the nature of the two audiences, the function of commentary as opposed to academic text, and the constraints of time on film.[2]

The articles by Watt and Kuehl prepare the ground for a closer consideration of the practical problems confronting the history-filmmaker, that is, the maker of *visual* histories, who must depend primarily on witnesses, photos, location shooting, and archive materials.

Two problems arise immediately. First, how does one handle the prephotographic era? The solutions to this problem are well known, if not terribly inspiring, and usually consist of using prints, reconstructions, historical and archeological sites, and a certain amount of "timeless" location shooting. This artifice demands an "as if" jump of the imagination—we look at today's bedouins or fishermen and are supposed to assume that's exactly how life was at the time of Jesus or Mohammed. Sometimes it works, but usually the self-consciousness of the method is all too obvious and gets in the way of believability. A second, and much more difficult, problem for the history-documentarist is to find a method for dealing with abstract ideas, whether about God, evolution, or democracy. John Pym discusses this problem at some length in his essay on Irish history, "Two Nations." As he indicates, the solutions are not very satisfactory, largely because the medium, by its very nature, demands the hard, concrete image and tends to oversimplify complex and involved matters.

Once one starts dealing with post-1840 history, the visual problems become somewhat easier. After Niepce, Talbot, and Daguerre, we have the photographic record, and after the Lumières, Dickson, and Edison, the film record. The visual record can, however, be both beneficial and problematic. Limitation of space prohibits extensive discussion of the subject here, but a few points are worth noting in regard to archive footage, which is a basic ingredient of so many documentary histories.

The first dilemma is that the archive footage which is visually most interesting may also be historically irrelevant. Thus, while tank battles of World War I may be fascinating to watch, they may provide little insight into the deeper meaning of the events. The second difficulty, seen more and more often on television, is the misuse and misquotation of archive film. This happens, for example, when stock footage of the 1930s is carelessly used to provide background to a film about the 1920s. The third, and possibly most serious, problem is the frequent failure of filmmakers to understand the biases and implications of the stock footage being used.

One example will suffice to illustrate this last point. Many films have been made about Jewish life in the European ghettos under Nazi rule. Most of the films use Nazi footage to portray the scene, as this is all that is available. For the most part, however, the footage is used as an objective news record, without any acknowledgment that the original film was shot with the express purpose of providing a negative and degrading portrait of the Jews.

The other side of the coin is that in a *visual* medium, the very absence of stock footage may lead to a serious distortion of history, as a subject or incident simply disappears. Again, one example is enough. Until the mid-1970s, many historians of the Holocaust implied that the six million Jews killed by the Nazis went to their deaths like "lambs to the slaughter." In fact, there were revolts and uprisings in over 110 ghettos and in the death camps—but these events were, of course, never filmed by the Nazis and so were, all too often, ignored by filmmakers and historians alike.

Often, too, visual history can be defective not because events or actions were physically unfilmable or politically undesirable to film (like the death camp murders), but because those in a position to do so thought the events were just not important enough to photograph. An example of this, pointed out by Jerry Kuehl many times, was the failure of newsreel operators to record the "iron curtain" phrase from Winston Churchill's postwar speech at Fulton, Missouri.

John Pym, in "Two Nations," discusses some of these archive problems and the presentation of war on film, centering on the portrayal of Irish history in the BBC series "Ireland: A TV History" and Thames Television's "The Troubles." Pym's article fascinated me because, among other things, it illustrates so clearly how two programs can take the same historical events and deal with them in completely different ways. He raises important questions on the structuring of film histories, alternative frameworks for history series, and the use or nonuse of the host narrator. He also discusses the use and implications of witnesses, an important issue for documentary in general.

It is interesting that today multiple witnesses are often used to recreate the sense of the events. Sometimes the witnesses are complementary, sometimes oppositional. In "The World at War," for example, the launching of a torpedo in the Atlantic sea battles was described first by German witnesses and then, in a supplementary way, by British witnesses who were on board the target boat. In "Vietnam: A Television History," however, we see frequent use of witnesses in opposition or contradiction. In the *America Takes Charge* episode, for instance, a raid on a Vietnamese village is described by an American soldier who took part and by a Vietnamese peasant, but their accounts of the same event are factually light years apart.

The use of witnesses is one of the key methods for bringing visual histories alive. Sometimes the witnesses merely provide coloring evidence, sometimes they provide the essential facts themselves. Usually a framework is set up to bring the witnesses within the audience's sympathies so that their stories will be believed. Pym shows exactly how manipulative this process can be by pointing out how Robert Kee, the narrator of the BBC series on Irish history, invites sympathy for one witness by the framing and gentleness of the questions, whereas the same witness appears awkward, hesitant, and totally alienated when recalling the same events in the Thames programs.

As mentioned, the witness is sometimes the sole authority for the facts, and therefore the *choice* of witness can be crucial where history is in dispute. Two series on the history of Palestine serve as good illustrations of the point. Both "Palestine: The Mandate Years," made by Thames Television, and "Pillar of Fire," made by Israel Television, deal with the flight of the Arab population from Haifa after 1945. In "Palestine," the incident is recalled by a former British army commander who is extremely hostile to the Jews and very sympathetic to the Arabs and who claims that the Arabs were forced to leave. In "Pillar of Fire," an Israeli witness, General Yadin, recalls how the Jews begged the Arabs to stay. Clearly, visual history is no less contentious than academic history.

Most of the history series made by network television rely on heavy narration to provide the central theses, with witnesses being used as gloss on the text. Independent filmmakers, however, have tended since the 1970s to move in the direction of *oral* history, that is, film history that depends almost entirely on witnesses and has a minimum of narration. The independent's canvas is more limited than the network's, with national politics and social history the dominant themes. Compared with network histories, the style is more personal, more compassionate, and more committed. The objective of many of the independent films is not merely to portray history but to involve the spectator in the process of growth and change.

The subject of independent filmmaking and history is broadly dealt with by Jeffrey Youdelman in "Narration, Invention, and History: A Documentary Dilemma" and again by Pat Aufderheide in her comments on *The Good Fight*. Both discuss the inadequacy of relying solely on witnesses as well as the more fundamental problems of independent history-filmmaking. The central difficulty is that many of the independents' films are simply inadequate as historical studies. Too often they present group biographies that never become serious historical analyses and present a highly romanticized view of history. Many of the films, like *Seeing Red*, about communism in the United States, and *The Good Fight*, about volunteers to the Lincoln Brigade in the Spanish civil war, are made from a left-wing point of view, which is no bad thing; however, they suffer from a serious defect in that they fail to analyze the realities of Soviet foreign policy before World War II, thus giving a very skewed image of history.

As a result of some of these practices, instead of having the past clarified and illuminated, we simply have a new mythologizing of history. This is, I think, extremely dangerous. Where the mythologizing is apparent, as in the independent films, the problems are minimal. But when the mythologizing is carried out on a larger, more authoritative scale, where it can be unperceived, then the dangers are far greater.

The series "The Unknown War," about the fighting on the Russian front in World War II, is one such case. Joshua Rubenstein's article "World War

II—Soviet Style" analyzes exactly how and where history was rewritten for the series. Rubenstein, a coordinator of Amnesty International, U.S.A., has no ax to grind, but sums up everything when he says at the end of his article, "The series does emphasize the magnitude of the conflict and the genuine suffering of the [Russian] people. Only the truth has been sacrificed."[3]

Though mythologizing is suspect, *de*mythologizing can be extremely important in getting a correct sense of the past. This happens constantly in literature, as, for example, in Nigel Calder's book *The People's War*, which removed some of the more blatant and cozy myths regarding English attitudes and behavior when facing the Germans in the early 1940s. This demythologizing was also one of the most vital functions of the film series "The World at War," especially in the reassessment of the Battle of Britain and the exploration of the reasons for using the atom bomb.[4]

Sometimes it takes courage to oppose the myths. In 1977, Albert Kisch of the Canadian National Film Board made a film about the Spanish civil war called *Los canadienses*, which I saw at a film seminar in the Berkshires. In his film, Kisch, like Orwell before him in *Homage to Catalonia*, suggests that atrocities were committed by *both* sides in the war. As a result, Kisch was viciously attacked by a predominantly left-wing audience, which could not accept this realistic, unromantic look at the first major antifascist fight.

Like *Los canadienses, The Sorrow and the Pity*, by Marcel Ophuls and André Harris, falls squarely in the demythologizing category. This four-and-a-half-hour film made in 1970 refutes France's heroic self-image as a nation of resisters in World War II. In consequence, it met with tremendous official antagonism and opposition when it was first released. James Roy MacBean's article "*The Sorrow and the Pity*: France and Her Political Myths" provides a perceptive look at the film and at its national reception. MacBean's view, which has a certain backing in France, is that Ophul's film does not pay full tribute to communist and worker resistance.

After practice and function comes the question of theory. The theoretical issues relating to the documentary history involve problems of interpretation and acceptability. In whose voice and with what authority does the documentary speak? What is its viewpoint? Why should one believe one view of history over another? Some of these questions were dealt with in Part I and also in Stuart Hall's "Media Power—The Double Bind" in Part IV. They are questions that cover all aspects of documentary, but they have a particular relevance to documentary and history.

It is often difficult to separate out the issues, but one of the most important points for consideration is the molding of interpretation and audience attitude around *accepted facts*. John Pym's "Two Nations" illustrates this problem, and the bias in the selection of witnesses has already been discussed. But three other series illustrate the problem even better. These are "Palestine: The Mandate

Years" (Thames TV), "Struggle for Israel" (Yorkshire TV), and "Pillar of Fire" (Israel TV).

The three programs all cover the same historical period—from the commencement of the British mandate in Palestine to the British withdrawal and the declaration of the independence of Israel in 1948—and they all cite the same historical events. But the emphases and interpretations vary enormously, as can be seen from the following example.[5]

In 1947, the British, despite warnings of retribution, hung three members of the Jewish Irgun underground group for organizing a mass jailbreak. A few days later, two British army sergeants were hung by the Irgun. In "Struggle," the hanging of the Jews gets a ten-seconds reference, while one and a half highly emotional minutes are devoted to the hanging of the sergeants. In "Palestine," no mention is made of the original execution of the Irgun members, but the murder of the sergeants—apparently without motive—is presented with a British Movietone News quote stating, "This hanging is the sort of cruelty once indulged in by the Nazis."[6] In the Israeli version, the death of the Irgun members is given extensive coverage, followed by a recital of the many warnings given the British that retaliation would follow.

It is quite clear from this comparison how different national and political viewpoints mold perspectives on the past. Some theorists, though, argue that such analysis and detailing are pointless, because all network television histories—at least in England—are at fault from an ideological standpoint. The best-known proponent of this attitude is Colin McArthur, whose views are set out at length in the BFI monograph *Television and History*.[7]

McArthur argues that all British television histories are damned because the filmmakers cannot free themselves from their bourgeois ideologies: they do not see the realities of history, they are obsessed with the history of great men, and they totally ignore such subjects as the history of labor, feudalism, and capitalism. He argues for the presentation of history from a Marxist perspective and cites the drama documentary series "Days of Hope," about a working-class family between 1916 and 1926, as one of the few decent presentations of history on British television.

McArthur's perspective, which is supported by the editors of the BFI's *Popular Television and Film*,[8] has already been discussed in Part I. A stinging attack on McArthur was, however, made by Jerry Kuehl in *Broadcast* magazine in 1978.[9] Kuehl maintains that McArthur's "revelations" about television processes are common knowledge among film practitioners, and that his central arguments are no more than jargonized nonsense, insofar as Marxist theoreticians are as much caught up in their ideologies as anyone else and, like others, never get outside their systems.

I basically agree with Kuehl that McArthur is elaborating the obvious. But I also support McArthur's call to widen the subject area of history documentary. I feel though that British television is moving in that direction, especially with films like *The Road to Wigan Pier*, about the labor movement in the 1930s, and Robert Vas's *Nine Days in '26*, about the General Strike of 1926, which is portrayed from a Trotskyite perspective and castigates not only the ruling class but also the leaders of the British trade unions.

Though I find McArthur's claims dogmatic and open to debate, the questions that he asks about ideology and voice do matter. These questions led me to choose Larry Lichty's article on "Vietnam: A Television History" to close this section. "Vietnam" is a thirteen-part television series made by WGBH-Boston, ATV (Associated Television, succeeded by Central Independent Television after a reallocation of British TV franchises), and France's Antenne-2.

In general the series was well received by American critics, including those of *Time* and *Newsweek*, who saw it as fair, brilliant, and objective, a series that gave the opportunity for both reconsideration and reconciliation. Some commentators, however, were quite critical. Norman Podhoretz, the neoconservative editor of *Commentary*, damned the series as presenting an oversanitized and highly idealized view of the North Vietnamese.[10]

Podhoretz was joined in his view by a right-wing group called AIM (Accuracy in Media), which had sufficient resources to produce an hour-long "correction" of the PBS series. AIM's film, entitled *Television's Vietnam: The Real Story*, criticized the original series for being a vehicle for left-wing propaganda and for presenting itself as the supreme and final authority on Vietnamese history. The first comment is highly debatable and the second totally unjustified, as the series, whatever its merits or demerits, had never claimed to be *the* history, but only *a* history, a good and fair but necessarily limited version of the events.

AIM then demanded from PBS the right to a public screening of its film. Feeling itself under attack, PBS yielded to the request, creating a situation almost without precedent in U.S. broadcasting history. PBS seemed to be yielding to political pressure of the worst kind.

The packaging of AIM's film by WGBH Boston in a two-hour broadcast was again seen by many liberal critics of PBS's weak-kneed policy as an occasion for either farce or tears. The first half of the broadcast was taken up by a film, made by the "Frontline" team, which discussed the ideals and politics of AIM and how it came to make *The Real Story*. This was followed by the screening of AIM's critique, which in turn was followed by a panel discussion. While there were no winners, there was clearly one loser: PBS, for having yielded on the principles of broadcasting independence and free speech.

The AIM critique went to an ugly extreme, but "Vietnam" obviously does raise the issues of concealed bias and of author's voice and credentials. The early episodes, for example, which were prepared by the British and French television teams, still have a slightly anti-American flavor, though this was evidently toned down after consultations with the films' advisers. I very much wanted to get close to the source in considering some of these questions, including how "Vietnam" came into being, so I specially commissioned Larry Lichty to write about the series. Lichty, now head of cinema studies at Northwestern University, worked as Director of Media Research for the whole project. His article discusses how the series was put together as well as the working and decision-making processes of the production team. Unfortunately, the AIM controversy arose too late in the production of this book for Lichty to include a comment on it in his piece.

Some topics in documentary are mulled over endlessly; others are relatively new. With regard to the relationship between documentary and history, the debate is only just getting started, thanks to a lot of obstacles having been cleared away over the past twenty years. Few people now dispute the fact that a serious presentation of the past is vital and important to television. Moreover, as the main issues have become more apparent, the latitude for interpretation has increased. Histories do not have to be definitive. "Palestine" and "Pillar of Fire" present radically different versions of the same event, but the versions do not have to be reconciled: each contributes to the endless historical debate.

If much has been achieved, what still needs to be done? Where do we go from here? In 1982 Jerry Kuehl proffered a few suggestions for the future in an article for *Sight and Sound*, "Television History—The Next Step."[11] Besides reiterating many of the points discussed in this chapter, Kuehl proposes two further guidelines for the future. First, visual history should incorporate into itself concerns about its own sources and methods. For example, in the "Palestine" series, American and British versions of the same newsreel story about an internment camp in Cyprus were juxtaposed, allowing viewers to judge for themselves the gulf between the two countries' versions. This was true also of the "Vietnam" series' presentation of the two accounts—one American, one Vietnamese—of a battle around a village, mentioned above.

Second, there needs to be a new frankness and modesty in the commentary, which is easy to call for but hard to see put into practice. "Questions about the provenance of film, or its significance, will become integral to programs in which it appears. There is more: commentary writers will not be expected to express certainties they do not feel, since an honest 'I don't know' carries more weight than a false 'This was how it was.' "[12]

If this openness can be adhered to, then, according to Kuehl, much of the falsity of documentary history can be avoided, particularly the complete and final summation of the subject under the words "there's nothing more to say." As he puts it, "All these measures have a single purpose: to treat the visual history of our century with the respect it deserves."[13]

I, for one, could not agree more. One needs to unravel and clarify history because it is the one subject that matters desperately. As Jeffrey Youdelman puts it, the importance of having a clear view of the past is to know how to interpret the present, act upon it, and thereby influence the future. And influencing the future is, of course, what documentary is all about.

Notes

1. Paul Smith, *The Historian and Film* (Cambridge: Cambridge University Press, 1976).

2. Kuehl enlarges on these points in a discussion about the making of "The World at War" in Alan Rosenthal, *The Documentary Conscience* (Berkeley and Los Angeles: University of California Press, 1980), pp. 37–53. The first four interviews in that book deal almost exclusively with documentary and history.

3. Joshua Rubenstein, "World War II, Soviet Style," *Commentary*, May 1979, p. 67.

4. See also the interview with David Elstein in Rosenthal, *The Documentary Conscience*, pp. 113–31.

5. For a fuller analysis of these three programs, see Alan Rosenthal, "Israel Documentary and *Pillar of Fire*," *Studies in Visual Communication* 8 (Winter 1982): 71–83.

6. Ibid., p. 81.

7. Colin McArthur, *Television and History* (London: British Film Institute, 1978).

8. *Popular Film and Television*, ed. Tony Bennett, Susan Boyd-Bosman, Colin Mercer, and Janet Woollacott (London: British Film Institute, 1981).

9. Jerry Kuehl, "Past Facts or Present Values," *Broadcast*, May 1, 1978, pp. 10–11.

10. Norman Podhoretz, "Vietnam: The Revised Standard Version," *Commentary*, Apr. 1984, p. 41.

11. Jerry Kuehl, "Television History: The Next Step," *Sight and Sound* 51 (Summer 1982): 118–91.

12. Ibid., p. 191.

13. Ibid.

History on
the Public Screen, I

Donald Watt

A certain experience of going to conferences where historians and professionals of the media—film and television—congregate has taught me that there are a number of fundamental "false problems" that have to be cleared out of the way before any intelligent discussion, let alone cooperation, is possible.

That this process should be undertaken is, I think, self-evident. For, at least on television, history has become big business. The Thames Television series "The World at War" was an enormous success, both commercially and in its public reception. The BBC series "The Mighty Continent," though received with mixed feelings by television critics (of whom more anon) and professional historians, was also a considerable success. The degree of the success of these two series can be measured in the immense sales enjoyed in each case by the book of the series. On the other hand one has such monstrosities as the BBC's series on the British Empire, which was even denounced on the floor of the House of Lords, or its equally appalling "Churchill's People," a series of historical playlets supposedly based on Winston Churchill's *History of the English-speaking Peoples*, in which central episodes of English history are reenacted as seen through the eyes of the "common people."

The first of these false problems (indeed the first two) can best be expressed in opposed propositions, as follows: The historian's main concern is accuracy; the producer of film and television is concerned with entertainment. The unspoken premise of the first proposition is that to be accurate is to be dull. The unspoken premise of the opposed proposition is that to be entertaining, it is necessary to distort or misrepresent. A good lie, so it is maintained, is always more entertaining than a dull truth.

The second set of propositions, in some sense, complements the first. They may be stated as follows: The historian (or more properly, the academic historian) is concerned only with words. Given his preferences he will lecture, and all the audience will see is a "talking head," that bogey of producers. The producer, by contrast, is really interested only in what appears on the screen, the visual impact of the medium. Given half a chance he will go after anything—provided that it is "good vision" (or good television)—irrespective of its relevance to the chosen topic. He will always prefer *art nouveau* "wallpaper" to the plausible, credible narrative.

To call these "false problems" is not to deny that they can exist. There are always unimaginative historians, just as there are always irresponsible rating-bound producers. Indeed, when collaboration between historians and makers of documentary films for educational or television purposes began, one could collect encyclopedias of horror stories wherever proponents of either camp could be found in Britain. But in the last decade there has grown up, as a result of mutual experience and a sequence of conferences, a convergence of minds and a mutual comprehension of the technical problems, at least at the level of the producer and the historian. The problems the historian faces with the media at the time of writing are usually created by the administrators and policy makers, not by the producers and the cameramen.

The subject of this essay, then, is the problems the historian faces with the media in the making of historical films of a nonfictional kind. This, of necessity, excludes all film but the purely educational, much of which is made for sale to public service or educational television anyway. Examples will be drawn mainly from the author's own experiences, insofar as these can be discussed without risking action for libel. But, like most if not all of the other contributors to this book,[1] the author feels that it is intensely important that the new media should be made use of and understood in all their aspects.

It is, of course, self-evident that the making of a nonfiction film or television program on a historical theme is as much an exercise in historiography as is the composition of a learned monograph, the editing of a collection of historical source materials, the writing of a historical best-seller, or the composition of an article for an illustrated part-work designed for a mass audience. All of these present their own problems of composition and presentation, from the precise form a learned footnote or the citation of a source should take, in the first, to the problem of how much of, for example, the first Moroccan crisis one can compress into two thousand words, in the last example.

It is equally self-evident that a historical statement made audiovisually is different from one made in writing. The tempo is different, there can be no recall, no flipping back of the page, no elaboration of parallel themes by footnotes or parentheses. Then too, there is infinitely more written evidence than visual material. Paradoxically, this is least true of ancient and medieval history, where the paucity of written material must be made up by the wealth of artifact and archeologically obtained materials. A series such as the BBC's recent "The Roman Way" illustrates how effectively this material can be used to enlighten and entertain (the use of Hollywood silent film of classical epics was a barely pardonable gimmick which neither added very much to nor subtracted very much from the total impact of the series). It is, however, characteristic of the problems presented by the visual evidence even here that it is at its richest for social history, and at its weakest on the political side. But the impact of certain film can be out of all proportion to its factual value. I know of few more effective ways of communicating the losses suffered by the frontline combatants in World War I than the panning shots of the military cemeteries employed, for example, in the much-criticized BBC series "The Mighty Continent." The real difficulty arises always in audiovisual historiography when the attempt is made to make a statement for which no visual material is available. This is a problem all historians and producers must face repeatedly and for which there is no universal solution.

The problems the historian faces with the media may best be described under the heading of curses. *Curse No. 1* arises because the media are administered by men of considerable sophistication, often highly educated, but of an education that in contemporary and recent history is usually a combination of out-of-date views and prejudices. It is embodied in the phenomenon of the amateur historian whose views were formed by the Left Book Club, an animal not tolerated for a moment in professional circles, who is rendered doubly intolerable by his monopoly access to the viewing audience conferred by the limited choice of television programs. One of the hardy perennials resulting is Paul Rotha's "Life and Times of Adolf Hitler"; another, equally objectionable, was the series on the Third Reich, "The Rise and Fall of the Third Reich," made on the basis of William Shirer's best-seller on the same theme, a book severely criticized for its restatement of old myths by every professional historian who reviewed it. I have written elsewhere of the combination of tendentious statement with verifiable inaccuracies exemplified by these two series and do not need to repeat myself here.[2] The BBC's action in rescreening the Rotha series showed a remarkable insensibility to criticism. Rotha's reputation as a maker of documentaries was, and is, considerable; but this should not be adequate excuse for reshowing, without comment, a documentary film of a historical rather than a contemporary nature, the only valuable historical contribution in it being the reproduction of Rotha's viewpoint, one forever imprisoned in the populist prejudices and half-truths of the British filmmakers' popular front.

Curse No. 2 arises from the element of finance. The budgets for the great historical television series such as ITV's "The World at War" and the BBC's "The Great War" and "The Mighty Continent" run of necessity into hundreds of thousands of pounds. The BBC has attempted to deal with this by dividing the cost with foreign agencies such as West German Television or the Time-

Life agency. This in itself already arouses problems of audience, since there is little experience or knowledge that a producer can assume to be common to British, American, and West German audiences. But the anxieties of the financial authorities can lead to other difficulties, such as, for example, the setting of a time limit for the making of the series that makes originality of thought or approach simply impossible. Four months was all that was given in one celebrated series for the unit responsible to produce the first program. A solution to the time-limit question recently produced is to engage a multiplicity of producers and writers, giving each a random allocation of programs from the whole—as it might be, programs one, five, eleven, and sixteen, irrespective of their having anything to do with each other—so instead of a single conception designing and unifying the various programs in the series, the series degenerates into a succession of individual programs united only by a title or possibly an outlook.

A third set of problems the heavy cost of historical series creates is the dissipation of know-how. The standard unit responsible for a historical film or television series consists of producer(s), writer(s), editors, musical contributors, cameramen, etc. It may or may not include a historical adviser. But much of the most essential work, the actual discovery of visual material, is the task of the lowly and underpaid researchers, often—too often—bright graduates fresh from university with degree qualifications only vaguely relevant to the subject of the series and only the remotest indications as to where to go for material. By the time they have finished the series they probably have amassed between them a very considerable body of knowledge of the available material. But with the end of the project the team is broken up and its members scattered to the four winds. So when, four or five years later, a Granada mogul, or a BBC deputy director, or whatever, strikes the desk with his open hand and says it is time for another historical epic, the whole process has to be begun again with a new team which has to learn the business from the beginning. The temptation, the necessity almost, of using again the same familiar material is obvious. Only the expertise, acquired on a shoestring, of the professional film archivists (which must include the invaluable catalogue of the Slade Film History Register), with their international connections, can save them from banal repetition or, most heinous of all faults, the misuse of material to illustrate something which it does not in fact depict.

Curse No. 3 of the media is the battle for ratings and the competition between the channels. The BBC is particularly open to accusation here. One remembers the deliberate placing of its highly publicized exercise in voyeurism, "The Family" (a slavish copy of an American original), so that it conflicted with the last five or so programs of Thames Television's "World at War" series; the reshowing of "The Great War" on a Sunday afternoon; the preemption of the normal time slot of the Tuesday documentary for "The Mighty Continent," which gave gratuitous offense to the fairly sizable audience of autodidacts and "concerned" who regularly watched the displaced program.

Curse No. 4 is the straitjacket of time. If a multiple-program series is envisaged, then it must for program-planning purposes consist of six, seven, nineteen, or twenty-six programs, since program planners always work on three months at a time, or rather on quarter-years of thirteen weeks each. Within this, each program has a fixed running time, usually of forty-five to fifty minutes or so (shortened on commercial television by the necessity of allowing for the insertion or addition of advertising material). This is not always too serious a problem for the producer, though it may offer a temptation to visual padding and it certainly sets problems of balance over the series as a whole. The worst sufferer is the Open University, whose time slot is severely limited to twenty-four minutes, far too short to deal adequately with the chosen subjects. Anyone who has participated in making films on historical subjects for the Open University will remember the agonies of cutting what seems an excellently balanced forty minutes or so down by half its length.

The worst curse of the media, however, is the contempt shown by the top brass for the taste and judgment of their audience. Despite the abundant evidence of their own statistics that there exists an enormous television audience for mildly educational material, especially on subjects connected with recent and contemporary history, war history in particular, they are petrified by the fear that if anything intellectually above the children's history book market is shown on their screens there will be a mass rush of viewers into alternative channels. The success of highly specialized general-knowledge programs such as "University Challenge" or "Mastermind" ought to have persuaded them that the large lay audience which they know to exist for films and series on historical subjects is intelligent enough to deserve respect. But the fear remains, to be expressed in such gimmicks as the introduction into serious historical programs of showbiz personalities carefully talking down to the audiences,[3] or the metamorphosis of a collective historical view into that of a single personality, as in Alistair Cooke's "America," itself a gorgeously produced exercise in amateur and myopic pontification by a writer-journalist whose ideological view of Anglo-America is one to which few professional historians would subscribe today.

This perhaps is the point to bring in another curse with which historians and media men alike have to contend: the absence of any serious and well-informed criticism of historical films and television programs. Television criticism itself is confined to the dailies, the Sundays, and the occasional weekly. Each paper or magazine usually employs only one critic, who is expected to cover everything from documentaries to drama, from "University Challenge" to "Top of the Pops," from "Yesterday's Men" to "Tomorrow's World." What respectable journal would expect one book reviewer to cover everything from *Winnie the Pooh* to Winston Churchill's *War Memoirs*? Yet this is what the television critic is supposed to do. Only one critic, Philip Purser of the *Sunday Telegraph*, has to the author's knowledge displayed any interest in the debate between producer and historian.[4] Alone among the weeklies, *New Society* has employed a leading professional historian, Douglas Johnson, to review series such as "The World at War" and "The Mighty Continent" on the basis of having seen more than two random selections from the entire series at a preview. It is the lack of a solid body of informed criticism that is most felt by the practitioners in the field of historical documentary. The *Journal of the Society of Film and Television Arts* is too much of a trade journal to supply this lack.[5] Nationally, perhaps, there is too small an audience or readership to keep a journal devoted to this field alive, but room might be found for something on an international scale if funds were forthcoming. At the moment, those who choose to use film or television for the making of historiographical statements have ony the praise or censure of the ignorant or the appraisal of audience research as a guide to their success or failure. The first is only of use or disadvantage when they are seeking to convince the bureaucracy of the feasibility or desirability of their tackling another historical theme. The second may be in addition a gratifying reward for the effort spent and the tension generated by the making of the program. But in answer to their questions it tells them little or nothing in detail as to variation in style and technique. With a multi-producer series like "The World at War" such mass approval is of little help to the individual producer.

In this it is easy to be cynical about the lot of the historical adviser. In many series he simply acts as a consultant: that is to say, he is consulted by the program researchers or the producer whenever they feel the need to do so but takes no responsibility for the final product. The historian who is inveigled into such a relationship is well advised to insist that his name be left off the credits or he may find himself held responsible by his professional colleagues for all the points on which he ought to have been consulted and was not. In some cases he simply functions as a means of internal persuasion. He will be asked to write a paper or a historical memorandum on suggested approaches or treatments, with which an ambitious aide may convince a reluctant department director to embark on a new enterprise or entrust it to him. He will often be lured, if unwary, into giving much unrewarded time and effort to the guidance of the plausible and ambitious, only to find in the end that the finished product incorporates all the received historical error against which he has given so careful a warning. He may find, too, that his name in the credits is being employed as a kind of British Standards Kitemark [mark of quality], a guarantee of the historical acceptability of the view to which the series or program on which he is advising is dedicated.

It is to this latter case that the remainder of this essay must be directed. The historian's criteria for judging a program from a professional viewpoint are three in number. First, the subject must be completely covered, within the limits set by the length of the program and the material. Second, the view presented of the subject must be objective within the acceptable definition of that term as understood by professional historians. It must not be *parti pris*. It must not be anachronistic, ascribing to the actors sentiments alien to the time and culture or condemning them for not recognizing values dear to the producer. It must not be ideological or slanted for purposes of propaganda. There must be no recognizable and obvious bias. It must seem to understand rather than to condemn. Third, the events described, the "facts" outlined, must be accurate, that is, in accordance with the present state of historical knowledge. Hypothesis, reconstruction, inference, are all legitimate, but only if they are presented under their own colors.

To ensure this, the historian rash enough to take on the post of historical adviser must insist on the right to vet the finished article in adequate time for alterations to be incorporated and distortions of statement or balance removed before showing. He must vet scripts before the film is dubbed. It would be advisable for him to be familiar with the shooting script and the producer's proposed manner of treatment. It is his job to be the conscience of the unit, to keep an eye on continuity and coverage, to stand back from the myriad and one day-to-day problems of TV shooting on location or of putting the film together in workshop and studio. He will find he has to be diplomat as well as heavy gun, the producer's ally in dealing with intervention from above. He must, if possible, deter the producer from using modern film to illustrate the past or film from fictional reconstruction as if it were actuality. He must have an accurate ear and memory for the kind of misstatement that creeps in through a commentator's ad-libbing. Lastly, he has to realize that it is an adviser's job to advise and that final responsibility lies with the producer. If he does not establish as early as possible where final responsibility lies, he is in for trouble later. (He would be well advised to keep a diary of his actions toward and arguments with the producer.) In the end he will still be regarded by those who notice his name among the credits as responsible for all with which they disagree. And he will long for a chance to make his own film to show how it should be done.

This is perhaps where another false problem arises: who should be dominant, historian or producer? Those who despair of ever getting the media to treat history responsibly tend to gravitate toward the British Inter-University History Film Consortium, an enterprise which conjoins the subscriptions of a number of university history departments so as to enable one of their number every so often to make its own film on a historical subject. Inevitably there is an element of home movie about the final product, even where it has been made in conjunction with a university department of film. The historian as amateur producer is no more satisfactory than the producer as amateur historian. And the pressures of academic life do not normally allow those who have made one film to make another within the time span in which they might learn from their own mistakes.

The producer-dominated series, on the other hand, leads directly to disasters such as that of the BBC's "British Empire" series, with its glaring omissions of central facts, its facile anti-imperialist prejudice, its reconstructions of the siege of Cawnpore and the demise of Ned Kelly on the cheap, its distraction by the contemporary televisual, and its general catalog of "awful warnings" for the future. The true relationship between historian and producer must be a kind of partnership, shading into symbiosis, where each understands, even if he cannot practice, the craft of the other. Audiovisual historiography is a bimedial art, like ballet or opera.

This ideal state has been most closely approximated by the producers of the Open University, whose profession it is to work with historians who cooperate by writing the script and selecting the material they wish to see incorporated into the film. This body of expertise is now being dissipated in turn, since the Open University's budget will not allow new series to be made: the constriction of the very limited time slot allotted by BBC-2's program planners is a source of constant frustration. Even here, the producers have to unlearn their BBC-instilled terror of the switch-off or switch-over. Early programs wasted valuable minutes establishing a locale—cameras panning around an archaeological site, for example.

With that the historian and producer still face the abiding problems of audiovisual historiography. What material is available? Is it to be used to illustrate a lecture, or should it be made into a silent film with a voice-over commentary, talking head, or mobile wallpaper? How do you make an essential point where no material exists? Do you use interviews with eyewitnesses or participants in the events you are describing? There was an excellent two-part series on Austria in World War II shown on West German television, made up almost entirely of selected eyewitnesses telling their story cut cleverly into each other so as to preserve the proper chronology. Can you avoid "bang-bang film" of the kind that might have been shot anywhere from Brest to Brest-Litovsk? Can you spot faked-up film (as the BBC documentary on the General Strike of 1926 most notoriously did not)?[6]

Each set of problems can only be resolved on the job itself, usually on the floor of the cutting room. There are enough and to spare without having to cope with the biggest problem of them all, the state of mind of those who direct the media, who cannot believe that waiting in front of their sets there is an educated, interested, mass audience, people unsure of their knowledge and avid for more, particularly if it will help them understand their own lives and lifetimes, and for whom there is no conflict between learning and entertainment, only between bad and good, pretentious and honest, programs. It is this amorphous and not easily defined lump of bureaucracy in the media that has created the present unsatisfactory state of audiovisual historiography in Britain, with its three equally, if differently, unsatisfactory types of material: the media epics, mutilated before birth by the top brass; the home movies of the British Inter-University History Film Consortium; or the straitjacketed expertise of the Open University, forever trapped in its twenty-four-minute time slots and starved of money to develop from its present level of expertise.

Notes

1. This essay was originally published in *The Historian and Film*, ed. Paul Smith (Cambridge: Cambridge University Press).

2. In *History* 55 (1970): 214–16; 58 (1973): 399–400.

3. For example, see *The Times* television critic's reaction to Mr. Benny Green's pictorial history of London, a two-part series made for Thames Television under the title "London: The Making of a City": "Looked splendid . . . a script which, when it did not drown every fact in cliché, was plain straightforward vulgar . . . an opportunity not lost but determinedly rejected by the producer who was his own writer; a deliberate and coldly calculated decision to ruin a good idea by trying to slice it so as to serve everyone" (*The Times*, Feb. 12, 1975).

4. See his entertaining account of a *rencontre* at Cumberland Lodge in the *Sunday Telegraph*, April 28, 1974.

5. See, for example, vol. 2, nos. 9–10 (1974), on "The World at War." *History* carries reviews of films but does not seem to be read at all in television circles.

6. See the letters of Frank Hardie and Paul Rotha in *The Times*, April 22, 1974, and the reply of Elizabeth Sussex, ibid., May 3, 1974.

History on the Public Screen, II

Jerry Kuehl

Relations between academic historians and producers of television documentaries have always been uneasy. Historians are maybe offended by the superficiality and incompleteness of programs made without their active collaboration, while producers resent efforts by academics to impose their standards and concerns in a field which may, they think, lie outside their area of competence. What lies behind this mutual unease is, I think, a serious failure in communication between the two professions. Each misapprehends the job of the other, makes wrong assumptions about what the other can or should do, and as a result is unable to appreciate fully either the other's achievements or his limitations. In the previous chapter Donald Watt examined this problem from the standpoint of the professional historian; I write as a producer of historical documentaries for mass audiences.

Let me say right in the beginning that what seems to me to be at the heart of the matter is the question of the commentary, which is an integral part of every documentary: who should write it, how should it relate to the film, to whom should it be addressed, and above all, what should it contain?

Most television documentaries are fifty minutes long. So let us consider just how much can be said in fifty minutes. BBC newsreaders, who are professionally trained to speak rapidly and comprehensibly, talk at about 160 words a minutes; this means that by talking *nonstop* they could deliver, in fifty minutes, a text not twice as long as this chapter. But in fact, as a rule of thumb, competent documentary producers begin to worry when a commentary takes up more than about a quarter of a program's length. In other words, a commentary of between one thousand and fifteen hundred words is quite long enough—any more, and the film is liable to become a kind of illustrated radio

444

program. It will appear to viewers as dense, overstuffed. They will be repelled, not informed. The consequence of this may be quite sobering to an academician: that is, whatever the writer wishes to say ought to be said in the equivalent of a single-page *New Statesman* article or a *fifteen-minute* lecture. There is no way around this. If he tries to say more, his audiences will understand less. They will, in time, simply switch off—figuratively or literally.

Once this point is taken, it is easy to see how inappropriate much academic criticism is. Consider for a moment the persistent academic complaint that historical documentaries invariably omit significant details or even major themes of matters which they touch. To take a particular instance, Thames Television's "World at War" series' introductory program, which dealt with domestic events in Germany from 1933 to 1939, was reproached, both in public and in private, for not dealing with events in Germany from 1918 to 1933. It was also reproached for not dealing with international affairs from 1933 to 1939, for not dealing with British domestic affairs from 1933 to 1939, and even, by one earnest correspondent, for not having examined the United States government's 1938 contingency plans for the mobilization of American industrial production in the event of war breaking out in Europe. All this in a program lasting fifty minutes.

The historian who wonders tartly why we omitted Stanley Baldwin from our account of prewar Germany should pause to consider what he would have included, and left out, in his own fifteen-hundred-word comprehensive account of the Third Reich (even if he were not limited by the necessity to confine his exposition to subjects about which film was available). That is, by misunderstanding the nature of the activity, the academic may find himself applying to it assumptions and expectations which have no hope of being fulfilled. Small wonder that professional television producers, for their part, so often think of academic historians as behaving like small children, helpfully offering their services as referees or peacemakers to Mommy and Daddy because they have not quite grasped that their parents are not really *wrestling*.

What I should like to do here is, first, elaborate on what I think conscientious producers of historical documentaries do try to do; second, discuss how and why academic historians are liable to misunderstand both their intentions and their achievements, and what the consequences of their misunderstanding may be; and third, offer a suggestion about what academic historians and documentary producers in fact should be able to offer each other.

First, what is it that television producers try to do? The first thing the good ones learn is that what they make are television programs, that is to say, works which should follow the rules of *television*—which are not at all the same as those which govern the production of learned articles or, indeed, purely literary works of any sort. The second thing they learn is that their audience is a mass audience—never fewer than several hundreds of thousands of viewers, and sometimes more than twenty million. Now, these two points—that television

is television and not something else, and that television is a mass medium—
may seem self-evident, but their implications are often misunderstood even
by many who earn their living in television. It is hardly surprising that academics
may fail to appreciate them.

One characteristic of television as a communication medium is that it offers
its audience virtually no time for reflection. It is a sequential medium, so to
say, in which episode follows on episode, without respite. This clearly means
that the medium is ideally suited to telling stories and anecdotes, creating
atmosphere and mood, giving diffuse impressions. It does not lend itself easily
to the detailed analysis of complex events; it is difficult to use it to relate
coherently complicated narrative histories, and it is quite hopeless at portraying
abstract ideas.

The reason is simply because there is no stopping en route, no feedback
between audience and program maker, which means that the viewer's interest
in any program is no more than the curiosity any audience has in the performance
of a storyteller, who invites his listeners to attend to what he says and tries to
hold their attention by all manner of devices, but does not invite, or even
tolerate, interruptions. It is, of course, true that there is no opportunity for
feedback in literary works, either; but it is possible to stop midway, to reread,
to reflect at leisure. It is also true that much effort has gone into trying to
minimize or overcome television's defective feedback mechanisms, but none
of the attempts made by such admirable agencies as the Open University are
very relevant to the problems of program making for general audiences.

It is not the fact that the skills the historians prize most are precisely those
which television can use least that is surprising, so much as the idea that
anyone should ever have thought otherwise—although it does become less
puzzling as soon as one takes into account the intensely literary and verbal
background of so many people who commission, produce, and publicly evaluate
historical documentaries.

A second point about the uniqueness of television as a medium relates to
commentary writing, and I have already touched on it. Commentaries are
intimately related to the images which they accompany, point up, explain, call
attention to, make sense of. Because of their brevity, they cannot be in any
real sense exhaustive or comprehensive. They need not even be coherent, in
the sense that they need not unambiguously argue that one thing or another is
the case. They do not lay down the line: they evoke. The one thing they cannot
do with any hope of success is to use as their models such literary forms as
the learned article, the public lecture, or even the popular journalistic review.
They are not an independent literary form.

Moreover, since a great many significant events, processes, decisions, were
never, could never, be filmed, the gaps in commentary may be dictated not
by the writer's conscious decision—as would be the case if he or she were
writing a brief article for a part-work—but by what is or is not available on

film. An example again: relations between church and state were very important to the leaders of the Third Reich and, it goes without saying, to ordinary Germans too. But very little film was ever made which even showed National Socialist leaders and churchmen together, let alone doing anything significant. So considerations of church and state were virtually omitted from our films on Nazi Germany—and from our commentary.

A third point focuses on commentary as well, but really involves the totality of the program: how much should it try to say, or at least mention? How much dare it leave out?

Historical documentaries do not exist in a vacuum. Nearly forty years after regular broadcasting began in this country, and with three channels transmitting over a hundred hours of programs a week, it is highly unlikely that a subject will be done for the first or last time ever. Yet just this kind of awesome prospect seems to brood over the producer and academic critic alike as they approach major undertakings. No one would seriously reproach Hugh Trevor-Roper for not including in his book *The Last Days of Hitler* a comprehensive account of the organization of the NSBO or of the Reichswehr (though if he were thought to be particularly knowledgeable about those topics, his admirers might well be disappointed if he never turned his attention to them). Yet this kind of reproach is regularly directed against documentary series, and even single programs, and it is more than just a quarrel with the producer about the relative importance of various elements in a story. From the producer's point of view the fear is that *this* is the only chance there will ever be to do something— so everything possible must be done. It is this desperate last chance to catch the moving train attitude that accounts for the presence of a great deal of bewilderingly superficial elements, as for instance the brief mention of the Polish question in episode 25 of "The World at War"—not long enough to be informative, yet long enough to be controversial and, almost certainly, offensive to those with knowledge of the matter, and there simply because it seemed inconceivable that a twenty-six-part series should totally omit any mention of Poland once it had been conquered by the Germans in the first reel of the second program.

Turning now to the second general consideration, that of television as a *mass* medium, a number of other special characteristics are apparent. The very numbers involved in programming for mass audiences are daunting. Any competent university lecturer alters the style and the content of his presentations, depending on whether he is dealing with a class of 150 first-year undergraduates, 25 third-year specialists, or a postgraduate seminar. And he also shapes his manner and matter depending on whether his post is a permanent one, totally free of student pressures, or whether he is teaching in an institution where student assessment of his performance has a bearing on whether he continues in employment. Academics assume, and rightly, a high degree of professional motivation on the part of their students: they are articulate and sociable; they expect to work in a systematic and sustained fashion, guided, if not positively directed, by their instructor or supervisor; they are verbally relatively skilled; they are young.

The audience to which a television producer addresses himself is not like that at all. A television producer has no students. The proportion of viewers who watch television as a part of their work is statistically trivial; the rest watch it to relax, to entertain themselves, only sometimes consciously to inform themselves. They are under no obligation to watch; they are not a captive audience in the sense that a university class or seminar is. They are unlikely to be highly educated—most of them in fact have had no more schooling than is required by law. Some are young, some middle-aged, some are old-age pensioners. Many are not articulate, they are all individuals, and there are at least twenty-four million of them.

It is insulting and wrong to think of this mass audience as uniform, homogeneous, ignorant; but it is equally unrealistic to think that its members will be or ought to be interested in a program intended to entertain or instruct a highly literate, highly educated minority. A producer making a documentary for such an audience could legitimately make assumptions about its cultural furniture which would leave a popular audience utterly bewildered. (Producers know that it is as dangerous to overestimate a mass audience's knowledge as it is to underestimate its intelligence.) To take a homely illustration: any serious account of the early years of National Socialist Germany must deal with the Roehm purge. To understand this, it is obviously necessary to describe the internal organization of the SA, its relations with Hitler, and its relations with the army. This background is not difficult to acquire from a handful of appropriate scholarly works. But it is quite unrealistic to expect that a working-class school-leaver, now working on a building site, would have an intimate knowledge of the intricacies of National Socialist infighting in the years before Hitler's accession to power. I cannot pretend that any of the films in our "World at War" series made luminously clear what the *Sturmabteilung* represented to the life of Germans living in the Weimar Republic, still less the transformation it underwent when the government fell into the hands of the National Socialists, but I suspect that had we been better at our jobs, we could have made such things clearer—and, moreover, that it was our job to make such things clear. Now, admittedly, there is an element of running with the hare and hunting with the hounds in what I am saying: claiming on the one hand that it is beyond the capacity of mass television to explain intricate relations between events and institutions, and on the other hand reproaching myself and my colleagues for being unable to do it *better*. So perhaps it would be more accurate to say that television's capacity to portray abstract notions is strictly limited and depends on striking a series of very fine balances between simplicity and precision. Believing that, I have little patience for producers whose film may have failed to impress viewers because they assumed that their audiences would be so intimately familiar with the persons and events that they need no more than say "SA" or "SS," and their entire audience would instantly grasp who they were and what their significance was.

There is a vulgar way of putting this: it is that a television producer has one bite at the cherry of audience interest. If he fails, then he loses his viewers, and that is the end of the song. The academic has repeated chomps at the fruit. If his audience fails to follow him, that is its own hard luck. If it does not understand, *it* is deemed to have failed, not the "producer": professors do not get fired when attendances at their lectures start to fall off. So the obligation that a responsible television producer has is to make his thought comprehensible to an audience about which he can assume nothing, so far as its degree of specialized knowledge is concerned. What he can rely on—and it is a pity that more producers do not take advantage of the fact—is a high degree of shrewdness, worldliness, and common sense. To put it in a slightly different way, to make a program for a mass audience is to make a program for an audience whose ordinary mode of apprehension is not literary. People who watch a great deal of television do not as a rule read many books; viewing and reading are for them mutually exclusive, not complementary, activities.

That means that for most of the audience "The World at War" was not a complement to the memoirs of Albert Speer, the learned volumes of Captain Liddell Hart, or the speculations of Mr. A.J.P. Taylor; it was *all they had.* Many of my colleagues are inclined to dismiss or simply not understand those whose education does not equip them for the task, or the pleasure, of translating Alan Taylor's flights of fancy into sober assessments. They, I believe, fail utterly to understand what their own job should be. It is not to furnish pictorial counterparts to the knowledge that their audience has acquired through its reading; it is to tell, and show—in a word, to *do* history for—people who do not, as a rule, read very much.

I confess that this understanding came late for me. An American ex-serviceman in his fifties told me after a projection of one of our programs how, through it, he had come to understand how his own job as a stoker on an American troop transport in the South Pacific helped shorten the war and so helped save Dutch Jews from extermination. My initial harsh reaction was to think, aghast, that if he had bothered to *read* even one popular account of the war in the past thirty years he would not have needed the film to reveal that to him. But a moment's reflection showed how wrong I was to think that way. The point was precisely that here was a man who did *not* enjoy reading books for pleasure or instruction, but who was pleased to use his eyes and his ears instead. No book about the war had struck his fancy—our films did. And our films were not made for book lovers who wanted more, they were made for film lovers who had little else.

If I am right about this characterization, then a great deal about the soured relations between academics and producers becomes clearer. Academics often think that their talents are ignored or misused because they have such a lot of knowledge at their fingertips (or in their file cards) which television producers perversely refuse either to acknowledge or to make use of. An academic views a documentary and asks its producer, "Who was your historical adviser?" The answer "I was myself" he finds an insult and an outrage. Yet, I would argue, there is no reason why it should be felt as such. No one forces producers to deal with historical subjects. If they do choose to make films about the past, it is because they want to, and the idea that historical studies are in such a state of anarchy and confusion that none except a professional historian has the qualifications necessary to thread his way through conflicting accounts of, or make public judgments about, the past seems to me to be arrogant and wrong. And even it were true, it would not change matters at all. Because, as a matter of logic, a producer incapable of making sound judgments about historical events because of his own inherent defects must also be incompetent to judge between the claims of rival historical advisers—unless of course the competitors were to speak with one voice, in which case there would be no problem in the first place. And the producer who knows enough to decide which of two or more competing advisers he is to trust clearly knows enough to form his own judgments without the supervision of any advisers at all.

What he does is turn to the same sources academic historians turn to: standard historical works, conversations with knowledgeable friends, learned articles, his own researches. Where the professional academic goes wrong is to think that the point of the producer's labor is to produce a work that will win the esteem of fellow historians: if it does not break new ground, if it does not contain new insights, then it is not worth doing. But this is simply not the case. Because it is the popular history that it is, television history is unlikely to be innovative. Let me give examples, once again, from our own series on World War II. I cannot think of a single program which contained doctrines unfamiliar to any competent practicing historian, though a great deal of what individual writers said and producers endorsed was novel, and offensive as well, to large sections of the viewing public. I do not simply mean—though it is true—that numbers of young people were surprised to learn that the Soviet Union fought on the side of the Allies during the last four years of the war, or that Britons of all ages were surprised to learn that Japanese troops had to acclimatize themselves to fight in the Burmese jungles, just as British troops did. What must have been incredible, judging from the correspondence generated by the programs, were, among others:

1. Our remarks about the contribution the Luftwaffe made to its own defeat in the Battle of Britain. Popular belief in this country has always been that the RAF defeated the Luftwaffe against all hope and expectation—not that the Luftwaffe's attempt to secure air supremacy over southern

England was a desperate gamble, almost inevitably doomed to failure from the start.

2. Our judgment about the magnitude of the Soviet contribution to Allied victory. Few viewers knew that at least twenty million Russians died, or that the bulk of Germany's forces fought on the eastern, not the western, front. Still less did they know that the Soviet Union was probably capable of defeating the Germans single-handed.

3. The idea that Hitler was a social reformer, whose destruction of the political power of the Prussian aristocracy and the military establishment made possible the emergence of a stable parliamentary democracy in postwar West Germany.

Now, none of these notions is incontrovertible, but no one could claim that any would outrage the sensibilities of conscientious professionals. They are the commonplaces of routine contemporary historical exposition; it hardly takes any special expertise to be able to grasp them or their significance. The expertise, it seems to me, comes in making them understandable to the mass audience. And that is not a historian's expertise.

There is another, less obvious, point. Historians see one of their principal tasks as that of conveying information (those with literary skill, of course, delight in conveying information pleasurably). But producers of programs for mass audiences—and in this they do differ from producers for adult education programs or for schools—must be more concerned to convey their own *enthusiasms*. The form that their best efforts take is not "Here are some things you all ought to know about the Battle of Stalingrad" but rather "We are passionately concerned about the Battle of Stalingrad. If you will watch our program, we will try to share with you some of our passion and some of our concern." This is not a sentiment which, in my experience, informs the pages of the *English Historical Review*.

I have not said anything so far about the producer's use of historical evidence, a matter of evergreen concern to academics. This is because I think it is of only peripheral interest. If producers were making films for an audience of professional historians, they would work in quite different ways. But their films are not densely packed arguments, and they neither need nor use the kind of *apparatus criticus* obligatory in scholarly articles or even textbooks. If there is a literary analogy, it is not the doctoral dissertation but the reflective essay in which nothing is said recklessly but in which the flow of the text is not burdened with a scholarly apparatus either.

It ought to be self-evident that competent producers are scrupulous in their use of film. They do not try to pass off feature films as newsreels or an interview made in 1960 as a faithful representation of the interviewee's views in 1970, but that is not because either the film or the interview is "evidence."

"Evidence" is something used in arguing a case. If all films argued a case, then the elements incorporated into them could properly be called evidence. But many documentaries do not argue a case—they explore possibilities, or they present alternatives, or they tell true stories. To misuse film in such contexts is not to fudge the evidence; it is simply to use film and interview less than honestly.

So far, I have been muddling prescriptive accounts with descriptive accounts—talking as if all producers were good and all good producers behaved the way I said they did, and as if all historians were on another side of a sharp dividing line. But perhaps this is the wrong kind of distinction to make. Some producers do make films (indeed, whole series) that are based on literary models, deploy arguments as if they were trying to convince a skeptical donnish audience, and introduce indifferently selected and irrelevantly deployed visual material. And, equally, some academics do exhibit a lively awareness of the limitations and resources of the television documentary, are careful not to confuse genres, and are capable of communicating with large audiences. In other words, the distinction is not between dons and academics on the one hand and professional producers on the other, but between those who are sensitive to the points I have raised about the world of the past and those who are not.

A final point. That there is academic discontent with the state of historical documentary seems to me to be obvious, and I have tried to account for some of its causes and consequences. What seems to be unfortunate is one form in which academic discontent has crystallized. Dissatisfied with what they take to be the superficiality, triviality, and incompleteness of popular accounts, concerned historians have begun to produce their own works. They have done so under difficult conditions with the help of devoted collaborators and on very small budgets. Their enterprise, and their ingenuity, deserve praise, but I fear that they have mistaken a profound characteristic of the medium for a simple defect in execution on the part of existing practitioners. So their work, far from breaking new ground, has only reproduced the worst faults of the kind of documentaries it has sought to replace. Films need a high ratio of visual material to commentary, and a low ratio of information to noise. In other words, trying to say too much is a recipe for not being understood at all, whether the subject is the Potsdam conference or the Spanish civil war. But this should not be construed to be a claim that there is no place for historical documentaries made by academics for academic audiences. What it does mean is that very careful thought ought to be given to what those documentaries ought to be like. Academic filmmakers ought to think not twice but three times before embarking on expositions of diplomatic encounters, analysis of abstract concepts, or complex narrative histories. I hope I have shown why. What they might consider instead is the production of films about historical topics which do not have wide popular appeal and of which no nonpartisan accounts yet exist: the internment of aliens in the United Kingdom during World War II, for example, or the persistence of British working-class hostility to Winston Churchill.

But in any event, I think that the universities would never wish to become major centers of documentary film production. Their efforts would be more valuable if directed to making filmed records of persons or events which would otherwise go unrecorded and, above all, to doing the sorts of thing they do best, traditionally. Rather than despising and dismissing popular television for being what it is, still less trying to replace the mass television history of our day with their own mandarin versions, they should concentrate on doing their jobs as historians as well as they can, so that the history they write will be as good as it can be, so that the popular accounts which we provide will be as true as they can be.

Narration, Invention, and History

Jeffrey Youdelman

In recent years, a significant body of social and historical documentary films has been created by politically conscious filmmakers using oral history interview techniques. These films capture for the first time the voice of people who have shared in the making of working-class history and culture. A common characteristic of this genre of documentary is its avoidance of voice-over and other forms of narration associated with the older tradition of documentary filmmaking. Such unanimity of purpose among contemporary filmmakers indicates the emergence of an esthetic operating from within a defined political trend.

At a workshop on the historical documentary held during the 1979 U.S. Conference for an Alternative Cinema at Bard College, filmmakers discussed their reactions to the voice-over narrator when asked by a history teacher if some form of voice-over commentary might serve as a useful means of supplementing the viewpoints of those interviewed. The suggestion was generally rejected as the filmmakers present summoned up their impressions of narration in older documentaries. The old films had that "detached, authoritarian male voice," said one filmmaker. "Yes, like the voice of 'The March of Time,'" added another. A third cited the narrator in the cold war TV program "I Led Three Lives."

Progressive filmmakers have just reason to reject these particular models, but they neither exhaust the vast possibilities for narration today nor represent the sum total of the past. Materially limited by the relatively primitive state of recording technology, the old documentary films rarely showed people talking. Yet the "substituted" soundtrack voices were not all like "The March of Time." Many of the filmmakers assembled at Bard, particularly those under thirty, had seen or read little of the documentary art of the thirties and forties. When Leo Hurwitz's *Strange Victory* (1948) was screened later in the conference, the audience was mesmerized by a style of filmmaking most had not seen before: a film composed by the now rejected method of montage, full of varied sequences, mixing newsreel and acted episodes. The film is held together by a narrative voice that assumes many styles and personas and by an overall structure that the writer Warren Miller described as "so complex it would require diagrams to explain it"—a structure that "gives the film the density of a poem."

The documentary voices of the thirties and forties that sought to identify with people's struggles were often strong, haunting, and lyrical. A rich cross-fertilization existed between literature and the visual arts, with close collaborations between writers, filmmakers, and photographers. Drawing on these talents, but exercising centralized artistic control, classical documentary directors like Joris Ivens could fashion fully composed films from outlines and scenarios. Spoken narrations were part of an orchestrated totality. "In filmmaking," Ivens wrote, "the writing, the words, are part of an interplay with pictures, sound, music, brought together in an editing that changes the quality of every component."

The texts of many writer-photographer collaborations of the thirties and forties spoke in a documentary voice that was rarely dull or detached. The writer often aspired to a collective voice—something not heard anymore, something that might sound "corny." Richard Wright's blues-based text for *12 Million Black Voices* (1941), describing Afro-American migration, evokes the tone of soundtrack narrations of the period:

"Don't do this!" we cry.
"Nigger, shut your damn mouth," they say.
"Don't lynch us," we plead.
"You're not white," they say.
"Why don't somebody say something," we ask.
"We told you to shut your damn mouth."
We listen for somebody to say something, and we still travel, leaving the South. Our eyes are open, our ears listening for words to point the way.
From 1890 to 1920, more than two million of us left the land.

Something in the current sensibility prevents filmmakers from turning to poetic forms. The old documentaries experimented with such things as rhythmic synchronization between the words, music, and images. In one segment of Willard Van Dyke and Ralph Steiner's *The City* (1939), the speeded-up montage of city bustle is matched by the increased tempo of Aaron Copland's music and Lewis Mumford's commentary. In Basil Wright and Harry Watt's *Night Mail* (1936), W. H. Auden's verse narration draws its rhythm from the momentum of the train wheels.

Joris Ivens, who began in the cine-poem tradition, saw the documentary as the "poetic pull" of film. *New Earth* (1934) examines the effects of a land reclamation project in Ivens's native Holland. After finally completing the arduous reclamation, the workers learn that "the grain is not for food, but for speculation," that "there is too much grain and not enough work." Ivens chooses the form of a satirical ballad to close the film:

> I would like to be in a country where
> the wind from the sea ripples over the wheat.
> In this land of fertile promise they ask for
> workmen to throw the wheat into the sea.
> There is too much grain in the fields.
> Bread seems to be a gift of the devil.
> One bagful brings too small a price.
> Throw half the harvest into the water.
> Throw it in, my boy.
> What a winter it will be.

The irony was not lost on a French censor who forbade a showing in a working-class suburb of Paris, reasoning that "many poor people live in these districts. After seeing this film, they would get ideas and march on City Hall and ask for bread."

Not all artists exhibited Ivens's closeness to or identification with the working class. Much of the documentary impulse of the thirties and forties is pervaded by a political liberalism which, while breathing verve, interest, and compassion into the art, does operate from a distance. Other artists attempted to use the folksy and lyrical "we the people" voices popularized by poets like Stephen Vincent Benet and Carl Sandburg. They looked back on Walt Whitman as the archetypal "democratic" American poet—the documentarist who cataloged the country, its cities, rivers, and mountains, celebrating the common people building America. This is the voice echoed throughout the narration of Pare Lorentz's *The River* (1937) as he takes us down the Platte, the Skunk, the Salt, the Black, the Minnesota, to where poor people, ruined by the Depression, try to make do with poor land. For Lorentz, the solution to their poverty lies in the coming of the Tennessee Valley Authority alone and not in any form of collective action by the valley's people, who are only fleetingly depicted in the film.

The Whitmanesque lines represent not just a literary form but a view of America. A more radical version of "we the people" is articulated by those artists who attempted to blend Marxism and populism by portraying the Depression years as the triumph of monopoly and privilege over a prior form of people's democracy. Probably no film of this period more clearly embodies the strengths and weaknesses of this radical populist voice than *Native Land* (1941), made by Paul Strand, Leo Hurwitz, and the Frontier Films collective.

Native Land began as an attempt to dramatize the revelations of the 1937 LaFollette hearings on the use of Pinkerton operatives and "labor spies" to smash the growing movement for industrial unionism—a story detailed in Leo Huberman's book *Labor Spy Racket*. Frontier Films eventually broadened its concept to include the wide-ranged assault on the masses of people. One powerful, early sequence culminates with Arkansas sheriffs gunning down a black and a white sharecropper who have just left an organizing meeting. The narration for the film is delivered in the rich and beautifully booming voice of Paul Robeson. Despite these progressive, antiracist aspects, despite the virtuosity and power of so much of the film, there is something disingenuous about significant parts of the narration Robeson delivers, a narration couched in an indiscriminate "we." It is by no means a classless "we." It is "we the people," but an identity shorn of contradictions and historical differences.

There is something of a lie in an Afro-American announcing that "we came to Jamestown . . . in search of freedom" without mentioning who came as freemen and who as servants; that "we established a Bill of Rights" without mentioning that the rich white men who wrote in this universal language disenfranchised the propertyless, women, and slaves; or that "led by Lincoln we fought a Civil War to extend these rights to the whole people" without scrutinizing Lincoln's differences with the abolitionists over the centrality of the slavery issue or his hesitancy about issuing the Emancipation Proclamation.

When I saw *Native Land* at the Pacific Film Archive in 1970, almost all of the younger members of the audience laughed at much of the narration and at the political assumptions and ideas behind it. One could say we were a bunch of hippies showing no respect for those who preceded us in the struggle; who were we to laugh at Leo Hurwitz, Paul Strand, and Paul Robeson? But I must defend the critical kernel within that ridicule, for many of the people sitting in that audience, whose consciousness was so much determined by the summers of urban uprising in America and by the anti-imperialist upsurge throughout the world, could see the thematic flaws. They could see that, ultimately, *Native Land* misinterpreted the struggles of its own time. While it provided populist gloom and populist hope, it rests on a false premise.

The overall theme of *Native Land* is that the Bill of Rights, the cornerstone of people's democracy, was being taken away by the forces of reaction. There is little hint of the capitalist state and its development. Like Walt Whitman, the filmmakers saw Democracy as the name of the social system, rather than as a particular, and always changing, form of bourgeois rule. They provide no real analysis of the precise relationship between class and national (racial) oppression in this empire/nation. In fact, they never considered America as an empire, which it was even in the late thirties. It is in an empire that the very notion of "we the people" most needs to be scrutinized. The attempt to sanitize Marxism ultimately gutted its message. *Native Land* calls not for decisive revolutionary change, but for a return to some period when the Bill of Rights worked—a time that never existed in our history. By 1968, a political generation had come into being which, despite all its theoretical weaknesses, knew the bankruptcy of Communist party chairman Earl Browder's assertion that "communism is twentieth-century Americanism."

The earlier generation of filmmakers believed in commentary, intervention, and invention. They believed in taking responsibility for the statement the film was making. The *cinéma vérité* critique of this style of filmmaking faults the filmmakers for not capturing actuality. Weighed down by bulky, immobile equipment, scenes often had to be carefully set up and "staged." Moreover, they have been criticized for presenting preconceived ideas and committing the terrible sin of lecturing. ("My main feeling about film," Richard Leacock said in 1960, "is that film should not lecture, and it's a terrible temptation to lecture. You have all that dark room before you, there is no other place where the eyes of the audience can go, so they have to keep watching.")

In the mid-sixties, Ivens was often asked what he thought about *cinéma vérité* vis-à-vis the old-style documentaries, particularly whether the new mode and style ruled out written commentary. Ivens's response was measured. "Cinéma direct," he told a 1965 interviewer, "is both indispensable and insufficient." The new technology gave "material authenticity" to certain parts of the film, for "it gives us the chance to hear the people in the film speak for themselves, and adds another dimension of physical reality. Even if it is a foreign language, the voices bring the film's subject closer, and give more evidence to judge what sort of man or woman is speaking." Yet overall, direct cinema was "insufficient because only commentary can express the complete, responsible, personal action—the involvement of the author, director or commentator." Ivens concluded that "in *vérité* people talk too much and the director too little."

In the old documentaries, the author's recourse to invention sometimes took the form of reenactment. Initially rooted in technological limitations, reenactment also rested on principle. It didn't occur to the old documentarists that such activities on their part were "manipulative." In fact, reenactment often proceeded with great care, and in some cases filmmakers lived for many months with the people they were filming. They learned about their subjects and created episodes meant to capture the essence of the situations and personalities. Reenactment usually involved the difficult task of directing non-professional actors, but the belief in the legitimacy of reenactment also extended to fictionalizing and using trained professional actors. Dramatic episodes were often interwoven with newsreel and other material. The key segment of *Native Land*, for example, involves the activities of a company "snitch." As played by Howard Da Silva, this character is presented in a realistically complex manner. The old documentarists did not have to search for the perfect *vérité* situation and did not limit themselves to a single technique. Filmmakers across the ideological spectrum could concur with the liberal British documentarist

Paul Rotha in asserting that every known technical device could be used, because "to the documentary director, the appearance of things and people is only superficial. It is the meaning behind the thing and the significance underlying the person that occupy his attention."

George Stoney's *How the Myth Was Made* (1979) points up some of the differences between the old and new documentaries. The film was motivated, Stoney relates, by his observation, while teaching at NYU, "that most of my students—all children of the sixties and *cinéma vérité*—are so dominated by that genre of filmmaking that they find it hard to open their minds to any other approach." As a result, "they miss the power and poetry of the earlier films while they fret about the veracity of details." *How the Myth Was Made* chronicles Stoney's return to his father's birthplace—the Aran Islands—to study how Robert Flaherty "staged reality" in *Man of Aran* (1934).

Flaherty is a well-chosen subject, because he embodies the seemingly contradictory aspects of the problem. He was able to make clear, well-crafted films using real people because he believed beyond question that artists choose and mold material according to their viewpoints. Having a viewpoint needn't preclude further investigations into the particulars of reality, or refinement, or changes in viewpoint. Flaherty's point of view, his thematic purpose, was literally a backward one—one seeking preindustrial man battling to survive against the natural elements: Nanook in the North, and the fishermen and community of the Aran Islands. So he ultimately sought to impose a mythic reality on the world before his eyes. He had to manipulate his "real people" to get them to do things they wouldn't ordinarily do.

Interviewing Aran Islanders who played in the film, as well as film people who worked with Flaherty, Stoney reconstructs how Flaherty went about creating many of the film's famous scenes. In illustrating the methodology of the classical documentarists, Stoney does not ignore the problem of manipulation. He shows how Flaherty created the climactic fishing in the storm scene by persuading the men to go out in a storm they would never normally fish in, and to use fishing implements which their grandfathers had used but which they themselves had long ago abandoned. To create his backward-looking view, Flaherty subjected the fishermen to great risk.

The desire not to manipulate, coupled with the avoidance of the older forms of artistic invention (including montage), has created a host of esthetic problems for contemporary filmmakers. The most important and most dramatic moments do not always take place spontaneously when the camera is ready to roll. A friend, on location doing a documentary portrait of two fourteen-year-old girls, wrote, "We've gotten a lot of nice things on film so far—but not the conflicts. The frustrating thing is that the problems are *there*—and not hidden either. It's just that we don't have them on film. So as the weeks pass, we are beginning to get extremely nervous."

Recourse to invention, filmmakers fear, might upset the hard-won trust they have been given by their subjects. My friend prefaced the difficulty about getting things one wants on film by describing how well integrated into the community the filmmakers had become, overcoming the initial reaction of being seen as social workers. The strength of many contemporary political filmmakers lies precisely in their ability to integrate themselves into the lives of people, and both the promise and difficulties are similar to other forms of political work and expression. The filmmaker, like the organizer, approaches a new situation with prior suppositions, a stance, and a theoretical orientation. This needn't be a form of closed-mindedness or dogma, for theory should be a guide to understanding the complexities of reality. It is not "manipulation" to say something "more" than the interviewees are saying. Such a belief, however, requires some form of narration or other device for supplying a fuller point of view.

Filmmakers today admit to giving little preparatory attention to such possibilities. The closeness they feel toward their subjects informs the composing and editing process. In editing, they first look to the words in the interviews, hoping to find key phrases which will articulate the viewpoint they want or the one closest to it. The desire for any narration usually comes when they find that the assembled footage doesn't quite say enough, that "facts and figures" are needed or that "transition" is lacking.

In the interest of nonmanipulation, the decision is sometimes made to use no off-screen narration at all, to let the story speak for itself without making its potential themes explicit. *Taylor Chain* (1980), the Kartemquin Collective's depiction of a seven-week strike at a small Indiana factory, combines scenes of worker camaraderie on the strike line and at a clubhouse with a series of union meetings at which the rank and file, the local leadership, and the international representative are at odds over the issues, strategy, and tactics.

A carefully constructed narrative, *Taylor Chain* does not hide behind *vérité* theory, but its makers clearly don't want to manipulate anyone—not even the audience—by drawing conclusions. Unlike such films as *Harlan County, U.S.A.* and *The Wobblies*, which seek commercial distribution, *Taylor Chain* is a "discussion film" aimed primarily at union audiences. According to a catalog description (which Kartemquin may or may not have written), it is hoped that "both membership and leadership will see some of their own dilemmas and frustrations as the story unfolds" and that "there are no heroes or villains." The film pretends not to interpret reality but only to present it for analysis, risking all on the quality and consciousness of post-screening discussion groups.

An audience which includes politically progressive union activists would most likely be able to subject the incidents in the film to critical analysis. They might criticize the international representative when, at a key moment and faced with rank and file objections, he proclaims, "I don't care whether you vote the contract up or down, I get paid by the union." They may well notice the ways the international rep tries to contain the strike within known and "legal" limits, playing by the rules, getting outfoxed by management moves, and always being surprised by the outcome: "I've never known a company to drop insurance before," he says when they do just that. More important, they might be able to put the story in the context of larger issues. They might know enough about labor history, of how the industrial unions, once all "illegal," were formed and of their subsequent development, to be able to fruitfully discuss what people involved in the union can do to change things.

Yet an audience could just as well not see or know these things. People might simply react by thinking that the union is hopeless and that it's a waste of time to be involved. When I saw the film at a Labor Film Conference for union people, audience response ranged from confusion over the film's purpose to the disgust of one union rep, who said, "I'd never show this." Kartemquin's leave-interpretation-to-the-audience strategy is an interesting attempt at minimalism—a long way from the fully composed, inventive, and explicitly thematic documentaries of the past. It raises the possibility that the reaction against voice-over narration could result in an abnegation of the role of the political documentarist.

Films that include other materials beyond the interviews and simple storyline take a step toward achieving a more explicit point of view. Connie Field's *The Life and Times of Rosie the Riveter* (1980), for example, attains a certain level of historical and cultural commentary by ironically juxtaposing the remembrances of its multiple narrators—five women who worked in factories during World War II—with rose-colored visions of the period presented in "March of Time" pieces. Another recent film, Deborah Shaffer and Stewart Bird's *The Wobblies* (1979), is technically the most cinematic of the historical documentaries. Built around a core of oral history interviews, it employs a wide variety of other materials: paintings, archival photos and films, old union songs, and a chorus of fifteen voices reading from working-class and ruling-class documents ("I can hire one half of the working class to kill the other," boasts Jay Gould). Many aspects of the organizing done by the Industrial Workers of the World (IWW) are covered, and many of the segments and episodes hold together quite well. Yet the overall thematic view is not all that clear, and at moments where more precise political analysis seems needed the film is somewhat evasive.

In an illuminating interview with Dan Georgakas (*Cineaste*, Spring 1980), Shaffer and Bird touch on some of the links between political analysis and the use of narration. Georgakas suggests that the reaction among progressive filmmakers against the "voice of God" narration has gone so far that filmmakers resort to some very awkward devices to avoid using a narrator. Shaffer and Bird explain that they hadn't realized they might need a narrator until the advanced stages of editing. Ultimately they chose one of the oral history informants—Roger Baldwin, a somewhat tangential and nonrevolutionary ally of the Wobblies—to also serve as the main narrator of the film. The filmmakers also state that they were unable to present such issues as the impact of the Russian Revolution, the demise of the IWW, and the ideological differences between the Socialist party, the IWW, and the Communist party as fully as they would have liked because the people interviewed were either reluctant to talk or incapable of substantive analysis.

Could these constraints have been overcome? In a section of the film exploring the effects of the Russian Revolution on the split in the IWW, the filmmakers interview Tom Scrivener who, as a Wobblie lumberjack, was present in the camps where the issue of "political action" was debated. According to Scrivener, one side would say, "Hell, the damned Ruskies beat us to it and had their revolution. We better study and learn from that," while the anarcho-syndicalists complained that the Bolsheviks were "just another bunch of damn politicians." The film then cuts to the anti-Bolshevik Roger Baldwin—the targeted "narrator" of the film—for his commentary on the ensuing raids and criminal prosecution of the Wobblies. The impression left by the entire section is that practically the sole influence of the Russian Revolution was to bring down repression on the IWW via the "Red scare" and cause its demise.

Do we owe this viewpoint to Scrivener's reluctance to get further into the issue or his failure to make critical distinctions? The best argument against this supposition lies in the existence of a mimeographed book Scrivener has written on his sixty years in radical movements, in which he uses the same words to describe the opposing IWW factions but carries the story forward by pointing out that "the great works of Lenin were to come in a short time into general circulation, which would soon change the picture." The changed picture included Scrivener's own progress from the IWW to the communist-led Trade Union Unity League and eventually into the Communist party, joining such former IWW leaders as Big Bill Haywood and Elizabeth Gurley Flynn. Unlike many of the veterans appearing in recent historical documentaries, Scrivener today remains a Marxist-Leninist—one who eventually left the Communist party to build a new "nonrevisionist" Marxist-Leninist party.

Cutting out Scrivener's communist background is, in fact, typical of the methodology of many recent films. Ex–Communist party members, and occasionally present members, pop up in a great many films. Politically and historically knowledgeable members of the audience can spot them, but their identity is hidden from the general audience. Such is the case with *Union Maids* (1976), a film by Julia Reichert, James Klein, and Miles Mogulescu featuring three wonderfully vibrant and enthusiastic women, two white and one black, who were active in the organizing drives of the thirties and are still politically aware and active today, and who collectively tell their story with conviction and humor.

Although they do offer important descriptions of the activities and feeling of radical organizers in the union struggles of the thirties, nowhere does the film explicitly probe any of their individual political affiliations. Is it the unwillingness of the women to talk? Such an explanation seems to be contradicted by an oral history anthology, Staughton and Alice Lynd's *Rank and File*, which includes an interview with Stella Nowicki, one of the women in the film. In the book, she talks openly about her work in a Young Communist League/ Communist party unit, about writing articles on Marxism for the party's mass paper for the stockyard and packing-house workers in Chicago, and a little about the party's factions inside mass organizations where strategy for the organizing drives was discussed.

The exclusion of this sort of material from the film denies its audience a knowledge of the historical role played by communists in the labor movement. The film audience, including those already interested in socialism, is kept from knowing exactly what socialism meant to people like Stella, how they organized around it and explained it, and how they viewed the relationship between militant trade unionism and revolutionary socialism. Any such information would be helpful in understanding and evaluating that work and historical period. The Lynds, at least, are more honest by pointing out, when introducing their subjects, that "most were some kind of socialist, many belonging at some point in their lives to an organized radical group. . . . Most of the organizers who were active in the 1930s were connected to the Communist Party." They were also honest enough to remind their readers that the people interviewed were "not selected at random."

Socialism in many of these historical documentaries is, therefore, often utopian and rarely "scientific." The IWW and the Communist party are nostalgically viewed as associations of heroic men and women. The filmmakers seem to feel that, in these times, it's enough for people to know that a past tradition of struggle, of people fighting against capitalist oppression, exists. The homages to the warriors of the past are loving, and love is important to the revolutionary process, but the films are rarely critical in any analytical ways. There is little attempt to sort out political and ideological tendencies, to show what exactly we should learn from the past. One gets the feeling that filmmakers share an embarrassment about the more recent historical past, the sixties and early seventies. With few exceptions—like Barry Brown and Glenn Silber's *The War at Home* (1980) and Joanne Grant's *Fundi: The Story of Ella Baker* (1981)—that period is rarely examined. Filmmakers seem to think that the upsurge of the sixties and seventies was a failure and that most answers lie further in the past, in simply recapturing a sense of the militance, camaraderie, and "closeness" to the working class.

The importance of having a clear view of the past is, of course, to know how to interpret the present, act upon it, and thereby influence the future. If we fail to be discriminating about what we think happened in the past, we're likely to be equally imprecise about the present. If we can't discriminate among politically conscious veterans, it will be harder to make sense of the beliefs of contemporary rank and file community people. In his review of Richard Boardman's *Mission Hill and the Miracle of Boston* (1979)—a film about the effect of land development and housing master-plans on a particular community—historian David Paskin finds that "ironically the very genuineness of the film is part of the problem." Although the filmmakers have gotten close to the people—living in the community, being wary of manipulation, and being able to capture real moments on film—they fail to take a critical enough stance. The filmmakers fail to draw a distinction "between the historical description and analysis of working-class beliefs and the critical judgment one places on those beliefs." While *Mission Hill* "succeeds wonderfully as a description of ethnic working class life," Paskin maintains it is foggy "as a political statement meant as a practical guide to action in Mission Hill and other urban communities" because it fails "to unravel the political implications of the internal beliefs of the community." Oral history doesn't quite speak for itself.

Current filmmakers, most of whom were politically nurtured in the sixties and seventies, seem both close to their subjects and unwilling to become spokespeople themselves. They have made it a principle to distrust all "outside" points of view—including their own. At the Bard workshop on historical documentary, one of the makers of a well-known film explained, "At first, we studied the various aspects of the issues, developing our own viewpoint. But we abandoned that. We didn't want to preach." The decision to shun narration and commentary is ultimately an ideological one. "Preaching" is considered by many to be authoritarian by nature, elitist and paternalistic. The fear of "preaching" stems from a rejection of what many filmmakers call "vanguard politics," particularly the Leninist notion that the working class needs to have political knowledge brought to it from outside. This attitude among filmmakers distorts the dialectic between politically conscious artists and the masses of people. The hundreds of radical filmmakers, as well as the thousands of Marxist academics, have done important work documenting our political past and present, unearthing working-class culture, and showing the links between daily life and politics. They all were created, in a sense, by the popular uprisings of the preceding period. Marxists are in the academy, for example, because those uprisings smashed at its walls. Swept forward by this wave, activists and artists are left to continue their work. It is fitting that they first go back to the people—to find out what is happening in people's lives, to find out the historical roots, the traditions and culture, to hear and record the veterans and the young. After taking from the people, however, after recording and transcribing, conscious political artists owe something more. What they owe is some leadership.

World War II—
Soviet Style

Joshua Rubenstein

This past year, a unique series of documentary films on World War II appeared on television stations in twelve major American cities. Entitled "The Unknown War," the series is based almost entirely on footage assembled by Soviet armed-forces photographers on the eastern front, with a good deal of film captured from the Germans themselves. Much of the material has never been shown before in the United States. While many Americans remember the major battles of World War II that took place in France or in the Pacific or in North Africa, the battles between Soviet and German tanks and infantry on the eastern front remain vague in memory, their decisive character forgotten altogether. For this reason alone, "The Unknown War" would seem to be a worthwhile project.

On June 22, 1941, the Germans invaded the Soviet Union with the most massive military force ever assembled: over four million men, 3,500 tanks, 3,900 planes, and 50,000 pieces of artillery. The Red Army virtually collapsed. Within six months, about four million Soviet soldiers were captured and three million were killed. Most of the Ukraine, including Kiev, was occupied. Leningrad was besieged, and Moscow itself was threatened. In November, barely five months after the invasion, Soviet troops paraded through Red Square on the anniversary of the Bolshevik revolution and then marched to the front; the Germans were near the suburbs.

Parts of the Ukraine and Byelorussia were occupied for three years, during which time the Germans shot over one million Jews. Leningrad remained under siege for nine hundred days. Almost half of the city's population, well over a million people, perished, mostly from hunger. There were incidents of cannibalism.

The German advance was not halted until it reached Stalingrad, on the banks of the Volga. Artillery and aerial bombardment destroyed the city, but the Red Army defended it block by block. Opposing infantry occupied different floors of apartment houses. Still, the Germans did not cross the Volga. From there, beginning in 1943, the Red Army pushed the Germans west, liberating the Ukraine and Byelorussia, the Baltic states, and then driving through Eastern Europe until the Red flag itself was unfurled above a gutted Reichstag in Berlin.

The twenty episodes of "The Unknown War" portray and document this terrible conflict, in which the Russians lost at least twenty million people, over 1,700 towns and cities, and with them 32,000 factories and 70,000 villages. The series, narrated by Burt Lancaster and edited by Isaac Kleinerman (the film editor for "Victory at Sea"), makes use of some extraordinary footage—corpses being dragged on sleds to the cemetery in Leningrad, pictures taken by the Germans of Jews stripping and falling into the ravine at Babi Yar—to create an often devastating visual effect.

Unfortunately, this effect is achieved at the price of historical distortion and falsification. Although produced at the initiative of an American company called Air Time International, "The Unknown War" accepts the official Soviet interpretation of the events it portrays—in particular the idea that the struggle against the Germans was a common effort on the part of the Russian people and their government and that sole blame for the dimension of the Soviet losses is to be laid on the fascists. In line with this, the script avoids mentioning events which Soviet authorities prefer to ignore; and where it does cover issues of controversy, it invariably adopts a point of view that coincides with official Soviet historiography.

Thus, in the first episode of "The Unknown War," the situation in the Soviet Union immediately before the war is described in idyllic terms. Under Stalin's leadership, "factories were given priority over creature comforts," but "workers learned as they labored." We are informed that "in the 1930s the quality of life was improving in the Soviet Union," as images of factory workers, farm laborers, and bustling urban crowds flash across the screen. The episode goes on to relate how Stalin tried to gain time to prepare for war by signing a nonaggression pact with Germany in 1939, but Hitler surprised him anyway two years later. In describing the initial, disastrous Soviet setbacks, the script does recall that Stalin ignored intelligence reports and that the country was caught by surprise, totally unprepared for the German invasion. But there is no mention of the actual situation in the country or of the magnitude of Stalin's responsibility for the disaster.

The Soviet Union of the 1930s endured one of the great terrors in history. During the forced collectivization of agriculture—referred to offhandedly by the television script—a million Ukrainian peasants were allowed to starve to death, while other peasants, the so-called *kulaks* who had a bit more land and livestock than their neighbors, were executed. In a version of "The Unknown War" done in book form, Harrison Salisbury recalls Stalin's admission to Churchill that the crisis over collectivization was greater than the strain imposed by the German invasion. No such admission occurs in the television series.

During the Great Purge of 1936–37, when millions of party members and ordinary people were killed, Stalin destroyed virtually the entire high command of the Red Army, including all division and brigade commanders. He created a mood of profound insecurity in the armed forces and in industry. No one wanted to make a decision or take the initiative for any project, lest he be accused of "sabotage." The purge is not mentioned in "The Unknown War."

The Soviet-German treaties of 1939 also contributed to Russia's collapse. "The Unknown War" gives no hint of the secret memoranda that accompanied the two treaties or of Soviet complicity with the Nazis until Hitler's betrayal in June 1941. The film shows scenes of Ribbentrop and Molotov signing the nonaggression pact in August 1939, with Stalin hovering over their shoulders. But the archives must also contain scenes of the banquet at which Stalin offered a toast to the health of Himmler, and Ribbentrop responded with a toast to Beria. This morsel of history has been excluded.

Stalin's diplomacy was a gross and immoral miscalculation. By dividing Poland with Germany and incorporating the Baltic states, Stalin created a mutual border with Germany that had never before existed. He knew that the treaties would allow Hitler to invade Poland, starting a general European war. But he hoped to stay out of it, while England and especially France kept the Nazis busy. The French collapse in June 1940 doomed Stalin's plans.

Still, he tried to bribe Hitler. The Soviet Union agreed to exchange information with the Nazis about Polish resistance units. Stalin gave the Nazis a naval base near Murmansk, on Soviet territory, where German ships could refuel and be repaired. Soviet ships reported weather conditions to the Luftwaffe while the Nazis were bombarding England. Stalin also gave Germany the right to transport strategic raw materials from Japan over the Trans-Siberian railway. None of this is acknowledged in the series.

As Solzhenitsyn remarks in *The First Circle*, all his life Stalin trusted only one man—Hitler—and that one let him down. As a result of that trust, the German invasion of Russia succeeded brilliantly. Five and a half million Soviet troops were taken prisoner in the course of the war. The television series makes pious remarks about their plight while ignoring the fact that they were betrayed by their own government. In October 1941 when Molotov protested their treatment at the hands of the Germans, Hitler responded by reminding the world that the Soviet regime did not adhere to the Geneva Convention on prisoners of war. The Swedish Red Cross offered to serve as a mediator between the prisoners and the USSR, but by then Stalin no longer regarded them as Soviet citizens; instead, they were traitors. The consequence, well known to the world but apparently not to the producers of "The Unknown

War," was that only a million Soviet POWs survived the war. These were forcibly repatriated by the British and Americans. Most were shot outright by Stalin or shipped directly to Siberia; only a small fraction returned to their families. By ignoring their fate, "The Unknown War" betrays them once again, with silence.

The Soviet Union was the only country in the war whose own captured soldiers took up arms against it. Under Gen. Andrei Vlasov, tens of thousands of Soviet POWs offered to fight the Soviet regime. Vlasov himself had been a highly praised commander in the battle for Moscow, and later was captured near Leningrad. In the closing days of the war, the Vlasovites, as they were called, found themselves in Czechoslovakia. They tried to surrender to the Americans but were rebuffed. As the Czechs were then revolting against the Nazis in Prague, one of Vlasov's divisions came to their aid, capturing the airport before advancing into the city. For a time, the Vlasov banner flew beside the Czech flag over Prague's city hall.

In his book version of "The Unknown War," Harrison Salisbury describes Vlasov's contribution to the fighting, but the televised series, although dwelling on the liberation of Eastern Europe by the Red Army, dismisses the capture of Prague with a single misleading and untrue comment: "The Americans liberated Prague from the west and the Russians from the east." In fact, the American advance was halted at Pilsen, the agreed-upon demarcation line. Czech partisan forces, aided by Vlasov, took the city. Soviet troops were held back from Prague, as they had been outside Warsaw and Budapest, to allow the Germans time to exhaust independent partisan movements that might make trouble for the Soviets in the future.

In addition to these major distortions of the historical record, "The Unknown War" commits a number of subtle half-truths that coincide with a peculiarly Soviet approach to history. We see a young Andrei Gromyko when he was the Soviet ambassador to Washington (from late 1943 to 1946), but we do not see the man he succeeded, Maxim Litvinov, who served as ambassador at the height of the war. Litvinov had been the first Soviet foreign minister; he was sacked from that position before the Molotov-Ribbentrop pact. He was Jewish, and it would have been awkward for him to negotiate such a treaty. A case was prepared against him by the secret police, but the German invasion changed Stalin's mind. Only then was Litvinov sent to Washington. Now he has been consigned to the memory hole, with the help of "The Unknown War."

An important dimension of the war that passes unnoticed concerns several small ethnic minorities, totaling about a million people, that were uprooted by Stalin: the Crimean Tatars, the Chichen, Ingush, Kalmyk, and Meskhetian peoples. The Tatars were accused of betraying the Soviet motherland. On one day, May 18, 1944, about two hundred thousand defenseless women, children, and infirm people were deported on trains and closed trucks to Soviet Central Asia. (The able-bodied men were in the army; the others were in labor camps.)

As a result of the deportation and the intolerable conditions they encountered, over half the Tatars perished. In 1967, the Supreme Soviet cleared the Crimean Tatars of the charge of treason. Even so, they are not permitted to return to their ancestral homes. Stalin committed such acts of genocide against several ethnic minorities, in effect exploiting the wartime crisis to pursue cruel population transfers. No episode of "The Unknown War" mentions these historical events.

Other facts must be similarly too "delicate" to mention. Several of the generals who had been arrested during Stalin's purge of the army in the late 1930s were released and returned to positions of responsibility after the German invasion. The final episode shows one of them, General Rokossovsky, commanding the victory parade in Red Square. His arrest goes unacknowledged.

Another episode dwells on a little-known battle at Malaya Zemlya in the Caucasus. It turns out that Leonid Brezhnev was a political officer there. (The series never explains why political officers accompanied Red Army commanders on all fronts.) We are also treated to several minutes of Brezhnev, now old, weary, and dignified, surveying the landscape of battle from a motor boat. One wonders who convinced the scriptwriters that Malaya Zemlya was a significant battle.

In its episode on the war in Poland, the show tells how Goebbels first accused the Soviets of murdering over fourteen thousand Polish reserve officers at Katyn forest near Smolensk. Then we learn that an investigative committee of Soviet citizens, including an army pathologist and the writer Alexei Tolstoy, with U.S. Ambassador Averell Harriman's daughter as an observer, concluded that the massacre was a German atrocity. The script, however, fails to inform the unwary viewer that every responsible Western historian regards the Katyn massacre as a *Soviet* atrocity. (The authors of the script apparently did not think to read the memoirs of Nadezhda Mandelstam or of Olga Ivinskaya, Pasternak's companion, to examine this particular Tolstoy's credentials.)

Harrison Salisbury's book version of "The Unknown War" provides much information that does not appear in the televised series and would not appear in present-day Soviet accounts of the war. Air Time International, the producer of the series, controls part of the rights to Salisbury's book; the still photographs in the book are from the archive that supplied the televised series. A note inside the book refers to the TV series. So it seems fair to assume that the producers are aware of the differences between Salisbury's text and the television script. Presumably Salisbury also recognizes these differences. How, then, did he, the author of *900 Days*, a masterful account of the Leningrad blockade, come to be associated with a script that coincides with Soviet propaganda?

And why has the National Education Association recommended this program for high school students?

The producers say they retained absolute "creative" control of the project, although in the February 25, 1979, issue of *Izvestia*, the Soviets announced that Roman Karmen, a Soviet cinematographer, directed the series with American help. The producers also claim that the Soviets have themselves agreed to show it to their own people in exactly the form it was produced. Hardly surprising, since from a Soviet point of view there can be nothing objectionable in this account of the war. The series does emphasize the magnitude of the conflict and the genuine suffering of the people. Only the truth has been sacrificed.

The Sorrow and the Pity: France and Her Political Myths

James Roy MacBean

Every country has its political myths. In *Le chagrin et la pitié* (The Sorrow and the Pity), however, filmmakers Marcel Ophuls and André Harris have prepared a mild but surprisingly effective antidote to one of the most highly cherished political myths of Gaullist France—the myth of *la résistance*. To a young, postwar generation of Frenchmen nourished on the edifying storybook image of occupied France as a network of *maquisards* rallying unanimously to the famous Appeal from London of General DeGaulle, it may come as a surprise to learn from *Le chagrin et la pitié* that this was not exactly the way it all happened; that in actual fact very few people heard DeGaulle's broadcast; that DeGaulle himself had very little popular following at that time; that *collaboration* with the Nazis was far more characteristic of the French nation as a whole than *résistance*; and finally, that by far the greatest percentage of the active *résistants* came from the ranks of French Communist party.

This is hardly the image the Gaullist regimes in postwar France have tried to cultivate. Consequently, although *Le chagrin et la pitié* was coproduced by the state-owned French television (along with the state-owned West German and Swiss networks), the film has been denied a television screening in France. (It has been shown on West German and Swiss TV.) According to *Le monde*, the decision to keep the film off French TV screens was taken by none other than Jacques Chaban-Delmas, prime minister under Pompidou, who passed on his orders directly to the ORTF television administration.

Moreover, in spite of having obtained first prize at the 1970 Festival of French-speaking Films at Dinard, *Le chagrin et la pitié* had trouble making its way into the commercial cinema circuit in France. Initially, it was booked only into two small Paris theaters frequented almost exclusively by students.

471

And when left-wing newspapers began publicizing the fact that the government had stepped in to prevent the film's being shown on television, the conservative newspapers tried to pass off the film as just another wild-eyed manifestation of misguided militancy, a by-product of May 1968.

In fact, however, *Le chagrin et la pitié* is anything but a militant film. Rather, it is a low-keyed, even bland, "liberal" examination of the Nazi occupation and the French collaborationist regime of Maréchal Pétain. Letting the extensive interview material and documentary footage speak pretty much for itself, filmmakers Ophuls (incidentally, Marcel is the only son of Max Ophuls) and Harris seem to have scrupulously avoided any hint of political editorializing. And in this they have succeeded so well that, aside from the prominence given to Pierre Mendès-France's pointed observations and personal reminiscences, the film seems remarkably devoid of any political *parti pris*.

What is ultimately most remarkable, then, about *Le chagrin et la pitié* is simply that such a politically vacuous film should be capable of stirring up such big political waves. (I even heard expressions of high-level concern in England that the BBC's television screening of the film in the fall of 1971 was likely to be considered such a provocative act toward France that it might jeopardize Britain's hopes of gaining entry into the European Common Market.)

As for the problem of censorship in France, the most significant aspect of the Pompidou government's suppression of this film is simply the revelation that even after DeGaulle, *not even* a subdued, reflective film like *Le chagrin et la pitié* is allowed to be shown widely to the French people. (Incidentally, it joins a long list of films—including *La religieuse, Le gai savoir, The Battle of Algiers*, and *Les cadets de Saumur*, to name only a few—that have been kept off the television and movie screens of France, either by direct government intervention or through pressure exerted on the government and the commercial movie exhibitors by right-wing lobbyists and agitators.)

Subtitled "Chronicle of a French Town under the Occupation," *Le chagrin et la pitié* focuses primarily on the occupation of the medium-sized provincial city of Clermont-Ferrand in the mountainous heartland of the French Massif Centrale, a locale chosen both for its proximity to Vichy (the capital of occupied France under the regime of Pétain) and for its importance as a center of underground resistance.

The choice of Clermont-Ferrand, however, is not without serious repercussions. Many French commentators have pointed out that this region is not at all representative of France as a whole; that, in particular, Communist party membership has always been disproportionately small in this traditionally anticommunist region; and that, consequently, unlike most other parts of France where the resistance was organized and carried out largely by Communist party members, Clermont-Ferrand's resistance was organized by an aristocrat, Emmanuel D'Astier de la Vigerie, and contained a much smaller communist participation than was normally the case throughout France.

The fact that this discrepancy is acknowledged in the film, it is argued, does not in any way correct or excuse the distorted picture of the phenomenon of resistance that the choice of Clermont-Ferrand entails. Moreover, it is particularly inexcusable that, with the exception of a few brief remarks by Communist party chief Jacques Duclos, the communist role in the resistance is simply mentioned in passing. And on one of the few occasions when it is brought up, the communists are disparaged as *"peu recommendables"* by a former Clermont *résistant* who declares himself a *monarchist*.

If the film's perspective on the resistance is vague and fuzzy, its perspective on the phenomenon of collaboration is much sharper and clearer. And the portrait that emerges is especially rich, since the collaboration is presented from the points of view of both the occupiers and the occupied. Throughout the film considerable attention is given to the reminiscences of the German occupiers. In fact, *Le chagrin et la pitié* begins with the edifying discourse of one Helmuth Tausand, former commanding officer of the occupying German forces in Clermont-Ferrand, as he delivers an extemporaneous little speech to his family on the occasion of the wedding of one of his children. And although the complacent, rationalizing "clear conscience" of the "man who simply followed orders" is transparent—and his capacity for arrogant self-righteousness downright objectionable—nonetheless, the film reveals enough striking parallels in the attitudes of the French collaborators to suggest that the two sides of the collaboration were really only two sides of the same coin . . . and that *fascism was the common currency of both the Germans and the French.*

Undoubtedly the most remarkable moment in *Le chagrin et la pitié* is the revelation of one Christian de la Mazière, a suave, socially prominent aristocrat, who tells why in his early twenties he enlisted in the "Charlemagne" Division of the German *Waffen SS*—a special division made up of some seven thousand young Frenchmen who were so won over by their occupiers that they chose to join the German army and were sent to fight on the Russian front. Mazière explains that, as an aristocrat who came from a family of French military officers, he could not help but admire the iron discipline and machinelike efficiency of the German army—so different, he emphasizes, from the sloppy and poorly trained French army!

The sight of those "blond, handsome, upright, barechested conquerors," he admits, was awe-inspiring and irresistible. Moreover, for him and for many young men from the aristocratic milieu, the defeat of France seemed almost a "Judgment of God"—something the nation had deserved for turning away from the old aristocratic values. Acquiescing to God's will, Mazière explains, meant joining forces with the German conquerors, who were seen to be His terrestrial agents.

And, as Mazière acknowledges, his political notions had been formed by the tremendous right-wing fear of the growing socialist sentiments of the *Front Populaire* movement in France and the fear of a communist victory in the civil war in Spain. The combination of all these factors, he concludes, made him what he was. When asked by the filmmaker if the term *fascist* would be inappropriate, Mazière amiably replies, "No, not at all inappropriate. I was a fascist, a young fascist, in those days."

But if Mazière's case is the most remarkable expression of French fascism in the film, this is only because it is the most extreme and the most frankly acknowledged. However, there are also innumerable indications in *Le chagrin et la pitié* of a more pervasive, although more passive, brand of fascism which attracted the French bourgeoisie to the paternalistic leadership of Pétain and to the authoritarian principles of the Vichy government's prime minister, Pierre Laval. (Incidentally, one of the most pathetic moments in the film occurs when Laval's son-in-law, the Count of Chambrun, tries to restore the reputation of his father-in-law by telling the filmmakers how kind Laval was to a man from the local village who had been held in a German concentration camp. Chambrun summons the ex-prisoner, who is now working for him as a laborer, and puts him on exhibition for the cameras, manipulating the old fellow like a puppet on a string, asking him to "tell these gentlemen all the kind things Monsieur Laval did for you.")

If the tone of the interview material tends to be exculpatory, the tone of several short films of Vichy propaganda that are included in *Le chagrin et la pitié* is strident and aggressive. Particularly revealing are the glimpses of the program organized by Georges Lamirand, Pétain's minister of youth and a zealous advocate of the fullest collaboration with Nazi Germany. Footage of Lamirand's racist, demogogic speeches to youth groups and of the militaristic youth camps he set up for French children would look right at home in Leni Riefenstahl's Nazi panegyric, *Triumph of the Will*.

Also disconcerting is the evidence presented in *Le chagrin et la pitié* of the virulent anti-Semitism that came to the fore in France under the Vichy regime. So pervasive was this "unofficial" anti-Semitism that the names of all Jewish actors and technicians were systematically blacked out on the credits of French films shown during the occupation. And in Clermont-Ferrand, as elsewhere in France, announcements began appearing in newspapers to the effect that such and such a merchant—one Monsieur Klein, for example—although bearing a name that could be mistaken as Jewish, did hereby assure his clientele that he was both 100 percent Aryan and 100 percent French. Finally, we are reminded by a Jewish scholar that on one infamous day in 1942, the Paris police not only carried out the occupiers' orders to round up all Jews over sixteen years of age from the *Vel d'Hiv* Jewish quarter of Paris but, in an excess of zeal (which even caused some momentary embarrassment to the German command), the French *flics* also rounded up four thousand Jewish children, forcibly separated them from their parents, and persuaded the Germans to deport them all to Nazi concentration camps.

Still another indication of the anti-Semitism that was rampant in occupied France is provided in the interview with Pierre Mendès-France, which dominates the first half of the film as Mendès-France gives a marvelously nuanced account of the troubles he encountered as a prominent Jew under the Vichy regime. Already a political figure of some stature, Mendès-France was put on trial by the Vichy government for supposedly having been a deserter when he sailed from Marseilles to Morocco to join the fighting forces of Free France, a move taken by his entire regiment. Arrested immediately upon his return to France and put on trial under extremely prejudicial circumstances, Mendès-France opened his defense with a simple statement of defiance: "I am a Jew; I am a Freemason; I am not a deserter. Let the trial begin." Found guilty and sentenced to six years in prison, he served only a few months of the sentence before making his escape by climbing over a prison wall—an escape, he adds, which was delayed for what seemed like an eternity by the inopportune presence on the other side of the wall of an amorous soldier and his all-too-hesitant girlfriend.[1]

Interspersed with the interview material in the opening half of *Le chagrin et la pitié* is some remarkable Nazi documentary footage depicting the debacle of the French defenders of the famed Maginot Line. One Nazi film presents long tracking shots filmed from a car as it drives past mile after mile of abandoned French vehicles lining both sides of the road—eloquent testimony to the chaos and desperation of the French retreat from the onrushing invaders. Another short propaganda film presents Hitler visiting conquered Paris at five o'clock in the morning, stepping out of his escorted jeep to climb the steps of the Church of the Madeleine, visiting the Arc de Triomphe, and receiving the Nazi salute in the early morning gloom from a contingent of Paris police.

One particularly odious piece of Nazi propaganda is a short film that depicts the conquering German army as discovering to their amazement that the great French nation, "supposedly one of the finest flowers of European civilization," was defended by an incredible potpourri of Turks, Arabs, black Africans, and Orientals—"a ragtag bunch of savages in French army coats"—whose exotic physiognomies are exhibited before the camera like so many specimens of prehistoric stages in the development of the blond master race.

To further round out the picture of the sad situation in the early days following the German invasion of France, Ophuls and Harris include some interesting material with Anthony Eden, whose measured comments, delivered in more than passable French, set forth the point of view of the British government in those troubled times. Of particular interest is Eden's description of the dilemma confronting England when it was feared that France—which had not only ceased fighting but had also, against all previous agreements with her allies, signed an armistice with Germany—might deliver her naval fleet into the hands of the Nazis. Acting quickly to prevent any such eventuality, the British navy made a surprise attack on the fleet of its allies (who, it was subsequently reported, were at that moment sailing to place themselves at the disposal of the British), sinking many of the ships and effectively disabling the rest. All in all, a most inglorious chapter in the saga of the war, Eden acknowledges, but one that must be considered in light of the fact that France was the only country in occupied Europe whose "legal" government practiced a policy of collaboration with the Nazis.

In the second half of this four-and-a-half-hour film, the focus shifts from the big events and the actions of prominent individuals to the choice that confronted the ordinary man of the street in occupied France, particularly in the streets (and nearby fields) of Clermont-Ferrand. Many individuals, of course, preferred to turn their backs on the choice and pretend it wasn't there. One bicycle racer–turned–bar owner tells the interviewers that the Germans couldn't really have occupied Clermont-Ferrand or he would have seen them— and, he declares, "I never saw a single German!" Newspaper photos, however, show this bicycle racer proudly accepting a trophy from the commanding officer of the occupying German army.

For others the choice was one of which accommodation to make and which not to make. An elderly hotel owner in Clermont whose establishment was commandeered by the occupying forces tells us that he and his wife decided that they would consent to house and feed the German soldiers but would not allow their premises to be used for prostitution. And where this latter issue is concerned, a former occupying soldier (now a farmer in Bavaria) gives us a pathetic reminder of the choice imposed on countless young girls in occupied France.

Some people, of course, tried to have it both ways, bending whichever way the wind was blowing. Near the beginning of *Le chagrin et la pitié* footage from the early years of the occupation shows Maurice Chevalier singing songs to the glory of Maréchal Pétain; then toward the end of the film we see Chevalier after the liberation, explaining (for the benefit of his English-speaking friends) that there are lots of foolish rumors floating about; that, for example, it isn't true that he made a singing tour in Germany at the invitation of the Nazis; that, in fact, he only sang "one little song" for the French prisoners of war, "just to cheer up the boys a little."

Perhaps most illuminating of all is the reunion of former *résistants* in a small rural commune just outside of Clermont-Ferrand, where the men recount the various excuses that were offered, after the liberation, by those who hadn't taken part in the resistance. "Quite a few of them said they had heard talk about a group of *résistants* and had wanted to join up, but didn't know where to go or whom to ask. Well, believe me"—the speaker pauses, making a gesture for the benefit of the camera—"this group of men right here is about the least well-educated group of men in Clermont-Ferrand, and none of *us* had any trouble finding out where to go or whom to ask!"

Eloquently indicative of the quiet courage and dignity of the lowest classes of French society is the story recounted by two Auvergnat peasants, Alexis and Louis Grave. While working for the resistance, Louis was denounced to the occupiers by an anonymous letter and sent off to Buchenwald. When he returned after the war, he immediately set out to discover who had denounced him. After a brief, discreet search, he determined that it was a certain neighbor. But now that he knew who it was, Louis didn't take any revenge. As he puts it, "When one has been beyond the scope of all justice, what good would it do to take justice into one's own hands, or even to turn things over to the 'official' justice?"

That it was invariably the lowest class of society—the peasants and, particularly, the workers—who rallied wholeheartedly to the resistance, is also the testimony offered by one Dennis Rake, a British secret agent who operated clandestinely in France during the occupation. "The workers were magnificent," Rake recalls with gratitude. "They would do anything to help our operations. They gave us our *bleus* [the blue coveralls worn by French workers]; they housed us, fed us, hid us from the Germans and the French police. Without the French workers and their organized resistance, we couldn't have accomplished anything."

When asked about the French bourgeoisie, Rake can only reply, tactfully, that they were "more or less neutral." Then, not wanting this observation to sound too damning, he adds, "I suppose it's only those who have 'nothing' who can afford to act on their convictions."

However, one of the very questions which *Le chagrin et la pitié* raises, at least implicitly, is whether the bourgeoisie in occupied France had any convictions at all—and if so, which ones? For the bourgeois owner of a prosperous pharmacy in Clermont-Ferrand, for example, "the important thing was to keep the store running." He explains that he had a large family to feed and a large house to heat, and that he needed a steady income to keep everything going. To make sure the Germans didn't just take over his house or his store—as he says they often did with people they didn't like—he just "kept quiet and minded my own business."

And when asked if he found those years of occupation a period of unrelenting hardship, he replies that it wasn't all that bad, that there were some good moments, like the year the Germans allowed them to reopen the hunting season, which had been canceled the preceding year. "*Alors*, here in the Auvergne, *vous savez*, we have a passion for hunting. And I can tell you, the reopening of the hunting season was an enormous consolation to us!"

In general, one of the most striking features of *Le chagrin et la pitié* is the pervasiveness of this capacity of the bourgeoisie to carry on business as usual while turning their backs on what was happening all around them or simply dividing their lives into a number of different segments whose interrelatedness they manage not to see. This departmentalizing attitude is reflected in the self-righteousness of the former German commander at Clermont, Helmuth Tausand, who blusters indignantly about the disgraceful behavior of the French resistance fighters. One day, he recalls, some of his men were marching down a country road near Clermont-Ferrand. They passed a handful of peasants who were planting potatoes. Just as his men marched past them, the peasants threw down their shovels, picked up rifles that were hidden in their bundles, and shot down the German soldiers. "That's not guerrilla warfare," he insists; "that's just plain murder. Real partisans," he adds self-righteously, "should wear badges or armbands to identify themselves."

But, as *Le chagrin et la pitié* reveals again and again, this departmentalizing attitude was just as characteristic of the occupied French, particularly of the French bourgeoisie, as of the occupying Germans. And, as Marcel Ophuls expressed it in a statement to the newspaper *Combat*, "the terribly bourgeois attitude of believing [that] one can separate what is commonly called 'politics' from other human activities such as one's work, family life, love, etc., this attitude, which is so prevalent, constitutes the worst possible evasion from life, from the responsibilities of life, that one can imagine."

Ultimately, *Le chagrin et la pitié* is not just a film about the occupied France of World War II. Relying extensively on interviews filmed in 1969, it is also very much a film about France today and the kinds of attitudes the French have about their own recent history. And although this film collapses the past and the present in a way that might recall Alain Resnais's *Nuit et brouillard* (Night and Fog), the effect is very different. For where Resnais's film about concentration camps is poetic and personal, very clearly the stylized work of an *auteur, Le chagrin et la pitié* is so unstylized, so pedestrian, that it seems almost *authorless*. Or, rather, one gets the feeling that the French people themselves were the only real *auteurs* of the film.

Normally, of course, this window-on-the-world approach serves to reinforce the bourgeois myths which the ruling class seeks to pass off as reality. But what makes this film so threatening to the ruling class is precisely that through the same window-on-the-world approach characteristic of bourgeois films, *Le chagrin et la pitié* manages to puncture some of the bourgeoisie's most cherished myths.

And where Resnais's *Nuit et brouillard* can be "read"—and passed off— as one man's very personal appeal to our conscience, *Le chagrin et la pitié* reads as a *self-incriminating* revelation by the French people themselves! Moreover, Resnais's collapsing of past and present is carried out in a way that points to the future. The tone of *Nuit et brouillard* is prophetic. It is the oracular tone of the artist-priest. As in Greek tragedy, the message is chilling but the medium is so exhilarating that the effect is cathartic. (Once again, however, the medium is the ultimate message.)

In *Le chagrin et la pitié*, however, the collapsing of past and present does not point prophetically to some vague but ominous future that awaits us like the *fate* of a tragic hero. The *temps* (time/tense) of *Le chagrin et la pitié* is neither the *mythic future* nor even simply the *demythified past*, but rather the *political present* which is the *temps politique par excellence*—the *continuous present* which teaches us to *think ourselves historically*. And in this respect, *Le chagrin et la pitié* has the very considerable merit of reminding us just how pronounced the narrow-minded bourgeois departmentalizing attitude was— and still is—in France . . . and just how disastrous were—and still are—its consequences on the political life of the French nation.

Note

1. In another humorous anecdote, Mendès-France recounts that at the close of his trial, one naive young man wrote to the lawyer who defended him asking for a transcript of the trial "in order," so the letter stated, "that I might personally call this matter to the attention of Maréchal Pétain, who obviously must not be aware of your case, for he would certainly not allow this miscarriage of justice to occur." The naive young man, Mendès-France reveals, was none other than Valéry Giscard d'Estaing.

Ireland—Two Nations
John Pym

The oral tradition, with roots in Gaelic Ireland, remains a powerful influence on, and contributory factor to, the course of Irish history. And it is only half a cliché to note, for example, as do both series I consider here, that Cromwell is still vividly remembered in Ireland. Although the fruits of pre-Christian Gaelic culture—other than those that can still be photographed—are hardly mentioned by Robert Kee, architect of BBC-TV's (in association with the Irish network RTE) "Ireland: A Television History," the tenets of the oral tradition have, subconsciously perhaps, gone some way to mold his approach to the ordering of a survey of Irish history from the twelfth to the twentieth century.

Kee's is, above all, "spoken" history—his listeners, like the poet's, are gathered at the hearth; and, while a modern television audience has not the patience for the intellectually warming delights of an epic tale wrapped in a skein of conventions and internal rhythms, it does expect another, modern sort of wizardry: that the teller of the tale appears not only to hold in his head, but also actually to *know*—like Lord Kenneth Clark and Dr. J. Bronowski—what he is talking about. The act of listening to this kind of "prestige" storyteller, and of watching him as well, requires for it to work a certain sense of audience wonderment, an unconscious submission to the story and the authority of the teller.

This is not to suggest that Robert Kee, a man who, on television at least, combines modesty with both gravity and urbanity, sets out to present himself as a sage. He wears his scholarship lightly; his is a serious, disinterested, but nevertheless primarily a popular, history. His modest purpose, suggested in the first episode, is to "ungarble" history. But the significance of the "story" itself is illustrated by the fact that the strongest of Kee's twelve episodes (a thirteenth, not seen at the time of writing, wraps up the series with a consideration of reactions to it) are those with the most coherent and vigorous narrative lines.

One of "Ireland's" episodes is given over entirely to the Great Famine of the 1840s, another to the life of Charles Stewart Parnell, another to the Easter Rising of 1916. To have devoted one quarter of a survey of eight hundred years to two relatively short periods of time and to one individual (albeit and his times) is not, in this case, so much an indication of the intrinsic importance of the Famine, Parnell, and the Rising—important though all three were—but rather, paradoxically, an acknowledgment of the primacy of the "story" over the television picture.

Although there is, of course, no mid-nineteenth-century movie film of the eviction of the poor or of starving children reduced to eating grass and berries, the Famine was, in a more fundamental sense, tailored for television "history." It has at its center a general truth that can be put in a sentence. Throughout the Famine, large quantities of food, other than potatoes, were being produced in and exported from Ireland. One remembers this: for once, it seems, there are no *if*s and *but*s. While not disavowing his television series, which he claims gives a different and in some way broader picture than his substantial published history of Ireland, *The Green Flag* (1972), Kee has pointed out that the medium gives scant encouragement to "conceptual" thought.

To present the Famine on television does not require conceptual thought. The potato crop failed not once, or twice, but *three* times; those, the majority, who relied on it as their only food starved to death by the hundreds of thousands; aid from England was pitifully inadequate; mass emigration followed. Detail these events in almost any way, and you have compelling television. Contemporary illustrations are judiciously used to suggest the plight of the Irish peasantry; but television, even here, has an opportunity: a gnarled hand cuts open a blighted potato, and the finality of the repeated failure of the potato crop is encapsulated in a single image. Cecil Woodham-Smith, the historian of the Famine, has like Kee described the "drama" of the catastrophe (and gone further than Kee in encouraging conceptual thought among readers), but there is no way of reproducing in print the effect of the actual *look* of a rotten potato.

Kee's difficulty in the pre-twentieth-century episodes was how to communicate ideas as opposed to a chronology of events—in the case of the Famine, how to render incomprehensible England's attitude: how was it possible that almost nothing of any substance was done to alleviate the suffering of the poor people of Ireland? His solution was to have English government policy personified by the figure of Sir Charles Trevelyan, the man most directly responsible for authorizing relief. He is portrayed by an actor, forever scratching away with a quill, looking ever more worried, hidebound by economic theory, fearful of the consequences of "giving" food to the destitute. This is fair enough as far as it goes; but the problem really is, is he not just another actor, a means in a sense of making do? This is not narrated history: we are no longer in thrall to the omniscient teller. "Here is something you ought to know, and I need this device to explain it."

In the case of Parnell another actor is used, but here, since Parnell holds center stage and Kee's role is for once that of interlocutor, the effect is somewhat different. We are held in thrall, but by Parnell himself. Instead of having him scratching stagily away, he is discovered in a black-and-white *Punch* illustration rising (quite convincingly) in the House of Commons from among his fellow-MPs, or in long shot, a figure of mysterious unknowability, strolling with Mrs. O'Shea across an expanse of grassy parkland. For Kee, Parnell is as interesting as a human being as he is as a political creature. Here is an insight into his political perspective; not necessarily wrong, but dovetailed to the medium of television. Why Parnell was incapable of seeing that his liaison with Kitty, a liaison he apparently regarded as quite "natural," would lead eventually to his political ruin is a question that intrigues Kee. Reduced, unfairly, to its most basic level, this is television soap opera rather than television history. This said, however, the episode on Parnell is fascinating because, in a sense, history and soap opera fortuitously conjoin.

It is in the episode on the Easter Rising that Kee's method comes into its own. Not only has the master storyteller led us with effect down the major byways of Irish nationalism and sketched the background with suggestive ease (if he hasn't told us everything, at least he knows it), but at last we have the live witnesses and the film: the climax that wasn't a climax; the climax in effect but not in actuality. (There is a sense of muddling dénouement in the episodes following the Rising—the Terror, the civil war, the almost unheralded birth of the Republic. The mood of these latter years, and of Kee's attitude, is best summed up, perhaps, by a former Irish minister, Noel Browne, when he wryly expatiates on the frustrations of attempting to govern with the archbishop of Dublin forever looking over your shoulder.)

In dealing with the Rising, Kee's authority is preeminent. It is not just that, as in the case of the Famine, the story itself is tinged with tragic irony or that the story tells itself, but rather that it can be personalized with such force. It is history recalled. It is also, importantly, spoken history recalled in human terms: Dublin is a city which can still be walked in comfort. The Rising becomes retrospectively a Great Event, enclosed in a prophylactic. Unlike, say, the civil war ("We were shot like rabbits," a Republican irregular recalls with undisguised bitterness from exile in Canada), those who fought in the Easter Rising—even if they didn't, strictly speaking, "fight,"— recall the past with a fondness born of official esteem. It is, for them at least, television history as celebration. This is not, of course, true for all those who recall its aftermath. James Connolly's daughter, bearing an uncanny resemblance to her father, describes in harrowing detail, on Irish archive footage, her last meeting with her father; and Tom Clarke's widow offers similarly grief-stricken testimony.

Kee's expository method throughout the series relies heavily on the dramatic moment: television works this way, the synthetic approach to exposition being too concentrated for the half-viewer, however enthralled. Kee chooses his dramatic moments with care. He has a taste for heroism, and the figure who in a way is seen, in almost abstract terms, as the touchstone of the Rising, the Great Event, is Michael O'Rahilly, *the* O'Rahilly. A founder of the Volunteers, O'Rahilly was opposed to the Rising; he was, however, in Yeats's phrase, "the man who helped to wind the clock and so came to hear it strike." (This being a spoken history, Kee is not averse to repeating the telling phrase or famous declaration.)

The reason the O'Rahilly comes to the fore in this television history is perhaps for the very unhistorical reason that he has such a handsome bearing and because he drove to the Rising in a De Dion Bouton car (a photograph of the burnt-out shell of which is subsequently shown). The story of his departure in the car and his farewell to his family is told by his niece, a woman of striking authority and a cast of mind not, one imagines, dissimilar to Kee's. She tells another incident about the death of a British officer, Colonel Fane, who having led his men straight into an ambush in Northumerland Road nevertheless drew his sword and won the admiration of the men who shot him dead, the irony of which one senses Kee approves. This incident finds an echo in the account of another eyewitness who describes the O'Rahilly's own death, leading a charge—well in front—from the Post Office down Moore Street. He crossed himself before expiring: something admirable in all this muddle.

Those who describe the Rising almost without exception enjoy doing so. They are up to a point conspiring with their questioner, the unseen Kee, in embalming the event. What we ultimately feel about the Rising, however, having watched and listened to Kee's account, has largely to do with what we subjectively feel about the witnesses, and what we feel about them depends partly on the conviction with which they present themselves. How far do you trust a man with rather wild mutton-chop whiskers as opposed to a man with short, neatly combed hair? In the end, as in the case of the paradox of the Famine, Kee turns back to simplicities, good television; the fact that the Rising burnt a place in modern Irish history was because the English were foolhardy enough to execute its leaders. This being spoken history, there is a fixing quotation: "It was like watching a stream of blood coming from under a closed door."

Kee's is, it must be said, a gentlemanly view of history. As an old "Panorama" hand he could, one feels, have spoken to Parnell, interviewed him, man to man, firmly but with discretion. His own feelings are only occasionally revealed: there is a reverential ring to a phrase like "the great Southern Irish regiments" (with reference to Irishmen fighting beside the English in the First World War); a distinct chill toward a man like Pearse, obsessed with his "blood sacrifice"; an admiration for Michael Collins. Irish history for Kee, striding hither and yon in suit and windbreaker, having learned his lines (or so it seems), is above all manageable. However bungled the rising, or bloody the reprisal, reason and a certain amount of order can be made to prevail.

Thames TV's "The Troubles," a five-part series written by the documentarist Richard Broad but drawing on the work of a collaborative team, uses many of the techniques of "Ireland: A Television History." Horses are made to clop, rifle bolts to snap, and cars to putter in what was once silent film. Archive footage is repeated: Carson reviews his followers, royalty arrives in Ireland in holiday mood (though "Ireland," thanks to the RTE connection, has annexed the anniversary interviews with the survivors of the Rising). Several of the same witnesses are called upon.

"The Troubles," however, as its Irish title suggests, is not a "television history," tailored as the BBC/RTE series was for transmission to a middle-of-the-road audience in both Eire and the United Kingdom (at the time of writing, Kee's handsome book-of-the-series is top of the best-seller list in Britain). "The Troubles" is partisan television, not so much in the sense that it takes sides as that its purpose is to fuel debate. It focuses on Ulster, providing a context for what has occurred there since 1969. Irish history becomes a prelude to this period.

The series is unified by a commentary spoken by an unseen actress, Rosalie Crutchley, who adopts a tone of uniform flatness, as if to banish through nonhumaneness any sense of sides being taken. (Kee, on the other hand, establishes his disinterested bona fides by his very *look*.) Subjectively, however, one should note that the effect of such a gray style of narration is to suggest that desperation is the keynote of *anything* to do with Ulster. "The Troubles" is not one man's view of history, it is rather a certain sort of consensus: Glen Barr, a Protestant, and Michael Farrell, a Catholic, both—at least on television, it seems—reasonable men, give their opinions on episodes in contemporary history in separate, book-lined rooms. Historians, notably Dr. A.T.Q. Stewart, of Queen's University, Belfast, are called to describe and interpret from various viewpoints. Witnesses are filmed in a careful pattern of close-ups, one from the right, the next from the left, against an anonymous dark background (as if the clothes and the posture adopted—Sean MacBride is almost grotesquely hunched in Kee's interviews—are in danger of in some fashion editorializing).

"The Troubles" is not on the whole a history of emblematic dramatic moments. The Famine passes in the course of a fast, one-episode summary of pre-1916 Irish history: the third failure of the potato crop, from which Kee extracted so much dramatic moment, passes unremarked. The effect is of a single broad wash. The camera pans along rows of blighted potato plants, without showing the actual rotten potato. A helicopter circles ruined buildings: history from the air, at a distance. Kee, for all the turgidity of the early episodes when there was little actually to show, favors wandering on the ground, standing on Vinegar Hill, pointing out what the extremity of the Pale looks like today.

A phrase such as "the great Southern Irish regiments" would be anathema to "The Troubles" team. The testimony of "individuals" is to be approached with caution. A person of apparent charm, Michael O'Rahilly's niece, when filmed in three-quarter length and interviewed by Robert Kee, whose point of view after eight episodes we have come to know, is a changed if not entirely different person in "The Troubles," where she is seen in close-up with her comments edited into much briefer time slots. She is, of course, still a "witness" in "The Troubles," but from time to time her testimony is curiously impersonal. Why, for instance, have her impart in a cut-away the information of Connolly's execution? She is in this instance not an individual but simply someone who was in Dublin in 1916: she stands in for thousands of others who heard, and were enraged by, the news that Connolly, too ill to stand, was shot sitting in a chair. No need here for information on the De Dion Bouton.

Another telling example of how the two series use their witnesses is the case of Vinny Byrne, a one-time member of Michael Collins's Dublin squad which was responsible for, among other acts of "terrorism," the murder in November 1920 of fourteen British undercover agents. When interviewed by Kee, he recounts in detail his part in the killing of two of these men, without remorse and even managing to lighten the description with a wry aside on the maid who opened the door to him and guessed what work he was on. He himself shot the two men in cold blood. The same killings are described, more briefly, in "The Troubles"; this time, however, sensing that his questioners are not perhaps so "understanding" as Kee, an indefinable sense of what can only be described as furtiveness creeps into his voice. He is not quite so self-assured. The coloring changes.

Both "The Troubles" and "Ireland" go figuratively out on the street for the representative voice. Both describe twentieth-century atrocities: the latter has an old, soft-voiced woman recounting, with unemotional resignation, the summary execution of a tubercular boy who had offered himself instead of his father; the former has an outburst from a woman, whose anger is as overstated as the other's was muted, describing a mutilated corpse. "The Troubles" has a distinctly grizzled former member of the Black-and-Tans describe the meaning of the burnt cork that hung from the trigger shield of his rifle ("We burnt half Cork, and we'll burn your house too"); "Ireland's" Black-and-Tan witnesses are carefully restrained (this, after all, is for Irish transmission). "Ireland" does not underplay the role of the auxiliaries and the Black-and-Tans, but characteristic of its approach to them (and of Kee's "dramatic moments" approach generally) is the long and detailed logistical description of the IRA's most successful ambush at Kilmichael, County Cork, when a flying column commanded by Tom Barry killed all eighteen members of a British patrol.

The factual history of Ireland's partition in the twentieth century as given by the two series is not substantially different, though Kee concludes his survey earlier than the Thames team does. Kee, however, has the edge in drawing the *distanced* moral from the straightforward narrative: he contrasts the un-hampered landing of guns at Larne in April 1914 for the Ulster Volunteer Force, and the landing of guns at Howth a few months later for the Irish Volunteers, an act the army firmly tried to prevent with resultant bloodshed. "The bitterness this caused at the very moment when nationalists were being thwarted over the fulfillment of their aspirations which the government had promised them, made the two conflicting attitudes to the Ulster problem more irreconcilable still." Quite so.

Where Thames's closer focus pays off, however, is in its marshaling of facts: its proof, by diagrams, electoral rolls, and maps, of the reality of Ulster gerrymandering. At one point, it shows part of the most telling documentary made in the 1950s detailing exactly who was housed where in the council property in the town of Fintona, County Tyrone: discrimination against Roman Catholic family after named Roman Catholic family is proved beyond doubt. This sort of primary evidence is crucial ammunition in any debate on the state of the province before the civil rights movement of the late 1960s gained momentum. (Kee shows part of the same documentary but substitutes his own comments.)

When, in "Ireland: A Television History," [former Irish prime minister and later president Eamon] De Valera is first heard actually to speak (in a surprisingly reedy voice), one senses history turning into current affairs. Kee, having mapped the background, begins to wind down. "The Troubles" embraces the challenge: the moment when De Valera, rather than being fortuitously caught by the camera addressing a crowd, directly addresses his television constituency, or when the hunger striker pulls himself up in bed to answer the one question allowed before the television camera.

The strength of the last two episodes of "The Troubles," where the "wit-nesses" are for the most part talking directly to the (archive) television camera, is in the peculiar, jolting effect of seeing yesterday's news as particularly bloody "current affairs." Running through the chronology of events in Ulster since 1969 (with the studious exclusion of the unfiltered "terrorist" perspective, Protestant or Roman Catholic) is, for once, to be forced into recognizing the reality of an ignored, low-intensity war. The picture is one of absolute gloom: the ungarbled past appears to offer no cause for future comfort.

We return, however, again to the difficulty of rendering ideas—or states of mind—on television. What people outside Ireland do not understand, Dr. Stewart explains, is that there is a set way to conduct a riot, there is a correct way, passed on, to burn a bus. This is real oral history as opposed to an evening in front of the television set. It is possible, as "The Troubles" does, to show a fireman shoveling up the remains of a victim of a Provisional IRA bomb, but it is another question altogether—even were it permitted—to lay open the thoughts of the bomber, the reason for the bomb having been planted, or to explain why the man who shot two undercover agents in cold blood in November 1920 undoubtedly feels as little remorse as his present-day counterparts. Television can show an incensed Brian Faulkner, having been thwarted in the Power-Sharing Assembly by Dr. Paisley, furiously loquacious, but what he *says* does not get to the heart of the matter. The past, on television, can be marshaled with some success, can be made manageable; but the present remains, for all its vividness, a largely unknown country.

The Good Fight

Pat Aufderheide

The 16mm camera and portable video equipment were part of the standard baggage of late-sixties radicals in the United States. Film, as a means to spur and accompany social change, often served as oral history, especially of blacks, women, and workers in civil rights, union, and political movements. The early results, including *Union Maids, With Babies and Banners, Children of Labor*, and *The Wobblies*, have become staples of the documentary circuit, and the second wave is now cresting, with the Oscar-nominated *Seeing Red* perhaps the best known.

The feature documentary *The Good Fight*, an oral history of Americans who fought in the Spanish civil war (more than three thousand American men and women fought on the Loyalist side), is a film that marks a high point in a particular style of documentary—the oral history narrative—and in a particular kind of history-from-the-left. Solidly credible throughout its ninety-eight minutes, and provocative long after viewing, it also has emotional moments that evoke laughter and tears.

The film's professional quality—this is an independent documentary to which the term "production values" can seriously be applied, despite its shoestring budget—has much to do both with the seasoning of the filmmakers and with their persistence. Codirectors Mary Dore and Noel Buckner were both directors of *Children of Labor* and have worked for public television. The third director, Sam Sills, a veteran of the 1960s independent film movement, worked on the documentary *Fundi*, about black activist Ella Baker. The three worked on *The Good Fight* from 1977 to 1983, with piecemeal funding to float the project.

The result is a remarkably sophisticated version of the now-familiar oral history film, superimposing on archival footage a trustworthy-sounding narrator (Studs Terkel in an anonymous third-person style) and interspersing the recollections of people who lived that history.

The legend of the Lincoln Battalion, part of an international outpouring of some forty-five thousand volunteers from all over the world (including escapees from fascist Germany and Italy) in the 15th International Brigade, is, like the history of the Wobblies and the early history of the CIO, one of the left's favorite heroic episodes. But it remains an unfamiliar story to most Americans. The left has never managed to maintain an institutional presence in American politics, nor has it maintained a consistent voice in American popular culture. Thus, its contributions to the American historical drama have become isolated in our ahistorically minded culture's past.

If history of and from the left has been shoved off the wide screens and best-seller racks, it is partly the left's own doing. Old leftists, often speaking out of and to small sectarian constituencies, told for-members-only stories or waged battles with competing ideologies by proxy. New leftists, rediscovering the excitement of politics, tended to selectively search the past for inspiration, celebrating the romance of dissidence rather than trying to establish that dissidence within a larger context. For instance, *The Wobblies* places the anarchist Industrial Workers of the World at the center of the epoch's political history, although the Wobblies' accomplishments were minor, if highly visible, next to the AFL's organizing and the political activities of the Socialist party. In both *The Wobblies* and *Anarchism in America?*, interviews with aged anarchists testify more to an enduring spirit of resistance than to the logic and consequences of any kind of political program.

It is hardly surprising, however, that enterprising new leftists who took up social-issue filmmaking in the late 1960s were drawn more to the romance of history than to history itself. Not only were they in rebellion against their immediate predecessors on the left, but they had little opportunity to learn much leftist history from standard sources. They certainly didn't get it from the popular media.

The achievement of *The Good Fight*, then, is particularly notable, given the blind spot mainstream history has for the Lincoln Battalion. Dore charges that the episode has been virtually "obliterated"; the monograph of historian Robert Rosenstone, who cowrote narration on this film, is an exception.

At the time, the battalion and the entire war itself were media blind spots. Cameras were there to capture the reality—and didn't. When a Republican, democratically elected Spanish government was overthrown in 1936 by a right-wing military backed by burgeoning fascist powers in Germany and Italy, European and American governments quietly looked the other way, participating in an embargo of military and economic aid to Republican Spain. Among the first to tell which way the wind was blowing were news agencies. British newsreels of the time, for instance, were strongly biased against the Republican cause, as is abundantly documented in Anthony Aldgate's monograph *Cinema and History: British Newsreels and the Spanish Civil War*. In the United States, when leftist film groups decided to put together agitprop films and couldn't find any news footage that wasn't profascist, they scraped together funds to send their own film teams over. While films like Joris Ivens's *The Spanish Earth* and Frontier Films' *Heart of Spain* struggled unsuccessfully for booking in theaters, Hollywood staged tearjerkers and morality plays in a mythical Spain. The result was typified by *For Whom the Bell Tolls*, which James Agee reviewed in disgust: "When f–sc–sts are actually mentioned, the one time they are, the context makes it clear that they are just Italians who, in company with German Nazis and those dirty Russian Communists, are bullyragging each other and poor little Spain, which wants only peace and quiet." This after a mass protest in the United States against the embargo, which had some media impact—a poll showed 75 percent of the American people in favor of lifting the embargo by the late 1930s.

The issue tore apart the intellectual community, and precipitated hot political battles in moviemaking circles (covered in Larry Ceplair and Steven Englund's superb *The Inquisition in Hollywood: Politics in the Film Community 1930–1960*). And yet Hollywood, ever resistant to politics, managed to produce six features about the Spanish civil war, none of which so much as mentioned the existence of the Lincoln Battalion or even addressed American "neutrality." (As was clear to the policymakers, neutrality under the circumstances meant helping the fascists.) The film that came closest to addressing these matters was *Blockade*, written by leftist John Howard Lawson—but then only in snippets. Henry Fonda makes a passionate speech asking, "Where's the conscience of the world?"—a righteous moral question, but not displaying much political insight.

If the populist-but-not-political strain in American pop culture militated then against making the Spanish civil war part of every schoolboy's knowledge, McCarthyism and the 1950s made that ignorance a certainty, because much of the mobilization of popular opinion about the war in this country was organized by the Communist party. At the time—it was the Depression—you didn't need to be a Russia-lover to notice that times were hard for workers and had to change. A million people passed through the party, many staying only long enough to join a few unemployed-worker demonstrations, others working on such projects as organizing the Lincoln Brigade. The question of Communist party involvement raised a lot of dust then, prompting author Archibald MacLeish to write, "the man who refuses to defend his convictions for fear that he may defend them in the wrong company, has no convictions." They were idealistic, passionate, urgent times, and it was unavoidable that the Communist party would play a role—a role that today is difficult to assess.

The challenge for any historian—and especially a historian working in the emotion-soaked medium of film—is to recapture the love and pain and above all the contingency of "then," while avoiding a triple threat: the mawkish sentimentality that gives a mirror image of Hollywood, the mindless cheerleading that is a counterpart of red-baiting, and the tedium that makes "our history" just as ploddingly earnest as anything dished up in civics class. The job is not only to recover good material, but to discover a new way for us to see it.

This film takes us partway there. It impressively balances the emotion and drama of well-told tales with a critical analysis of those tales' context. And if it doesn't give us a new way of seeing, it does a far better job working with traditional styles than many recent films have—indeed, than much of what is turned out as narrative history for public television consumption on less-hot topics.

Like *Seeing Red*, the film draws its great strength from its eleven interviews with old leftists, who are as good as commercials for the good life through leftism. As one woman says, "I've done my part, but I'll never be old." Just as he did in *Seeing Red*, longshoreman Bill Bailey steals the show every time he gets on camera, with his gruff frank tones and his vivid, earthy stories. True, maybe the filmmakers just got the best and the brightest, and they did have 125 taped interviews to choose from by the time they were done researching. But if out of 125, say, accountants, you could find eleven this interesting, it would be a hell of a recommendation for a career in accounting.

Everyone will have personal favorites among the eleven, but no one will leave without a burning image of young Evelyn Hutchins. Her old photos show a blonde, angular-featured woman with an elegant way of wearing khaki, standing next to the ambulance she had to stare down a local brigade board to be allowed to drive. (The machinery was regarded as too complicated for a woman.) "Women have always worked hard. Don't forget that," she says today with the same kind of asperity that must have shamed the board into shelving their objections.

Everyone will have favorite stories too, many of them classic what-I-did-in-the-war tales, and some offering a rare angle. For instance, several volunteers recount how they told—or didn't tell—their mothers they were going off to someone else's war. (Too few returned; the brigade had about a 70 percent mortality rate.) One surefire favorite story has to be the response of wounded soldiers to a hospital visit by pompous, exhortatory dignitaries. One veteran recalls that one day, after a particularly long-winded call to further heroism by then American Communist party president Earl Browder, the men burst into song. "We're a bunch of bastards," they sang to entertain their guests, "and we'd rather fuck than fight for liberty!" When Browder misinterpreted their pique as low morale and threatened to order them all home, they cheered him on. The man could not take a joke.

The film doesn't take these characters at their face value, nor does it settle for the indisputable color of the well-told war story. Both narration and interviews search behind the anecdotes. We find out why they went, and why they stayed in conditions where they sometimes fought without weapons, where they bathed every several months (Bailey remembers a camp song about lice that chorused, "I retreat but they advance . . ."), and where in a single battle two-thirds of the participants might die.

Many were moved by simple injustice, or as Ed Balchowsky puts it, "I didn't need politics to see that people were being oppressed in Spain." Some were terrified by the rolling advance of fascism and foresaw a global struggle if Spain fell. Some believed the party's workers-of-the-world-unite logic. As Bailey says, "That was your brother over there in Addis Ababa." Evelyn Hutchins remembers that Republican Spain was a ray of hope in a season of ugly news, it was a place where children were going to school free and women were voting. Some stayed because the international brotherhood line turned out to be true. "There's something very emotional, powerful, when you find a way to connect with people," says a nurse. "It's a reason for living." The two blacks interviewed say that in Spain people treated them with dignity, as individuals. Some stayed to prove themselves—Americans had a soft image in the brigade. But all of them were in "first love," doing what they knew was right.

So not the least interesting part of the film is their talk about retreat and then defeat. "It makes you ask that question, is it possible to win the good fight?" one says bleakly. Yet they do weather these and other horrors, and by the end of the movie two veterans are seen heading off on the spur of the moment to picket Nazis in Skokie.

Still, these are not just spunky old folks who used to be idealistic young folks. These are people who had and have respect as well as criticism for the organization that made their part in the Spanish civil war possible. And in both narration and interview the film reveals some of the foibles and weaknesses of the party—the male chauvinism Hutchins experienced, the blowhard rhetoric, the irritating decision to appoint "political commissars" to keep order among the troops. And it also shows why both the Communist party and the Soviet Union were widely respected in Spain. For one thing, only the USSR was delivering any concrete aid to the embattled Republicans, and that meant that Americans got rifles. It also made them think that the USSR had values they shared.

Like all the recent history films, *The Good Fight* skirts the devastating long-range effects on the American left of the Communist party's close liaison with Russia, a liaison that not only left many Americans feeling that communism was (despite the slogans) un-American but also trapped the American Communist party in political strategies and tactics that had nothing to do with American political reality. But this avoidance is far more acceptable in a film like *The Good Fight* than in *Seeing Red*.

Seeing Red is an insider's history of Communist party activists from the era of the party's heyday in America, the Depression. The new-left filmmakers Julia Reichert and Jim Klein set out to find what inspired activists of then to "stay political all their lives," and their film reveals with captivating charm the charisma and energy of their sources. But, hewing closely as the film does to its sources' perspective, it limits itself to the party members' and former members' own self-criticism: the context of *Seeing Red* is the context of its spokespersons. Not only does a group biography never become history, but the deeper question of how most Americans to this day regard the Communists' experiences (not their characters) as illegitimate cannot be addressed.

Seen from the new-left perspective, the old Communists become zestful senior citizens with colorful pasts—which helps explain *Seeing Red*'s generally positive reception in the American mainstream. A public that prides itself on tolerance can tolerate the notion that old ex-Communists can be people too (although even this is an achievement, given the devil-imagery surrounding communism in twentieth-century American media). But the party members only become important on the historical landscape if their programs and policies had effects. *Seeing Red* lets them judge themselves in that regard. The film also encourages the ahistorical attitude of the viewers, most of whom had no notion that the Communist party played a historical role. The question boils down to whether or not the party members are inspiring, vital people. And they are.

The Good Fight tackles a different problem; it analyzes not the life histories of communists, but a historical episode. It evokes the many reasons why and how people found themselves in the Lincoln Battalion, which wasn't limited to communists. The comments of different individuals provide perspective, and the narration guides viewers as well. The period is evoked so well that viewers can not only imagine their own reactions to events but also imagine the different reactions of others around them. In the story told in *The Good Fight*, the long-range role of the Communist party in the United States stands to one side of the Lincoln Battalion's mobilization and demobilization.

The Good Fight is an unpretentious, humane rendition of a contentious historical episode. Studiously avoiding even minimal play with film form, it is not far in concept from a lecture-slide show. The simple format has the great advantage of letting us sit on the filmmakers' shoulders while they get the raw data for their essay-narrative, and we are in on the best parts. This cool, reasoned approach marks among other things the difficulties of making popular history on political issues in America today. The tone and style establish the filmmakers' credibility and allow for the (unfortunately necessary) assumption that viewers may be entirely ignorant of the era. Documentaries made at the time were, ironically, more formally daring, using the medium itself to expose ways of thinking. Today, documentaries on any other subject have more license to experiment—only that dread moment when the Red Menace was still a public presence is still taboo. For instance, reenactment—an ever more fashionable option that the Cubans, among others, are playing with—was recently used in *When the Mountains Tremble*, a film about political turmoil in Guatemala. And the joys and ironies of fast-cut, narration-free montage made the antinuclear *Atomic Cafe* into a mainstream must-see.

With *The Good Fight*, the oral history film on subjects purged from orthodox history books has come of age. The film may originate on the left, but it is not partisan. It is history with the people left in it, rooted in, not towering over, their landscape. If others follow its example, we may yet see the kind of formal experimentation that happens when the limits of *cinéma vérité* and voice-over narration have been reached.

"Vietnam: A Television History": Media Research and Some Comments

Lawrence W. Lichty

I began studying the coverage of the war in 1967 and for that purpose visited Vietnam as an observer in the summer of 1968. At that time, I had been teaching broadcasting history, documentary film, media effects, and related courses for three years as a professor at the University of Wisconsin. Vietnam became one of my major research interests. With a number of colleagues I did analyses of the network evening news coverage of Vietnam, television news anchor reporting of the war, TV documentary and public affairs programs, a number of independent, government, military, USIA, and foreign films, and films about the use of television by Presidents Johnson and Nixon.

In early 1977, filmmaker Richard Ellison and journalist Stanley Karnow first discussed what was to become "The Vietnam Project." Ellison had been a producer at CBS and worked for PBS and Time-Life Films. After talking with a friend at NBC News he began planning a TV documentary series making use of the millions of feet of network newsfilms from Vietnam. At about the same time, Lawrence Grossman, then president of the Public Broadcasting Service (PBS) asked Stanley Karnow to write an outline for a series on the Indochina wars. A correspondent in France and Asia for *Time* and the *Washington Post*, among other publications, Karnow had reported on Vietnam for nearly thirty years. Then in May 1977, executives of public station WGBH-TV Boston also proposed a Vietnam series to be produced there. The three projects were joined.

When I first met Dick Ellison in the spring of 1978 I was on leave from the University of Wisconsin as a fellow at the Woodrow Wilson International Center for Scholars, where I was continuing my study of the TV coverage of the Vietnam war. We were convinced, as Dick later wrote, "that the United

States stood in need of a full-scale television history that would deal with Vietnamese culture and traditions, the century of French colonial domination of Indochina, the eight-year war between the French and the Vietminh, and of course with the American involvement that has no official name, which we have come to call the Vietnam war."[1]

Ellison, Karnow, and WGBH (with National Endowment for the Humanities and PBS support) sought funding for the project in all the usual ways. We were most often told we were too early—the wounds had not healed—it could not be done. Or we were refused because it was too late—it was over and should be forgotten. Six years later, with the Vietnam Memorial one of the most popular tourist attractions in Washington, the growth of a new "patriotism" in the United States, and increased recognition of and understanding for the Vietnam era vets, it now seems hard to believe that few were interested in a major historical series about Vietnam. Dick Ellison has often said that the hardest part of producing the series was raising the money. Indeed, because of production delays due to funding problems, the thirteenth episode was still being edited when the first episode went to PBS in October 1983: two books and other materials related to the series had been published and nearly all the publicity and TV listings taken care of, but the narration for the last episode was finally recorded less than four weeks before it was to be broadcast.

In 1980, after the Corporation for Public Broadcasting refused us the necessary start-up money, a big boost came when Associated Television (ATV, later Central Independent Television) in Britain agreed to coproduce the series. (ATV and WGBH had been associated on earlier documentary projects, including the controversial *Death of a Princess*.) Coproduction with the British company was necessary for financial reasons. We had had difficulty raising money in the United States, not solely, I think, because of the controversial nature of the history of the Vietnam war—finding adequate funding is simply a typical problem of documentary production in this country. At a PBS preview of the series for TV critics in the summer of 1983, an executive of one large corporation, a big funder of PBS programming, stated that his company just did not consider giving money for public-affairs (meaning controversial) programming.

Coproduction with the French was necessary to assure access to valuable archives there. Production companies in other countries were approached, but none would agree to join—preferring (as one European national broadcasting company executive told me later) to purchase rights to run the series later, since that would be less expensive.

Through all of this, Peter McGhee, program manager of national productions for WGBH, and Richard Creasey, head of documentaries at ATV, maintained their faith in the project, putting themselves and their organizations on the line. There was never a written contract between ATV/Central and WGBH. The original understanding was that the British would produce three episodes, but that number was increased to four when we failed to gain additional U.S.

financing. In the end, the ATV production team did the preliminary work on a fifth program that was later taken over by producer Drew Pearson at WGBH.

Initial money for research came from WGBH, ABC-TV, PBS, and the National Endowment for the Humanities. Preliminary research took two forms: a detailed analysis of one historical "turning point," the death of President Diem (which became part of the third episode), and a series of seminars. With that money Ellison and Karnow also did the first interviews, with the aims of preparing a demonstration segment to aid in further fundraising and of recording some of the key participants of advanced age. Among these were interviews of Henry Cabot Lodge and Maxwell Taylor (and by careful examination of the completed programs you can see that, unlike the later interviews, they were recorded on videotape, not film).

Martin Smith, who had worked at BBC and was a producer-director on the "World at War" series (Thames-TV), and Bruce Palling of ATV moved to Boston in the summer of 1980 and stayed on for two years during the production of the four episodes for which they were primarily responsible. In the case of the French partner, Antenne-2, it was agreed that they would provide three programs on the French period in Indochina. Those three hours were eventually incorporated with other footage and edited into the first two episodes of the series. This allowed WGBH to produce another program, *Homefront U.S.A.*— not included in the original outline but one we thought very important.

A five-week period of intense preparation in October and November 1980 included lectures and other presentations by more than thirty academics, military historians, journalists, and other experts, most of whom were among the fifty-five series consultants.[2] Subjects ranged from the archaeology, ancient history, and French colonial period of Vietnam to the role of women in Vietnamese society, World War II and Vietnam, the cold war and the Geneva agreements, the 1968 Tet offensive, Washington decision making, the role of the media in covering the war, and even the portrayal of Vietnam and Vietnam vets in motion pictures and fiction. These seminars were attended by producers and most of the other production staff associated with the series, including some college student interns. At the last seminar I showed all or part of more than thirty documentaries about Vietnam and twelve hours of excerpts from network evening news coverage.

My title on the series was Director of Media Research, one that, to the best of my knowledge, had not been used before in a documentary production. The word *media* reflects the fact that we depended on audio- and videotape and photographs and that we researched in all media—not just film. More important, virtually every person working on the series was a "researcher." For each episode the producer and associate producer spent most of their time on research—reading, conducting preliminary and filmed interviews, reviewing archive film and the film researcher's notes, and checking again and again to see that all this information was carefully arranged. We used interns and depended heavily on many journalists and academics who had studied specific aspects of the Vietnam era.

Content Analysis and Film Research

The analysis I had done, with colleagues, of the network evening news and documentaries included such details as location, military unit, subject matter, interviews, and, of course, network, reporter, and date. Further, our coding of news stories, anchor reporting, documentary subjects, and guests on interview programs had familiarized us with much of the material we would eventually use as the "compilation" part of "Vietnam: A Television History." In all we had coded more than ten thousand network evening news reports and some two thousand network documentary, information, and public affairs programs, and we had viewed more than five hundred other documentaries, both domestic and foreign. After we started film research we added about six thousand other "titles" from cut films made by the military (most at the army film archive in Tobyhanna, Pennsylvania, since removed to Norton Air Force Base).

At the seminars described above, an outline was developed of nine episodes that could be done with available funding and of an additional four episodes we hoped to fund eventually. The intensive research to prepare for interviews in Vietnam started before those sessions and continued afterward up until two months before on-location filming was to start. The main objective was to find principals and observers of the important events in the war. Here the previous film research was very useful.

For example, one of the most controversial Vietnam news reports on American television had been an August 1965 CBS Evening News story by Morley Safer. The footage included shots of a Marine holding a cigarette lighter to the thatched roof of a hut and of a flamethrower igniting other dwellings in a village called Cam Ne, very near the big U.S. air base at Da Nang; it also included shots of several women who lived in the village. The incident inspired several articles on TV coverage of the war, including one in *Newsweek*; it sparked a controversial exchange of letters between CBS News president Fred Friendly and assistant secretary of defense Arthur Sylvester and phone calls from President Johnson to Dr. Frank Stanton of CBS; and it later led to a congressional hearing on press coverage of Vietnam. (A brief discussion of the furor can be found in David Halberstram's *The Powers That Be*.)

When producer Martin Smith discussed arrangements for filming with Hanoi officials, he gave them 8×10 stills of the women filmed in that fifteen-year-old CBS report and asked for help in locating them. During the filming trip in early 1981, Smith and producer Elizabeth Deane were able to visit Cam Ne, and they interviewed several of the women and also filmed a former Viet

Cong guerrilla who still lived in the village. This segment is in episode 6, *America's Enemy*. It tells the story of that day in 1965 through contemporary interviews with USMC Col. Ray Snyder, then a lieutenant, who led the Marines into the village, and with Sgt. Thomas Murphy. In addition to the interviews, this segment was based on that Marine Corps unit's postoperation reports, on file at the Marine Corps Historical Center, Washington, and the CBS film was supplemented with color film of the action from the USMC film archive. In this way we brought perspective to bear on the story of one part of one day in a war that lasted thirty years.

The development of episodes and detailed program outlines was done in, I think, a fairly normal manner. Ellison, Karnow, and I discussed the specific outline for each episode with its producer and associate producer, with some input from the producers of other episodes. Six different production teams worked on the thirteen episodes: Judith Vecchione and Karan Sheldon were producer and associate producer for the first two episodes, which incorporated the material developed by French producer Henri de Turenne and researcher Serge Gordey. Producer Austin Hoyt and associate producer Marilyn Hornbeck Mellowes produced two episodes, and Elizabeth Deane and Judith Vecchione produced three. All four are WGBH "regulars." Martin Smith and associate producer Bruce Palling, with editors who came from England to WGBH, were responsible for four episodes. The teams of Andrew Pearson and Tuggelin Yourgrau, and executive producer Richard Ellison and Kathryn M. Pierce, each produced an episode.

Since my primary purpose in this short piece is to discuss our media research for the series, let me briefly note how we kept track of film and videotape as we ordered it. Using a system similar to the one I used to study network TV coverage, Kenn Rabin, our patient, cooperative, hard-working and incredibly responsible archivist, established a set of categories to record and recall each piece. As each "story" was ordered from an archive, processed, and received we entered date, caption, source, subject, edge numbers, and other technical information. It was not a complicated system, but by keeping it up to date— processed by Pat Venus in Austin, Texas—we had regular computer printouts listing all the film we had in each category. To the best of my knowledge, we never ordered the same film twice—even though we had twelve different film researchers working in four major locations over more than three years.

The keys to film research are two: the film researcher's notes, kept on the story cards, and the cataloging and checking by the film archivist. As film researchers worked in various archives, their detailed notes for each "story" viewed and their general impressions were fundamentally important. When each piece of film work-print or videotape was received at WGBH, Kenn Rabin reviewed it, which often meant more checking with experts. No one was allowed to touch any piece of film until Kenn had checked it for film quality and archival accuracy—the most complete and accurate information at this stage is crucial.

Chief among the film researchers were Raye Farr (also of "World at War"), Janet Hayman (experienced as a researcher on several other series and a film producer), Bradley Borum, Kay Matschullat, Margot Edman, and Mavis Lyons Smull. Of course, we often drafted friends and researchers at different collections to help us find specific pieces of film. For example, after we examined some home movies made by an American adviser in Vietnam in the 1950s, his son remembered that a TV program had been done at the Michigan State station on training civilian police in South Vietnam. A former family babysitter of ours, now living in East Lansing, spent several days with employees of the station in a warehouse searching for the film but could not find it. One final check turned it up—in the station's regular film library. After receiving her report, Ellison saw and obtained the film. That sequence is in episode 3, *America's Mandarin*. We all used friends or just asked people working at libraries and archives to help us.

Film Sources

In all, the film and videotape we collected came from about ninety different sources—a total of fourteen hundred different "stories" (individual newsfilm reports, documentaries, TV programs, the film elements of network programs within live broadcasts, and so forth). The archive film ordered for the series would run more than one hundred hours. About half of everything used came from the three American TV networks—ABC, CBS, and NBC. An eighth was from U.S. military sources.

The largest single source was Sherman Grinberg Libraries, a New York film archive, which supplied about 40 percent of all the compilation film, mainly from ABC News footage. Early in the development of the series, Dick Ellison negotiated an agreement with ABC News that gave us use of their newsfilm free of licensing fees, and ABC also gave the project a start-up grant of $50,000. In exchange, ABC received an option to negotiate the broadcast of some materials from the series at a later date. (In doing film research at Grinberg we of course paid the usual viewing fees at Grinberg and all lab and other expenses.) Years later, ABC exercised its option by airing one of the programs, episode 4, *LBJ Goes to War*, as part of the regular ABC Friday-night program "Nightline." Since this was done the week before "Vietnam" premiered on PBS, it turned out to be good publicity for the series as well.

During most of the Vietnam war period, ABC had not kept its own film library but had turned materials over to Grinberg. This meant not only that many of the outtakes (parts of the film not used) were saved, but also that footage was more accessible and in better condition than CBS or NBC newsfilm, which was often reused in documentaries and news broadcasts. Since many of ABC's outtakes, as well as stories that had never been broadcast, were available at Sherman Grinberg, we often found additional interviews and the long shots and variety of angles we needed for editing. In sum, without the access to the ABC materials at Grinberg, and without the waiver of rights fees (especially since financing was so short), I doubt that the series could have been done. After ABC the next most important single source was CBS News. Since I had kept track of the reporting of all the network correspondents, we could sometimes check with the original reporter or camera crew to confirm or get additional information on a story. We generally did this in the process of vetting virtually every piece of film as we received it.

Martin Smith, on the research trip to Vietnam in the autumn of 1980, spent more than a week in Hanoi on film research. He obtained about two and a half hours of material from the Hanoi Documentary Studios and the army film archive, but these sources yielded only 2 percent of the film used in the thirteen programs. It was difficult to get accurate material from the North Vietnamese: it was in short supply, inadequately preserved and catalogued, and usually avowedly propagandistic.

In addition we used film from Britain, Japan, Poland, Russia, France, Belgium, and East and West Germany, as well as "captured enemy" film available in various U.S. archives.

Checking and Changing

First and foremost, the project was a team effort. Editing teams (usually three at a time) worked in adjoining rooms—we ordinarily edited only two episodes at any one time. The producer of each episode wrote out repeated draft "scripts" (outlines of the film material and suggested narration) that were critical to the editing. The entire production group (all producers and researchers working on the series) was involved from the first assembly of materials through five or more versions of each program to the final edit.

I will not dwell on it here, but it may be important to note that these sessions were often angry and gut wrenching. It may sound like a cliché now, but the Vietnam war *was* political and emotional, and we seemed to repeat every argument. Agreement on the choice of a shot or the positioning of a sequence would involve such considerations as the provenance of the film, its historical context, and, as a practical matter, the cost of using a particular source. On several occasions I called network correspondents or cameramen and asked them to recall a story they had done a decade before, and they retrieved their records or notes from attics, basements, and files to help. The central question never changed: What is the *evidence* that supports showing or saying this?

I have been told of rumors of "editorial differences" among our French production unit, our British colleagues working with us in Boston, and those already at WGBH or who moved to Boston to work on the series. But I did not notice any consistent, generalized differences in our points of view. For the first two episodes, the French provided about three hours of material. But the producer and associate producer of these episodes, Judith Vecchione and Karan Sheldon, also did research, conducted their own preliminary and filmed interviews and had others done in Europe, and got additional footage in the United States and in Europe—in short, they followed precisely the same process that the producers of all the other episodes followed.

Martin Smith and Bruce Palling of ATV/Central were at WGBH throughout the production of their episodes. We all met and worked together nearly every day. Consultant academics, military experts, and GIs reviewed all the episodes, regardless of who produced them. Each part was reviewed by all the staff—American and British—on board at the time.

All of our offices and film editing rooms were within a few feet of each other. We talked every day and late into many nights, and our conversations (at least the ones I was in) were almost exclusively about Vietnam and the production in progress—but, as is common in journalistic circles, the second most important topic was food and good places to eat around the world.

There were certainly many "editorial" differences—based on what we knew, where we had been, and so much more. No single episode had an individual, different editorial view, though: each production team was subjected to virtually the same process described here.

The "history" (as best we could review, learn, and understand it), the evidence we could find in the film documentation itself, and the interpretations of those we interviewed guided each choice. We did not fit any story or interpretation to the film we had—we sought the film evidence for what we thought were the central points to understand. Whatever errors there may be are not errors of complicity but are simply based on our own lack of knowledge. The two basic questions over which we argued most were, do we have the history-conception-evidence correct? and, are we using the correct film-interview-narration material?

Each episode was viewed in several rough forms by series consultants and others. We asked Vietnam veterans and military historians to check us on various details. For example, Karan Sheldon and I learned some of the history of the M-16 after a GI noticed one in our segment on the 1963 coup against Diem—several years before the American army used that weapon in Vietnam. We discovered that an earlier model of the M-16 had been carried by Diem's palace guards, so we knew the film was authentic.

An early cut of the Tet episode was viewed in my basement by Peter Braestrup (*The Big Story*), Don Orberdorfer (*Tet*), Herbert Schandler (*The Unmaking of a President*), and Vincent Demma (an expert on the period from the Army Center for Military History). A later version it was reviewed again by experts on the U.S. military and political history, experts on public opinion, and those experts most familiar with the South and North Vietnamese.

When possible, we assembled as many of our advisers as possible in one place (Boston or Washington), showed an episode, and held a discussion—occasionally lasting five or six hours. One of the episodes was seen by about twenty GIs invited to WGBH. Other series consultants were sent videotapes or scripts for review. The oral and written comments of each were assessed against what we considered the best evidence we had for each part of each episode. These comments were also helpful in the process of polishing the final narration script to explain and provide context for the interviews and archival film.

The narration was finished, after the film was "frozen," by each episode's producer and associate producer with Ellison, Karnow, and me in marathon viewing (and arguing) sessions before negative editing and post-production. Frequently we would contact several outside experts—usually from among our consultants—to help decide on a single word. As an example, we deliberated several hours before writing this line in the episode describing Dien Bien Phu: "They [Eisenhower and others] studied alternatives, including the possible use of tactical atomic weapons." The argument was over *studied* as opposed to *considered* or some other verb. Late at night we called Professor George Herring of the University of Kentucky, an expert on the period. And so we reached a decision.[3]

Then at the last moment, while adding sound and recording the narration, we might check and recheck a point.

As with any similar series, the media research was only a small part of our production. Interviews and research from books and other traditional sources were just as (or more) important. Phone calls to hundreds of observers, experts, and journalists who had reported on events provided many leads. For each episode, fifty to seventy-five people were interviewed initially to get the eight or twelve eventually seen on the screen. We decided early on that the series would show only observers giving first-hand accounts—that is, we filmed "participants" rather than journalists or academic experts.

The above is almost exclusively about the compilation part of the production; one-third of all the material in the series was from more than one hundred original filmed interviews. The proportion of each episode given to "talking heads" varied from about one-quarter to nearly half.

The production of some episodes stretched for more than nine months; others were done more quickly. Most were edited on an eleven-to-eighteen-week schedule, not including soundtrack work. The series did not use music that was not on the original sound track (except for the opening titles and end credits)—that is, we did not use any composed or "atmospheric" music.

Sound effects were added when only silent film was available (as with much of the military footage), but in all cases we checked carefully to find the authentic sound.

Twelve episodes of the series were seen first in Britain on channel 4, beginning April 11, 1983. The first episode in the series was modified slightly to appeal to the British audience (with more on the British role in 1945), and the narration of the entire series was by British voice. In the United States the series began on PBS on October 4, 1983, and continued through December 20 with episode 13, *Legacies*.

Five episodes of "Vietnam: A Television History" were measured by the Nielsen National Television Index on the first run—all five placed among the ten highest rated public-affairs programs on PBS to date. It thus became the most-watched public-affairs series ever to air on public television. Episode 1, the highest rated, had a cume rating of 8.7, meaning that nearly 9 percent of all American households were tuned into the program. The largest demographic category was men 35 to 49 years old—21 percent of the audience for the series but only 9 percent of the U.S. population. A second run on PBS during the summer of 1984 had an average rating of 2.3, a 4 percent share in the five largest markets.

About two hundred colleges paid for a license to record the series off the air for credit courses in the fall semester of 1983, for a total of about five thousand students. And we know that many other teachers used the series as part of history and other classes. A shorter version will also be available on videotape for school use.

Acknowledgments

I gratefully acknowledge financial and other support for my research provided by the University of Wisconsin, Madison, and by the Woodrow Wilson International Center for Scholars. Sandra, Belinda, and Laurel sacrificed most. I appreciate the help and support of those who worked with me, some named here, others not, and still others who helped on the series whom I never met.

Dick Ellison, Martin Smith, Stan Karnow, Kenn Rabin, Mal Topping, and Doug Gomery aided me by reviewing versions of this essay, but the conclusions and mistakes are mine.

Notes

1. Steven Cohen, ed., *Vietnam: Anthology and Guide to A Television History* (New York: Alfred A. Knopf, 1983). This book has a short history of the project and an introduction with

some information on television documentary. Stanley Karnow's *Vietnam: A History* (New York: Viking, 1983) is the companion book to the series.

2. The series consultants are listed along with other information on the series in *A Guide to Vietnam: A Television History* (newspaper supplement), edited by Stanley Karnow and Lawrence W. Lichty, WGBH-TV, 1983.

3. For an account of this event, published after the episode was completed but showing the results of Herring's study, see "Eisenhower, Dulles, and Dienbienphu: 'The Day We Didn't Go to War' Revisited," *Journal of American History* 71, no. 2 (1984): 343–63. Our problem was to try to convey twenty pages of careful research in a word.

Bibliography

Bailey, George A. "Interpretative Reporting of the Vietnam War by Anchormen." *Journalism Quarterly* (Summer 1976).

———. "Television War: Trends in Network Coverage of Vietnam, 1965–1970." *Journal of Broadcasting* (Spring 1976).

Bailey, George A., and Lawrence W. Lichty. "Rough Justice on a Saigon Street: A Gatekeeper Study of NBC's Tet Execution Film." *Journalism Quarterly* (Summer 1972).

Carroll, Raymond L. "Economic Influences on Commercial Network Television Documentary Scheduling." *Journal of Broadcasting* (Fall 1979).

Hoffer, Thomas W. "Broadcasting in an Insurgency Environment: USIA in Vietnam, 1965–1970." Ph.D. dissertation, University of Wisconsin, 1972.

Kautz, Sandra N. "President Johnson and President Nixon: Their Use of Television and the Relationship to Gallup Poll Ratings." M.A. thesis, University of Wisconsin, 1973.

Lichty, Lawrence W. "The War We Watched on Television." *AFI Report* (later *American Film*) (Winter 1973).

———. "Getting Down to Specifics." *[MORE]* (Dec. 1973).

———. "The Night at the End of the Tunnel." *Film Comment* (July–Aug. 1975).

———. "Comments on the Influence of Television on Public Opinion." In *Vietnam as History*, edited by Peter Braestrup. Washington, D.C.: University Press of America, 1984.

Lichty, Lawrence W., and Murray Fromson. "Comparing Notes on Television's Coverage of the War." *Center Magazine* (Center for the Study of Democratic Institutions) (Sept.–Oct. 1979).

Part VI
Images of Society

Introduction

One of the hopes we pin on documentary is that it mirror the changing nature of the society within which it exists. It should reflect, draw attention to, and focus on emerging issues, thus helping to define the political and social agenda of the times.

The commercial networks do not perform this function particularly well, especially now, when their interest in documentary is declining. Here and there they have turned their attention to such issues as drugs, youth crime, homsexuality, or police corruption, but in general these efforts are mere drops in the bucket. Instead, the networks have concentrated on hot-item news and current-affairs documentaries—the biggest political story, the latest crisis in the Middle East, the state of the presidency, the military industrial complex, and so on.[1]

The presentation of a broader vision of American society has, for the most part, been left to the public broadcasting stations and to independent filmmakers. They are the ones who have provided the deeper, more personal, more subtle portraits of ourselves and our relationship to society, who have helped us to see a little more clearly where we are going and what is at stake in the world around us.

Through the 1970s and mid-1980s, the cameras of PBS and the independents have covered a wide and exciting spectrum of subjects. Fred Wiseman has surveyed many American cultural institutions. Educational television has looked at farmers, banks, migrant workers, artists, and musicians. The subtleties of human relationships were explored in *An American Family*, *Grey Gardens*, and *Best Boy*, to name only a few films in an extremely rich area. Society's attitude toward its children was considered in *Your Child—My Child*; *Say*

Goodbye Again looked at divorce from a child's point of view; and Josh Hanig and Denis Hick's *Coming of Age* provided sensitive insights into black and white teenagers' views of each other. *Soldier Girls* focused on women in the army, and two kinds of societal confrontations were considered in *Harlan County, U.S.A.* and *The War at Home*.

This brief outline is not provided merely for the sake of a listing, but rather to suggest the richness and variety of issues that have been covered and explored outside the realm of the commercial networks in the past decade and a half. Four new topics clearly dominated American noncommercial documentary in the 1970s, however: the Vietnam war, the women's movement, personal and family relations, and the broad face of America and its institutions. Interest in these issues continues into the 1980s, and in the meantime new concerns and new trends in society have generated new subjects for discourse.

The Vietnam war as a documentary subject illustrates well the change in direction and focus over the past fifteen years. In the early 1970s, films like de Antonio's *In the Year of the Pig* and Peter Davis's *Hearts and Minds* focused on the root causes of the war and the escalation of U.S. military involvement. WGBH's "Vietnam: A Television History," aired in 1983, covered much the same area but used its last two programs, *The End of the Tunnel* and *Legacies*, to consider postwar feelings and the ramifications of the war for both Vietnam and the United States. As the events of the struggle have faded, the cameras have delved increasingly into the war's human costs: William Couturier's *Vietnam Requiem*, for example, looks at Vietnam veterans who have turned to crime, while Dorothy Tod's *Warriors' Women* examines the plight of Vietnam war wives.

Like the Vietnam war, interpersonal communication continues to provide a fruitful subject of documentary interest. Thus, the year-long shooting of *An American Family* has been followed by Ed Pincus's *Diaries*, an exploration of Pincus's own marriage shot over four or five years. And in the tradition of *Grey Gardens*, which delved into the intricacies of a mother-daughter relationship, Ira Wohl's Academy Award–winning *Best Boy* looked at the complex relationship between two aging parents and their fifty-four-year-old mentally retarded son.

The main aim of this section is to consider in greater depth three documentary areas of continuing social significance. One of these areas is Women's Liberation, for some years a central issue for documentarists; the other two topics, the war in Central America and nuclear disarmament, are relative newcomers to the documentary scene.

Before coming to particular themes, however, I want to discuss two theoretical issues that lie at the heart of the documentary problem. The first concerns just what documentary films really tell us about society. Do they truly have the educational and social function we claim they do, or are we merely deluding ourselves as to their significance? The second issue has to do with the problem of cultural misunderstanding between filmmaker and subject. Both of these topics have been mentioned in passing in this book, but they are tackled head on in this last section.

Brian Winston's article "Direct Cinema—Third Decade" uses the PBS series "Middletown" and the BBC series "Police" to launch a major attack on *cinéma vérité* in the 1980s—which could be going nowhere, in Winston's opinion—and on the irrelevance of a lot of documentary filmmaking. He asks two basic questions: Do the films in these series illuminate our understanding of society? and, Do they have social relevance? His answer is Yes for "Police" and No for "Middletown."

When "Middletown" was broadcast in 1982, executive producer Peter Davis stressed repeatedly the broad sociological significance of the series. He claimed that within the context of community life, "Middletown" explores those standard experiences which shape our sensibilities as individuals and as a nation. Commenting on Davis's statement, *New York Times* critic John O'Connor wrote, "[Davis] may be absolutely right, but the proof is not established in the scattered, not necessarily typical vérité portraits of this television project."[2]

O'Connor particularly disliked *Seventeen*, the one program Winston had admired, claiming that it told little about education in America. But one film cannot be expected to do everything. I see *Seventeen* as an immensely powerful statement about teenagers and growing up in America, but I also feel that it should, for maximum effect, be screened together with a *vérité* film like Wiseman's *High School* and a more sociologically based film on education such as Arthur Barron's *Sixteen in Webster Groves*. I suspect that all three films would gain added nuances and dimensions by being screened in a context that allows each film to bounce off and add to the perceptions of the other two.

Winston's praise is saved for Roger Graef's thirteen-part series "Police," based on months of *vérité* shooting with the British Thames Valley police force. It is interesting to compare Graef, who is known for his studies of the way power works in institutions,[3] to Wiseman, for although the two men tackle similar topics and issues, Graef's films seem quite focused and penetrating, whereas Wiseman's have a diffuse, somewhat ambiguous quality. Winston sees in Graef a tremendous attention to the footnoting of the social process. In practice, it may just be that Graef and cameraperson Charles Stewart have sharper eyes than the "Middletown" filmmakers for what is really socially relevant.

The second main theoretical subject dealt with in the section is that of cultural misunderstanding. At issue is the relationship between the filmmaker, with a particular set of cultural expectations, and the people being filmed, who have their own cultural perceptions—and then the audience enters in, with a host of viewpoints and understandings affecting interpretation of what is being presented. That is, most filmmakers inevitably react to a strange society from their own cultural vantage point and interpret it in that way to the audience back home. But the filmmaker may have totally misread the codes of the society, the meaning of people's actions and relationships as seen by the subject society itself.

I have used two film reviews to cover this topic: they play off each other and between them illustrate most of the central dilemmas. Umberto Eco's "De interpretatione" looks at the furor caused by Antonioni's film on China, which Antonioni considered a warm, supportive tribute to modern Chinese society, whereas the Chinese rejected it as a semifascist affront. Todd Gitlin's review of Louis Malle's "Phantom India" examines a similar phenomenon. Malle spent months making six films on India for the BBC, only to have them rejected by the Indian government as a muddleheaded, insensitive picture of life on the subcontinent.

Cultural misunderstanding obviously shades at times into questions of un-acceptable criticism and political interpretation, and separating the issues can be difficult. Antonioni's film was unacceptable to the Chinese because of its cultural misperceptions. Though this was partly true of Malle's series, his films had the added problem of presenting a true, but negative, face of India that was *politically* unacceptable to a propaganda-conscious government wishing to improve its overseas image.

Susan Sontag's work in Israel provides a further illustration of the thorns and thickets into which the "stranger" filmmaker can fall. In 1973, Susan Sontag made *Promised Lands*, shot in Israel in the months following the Yom Kippur war. The film was greeted in the United States as one of the finest portraits of Israel ever made,[4] but the Israelis, for their part, said the film was uninformed, full of clichés and stereotypes, and totally lacking in any feeling for the subject.[5] What differentiated Sontag's film from Malle's "India" and Antonioni's *China* was that a propaganda war over Palestinian rights was being fought in the American media, and the Israelis objected to such a simplistic, hurried film serving as a major informational tool for an uninformed audience.

U.S. involvement in Central America may be to the 1980s what the Vietnam war was to the 1960s and 1970s, a subject for confusion, division, anger, and explosion. As with Vietnam then, the issues of Central America today get short shrift in the commercial networks. Once more, news and anecdote take the place of background and in-depth analysis.

The subject of documentary film on Central America was covered in some detail in the 1984 anthology *Show Us Life*, edited by Thomas Waugh.[6] Since the third section of that book gives an excellent overview of the subject, I include here only one article on the topic, a discussion of *When the Mountains Tremble*, a film by Pamela Yates and Tom Sigel.

Pamela Yates describes the problems and dangers of an independent filmmaker covering the unknown war in Guatemala. *When the Mountains Tremble* follows a fairly conventional TV documentary style, but three things set it apart. First, there is a sense of passion, commitment, and concern on the part of the filmmakers for their subjects that is comparatively rare in network TV. Second, the filmmakers were not content simply to show *vérité* footage of a war but looked for a binding motif as well. This is provided by a young Guatemalan woman, Rigoberta Menchu, whom they film in limbo in a studio and who appears throughout the film to tell of the cruelty and oppression her family endured. Her story provides the spine of the film. And third, the film digresses from a standard style in the use of two reenacted dramatic scenes involving American and Guatemalan officials, based on declassified U.S. documents.

In her strength, courage, and choice of the political arena for her filmmaking, Pamela Yates is typical of many of the women described in Patricia Erens's article "Women's Documentary Filmmaking: The Personal Is Political." Erens has written extensively on women's issues,[7] and her article provides an excellent and comprehensive view of the last twenty years of women's involvement in documentary. In a clear and elegant style she details the most important women's films that have been made since the late sixties and describes the filmmakers themselves and their considerations in making their films. She also provides a brief review of the current state of feminist criticism as well as a few practical words about film distribution and locating major works.

Today's films by women embrace every subject and style, from Barbara Kopple's *Harlan County, U.S.A.* to Meredith Monk's experimental *Ellis Island*. One woman who combines a great concern for women's issues with highly developed filmmaking skill is Michelle Citron. Her work, which seems to point to new paths for the future, is well analyzed in Linda Williams's article on Citron's *What You Take for Granted*, a film that is particularly compelling because of its combination of an interesting subject—that of women in jobs traditionally dominated by men—with a willingness to take chances with film forms.

What You Take for Granted presents a fascinating amalgam of drama and pseudodocumentary styles that continually deceives and bewilders the viewer. In the beginning, the film appears to be a standard documentary based on lengthy interviews; gradually it becomes clear that it is actually fiction. In the end, however, this very mixture of forms, and the confusion it creates in the viewer, help to provide a deeper understanding of the subject than that obtainable by using the standard documentary techniques.

Citron's experiments with form can also be seen in another film of hers, *Daughter Rite*, which deals with mother-daughter relations. Again, as in *What You Take for Granted* and *David Holzman's Diary*, the boundaries between fact and fiction are not clear-cut. Both Citron's films are, in the end, fictions, but in their choice of subjects, their dependence on research and interviews, and their experimentation with form, they raise interesting possibilities for the future of documentary.

To round out the topic of personal liberation I chose Lee Atwell's review of *Word Is Out* and *Gay U.S.A.* Both films, dealing with Gay Liberation in the mid-seventies, were landmarks of their kind. Atwell covers the making and the results of the films and discusses the hopes of the filmmakers that their work would help change attitudes and opinions.

Of all the films that followed *Word Is Out* and *Gay U.S.A.*, the most provocative has been *Improper Conduct*, by Nestor Almendros and Orlando Jimenez-Leal, which deals with the harassment and difficulties of homosexuals in Cuba. This film was severely attacked by critics from the American left, such as Ruby Rich. Almendros's own defense of *Improper Conduct* finally appeared in *American Film*,[8] where he agrees that he intended the film to go beyond the persecution of gays and to make a comment on the overall repression of Cuban society—a statement that is difficult for the American left to accept quietly.

The nature of personal relationships, personal expression, nurturing, love, and growth are the immediate concerns of our everyday lives, but they are framed against a belief in the future, the belief in a better, saner, healthier world. The possibility of nuclear war, with the devastation and destruction of all civilization that it implies, puts all these beliefs and hopes in doubt. Nuclear warfare is clearly the most pressing issue of our age, and yet it was. for a time, almost completely ignored by television and filmmakers: very simply, it was taboo as a discussion topic. One can only conjecture as to why there was such silence—probably out of fear that a subject of such terrifying dimensions would alienate sponsors, advertisers, and governments and would cause panic and resentment among audiences.

The situation has altered in the past ten years, and as we have approached and passed the fortieth anniversary of the bombing of Hiroshima films have proliferated on all aspects of nuclear warfare. *The Day After Trinity* and *A Is for Atom, B Is for Bomb* dealt with the careers of Robert Oppenheimer and Edward Teller, the development of the atom and hydrogen bomb, and the nature of scientific responsibility in the growth of such weapons. *Atomic Cafe* and *No Place to Hide* both discuss changing American attitudes toward nuclear warfare, and *Ten Minutes to Midnight* focuses on Dr. Helen Caldicott's campaign against the spread of nuclear weapons. Although scores of films have been made on the subject in England and Europe as the voice of antinuclear demonstrators has grown stronger, the most moving film on the subject still must be Robert Vas's *Summer of Hiroshima*, which looks at nuclear war through the eyes of Japanese atom-bomb survivors.

To introduce the subject of film and nuclear war, I have used Erik Barnouw's article *Hiroshima-Nagasaki, August 1945*. Like Vas's film, *Hiroshima-Nagasaki* goes back to the earth-shattering events of 1945. It is a short black-and-white film made at Columbia University under the supervision of Erik Barnouw, based on archival footage shot originally by Japanese camerapersons. It shows simply and horrifically the devastating effects of the two atomic explosions on both human beings and a city structure. Like *Dark Spring*,[9] it was assembled from footage that had for years been kept from the eyes of the public by successive American governments.

Besides describing how *Hiroshima-Nagasaki* came to be made, Barnouw's article raises two important points relating to secrecy and network attitudes. For years, various administrative rulings kept the Hiroshima footage under close wraps. Why? What was the purpose of keeping such dynamic material hidden when it was surely in the public interest for it to be made available? Barnouw tentatively suggests that officials feared that screening the material would lead to a public horror at the events shown so great as to hamper U.S. ability to develop the hydrogen bomb.

Barnouw's second point concerns the attitude of the networks. When *Hiroshima-Nagasaki* was finished and given a press screening, not one commercial network official bothered to attend—the film had been made by a nonnetwork person and therefore could not be used. That the film might have been of major public importance was obviously a secondary consideration. Only when UPI hailed the film as worthy of serious attention did the networks finally deign to view it, but they continued to claim they had no use for it.

One film above all others merits attention in the discussion of television and nuclear war, and that is Peter Watkins's *The War Game*. This drama documentary tells the story of the commencement of hostilities between Russia and the Allies, the use of an atom bomb on a small town in England, and the horrifying aftermath of the explosion. The film was made in 1965, and although it had a fairly wide theatrical distribution throughout the late 1960s, the BBC considered it too realistic and frightening for television airing and so shelved it. It received its first English television screening only in 1985.

Nearly twenty years after its production, Watkins's work inspired three films that follow a path very similar to *The War Game*. ABC's *The Day After*, with Jason Robards, is a soap-opera version (and unrealistically mild) of how nuclear warfare comes to America. Not a very good film, it nevertheless stirred up tremendous controversy, bringing out both anti- and pronuclear war activists. A considerably better feature, *Testament*, directed by Lynn Littman, was shown in theaters at about the same time but was unable to obtain a network broadcast. For its part, the BBC film *The Thread* (1984) is the closest of the three to Watkins's original. *The Thread*, another drama documentary in the realistic Ken Loach tradition, avoids the use of major stars and, like *The War Game*, intersperses facts and figures with drama as the story progresses. In this case, the film commences with the dropping of a hydrogen bomb on the city of Sheffield, and it closes thirteen years later with glimpses of the birth of the first postholocaust generation.

Given the interest in the subject and the increasing public debate on nuclear warfare, a discussion of *The War Game* seems the perfect way to close the book. I met Watkins fifteen years ago in Toronto, when he was choking with rage at media secrecy. This comes out in the interview, and I have also reprinted my introduction to our discussion, which may be useful to show how Watkins and his film were both seen at the time.

My use of the Watkins interview is similar to my use of Fred Friendly's extract on the McCarthy film. I want the reader to recapture history—to see that there have been forerunners and pioneers. Watkins's film took immense courage. He made it against tremendous opposition and believed in his convictions enough to cut the umbilical cord binding him to the BBC when they refused to show his film. I believe that Watkins represents an example to all filmmakers. He is one of those who burned and still burns with what Robert Vas once called "the burden of the message that must get out," the message that must be transmitted whether the audience wants to hear it or not. Watkins accepted that as a challenge he had to face, whatever the consequences. Only today are we beginning to appreciate how well he took up the gauntlet for all of us.

Notes

1. There are obviously a number of exceptions to this sweeping statement, mostly in local programming. Thus, WCBS New York ran an excellent investigatory series for years under the title *Eye on New York*.

2. John O'Connor, *New York Times*, April 4, 1982, p. 17.

3. For a fuller discussion of the work of Roger Graef, see the interview with Graef in Alan Rosenthal, *The Documentary Conscience* (Berkeley and Los Angeles: University of California Press, 1980), pp. 171–81.

4. Edward Grossman, "Susan Sontag's Israel," *Commentary*, Oct. 1974, p. 78.

5. For a fuller discussion of *Promised Lands*, see Alan Rosenthal, "Promised Lands," *Film Library Quarterly* 10, no. 1/2 (1977): 51–56.

6. Thomas Waugh, ed., *Show Us Life* (Secaucus, N.J.: Scarecrow Press, 1984).

7. See, in particular, Patricia Erens, *Sexual Stratagems: The World of Women in Film* (New York: Horizon Press, 1979).

8. Nestor Almendros and Orlando Jimenez-Leal, "Improper Conduct," *American Film* 9 (Sept. 1984): 18, 70.

9. This was the case also with the film *Dark Spring*, which uses 102,000 feet of color footage of Hiroshima and Nagasaki shot in 1945 by an American film crew that was part of the U.S. Strategic Bombing Survey.

Direct Cinema: The Third Decade

Brian Winston

Richard Leacock recounts that Flaherty used to liken the processes of documentary filmmaking to old-style whaling expeditions from New Bedford. A captain would interest investors in kitting out a ship and would then disappear for maybe years on end. Eventually he would return to port, and there on the quay the investors would be waiting. "Hell of a good sail," the captain would shout down from the bridge. "Sorry, no whales."

That Flaherty, who loved the climactic death of great sea creatures the way producers of old-time serials loved tying heroines to railway tracks, should choose a whaling metaphor ought not to surprise. But the image is even more apposite now in the age of direct cinema than it was in his day. Flaherty could, by research, script, and reconstruction, guarantee that whales would at least be sighted. Today's documentarists, inhibited by the dictates of nonintervention and averse to the rigors of extensive research, can easily sail straight past any subject—and frequently do. Direct cinema, the source of the dominant documentary style, is now entering its third decade. It seems fair to ask, How is it doing?

Take two recent major whaling expeditions. One, "Middletown," the brainchild of Peter Davis, was a series of films and tapes executed by various hands and aired last year on American public television. The other, "Police," made by a team led by Roger Graef and Charles Stewart, was transmitted at much the same time by the BBC. None of the films of these series were *cinéma vérité*, for all that they were everywhere so described. *Cinéma vérité* is a style of documentary that deliberately draws attention to the processes involved in the making of the film. It was invented, as its name clearly indicates, in France. All it has in common with the American school of "direct cinema" is equipment.

Direct cinema is the exact opposite of *cinéma vérité*. It seeks more completely than any previous mode of documentary production to hide the processes of filmmaking—to pretend to an unblinking objectivity supposedly similar to that possessed by a fly on the wall. "Police" is in a pure direct cinema mode. "Middletown" is in a less pure but more common variant of the style. Neither is *cinéma vérité*.

The six segments of the "Middletown" series (only five of which were publicly seen) looked at first sight like nothing so much as reruns of the great early direct cinema films. Here, as in the Leacock/Pennebaker *Primary* (1960), was the close-up on the political campaign. Here, as in Lipscomb's *Mooney v. Fowle* (also known as *Football*, 1961), was the high school sports event. Here, as in Wiseman's *High School* (1969), was the teenage subculture. After twenty years it seemed as if direct cinema had exhausted America. It was now doomed, as with a grade school essay entitled "What I did on my visit to the Midwest," to endless repetitions; not perhaps so inappropriate in this context, given that Xerox Corporation was the series underwriter.

But this was only true of the first sight. For "Middletown," except for two of its episodes, was not really direct cinema at all but an ersatz variety developed in televisionland on both sides of the Atlantic which can best be called *vérité*. This is a bastard form that reduces the rigor of both direct cinema and *cinéma vérité* practice to an easy amalgam of handheld available-light sync shooting. *Vérité* films contain such material, but they can also use all or any of the elements of more traditional documentaries, such as commentary and interviews. Thus it is that the dominant documentary style is not direct cinema itself but is rather derived from it. The subtlest deception occurs when, as with four of the "Middletown" episodes, only interviews are added to the mix. The impression is then given that direct cinema, implying months of filming, huge amounts of footage shot, minimal contact with subjects, is being used; but in fact, *vérité* is at hand—which means the usual visiting TV professional firemen in the usual five-star hotels, set-up interviews (ever seen an unset-up interview?), and careful harboring of resources so that only certain moments in any given situation are covered. Direct cinema might have promised more than it could ever deliver, but *vérité* debases that promise by playing an even greater confidence trick on the audience.

In "Middletown," apart from the episode directed by Leacock himself and the banned segment done by his ex-pupils Joel DeMott and Jeff Kreines, the rest were testimony to how far the *vérité* rot has set in. In these films (and in Leacock's contribution) the use of interviews, or situations so close to interviews that it would be positively Jesuitical to claim them as noninterventionist, is the big clue to the presence of *vérité*. *Cinéma vérité* has never caught on in the Anglo-Saxon world, being too reflexive and experimental. Direct cinema has now been tainted so that it is just as much an endangered species.

That the "Middletown" films and tapes by and large failed to advance the art of documentary would be of little importance had they illuminated our understanding of the society they sought to portray. But what we got, with the exception of the Kreines and DeMott piece to which we shall return below, was a tired rehash of what have now become the documentary clichés of Middle America. The series, although the high spot of last year's U.S. output, would barely warrant attention did it not encapsulate a whole slew of problems summed up, neatly and elegantly, by its title. Each episode contained the opening credit "From the Middletown Studies," referencing a classic work of American sociology, *Middletown* by Helen and Robert Lynd, published in 1928 and added to, as *Middletown in Transition*, in 1937.

What documentaries actually do—what is within the frame—is often at odds with what they are supposed to do—what rhetoric surrounds their production and exhibition. Today's practitioners, at least sophisticated practitioners, acknowledge the impossibility of the objectivity implied by classic documentary rhetoric. They speak instead to the inevitable subjectivity of their actual practice. But the context remains unchanged: the classic notion of objectivity and observation is still what most people mean when they think of documentary. In these circumstances, too many documentarists, by less sophisticated utterance or genuine ignorance, are quick to want to have their cake and eat it.

"Middletown" is a classic example. A series of, by and large, predictably personal, idiosyncratic, and nonrepresentational (in any sociological sense) films and tapes is forced to assume, because of the title given it, a weight which it can in no way carry. Peter Davis, normally a lucid human being, justified the choice of title in this way: "We tried to locate certain universal human coordinates in specific stories, and we were inspired in the first place by our sort of 'grandparents' in this kind of study, Robert and Helen Lynd. And their study is about 'Middletown.' So is ours." This apparently is the sort of talk you need to master if you are to pull in the few millions it now takes to make such a series in America. It's the kind of talk that impresses public television funding agencies and the great private corporations. That Davis was uttering these justifications as the Lynds' masterpiece was celebrating its fiftieth anniversary must only have added to the general "sexiness" of the idea.

Such sexiness necessitates the title. "Middletown is utterly typical in this, for the world of documentaries is a world of city symphonies, married couples, American families, police, and sailors. But this search for universality takes its toll. First there is the traditional cost. Documentaries exist in free-fall between the general and the particular. Every last Inuit, industrial worker, deepsea fisherman, etc., must stand on the screen both for himself and for a class of persons of his type. The actual image is of one particular person; the rhetoric of the title and the genre is of a tribe. So parts come to stand for wholes, and this synecdoche is needed if a claim of social relevance (which is essential to justify driving the Inuit, or what have you, crazy during the filming) is to be sustained. "Middletown" piles synecdoche on synecdoche. Not only do the individuals in the six segments stand for those classes of individuals, but Middletown itself stands for America—"the universal human coordinates" coordinate not because of what is filmed but because of the context in which such filming is viewed. The actual films take second place to the sustaining rhetoric, the context created by the public television channel, its documentary slot, and, above all, a title that establishes for the viewer exactly what sort of work is intended. (Films are never called "Six Days in the Life of Mr. and Mrs. Bloggs of Acacia Avenue" or "Events Observed During a Facilities Visit to a Military Establishment by Me and My Crew When We Happened to Have the Camera Loaded.")

But "Middletown" adds to this normal cost by a second specific problem. Calling a series of documentaries after a classic sociological study makes explicit the usually hidden sociological legitimations of such films and invites comparison between the screen and the book. In this case, without prejudice to the value and limitations of positivist sociology, the comparison is disastrous to the films. In short, the books tell us much we didn't know and the films tell us little. We might feel sorry for some of the protagonists, not least because they were foolish enough to allow the cameras in, but such empathy cannot justify the exercise, never mind the title. Indeed, the title, so necessary one supposes for getting the series made, actually works to reduce the validity of the better episodes.

Leacock's Middletown whale, for instance, *Community of Praise*, deals with the practice of Fundamentalist Christianity. Beyond the major danger of the direct cinema approach, which is that filming the surface of things reveals the surface of things, Leacock has another problem. His episode must stand for religion in Middletown, yet his family is utterly atypical—speaking in tongues, falling over, and the like. Were this then Leacock's own essay, one would simply be worried about the stereotyping of this family. That the mother had a big-city background and a degree—facts which would work against this stereotyping—I learned from Leacock himself, not his film. And the elements of the film that are surprising, nonstereotypical, look like nothing so much as sins of omission. For the family says nothing of racism, anti-Semitism, or the rest of the bigotry associated with this faith. But, then, the real wonder of the film is that Leacock liked his subjects. He proceeds throughout with the air of a man who can now say, "Some of my best friends are Holy Rollers."

Compare this with the Lynds' account of religion in Middletown. Fundamentalism of the sort Leacock concentrates on takes its place amid the thirty-four organized religious groups the Lynds discovered. Their approach to the question of religious practice also related attendance and belief to class. They found two classes in Middletown—the business class and the working class—and of the 43 percent of the inhabitants who worked, seven out of ten were employed workers and three belonged to the business class. This is where the Lynds start, with what they call "the long arm of the job." I am not arguing that it was Davis's task to update such statistics, much less systematically include them in the films. But in any supposed portrait of a modern community, is it too much to ask that some sense of the world of work and business be given?

As is usual on American television, "Middletown" has almost nothing of work in it. The episode ostensibly devoted to trade, *A Family Business*, was about an ex-Marine officer and his umpteen kids tottering on bankruptcy running a pizza parlor. At the climax, one son says that Dad can close up the place without worry because, hell, they can all find jobs. Whether they can or not in a severely depressed Midwest is simply never dealt with by the series. Neither are employment and unemployment mentioned in the episode devoted to the town's politics, which are observed during the drama of a mayoral election campaign concentrating almost entirely, in the American fashion, on personalities.

As with work, so with race. Apart from the DeMott/Kreines film *Seventeen*, there is no mention of race. In *Community of Praise*, the Fundamentalists, all white, are led in prayer by a black preacher—the sociology of which screams to be explained. It isn't. *The Big Game* is a video effort of which about a third is nothing more than coverage of the high school basketball game with voice-over commentary taken from the local radio station (there's purity for you). Blacks figure, for the only time in the publicly seen episodes, but, despite the use of interviews, their situation is not examined.

The result of this eclecticism is that one can learn more of Middletown from the Lynds' footnotes (what a school dance cost, how you had to take the girl to the dance in a taxi if you didn't have a family car, whose kitchen lights were on at 6:00 A.M. of a winter's morning) than one can from the whole transmitted series. Davis has failed to find ways of dealing with such Lynd topics as "Food, Clothing, and Housework." Instead, we have the sections of the book that can be turned into dramatic movies, the rites of passage—marriage, the big sports game, impending bankruptcy, graduation, interracial sex, faith healers: the "sexy" bits. Thus it is that documentaries "look at the world and run away from its social meaning."

Middletown, as the Lynds were at pains to hide but as is now well known, is Muncie, Indiana. Thanks in part to them, this is now a town so average that a large sign on an approach highway proclaims it as "Modeltown, America." Its big attraction is that its demographic typicality is embodied by a group of folks who are friendly to strangers, real friendly. They will apparently entertain sociologists or camera crews at the drop of a hat. But Middletown was subjected to this latest invasion of investigators without those investigators in any way coordinating their efforts. At no time were the filmmakers called together to discuss the implications of making such a series under such a title; they were not even apparently required to read *Middletown* itself.

The result is a mishmash of styles and techniques that speak well to the current state of direct cinema. Leacock and his assistant, Marisa Silver, moved into Muncie and made their film there. The film contains acknowledgments of the camera's presence, some interview material, but is largely in the now classic direct-cinema style. DeMott and Kreines, normally based in Alabama, moved in too. They are, after the fashion of top students, even more rigorous than the master. They work, turn and turn about, solo. *Seventeen*, the unseen episode, is by happy accident, then, the purest expression of direct cinema (containing acknowledgments of and a few questions from the camera), and the only attempt in the series to deal with the working class, white and black. The other four programs were the usual mix of interventionism and self-effacement.

Their fly-on-the-wall conceits begin to look odder and odder to me. Two people sit in the front of a large American car, both in profile, and talk to each other. I am now so conscious of the camera that all I can think of is Eliot's query, "Who is the third who walks beside you?" (never mind the fourth sitting in the back with the tape recorder). These episodes all had big crews— seven production assistants on *The Big Game*, a grip, a gaffer, a best boy, and four production assistants on *A Family Business*. One is reminded of Paul Rotha's thought: "It is strange that these many and varied efforts to realize and solve the problem of people in documentary are marked by an increasing, and perhaps dangerous, return to theatricalism. Having been freed from the banalities of the story film, having been developed along fresh and stimulating lines, documentary may now present the sad if faintly ironic spectacle of returning, in spirit if not in material, to the studio."

For the direct-cinema episodes of "Middletown," the pretension of the title remains a key problem, and the difficulties of penetrating beyond the surface still loom large. For the four *vérité* segments, the pretense of sociology seeks to mask a mass of haphazardly researched, unimaginatively chosen topics. Behind the appearance of objectivity lies, instead of the rigor of yesterday's direct cinema (warts and all), a mélange of styles and techniques, each more elaborate, complex, and, above all, phoney than the last. The mundane, in these circumstances, will remain an undiscovered country.

Davis, an alumnus of American television's most distinguished documentary series, "CBS Reports," and maker of the antiwar film *Hearts and Minds* (1974), might seem in "Middletown" to be following in the footsteps of those documentarists who were influenced by the "mass observation" movement of the 1930s. But it turns out that only surrealists really want to know what every last person is doing at six o'clock of a Saturday night. The rest of us, Davis included, are more interested in the extraordinary, or we are attracted to unexceptional folk only in exceptional circumstances—the moments of crisis. Then and only then do ordinary lives become sufficiently theatrical to sustain a documentary film.

Roger Graef, who comes from the theater, has seldom been seduced into attempting to illuminate the ordinary. Instead, over the past decade he has concentrated in a series of remarkable films on the portrayal of power. This is not to say that he treats power as if it were deviance—as his colleagues for the most part tend to treat poverty and misfortune. Rather, he has substituted the frisson to be had from watching normal but usually secret behavior for the frisson of watching deviance. For this subject—the observation of the hidden workings of power within institutions—Graef uses the purest of direct-cinema modes. In the hands of his long-time collaborator, Charles Stewart, the style of these films is minimally interventionist. Graef, however complex the topics, still eschews interviews and narration. Interested in institutions, he avoids the private domain almost entirely, and also avoids thereby the pitfalls of the dominant "victim" documentary.

To deal with the powerful rather than the powerless in society, Graef has elaborated the rules of direct cinema. His films crucially depend on a proper, not to say handsome, level of support from the broadcasters for whom he normally works. Time must be allocated for research and filming way beyond the *vérité* norms they are used to, even beyond the larger expectations of direct cinema. This means that Graef's claim to be making a "film of record" can be better sustained. But a film of record depends on more than the largesse of producers. It can be attempted only if very limited canvases are tackled. Graef delineates these by observing, within the complexities of the organization, just one small singular activity, one issue. In the nature of the case he sometimes is not in at the very beginning, but he always has enough time to wait for a resolution. The crew ask to be informed of all developments relevant to the one issue agreed upon as the film's subject. They bind themselves to secrecy until the film is made. The subjects, the powerful, are allowed to view a fine cut for the purpose of checking accuracy only; not for Graef the release form whereby the documentary filmmaker all too often joins the rest of society in exploiting the victim.

The U.S. Senate, the British Parliament (at least peripherally), EEC head-quarters, British Steel, Hammersmith Borough Council, Occidental Oil, and the Communist party of Great Britain are among the doors that Graef had managed to get behind. And last year he turned to the police.

Like the subjects of the "Middletown" series, watching the police at work has become something of a direct-cinema cliché, from Wiseman's *Law and Order* (1969) to the Raymonds' *Police Tapes* (1977). But "Police" achieved exactly what the publicly seen episodes of "Middletown" missed: it illuminated. It did not do this, of course, by presenting an abstracted and sociological picture of its subject replete with statistics. It was more like that aspect of the

Lynds' work that best reflects the power and accuracy of their observation. "Police" was a series of Lynd-style footnotes elevated into an informing and well structured set of texts. In this it did perhaps all that documentary can do—it fleshed out with vibrant images the bare bones of a social situation which its audience understands from lots of other sources.

What justifies dealing with this topic again is the sense, perfectly caught by the series, of the dilemma of the modern British policeman. On the one hand he has the traditional self-image of public guardian, the man who helps little children across the street; and on the other hand he has a more modern vision of himself as a besieged defender of law and order facing a rising sea of barbarism. This modern copper wouldn't help any children across the street, because he knows they are nothing but momentarily quiescent rioters. It was perhaps this schizophrenia that allowed the senior officers of the Thames Valley force to agree to Graef's system of filmmaking and to permit transmission of the results.

A drunken phone call threatening a dog evoked from the police a "Hill Street Blues" response, flak-jackets and sharpshooters in goodly numbers— even, to lead this embattled team, a quiet-spoken, upper-class military chap. That the police have such tactical units comes as little surprise, but that one is stationed about ten miles from the quiet Oxfordshire field where I used to live astonished me. It clearly was still a bit of a novelty to the two senior policemen involved in the operation. As they walked into the range of their own guns to talk the supposed offender out of his lair they were wryly commenting on the dangers of friendly fire.

The strain between the old and the new in this sequence was expressed in glances, the looks the ordinary policemen gave each other when confronting the tactics of the Clausewitz now recruited to their ranks. Catching such minutiae is what makes the footnotes vivid; it is what justifies the film as a whole. And thanks, not least, to the mismatch between the lens's angle of view and the human angle of vision, it is by no means an automatic function of the equipment to capture this sort of detail. One needs, like Stewart and the second cameraperson, Diane Tammes, to have independent eyes. (Following the advice of the tactical group, by the way, cost the police £40 for breaking the drunk's door down without a reason.)

By dint of these footnotes, a coherent picture of the society in all its richness emerged. I can think of few better texts on the realities of class in Britain, for instance, than the episode wherein the CID [Criminal Investigation Division] lie in wait for a band of expected thieves at the Duchess of Marlborough's country home. One officer, a Cockney lad, took most of the film to get to the correct form of address. His first try, "Lady Marlborough," was curtly corrected to "It's the Duchess of Marlborough, actually." Thereafter he tried the odd "Madam" and even "Er, er, Duchess" before he finally achieved "Your Grace." (The thieves did not show.)

If this was the attractive and somewhat charmingly comic face of the old-style police, the social significance of the series was the exposure of their up-to-date aspect. *A Complaint of Rape* had three officers interrogating a woman who claimed to have been raped. The style of questioning—hostile, overbearing, and insensitive to a painful degree—caused a public outcry. In this it was not little aided by the fact that Mrs. Thatcher was already in full voice about a series of judicial decisions letting rapists off with scandalously light sentences. The impact of the film was immediate. Officers were demoted and reforms promised, including a special rape unit staffed by policewomen.

The underlying assumption of most social documentaries is exactly that they shall act as agents of reform. That they almost never do is conveniently forgotten when justifications for invasion of privacy, voyeurism, or general disturbance are trotted forth by documentarists. An external factor, as in this case with the accident of all those rape stories in the papers, is needed to make the film "work" in this way—and even then it is a rare occurrence. Whether film should have this power or not is another matter, for who mandates the filmmakers as reformers—who pays them and who benefits from their efforts? *A Complaint of Rape*, though, seems to lie among the most clear-cut of such cases. The BBC and the rulers of the Thames Valley police, for whatever internal reasons of their own, clearly licensed Graef to proceed.

The public discussion that followed transmission was, needless to say, more interested in the usual and largely irrelevant agenda of documentary "problems"—the "problem of performance" commanding much attention from editorial and feature writers. "The 'cinéma vérité' [this is the *Guardian*, of course] approach used here invites the assumption that we are viewing the whole truth; but this is not necessarily the case at all. It is dangerous to extrapolate and generalise from situations which must be influenced, to some degree, by the presence of a television camera and crew." It is obviously more interesting to deal with the notion that the police were acting up for the camera than it is to tackle the vexed relationships of pro-filmic to filmic event and the all-important impact of the editing process.

The suggestion here is that the police were modifying their behavior for the camera, but it is just as likely that they were doing no such thing. Indeed, the most obnoxious of the three detectives involved kept dismissing the woman's fears of reprisal from her attackers with the phrase "This is not 'Starsky and Hutch.' " I thought his manner, and the manner of all the "modern" officers in the series, was very much "Starsky and Hutch." I got the impression that their role models were media-generated and that, in effect, they probably behaved like the heroes of a TV cop show all the time. Actually having a camera present for once made little difference, beyond revealing this disturbing characteristic to the rest of us. And although this personal police style clearly does not apply to other situations, in these, too, the question of the camera encouraging performance is almost always irrelevant. When Leacock claims that, with current equipment, the event can be more important than the filming, he speaks, for most of the situations filmmakers of his type are interested in, nothing but the truth.

For most people, Graef's films are quite simply evidence. For all those who thought the evidence suspect, there were others, equally curious, seeking to determine the truth of the woman's tale on the basis of the screen alone. This sort of response is not uncommon with Graef movies. It is one of the major factors that mark him off from other documentarists, for the commonest reaction to vexatious material is always to claim that the filmmakers fixed it in some way. With Graef films that never happens, and the controversies, which are not infrequent, turn—as in this case—on the substance of the events filmed rather than on the filming.

The banned "Middletown" episode *Seventeen* was not so lucky and therefore is more typical. Xerox Corporation did not like *Seventeen*, and neither did the executives of the American public television system. The usual charges of reconstruction, intervention, and incitement were hauled out. But the filmmakers, lacking Graef's elaborate work code and dealing with a broad topic which took them to a variety of people and settings, could not easily rebut such accusations. The controversy also encompassed the language used in the film. Working-class kids use foul language and drugs, smoke grass, talk about sex, and don't study much. Apparently, Xerox would have us believe, they only behave like this in the presence of a camera when encouraged to do so by passing filmmakers. Or, if that is a little far-fetched, an alternative scenario has the filmmakers themselves seeking out that small minority of kids who do these things.

Given the Alice in Wonderland quality of the "sociology" of the transmitted episodes, this sudden demand for accurate representation, this appeal to the court of the typical, is a little astonishing. The actual problem with *Seventeen* is not its language (except for one sequence which could easily have been "cleaned up" for transmission). Bad language was heard on some other shows and is anyway not unknown on public television in America. What got up Xerox's nose was the fact that, during the course of filming, the chief protagonist, a white girl, started going with a black boy. Interracial dating was the real, if somewhat obscured, issue. The result was a public debate notable chiefly for its hypocrisy.

The irony is that, alone of the "Middletown" series, *Seventeen* had, to quote Grierson, "documentary value." It shared with "Police" the power to inform. The potential for such interracial relationships in a midwestern high school, their effect (a cross was burned on the girl's lawn, but the whole family took that, to my surprise, more or less in their stride), the attitude of the boys and girls involved—all this was new, a Lynd footnote of the best type. The film filled in this broad theme with illuminating detail: that teenagers in Muncie hold beer parties of utter raucousness under the supervision of their parents; that parents will turn out to witness a threatened gang fight, involving their own kids, in the spirit of attending a sports event. And amidst the bad language, I learned much talk that was new. "Crank that jammer," for instance, apparently means "turn up the radio"—this during a sequence in which a boy mourns the death of his best friend in a car accident by asking a local station to play "Against the Wind."

Seventeen and "Police" are examples of direct cinema's best. By all the requirements of the Griersonian tradition they are fine pieces of work. Their limitations and difficulties are, then, the limitations and difficulties of the entire tradition.

Take "victims." In "Police," Graef's usual focus on the powerful involves victims as the police "props," as it were. The rape victim, her identity carefully concealed by a crew who never filmed her face, was discovered, no doubt at some expense, by the *News of the World.* According to that paper's account, the woman was upset by the cameras, although the language she uses in the newspaper interview seemed to me sufficiently at odds with her performance in the film to call into question the trustworthiness of this testimony. Nevertheless, she was there to be found by the Sunday press. The point remains that although she was clearly a victim of the police, she was also, in some sense, a victim of the crew. In this case, however, the justification is quite straightforward. Balancing the treatment she was seen receiving at the hands of representatives of the state is the public's right to know. This right often seems too close to voyeurism to mean very much, but here, as subsequent events demonstrated, it had real substance. The other victims in the series cannot be so easily accounted for—the parade of drunks, pop festival attenders, petty criminals, are all part of contemporary documentary's obsession with the halt and the lame. That "Police" was a hit television series, one of the rare examples of documentary escaping from the ghetto of small audiences, exacerbates the problem.

Seventeen raises the same issue. I feel the value of the film is self-evident, yet its topic is contentious, and its transmission could have haunted the participants. Kreines and DeMott had thought about this and were at ease because the girls they featured had all, by the time of the planned transmission, moved away. Of course the controversy wrecked this strategy: it had the effect of a self-fulfilling prophecy, creating in advance of transmission exactly the furor that was supposed to be the danger if the show went out. The local station was especially effective in this, calling in children for cross-examination, summoning Muncie's great and good to private screenings, and generally making sure that all concerned in *Seventeen* would regret their part in the venture.

All "Middletown," to one degree or another, dealt with victims. The pizza parlor owner is now publicly inscribed as a failure. The film will circulate like that other study of midwestern entrepreneurial incompetence, *Salesman* (Maysles, 1969), in perpetuity. The divorced pair who remarry in another episode also have a wedding album they might live to regret. If there is any public right to know here I find it hard to detect. And the acute limitations of that right should not be forgotten. While the Maysles brothers' Bible salesman film is freely available for screenings, the two films they made about powerful figures, *Meet Marlon Brando* (1965) and *Showman* (1962), the portrait of Joe Levine, are not to be seen, for both have been padlocked in the Maysles' vaults by high-powered lawyers acting for the subjects concerned. In fact, *Seventeen* is the only one of the "Middletown" films for which a public right-to-know case can be made. It is all too typical that the banning hinged on quite other and irrelevant issues, issues that could have been better used to prevent the transmission of some of the other episodes.

The direct-cinema style has made the problem of documentary subjects' rights acute, exactly because it allows the filmmaker far greater opportunity to lurk and pry. Let Harold Williamson, writing in the *Listener*, stand for the majority of filmmakers. Williamson has the dubious honor of contributing to the early "Man Alive" series, which, you might recall, came closer than any other to importing the standards of the yellow press to British television on a regular basis. He had the idea of approaching some of his victims from this period again. "For a long time after the programme went out—sometimes for years afterwards—they had been got at by neighbours, or family, or colleagues who, for one reason or another, were angered, outraged, ashamed, envious or offended by their television broadcast to the nation." He tells of fear, loss of jobs, forced house moves. On the plus side, he has a rector who turned his crypt into a pub and was visited by the Queen Mother!

Some people agreed to work with him again. "They all needed coaxing to tell their stories, but, in the end, they decided to trust television again because, all of them said, someone might benefit from their experiences." This "someone" is to my mind as mythic a beast as the chimera. I regret that the silver-tongued Williamson and all his equally glib colleagues are able to coax anyone before their cameras.

If the accepted standards of documentary morality urgently need to be examined, the same is no longer true of the other major problem. Direct cinema promised to deliver observation, pure and simple. But the need creatively to manipulate reality for the purposes of storytelling did not go away—and that at least is now better understood. The third decade of direct cinema finds the debate about ethics as attenuated as ever, but the issue of objectivity is at last being seriously addressed.

It is a pity that currently fashionable theoretical approaches to the documentary, while quite properly insisting on the ideological complicity of the idea of observation, nevertheless fail to take account of the social context in which these films and tapes exist. This is a sort of backlash. It is being argued that because no film can be made without mediation, and all films claiming to be observational are inherently dishonest, we can learn nothing from them. Current criticism would thus deny even the force of a Lynd-like footnote to direct cinema. But there is a jump in logic here. For to argue that, say, the effects of "Police" are an accident, since the films' obsession with surface leaves no possibility of analysis, is to deny the audience the chance for such analysis. It is to claim, as a species of radical naif, that people watching "Police" know nothing of policemen and can therefore reach no conclusions about the films.

The limits of this can be seen in the response to a recent fashionable documentary. People by and large know little of Spanish Harlem and are therefore prepared to find in Chris Menges's *East 103rd Street* a depth of analysis that is denied Graef. Since *East 103rd Street* is but another beautifully shot and exquisitely edited beached direct-cinema/*vérité* whale, in which the stereotypical victim-subjects obey such fundamental dramatic conventions as not speaking their own language and magicking soft drugs into hard, I find it hard to see it as a more responsive and revealing text. What is revealed, however, in the critical acceptance of *East 103rd Street* is the importance of building into our understanding of how documentary works some assessment of the viewers' own knowledge or ignorance of the topic at hand.

The cost, then, for our greater understanding of the limits of objectivity is a *reductio ad absurdum* of the camera's ability to record. It is clear that the direct-cinema practitioners have brought this upon themselves. They have not distanced themselves from the previous Griersonian rhetoric. Indeed, they have claimed to be the only true believers in the great tradition. They are not careful about the continuing effect of their work on the people they use as subjects. They are unprepared to address the paradox of their own reputations as filmmakers (or artists) against the supposed transparency of their fly-on-the-wall techniques. They will not acknowledge the essential work of fictionalization that goes on in the cutting room. The result is that direct cinema has been sailing away on whaling expeditions without proper charts, seeking quite the wrong sort of beasts. The crisis of documentary is therefore deepening. The danger is that film's ability to tell us anything of the world will be lost in the wreck of the direct-cinema idea.

De interpretatione; or, The Difficulty of Being Marco Polo: On the Occasion of Antonioni's China Film

Umberto Eco

What happened in Venice last Saturday fell somewhere between science fiction and comedy *all'Italiana*, with a dash of western. In the wagon ring, desperately resisting, were Ripa di Meana and the Venice Biennal Exposition officials. Around them galloped Chinese diplomats, the Italian foreign minister, the Italian embassy in Peking, the Italian-Chinese Association, the police, the firemen, and other Sinophiles. The story is noteworthy: China was protesting the imminent showing of Antonioni's documentary *Chung Kuo* at the Fenice. The Italian government had done everything possible to prevent the showing; the Venice Biennal Exposition had resisted in the name of the right to information and to artistic expression; at the last moment the Venetian prefect, coming to the aid of Peking, discovered that the Fenice was unusable as a movie hall (after having done nothing but run films there for a week). Meana let leak at a press conference a few well-chosen words of "pity" for the prefect, "forced into such a vile business," and got on the phone to his colleagues. Within half an hour he freed the Olimpia movie house, where Barbra Streisand was fleeing, pursued by a herd of cattle. Here the screening took place while police held an enormous, tense crowd at bay in such a way that no incident could give the prefect (their direct superior) the pretext to call off even this last expedient. Antonioni, nervous and troubled, was once again suffering his very personal and paradoxical drama—the antifascist artist who went to China inspired by affection and respect and who found himself accused of being a fascist, a reactionary in the pay of Soviet revisionism and American imperialism, hated by eight hundred million persons.

Now the Biennal Exposition did with firmness and dignity what should have been done long ago: it gave us all the chance to see and resee the three

530

and a half hours of incriminated documentary, so that we can finally open a political and aesthetic debate around it.

What is Antonioni's *China*? Those who saw it on television remember it as a work that manifested, from the start, an attitude of warm and cordial participation in the great event of the Chinese people; an act of justice on television's part, which finally revealed to millions of viewers a true China, human and peaceful outside of the Western propagandistic schema. All the same, the Chinese have denounced this film as an inconceivable act of hostility, an insult to the Chinese people.

It had been said that Antonioni's film would be only a pretext, a *casus belli* chosen by a Peking power group to advance the anti-Confucian campaign. But even if that were true, the fact remains that a *casus belli*, to work, must be credible: a world war can be started because of the murder of an archduke but not because of the murder of a footman. Where is the archduke in Antonioni's documentary?

It is necessary, then, to see the entire work from a different viewpoint: not from an Italian point of view, but from a Chinese point of view. This is not easy, since it amounts to activating all one's own anthropological antennae, alerted by the fact that words and images acquire different meanings according to the cultures that interpret them. Saturday night I was favored by the fact that I could see the film while a young Chinese movie critic from Hong Kong—who saw, and still sees, this work rigidly and polemically, identifying himself with the values and culture of People's China—provided a shot-by-shot commentary on it.

Now, it is certain that serious ideological objections can be advanced against Antonioni's work. A Western artist, particularly inclined to plumb the depths of existential problems and to emphasize the representation of personal relationships rather than abstract dialectical problems and the class struggle, speaks to us about the daily life of the Chinese within the revolution rather than showing the revolution as the moment of a primary contradiction, within which poles of secondary contradiction open up. Furthermore, a director capable of speaking with masterly skill by stressing the inessential, the secondary episode charged with multiple meanings and subtle ambiguities, has been watched by an audience that knows best great frontal oppositions, symbolic characterizations in clear ideological cipher. Here is enough to start a serious debate about the ends and means of revolutionary art, and it is not valid that Antonioni simply defend the rights (for us, uncontestable) of his poetic vision, of his artistic eye's special interpretation; another aesthetic, as a given fact, opposes him, an aesthetic that seems to negate the rights of art, an aesthetic that in reality reaffirms them in a way foreign to Western tradition. If this were all, a splendid chance for confrontation would have presented itself, and *China* would have become the basis for mass showings followed by political debate. Instead, *China* unleashed an almost physical reaction, a violent and offended rejection.

And there is something more. The *China* question reminds us that when political debate and artistic representation involve different cultures on a worldwide scale, art and politics are also mediated by anthropology and thus by semiology. We cannot open a dialogue on identical class problems among different cultures if we do not first resolve the problem of symbolic superstructures through which different civilizations represent to themselves the same political and social problems.

What discourse did Antonioni address to the Western public with his film? In a few words, I would say the following: "Here is an immense and unknown country that I can only look at, not explain in depth. I know that this country used to live in immensely unjust feudal conditions, and now I see the beginning, through daily struggle, of a new justice. To Western eyes this justice might have the look of a diffuse, austere poverty. But this poverty establishes a possibility of dignified survival, it reinstates persons who are calm and much more human than we are, at times it comes close to our ideal of serenity, harmony with nature, affection in personal relationships, tenacious inventiveness which resolves with simplicity the problem of redistribution of wealth in an often greedy territory. I am not so much interested in seeing those cases where the Chinese were able to construct industries like Western ones; we know that they have the atomic bomb: but it seems to me more interesting to show you how they were able to construct a factory, or hospital, or child-care center from a few scraps, in working conditions based on reciprocal respect. I want to tell you how much sorrow and how much work that task cost, and suggest to you the measure of happiness—different from ours—that all that could encompass, perhaps also for us."

All this entailed the search for China as a potential utopia by the frenetic, neurotic West; and the use of categories that for us assume specific values, where when people say "*arte povera*" they mean a kind of art delivered from the frenzy of jargon required by the commercial gallery circuit, when they say "*medicina povera*" they mean a medicine that substitutes the rediscovery of the relationship between human beings and herbs, and the possibility of a new, popular knowledge for the poisoning of our pharmaceutical industries. But what meaning can the same words have for a country where "poverty" meant, only a few decades ago, death by starvation for entire generations of children, class genocide, sickness, ignorance? And where the Chinese see a suddenly acquired collective "fortune," the film commentary speaks (in my opinion) about a serene and just "poverty." Where the film means "simplicity" for "poverty," the Chinese viewer reads "*miseria*" and failure. When his Chinese escorts told Antonioni, with pride, that a refinery had been built from nothing, using scavenged material, the film emphasizes the miracle of "this humble factory, made with discarded materials"—and Western taste for the ingeniousness of *bricolage*, to which we currently attribute aesthetic value, is at play in this linguistic formula. But the Chinese see in it an insistence on an "inferior" industry, just at the historical moment in which they are successfully closing their industrial gap. When the film celebrates, today, fealty to the past and proposes a model of integration between development and tradition, the Chinese (engaged in a struggle to destroy an unjust past) see in it a praise of feudalism and an insinuation that nothing has changed.

The root of the misunderstanding becomes evident in a theatrical presentation that Antonioni shoots at the end of his documentary: smiling Chinese athletes, dressed in vivid colors, guns slung on their shoulders, make their way up tall poles with acrobatic energy. This is revolutionary China, which presents a strong picture of itself. But Antonioni's film presents a tender, docile picture. For us, gentleness is opposed to neurotic competition, but for the Chinese that docility decodes as resignation. Antonioni explores with realistic gusto the faces of the old and of children, but Chinese revolutionary art is not realistic, it is symbolic, and presents, in posters as in film, an "ideal type" that goes beyond ethnic characteristics (as if Sicilians decided, and with good reason, to represent themselves only through the faces of Sicilians of Norman ancestry, blond and blue-eyed). And doesn't it occur to us Italians to feel betrayed when a foreign film depicts us with the faces of Southern immigrants or Sardinian shepherds in costume, when we tend to identify our country with freeways and factories? The narration states (and it is a positive thing in our eyes) that the Chinese surround suffering and sentiment with shame and reserve. And a culture that rewards dynamism, enthusiasm, and extroverted competitiveness reads "reserve" as "hypocrisy." Antonioni thinks about the individual dimension and speaks of suffering as an ineradicable constant in the life of every person, tied to passion and death; the Chinese read "suffering" as a social ill and see in it the insinuation that injustice has not been eradicated, but merely covered up.

Thus we see how the by now famous criticism in *Renmin Ribao* could consider the shot of the Nanking bridge as an attempt to make it appear distorted and unstable, because a culture that prizes frontal representation and symmetrical distance shots cannot accept the language of Western cinema which, to suggest impressiveness, foreshortens and frames from below, prizing dissymmetry and tension over balance. And the shot of Peking's Tien An Men Square is seen as the denunciation of swarming mass disorder, while for Antonioni such a shot is the picture of life, and an ordered shot would be the picture of death or would evoke the Nuremberg stadium.

Antonioni shows the vestiges of feudal superstition, and then immediately afterward he shows students returning to work in the fields, spades slung over their shoulders; the post-1968 viewer thinks that that is justice: the Chinese critic sees another logic (today, too, students work hard in the fields as they did in the past) and becomes indignant. Also, cutting is a language, and this language is historical, linked to different material conditions of life; the same shots portray different things and different persons. The same thing happens with colors, denounced by the Chinese as unbearably pale and cold, and rightly so, if you compare a film like *Red Detachment of Women*, where extremely bright colors acquire a precise linguistic value and directly symbolize ideological positions.

I could go on at length and point out that the dialogue between peoples (and between persons of the same class who live in different cultures) must be sustained by a historical and social conscience of cultural differences. We must not blame Antonioni for this, since he made a film for the Western public, but perhaps he might have realized that the film could not remain a work of art and would immediately acquire the weight of a diplomatic note—in which every word is fraught with ambivalence. But the consultants of People's China should have realized it too, since they showed Antonioni the places and the things to film, insisting on the peaceful aspects of their society, and it took a year for them to be denounced by other critics, who in their turn are now displaying remarkable ethnocentrism and showing themselves incapable of seeing the different effects that the film can have within and outside China.

But perhaps the greatest responsibility rests with the Italy-China Association, whose task is precisely that of mediating these misunderstandings, supporting on more than one level of "translation from culture to culture" the cause of understanding among peoples: in transferring the Chinese protest bodily into Italy it acts objectively as a factor of misunderstanding, it widens the gap and foments a reactionary game (which enlists willing ministers, prefects, police superintendents, and old-school diplomats, for whom it is valuable that the Chinese remain yellow, treacherous, mysterious, and pig-tailed).

Finally, if useful mediation had been undertaken, then we would have been able to clarify the grossest misunderstandings. For example, the notorious scene of the pigs over which—for pure reasons of sound mix—a musical fragment is inserted. Unfortunately, this fragment happened to be more or less the equivalent of our *Fratelli d'Italia*, evoking in the Chinese viewer the same reaction that a bishop might experience seeing an embrace accompanied by the hymn *Tantum Ergo*. But at the editing table, it seems, there was a consultant from People's China who realized nothing and told no one about the blunder. And then there is the fact that the narration, trying to be dry and objective, leaves too much room to isolated words, which thus acquire a disproportionate value: when it is said that a certain restaurant (rather modest from the outside) is the best in the city, probably it was meant that it served the best food, but the viewer could infer that there are not more imposing restaurants. And when a historical truth is related, such as the fact the modern Shanghai was built urbanistically by colonial powers, a handbill distributed by the Italy-China Association translates (to tell the truth, without justification) that industrial Shanghai was built by People's China "with the help of the imperialists." All these are nuances that Antonioni could have easily avoided if only someone had brought them to his attention. But by now the situation has deteriorated beyond repair.

Now Chinese and Sinophiles have become rigid in their rejection. Antonioni has closed himself up again in his personal sorrow of the-artist-in-good-faith and accepts only with difficulty the idea that from now on the debate will go far beyond his film and will involve on both sides—apart from political questions that elude us—unexorcised phantoms of ethnocentristic dogmatism and aesthetic exoticism, and symbolic superstructures that obscure material relations and delay the course of history. The Venice Biennial Exposition pointed out a way and reopened critical discussion. We hope that this will not be in vain.

Already last Saturday evening, after the showing, a more open debate was in the air, beyond the scandal mongering. And to illustrate the fact, journalists' eyes were fixed on Antonioni and the young Chinese critic, who, at two in the morning around a restaurant table, were polemically exchanging ideas and impressions. And in the corner, ignored by everyone, a young woman with soft, sensual eyes was following the discussion, accepting the fact that more important considerations were in play and that the protagonist of the evening was the Chinese. Her name was Maria Schneider, but few would have recognized her.

Translated by Christine Leefeldt

"Phantom India"

Todd Gitlin

As bewildered radicals, lacking in political (or any other) faith in the Nixon era, cast about for ways of understanding the world that promise to transcend, or at least evade, intolerable reality, it is natural that we once again encounter the East. Perhaps it began with the romance with the Vietnamese revolutionaries, so hard to avoid when one has been in contact with them: What do they have that we don't? How do we explain their tenacity as against our impatience, their calmness under fire as against our paranoia, their optimism as against our despair? But the new journeys to the East have deeper roots than a passing political alignment; they flow from the revolt against materialism and technological reason and from the communal—even spiritual—urges that once found a home in the movement and are now looking for more viable and less fratricidal places to rest. Increasingly, what remains of the movement of the sixties divides between those for whom the East is Red (China is near and getting nearer all the time) and those for whom the East is God or Void, the "bou-oum" of the Malabar Caves come home to roost. In any case, passages to India these days are as common as trips to inner space; indeed, they sometimes feel like *Drang nach Osten*. And they are just as complex, just as subjective, just as burdened by the personal and social past.

Louis Malle's "Phantom India" is a documentary in seven parts, lasting a total of almost six hours; it has been shown both on television and in theaters, and it comes to this country at a good time. Malle's passage began, he says, as a flight, a diversion; it became a quest. It is the classic *Bildungsroman*; and if Malle's ideas are finally inadequate to the camera, as the camera is finally inadequate to the material it seeks to record, he has still given us a useful first approximation to an honest Westerner's India. He refuses to let us have our simple Indias: he confronts the mystic with human wretchedness and exploitation, and the Marxist with undeniable spirituality. As long as the film can sustain this negative capability, this juxtaposition of the uplifting and depressing, it is a useful antidote to easy attitudes.

Malle begins, like a good French intellectual, with his self-consciousness. The first fifty-minute segment is called, appropriately, *The Impossible Camera*, and it examines the nature of film, as James Agee explored the nature of writing in *Let Us Now Praise Famous Men*. A peasant woman says the camera is an evil eye; Malle is embarrassed but goes on filming. "To them we are men from Mars. . . . Our camera is a weapon and so they are afraid of us." Of others he says, "They dance, I film, that's all there is to it." He denies he is selecting material; he is "just following the camera." Apparently it is not hard, in India, to blunder into the bizarre and the unspeakably sad. Workmen make 150 bricks for one rupee. There is a long, exquisitely disgusting segment of vultures feeding on the carcass of a water buffalo: a metaphor, communicated by the camera's very steadiness, for the otherness of Indian reality. This in itself is a nice departure from the usual nervousness of the documentary camera. "When I look at the scene today," Malle says in his narration, "I realize we reacted according to our culture. For us it was tragedy, but for the Hindu it was only an everyday occurrence . . . a metaphor for life and death." Shortly after this ugliness—by using the word I reveal my culture; so be it—Malle shows us the ugliness of petty capitalism, "the old story of exploitation." But there is clearly something extraordinary in this Indian material: of the Indians Malle says, "They live in the present, without past or future." Whether Malle means this is in the laudatory sense of the counterculture is not clear, but he is at least intrigued. "So, here's your film," he concludes. "On the one hand, my little dream world; on the other, the harsh economic facts. Almost always the harsh reality comes out on top."

Malle seems aware of the risk he is taking, steering between total acceptance and his Cartesian skepticism. A risk is best illustrated with foils, and these Malle finds. Two French hippies have come to India in pursuit of holy mystery—and hashish. Two weeks later he meets them again. They can't cope with the climate, they have headaches and are constantly throwing up. They have decided to go back to France; their parents sent them the air fare; they didn't want to be treated in an Indian hospital. And then there is the Italian hippie who came to India to find what was missing in his intellectual life. He was looking for Gandhi, "but Gandhi and Gandhi's ideas are gone."

The first segment of "Phantom India" is the most successful precisely because it acknowledges that the camera is "impossible." Not being willing or able to penetrate the Indian consciousness, and not being satisfied with travelogue, Malle uses his own consciousness as the foil for Indian reality. The tension between his consciousness and the filmed material is what makes the film interesting: the narrative intervenes to avert travelogue whenever it rears its head, whenever the camera becomes too naive. Since his short sojourn prevents the kind of tension between opposed consciousnesses that animates a novel like *A Passage to India*, Malle resorts to another order of tension; this immediately sets his film apart from such superficial travelogues as Antonioni's TV film on China. But Malle's choice imposes a great burden on his own consciousness; should his ideas solidify and lose their suppleness, the film degenerates into a futile interplay between static images and stale ideas. This is ultimately what happens. India's demands on Malle's sensibility become too much for him, and he resorts to self-contradictory cliché. We can admire the audacity of his attempt and at the same time recognize that he was defeated. Susan Sontag and Mary McCarthy have written astonishing books on North Vietnam precisely because the Vietnamese reality opens them like wounds: opens them to the limits and costs of their own exquisitely Western consciousness. Malle opens himself just so far and then slams the door.

In segments two through seven, Malle repeatedly falls back on his subjectivity, but now that we are alerted to the fact that he insists on that subjectivity, it proves less interesting. He finds himself in a Madras crowd celebrating a temple. His fear melts into ecstasy. "For a time I forgot who I was." Rationally he knows this is the opium of the masses, "but for five hours I lived by instinct, not reason. Time vanished." This tells us more about Malle than about the meaning and configuration of the ritual, but not much about either: for might he not lose himself in a political demonstration as well, let's say, or a Catholic mass? Finally, he says, "we were intruders in a world to which we could never belong," but by then the point is obvious. In this manner his consciousness disengages from India. He becomes a shower and teller, no longer a film essayist—and, granted this is a difficult form, rarely achieved— he is reduced to pure *vérité*. At the beginning of segment four he tells us he spent whole days without shooting: "It was no longer important." What had become important, presumably, was the journey of Malle's psyche; but he does not let us in. (A similar thing seems to have happened to Allen Ginsberg in his *Indian Journals*; Ginsberg has a vocabulary and method for defining his subjectivity, though, so the book becomes interesting as a representation of Ginsberg. But Malle withdraws his psyche from our view, leaving us with prettified images.)

With the disappearance of Malle's tension with his images there appears Malle the commentator, the producer of opinions. He does not play his sensibility off his images, but presents his attitudes, mostly political. Some of these are interesting and some are execrable, some I happen to agree with and others I happen not to. The worth of his attitudes—and I will get to them in a moment— is somewhat beside the point. The point is that the attitudes are no longer grounded in Malle's journey and become a way of extricating himself from it. I do not mean this too harshly: it may be that the reality of India for a basically rationalist Westerner is so bizarre and .imponderable that it would throw anyone back on attitudes. But this lessens the film, reduces it from that very difficult film essay to a travelogue with superimposed opinions. The camera has become all too possible.

One consequence of the creeping possibility of the camera—perhaps the filmmaker's bane—is that India is oddly despiritualized. The very clarity of images, the separateness of shape and color, is at odds with what F.S.C. Northrop called the "undifferentiated aesthetic continuum" of the East. (In her essay on North Vietnam, Mary McCarthy also wrote very convincingly about the Western novelist's consciousness, which makes much of differences between people, places, situations, moods, appearances, and the Vietnamese "collectivist"—but also Buddhist—insistence on underlying unities.) To show the odd contortions of a Yogi is not to enter into the consciousness of the Yogi. Without being able to enter, Malle falls back on mere opinions. Presumably he is very skeptical of the ashram's claims to be ushering in world peace, as he has every right to be; but this is to shortchange the Yogi, who has, perhaps, his own definition. To dispute the definition is one thing, and permissible, but it is all the more compelling to do so when the consciousness can be entered into on its own terms—if only to extricate oneself from it. When E. M. Forster, at the end of *A Passage to India*, tells us that the Indian and the Englishman must go their own separate ways, this is credible and meaningful precisely because we have entered the skulls of both men. Malle's judgments about the political future of India are easily discounted because he does not ground them in his own human experience.

A major exception to this lack in Malle's approach is the fifth segment, *A Look at the Castes*. He *shows* us, with images, precisely what he found objectionable about the caste system, and uses narration to extrapolate from images. Thus, the untouchable children, who are not allowed to eat food in the village school, *look* unhappy. The caste system emerges as the foundation of Indian spirituality, or at least a system logically inseparable from the fabric of Indian religious ideas; Malle could have said more about the basis of Hinduism in the belief in inescapable *karma*, which logically justifies caste. This segment ends with Malle's most pointed political critique of Indian "democracy." He shows us a village meeting which looks, at first, impeccably democratic. The villagers in attendance seem involved. "At first," says Malle, "I was much impressed. I was seeing direct democracy in action." But he observes that untouchables and women are not present. The meeting turns to consider an important matter: the village headman has been accused of embezzlement. The inquiry gets nowhere. It turns out that the local civil servant, in charge of such matters, is a friend of the headman. "I gradually perceived that beneath the cloak of democracy is an institution that belongs to rich farmers." The observation is grounded in—though not wholly determined by—the observed images: the tension between narrative and image returns.

The next segment, *On the Fringes of Indian Society*, reveals the fragility, even the repulsiveness, of some of Malle's ideas. A group of intermarrying Jews is called "decadent" because they sequester themselves from the rest of Indian society—an odd word, to say the least, considering that some eighteen hundred caste divisions also sequester themselves and are not called decadent for that reason. After a short visit to the ashram of rich Western devotees who believe themselves saviors of the world—"Maybe they're right," says Malle in the depths of his confusion—he takes us to what he calls an "ideal society of villagers." They have no war, no laws, no weapons. The eight hundred of them have resisted missionaries, the English, tourists—and filmmakers. They have, Malle says, "sexual freedom." The women are sexually "initiated" by "experienced" men at age thirteen—he does not say how the men are "initiated." Women are apparently common property, and are given to kissing the feet of men—but not vice versa. Malle does not comment on this inequity in what he calls a "perfect society": he merely nostalgically observes that the villagers will soon be evicted, as their land has been taken for turpentine cultivation. Later on, he interviews a Western-trained economist and refers to her, condescendingly, as "this very pretty young woman." With such images of "the ideal society" versus "decadence," it is fair to say that Malle should not allow himself to indulge his attitudes.

The last segment deals with Bombay, but too briefly. "The dire poverty of India you can never get used to," but Malle shows us little of it, and his color camera prettifies even those who sleep on the pavement. In his *Calcutta*, made from the footage shot on the same trip, we of course see plenty of poverty, but in "Phantom India" Malle pays little attention to the Indian millions who live and suffer in cities. Having finally penetrated Bombay, he is already preparing to wrap up the film. And here the thinness of his attitudes, already severely stretched, breaks apart. The masses are wretched. Right-wing demagogues thrive. The communists, rigidly trained by the British party, hopelessly middle-class and splintered, are out of touch with Indian culture: "They need a Mao Tse-tung."

What is left to say? The traditional society, Malle sums up, is doomed by inevitable industrialization, "which brings with it the exploitation of man by his fellow man." He has just observed that the new bourgeoisie is "comfortable enough to feel nostalgia," yet here is Malle indulging in the same. To argue that it is industrialization that brings exploitation is to forget his own earlier observations on the horrors of the caste system, on the exploitation of peasants, the poverty and starvation that everywhere leer at the Western optimist. Pressed to produce a moral, a message, Malle falls back on the classical mistake: if the new is bad, the old must be good. The wistfulness of his call for an Indian Mao dissolves in a soup of back-glancing. This is an understandable response to the sheer horror of the Indian present, but it does not clarify Indian possibilities.

It is no wonder that American middle-class viewers talk afterward in the lobby about how nice it would be to visit India.

Perhaps, as a friend of mine says, all political films fail—fail to generate action, or even understanding, in accord with the desires of the filmmaker. But they should at least clarify choices, help us to understand the stakes and the risks of each choice, and if ambivalence is the final feeling, then let the audience make the most of it. Such ambivalence must be fertile, rich, and clear. Malle's too often is not. The medium has lent itself to travelogue, which has overwhelmed whatever the message was supposed to be. And yet the travelogue of faces and settings is itself untrue to the spirit of India, except insofar as it points to the otherness of the phantom. Malle therefore ends up with neither his own consciousness nor India's. That images are too clear for the reality, and the ideas not clear enough. To the extent that Malle's vantage point is explicit, it is stale with nostalgia for an idea that is either impossibly vague or tendentious. After six hours of film, Malle's conclusions remain vague and flabby.

The difficulty is perhaps with the form Malle has adopted. Documentary without point of view must rest, for its force, on the capacity of consciousness to distill sharp conclusions from the material. Granted, this is difficult when the camera is invading an alien reality—indeed, a reality that does not claim even to be "real." Malle is at his best in extracting meaning, or meaninglessness (another form of meaning), from detail. Here his consciousness is interesting enough to make his reactions plausible, to take us into them. We may then, if prohibited from entering into Indian reality, still enter into Malle's consciousness, identifying with the agonies of the filmmaker who tries to make sense of the ineffable. Perhaps it is not only the camera that is impossible, but conclusion itself. If that is so, Malle should have had the courage of his lack of conviction. Instead of grasping at straws, he should have thrown up his hands.

When the Mountains Tremble: An Interview with Pamela Yates

Alan Rosenthal

How to present history on film is one of the key problems obsessing documentary filmmakers. In essence the problem has two different aspects—how to assess and evaluate the past, and how to help understand the present and possibly change the future.

The assessment of the fading past can be seen in all the histories and revisionist histories of the Second World War, from "Victory at Sea" and "The Churchill Years" to "The World at War." It is arguable that the further history recedes, the easier it is to deal with. Thus WBGH's Vietnam series of the early eighties was, in a sense, more difficult to handle than documentaries of the 1939–45 European conflict because of the continuing immediacy of the pain, the wounds, the conflicts, and the controversies.

During the late sixties and early seventies, the confrontation with history, for most American filmmakers, came through their feelings about the Vietnam war. Today this has largely been replaced by a confrontation with the issues of the wars in Central America, giving urgency to the second part of the documentarist's problem—how to understand the present and do something about the future.

The filmmakers covering the wars, repressions, and revolutions of Central America range from commercial network and PBS crews to independent North American and European sympathizers with the revolutions and to Central American filmmakers themselves. They speak to different audiences, they use different methods, and they represent a variety of political views. Many of the complexities and problems of their films have been perceptively dealt with by Julia Lesage in her article "For Our Urgent Use: Films on Central America."[1]

Pam Yates's experiences are emblematic of those gone through by filmmakers working in areas where guerrilla struggles are in progress, and she brings to the situation an unusually rich background. In the discussion below, we focused on her most recent film, *When the Mountains Tremble*, which is about contemporary Guatemalan history. The spine of the film is provided by the experiences of Rigoberta Menchu, a Christian Indian. Through the threads of Rigoberta's story we feel the richness of the culture, the courage of her people, and the tragedy of greed, corruption, and repression in Guatemala. Most of the film is shot *vérité* style by Yates and Thomas Sigel, the film's codirector. Part of the filming is done from the government side, but the major experience of the story is seeing the conflict through the eyes and experiences of the Indian peasants and guerrilla fighters.

There are a few stylistic breaks in the film. First, there are two dramatic reenactments near the beginning of the film, one involving an American ambassador and Guatemalan officials, another portraying a CIA officer. Both episodes are based on American documents and establish the importance of U.S. commercial interests in Guatemala. Both scenes have also been fairly heavily criticized by purist critics.

The second stylistic break relates to the filming of Rigoberta Menchu herself. She is filmed in limbo in a studio and describes both the decimation of democratic hopes in Guatemala and the murder of her family by the security police. As the film expands to cover the activities of the government and the guerrillas, so Rigoberta's story becomes the story of her people.

It seems that people define themselves by their choices. Why did you choose Latin America as a subject for filmmaking?

Well, I was working as a freelance photojournalist in the early seventies for a newspaper in Massachusetts when the Puerto Rican migration moved up from New York through that area of New England. No one on our newspaper spoke Spanish, so I decided to take a short leave of absence and go to Mexico to learn Spanish. While I was there, I began to shoot photos for a Mexican newspaper, and two months turned into two years.

That was thirteen years ago. Since that time I've spent about half my life in Latin America.

When I began to work in the film industry as a sound engineer, I got most of my early jobs because I was bilingual in Spanish and English. That meant I was able to spend a lot of time in Latin America. Then, when the war started against Somoza in Nicaragua in 1978, I began to spend even more and more time. And that's how I really became known for the work I did in Central America.

Did you come to this work with any strong political preconceptions? Had there been a strong political element in your background?

Not beyond what most Americans of my generation experienced, which was coming of age in the United States during the Vietnam war, which as high school students taught us to question the very principles that our government said it stood for: peace and democracy. We were organized to stop the war, knowing that most Americans were opposed to involvement in Vietnam.

Can you tell me about the origins of When the Mountains Tremble?

My partners in Skylight Pictures, Tom Sigel and Peter Kinoy, and I wanted to make a film about Guatemala. It was a challenge to us. We're a cinematographer (Sigel), sound recordist (myself), and editor (Kinoy). We all worked freelance and then came together with our skills and equipment to form Skylight Pictures.

We wanted to make a film about Guatemala because none had been made, and we knew that one of the reasons none had been made was because over twenty-five Guatemalan journalists had been killed in the three previous years, and international journalists were being prevented from going into Guatemala. Having already filmed in Central America for three years, we wanted to bring all our knowledge, skills, and emotions to the least-known country, Guatemala. And we felt, through everything we knew about Guatemala, that there was an incredible story to be told there.

We tried but could never raise the necessary money, so we decided to go to the networks with this idea. We went to the three commercial networks and to PBS. Two of the networks, ABC and CBS, wanted to do the film with us, and we decided to go with CBS because they had a better reputation for doing straightforward documentaries, especially in the "CBS Reports" units. And that's how it started.

After some discussion CBS then said, "But *you* can't produce this film. We're going to send a CBS producer with you." So we said, fine, and became the associate producers—even though we had worked in the area far longer and spoke Spanish. The producer we actually ended up working with, Martin Smith, was very good. We were able to teach him a lot about Central America, and he was able to teach us a lot about producing for television and how to reach an American audience.

One interesting thing is that prior to all this we had done another film, *El Salvador, Another Vietnam* (which was seen widely in the United States and Europe and was nominated for an Oscar). This slightly frightened CBS. They were afraid to send us with Marty because we were going to be both crew and associate producers, which is a little bit unusual. CBS was afraid that the Guatemalan government would know we had done the El Salvador film and would stop us at the airport and prevent the whole crew from going in. So CBS said to us, "Okay, you can do the guerrillas and the left, and we'll do the government and everybody else who's above ground. And we'll have two crews, and that's how we'll solve it." We said, "No. We're either going to do everything or we're not going to do anything," and CBS had to agree. So we ended up going into the country a few months before the elections in 1982. That's how we were able to get in. They knew they had to open it up to international journalists.

In the end we shot two films for CBS. One called *Central America in Revolt*, in which we did the Guatemala section. And later another hour for "CBS Reports," called simply *Guatemala*.

During the most dangerous and secret parts of the filming, no CBS producers or correspondents were present. These were the most exciting, newsworthy scenes, which then belonged to us as independent filmmakers. On our return to New York, we viewed the material and decided we owned a lot of unused film, and we thought, well, we're going to go back to Guatemala now that we have the experience under our belt, and we're going to do the film we originally wanted to do. Because the Guatemalan story, with its Indian roots and historical importance, can never really be told in a network format. It needed a partisan approach with a healthy dose of dream realism à la García Márquez.

Where did you think your film would differ from a network report?

I think many television reports are moving slide shows. There's wall-to-wall narration over everything, telling you what you're seeing, how to see it, and who the people are. There's not very much lyricism. The producers are prevented from doing certain things by journalistic constraints, like adding additional music that doesn't emanate from the scene. And they're so obliged to tell a balanced story. To our way of filmmaking, a balanced story can be a confusing story. All controversy, provocative ideas, are diluted. Experts speak, but not those who are most affected: the powerless.

This notion of objectivity also means that you distance yourself and the audience from the people you're filming. We wanted to make a film which would actually draw Americans closer to Guatemala, not distance them in a dry, educational—that is, boring—way.

Also, in most network pieces there's a correspondent who becomes the centerpiece of the film. We wanted to avoid that by featuring a Guatemalan in a dramatic role, which is essentially how Rigoberta Menchu is used in *When the Mountains Tremble*.

How did you eventually raise the rest of the money?

From individuals, church groups, foundations, and finally we were able to get finishing funds from the Corporation for Public Broadcasting.

We presented them with a proposal, and we also cut together a ten-minute pilot, which was a short film in and of itself. It's always been our strength at Skylight, with an editor like Peter Kinoy, to make good pilots, ones that are dramatic and fun to look at, and that have a high success rate in raising money.

How did you find Rigoberta? When did you decide to build the film around her?

We met her when she came to speak at the United Nations before the General Assembly. We knew that our main problem in the editing of *Mountains* was that we had very few central characters, and we had no one, central character to act as the thread to weave the film together. And then, about three days after I met her, I knew that she would be the best choice. Then it was Tom's idea that we film her in isolation the way we did, to give her that storytelling quality, to separate her from the bulk of the documentary filmmaking, and to represent her as the voice of the Guatemalan people.

We also filmed her this way because we're moving toward a combination of drama and documentary forms, and Rigoberta's role was another way of experimenting with that.

Did you shoot her before you started the editing? Afterward?

At the very beginning, before we really had an assemblage. She came and looked at all the footage with us, and we discussed the kinds of scenes we were going to put together. Of course, we knew her whole story. We had tried to gather every article that had been written about her, and we also had many long conversations with her. Then she sat down and wrote the script, her own personal story, over a period of three days. Afterward we went into a studio and filmed her.

Can you tell me about the organization and logistics of the filmmaking?

We wanted to talk to all of the motive forces involved in the Guatemalan conflict. We knew from our previous experience that an American audience would not accept a film unless that had been done. So we actually filmed almost all the government side first, and got the film out of the country, and then we went on several trips with the guerrillas into the Indian highlands.

Did the government know you were going to film the guerrillas?

No. If they had known, we would have been declared enemies of the state and either killed or expelled.

But how did you accomplish it?

We made contact with the guerrillas before we went into the country, and we were given a time and a place, and instructions on how to meet a contact of theirs. When we met the contact, we started a whole series of meetings about what we wanted to film, how we were going to achieve it, and where they were going to take us.

This working on both sides of the line made for interesting contrasts. The general oppression is so intense in Guatemala that you just can't ask someone their candid opinion, because they won't tell you. At least not above ground in the capital.

But when we went with the guerrillas, it was like crossing an invisible line. All of a sudden, everyone would tell you anything you wanted to know. They were very free about how they spoke, whether it was for or against the guerrillas. And to me that was a revelation. A once-in-a-lifetime journalistic experience.

Didn't the government question what you were doing? They knew you were in the country, that you hadn't left, and you suddenly disappear, then what? Where were you?

Well, the Guatemalan government had other concerns besides journalists at that time. For instance, they were very interested in getting as much exposure in the United States as possible, because it was before Reagan had decided that he was going to reopen military sales to them. The Guatemalan government didn't see us as posing any threat, and when we went on the secret trips we tried to leave when there were a lot of journalists in the country so that our absence wouldn't be noticed.

What were the main difficulties of filming, technical or otherwise?

The main difficulties were keeping a high level of credibility with the Guatemalan government; going for very long periods of time without being near electricity; keeping our equipment clean; keeping safe; keeping calm; all the time being aware of everything that was going on around us.

History moves very fast in Central America. When we went into the Indian highlands, we decided to take more equipment rather than less because we wanted to film all sides with an equal level of technology. For example, we took a tripod. Now, a tripod is a real luxury to carry over hundreds of miles. Tom wanted to take it because it meant he could do certain kinds of shots that we had done in the city. I took radio microphones, which are very fragile. We outfitted backpacks with foam in order to carry all this equipment. And we took one change of clothes.

How did you gain the trust and confidence of the guerrillas?

A few things helped us. One was that their leadership had seen *El Salvador: Another Vietnam*. That film was used as a fundamental tool in catalyzing a movement to stop U.S. intervention in Central America. So that was our introduction.

The second thing was that they, just like the Guatemalan government, wanted to speak to Americans and put their case before them. We were introduced to the opposition by people who were trusted by the guerrillas, so they in turn trusted us. We spoke Spanish and we had access to the networks (big audience) as well as independent exhibition (important, active audiences).

What I like very much in the film is its style. It isn't just polemic or propaganda. You feel people as human beings, as having lives, dimensions. And a large part of that comes through really looking at them. You're really looking, you have time to pause and you're seeing and you're feeling. Was that very deliberate as a camera style?

Yes. It was. The way we make films is by knowing and reading all the available material and by talking to as many people as possible before we embark on the production. So in many senses every frame of the film should reflect what you've been able to gather about a situation, about a country. You know the frame where the general is sitting in front of the camera with sunglasses on and a bodyguard behind him? You see the general's head, and just the bodyguard's waist and his pistol behind him. Those kinds of frames come from a certain knowledge about visual relationships that point to a political relationship.

Making a film as a narrative means that you have to look at people. And in Guatemala you're drawn to look at people anyway because they are so beautiful and the clothes they wear are so unusual. Even though they're very poor, the Indians have a really remarkable sense of beauty integral to their culture.

In a number of your films you've shot battle skirmishes and fighting. There must have been times when you were in danger? What was happening inside yourself?

Let's see, was I afraid? I'm always afraid in battles. The first and second confrontations are usually the worst. After that, you get more used to it. It's like acquiring street smarts. You know, people in Iowa would think growing up in New York terrible. "On the streets of New York, aren't you afraid? Aren't there criminals around every corner?" You learn how to conduct yourself in battle, in crossfire, what you can do, what you can't do, what weapons are being used, what their effect is, where the fire's coming from. You can't control a combat situation, but at least knowing the ropes helps assuage the fear.

What is the hardest thing, say, emotionally, for you during the filming?

Overcoming the fear inherent in making good films in Central America. Not the fear of battle so much as the fear of what could happen. The fear that seizes you when you go on a night trip with the guerrillas. The fear of being picked up by the paramilitary death squads, or feeling that someone is watching you all the time. Just not knowing from minute to minute what is going to happen to you or when the government is going to find out what we are really doing.

In the film, your sympathies come out very much on the side of the guerrillas. Did you consider portraying the other side in a more logical, more emotional, more sympathetic way? Were there voices that you dropped? And was there any slanting, conscious or unconscious, of the people you interviewed?

We tried to interview everyone, from moderate politicians to church to armed forces, to government to guerrillas. But in Guatemala, the government has been characterized by Amnesty International as one of the worst abusers of human rights in the hemisphere. And they are. It's hard to characterize the head of the armed forces, after you've seen massacre after massacre, in any other light than the one we did in the film. I mean, if you were in Germany from 1935 to 1940, how could you present a balanced picture of what Hitler was doing? There's no way morally you could have, especially if one knew then what we know now, or if one had enough foresight to see it coming. That's what we hope to achieve with *Mountains*, vis-à-vis Guatemala specifically and Central America generally. We are trying to show what history was, is, and may be. "May be" in the sense that each person can influence history.

The film has a very logical drive and thrust to it—the story holds together very well and its unfolding seems inevitable, as if it could have been done no other way. Were there major scenes that you had to drop, that you regret, that were left out?

There were many, particularly some of the scenes people risked their lives to help us get. We weren't able to include them in the final film because a lot of them are testimonies of torture and murder by the Guatemalan armed forces, and we just felt the audience could only take so much of that. Luckily, because we did the two television programs as well as a video short for use in U.S. congressional efforts, we were able to make use of them. We tried to have a linear, narrative structure to the film, so that Americans would understand why somebody like Rigoberta actually was in favor of armed struggle. Our idea in the film was to build it logically, through the different progressions of frustrated struggles for democracy to the inevitable conclusion of the armed struggle.

Were you conscious of the very gentle, very human way the women guerrilla recruits are shown in the film? Was there a conscious attempt to get shots that would show them in that way? The women are soldiers but still seem very tender and feminine.

Yes, I like those scenes with the young women recruits. If you see the rushes themselves, you see the girls are giggling to death. And they're flirting with the person who is our translator. It's a phenomenon I've seen many times in Central America among teenage combatants—they combine tender and childlike qualities with a very serious and sophisticated understanding of what they're doing, why they're fighting. They are wise in a way beyond their years.

Many of the people in the film tend to become symbols, to become voices larger than themselves. And there is a danger of being simplistic. Do you think film critics or American analysts of Guatemala will have difficulties with any of this or with the politics of your film? With any of the political descriptions of the film? Or would they basically agree with them?

They would think the film reflected Guatemalan reality. But I think, like you, they would say it's a little too simplistic. It's too black-and-white and no grey areas. To our way of thinking, in making films the most important thing is to tell a good story—to reach an audience through the telling of our story. And that means, even in the documentary, taking certain dramatic liberties. Since there were no films about Guatemala, we decided to tell the story through Rigoberta with a definite point of view. Hopefully other films will come along about Guatemala and will explore certain sections of what we tried to cover (for example, the church) and show more of its complexity. But we chose to make a general film about Guatemala because one didn't exist. At the same time, one has to be very careful not to put everything in one film. You also want to tell a very good story, not spew facts and figures. And I think that may be an area the political analysts would have trouble with. But most filmmakers and viewers won't.

When we were talking earlier you said that occasionally you have had difficulties with left-wing criticism of the film. I'm curious as to why.

Well, like most critics, they don't feel they've justified their role in society until they've criticized something. We made the film for an American audience, most of whom know little about Central America or who have never been to Central America or who have been there only as tourists. So they knew little and are confused about the role of the United States in Central America and the war there. The sign of a good political filmmaker is if he or she thoroughly understands the subject, thoroughly understands the audience, and then moves the audience a little closer to the subject. Then one has accomplished something!

But the left-wing critics want a more complex analysis, and because we didn't always cover the political situation in depth, political analysts and film critics of the left have criticized our film. They've said that we have an unblinking admiration for the guerrillas. They've been very narrow-minded in terms of documentary film form, arguing that the dramatic sections ruin the film. And even though the film has had a great response theatrically, there still hasn't been that much publicity or interviews with magazines such as *Cineaste* or *Jump Cut.*

About six months have passed since you finished the film. Looking at it today, do you see anything you would have done differently?

I think I would consider doing the dramatic section a little differently, but I'm really glad we did it. At the moment it doesn't work in and of itself because there are so many different elements competing in the first reel.

I'll tell you one thing we did change. When people first saw the film they were really confused, because of the dramatic section, about who was real and who was an actor. So we had to put a title card at the beginning of the film explaining that all of the people and events in the film are real except for two reenacted scenes which are based on recently declassified U.S. government documents.

There is one other point we've had second thoughts about and that's the tone of the voices we use in some of the voice-overs. We were really undecided whether to do voice-over in English or subtitle the film. We wanted to subtitle it because it's a more purist approach. But we also knew that Americans hate subtitles, and since film is a visual medium, we didn't want people to read the film. We wanted them to watch the film. So we made a stylistic decision that all of the action sequences would be subtitled. And all of the sequences with people speaking directly to the camera would have voice-over in English.

There's nothing else really that I would do over again. You know, we spent a year and a half crafting the film, and everything in the film is very, very well thought out. That's one of the pleasures of working as an independent filmmaker. You're not working for an executive producer, and consequently you have a certain kind of freedom. No one's telling you what to do and what not to do. And I think that's why we decided to make these kinds of films. We've worked so much producing and shooting for television requirements that in our independent work we want to do films that have much more passion.

One hopes that these kinds of films will bring about change, though what documentary does is absolutely undocumented. What would you like this film to do?

Well, I'd like the film to help organize Americans to stop U.S. intervention in Central America. And also, in doing that, to aid in the organization efforts for social change in the United States. These two fundamental reasons were why we made the film. I think one of the reasons the films [*When the Mountains Tremble* and *Nicaragua: Report from the Front* were being shown together] have been so successful theatrically is because when they were released one of the strongest political movements in the United States was for peace and against intervention in Central America. That movement was where we drew our inspiration for the making of the films. And now that we've made the films we're giving them back to that movement.

In other words, in every city we open in, part of the formula for success is making sure that there is a grassroots campaign and that the groups have access to the theater to talk to people about the local work, to sell their literature, to get more people active. So it's been kind of a give-and-take thing. The film wasn't developed in isolation. And we hope that it will add to the movement for peace. We hope that when people come out after the film is over they will have had an emotionally compelling experience that makes them think or feel that the people of Central America and the people of the United States have more in common with each other than we each have with our respective governments (with the exception of Nicaragua).

Have you made any attempts to show the films to government circles?

Sure . . . especially *Nicaragua: Report from the Front*. We've shown that a lot to Congress people. As a matter of fact, there are several parts of that film that have been officially entered into the Congressional Record, by those Congress people who are against giving aid to the Contras.

How was Nicaragua: Report from the Front *put together?*

Originally we went to film the U.S. military maneuvers in Honduras for Haskell Wexler's dramatic film *Latino*. The purpose was twofold: to shoot all footage in Super 16mm for inclusion—by blow-up—in his 35mm footage and to get as much information as possible for research, dialogue, costumes, art direction, and so forth. But since our research and perseverence yielded a scoop, we first broadcast the material as a series of news stories on the CBS Evening News.

Up to that point, the Contras were just a rumor. Everyone knew they were there, but no one had seen them or could get to them—or could prove the connection between the U.S. military and the Contras, prove that there actually was American aid going to the Contras.

After we put the program on the CBS Evening News, we had masses of footage left over, maybe thirty hours of very good footage. And we decided to do something with it, especially because many of our friends kept persuading us to make a half-hour film out of it all. So we turned all the footage over to Deborah Shaffer and two coproducers, Ana Maria Garcia and Glenn Silber, who directed *El Salvador: Another Vietnam*. They raised the rest of the money, did some shooting in the States, and put it together in three months. That way, Skylight Pictures was able to open both films together.

That joint opening was important because although people know that the United States is involved in Nicaragua, they don't know there is a civil war going on in Guatemala. A lot of people come to the theater because of the news hook of Nicaragua. And so the combination of the two films has been better than either of the films alone. And also they're stylistically very different.

Was there any time in the filming where you felt awkward? Something you wanted to do but felt that you were too deliberately pulling it out of somebody, an interview or shot or situation?

I felt that one time, and that was in the Nicaragua film. We snuck into Nicaragua from Honduras with a Contra patrol, who then wanted to make sure that we were involved in combat, that we shot combat. And they wanted to set up ambushes so that we would be able to film them. I really stepped away from that. I knew that they'd do it anyway, but I also felt that they were doing that action for us to film. I didn't wish anyone's death merely so that we could capture it on film. I was absolutely opposed to that.

There was one other difficult occasion in *When the Mountains Tremble*—that was the funeral of the community organizer, Luís Godoy, which was a very tricky situation. The way we found him was to go every morning at five o'clock to the firemen's main office in Guatemala City. We did this because at dawn people who found bodies would call the firemen's office and they would come and pick up the bodies. So we went out with them on several of those calls, and that's how we came across Godoy's body. His neighbors were so emotionally upset at this death, because he was a very important community leader in that poor neighborhood, that they said things to us which could endanger their lives. Especially considering everything was said full-face to the camera. So we asked them, "Are you sure you want to be filmed?" And they said "Yes, yes, yes."

We followed the story all the way through the funeral, and we went back to the neighborhood a few days later and asked them again if they still wanted to be in the film—because we knew that if the film came out in the States anybody could have access to it and their lives could be threatened. And they still said "Yes." And we said, "Well, if you change your mind, here's our address in New York. And write to us and we'll take you out of the film." But they never did. People have to make decisions for themselves about when and how they're going to be heroic, and you just have to let them be able to make that decision. Make sure you've given them all the options to do that, don't just capture them in an emotionally charged situation.

What in the end does When the Mountains Tremble *mean to you?*

One thing that people always ask is, "Well, what about your point of view when you went there? Did you go there with a preconceived idea of what you wanted to do?" What I have to say is that *When the Mountains Tremble* is actually a compilation of over a decade of experience in Latin America. And I think that the film reflects everything we've come to know of the way certain systems and cultures operate. So we may have gone into this film knowing that we were going to explain certain things. But other things we absolutely did not know we were going to face. It's really been a combination of facing the unexpected and also using our experience and perception of covering Central America for about five years, and developing a way of understanding and communicating what we know about Central America. And here I speak for all of us, because *When the Mountains Tremble*, as well as *Nicaragua*, is very much a joint effort, a combination of the different strengths of Tom Sigel, Peter Kinoy, and myself. It's also the result of the effort of people we dedicate the films to: the thousands of Central Americans who risked their lives in order that we might tell their story.

Note

1. Julia Lesage, "For Our Urgent Use: Films on Central America," *Jump Cut*, no. 27 (1982).

Women's Documentary Filmmaking: The Personal Is Political

Patricia Erens

Prior to the 1970s, women's involvement in documentary filmmaking was appallingly limited. Only a handful of American women worked in the field, including Helen Levitt and Janice Loeb, who along with film critic James Agee made *The Quiet One* (1949); Joyce Chopra, who worked with Richard Leacock on *Happy Mother's Day* (1963); Shirley Clarke, who filmed *Portrait of Jason* in 1967; and Charlotte Zwerin, who received cocredit with the Maysles brothers beginning with *Salesman* (1969). In the first edition of Lewis Jacobs's *The Documentary Tradition*, published in 1971, the only women to receive detailed treatment apart from Levitt and Loeb were the Europeans Esther Schub and Leni Riefenstahl.

A Longer Tradition in Europe

In almost all cases, the American women worked in conjunction with men, failing to distinguish for themselves a unique personal vision. In contrast, European women can be credited with major contributions to the field of documentary filmmaking. In 1927, Soviet filmmaker Esther Schub produced the first compilation film (composed of reedited archival footage), *The Fall of the Romanov Dynasty*. More celebrated is the work of German director Leni Riefenstahl, whose two controversial documentaries, *Triumph of the Will* (1935) and *Olympiad* (1938), are milestones in film history. During the 1950s, Marta Meszaros began making documentary films in Hungary, and Agnes Varda, Nelly Kaplan, and Nicole Vedres all did shorts in France. All four subsequently moved into feature-length filmmaking, and all, apart from Vedres, shifted to fiction. During the 1960s, Mai Zetterling, a Scandinavian, made documentaries, and later she too directed narrative fiction. Both Varda and Zetterling have continued to evidence a concern for documentary filmmaking, Varda in her *Daguerreotypes* (1975) and *Walls Walls* (1980) and Zetterling in the segment she filmed of *Visions of Eight* (1973).

A Time for Change—
Consciousness-Raising Films

With the rise of the women's movement at the end of the 1960s, American women moved into documentary filmmaking in ever increasing numbers, entering the previously male-dominated domain from two directions. The first group were women already working within the film industry, as independents, as artists, or as editors, who were stimulated by the greater opportunities now being offered and who chose to explore their own consciousnes on film. The second group came from within the women's movement. These women saw film as a tool for raising consciousness and implementing social change; they had a message and a wish to treat subjects of importance to women that male filmmakers had so far ignored. In order to learn the necessary skills, they took classes or joined cooperatives where training was available.

One attraction of contemporary documentary filmmaking has been the availability of low-cost, lightweight equipment, which did not exist prior to World War II. Although women did not immediately take advantage of this new technology, the women's movement gave them the impetus to tackle new skills. Furthermore, since fewer technical skills and less capital are necessary to produce a documentary than to produce narrative fiction or an experimental work, women were able to compete on a more equal footing than would have been possible in Hollywood-style filmmaking. The first feminist films, not surprisingly, were straightforward in their approach and somewhat limited in their conception.

The first four films to have an impact and to establish a new direction for women all emanated from the women's movement and were released in 1971. Kate Millett's *Three Lives*, produced by an all-woman crew, is a dialogue with three women: a middle-aged, married chemist, a thirty-year-old divorcée, and a twenty-one-year-old lesbian. Judy Smith's *The Woman's Film*, produced by San Francisco Newsreel, a group devoted to providing alternative visions to both Hollywood and commercial television, focuses on working-class women who talk about their oppression and the need to work together for positive change. *Janie's Janie*, by Geri Ashur, follows the life of a young welfare mother as she emerges as a woman with her own identity. *Growing Up Female: As Six Becomes One* developed from the experiences of Julia Reichert and James Klein during a course they taught at Antioch College on Media for

Political Change. In this work they explore the lives of six females ranging from age four to age thirty-five and analyze the socialization process that shapes all females in our society.

In addition to these four early films, Amalie Rothschild directed *Woo Who? May Wilson*, a film about an older artist in the process of building a new life, and *It Happens to Us*, a series of interviews with women who have had abortions. Both were released in 1970, and both pointed to new directions for feminist filmmaking.

Remaking Women's Image— Film Portraits

These films all had in common a concern for women and women's issues. Women and their environments were made visible in a new way. By eliminating the omniscient male narrator, women could speak in their own voices and validate their experiences. This was especially true of ordinary women whose stories are presented by direct interview or personal monologue—a natural outgrowth of the *cinéma vérité* techniques of the 1960s. As a group, these early works offered several approaches to feminist film practice and established a pattern that became the dominant mode in the first part of the decade.

In documenting the lives of ordinary women, the films emphasized a message that would later echo through much feminist writing: the personal is political. As woman after woman speaks of expectations (her own and others), of sacrifices and choices, of options (open and closed), we can reconstruct an entire record of women's social history. By allowing each woman to tell her story, filmmakers not only restored to women their own voices but in some cases also created positive role models.

It was not long before the consciousness-raising films developed into full-fledged film biographies. So many were produced that it is possible to treat them as a separate subgenre of women's documentary. Following on the heels of *Three Lives* and *Janie's Janie* there appeared probing studies of contemporary women; some had made outstanding contributions to their various fields, others had lived lives away from the limelight; some were well known, others forgotten. These works grew out of a reexamination of women's contribution to history, art, science, politics, and other arenas. At first the women chosen for valorization were names familiar to the general public, but gradually films appeared about less recognizable figures. Among the most popular film portraits were *Angela Davis: Portrait of a Revolutionary* (directed by Yolande du Luart, 1971), *Gertrude Stein: When This You See, Remember Me* (Perry Miller Adato, 1971), *Antonia: A Portrait of the Woman* (Judy Collins and Jill Godmilow, 1974), *Chris and Bernie* (Bonnie Friedman and Deborah Shaffer, 1974), *Yudie* (Mirra Bank, 1974), *Never Give Up: Imogen Cunningham* (Ann Hershey, 1975),

Elizabeth Swados: The Girl with the Incredible Feeling (Linda Feferman, 1977), *Love It Like a Fool*, a film about Malvina Reynolds (Susan Wengraf, 1978), *Lady Named Baybie* (Martha Sandlin, 1979), *Fundi: The Story of Ella Baker* (Joanne Grant, 1981), *Where Did You Get That Woman?* (Loretta Smith, 1983), and *Doctora* (Linda Post and Eugene Roscow, 1983). Because of the frequent use of direct camera address, these works created a form of auto-biography in which each woman narrated her own life.

More recently, black women and other women of color have begun to chronicle their history and cultural contributions. Among those who have created film portraits of blacks are Madeline Anderson, *Clementine Hunter, Artist* (1976); Ayoka Chenzira, *Syvilla: They Dance to Her Drum* (1979); Carroll Blue, *Conversations with Roy deCarava* (1984); and Barbara Mc-Cullough, *Horace Tapscott* (1984). Among the films by and about minority women are *Chicana* (Sylvia Morales, 1979), *Annie May: Brave-Hearted Woman* (Lan Brooks Ritz, 1980), *Mitsuye and Nellie* (Allie Light and Irving Saraf, 1981), *La Operación* (Ana Maria Garcia, 1982), *Nisei Soldier: Standard Bearer for the Exiled People* (Loni Ding, 1984), and *Mississippi Delta* (Christine Choy, Worth Long, and Allan Siegel, 1984).

As film portraits developed, several filmmakers began to use cinema as a means of examining their own lives and relationships, replacing the traditional journal, diary, essay, or novel. Those women who made autobiographical works include Joyce Chopra and Claudia Weill, *Joyce at 34* (1972); Miriam Weinstein, *Living with Peter* (1973); Amalie Rothschild, *Nana, Mom and Me* (1974); and Liane Brandon, *Not So Young Now as Then* (1974).

Another form of film portraits are those works that examine groups of women in specific situations, some limited to traditionally female spheres, others stimulated by the uniqueness of the environment. In the main, these films have utilized a *cinéma vérité* technique. Recent entries include *Soldier Girls* (Nick Broomfield and Joan Churchill, 1981), a film on women in the military; *P4W: Prison for Women* (Janis Cole and Holly Dale, Canada, 1982); *Coalmining Women* (Elizabeth Barret, 1982); *Miles to Go* (Deborah Boldt and Sarah Stein, 1983), a view of eight women on a wilderness expedition; and *Gold Rush Women* (Vivian Kleiman, 1985). The best of these works reveal something of women's condition and raise questions about a sexist society.

The area of film portraits has provided a prodigious quantity of work. However, given the number of outstanding women past and present and the fascinating stories to be told about the lives of ordinary women, this subgenre is bound to provide rich material indefinitely.

One of the best known film portraits is *Union Maids* (Julia Reichert, James Klein, and Miles Mogulescu, 1976), a documentary telling the story of three union workers. Using an interview format and historical materials, the filmmakers attempted to reconstruct a history of women's involvement in labor organizing.

As an effort to produce women's history, it is a bridge to the next group of films under consideration.

Toward an Analytic Cinema— Women's History

Also developing from the roots of consciousness-raising films, but following the model established by *Growing Up Female* and *The Woman's Film*, were works that dealt with women's history. Like consciousness-raising films, these films used direct interviews and other *cinéma vérité* techniques, but in addition, a female narrator raised questions, provided information, and established a social context. Stimulated by increased knowledge of individual women's lives thanks to a surge of research and publishing and the growing attentiveness in feminist theory to the historical and social situations of women and events, filmmakers felt the need to utilize alternatives to *cinéma vérité*–type films. Often this meant taking a historical approach to an issue, although several works deal with contemporary issues. These films, then, are set apart from the film portraits by their analytic style, their historical perspective, or both.

One of the first films to treat women's history was Helena Solberg-Ladd's *The Emerging Woman* (1974), produced as part of the International Women's Film Project. It provided a historical perspective by using old engravings, photographs, newsreels, and other film clips to document women's struggle for equality and to highlight the accomplishments of outstanding women. Later films adopted these techniques too. By focusing on little-remembered events, the filmmakers were putting women back into history, creating a woman's history, and making connections with contemporary feminist activities.

It is in the area of women's history that filmmakers have made some of the most enduring and valuable contributions. These works, characterized by a compilation structure using historical materials, often in combination with direct interview, and dominated by a narrator (or narrative technique) who sets the tone and direction of the material, have expressed most successfully and forcefully the tenets of the women's movement.

Two outstanding examples of this technique are *The Chicago Maternity Center Story* (Kartemquin Films, 1976) and *The Life and Times of Rosie the Riveter* (Connie Fields, 1980). The first work chronicles the efforts of a group of women to save a home delivery program in Chicago. Filmed in two parts, part one offers a *cinéma vérité* record of the lost struggle and an intimate view of a home delivery; part two, an analysis of health care in America, raises many questions central to feminism. *Rosie the Riveter*, a documentary about American women, especially during World War II, presents a look at women's contribution to the war effort and offers an insightful analysis of how government and, through extension, advertising work to manipulate women into and then out of the work force. The film also allows women to speak out about their own feelings concerning work, economics, race, and class.

Other history projects which attempted to reexamine the record and reconstruct events from a female perspective include *Great Grand Mothers: A History and Celebration of Prairie Women* (Anne Wheeler and Lorna Rasmussen, Canada, 1976), a chronicle of the nameless women who crossed the prairie and settled the frontier, and *With Babies and Banners: The Story of the Women's Emergency Brigade* (Lorraine Gray, 1978), a documentary about the 1937 General Motors sit-down strike in Flint, Michigan, that weaves the story from the memories of the women who lived through the events.

Educational Needs—
Films on Women's Issues

Following Rothschild's pro-abortion film *It Happens to Us* (1970) came scores of films that covered basic women's issues like health, childbirth, work, divorce, self-defense, day care, rape, and organizing. Although the filmmakers use a variety of techniques, these works all have a common aim: to provide necessary information on vital subjects. Like many of the first consciousness-raising films, some of these works now appear dated, but here it is because much of the information presented has since become widely known and because issues have changed. It must be remembered that each of these works was relevant at the time, and several were enormously influential. *It Happens to Us*, for instance, was part of the campaign to win abortion rights for women, a struggle that was won with the Supreme Court decision in 1973.

The list of films on women's issues is long. A selection of titles includes *Self-Health* (San Francisco Women's Health Collective, 1974), *Rape Culture* (Cambridge Documentary Films, 1978), *Healthcaring: From Our End of the Speculum* (Denise Bostrom and Jane Warrenbrand, 1977), *The Double Day* (Helena Solberg-Ladd, 1976), *Good Day Care: One Out of Ten* (Barbara H. Martineau and Lorna Rasmussen, Canada, 1978), *This Film Is About Rape* (Bonnie Kreps, Canada, 1978), *We Will Not Be Beaten* (Transition House, 1978), *Killing Us Softly* (Jean Kilbourne, 1979), *Right Out of History*, on the making of *The Dinner Party* (Joanna Demetrakas, 1980), *Love, Honor and Obey* (Christine Choy, 1981), *The Last to Know* (Bonnie Friedman, 1981), *Not a Love Story* (Bonnie Klein, Canada, 1981), *What Would You Do with a Nickel?* (Cara Devito and Jeffery Kleinman, 1982), *Hookers on Davie* (Holly Dale and Janis Cole, 1984), *Rated X* (Lucy Winer, 1986).

The most recent works in this category have provided analytic and historical contexts for the issues they raise; thus, the boundaries between these works and the films on women's history can become somewhat blurred. Further, apart from serving as informational sources, many of these documentaries also urge change and suggest solutions.

In an additional subcategory are many films that treat lesbian concerns. The intent here is twofold: to provide education on lesbian issues, and to provide consciousness-raising for lesbians in the manner of the first feminist films. These films run the gamut of styles and techniques. Among the best known are *Holding* (Coni Beeson, 1971), *In the Best Interest of the Children* (Iris Films, 1977), *Word Is Out* (Mariposa Film Group, 1978), *If She Grows Up Gay* (Karen Sloe, 1983), and *Before Stonewall* (Greta Schiller, 1984).

Questioning the Medium's Message—Feminist Film Criticism

Even with the first flush of success, feminist critics were beginning to ask questions about the appropriation of *cinéma vérité* methods with its presumption of unmediated "truth"—a presumption that may actually mislead viewers by implying that the person or situation portrayed is representative of the people or circumstances being discussed.

Also problematic was the tendency of many viewers to identify with the protagonist in the film (as readers do when reading nineteenth-century realistic fiction), becoming absorbed in the screen images and ignoring the larger social issues. In a perceptive article entitled "Documentary, Realism, and Women's Cinema," published in the now defunct *Women and Film*, Eileen McGarry raised questions about capturing "real" women on film and commented on the tendency of *cinéma vérité* simply to perpetuate female stereotypes. She ended her analysis with a quote from British feminist critic Claire Johnston: "If women's cinema is going to emerge, it should not only concern itself with substituting positive female protagonists, focusing on women's problems, etc.; it has to go much further than this if it is to impinge on consciousness. It requires a revolutionary strategy which can only be based on an analysis of how film operates as a medium within a specific cultural system."[1]

These questions were very seriously taken up in several articles during the late 1970s. In opposition to McGarry's expressed concerns with regard to *cinéma vérité*, feminist film critic Julia Lesage felt that the deliberate use of a traditional "realist" documentary structure could be appropriated by women in a subversive manner to challenge the status quo and to present women's bodies, women's voices, and women's domestic space in a new way. In "The Political Aesthetics of the Feminist Documentary Film," Lesage states: "The Feminist documentaries represent a use of, yet a shift in, the aesthetics of *cinéma vérité* due to the filmmakers' close identification with their subjects, participation in the women's movement, and sense of the films' intended effect. The structure of the consciousness-raising group becomes the deep structure repeated over and over in these films. . . . Either the stance of the people filmed or the stance of the film as a whole reflects a commitment to changing the public; and for this reason, these filmmakers have used an accessible documentary form."[2]

Despite Lesage's defense of women's *cinéma vérité* as a means of asserting political and sexual difference, other critics objected to its use in the presentation of history. In "Feminism, Film, and Public History," published in *Radical History Review*, Sonya Michel addressed issues relating to historical accuracy and subject typicality. "From a historian's point of view, however, these privileged subjects can become problematic if a film limits its perspective by relying on them as the sole or even primary informants. While oral history subjects are frequently both engaging and uniquely informative, their accounts of historical events or periods can be partial, fragmentary, idiosyncratic and sometimes—deliberately or unintentionally—misleading."[3]

Similar reservations were raised on the pages of *Screen* in an article by Noel King, "Recent 'Political' Documentary: Notes on *Union Maids* and *Harlan County, U.S.A.*" As King points out, "any strategy which locates evidence/history unproblematically in the human, the natural, means that history is held to reside in the subjectivities of its participants," resulting in a form of "humanism which constructs historical narrative as the actions of historical persons."[4]

In the United States and especially in Britain, many women have responded to these issues. Several women practitioners began to question the relationship between film theory and film practice. Questions arose (also in the area of narrative filmmaking) concerning the need for new forms, forms that would emphasize a feminist consciousness and ensure an alert, responsive audience. Their aim was not simply to replace the male voice with a female voice; they wanted to break down the traditional, passive way in which films are viewed.

Furthermore, many women felt it important to devise a cinema that presented individuals within the context of a complex social structure and at the same time that critiqued the process of image making—an urgent need in the light of the way women have been stereotyped and their bodies co-opted to sell products and to provide sexual pleasure for men.

The Seeds of Invention—
Women's Experimental
Documentary

As a result of these concerns, many women began experimenting with new forms and techniques in an effort to break down the traditional boundaries between documentary, narrative, and experimental film. Several filmmakers incorporated documentary techniques into their fictional films or created narratives that mimicked documentary forms. *Not a Pretty Picture* (Martha Coolidge, 1974), for example, reenacts a high school rape using actors; then Coolidge discusses the filming of the act, what feelings it produced in the actors, and how the filming revived the original emotions of this autobiographical event. *Daughter Rite* (Michelle Citron, 1979), about mother-daughter relationships, is a narrative fiction that imitates *cinéma vérité* techniques to question the use of "truth." Intercut with acted scenes are reprocessed home movies. *Scream from Silence* (Anne-Claire Poirier, Canada, 1979), about rape, is another fictional film, but it is intercut with scenes of a director and editor discussing how to present the event without sexual exploitation. The film also includes documentary footage of a clitoridectomy. *Song of the Shirt* (Susan Clayton, Britain, 1979) focuses on women textile workers, especially in the 1830s and 1840s, and utilizes acted scenes, written texts, video material, still photography, graphics, and acted improvisation. This film attempts to investigate how history is written and the means by which it is represented.

Several other works have used experimental techniques as well. *Anything You Want to Be* (Liane Brandon, 1971), for example, uses experimental editing techniques to help women think about new roles and occupations. In *Betty Tells Her Story* (Liane Brandon, 1972), Betty tells of losing a dress that made her feel very pretty. First she tells it as an adventure story; then it is repeated with more insight, revealing her true pain. *Penthesilea* (Laura Mulvey and Peter Wollen, Britain, 1974) presents five segments filmed in different styles, all of which relate to the Amazon myth. Included is a filmed performance and clips from an early suffragist movie. *Woman to Woman* (Donna Deitch, 1975) uses interviews in conjunction with news clips, advertising, and images of art and sculpture to make its statements. Margie Keller's *Misconception* (1976), a film about childbirth, suggests a home movie in its personal approach to documentary. *The Night Cleaners* (London Women's Film Group, Britain, 1975) examines the relationship between sexual oppression and class exploitation. *Riddles of the Sphinx* (Laura Mulvey and Peter Wollen, Britain, 1977) uses innovative camera movements and documentary footage of a young working mother in Britain. In *Rape* (JoAnn Elam, 1978), several rape victims discuss their experiences and take turns doing the filming. The filmmaker intercuts scenes with humorous or associational images.

Recent films include the creative *ClothesLines* (Roberta Cantow, 1981), about women's work; *What You Take for Granted* (Michelle Citron, 1983), a fictional film about professional and working-class women that utilizes pseudodocumentary interviews; and *Born in Flames* (Lizzie Borden, 1983), a futuristic, documentary-style look at one woman's revolution.

These films have caused interest and controversy in film communities; the major objection to *some* of them is their difficulty for working-class women (often the intended film audience) and others unfamiliar with experimental techniques, who feel alienated by the somewhat elitist approach. The issues of form and film practice continue to be areas of lively debate among feminist filmmakers.

The Alternative Distribution Network

Women have been quick to realize the importance of alternative means of exhibition and distribution. Many of the films made over the past decade and a half have been produced with women's audiences in mind and have been shown in situations that allowed for discussion. These films promote consciousness-raising and help in organizing.

To make these films available, women have established their own distribution companies. First on the scene were New Day Films and Women Make Movies. Founded in 1972 by Liane Brandon, James Klein, Julia Reichert, and Amalie Rothschild, New Day is dedicated to distributing feminist films about men and women. Owned by the filmmakers themselves, the works are produced independently and distributed cooperatively. Members are added each year by vote, and the group now numbers thirty. Women Make Movies, also founded in 1972, is a feminist media organization set up to teach film skills and to distribute films and video tapes. Included in their catalogue are works about women prisoners, rape, and health care.

In addition, several other distribution companies have emerged. The largest was Serious Business Company, founded by filmmaker Freude Bartlett and devoted to films by and about women.[5] Iris Films—founded in 1975 as "part of the movement of women to regain, define, and create our own culture"— distributes films on day care, women in prison, rape, and lesbian issues. Third World Newsreel, an organization dating back to 1969, handles several titles related to women. Kartemquin Films functioned as a cooperative during the 1970s and now distributes several works relating to women. Cambridge Documentary Films both produces and distributes films and has dealt with many of the most important feminist issues of the decade. During the 1980s, many documentaries by women are being distributed by First Run Features and Direct Cinema, Ltd.

Beyond Feminism— Political Filmmaking

In addition to the films discussed above, many individual women have created works that cannot be classified strictly as feminist, dealing with subjects in a broader realm of issues. Included are works like *Attica* (Cinda Firestone, 1973), *Promised Lands* (Susan Sontag, 1973), *Grey Gardens* (David and

Albert Maysles, Ellen Hovde, Muffie Meyer, 1975), *Harlan County, U.S.A.* (Barbara Kopple, 1976), *Rising Target* (Barbara Frank, 1976), *Number Our Days* (Lynne Littman, 1976), and *On the Line* (Barbara Margolis, 1976).

More recently, women have taken up issues related to leftist politics, the struggles in Central America, environmental control, and the campaign to prevent a nuclear holocaust. For some, this is a return to political commitments that preceded feminism; for younger women, it is a development nurtured by feminist awareness. Among the socially motivated films directed or codirected by women are *The Wobblies* (Deborah Shaffer and Stewart Bird, 1979), *From the Ashes: Nicaragua Today* (Helena Solberg-Ladd, 1981), *Eight Minutes to Midnight* (Mary Benjamin, 1981), *Roses in December: The Story of Jean Donovan* (Ana Carrigan and Bernard Stone, 1982), *If You Love This Planet* (Terri Nash, 1982), *Nicaragua: Report from the Front* (Deborah Shaffer and Tom Sigel, 1982), *In Our Water* (Meg Switzgable, 1982), *Blood and Sand: War in the Sahara* (Sharon Sopher, 1982), *America: From Hitler to M-X* (Joan Harvey, 1982), *Seeing Red* (Julia Reichert and James Klein, 1983), *When the Mountains Tremble* (Pamela Yates and Tom Sigel, 1983), *The Freeze: An Overview of the Arms Race* (Barbara Zheutlin, 1983), *The Good Fight* (Noel Buckner, Mary Dore, and Sam Sills, 1984), and *Plant Closing in the American Workplace* (Barbara Kopple, in progress).

Furthermore, several women who began as documentarians have now moved into fictional filmmaking. Most prominent is Claudia Weill, who did several short feminist documentaries, including *The Other Half of the Sky: A China Memoir* (with Shirley MacLaine, 1974), before directing *Girlfriends* and *It's My Turn*. Joan Micklin Silver also gained her training in documentary work before she directed *Hester Street, Between the Lines*, and *Chilly Scenes of Winter*. More recently, Mary Lampson, who worked with Emile de Antonio on *Underground*, has made a short narrative film entitled *Until She Talks*, and Linda Feferman completed *Mother May I?*. Likewise, both Donna Deitch and Mirra Bank, who produced early feminist documentaries, have completed commercial features: Deitch with *Desert Hearts*; Bank with *Enormous Changes at the Last Minute*, which she co-directed with Ellen Hovde. Actress Lee Grant has directed the documentary *The Wilmar 8* (1980), about a strike for equal pay by eight bank workers, and the narrative *Tell Me a Riddle*, based on the novella by Tillie Olsen. And currently, Martha Coolidge has moved from independent filmmaking to Hollywood, serving as director of *Valley Girl* and *The Joy of Sex*, and Joyce Chopra has made a similar move as the director of *Smooth Talk*.

Like all documentary filmmaking, women's documentaries follow several models. In addition to differences in form and content, each subgenre is characterized by an appropriate style and technique, dictated in part by the film's purpose and intended audience. Thus, the first consciousness-raising films were utilized to promote discussions among women; the film portraits created new images, highlighted women's accomplishments, and created role models; women's history films offered reinterpretations of the past from a feminist perspective; films on women's issues provided essential information on a variety of subjects; and experimental documentaries investigated the medium itself.

Films often address several purposes simultaneously, using a mixture of techniques and styles—*cinéma vérité*, the direct interview, and historical compilation. The best films are those that seek to expand their subjects, by providing an analytic context within which the viewer can place the material offered or by challenging our normal perceptions of the world (including film). These works represent the most sophisticated contribution of feminist thinking.

Although women are finding increased opportunity to move into mainstream documentary filmmaking, most carry with them an artistic and mental set honed by feminism and the changes it has wrought in the lives of women in the past twenty-five years. The sheer number of women working in the field today, as compared with the early 1960s, speaks to the success of the women's movement. Although few women are now turning out consciousness-raising films, scores are committed to feminist filmmaking, and almost all have enriched the field by bringing to documentary a new sensitivity, by asking the unasked questions, and by training their cameras on previously invisible subjects.

Notes

1. Eileen McGarry, "Documentary, Realism, and Women's Cinema," *Women and Film* 2, no. 7 (1975): 50–57.

2. Julia Lesage, "The Political Aesthetics of the Feminist Documentary Film," *Quarterly Review of Film Studies* (Fall 1978): 507–23.

3. Sonya Michel, "Feminism, Film, and Public History," *Radical History Review* 25 (1981): 47–61.

4. Noel King, "Recent 'Political' Documentary: Notes on *Union Maids* and *Harlan County, U.S.A.*," *Screen* 22, no. 2 (1981): 7–18.

5. Films can still be obtained by writing to Serious Business in Oakland, California. They will put people directly in touch with the filmmakers.

What You Take for Granted

Linda Williams

A fire fighter releases a powerful gush of water from a hydrant, a welder climbs a girder, a tense pilot scans the sky. With these images of tough, satisfying, useful work, Michelle Citron begins her new film *What You Take for Granted*. The images may be clichés, the stuff of TV beer commercials, but the idea of hard work and Miller Time camaraderie and relaxation after a job well done is a compelling one in our culture. Citron's images are different, though. Unlike the macho men of the beer commercials, the fire fighter, welder, and pilot are all women. And for them, the work, the camaraderie, and the relaxation are much more difficult matters.

Citron examines the contradictions of these opening images in a multilayered work that situates itself in the gray areas dividing fiction and documentary. Weaving together these two different forms, *What You Take for Granted* offers a novel look at women who work in jobs that have traditionally been dominated by men.

Except for biographies and dramas of the rich and famous or an occasional union drama or fantasy (*Coalminer's Daughter, Norma Rae, Nine to Five, Silkwood*), it is remarkable how few Hollywood films have taken women and their work seriously. This is in contrast to the many films that take the importance of men's work, as the film's title says, "for granted." By concentrating on the vanguard of women who have broken into the kinds of jobs our culture values, the film gives the clichés of male-dominated work a new vitality. But except for the brief opening and closing sequences that actually show women working, the bulk of the film is concerned not with the image of women at work but with what the work really means to them. We see women workers of all sorts reflecting on their jobs and confiding their mixed exhilaration and frustration at entering the demanding arena of male competition.

Anyone who has seen Citron's previous film, *Daughter Rite*, will recognize a similar approach, one that is distinctly Citron's own. Women talk, even complain, directly to the camera about the difficulties of a relationship to an absent figure. In *Daughter Rite*, that figure was an off-screen mother, and the women talking were her daughters: in an apparent documentary interview, two sisters talk about their mother to us and with one another; elsewhere, in voice-over narration, another daughter speaks of another mother over images of edited home movies of a woman and her two daughters. The effect of the film is to build, not an individual story about the daughters, but a composite picture of daughters trying to sort out their relationship to their mothers. The real subject of the film is absent. "Mom" herself has no voice except through the alternately idealizing and vilifying voice of the daughters—though it becomes clear in the course of the film that in talking about a figure so close to them they are also talking about themselves.

In a sense, Citron's new film is the flip side to *Daughter Rite*. In talking about their relationship to the male world of work—the bosses and male co-workers whose approval they seek—the women in the film are also talking about their relationship to their fathers. Like the Mom of *Daughter Rite*, this composite image of the father structures the film in his absence. And like her, he too is alternately idealized, vilified, and—to a lesser degree—internalized by the "daughters" who obsessively talk about him. But where the dramatic conflicts in *Daughter Rite* revolve around the daughter's symbiosis with a mother she was too much like, here the dramatic conflicts revolve around the frustrations of fitting into a mold of behavior demanded by the much more distant figure of paternal authority.

What You Take for Granted begins with a collage of interviews in which women of various races and classes talk about their work. Their jobs range from truck driving, carpentry, and cable splicing to sculpture, teaching philosophy, and practicing medicine. What they share is the common desire to escape the poor pay and powerlessness of traditional women's work, whether for purely practical reasons (a carpenter explains that for her the choice was between "shit woman's work for shit pay or shit man's work for more pay"), as a means to self-expression (a feisty iron sculptor speaks of her joy working with materials that are "obstinate and obdurate"), or out of a desire to do good (a doctor speaks of her identification with the kindly doctor–father figure of a TV doctor series).

All of these women have "made it" in the man's world of work; all are proud of their accomplishments and know that it will be easier for the women who come after them. But as highly visible minorities, as the token women who are there partly to prove the democracy of a system that is not democratic enough to accept them *as* women, each has had to accommodate her identity to a foreign system of values. Some, like the doctor, who has learned not to smile, have simply repressed their gentle side to compete effectively with men. Others, like the aggressive truck driver, have learned to take whatever male co-workers dish out without compromising their values. Still others, like the ever practical carpenter, choose to play the role of the "nice girl" who is shocked by foul language in order to avoid the greater abuses that come with being "one of the guys."

Thus, Citron's film investigates the price women have to pay to be admitted into the male world of work. The investigation is carried out on one level by apparent documentary interviews in which the women simply tell us, in engaging anecdotes, the personal stories that typify the experiences of so many women in their situation.

Documentaries, except those that focus on the remarkable person or situation, have always claimed to represent the most truthful and typical aspects of human experience. But there is often a very fine line between the camera capturing the typical event, or account of an event, and the fictionalized staging of that event. Once the camera is present, the event becomes a performance, staged either by the subject or by the director—and if by the director, the camera can easily intrude on the more revealing acts and gestures of unsuspecting subjects.

Much recent feminist documentary has chosen to avoid directorial staging as too intrusive and controlling, preferring to collaborate with the subjects in sympathetic interviews that give interviewees as much control over the image and its content as possible. Citron has taken this tactic a step further. Acknowledging that all documentaries are fictions of a sort, Citron has used actors to impersonate the subjects interviewed in her film. The result is a uniquely engaging blend of fact and fiction.

Is what these subjects tell us any less true because of Citron's technique? In a way it is more true, because more typical, based as it is on interviews with many more women workers than could possibly be included in the film, as the credits reveal. But more important, the strategy allows the kind of condensation of issues and themes that can only be achieved in a scripted fiction, while retaining, through improvisational acting, the documentary style of real people groping to express their experiences. This intentional blurring of the already blurred area between documentary and fiction has another advantage: it allows Citron to develop a fictional elaboration out of the "facts" of the documentary.

The elaboration begins in a highly contrived meeting between two of the subjects of the documentary. The truck driver has cut her hand; the doctor, in a most unlikely house call, tends to it and stays to cook dinner. As they make their first tentative efforts to get to know one another the doctor asks, "So, what's it like to drive a truck?" In answer the film cuts to another "interview" with the truck driver, who talks of her excitement at her job and the "good feelings" she gets from customers, then to the sculptor, who talks of winning a prize, and then to the philosophy professor, who talks of being judged by men who are not her peers.

Thus the film weaves social document with private drama, expanding on the unique experience of the individual drama with a collage of related interview experience that gives a rich texture to the entire work. While the women in the interviews *tell*, in rational, public voices, of their difficulties dealing with a system of male authority whose rules are foreign and oppressive, two of these same women *show*, in the private dynamics of their developing friendship, the more subtle ways in which male authority affects their relationship to one another.

Anna is a gregarious and volatile working-class truck driver who has brashly pioneered work for women truckers at her company. Dianna is a comparatively repressed and ladylike middle-class doctor who has played the game more conservatively in her efforts to gain acceptance in the doctor club. To this extent they are typical of their jobs and class. But in another sense they are not. Anna fits the stereotype of a leather-jacketed, butch trucker, but it is the more ladylike doctor who turns out to be gay. Just what Dianna's gayness means to her is not explored in the film, not because the film represses it but because Dianna, in her role as competent and confident doctor, does not appear to be prepared to deal with her sexuality at all—at least not in her relationship with Anna.

As Anna and Dianna's friendship develops, in narrative scenes that punctuate the interviews, it becomes apparent that Dianna has arrived at her position of relative power and authority by living up to the expectations of her own father. So much of her life has aimed at making herself acceptable to paternal authority that she has closed off some of the more vulnerable aspects of her personality, including, the film implies, her gay identity. A particularly revealing scene shows her pain as she listens to the voice of her father on the phone, presumably telling her to accept a position that will not interfere with marriage.

Unlike Anna, who suffers in her job for being too aggressive and is thus passed over in a promotion, Dianna has accepted male authority and suffers in the repression of her private life. Happily for the film, Dianna's career "success" and Anna's career "failure" are not there to draw moral lessons about the price of success, the integrity of failure. As the interviews show, many other women have made many other kinds of accommodations to male authority, ranging from angry threats of violence to playing the good little girl. The fiction is just one instance of how women's relationship to paternal authority reverberates in their private lives.

Nevertheless, there remains a touch of the overschematic in Citron's manipulation of the material. One problem is that the fictional narrative sections illustrating Dianna's cautious repression and Anna's volatile acting out do not offer enough of the dynamic of their relationship; another is that this relationship does not contrast enough, thematically or emotionally, with the pseudodocumentary material. The result is a film with many fascinating insights into work and work's effect on women's relationships across class boundaries, but none of the instant electricity and recognition of *Daughter Rite*'s approach to the mother through the anger and love of her daughters.

Perhaps significantly, *What You Take for Granted* has no formal equivalent to the intimate voice-over of the home-movie sections or the high melodramatic notes of some of the sister scenes. It is as if the subject of this new film—women's relation to work and hence to the implied authority figure of the father—put a damper on Citron's own emotional resources. Where *Daughter Rite* is alternately angry and loving, liberated and locked into deadly patterns of repetition, and the absent mother is always felt as a powerfully determining presence, the absent boss-father who structures this film is simply too distant, too abstract, to be felt as a powerful force in these women's lives. Undeniably he *is* such a force, as the pseudodocumentary interviews wonderfully attest, but he is not felt emotionally. Citron's new film, then, is somehow not as urgent an expression of long-repressed aspects of women's lives as was her earlier film.

What You Take for Granted remains, however, an enormously important work of feminist documentation and feminist fiction precisely for the ways these two forms give resonance to one another. As the fictional story grows out of the documentary interviews, and as two of the subjects of these interviews become actors in the fiction, it becomes clear that neither form is exactly what it seems. The fiction is acted and shot in an improvisational *cinéma vérité* style that connotes documentary. The supposed documentary sections are in turn more polished and rehearsed than interviews usually are. Audiences first accept, then question the documentary "truth" of the interviews. Although the straightforward feminist documentary, representing real women and real concerns, has been an important way for women audiences to recognize aspects of their lives not otherwise given cinematic representation, the documentary forms privileged in this type of representation have tended either to heroicize their women subjects or to shape the events of their lives into overly neat narrative resolutions (e.g. *Antonia: Portrait of a Woman, Union Maids, Janie's Janie*). Both tendencies are highly fictionalized shapings of real events.

Citron's film does not set out to confuse its audience as to the fictional or documentary nature of its materials. Rather, it plays on the audience's recognition of the many shades of difference between, on the one hand, real lives shaped by documentary techniques into partial fiction and, on the other, fictional representations based to varying degrees on reality. Neither a total fiction that the audience can unproblematically enter into and identify with, nor a true document that speaks an unquestioned unitary truth, *What You Take for Granted* interrogates the filmic process of representation while also allowing the presentation of a wider range of personal and political issues than either documentary or fiction alone could offer.

Word Is Out and Gay U.S.A.
Lee Atwell

Historically, the cinematic image of the homosexual, which has only come into focus within the last decade, has consistently suffered from stereotypical distortion, derision, and condescension. As minority members who have never been in control of their public image, gays have witnessed in narrative fiction film an almost systematic attempt to devalue, while giving token recognition to, their lives and feelings. If television responds on occasion with a sympathetic episode, movies are largely content with liberal notions of obvious "fairies" for humorous relief or, worse, unhappy psychopathic villains, reinforcing ignorance and prejudice among what Christopher Isherwood terms "the heterosexual dictatorship."

In the field of documentary, or *cinéma vérité*, where the index of reality is somewhat more reliable and where we at least have the advantage of experiencing not actors impersonating gay types but the real thing, isolated examples have failed to have any significant impact. In *The Queen*, Frank Simon penetrates behind the facade of male drags participating in a beauty contest, while at another extreme, Rosa van Praunheim's *The Homosexual Is Not Perverse but the Society Which Produces Him* offers a cynical, candid glimpse into the S&M/motorcycle/leather faction of the macho gay world, and Shirley Clarke's feature-length interview with a black male prostitute, *A Portrait of Jason*, conveys an unsparing, unpleasant confessional vision.

Diverse and positive images of gay persons were not forthcoming for two basic reasons. First, in spite of the clarion call "Out of the Closets" by liberationists, large segments of the gay populace feared any sort of public exposure that might mean loss of jobs, friends, or family support. Simply getting an openly gay woman or man to appear before a camera was a primary difficulty. And second, the difficulties in financing a nonsensational (noncommercial) treatment of the subject were virtually insurmountable.

The first work reflecting the otherwise extremely vocal politics of Gay Liberation was a highly professional student production, *Some of Your Best Friends* by Ken Robinson of the University of Southern California. Employing a *cinéma vérité* format, Robinson captured the spirited genesis of the movement in New York and Los Angeles, interviewing up-front participants about feelings and experiences of oppression and freedom. Especially memorable is a Los Angeles man walking through Griffith Park, relating his entrapment by a local vice officer and his plans to defend himself in a court trial (which he subsequently won). A gay contingent is seen confronting a psychiatric convention, challenging its oppressive advocacy of aversion therapy with a rousing debate. Representatives of a New York homophile organization are shrouded in shadow to protect their identity while the bright shining faces of the street folk project pride, prominently including women as well as men.

Six years were to pass, however, before other gay filmmakers were to significantly take up the direct-cinema approach begun by Robinson. Though financial support was still virtually nonexistent for pro-gay films, the rising tide of anti-gay propaganda, spearheaded by Anita Bryant's Bible-thumping crusade, provoked social consciousness and a revitalization of the movement throughout the land. A highly sophisticated quality gay news medium began to unite divergent forces into political cohesiveness, and at the same time the awareness of a need to communicate prompted socially conscious filmmakers to action. Their efforts resulted in two unique and exceptional human documents, *Gay U.S.A.* and *Word Is Out: Stories of Some of Our Lives*. Both films employ the interview as a fundamental technique, but their production circumstances and organization of material differ distinctly in spite of occasional parallels.

In 1975, Peter Adair, then a producer for San Francisco's KQED, had become dissatisfied with the quality of his work there. "I felt that I needed to make films that were of value to me . . . I wanted to get into some sort of social filmmaking. I started with the issue that concerned me most—that was rights for gay people." He envisioned a short film to be used as a teaching aid for college and professional groups, made of interviews with diverse individuals. But after two years of perseverence, Adair discovered foundations were unresponsive to such a project, and he finally resorted, like the makers of *Gay U.S.A.*, to private and individual investors. He joined forces with his sister, Nancy, assistant cameraman Andrew Brown, sound editor Veronica Selver, New York filmmaker Lucy Massie Phenix, and Rob Epstein—and the Mariposa Film Group came into existence. With the expansion of the group came the decision to enlarge the scope of the work. What had begun as a modest presentation of positive role models for gay people became a much larger sampling of the vast range of America's gay population.

Every attempt was made to engage filmmakers and participants in a collective expression, decentralizing all procedures from shooting to editing. In preparation, the members "preinterviewed" on videotape two hundred persons from various sections of the country. The team then collectively viewed this material and selected twenty-six women and men whom they returned to film. As Teresa Kennett notes in *The Reel Thing*, certain ground rules were agreed on by the Mariposa Group. "The setting for every interview was worked out very carefully between subject and filmmaker. Choice of location and 'props'—photographs, pets, clothing, etc.—was made on the basis not only of what looked good visually, but of what was meaningful to the interviewee. Making the subject feel at ease was of utmost importance; to this end a stationary camera setup was decided upon, thus eliminating any extra distraction. And since whoever operated the camera also conducted the interview (usually with only one other person on sound) it was possible to develop real unbroken communication between interviewer and interviewee." In addition to the interview material, several hours of *vérité* footage were filmed, depicting working and living situations of the subjects and songs performed by Trish Nugent and the gay rock band Buena Vista.

Four of the Mariposa Group spent over a year editing various cuts down from approximately fifty hours of material. From time to time cuts were screened for predominantly gay audiences, with responses solicited in questionnaire form. Thus, the larger community was able to participate in determining the actual final content of the film. In this process it soon became evident that the large amount of cutaway material detracted from rather than amplified the succession of interviews, and in the final 135-minute version, its presence is minimal. This undoubtedly accounts for the strength of the film's emotional and psychological impact, as well as for its structural and conceptual weaknesses.

Word Is Out is divided into three broad sections: "The Early Years," "Growing Up," and "From Now On." The rather vague nature of these arbitrary categories becomes evident as each section unravels, prefaced by an introductory montage of the personalities included in each segment. Although the interviewees have been carefully chosen to display a richly diverse and contrasting series of views and life-styles, no apparent structural pattern emerges in the editing scheme. Individual interviews are broken up and reappear from time to time, often being used in more than one section, as remarks seem generally relevant to the broad category.

The static stationary camera angle is consistently a frontal medium-close to close shot, giving the impression of a talking portrait in which the subject directly addresses the camera/audience, creating an intimate, engrossing and often emotionally charged rapport between subject and viewer. However, in a film of two-hours-plus duration, variety and contrast are essential to retain the viewer's interest, regardless of how riveting the interview material is assumed to be. In the final analysis, though each individual shot has its own mood, composition, and dynamic center, it is an isolated unit that only marginally relates to the other units that make up the framework.

In addition to the gay musicians, who are seen at random intervals in studio and in concert performances, three sequences deviate significantly from the armchair interview format, giving a much-needed variation in the cinematic space. Elsa Gidlow, 79, the oldest member of the cast, is seen in her Northern California home talking with three young women about lesbian politics and her feelings about appearing in the film. Suddenly, for the first time we see the faces of interviewer(s) and interviewee in the same space, engaged in a conversational exchange, while the handheld camera freely moves from face to face. Similarly, after we have become familiar with a blond lesbian named Whitey who lives in a Northern California cabin, we see an early-morning excursion in which she and her friends saw off a section of a giant tree that is threatening her domicile. The operation, shot from a variety of angles, is successful, and audiences invariably cheer and applaud this rustic interlude. Following interviews separately and together with lesbian mothers Pam Jackson and Rusty Millington, we see a beautifully filmed sequence in which the two women play touch football with Rusty's children on a beach and serve a picnic supper, during which one of the children is interviewed. Other cutaway material, such as the film's self-proclaimed drag queen, Tede Mathews, frolicking with children at a playground or the middle-aged couple Harry Hay and John Burnside picking berries together in the countryside, displays a charm that is more poignant than their speech.

In spite of its diversity of ethnic and sexual types, it would be a mistake to draw anything other than superficial sociological arguments from *Word Is Out*, which is only a bare suggestion of the variety of gay life-styles. Brooklyn professor Betty Powell, one of the film's most articulate speakers, emphasizes, for instance, that she should not be taken as in any sense representative of black lesbian feminists (though she is in fact the only one to appear in the film).

Nevertheless, certain patterns begin to emerge in the selection of material that assert a strongly middle-class value structure. The large number of stable couples suggests an ideal of traditional matrimonial bliss. Only one person speaks up for the single, casual-sex status that characterizes vast numbers of gay people. Although only one speaker, a vice-president of a New York corporation, defines himself as a conservative ("I feel that radicals are necessary and I feel that we are necessary"), the majority of persons interviewed can be categorized as politically conservative, especially those whose formative years preceded the sixties and Gay Liberation. Comedienne Pat Bond, a middle-aged ex-WAC who talks of communal, role-defined lesbian life in postwar years and recounts the terrors of the army's inquisition during the McCarthy period (which resulted in five hundred dishonorable discharges), is nevertheless nostalgic about the past. Although she sees the necessity of gays coming out publicly now and finding a new sense of identity, she misses the butch/femme role dichotomy and the secrecy of "the Little Orphan Annie decoding society" of her early years.

The film's final section, "From Now On," tends to focus on the more radical dimension of gay politics, and its most eloquent and persuasive arguments are presented by lesbian feminists Betty Powell and Sally Gearhart. Powell, who is a member of the National Gay Task Force, tells of coming out of a heterosexual marriage and realizing her love for a woman through the women's movement. Her assertion that "lesbians and gay men have a great deal to offer in terms of restructuring the world culture" is more fully articulated by Sally Gearhart, who asserts that all humans are born with a bisexual potential, but from the moment they are born they are made half-persons by society's strict programming of appropriate gender behavior and attitudes. Gays tend, on the other hand, more toward a natural balance of male and female in one person. This is, of course, an ideal, and the film's inclusion of stereotypical dykes like Pat Bond (who quaintly classifies herself as "femme") and effeminate men like Roger Harkenrider (who honestly admits to archetypal "faggoty" behavior) suggests the infinite complexity of sexual role-playing in the gay world. On the other hand, there is a typically male model present in Donald Hackett, a black truck driver, and a female model in Linda Marco, an attractive former "American dream daughter," both of whom came out from heterosexual marriages (another significant pattern in the cast). It is also interesting to note that while the film's most cogent intellectual arguments come from women, its strongest emotional moments emerge from men. Probably the most memorable is George Mendenhall's tearful reminiscence of a male opera singer named José encouraging men in the gay bar to sing "God Save Us Nellie Queens" in the fifties, when San Francisco police mercilessly harassed gays. More deeply touching is the confession of young David Gillon: "In high school I thought I was just one of those people who could never love anybody. When I fell in love with Henry, it meant I had incredibly deep emotions—it meant I was human."

Like *Word Is Out*, *Gay U.S.A.* is also a collective production, made by a large number of persons under the banner of Artists United for Gay Rights, and a considerable part of the work is made up of interview footage. But the point of view and structure are radically different.

Rather than being assembled by democratic communal decisions over a five-year period, *Gay U.S.A.* was filmed largely on one day: June 26, 1977; and, apart from actual materials, it was created with donated talent and labor from a vast number of individuals, all coordinated by one filmmaker who conceived the project and gave it its final creative form: Arthur Bressan, Jr.

In the angry wake of the defeat for gay rights in Miami on June 7, Bressan, who had begun to establish his gift as a director in the gay porno circuits, joined in the San Francisco evening demonstration that grew spontaneously. "My movie camera jammed in front of City Hall. I stood there and felt the energy swirl around me. If this was 'defeat,' what would Gay Freedom Day be like?" Bressan began to "cinematize" the approaching spectacle in his mind, and gradually the idea emerged of forming units of six cities (ultimately, San Francisco, San Diego, New York, Chicago, Houston, and Los Angeles) and using the parades as metaphors for an emerging gay consciousness in America.

The material Bressan eventually received, though varying in quality, was largely overwhelming. The San Francisco parade, made up of almost 250,000 participants from many parts of California and the United States, was captured in its diverse splendor by eight camera crews at varying distances from the swirling tide of humanity, with sync interviews filmed against the constant flow of marchers and observers. However, by cutting from San Francisco to New York to Los Angeles to Chicago and back, the film gives the impression of a united, growing struggle against conformity, bigotry, and oppression from coast to coast. Before discussing the structure of *Gay U.S.A.*, however, it is important to assess the nature of the materials of which it is constructed.

In *Word Is Out*, one has the impression of distinct, unrelated, reflective, private experiences being expressed; in *Gay U.S.A.*, one is confronted with persons caught up in the communal excitement of the "politics of celebration," in which spontaneous feelings and attitudes are highly charged. Certainly, *Gay U.S.A.* is the first film ever to fully capture the intense anger, joy, and love embodied in these very public expressions of freedom. In addition to the sync interviews, Bressan amplifies the 1977 material with historical footage of the first Christopher Street Parade in New York in 1970 and of subsequent parades in Los Angeles and San Francisco leading up to the present; slides, still blow-ups, and "found" footage of civil rights marches and Nazi parades are also interpolated in the film's elaborately edited finale.

Before making a total commitment to film, Bressan lectured on history, philosophy, and American civilization in New York, and his avowed primary cinematic models, Frank Capra and Sergei Eisenstein, reveal his strong personal political stance. His admiration of Capra's social criticism, the individual confronting the political establishment, is tempered by a collective spectrum of values. "Politics is a dangerous game for a filmmaker," says Bressan. "It's double jeopardy when it's a low-budget film. You can't afford second thoughts. And political winds are always changing. I was lucky. I got solid political advice from people in the Bay Area—and long distance help from Houston, Chicago, New York, and Boston. The rest I trusted to good intent and the margin for error audiences allow when they're feeling kind." In *Gay U.S.A.*, Bressan orchestrates a richly diverse spectrum of faces, opinions, and life-styles: lesbian lovers, sympathetic straight families, drag queens, gay professionals, children and youths, gay women, ex-prisoners, dykes on bikes, blacks, school teachers, Asiatics, anti-gay dissenters, and critics of every social, economic, political, and religious persuasion.

From Eisenstein Bressan has evolved a system of montage that is composed of dialectical oppositions in both sound and image. The lengthy pretitle sequence begins with a series of black-and-white stills of the San Francisco March underscored by a series of voice-overs. A New Yorker: "I think it's at least double what it's been in the past. As we expected, there's new militancy in the gay movement and it's here today." A black male: "I'm not prejudiced or anything like that, but when they come in the street and mess with normal people . . . " An elderly Jewish male: "I'm surprised to see so many women in the parade . . . there must be an awful lot we don't know about." A Puerto Rican male: "I have two beautiful children, both boys—seven and nine years old. If they grow up to be gay I'll love them as much as I love them now." A deep-voiced Southern male: "I think they're *nuts*," followed by what sounds like a shrewish Brooklyn housewife, "We understand they have a problem. We want them to be cured, we don't want them to go on living in sin." A proponent for repealing laws against gays is juxtaposed with an anti-abortionist who supports Anita Bryant and flatly admits, "I'm not for gay rights." A young male gay Catholic: "The reason we're staying in the church is to protest its policies against gay people," followed by a fundamentalist who claims, "Homosexuality is condemned by Christ in the Bible as an unnatural way of living." This negative pseudoreligious/pseudoscientific diatribe, which introduces the film's first actual synchronized interview, is counterbalanced visually with individual and collective images of happy, smiling faces united in a common struggle that belies the thrust of the opposition. Positive gestures and statements from gays and friendly nongays give the work a spirited tone of debate that reveals much spontaneity and healthy thinking in this tribal gathering.

Image and sound continue to combine moments of frivolity and seriousness, one of the features of these large demonstrations which Bressan uses to great effect. A quip by a Florida gay about California orange juice is, for instance, set against a unisex figure covered in funeral black holding a prominent cardboard sign: "I am the homosexual you are afraid to see." One is constantly aware of the mixture of humor, sometimes of a bizarre, extravagant nature, with a truly painful, sometimes tearful struggle in the face of a hostile environment, which gives us a unique insight into the dimensions of human courage combating ignorance and superstition. The pretitle sequence ends with a brief statement by two tiny boys, about nine or ten. The older places his arm around the other and says, "I can probably speak for all the kids in the United States—and my brother even. We all believe in equal rights for kids . . . I think that should be made into a law too."

With the brightly punctuated titles we realize that we have been witnessing a preparatory overture and that the parades are beginning. The "Dykes on Bikes" lead off the procession down San Francisco's Market Street, followed by thousands of women sporting banners: "We are your teachers," "Gay, Alive and Healthy," and "Remember the Witch Hunts," against a strong ballad, "Reflections" by Marjie Orten, on the track. Breaking into the procession is the second long sync interview, with two lesbians from northwest Kansas, one of whom was married for 15½ years before coming out in the army reserves in Alabama. She tells of losing jobs because of being gay and finally, out of desperation, leaving for the coast with her lover.

The pace picks up its rhythmic momentum, however, with a three-part "Are You Gay?" sequence, beginning with an aerial view that yields to a handheld tracking camera cutting from response to response, from yeas to nays, from "I don't think I can classify myself" to "That's none of your business." The flow of responses is an introduction to the next sustained interview, shot against the constant movement and sound of the parade. Its subject is a handsome businessman, dressed in a three-piece suit, sixty years old but looking easily twenty years younger, who talks about coming to San Francisco after World War II. He speaks positively about the parade as a "show of individualism and people power that we saw in other minority movements back in the fifties and sixties." His interview continues as a voice-over, a springboard for a visual recap of the history of Gay Liberation and its public manifestations. As he remarks that "parades have changed over the years as gay consciousness has changed," we see black-and-white footage of the boarded-up Stonewall Bar and demonstrators preparing for the first Gay Pride March in June 1970, intercut with views of the first march on Hollywood Boulevard—indicating the celebratory quality of "coming out" that such events began to signify. As the sequence gains momentum, verses of James O'Connor's upbeat ballad "Great Expectations" are interwoven with further interviews, climaxing in the intercutting of a 1972 view of the San Francisco march—thirty stories above the City Hall plaza—with an identical composition from 1977; a movement grows from about two thousand people to approximately one hundred thousand.

As the crowds pass by, one observer says, "This parade is bigger than any one reaction," a statement that accurately describes the kaleidoscopic vision imparted by *Gay U.S.A.* Following positive and moving images of men and women affectionately gathering in Central Park, a debate is heard between a constitutionalist and several Fundamentalist Christians. The former argues that churches have always backed repression: war, witch burning, the Crusades, and the Spanish Inquisition, while the Fundamentalist blandly asserts that the Bible says sex, aside from procreation, is "degrading, decadent, weakening, childish" and, astonishingly enough, that "man was not intended to enjoy his senses"! But his opponent argues for a separation of church and state. "It's right there in the Constitution—freedom of religion. And you can't have freedom of religion if you have religion in the law."

Although the tone of Bressan's film is primarily positive, the inclusion of dissenting opinions offers the viewer a climate of dialectic in which prejudices may be questioned. Even in a city that traditionally is "open" for gays to pursue a free and equal life in diverse ways, there still are elements of intimidation and violence. Just days prior to the 1977 San Francisco march, Robert Hillsborough, a handsome young man, was brutally stabbed on the streets by a trio of youths. Bressan has dedicated *Gay U.S.A.* to him and closes the film with a spontaneous floral remembrance on the steps of City Hall seen from an aerial view. Several young men recount experiences of being called "fag" by black men on the streets. But the anger that emerges is channeled back into creative impulses in Pat Parker's unforgettable recitation of her poem "For the straight folks who don't mind gays but wish they weren't so blatant," which should give many self-righteous heterosexuals plenty of food for thought.

Bressan's feeling for ideological and aesthetic contrast extends to differences within the gay community itself. The notion of drag is viewed with disfavor by a woman who sees it as degrading to women. "I don't pretend to understand what motivates the men to do that but I know that the whole society mocks women at the same time that it pushes them into that role"—meaning the stereotype of femininity. Her interview is intercut with the positive view of an intelligent, bearded youth in a sequined drag costume. He contends that "drag is just the tool that you use to express who you are in terms of clothes." He personally finds a political sentiment in wearing women's clothing, which makes him feel like a whole rather than a half-person. Again the interview becomes a voice-over that leads to the film's most complex constellation of ideas and imagery. A parade float featuring blow-ups of the faces of Stalin, Hitler, Anita Bryant, a Ku Klux Klan member, and Idi Amin is intercut with Nuremberg rally footage from Leni Riefenstahl's *Triumph of the Will*, as the young man notes that "in fascist societies, people are taught to dress alike, to act alike, to perform alike, as opposed to following their inner needs. When you look at mass demonstrations in totalitarian societies, I mean where you see as many people as there are here, you don't get a sense that these are real people . . . I mean you see herds of sheep." Bressan's brilliant juxtapositions clearly demonstrate the lack of individuality that his subject sees as the basis of stereotyping in racism and sexism, and precisely how this is refuted by the diversity of the gay marchers. Suddenly another voice informs us of the history of "The Pink Triangle," a mark used by the Nazis to designate homosexuals, who died by the thousands in the concentration camps—with a visual evocation of the past, dissolving into the present and back to a historical truth.

This chilling reminder of past persecution shifts quite naturally into a positive, major key with the "Gays in History" sequence, in which an interviewer asks various persons, "If you could invite one gay person from any period in history, who would you like to see here today?" The answers are interesting: Alexander the Great, Sappho, and Diana the Huntress, Jesus Christ, Herman Melville, André Gide, and Bessie Smith. Countless other names are cited as the parade floats by with pride and dignity.

Word Is Out and *Gay U.S.A.* are unique documents in the history of cinema because they represent, for the first time, a truly open response to the world of a vast and extremely divergent human minority that is now on the move to secure its human rights and full participation on an equal basis with the heterosexual majority. Each film speaks with a voice long denied the access to the media which has been granted other minorities, and one which will no longer remain silent in the face of bigotry and oppression.

Ironically, although these films are largely intended to educate nongays about the realities of gay existence, they have so far been seen chiefly by predominantly gay audiences in metropolitan areas. While *Word Is Out* is greeted with a calm, reflective response, *Gay U.S.A.* tends to generate a spirited air of celebration and an emotional "high" that can be felt by any viewer sensitive and open to feelings. There is no question that these films, if seen by large numbers of people, could prove to be highly effective tools for social change, for a revolutionary transformation of consciousness and an acceptance of sexual, as well as religious and political, differences that might lead to a true "liberty and justice for all." Meanwhile, the struggle to be heard continues; those of us who refuse to listen may be seen as part of the problem, and those who elect to listen with patience and openness may prove to be part of the solution.

Hiroshima-Nagasaki:
The Case of
the A-Bomb Footage

Erik Barnouw

It was in 1970, a quarter of a century after the footage was shot, that the documentary film *Hiroshima-Nagasaki, August 1945* had its premiere and won an audience—an international one, as it turned out. In recounting the origin and history of this film I want to emphasize the extraordinary twenty-five-year hiatus. It seems to me to have implications for filmmakers and film scholars and perhaps even for the democratic process itself.[1]

I become involved in this story in its later stages, as producer of the 1970 compilation documentary, and this involvement came about almost by accident. Before I explain how this happened, let me go back to the beginning of the story, as I have been able to piece it together over the years.

In August 1945, after the two atom bombs had been dropped on Hiroshima and Nagasaki, a Japanese film unit named Nippon Eiga Sha was commissioned by the government to make a film record of the effects of the devastating new weapon. Nippon Eiga Sha was a wartime amalgamation of the several newsreel and documentary units that had existed before the war. They had been nationalized for war purposes.

The man entrusted with the making of the film was Akira Iwasaki, a film critic, historian, and occasional producer. The choice of Iwasaki for the assignment was significant. During the 1930s he had been the leader of a leftist film group called Prokino. or Proletarian Film League, similar to the Workers' Film and Photo Leagues in the United States. Being antimilitarist, Prokino had been outlawed shortly before the war, and some of its members had been jailed under a preventive-detention law. Iwasaki himself had spent part of the war in prison. The fact that he had regained standing and was given the film assignment reflected the turbulent situation in the final days of the war, and the extent to which the military had already lost status.[2]

Because of the breakdown of transport and the difficulty of obtaining adequate supplies, it took the Nippon Eiga Sha film crews some time to reach their locations. But they were at work in Hiroshima and Nagasaki when the American occupation forces arrived. What happened then has been described by Iwasaki. "In the middle of the shooting one of my cameramen was arrested in Nagasaki by American military police . . . I was summoned to the GHQ and told to discontinue the shooting." The filming was halted, but Iwasaki says he re-monstrated and "made arguments" with the occupation authorities. "Then," he writes, "came the group of the Strategic Bombing Survey from Washington, and they wanted to have a film of Hiroshima and Nagasaki. Therefore the U.S. Army wanted to utilize my film for the purpose and changed its mind. Now they allowed me—or better, ordered me—to continue and complete the film."[3] During the following weeks, under close American control, much additional footage was shot. All was in black-and-white; there was no color film in Japan at this time. As the shooting progressed, the material was edited into sequences under the overall title "Effects of the Atomic Bomb." There were sequences showing effects on concrete, effects on wood, effects on veg-etation, and so on. The emphasis was on detailed scientific observation. Effects on human beings were included, but sparsely. Survivors on the outer fringes of the havoc were photographed in improvised treatment centers, but here too the guiding supervisory principle was scientific data-gathering rather than human interest. The interests of the camera teams were to some extent at variance with this.

The edited material had reached a length of somewhat less than three hours when the saga entered a new phase. Occupation authorities suddenly took possession of the film—negative, positive, and outtakes—and shipped it to Washington. Film and all related documents were classified SECRET and locked away, disappearing from view for almost a quarter of a century. Most people, including those in the film world, remained unaware of its existence. Apparently a few feet were released for army-approved uses, and the project was briefly mentioned in *Films Beget Films*, by Jay Leyda, published 1964, a book that began as a memorandum for the Chinese government on the values of film archives.[4] But whether the earliest Hiroshima and Nagasaki footage still existed was an American military secret. With later color footage of the ruins making an appearance and to some extent satisfying curiosity, the missing footage did not become an issue in the United States.

Until 1968 I was oblivious to its existence. But early that year, a friend, Mrs. Lucy Lemann, sent me a newspaper clipping she had received from Japan which excited my interest. It was from the English-language *Asahi Evening News* and reported that the footage shot in Hiroshima and Nagasaki in 1945 by Japanese cameramen had been returned to Japan from the United

States and that the government would arrange a television screening "after certain scenes showing victims' disfiguring burns are deleted." The items also stated that the film would later be made available on loan to "research institutions," but it added: "In order to avoid the film being utilized for political purposes, applications for loan of the film from labor unions and political organizations will be turned down."[5]

I was at this time chairman of the film, radio, and television division of the Columbia University School of the Arts and had organized a related unit called the Center for Mass Communication, a division of Columbia University Press producing and distributing documentary films and recordings. Naturally the clipping seemed to demand some investigation or action. Mrs. Lemann was a contributor to the World Law Fund, and at her suggestion I wrote for further information to Professor Yoshikazu Sakamoto, professor of international politics at the University of Tokyo, an associate of the fund. His prompt reply said that the Japanese had negotiated with the U.S. Department of State for the return of the film, but the Department of Defense was thought to control it. The material sent to Japan was not the original nitrate film but a safety-film copy.

Somewhat impulsively, I wrote a letter on Columbia University stationery, signed "Chairman, Film, Radio, Television," addressed to "The Honorable Clark M. Clifford, Secretary of Defense," with the notation that *cc*'s should go to Secretary of State Dean Rusk and to Dr. Grayson Kirk, president of Columbia University. The letter asked whether Columbia's Center for Mass Communication might have the privilege of releasing in the United States the material recently made available for showing in Japan.[6] I felt a bit flamboyant in this but sensed I had nothing to lose. I scarcely expected results.

To my amazement, a letter arrived within days from Daniel Z. Henkin, deputy assistant secretary of defense, stating that the Department of Defense had turned the material over to the National Archives and that we could have access to it there.[7] So it was that early in April 1968 I found myself with a few associates in the auditorium of the National Archives in Washington looking at some two hours and forty minutes of Hiroshima and Nagasaki footage. We also examined voluminous shot lists in which the location of every shot was identified and its content summarized and indexed. Every sheet bore the classification stamp SECRET, but this had been crossed out and another stamp substituted: NOT TO BE RELEASED WITHOUT APPROVAL OF THE D.O.D. There was no indication of the date of this partial declassification. We guessed that some routine declassification timetable had taken effect but without public announcement. Perhaps we were merely the first to have inquired about the material.[8]

Some in our group were dismayed by the marginal quality of much of the film, a result, perhaps, of the circumstances under which it had been shot and the fact that we were looking at material some generations away from the original. But this quality also seemed a mark of authenticity, and it seemed to me that enough of the footage was extraordinary in its power, unforgettable in its implications, and historic in its importance to warrant our duplicating all of it. A grant from Mrs. Lemann to Columbia University Press made it possible to order a duplicate negative and workprint of the full two hours and forty minutes, along with photostats of the priceless shot lists. During the summer of 1968 all this material arrived at Columbia University from the National Archives, and we began incessant study and experimentation with the footage, with constant reference to the shot lists and other available background information.[9]

The footage contained ruins in grotesque formations and endless shots of rubble. At first we were inclined to discard many of the less striking rubble sequences, but when we learned that one had been a school (where most of the children had died at their desks), and one had been a prison (where 140 prisoners had died in their cells), and another had been a trolley car (whose passengers had evaporated, leaving in the rubble a row of their skulls and bones), even the less dramatic shots acquired new meaning. Eventually a montage of such rubble shots, linked with statistics about the people annihilated or injured and the distance of each location from the center of the blast, became a key sequence in the film.

The paucity of what we called "human-effects footage" troubled us deeply. We felt that we would have to cluster this limited material near the end of our film for maximum effect, but meanwhile we resolved on a sweeping search for additional human-effects footage. We wrote to the Defense Department asking whether additional material of this sort had perhaps been held back. The Pentagon's staff historian answered, assuring us that nothing was being held back and adding: "Outtakes from the original production no longer exist, having probably been destroyed during the conversion from acetate [*sic*] to safety film—if they ever were turned over to the U.S. Government at all."[10] This curious reply made us wonder whether footage such as we hoped to find might still exist in Japan or might be held by people in the United States who were in Japan during the Occupation. Barbara Van Dyke, who became associate producer for our film, began writing letters to a long list of people, asking for information on any additional footage. In the end this search proved fruitless; we found we had to proceed without additional human-effects footage.

One of those to whom she wrote was the Japanese film critic and historian Akira Iwasaki, the original producer. His name was not mentioned in documents received from the Defense Department or from the National Archives, but he was suggested by the writer Donald Richie, a leading authority on Japanese cinema, as a likely source of information.[11] Iwasaki did not reply to our inquiry; he explained later that he had doubted the "sincerity" of our project.

Van Dyke's search did produce one extraordinary find. One of the occupants of the observation plane that followed the *Enola Gay,* the plane that dropped the bomb, to Hiroshima was Harold Agnew, who later became head of the Los Alamos Laboratory. As a personal venture he had taken with him a 16mm camera. The very brief sequence he brought back provides an unforgettable glimpse of the historic explosion and the shuddering impact of the blast on the observation plane itself, which, for a moment, seems likely to be blown to perdition. From Mr. Agnew we acquired a copy of this short sequence.

Our first rough assembly was some forty minutes long, but we kept reducing it in quest of sharper impact. What finally emerged, after more than a year of experimentation, was a quiet sixteen-minute film with a factual, eloquently understated narration written by Paul Ronder and spoken by him and Kazuko Oshima. Ronder and Geoffrey Bartz did the editing, with musical effects by Linea Johnson and Terrill Schukraft. We consulted at various stages with Albert W. Hilberg, M.D., and historian Henry G. Graff. We were not sure the film would have the effect we hoped for, but our doubts were soon resolved.

After several small screenings we arranged a major preview at the Museum of Modern Art in February 1970, to which the press was invited. The auditorium was jammed, and at the end of the showing the audience sat in total silence for several seconds. We were at first unsure what this meant, but the comments soon made clear what it meant. Later that day the UPI ticker carried a highly favorable report that treated the film as a major news event, mentioning the address of the Center for Mass Communication and the print sale price, $96. Two days later checks and orders began arriving in the mail and continued, without promotional effort on our part, at the rate of a hundred a month. In five months almost five hundred prints were sold to film libraries, colleges, school systems, clubs, community groups, and churches. Every screening seemed to bring a surge of letters and orders. Foreign sales came quickly.

Two things amazed us: the electric effect on audiences everywhere, and the massive silence of the American networks. All had been invited to the press preview; none had attended. Early in the morning after the resounding UPI dispatch, all three commercial networks phoned to ask for preview prints and sent motorcycle couriers to collect them, but this was followed by another silence. By making follow-up phone calls we learned that CBS and ABC were "not interested." Only NBC thought it might use the film, if it could find a "news hook." We dared not speculate what kind of event this might call for.

The networks' attitude was, of course, in line with a policy all three had pursued for over a decade—of not broadcasting documentaries other than their own. We at Columbia University were outraged at the network policy.[12] We had half expected that the historic nature of the material would in this case thrust it aside, but we were for the moment too busy filling nontelevision orders to consider any particular protest or action.

Then a curious chain of media phenomena changed the situation. On 5 April 1970, the Sunday supplement *Parade*, which generally gave its chief attention to the romantic aberrations of the mighty, carried a prominent item about *Hiroshima-Nagasaki, August 1945*, calling it unforgettable and necessary viewing for the people of any nation possessing the bomb.[13] This apparently caused the editors of the Boston *Globe*, which carried *Parade*, to wonder why television was ignoring the film. They made phone calls to nuclear scientists and others, asking their opinions on the matter, and reached several who had attended our previews. The result was a lead editorial in the *Globe* headed: HIROSHIMA-NAGASAKI, AUGUST 1945—NOT FOR SENSITIVE U.S. EYES. It quoted Dr. S. E. Luria, Sedgwick Professor of Biology at Massachusetts Institute of Technology, who described the film as "a very remarkable document," adding, "I wish every American could see it, and particularly, every Congressman." Norman Cousins described himself as "deeply impressed." The *Globe* ended its editorial with a blast at the networks for ignoring the film.[14] *Variety*, the show-business weekly, was interested in the *Globe*'s "needling" of the networks and featured the issue in a special box in its next edition.[15] This brought sudden action from National Educational Television, which a few days later signed a contract to broadcast the film in early August, twenty-five years after the dropping of the bombs. No sooner had the contract been signed than NBC announced that it wanted the film for use on its monthly magazine series, "First Tuesday." When Sumner Glimcher, manager for the Center for Mass Communication, explained that the film was committed to NET, he was asked if we could "buy out" NET so that NBC could have the film, but we declined to try.

As the issue of a U.S. telecast was moving to a resolution, we were aware of parallel, and apparently more feverish, developments in Japan. Our first inkling of what was happening in Japan came at the Museum of Modern Art preview, where we were approached by a representative of TBS (Tokyo Broadcasting System), one of Japan's commercial systems, with an offer to purchase Japanese television rights. To be negotiating such a matter seemed strange in view of the Japanese government's announced plans for a television screening, but the TBS man was persistent and eager, and we finally signed an agreement authorizing a telecast, with an option to repeat. The telecast took place 18 March 1970, and the option to repeat was promptly exercised. We gradually became aware, through bulletins from Japan, of the enormous impact made by these telecasts. The government-arranged showing had taken place earlier over NHK, the government network, but had included little except rubble. Human beings had been excised "in deference to the relatives of the victims," but this action had brought a storm of protest. It was against this background that TBS had negotiated for our film. It also gave our film, which made use of everything that NHK telecast had eliminated, an added impact. Professor Sakamoto of the University of Tokyo began sending us voluminous translations of favorable reviews and articles, one of which paid special tribute to Columbia University for showing the Japanese people "what our own government tried to withhold from us." The reviews included major coverage in a picture magazine of the *Life* format. Viewing statistics were provided. The *Mainichi Shimbun* reported that the film "caused a sensation throughout the country," while in Hiroshima "the viewing rate soared to four times the normal rate."[16] The *Chugoku Shimbun* reported:

> At the atomic injury hospital in Hiroshima last night, nine o'clock being curfew time, all was quiet. Only in one room on the second floor of the west wing, the television diffidently continued its program. . . . They had obtained special permission from the doctors. . . . The first scene was of ruins. "That's the Aioi Bridge." "That's the Bengaku Dome." The women follow the scenes. Even the Chinese woman who had not wanted to see is leaning from her bed and watching intently. . . . The scene of victims which has elicited so much comment is now on. "That's exactly how it was," they nod to each other. However, when the film was over they contradicted their words and said, "It was much, much worse."[17]

A letter came from the mayor of Hiroshima. The city would mark the twenty-fifth anniversary of the bomb with a major observance including a long television program, and wanted to include material from our film.

The most gratifying response came from Akira Iwasaki, who after a lapse of almost twenty-five years had seen his footage on television. His role in the project was not credited, and he might have been expected to resent this, but no sign of resentment appeared. He wrote us a long letter expressing his gratitude and appreciation for how we had used the material. He also published a long review in a leading Japanese magazine, describing his reaction.

> I was lost in thought for a long time, deeply moved by this film. . . . I was the producer of the original long film which offered the basic material for this short film. That is, I knew every cut of it . . . yet I was speechless. . . . It was not the kind of film the Japanese thought Americans would produce. The film is an appeal or warning from man to man for peaceful reflection—to prevent the use of the bomb ever again. I like the narration, in which the emotion is well controlled and the voice is never raised. . . . That made me cry. In this part, the producers are no longer Americans. Their feelings are completely identical to our feelings.[18]

The impact of the film was further illuminated by a bizarre incident. At my Columbia University office a delegation of three Japanese gentlemen was announced and ushered in, all impeccably dressed. One member, introducing the leader, identified him as a member or former member of the Japanese parliament, representing the Socialists. The leader himself then explained that he came on behalf of an organization called the Japan Congress Against A and H Bombs, also known as Gensuikin. In this capacity, he had three requests to make. First, as a token of appreciation for what we had achieved with our film *Hiroshima-Nagasaki, August 1945*, would I accept a small brooch as a gift to my wife? Puzzled and curious, I accepted.

Second, would I consider an invitation to speak in Hiroshima on the twenty-fifth anniversary of the dropping of the bomb, in the course of the scheduled observances? I hesitated—the suggestion raised endless questions in my mind, but I said I would consider. The leader seemed reassured and said I would receive a letter.

Then came the third request. Would he be permitted to purchase six prints of *Hiroshima-Nagasaki, August 1945*? I explained that we sold prints at $96 for nonprofit use, making no discrimination among buyers; anyone could buy. With an audible sigh of relief, he suddenly unbuttoned his shirt, ripped out a money belt, and produced six pristine $100 bills. Accustomed to dealing with checks and money orders, it took the office a while to round up the $24 change. We handed him the six prints. One member of the delegation had a camera ready; photographs were taken, and the group departed. But a few days later we received a letter from another organization with a very similar name—the Japan Council Against Atomic and Hydrogen Bombs, or Gensuikyo. It wished the right to translate our film into Japanese, without editing change. Again we wrote to Professor Sakamoto of the University of Tokyo for enlightenment. Again he responded promptly.

> The movement against atomic bombs had been split into two groups since early in the 1960s, the immediate cause being the difference in attitude toward the nuclear tests carried on by the Soviet Union. The Japan Congress Against A and H Bombs, which politically is close to the Social Democrats, is against all nuclear tests, regardless of nation. The Council Against Atomic and Hydrogen Bombs, the other body, is close to the Communist Party, and is opposed to nuclear tests by the United States but considers tests by the Socialist countries undesirable but necessary. . . . The Council is a somewhat larger organization than the other. Many efforts have been made in the past to merge the two bodies but none have been successful to date.[19]

In the following weeks we were bombarded by both congress and council with cabled requests about prints, translation rights, and 8mm rights. To our relief, the issue was resolved, or apparently resolved, by another news item from Professor Sakamoto. He reported the revelation that in 1945 a Nippon Eiga Sha technician, fearing that the American military would seize and remove the footage, had secreted a duplicate set in a laboratory ceiling. He had now made this known.[20] From then on we referred Japanese inquirers to this "newly available" resource. Apparently the Defense Department's suspicion, expressed in the letter from the Pentagon historian, had had some validity.

On 3 August 1970, *Hiroshima-Nagasaki, August 1945* had its American television premiere over National Educational Television, giving the system one of its largest audiences to date. "Hiroshima Film Gets Numbers," *Variety* reported.[21] NBC's "Today" program and the CBS Evening News with Walter Cronkite had decided, at the last moment, to carry news items about the event, using short clips and crediting NET and Columbia University. NET's Tampa Bay outlet did a delayed telecast via tape, after deleting some of the "human-effects footage." So far as we could learn, all other stations carried the full film. The telecast won favorable reviews across the nation, acclaiming NET's decision to show it.

To my disappointment, NET coupled the film with a panel discussion on the subject "Should we have dropped the bomb?" It was an issue I had resolutely kept out of the film, even though most members of our group wanted the film to condemn Truman's action. I did not myself see how President Truman, in the situation existing at that time, could have refused a go-ahead. But this seemed to me irrelevant to our film, a bygone issue, already endlessly discussed. To center on it now seemed to me an escape into the past. To me, the Hiroshima-Nagasaki footage was meaningful for today and tomorrow rather than for yesterday.

During the research for my books on the history of American broadcasting, especially *The Image Empire*, I became chillingly aware of how often in recent years men in high position have urged use of atomic weapons. French foreign minister Georges Bidault has said that Secretary of State John Foster Dulles, during the Dien Bien Phu crisis, twice offered him atom bombs to use against the beleaguering Vietnamese forces, but he demurred.[22] Oral histories on file at the Dulles Collection in Princeton make clear that Dulles made the offer on advice received from the Joint Chiefs of Staff. Apparently Bidault's refusal (not President Eisenhower's, as some writers have assumed) averted another holocaust. During the Quemoy-Matsu confrontation, use of an atomic bomb was again discussed.[23] In 1964, Barry Goldwater felt that use of a "low-yield atomic device" to defoliate Vietnamese forests should be considered.[24] (He later emphasized that he had not actually recommended it.) More recently there has been widespread discussion of proposed world strategies based on "tactical" nuclear weapons—a term meant to suggest a modest sort of holocaust but actually designating bombs equivalent in destructive power to the Hiroshima bomb. A more advanced bomb now equals 2,500 Hiroshima bombs, as our film makes clear. Victory with such weapons would only win an uninhabitable world.

Such proposals can only be made by people who have not fully realized what an atomic war can be. When I first saw the Hiroshima-Nagasaki footage, I became aware how little I had comprehended it. Yet this footage gives only the faintest glimpse of future possibilities.

Why, and by what right, was the footage declared SECRET? It contains no military information, the supposed basis for such a classification. Why, then, the suppression? Why the misuse of the classification device? The reason most probably was the fear that wide showing of such a film might make Congress less ready to appropriate billions of dollars for ever more destructive weapons.

I produced the short film *Hiroshima-Nagasaki, August 1945* with the hope that it would be seen by as many people as possible on both sides of every iron curtain. If a film can have the slightest deterrent effect, it may be needed now more than ever. Fortunately, it is achieving a widening distribution.

Although I did not accept the invitation to the 1970 Hiroshima observances, I have visited Japan twice since then, had long talks with Akira Iwasaki, met one of the cameramen in his 1945 unit, and visited the generously helpful Professor Sakamoto. I continued to correspond with Iwasaki until his death on 16 September 1981. In 1978 he published in Japan a book whose title can be translated as *The Occupied Screen*, dealing with various aspects of the relations of the Japanese film industry to the American occupation. One long chapter concerns the production of the Hiroshima-Nagasaki footage, its suppression, the disputes concerning it, and the eventual emergence of the footage in *Hiroshima-Nagasaki, August 1945*.[25]

Notes

1. *Hiroshima-Nagasaki, August 1945* is now widely available. Primary distributor is the Museum of Modern Art, 11 West 53rd, New York, N.Y. 10019, which offers prints for life-of-the-print lease or per-day rental. Per-day rentals are offered by many film libraries—more than one thousand prints are in circulation. The film's history was discussed by the author in a public lecture in Philadelphia, 11 February 1980, at the Walnut Street Theater; the present report is based on that lecture.

2. Interviews with Akira Iwasaki, Fumio Kamei, Ryuchi Kano, in Tokyo, February 1972; Iwasaki, "The Occupied Screen," *Japan Quarterly* 25, no. 3 (July–Sept. 1978).

3. Letter, Akira Iwasaki to Barbara Van Dyke, 15 March 1970, Hiroshima-Nagasaki file, Barnouw Papers. All letters, memoranda, and press excerpts quoted in the present report are available in a file of some three hundred items deposited with the Barnouw Papers in Special Collections, Columbia University Library. Photocopies of the entire file have also been deposited at the Museum of Modern Art, primary distributor of the film, at the Motion Picture, Broadcasting, and Recorded Sound Division of the Library of Congress, Washington, and at the Imperial War Museum, London. The file will be referred to hereafter as "HN file."

4. Jay Leyda, *Films Beget Films* (New York, 1964).

5. *Asahi Evening News*, 26 Jan. 1968.

6. Letter, 8 March 1968, HN file.

7. Letter, 19 March 1968, HN file.

8. The lists were on large file cards, cross-referenced for such topics as "Atomic: Physical Aspects," "Shadow effects," "Shrine," "Debris," "Civilians: Jap." Copies of fifty-three such cards are in HN file.

9. The two hours, forty minutes of *Effects of the Atomic Bomb* held in the National Archives were in the form of 35mm acetate preservation material made from the original, which was on unstable nitrate and no longer existed. We worked from 16mm material made from the National Archives holdings.

10. Letter, R. A. Winnacker to author, 27 June 1968. The word *acetate*, used in error, should have been *nitrate* (HN file).

11. Donald Richie, coauthor with Joseph L. Anderson of *The Japanese Cinema* (Rutland, Vt., and Tokyo, 1959) and longtime film critic in Tokyo, with occasional service as visiting film curator at the Museum of Modern Art, New York.

12. For genesis of the policy, see Erik Barnouw, *Tube of Plenty* (New York, 1975), pp. 269—70.

13. *Parade*, 5 April 1970.

14. *Boston Sunday Globe*, 5 April 1970.

15. *Variety*, 22 April 1970.

16. *Mainichi Shimbun*, 20, 22 March 1970.

17. *Chugoku Shimbun*, 19 March 1970.

18. Akira Iwasaki, "It All Started with a Letter," *Asahi-Graph*, 3 April 1970.

19. Letter, Professor Yoshikazu Sakamoto to author, 4 May 1970, HN file.

20. Letter, Sakamoto to author, 8 June 1970, HN file.

21. *Variety*, 5 Aug. 1970.

22. The Bidault statement is in Roscoe Drummond and Gaston Coblentz, *Duel at the Brink: John Foster Dulles' Command of American Power* (Garden City, N.Y., 1960), pp. 121–22. Bidault repeated the statement in the Peter Davis documentary film *Hearts and Minds*.

23. Statements by Nathan Twining and George V. Allen in Dulles Oral History Collection, Princeton University, re Dien Bien Phu and Quemoy-Matsu deliberations.

24. The Goldwater statement was in a 1964 ABC-TV interview with Howard K. Smith and became a major focus of the 1964 presidential campaign won by Lyndon B. Johnson.

25. Iwasaki, *The Occupied Screen* (translation of Japanese title), pp. 14–17 and 110–209, deal with the Hiroshima-Nagasaki film. A segment of *The Occupied Screen* dealing with other aspects of the period appeared in translation in *Japan Quarterly* 25, no. 3 (July–Sept. 1978).

The War Game:
An Interview
with Peter Watkins

Alan Rosenthal

It may be the most important film ever made.
Kenneth Tynan, *The Observer*

The War Game was produced and directed by Peter Watkins in 1965 and was denied a television screening by the BBC in 1966 as a result of a directive by the then director general of the BBC, Sir Hugh Greene. But in spite of Sir Hugh Greene's restrictive policy, the BBC finally bowed to pressure and released the film for theatrical but not television screening.

The War Game starts with a series of maps showing the vulnerability of England to nuclear attack. It then suggests an international crisis that culminates in a Berlin confrontation between the Russians and the Americans. As a result of the crisis the allies use tactical nuclear weapons in Europe, which in turn provokes the Russians to drop atom bombs on England.

What follows is a hellish evocation of disaster. Carefully prepared civil defense plans prove futile and useless; children are blinded, firestorms rage, and the dead lie in the streets. After a while there are hunger riots; police are assaulted, and food thievers are shot by execution squads. It seems, in fact, as if civilization is disintegrating.

The style of the film is highly composite. Live interviews are mixed with carefully staged vignettes; the beginning of a storyline is broken by comments quoted from religious and scientific personalities; grainy newsreel camerawork suddenly gives way to the smoothest of Hollywood set lighting. In theory, it shouldn't work; in practice, it all blends together as a unified piece of art.

Although defenders of the film saw it as an authentic vision of catastrophe, it was damned by many British dailies and written off as a grossly distorted message by the British right wing. Watkins was charged with failing to show hope and the resilience of the human spirit. He was also accused of being too harshly realistic and (worst of all) of propagandizing for nuclear disarmament in the crudest possible way.

All art, however, is propaganda in one form or another, and to seek "objectivity" in a film about the atom bomb seems to me to be a red herring. Watkins was presenting a personal vision based on well-researched facts which few critics bothered to challenge. Moreover, a great deal of the criticism very definitely exhibited an ostrichlike approach to life, which Bertrand Russell commented on as follows in his autobiography: "Those who try to make you uneasy by talk about atom bombs are regarded as troublemakers, . . . as people who spoil the pleasure of a fine day by foolish prospects of improbable rain."

In reviewing the whole situation, it seems a pity that *The War Game* led to Watkins's resignation from the BBC. It was unfortunate because the BBC in the past has been relatively open to the dissenting voice and the individual opinion (certainly far more so than the commercial networks in the United States) and would have seemed to be the ideal place for Watkins to work out his own personal and committed brand of filmmaking.

Since 1966 Watkins has trodden a varyingly successful path in feature films, with the direction of *Privilege* and *The Gladiators* to his credit. At the time of writing (November 1970), he was engaged on a series of films dealing with key events in American history, such as the Civil War, and their relevance today.

This interview took place on a freezing Sunday morning in Toronto. Time was very limited, and because James Blue had already covered a lot of the shooting details of the film in an excellent interview with Watkins published in *Film Comment*,[1] I decided to concentrate my questions on the preliminary research rather than on the filmmaking itself.

What was your background prior to entering the BBC?
I wanted to be an actor, but my drama training stopped when I did my national service. I came out of the army in 1956 and, for no reason at all, suddenly decided to become a filmmaker. I saw somebody using an 8mm camera, and I guess it excited me—I can't remember why. It all happened in about a week, and I stopped trying to become an actor and began the long, dreary, uphill trail of getting into the film business. First I became an assistant producer in an advertising agency, doing commercials. I then became an assistant editor and finally a director about seven years later in a London sponsored documentary unit. That was the professional side of it. However, about once a year I spent all my money and made an antiwar film. A couple of them won amateur film awards and were shown on television.

By that time I was getting a little fed up with England, and as my wife is French I decided to try and get some work in France. I bashed away with nothing happening for five months, then decided to apply to the BBC. Luckily,

I was saved from some of the hapless formalities that you have to go through in joining the BBC, as Huw Wheldon had seen an amateur film of mine called *The Forgotten Faces*. This was a reconstruction of the Hungarian uprising of 1956 which had been shown on television, and Wheldon had liked it. So I became one of the first of the new wave of people who were taken into the opening of channel 2. As it happened, I never worked in channel 2; I stayed in channel 1, was a production assistant for a year, and then I said I would like to make a film about the battle of Culloden.

Was much supervision given on what was, after all, your first film for the BBC?

They let me do it completely on trust and on my record of amateur filmmaking. I had read a very interesting book on the battle, thought the scope of the subject tremendous, and Huw Wheldon said, "Well, just do it." I don't think he had time or particularly wanted to read the script; he just let me do it. It was completely subjective, of course, as those were the golden days of documentaries; I am not sure that the freedom I had exists any more. But it was marvelous at that time. Unfortunately, Huw Wheldon went up to his high position, and the situation has changed.

Your history of antiwar films seems to indicate that The War Game *wasn't a sudden inspiration but was the result of development over a number of years.*

Well, way back in 1961 or 1962, like most people in England, I was an observer of the Campaign for Nuclear Disarmament. I felt very strongly about the issue but didn't join the campaign because, although I agreed with their objectives, I disagreed with their strategy. Those were the days before I joined the BBC, and I had an idea for an amateur film about a group of atom-bomb survivors in a cellar. I wanted to do face-to-face interviews of what they had been through and that sort of thing. Anyway, it sort of lay there ticking for a number of years; but as soon as I had done *Culloden* I raised the subject with my boss.

At that time I was a good boy in the eyes of the BBC. *Culloden* had been well received, and I had a certain amount of rope given to me. By that stage I suppose I must have abandoned the cellar idea and broadened the whole to include the wider effects of a nuclear attack on England. Wheldon was a bit worried about it but said, "Okay, I'll have to put this to the higher-up people, and they'll probably want to see a script." So it went through to this upper echelon, but they really didn't approve of the thing until five days after I had started shooting, when their reaction was, "Well, we'll wait and see it, and then evaluate it afterwards, because it may be difficult." It was left on a very vague basis.

One of the striking things about The War Game *is the amount of research it must have involved. Was the information on which you based your script readily obtainable?*

The more films I do, the more I research. It's a growing pattern. I tend to put more and more emphasis onto the solid basis of research. With *The War Game*, I had to do a great deal of original research because nobody had ever collated all the information into an easily accessible published form. Quite a lot of books had been written on the effects of thermonuclear bombs, but very few of these had ever been seen by the public.

You must realize that there are an infinite number of books published, which the public can get at, on a normal historical subject like the American Civil War. In contrast, there is an extreme dearth of literature available to the public about the Third World War. What literature there is, is stacked up on the shelves of the American Institute of Strategic Studies and those sorts of places and is never read by the public. So it was an extremely esoteric subject for a filmmaker to delve into and quite hard to find basic facts.

Did you employ a research team?

No, not really. I did it all myself and mounted the research in several different areas, such as technical and sociological. On the technical side I went to Germany and tried to get the essence of Berlin, the Berlin Wall, and the situation there, because even before I started writing, I had an intuitive sense tht I would need a hypothetical "bust-up" place, and in 1965 Berlin was a little warmer than it is now. But as I always say to people, the flash point is really immaterial. The point is what happens when the war comes. After Berlin, I met with professors, biologists, physicians, and radiologists from London University. I also met with people from the London Institute of Strategic Studies, and I did research into the payload of rockets, the effects of fallout on white and red blood corpuscles, the effect of radioactivity, and the like.

It was all immensely complicated—the amount of force required to fling a brick three hundred yards in how many seconds, the amount of thermal heat required to melt an eyeball at this and that distance. I read reports from Hiroshima, Nagasaki, and Dresden and found that, though there is plenty of technical material, the emotional effect of an atom bomb on people has been much less thoroughly investigated.

When the various places supplied you with pamphlets, did they want to know your motives or anything like that?

You have to differentiate here between people in general and governmental bodies. The experts, the professors and so on, were extremely cooperative and very interested. A few were a little skeptical of an amateur blundering into their domain, but they freely supplied what little information they had. The governmental bodies were different. In general they said No.

I made formal approaches, realizing that I was rather putting my head in the lion's mouth; but I thought, what the hell, I've got to try it all ways round. So I went to the Home Office—I think the A.G. 4 branch was the department in charge within the Ministry of Civil Defense—and I said, "I would please like to know . . . ," and I gave them a long, long list of questions about civil defense preparation in Britain. I said, "I want to know your placings and the amounts of your stockpiles; I want to know your withdrawal policies; I want to know who are going to be regional senior government officers." It was a long, long list of questions. A few may have touched on semisecret data, but I am sure that 80 percent of the answers came within the realm of information that should be available to the public.

The BBC sort of gingerly supported the request for this information, but the Home Office was rather taken aback. Then there was silence for three weeks before I was called into a BBC office and told, "We're afraid you are not going to get this information, and we believe it's best for you not to push the point." In other words, something appeared to have happened between the BBC and the Home Office. I can't be sure of this, but I think the BBC was told to cooperate in persuading me not to obtain this information. But then what happened later was worse, because the Home Office withdrew all official help.

At that juncture I was in the process of asking for help from the various branches of the Kent Auxiliary Fire Service, the main fire service, the civil defense, and the police. This went right down to the sort of nitty-gritty of technical help in supplying the radioactive meters, civil defense uniforms, rescue packs, ambulances, police information, and so forth. The Home Office put the clamp down on that immediately and told everyone to have absolutely nothing to do with me and to give me no help whatever, of any shape, size, or form. So, in most of the places I went people said to me, "Sorry, we've been told not to touch you."

The only group that helped me voluntarily after that was the Fire Service, which appeared to me to be the only group or agency in England that had and has a realistic approach to the effects of a nuclear attack. They were the only people willing to talk to me and willing to supply me with the needed bits and pieces of equipment. They said, "We've been told not to, but we realize this is an important subject." They didn't say, "Look, if a nuclear attack comes, we'll mop it up easily in England." They took the reverse approach, because they had had to deal with the small-scale fire storms in Kent during the Second World War. They had seen the ravages of a mass incendiary raid, and they knew that a nuclear attack would be infinitely worse. They knew of the terrible toll in the fire storms in Dresden. These practicing technicians were the weak link in the official "happiness bureau." They knew what it would be like, and they helped me. And they did it unofficially. Officially, there was a complete clampdown.

How much time did you put into research?

I suppose the amount of actual pure research, of bashing around and talking to these radiologists—rushing out to Oxford to meet a man who knew about the "Honest John Rocket" in Germany and meeting people doing strategic studies here and there—probably ranged from November 1964 until January or February 1965. It took about three months. I shot the film in April 1965, but I kept on researching up to the end, so you could say solid research was about two to three months, while there was some polishing during the period I was writing the commentary.

You mentioned doing sociological research as well as technical probing. Would you mind going into that a little more?

The sociological background to a third world war was just as important to me as the technical research, but here the research was more in terms of people than books. I went to see from thirty to fifty people, ranging from poets and sculptors to conductors, composers, writers, producers, and so on. I wanted to hear what they felt about the silence on the whole subject of the effects of nuclear war, and what they felt about their part as intellectuals in contributing to the silence. I just wanted to feel the response, which was quite an experience. In fact, one day I'd like to write a book about it. These meetings were the most interesting and moving part of the research, and the responses I obtained were continually fed back into the film.

At what stage did you begin trying to formulate a script?

Script is something I can't be very exact with you about, as I am not very exact about it myself. I wrote a document which was about half the size of the London telephone directory. It was tremendously detailed; I believe it was quite authoritative and, apart from anything else, presented a complete indictment of British civil defense by showing the futility of their planning and methods.

Did the script go through many versions before you were satisfied with it?

Yes. Originally it was much more padded and there were many more incidents. I wanted to follow many more individuals. I seem to remember I had a man in Kent who was working in a factory, but I can't remember what he did. There were also various other individuals, like the doctor, who are now in the film not really as characters but just as human beings caught up in the holocaust. I hadn't developed their characters much more in the original script, but I had placed them with much more regularity throughout the film. We kept going back to them, characters like the police inspector, and they provided a continuing thread.

How close did you work to your final shooting script? Was it a guide or a bible?

The script was overly long and immensely complicated. It had everything in it, almost too much. It certainly had all the logistics of the attack and why the English civil defense couldn't pick up the pieces. It had all this but was far too long, and it was in the back of my mind rather than in the forefront during the shooting. In this kind of a situation you have three or four weeks to make the film, and you just try to extract the essence of what you're doing while facing the daily problems.

What kind of problems—artistic, logistic . . . ?

You are constantly having to grapple with "Has Mrs. Brown gotten up this morning?" "Who's going to come and be the warden for this street?" "Has Mr. Baker caught his train for Tunbridge?" "Are the police going to let us use this street?" "That guy over there, knocking down that house, is he going to stop acting half mad?" "Is it going to stop raining?" "Is the hotel going to supply lunch for the cast?" All these things were part of the filmmaking. It was a hard, bloody fight, going on for weeks, with a lot of the niceties of the script just going down the drain. When you've got a long document like I had, even more goes down the drain. What you are continually trying to do is hold on the essence of the whole thing. You are having to deal with a myriad of contingencies while you're filming, while at the same time you're doing a stripped-down précis of the script and praying to God that you're retaining a structure, even if it's changed from your original concept.

How limited were you in your budget?

That's an interesting question. No one ever stated precisely how much I could have. I seem to remember that they sort of drew the line at about £12,000, but you must remember that BBC costing is extremely complicated. They have an above-and-below-the-line system, which means in fact that nobody ever knows what you're spending. Quite a lot of overheads are charged to the BBC. I think that they said that the above-the-line costs would be £12,000. It was said that I spent £20,000, but nobody ever told me whether the extra £8,000 was above-the-line or whether it was an expression of the BBC's overheads.

One is struck and overwhelmed by the sense of factual reality in The War Game, *the veracity and truth of the actors, which makes part of the film look like a newsreel. This realism was also one of the most brilliant things about* Culloden. *How do you achieve these results?*

It doesn't happen by accident. My drama training helped somewhat, but I really think that a large proportion of the realism is due to the fact that I try to make my films provide a common experience for the people in them. Both *Culloden* and *The War Game* are films made in unusually adverse conditions. For me, they are practically pure conditions, as I think this is what filmmaking is about. When you do a film like *Culloden* or *The War Game*, people have literally to stand in the gutters, in the howling wind for hours on end, fed probably on beans and a hamburger.

In *Culloden*, people were standing in fairly good reproduction Highland costume, which meant a plaid, probably a pair of jockey shorts underneath, and something on their feet—and that was it. They then walked for the best part of two weeks in the biting wind, in the rain, over moors more than a foot deep in water. And something built up between them. A similar kind of thing happened in *The War Game*. And all this is done out of enthusiasm. The people aren't paid, or are paid only token amounts.

How do you approach these people? How do you get your participants?

There are various ways. A bad way, which still works, is to advertise in local papers that you're making a film and are going to have a mass meeting for people who are interested. The other way is to approach local cine and dramatic groups, of which we have a lot in England, or to go to the schools and universities.

I usually start the ball rolling by having a mass meeting in town, at which there might be two or three hundred people from different drama groups and the like. I then get up on the platform and talk for two or three hours. I tell them why I'm making the film. I try to get them involved in the subject and to understand its importance. I try to get them to understand its connection with them as human beings and what might be the worth of the collective experiences of making a film on the subject. I then usually terminate the meeting and try to meet every single one of these people individually.

I have an idea of the sort of people I am trying to cast, but it has to be immensely flexible. If I see a guy who I think might be a good policeman, I make a note of that. I talk to each person for about ten minutes or a quarter of an hour—it depends on the number of people there and on the time pressures. Then the thing narrows down a little. People drop out; other people stay with you. In *The War Game*, I built up an aggregate of about four hundred people who stuck with me the whole time. Not one was a professional actor, and fewer than half had ever played in front of a camera before.

How do these people get this realism? How does somebody just simply cry?

You can't just pull a man in from a job and say, "Okay fellow, I want you to suddenly become involved in a nuclear war, and I want you to give me a very stark realism which has to come smacking across as if you were actually caught in those circumstances." That doesn't just happen in five minutes. You have to get to know the chap, you have to pull him into the communal thing of making films.

Filming is the most god-awful boring thing for people who are in it, at least in this sort of film where they have to stand around for hours on end watching you grapple with the problems, waiting to do their little bit as a policeman. Maybe you've told Mr. Brown, "Now you've gotta be here at half past nine on Monday," but at half past two on Wednesday you still haven't filmed him. You have to pull people through all that; and what holds them might possibly be my personality, but it certainly has to do with what you have impressed on them as the meaning of the subject.

What also comes through is their desire as a person to express themselves; and when you make my sort of film, you find yourself unexpectedly tapping this. It's a collective "thing," plus what you say to them just before you start running the camera, or you talk to them the night before—something like, "You're going to be a nurse and I want you to think about holding a child, and it's dying." And you go through this, and you maybe act it for them, maybe you don't—but I try essentially to let them come out with it themselves, which they usually do on the first or second take.

I must emphasize that there's no pat answer to this; it's part of a collective experience. It may have come from something generated for them over a couple of meetings or the collective thing of two or three weeks of filming. What matters is getting people involved in a human experience or emotion and letting it develop and flower in the particular way you need. I have also found that using nonprofessionals in this sort of film is usually a little better, because professionals often bring in a tremendous art and craft and technique which spoils the naturalism. But it's a difficult problem. There are no rules.

You've got a number of comments in the film about what people think of carbon 14, or whether we should bomb Russia in retaliation for their dropping a bomb on us. Were these comments written into the script, or are they real off-the-street reactions?

That's one of the main questions that's been asked over the past few years, and I can understand why. People know that the film is a reconstruction; therefore, they probably say, "Ah, he's reconstructed this." Yet the carbon 14 sections and the "retaliation against Russia" section are the only ones that *aren't* reconstructed. In other sections I've got people playing churchmen or strategists; what they say is what I heard and learned talking to churchmen and strategists during the research. But the statement of the women in the street talking about carbon 14 and retaliation are completely genuine from members of the cast.

One morning I got the cast together and said, "I want to do something a little bit different for the next couple of hours, but I'm not going to tell you exactly what it is." My cast were housewives from Gravesend, and they looked at each other thinking, "Oh, God, what's he going to do with us now"—this was after they had been thrown out of windows and trapped in fires for the sake of the film in the last two weeks. Then I took them aside, one by one, and said, "Okay, now I'm going to ask you questions, I want you to answer me whatever way you feel. Just say whatever you think." And for a moment they became what they really were—ordinary lay members of the British public. I asked these questions about fifty feet away from the main group; no one could hear what I was saying. And those questions and responses—particularly the responses—are perhaps the biggest single indictment in the entire film of the way we are conducting our society and of the lack of common public knowledge of the things that affect humanity.

Could we move into the technical area and directorial decisions?

Technically, the film was very difficult to make and was shot at a ratio of about twenty to one. I think if we discuss the firestorm sequence, that will sum up for you many of the difficulties of the film and the problem of obtaining a kind of documentary authenticity.

A firestorm is very different from an ordinary fire; it's an all-consuming tornado, and it was very difficult to create that effect.

THE WAR GAME
The Fire Storm

Picture	*Sound*
Firestorm sequence Buildings on fire	COMMENTATOR: Rochester in Kent. Now two square miles of fire resulting from the heat of a thermonuclear missile which exploded "off-course" from London Airport, 3½ miles from this position.
Firemen	This is the unknown phenomenon which could perhaps happen in Britain following a nuclear strike against certain of our cities. This happened after the bombing of Hamburg, at Dresden, at Tokyo, and at Hiroshima. This is what is technically known as a firestorm.
Fire alley	Within its center the rising heat from multiple fires caused by both the heat flash and the blast wave upsetting stoves and open furnaces is sucking in ground-level winds at speeds exceeding one hundred miles an hour. This is the wind of a firestorm.
People running/ bowled over Woman in fire storm	WOMAN: "I saw a man being caught by a great gust of wind, tore the coat right off his head . . ."
Close-up of man with gasmask	
Caption	NEWSREADER: During a recent meeting of the Ecumenical Council at the Vatican, a bishop told the press that he was sure "our nuclear weapons will be used with wisdom."
People bowled over by wind Bishop	"I believe that we live in a system of necessary law and order—and I still believe in the 'war of the just.' "
Car burning Car explodes	COMMENTATOR: Within this car a family is burning alive.
Brooks	Charles Brooks, chief fire officer of Chatham. Already three of his appliances have been smashed, gutted, or overturned.

| Firemen—roof explodes | Already seventeen of his sixty firemen have been crushed, hurt, or killed by flying debris. |
| Firemen collapsing | This is a firestorm. Within its center the oxygen is being consumed in every cellar and groundfloor room, to be replaced by the gases of carbon monoxide, carbon dioxide, and methane. Within its center the temperatures are rising to 800°C. These men are dying—both of heat stroke and of gassing. |

We were working in an old barracks that was about to be pulled down and that gave us the impression of large buildings which might vaguely be taken for office blocks. We put white magnesium flares in all the windows and then built up the fire behind. For the soundtrack we tried a mixture of fire, volcano, and other things, all treated very coarsely. I then brought down a friend of mind, a stunt man, to help me with the management of the people caught in the firestorm.

We put a mattress down and got the people to sort of run and pick themselves up off the mattress. It's extremely difficult, and it doesn't work completely—but it works. As you are running, you have to suddenly feel yourself caught and turned by an air current. To achieve this we started pulling them with wires, but we finally decided not to do that, as we thought it would hurt them. We also thought it would look false. So everything is actually what they do themselves, plus the cutting of the best sort of positions. We also helped the effect by having flares roaring in the background and putting two fans quite close to them to whip bits of shredded paper and flour across so that you get the visual impression of a sudden whipping across of something. As they ran to a particular spot where their mattress was, the white bits of paper would whip across and catch them, that would be their cue for letting themselves be caught in it and turned. That's just a small example of the solution to a technical problem; it really has nothing to do with filmmaking, but it's what that nutty film is about.

As far as camera techniques are concerned, well, obviously we were letting people shout, letting them distort the microphone, and letting them deliberately butt into the camera. What we were trying to do was create a sort of total emotion, or total involvement, which affected us as well as the actors. I would give the cameraman specific directions, but obviously things would often be happening very suddenly and he'd be on his own.

Did you use any stock shots?

Every single frame in that film is us. We put the film through a particular process to try and get it to look as if it had been grabbed out of archives of twenty years ago. I forget how we did it; it was a case of getting a dupe negative, then getting a particular harsh-grain positive and reprinting from the positive—that accounts for that extreme contrast in look in a lot of the film. That was obviously deliberately sought after and finally achieved by us and by the laboratory, which did very well.

There was one scene where a rocket goes off. Was that your rocket?

Yes. My art director went out and built a bit of a rocket. He was able to wheel the thing up the ramp just about three feet, and at that point I'd bring the camera up so that it was near the top of it. The rocket and every other single inch in that film is us. Some of it, I must admit, is not done as well as I would have liked, but it's all us, with all its faults. It's all us, every foot of it.

1. *Film Comment* 3, no. 4 (1965).

Index